Messerschmitt Bf 110/Me 210/Me 410

An Illustrated History

Messerschmitt Bf 110/Me 210/Me 410

An Illustrated History

Heinz Mankau & Peter Petrik

Schiffer Military History
Atglen, PA

Book Design by Ian Robertson.
Translated from the German by Don Johnston

Library of Congress Catalog Number: 2002115014

This work was originally published under the title *Messerschmitt Bf 110 - Me 210 - Me 410, Die Messerschmitt-Zerstörer und ihre Konkurrenten*, by Aviatic Verlag.

Printed in China.
ISBN: 0-7643-1784-9

We are interested in hearing from authors with book ideas on related topics.

Published by Schiffer Publishing Ltd.
4880 Lower Valley Road
Atglen, PA 19310
Phone: (610) 593-1777
FAX: (610) 593-2002
E-mail: Info@schifferbooks.com.
Visit our web site at: www.schifferbooks.com
Please write for a free catalog.
This book may be purchased from the publisher.
Please include $3.95 postage.
Try your bookstore first.

In Europe, Schiffer books are distributed by:
Bushwood Books
6 Marksbury Avenue
Kew Gardens
Surrey TW9 4JF
England
Phone: 44 (0) 20 8392-8585
FAX: 44 (0) 20 8392-9876
E-mail: Bushwd@aol.com.
Free postage in the UK. Europe: air mail at cost.
Try your bookstore first.

Contents

Foreword 7
Bf 110 Chronicle (with the FW 57 and Hs 124) 9
Ar 240 Chronicle 83
Me 210/410 Chronicle 89
Overview of the Types 153
The *Luftwaffe's* Tactical Guidelines for the *Rüstungsflugzeug II* (1932) 154
The *Luftwaffe's* Tactical Guidelines for the *Rüstungsflugzeug III* (1934) 155
Unrealized First Generation *Zerstörer* Projects 155
Ago Ao 255 155
Dornier Project 156
Gotha's Project 3001/3002 156
Heinkel's Project 156
FW 57 156
FW 57 V1, 1936 *Zerstörer*, 1937 Multi-Role Aircraft 157
Hs 124, 1936 *Zerstörer*, 1937 Multi-role Aircraft 157
Hs 124 V1, 1936 *Zerstörer*, General Assessment 158
Hs 124 V2, 1936 *Zerstörer*, 1937 Multi-Role Aircraft 158
Hs 124 V3, 1936 *Zerstörer* and High-Altitude Strategic Reconnaissance Aircraft, 1937 Probable Strike Aircraft 159
Hs 124, Bomber, Strike Fighter, Strategic Recce (1937 Proposal) 159
Bf 110 162
Bf 110 V1 162
Bf 110 V2 164
Bf 110 V3 164
Bf 110 A *Zerstörer*, Heavy Fighter 165
Bf 110 B *Zerstörer*, Heavy Fighter 166
Bf 110 C *Zerstörer*, Heavy Fighter 172
Bf 110 D 180
Bf 110 E 186
Bf 110 C through E, Night Fighter 194
Bf 110 C through E, DB 601N Powered Aircraft 195
Bf 110 C through E, Tropical Equipment Fitted Aircraft 196
Bf 110 C through E, Me 321 Tow Aircraft 197
Bf 110 C through E, Strike Aircraft 200
Bf 110 F 203
Bf 110 G 211
Bf 110 H 230
Heavy Fighter Tactical Technical Requirements (1936/37) 233
Kampfzerstörer Technical Guidelines from 7 Aug 1942 234
Ar 240 234
Ar 240 V-1 and V-2 235
Ar 240 A 236
Ar 240 B 241
Ar 240 C 242
Ar 240 D 244
Ar 240 E, Special Bomber 244
Ar 240 F *Kampfzerstörer* 245
Ar 440 A 245

Me 210 247
Me 210, Drafting the Project 247
Me 210 V-1 Through V-4 249
Me 210 V-5 Through V-16 252
Me 210 V-17 and Other Prototypes 254
Me 210 A 254
Me 210 B, Recce Version of the Me 210 A 278
Me 210 C 278
Me 210 D, Recce Version of the Me 210 C 281
Me 210 E-1 (1941/42), *Zerstörer* and Dive Bomber 281
Me 210 F, Recce Version of the Me 210 E 281
Me 210 S-1 (1942), Strike Aircraft 282
Me 210 S-2 (1942), Strike Aircraft 282
Me 210 Trainer 282
Me 310 282
Me 410 283
Me 410 A 283
Me 410 B 302
Me 410 C 310
Me 410 D 312
Me 410 H, High-Altitude *Zerstörer*, Torpedo Bomber, Bomber 314
Me 410 with 1 or 2 TL 314
Me 610 *Zerstörer* 316
Li P 10, Tailless Counterpart to the Me 210/410 317
Me 329, Tailless Counterpart to the Me 210/410 317
Me 410 Conversion Kits (as of 15 May 1944) 319
Variants, Serial Numbers, Quantities 323
Prototypes and Testbeds 328
Zerstörer Engines and Powerplants 347
Definitions 347
Engines for the *Zerstörer* Prototypes: 347
Jumo 210 347
DB 600 348
BMW 132 Dc, Radial (carbureted), from 1937 348
First-Generation *Zerstörer* Engines: 349
Jumo 210 349
DB 601 (from 1937) 349
Second-Generation *Zerstörer* Engines: 349
DB 601 349
DB 605 349
Junkers Jumo 211 350
Junkers Jumo 213 351
DB 603 351
Third-Generation *Zerstörer* Engines: 352
Junkers Jumo 213 352
DB 603 352
Standard Powerplants 354

Bibliography 355
Books 355
Magazines and Publications 356
Test Reports and Meeting Minutes 356
Manuals, etc. 357
Conclusion 359

Foreword

Based on numbers alone, the Bf 110, Me 210, and Me 410 would not make the top of the list for the German *Luftwaffe*, yet with approximately 6000, 500, and 1300 built of each type, the three designs were not exactly rarities, either. Although having been discussed in several magazines, publications, and books from the 1950s onward, the information on these types has proven to be so contradictory and in many cases downright erroneous that Peter Petrick and I felt it appropriate to tackle the subject anew.

It is not our intention to take our colleagues to task here, for ultimately we owe our gratitude to authors such as Nowarra, Lange, Green, etc. for bringing to light the available facts at an early stage. Wartime conditions, however, led to many documents being destroyed or inaccessible, meaning that of necessity the history of these aircraft types would never be complete. Nevertheless, we would have liked to see these writers at least acknowledge any gaps in information and not simply have filled them with speculations. Further inconsistencies stem from the time period in which the evidence was obtained. For example, following a redesignation campaign the designation Bf 110 D-1 was initially applied to a reconnaissance version in order to indicate a variant of the Bf 110 D-0 built by Focke Wulf.

We began collecting materials more than twenty years ago, and in doing so were given much assistance from eyewitnesses, authors, and collectors. Special thanks go out to Messrs. Theodor Morr and Willy Radinger for their valuable help, as well as to Messrs. Georges van Acker, Rick Chapman, Hans-Peter Dabrowski, *Dipl.-Ing.* Karl Kössler, Dr. Jörg Armin Kranzhoff, Bruno Lange (+), Heinz J. Nowarra (+), Hans Redemann (+), Hanfried Schliephake, Gerhard Stemmer, Christiaan Vanhee, Andreas Weber, and Gerhard Winterer. For the most part, the photos used in this book come from former *Luftwaffe* members or out of the manuals. The quality of the latter source is poor, as these were crudely printed on cheap paper.

We also made use of documents from the *Deutsches Museum* in Munich, the *Bundesarchiv* in Freiburg and Koblenz, and the WAst, Berlin. The *Deutsches Museum* in particular has thankfully expanded its collection inventory over the last few years, making it possible to determine the facts in many cases for the first time. The *Bundesarchiv* in Freiburg charges 0.80 DM for a single page copy and 40 DM for a photo reproduction. In addition, there are shipping and handling costs to deal with. This fact may explain why the still unpublished treasures of this institution so rarely see the light of day. The *Deutsches Museum's* photo reproduction costs are similar.

In 1981/82 I made a first attempt at describing the Me 210/410 in *Modell Magazin*. As I subsequently discovered, the articles contained several errors, including missing information and, what more importantly, chronological inconsistencies. In order to avoid making a similar mistake in this publication, I have chosen to portray the histories of the types in the form of a chronicle. The basis for this approach was the minutes from meetings held either at or within the ministry of *Generalfeldmarschall* Milch. These minutes, transcribed during the period when he was the *Generalluftzeugmeister* of the *Luftwaffe*, are available from the *Bundesarchiv* in Freiburg in the form of microfiche files. Approximately 8000 pages were reviewed for this book. In these minutes, the specific aircraft were often only briefly mentioned, either as part of a list or, more often, within the framework of a discussion. I have reproduced the brief references word for word, and in other cases I have paraphrased the statements insofar as they relate to the relevant types. As with any discussion, the statements made by the participants will not always be understood by someone reading the quoted excerpts, particularly when the discussion centers around written documents which the participants had available but were not included in the minutes.

It is also important to note that the discussions at the office of the *Generalluftzeugmeister* addressed problems, yet often provided no solutions. This was because the important decisions were reserved for *Reichsmarschall* Göring.

I have also included other relevant details within this framework. This seems to me to be the most effective way of ensuring a proper chronological order.

In limiting our scope, it made sense to us to include the contemporary designs of the FW 57, Hs 124, and the Ar 240, and thereby show why the RLM decided to acquire Messerschmitt types. Other aircraft types, although they may have fit well into the theme of this book, have been left for later publications so as not to step outside the framework. These include the Ta 154, which the RLM hoped to have produced as a supplement to the Bf 110 by using readily available wood materials and the Jumo 211 engines freed up with the cessation of Ju 88 and He 111 production, and the Do 335, which began its brief career as a high speed bomber, yet was ultimately planned as a successor to the Bf 110 and Me 410.

Over several years, Peter Petrick has collected factory markings and serial numbers for the Bf 110, Me 210, and Me 410. Mr. Gerhard Stemmer deserves special recognition here for his assistance in this endeavor. Although it was originally our intention to include the results of this work, space constraints preclude such a listing. Documenting individual aircraft with serial numbers, factory registration, unit markings, and disposition would have been a 150 page work in and of itself. However, the included listing of serial numbers and quantity is the result of these efforts.

Bf 110 Chronicle (with the Fw 57* and Hs 124)

The following events are derived in the main from notes taken by *Generalfeldmarschall* Erhard Milch. A large portion also stems from other documents from the *Reichsluftfahrtministerium*, either those which the authors had direct access to or those which have been cited in literature dealing with the subject (procurement plans, etc.). The latter sources are indicated by "GL" for *Generalluftzeugmeister*, "RLM" for *Reichsluftfahrtministerium*, "Mtt" for Messerschmitt AG, "GWF" for Gothaer Waggonfabrik, and "Ar" for Arado.

2/22
The *Entente* permits Germany to resume building aircraft on a limited basis beginning 5 May 1922.

4/14/22
The Ambassadors' Conference provides the Reich Government with the "Conceptual Guidelines," which describe what types of aircraft can be built and operated in Germany. Construction of military aircraft is ruled out.

1/1/23
Germany regains the authority to exercise control of its airspace.

1/11/23
Five French divisions, together with Belgian troops, march into the Rhineland in order to force Germany's compliance with reparation payments, which Germany can no longer make due to inflation.
The result of this conflict is that the Reich Government drops its resistance to active military aviation in the *Reichswehr* and approves the acquisition of aircraft.

1923
Heinkel produces the first military aircraft, the HD 17 and HD 33, in violation of the "Conceptual Guidelines."

1924
Subsidized by the *Reichswehr* Ministry, the civil "Sportflug GmbH" becomes a training tool for military pilots.

4/1/25
The Deutsche Verkehrsflieger-Schule (DVS) is established as an expansion of the Sportflug GmbH, where only training in small aircraft is provided. The DVS, on the other hand, offers military pilot training up to the B2 class license.

1925
Within the *Reichswehrministerium* and the developmental departments of the *Heereswaffenamt* there now begins preliminary work on the establishment of a new German *Luftwaffe*. A test center is established in Rechlin, ostensibly for the *Reichsverband der Deutschen Luftfahrtindustrie* (German Aviation Industry Federal Union).

5/26/26
The restrictions of the "Conceptual Guidelines" are lifted. This clears the way for development of state-of-the-art military aircraft.

1927 to 1929
The *Reichswehr's* aviation rearmament planning enables the introduction of an invitation to tender program for aircraft and engines. Requirements for the first developmental series are issued.

* *Officially the aircraft was designated FW 57 throughout the 1930s, since the company title derived from two separate names. However, the designation Fw 57 could also be found in contemporary magazines, books, and company documents. Sometime around 1940 the Fw appellation won out within RLM as well.*

5/27
Tasking for development of new powerplants calls for both water and air-cooled lightweight engines rated up to 2000 hp, with compressor systems and variable-pitch propellers, enabling flights up to altitudes of 10000 meters.

1927
The Bavarian Government and the *Reichsverkehrsministerium* encourage the Messerschmitt G.m.b.H., heavily in debt at this point, to form a joint interest partnership with the Bayerische Flugzeugwerke A.G.

1928
During the spring the *Reichsverkehrsministerium* begins negotiations for purchasing controlling interest in the BFW's company stocks, something which also piques the interest of the Heinkel company. On 5/15/28 Willy Messerschmitt sends a letter to prominent persons in the aviation industry which, in particular, levies criticism against Ernst Heinkel and his designs.

1929
The *Heereswaffenamt* issues specifications for inverted piston aircraft engines with a cylinder displacement of 20 to 30 liters. The inverted design is specified to offer significant forward visibility for single engine aircraft. These specifications lead to the water-cooled inline Jumo 210, DB 600, BMW 116, BMW 117, and the air-cooled BMW and SAM 322 radial engines. (As BMW is at full operating capacity supplying radial engines, the BMW 116 and BMW 117 engines are not put into production. In 1936/37 the RLM directs BMW to cease further work on water-cooled powerplants.)

3/5/30
During the flight of a Messerschmitt-designed M 24 operated by the Deutsche Verkehrsflug AG, the last fuselage bulkhead breaks at the aft anchor point for the tailfin. Although the airline reports the matter to the DVL, the latter maintains that existing regulations are sufficient.

10/6/30
An M 20 b airliner crashes when the vertical stabilizer breaks off. Cause of the accident is initially attributed to operator error.

4/4/31
Another M 20 b crashes due to the vertical stabilizer breaking off.

4/16/31
Theodor Croneiß, of the Deutsche Verkehrsflug AG, writes to the DVL that the crashes of the two M 20s could have been prevented if the findings of 3/6/30 had been acknowledged. Looking back, the two crashes were not caused by pilot error, but by a breakage of the empennage. The DVL's regulations are not sufficient, as they do not take into account dynamic stress.

Spring 1931
After the two Messerschmitt designed M 20 airliners are determined to have crashed due to a design flaw (breakage of the vertical stabilizer due to inadequate dimensions), Lufthansa (under the direction of its CEO Milch) blocks the contract for a further 10 aircraft of the type. As a result, the Bayerische Flugzeugwerke (BFW) finds itself in a serious financial situation, and Milch's impression of Messerschmitt is and remains negative until the end of the war.

6/1/31
After merger talks with Heinkel and Dornier prove unsuccessful, BFW files for bankruptcy at the Augsburg district court.

2/1/32
A *Reichswehr* planning study calls for a *Luftwaffe* with an inventory of 1056 total aircraft by 1938.

6/28/32
A decree is issued calling for the establishment of a *Luftwaffe* within the new peacetime army.

8/10/32
The "Organizational Foundations for the Establishment of Air Forces" are worked out.

8/14-15/32 through 8/25/32
An article appears in the *Völkischer Beobachter* questioning the single-spar design in light of the several accidents involving Messerschmitt sport planes (wing failure of the M 29, leading to the type being banned). In a subsequent discussion, the *Führer's* adjutant, Rudolf Hess, takes a vehement pro-Messerschmitt position and even insinuates sabotage, while notable German designers such as Siegfried Günter attribute the breakages (wings and other components were fractured) to the light design methods employed by Messerschmitt. They point to the fact that other aircraft having the same layout, such as the *Sausewind*, can fly safely, and imply that Messerschmitt puts lightweight design above safety. Günter claims that it is irrelevant whether Messerschmitt aircraft met the DVL's structural requirements. These are, he believes, only general minimum standards that a designer must exceed, particularly in view of static and dynamic loads that have yet to be fully researched.

10/32
At the beginning of the month there appears another article, this time in volume no. 9 of *Flugkapitän*, which deals with the crashes of the Messerschmitt aircraft. *Prof.* Georg Madelung, former member of the board of the *Deutsche Versuchsanstalt für Luftfahrt*, professor at the technical college in Stuttgart, and Messerschmitt's father-in-law, takes the view that there were those behind the article who wanted to eliminate the Messerschmitt company and were using methods which would necessitate the involvement of the public prosecutor. He further speculates that those who would engage in such organized lies are also capable of other crimes, and indicates the possibility that someone may have tampered with the rudders of the two M 20s and the wings of the two M 29s that had gone down. In view of the happenings in the spring of 1931, Fritz Hille and Ernst Heinkel of Ernst Heinkel AG take particular umbrage at these remarks. These events are the cause of the enmity between Ernst Heinkel and Willy Messerschmitt.

10/7/32
Robert Lusser, who at this point still worked for Ernst Heinkel AG, determines that the M 29 crashes can be traced to weight-saving measures applied to the horizontal stabilizer, these being an undamped design lacking a counterbalance and using an extensive aerodynamic force offset. This arrangement, which probably had the aerodynamic force offset too great, leads to certain maneuvers causing the plane to porpoise so violently that the wings fracture. Lusser goes on to state that this matter had been cleared up in principle as early as the beginning of August, and for Prof. Madelung in September to offer up sabotage as an explanation was sheer demagogy.

The events mentioned above reveal a fundamental difference in the design philosophies of Messerschmitt and his contemporaries. Whereas Messerschmitt designed his aircraft to be as light as possible in order to squeeze out superior performance, his competitors chose a safer route. As a result, Messerschmitt machines exhibited consistently better performance characteristics, but crashed much more frequently and demanded better trained pilots.

10/32
The tactical requirements of the *Reichswehr* for the 1933-37 armament period are laid down. These include the "*Rüstungsflugzeug II*," a single-engine, two-seat fighter, reconnaissance aircraft and light bomber.

1932 (Ar)
At Arado, studies are conducted involving a powered drive system for pivoting a 2 cm Oerlikon cannon. Calculations show that power available to aircraft at the time is not sufficient to operate a pneumatic or hydraulic drive system.

11/11/32
A report on the "inadequate state of the *Luftwaffe's* personnel and material resources" calls for the acquisition of a further 83 single-seat fighters to complement the existing 41 in inventory, plus another 12 Albatros L 84 two-seat fighters. In this case, 12 aircraft equal a squadron.

1/30/33
Hitler is named as *Reichskanzler*.

1/31/33
Hitler persuades Erhard Milch to become secretary of state of a newly created aviation ministry.

2/2/33
Hermann Göring becomes *Reichskommissar der Luftfahrt*, or commissioner of aviation.

4/27/33 (RLM)
The *Luftfahrtkommissariat* (Commission of Aviation) becomes the *Luftfahrtministerium* (Ministry of Aviation). The *Technisches Amt LC* (Technical Department of Aviation), also known as the "*C-Amt*" and with overall responsibility for technical developments, becomes an independent body in the process. It is chaired by Aviation Minister Göring and Secretary of State Milch.

5/10/33 (RLM)
War Minister Blomberg directs the Central Flying Command Staff under *Oberst* Bohnstedt to become subordinate to the Ministry of Aviation. This is considered the birth of the *Luftwaffe*.

6/19/33 (RLM)
In a meeting between *Oberst* von Reichenau and Secretary of State Milch, it is agreed that by the end of the first rearmament phase in the summer/autumn of 1935 the air fleet is to consist of approximately 600 aircraft (51 squadrons), to include two fighter wings of 36 aircraft each (for a total of six squadrons).

7/8/33 (RLM)
The massive aircraft construction program necessitates the inclusion of the Bayerische Flugzeugwerke. Seiler, a financier, seeks out the RLM secretary, Milch, to request that the company be given another chance. Seiler persuades Milch to agree, but the latter makes no secret of his dislike for Willy Messerschmitt. He considers him to be a capable aircraft designer, but with character flaws, and notes that he did not make an appearance following the crashes of the Lufthansa planes. Milch believes that Seiler will only meet with ingratitude from Messerschmitt for his efforts.

7/12/33 (RLM)
Plans now call for the *Luftwaffe* to include just 26 squadrons, although the six fighter squadrons will be retained.

8/24/33 (RLM)
The RLM is reorganized. *General* Wever is appointed as successor to *Oberst* Bohnstedt as Chief of *A-Amt* (Chief of General Staff). Wever has been influenced by the air war theories of the Italian general Guilio Douhet and the Frenchman Camille Rougeron, who believe that bombers will play a decisive role in any war.

8/28/33 (RLM)
On the orders of the aviation minister, the number of fighter squadrons for the second rearmament phase to 1935 is reduced to three. The five bomber and five auxiliary bomber squadrons, on the other hand, are adjusted to 16 bomber and one auxiliary bomber squadron.

1933/34 (Ar)
In a study begun in late 1933, Arado's Walter Blume discovers that two gun turrets, each with a single MG FF as a bomber's defensive armament, would increase the airplane's weight by approximately 1000 kg and re-

quires an engine output of around 620 hp to maintain 450 km/h at an altitude of 4000 m.

1934 (RLM)

As part of a study of possible tactics in a future offensive air war, the *Luftwaffe's* command staff develops its thinking with regard to the employment of new weapons types. A twin-engined multi-seat aircraft—about the size of a light bomber—is drawn up, with heavy concentrated cannon armament in place of ordnance. The guns would be either fixed or rotating, and the mounts or turrets would cover the air ahead of and above the aircraft, as well as having a limited lateral arc of fire. According to the study, these planes would fly in close formation ahead of an attacking bomber formation and clear a wide path through the enemy's defenses. Technicians fear that the type would be too heavy and unmaneuverable for its intended role and slower than the bombers it was designed to protect. Göring decides in favor of the *Zerstörer* (lit. "Destroyer"), and in the future calls it "his" weapon.

Early 1934 (RLM)

The *Luftwaffe's* tactical guidelines are modified. The *Rüstungsflugzeug III* (1934) replaces the *Rüstungsflugzeug II* (1932).

Early 1934 (Mtt)

Willy Messerschmitt and project chief Robert Lusser meet with the RLM on the topic of the "*Zerstörer*." Discussions include the general specifications and the appearance of the new aircraft, which within the company is designated project number 1035. Following these meetings, Willy Messerschmitt submits Memorandum P 1035 to the RLM, which not only offers a *Zerstörer* design, but also a derivative high altitude strategic reconnaissance platform and a bomber. The variants differ fundamentally only in the fuselage.

The Henschel developmental team around *Dipl. Ing.* Nicolaus, in view of the restrictive technical requirements specified by the RLM, anticipate no real advantage of a bomber destroyer over a traditional bomber, for neither the engine performance, nor the dimensions or the weights can justify the type. The engineers later assess the tactical requirements of the General Staff to be so inaccurate that a performance parity or superiority with the bombers could not have been expected from the outset. While Messerschmitt hopes to meet the various role requirements by using different fuselage designs, Henschel gets the idea to simply modify the nose sections.

The layout as a *Zerstörer*, strategic reconnaissance aircraft, and bomber is a feature of all the design proposals and not just a Messerschmitt speciality. It is not known whether the idea of using the basic aircraft type for three roles came from within the RLM itself or was introduced by one or more companies, but the concept had become well established by the time of the *Rüstungsflugzeug II* in 1932.

A popular view in postwar literature is that Messerschmitt paid little attention to the established guidelines and surprised the RLM with a new interpretation, and the Bf 110 was therefore not impacted when the unsuitability of the bomber destroyer concept became apparent.

In view of the tense situation between Willy Messerschmitt and Erhard Milch and the total dependence of the Bayerische Flugzeugwerke on Luftwaffe contracts, it seems highly unlikely that anything took place in the Bayerische Flugzeugwerke's developmental department which had not been precisely coordinated with the RLM. The BFW's unique approach was known to, and desired by, the RLM from the beginning. What is more likely, then, is that the obvious dimensional and conceptual differences between the FW 57, Hs 124, and Bf 110 types was due to the RLM and the General Staff not yet having finalized on the shape of the type, and hoped to find the best approach based on the evaluation results from the three proposals.

5/25/34 (RLM)
For the third buildup phase, The aviation minister determines that by 10/01/36 15 wings (45 squadrons) of bombers and 7 wings (21 squadrons) of fighter aircraft are to be established.

6/34 (RLM)
The command staff directs LC II, the technical development branch, to develop the bomber destroyer concept further. The request for tender goes out to the companies of AGO, the Bayerische Flugzeugwerke, Dornier, Focke-Wulf, Heinkel, and Henschel. AGO draws up the Ao 225 project, a twin-engined low-wing design powered by the Jumo 210 and apparently armed with four 2 cm machine guns. Gotha produces the 3001 and 3002 projects, twin fuselage designs with DB 600 engines housed in the fuselage driving the propeller via an extended shaft. These authors have no detailed information on the Heinkel and Dornier projects. The projects of BFW, Focke-Wulf, and Henschel give rise to the Bf 110, FW 57, and Hs 124, respectively.

7/34 (RLM)
The ministry approves a program calling for the construction of 4021 aircraft by the end of September 1935.

The Ministry of Aviation issues a contract to the companies of the Bayerische Flugzeugwerke (BFW), Focke-Wulf (FW), and Henschel (Hs), along with the *Erprobungsstelle* (E-Stelle, or Test Center) for the development of the *Zerstörer*. Each are to construct three prototypes and five preproduction versions to be used for evaluation, and potentially as the pattern ready for full-scale production. Planned engines are two 20 liter powerplants (Jumo 210). Mockups are to be ready by 2/35 and the first aircraft by 2/36.

These companies were certainly not caught unawares by this contract and had, as shown earlier, already begun preliminary work. Nevertheless, it is an amazing feat to work out an entirely new concept and develop it to the point where a mockup could be unveiled within the space of just seven months. It also took considerable effort to be able to complete construction and have the prototypes built within another year, particularly when one considers that these prototypes were not only intended for testing within the companies, but would also be evaluated by the E-Stelle. During the design phase, the issuer of the contract (the RLM) closely followed developments and introduced a number of changes.

Spring 1935 (press release)
The RLM issues requirements for a new high-speed bomber, armed with just a single machine gun and able to carry a 500 kg bomb load at a speed of 500 km/h. Cruising speed is to be 450 km/h. The invitation to tender is extended to Junkers, Messerschmitt, Henschel, and Focke-Wulf. Some sources claim that the tender request was issued in the spring of 1936.

Mid-1935 (based on the recollection of Ernst Zindel, the designer responsible for the Ju 88)
The sport aviatrix Marga von Etzdorf makes an extended information tour of the USA, which she probably carries out at the behest of the RLM. Visits several aircraft companies and reports on her observations, to include those of a high-speed, medium sized bomber she sees at the Glenn L. Martin Company that is capable of attaining 450 km/h. Junkers and other companies embrace the concept.

8/35 (based on the recollection of Ernst Zindel)
Under the direction of *Dipl.-Ing.* Quick, the design bureau at Junkers develops the initial projects for a high-speed bomber capable of 500 km/h and able to carry a payload of approximately 1000 kg. Shortly thereafter the RLM issues a contract to determine the feasibility of building a bomber with a medium payload capability which would only be marginally slower than the fighter types then being introduced.

This reveals that the RLM was aware of the problem issues regarding the bomber destroyer concept and now wanted specialized types. The companies of BFW and Henschel therefore attempted to accommodate this change in tack with the bomber destroyer designs then in development. The Bf 110 subsequently became a pure Zerstörer, complemented by the Bf 161 high-speed bomber with wider fuselage, a type which was turned into a reconnaissance platform in late 1935. The Hs 124 was too large to be a Zerstörer, and— like the Bf 161—had too small an internal bomb bay to be a high-speed bomber. As a result, its development progressed along the lines of a light bomber or strike aircraft. The FW 57 proved to be a flawed design, being too large and above all too heavy, and was finished as a training exercise in metal aircraft design without any hope of entering production. In answer to the high-speed fighter request for tender, the BFW developed the Bf 162 and Henschel the Hs 127, both of which built upon the work of the bomber destroyer. Both, however, had no chance of survival in comparison with the Ju 88. Zindel recalled a discussion with the RLM regarding the wing sizes selected. The RLM preferred a smaller wing, since this approach offered higher speeds, and referred to the Bf 162 with its wing surface area of approximately 38 m^2. Zindel countered with the conviction that even the 52.5 m^2 of the projected Ju 88 would still give a wing loading of 160 kg/m^2 and would cause problems when introduced into field units. By the time the Ju 88 entered production, 200 kg/ m^2 had been achieved, and Zindel's team was quite pleased at having chosen the larger wing. Messerschmitt more than anyone catered to the contemporary trend of small wing design, an approach which later led to serious troubles with the Me 309 and Me 410.

8/35
According to the Aircraft Development Program of 11/1/35, the BFW's contract is expanded to include a high-speed bomber with a wider fuselage (Bf 110 V4), a derivative of the *Zerstörer* type. Completion of the mockup is projected for December 1935. A decision on further development would follow afterwards. The Bf 110 V3 is to be powered by the DB 600.

8/29/35 (RLM)
Luftwaffe planning calls for the establishment of 204 squadrons by 10/1/38, of which 90 are to be bomber, 6 auxiliary bomber, and 45 are to be fighter squadrons.

11/1/35 (GL)
The aircraft acquisition program orders the development of three prototypes and five pre-production aircraft each of the Bf 110, FW 57, and Hs 124 during the period 1935-1937. The BFW and Henschel aircraft are mainly planned to utilize the Jumo 10 (210), while the FW 57 V1 is to be powered by the RR Buzzard and the FW 57 V2, FW 57 V3, and the Bf 110 V3 will be fitted with the DB 600. Within this program, the FW 57 is no longer being considered for acquisition, i.e. even before its first flight. No decision is yet made on the role of the Bf 110 pre-production series and its powerplant. A new acquisition is the Bf 110 V4 high-speed bomber with wider fuselage and powered by the Jumo 10. A decision on further construction would be made following the completion of the mockup in December 1935.

11/35 (GL)
The RLM determines the Bf 110 is to be used as a *Zerstörer* and calls for further development of the high-speed bomber mockup (Bf 110 V4) as the Bf 161 high altitude reconnaissance aircraft with wider fuselage. The RLM considers the Bf 110 mockup as suitable for a bomber role as well, and provides the BFW with additional technical requirements for the high-speed bomber. The number of pre-production aircraft is increased to seven. The DB 600 is selected as the engine for the FW 57 V1.

11/8/35 (LC II)
Memorandum to the main office re: correspondence and memos from the Bayerische Flugzeugwerke

Effective 6 November 1935 it is requested that all correspondence and messages of the Bayerische Flugzeugwerke which refer to the outdated designation of "Me" (e.g. Me 110) instead of "BF" (e.g. BF 110) for their aircraft types are not to be accepted and should be returned to the Bayerische Flugzeugwerke with the relevant explanation. This measure is necessary in order to ensure consistency within the Air Ministry for type designations of aircraft manufactured by the Bayerische Flugzeugwerke. It is requested that such memorandums and correspondence not be put into circulation beforehand, and if necessary have the filing rooms within the individual departments return the materials without logging them. I.A. Lucht

1/1/36 (GL)

Planned types for the aircraft development program are the Bf 110, Hs 124, and FW 57

Tabelle 1: Auszug aus dem Flugzeugentwicklungsprogramm vom 1.1.36

Gerät mit Musterbezeichnung	Firma	Aufgabenstellung bei der Entwicklungsgruppe	Aufgabenstellung an Industrie	Fertigstellung von Attrappen	1. Flugklartermin	Erprobungsabschluss einschließlich Mustererprobung / Einführungsreiferklärung bei 0-Serie
Bf 110 –V1 2 x Jumo 10	B.F.W.	6.34	7.34	2.35	2.36	12.36
Bf 110 –V2 2 x Jumo 10	B.F.W.	6.34	7.34	2.35	3.36	12.36
Bf 110 –V3 2 x DB 600	B.F.W.		8.35	12.35	5.36	3.37
Bf 161 Höhenfernerkunder mit breitem Rumpf 2 x Jumo 10	B.F.W.		8.35	11.35	7.36	
Bf 110, Bf 161 0-Serie (7 St.) Motor ?	B.F.W.	6.34	7.34		2.36	1.37
FW 57 – V1 2 x DB 600	FW	6.34	7.34	3.35	6.36	4.37
FW 57 – V2 2 x DB 600	FW	6.34	7.34	3.35	7.36	4.37
FW 57 – V3 Zerstörer und Höhenfernerkunder 2 x DB 600	FW	6.34	7.34	3.35	8.36	4.37
FW 57 A-0 0-Serie (5 St.) 2 x DB 600	FW	6.34	7.34			3.37
Hs 124 – V1 2 x Jumo 10	Henschel	6.34	7.34	11.34	6.36	4.37
Hs 124 – V2 2 x Jumo 10	Henschel	6.34	7.34	3.35	7.36	2.37
Hs 124 – V3 Zerstörer und Höhenfernerkunder 2 x Jumo 10	Henschel	6.34	7.34	12.35	8.36	3.37
Hs 124 A-0 0-Serie (5 St.) 2 x Jumo 10	Henschel	6.34	7.34			3.37

Zerstörer types (see table 1 opposite page).

1/36 (Mtt)
At the *Aerodynamische Versuchsanstalt* (AVA, or Aerodynamic Test Facility) at Göttingen, a model of the Bf 110 is examined which, in actuality, is nothing more than a Bf 109 with engines mounted on the wings. These authors speculate that this configuration was done in order to be able to carry out performance estimates with regard to the additional drag imposed by the engine nacelles. It appears highly improbable that this was a preliminary design for the Bf 110, since the proportions between the nacelles and fuselage were not equidistant. Furthermore, the Bf 110 mockup had been completed almost a year earlier, and the first test flight of the type was imminent.

5/12/36 (Mtt)
With Dr. Hermann Wurster at the controls, the Bf 110 V1 takes off from Augsburg on its maiden flight. It is assigned serial number 868 and is later registered as D-AHOA.

The armament question was proving so difficult for the companies that none of the first prototypes were fitted with the final weapons configuration. All were unarmed, and the planned weapons layout had only been rendered in mockup form. The roundish nose of the Bf 110 V1 leads one to conclude that the weapons configuration was initially conceived differently than actually implemented on production types.

6/36 (Focke-Wulf and Henschel)
The FW 57 V1 and Hs 124 V1 also take to the air for the first time.

6/4/36 (RLM)
Göring decides to replace *General* Wimmer, Chief of the Technical Office, with *Oberst* Udet.

The next few years reveal that Udet was the wrong man for the job. With regard to the development of aircraft, engines, etc., he made a series of poorly judged decisions which ultimately proved fatal for the Luftwaffe. Udet was known as a friend of Messerschmitt and supported him. But he did not, as claimed by Heumann, allow the Bf 110 into the competition after the fact. There is also little basis for the belief that his influence was responsible for the decision in favor of the Bf 110. The decision had already been made by the time he assumed office, and the concept upon which the Hs 124 and FW 57 were based had lost considerable support by then.

Top.
The FW 57 began flight testing in June of 1936. (Handbuch der Luftfahrt, *Focke Wulf*)

Above:
The Hs 124 V1 also flew in June of 1936. (Flugsport, *Henschel*)

Left:
The maiden flight of the Bf 110 took place on 12 May 1936. (Radinger)

10/24/36 (Mtt)
The Bf 110 V2 (W.Nr. 869, D-AQYE) flies for the first time from Augsburg.

11/1/36 (GL)
Procurement plan No. 4 calls for the following deliveries between 10/36 and 3/38:

Bf 110: B.F.W.: 74, beginning from 4/37, and continuing from 3/38 at a rate of 10 per month
GWF: 30, beginning from 11/37, continuing from 3/38 at a rate of 10 per month
Bf 161: B.F.W. 19, beginning from 9/37
Bf 162: B.F.W. 27, beginning from 6/37
FW 57: FW 13, from 6/37 through 12/37
Hs 124: Hs 13, from 7/37 through 1/38

The delivery numbers for BFW are broken down into a group of 12 aircraft, to be supplied from 4/37 through 10/37, and a second group of 62 aircraft with deliveries beginning in 7/37. The authors believe that the first group was composed of Bf 110 Bs and that, according to this plan, only Bf 110 Cs would be supplied from 8/37 onward.

In this procurement plan the quantity of aircraft on order effectively burst its banks. For example, in addition to the high number of standard types like the He 111 and Bf 109, etc., the plan included 7 Ago 192, 7 Ar 81, 15 Ar 95, 7 Ar 197, 19 Bf 161, 27 Bf 162, 10 Bf 163, 10 Fi 157, 7 Fi 158, 6 Fi 167, 7 FH 104, 10 FH 201, 13 FW 57, 18 FW 159, 10 FW 186, 11 FW 187, 7 FW 259, 7 Go 146, 10 Go 149, 55 He 245, 15 He 112, 5 He 116, 12 He 118, 7 He 119, 13 Hs 124, 17 Hs 127, and 3 Kl 26 aircraft types. One gets the impression that the Generalluftzeugmeister hoped to avoid offending any of the companies and wanted to buy a couple of every aircraft in development.

12/16/36 (RLM)
The RLM decides to cancel the majority of the above-named developmental projects, including the Bf 161, Bf 162, FW 57, and Hs 124.

Late 1936 (RLM)
The tactical/technical requirements are drawn up anew. This results in a successor to the Bf 110 being conceived. Thus it is clear that, contrary to the claims of several authors, the resulting Me 210 was in no way spawned from the poor experience (many even state its combat experience) with the Bf 110.

12/24/36 (Mtt)
Dr. Hermann Wurster flies the DB 600 powered Bf 110 V3 (*W.Nr.* 870, D-ATII).

1/11/37 (GL)
Presentation on an increased acquisition program, which now calls for a total of 184 Bf 110s instead of the original 104, to be delivered by 4/1/38.

On its first flight the Bf 110 V3 already exhibited the DB 600 engine and the box-like radiators. (Lange, Messerschmitt)

1/20/37 (GL)
During a meeting on development at the LC II; department chairman *Major* Junck decides that the Ar 96, Do 19, Fl 184, Fi 157, FW 57, 186 and 61, Hs 124 and 127, He 119, Ju 89, EF 61, and Bf 163 types, if not already classed as such, are in the future to be designated as SV types (design studies).

3/21/37 (GL)
Procurement Plan No. 5 envisions the delivery of 160 Bf 110 *Zerstörer* types from 2/38 through 8/38, and continuing at a rate of 30 per month. The Bf 161, Bf 162, FW 57, and Hs 124 are dropped.

7/1/37 (GL)
Procurement Plan No. 6 calls for the delivery of a total of 53 Bf 110s with Jumo 210 engines, beginning from 1/38 and continuing through 6/38. 489 Bf 110s with the DB 601 powerplant are to be delivered between

4/38 and 3/39, continuing at a rate of 60 per month thereafter. The Bf 110 *Zerstörer*/destroyer classification is now dropped in favor of the term "heavy fighter."

1/1/38 (GL)
Procurement Plan No. 7 calls for a total of 86 Bf 110 Bs with Jumo 210, beginning in 4/38 and continuing through 2/39. The Bf 110 C with DB 601 engine is to be built in a quantity of 190 from 10/38 through 2/39. This delivery plan is the first to include the Bf 109 C with fuel injected Jumo 210 G engine.

4/19/38
Dr. Hermann Wurster's flight log makes reference to the Bf 110 B V7 with factory registration number of 917 and the Bf 110 B-01 (918).

7/11/38
The Bayerische Flugzeugwerke is renamed the Messerschmitt AG. From this point on the company's new developments are designated with the abbreviation Me; in official documents the old developments remain Bf, although the Me 109 and Me 110 are often openly referred to in speaking and writing.

8/15/38 (GL)
Procurement Plan No. 8 calls for a total of 82 Bf 110 Bs with Jumo 210 G from 4/38 through 4/39. This is the first delivery plan identifying the Jumo 210 G fuel injection engine in conjunction with the Bf 110, and this even for those aircraft already delivered. From 1/39 through 3/40, plans call for a total of 990 Bf 110 Cs with the DB 601 powerplant, continuing at a rate of 100 per month.

9/20/38
(Letter from Göring to Udet and Milch)
Göring writes: "The heavy fighter is to be developed so that its range is able to cover England."

This may have been the reason for the development of the D-series.

11/7/38 (*Luftwaffe* General Staff)
The General Staff approves an armament plan effective from the autumn of 1938 through the spring of 1942. This plan calls for: 40

In addition to the three V prototypes, during the summer of 1938 there were only seven of the early null series of the Bf 110 A, all of which were unarmed. (Heumann, Messerschmitt)

bomber wings; 10 maritime bomber wings; 16 *Zerstörer* wings; 12 *Stuka* wings; 10 tactical reconnaissance groups; 23 strategic reconnaissance squadrons; 36 ship- and carrier-borne squadrons; 1 strike wing; 4 transport wings; and 16 fighter wings. The 16 *Zerstörer* wings are to comprise Bf 110 and Me 210 aircraft, to include a minimum of 7-8 wings of Me 210s.

This plan was never implemented, since it could not be realized by the prevailing industrial and raw materials conditions. It does show, however, that the Luftwaffe's leadership viewed the Luftwaffe as an offensive instrument. Defense would occur when the bombers destroyed the enemy's means for launching an attack on the ground. In the leadership's view, any remaining forces which could attack from the air would be dealt with by relatively weak fighter units on the border or by anti-aircraft or fighters at the site being protected. Accordingly, this plan contains a comparatively low number of fighters. The Zerstörers *would accompany the bombers and count as an offensive weapon. It was not until air superiority had been lost for a good while that efforts were made to take the defense of the Reich seriously.*

12/13/38 (GL)
The *C Amt's* program contains 3200 *Zerstörer* by 4/12 (this is about 300 shy of the requirement, taking into account the industry's switch from the Bf 110 to the Me 210)

At this point in time a wing consisted of three groups, with three squadrons each. The squadron had 12 aircraft, meaning that 16 *Zerstörer* wings contained 1728 aircraft (not counting reserves). It is not clear to the authors in what context the above-named figure—virtually double the amount expected—is made in reference to the wing strength and number.

12/31/38 (GL)
According to Procurement Plan No. 10 a total of 37 Bf 110 A/Bs have been delivered, including four produced by Gotha. By June of 1939 another 58 Bf 110 Bs are to be produced by Gotha. The delivery plan also shows that Messerschmitt was to begin production of the Bf 110 C in February 1939, with Miag and Gotha following in April 1939 and Focke-Wulf in May 1939. By April 1940 Messerschmitt's monthly output is to be 20, Gotha and Miag's 16, and Focke-Wulf's 10 per month. It is planned that 1222 Bf 110 Cs are to be produced by the time production ends in March 1941.

4/1/39 (GL)
According to Procurement Plan No. 11, 47 Bf 110 Bs and 8 Bf 110 Cs have been delivered. By the expiration of the plan on 4/1/42, a further 48 Bf 110 Bs and 1324 Bf 110 Cs are to be produced. The planned total is therefore 95 Bf 110 Bs (including 7 Bf 110 As) and 1332 Bf 110 Cs.

5/39 (RLM)
A draft description of the fixed and traversible armament (L.Dv.578/1) outlines the fitting of four MG 17s, two MG FFs, and 1 MG 15 for the Bf 110 B, C, and D-0 series.

7/3/39 (Rechlin)
A Bf 110 with a 3 cm MK 101 cannon is shown to Hitler at Rechlin. The machine is a Bf 110 B-1 with factory serial number 928 and registration code D-AAPY. Hitler is impressed with the cannon and says, "I believe this is an extraordinarily important weapon, because I don't think we could ever have enough heavy weapons."

7/7/39
The Bf 110 B-1 is withdrawn from combat units in the summer of 1939 and transferred to flight training schools. Chief of Training reports the acquisition of Bf 110 B-1s on 7 July.

Those Luftwaffe *aircraft not previously given military registrations were assigned such in 1939, such as this trainer with the code "WL". (Petrick)*

7/20/39 (GL)
Göring orders: "manufacture of the 3 cm airplane cannon is to be accelerated at all costs."

8/15/39 (Rechlin Test Center)
The *E-Stelle* states in an engine test report for the Bf 110 C: "The powerplant of the Bf 110 C in no way meets the conditions expected of a modern engine system. One problem in development was the circumstance in which an aircraft designed to accommodate two 20 liter engines then had to be fitted with two 30 liter engines without any modification to the airframe. The system can be considered suitable for operations once the deficiencies outlined on the page opposite have been rectified."

8/27/39 (Henschel)
Henschel publishes specification No. 33, which offers the Hs 124 as a multi-role aircraft (bomber, strike fighter, and long-range reconnaissance aircraft) based on the Hs 124 V2 with BMW 132 Dc engines. The selection of weapons and equipment on offer indicate that this aircraft would be offered to foreign nations.

8/31/39 (*Chef Genst. Lw Gen Qu. 6. Abt.)*
The *Luftwaffe* has 27 Bf 110 Bs and 68 Bf 110 Cs in its front line inventory. Of these, 23 Bf 110 Bs and 59 Bf 110 Cs are operationally ready. The *Zerstörer* wings are stocked with 36 Bf 109 Cs and 277 Bf 109 Ds.

9/39
The Bf 110 C-1 is used in Poland, serving with *Geschwader* I.(Z)/LG 1, I./ZG 1, and I./ZG 76. Due to the limited opposition in the air, they seldom are called upon to fulfill their roles as bomber escort and as *Zerstörer* against enemy bombing raids. The aircraft are therefore also employed in the ground support role. Some kills are made, but some aircraft are lost as well. The Bf 110's expected inferiority in dogfighting single-engined fighters is confirmed for the first time.

10/25/39 (GL)
The aircraft acquisition program now calls for a total of 1850 Bf 110 Cs.

11/26/39
(Jagdgeschwader 2, "Richthofen")
A report is made on evaluating the Bf 110 in the night fighting role. Aside from a few minor shortcomings, the Bf 110 appears to be a type well suited for night fighting. The main sticking point is the type's lack of instrument flying capability.

At this time production shifts from the Bf 110 C-1 to the C-2.

12/18/39
The Bf 110 proves effective in countering a British bombing raid over the North Sea. I./ZG 76 shoots down 9 out of 22 attacking Wellington bombers.

This Hs 124 met the specifications for the multi-role design proposed in August of 1939. (Deutsches Museum, Munich)

4/40
During the operations against Denmark and Norway, *Zerstörer* crews (from I./ZG 1 and I./ZG 76) score kills while acting in their intended role. The aircraft are mainly employed against ground targets. Nevertheless, here too *Zerstörer* are lost in combat against antiquated single-seat fighters. The *Luftwaffe* loses 25 Bf 110s in Norway, although not all of these are in air-to-air combat.

The first Bf 110 D-0/B, with a belly tank capable of being swapped out for two ETC 500 racks, is completed at Messerschmitt and delivered to the Rechlin Test Center.

5/10/40 through 6/25/40
ZG 1 and ZG 26 see action in the attacks on Holland and Belgium. Losses are low. After the capitulation of the Dutch armed forces, these two units reinforce LG 1 and ZG 76 during the French campaign. In combat against modern enemy fighters the type suffers heavy losses for the first time. Particularly over Dunkirk, where several *Zerstörer* are lost in combat with Spitfires. From a total of 355 Bf 110s available, the *Luftwaffe* employs 248 in this campaign. 57 Bf 110s are lost.

5/17/40 (GL)
The increased amount of aluminum now coming from Norway is to be used in part for a rise in production. *Genst.6.Abt.* proposes the following prioritization: 1. Ju 52, 2. Bf 110, 3. Bf 109. The ratio of increased deliveries of the Bf 109 and Bf 110 is projected at 1:2 in favor of the latter.

5/24/40 (GL)
GL announces that 1000 601 N engines will be built by 1/1/41. In addition to installation in the Bf 109 F-1 and F-2, the GL also explores the possibility of installing the type in the Bf 110. Deadlines are announced.

Prioritization of Repair Aircraft for June
LC 2/V proposes three levels of priority for carrying out repair works:

1) Aircraft that require a total concentration of prioritization resources (Bf 110 C/D and others)
2) Aircraft that can be rebuilt during the normal course of production (Bf 110 B and others)
3) Aircraft to be repaired only when the re sources are not required elsewhere.

5/31/40 (GL)
With 1000 601 N engines anticipated by 1 January 1941 (of which approximately 350 are to be put in reserve), only the Bf 109 F-1 and F-2 series can be fitted with the powerplant in accordance with Procurement Plan No. 17. Later production of the 601 N for the Bf 110 will be explored at a subsequent time. The General Staff asks for a report on the state of armor for the Bf 109 and Bf 110.

6/7/40 (GL)
In the new program, the Bf 109 and Bf 110 are to be powered by the 601 N engine. 100 metal 300 l fuel tanks are fitted to the Bf 110 D-0 for I./ZG 26.

6/14/40 (GL)
Bf 110 program change. Ratio of Bf 110 C deliveries to Bf 110 D deliveries is dropped from 3/5 to 2/5. This change presupposes that fuel tank pumps will become easier to acquire in the future.

6/20/40 (Rechlin)
The test center publishes a range table for the Bf 110 D-1. This has neither a fuselage tank nor bomb racks.

6/25/40 (GL)
The General Staff orders the acquisition of the D version of the Bf 110, three out of five with bomb racks and two out of five with the *Dackelbauch* fuel tank. *LC 21* asks that the General Staff research the possibility of dropping the *Dackelbauch* requirement altogether, instead fitting all Bf 110s with two external tanks beneath the outer wing panels. The General Staff can reach a decision only after 4-6 more weeks of front-line studies.

This involves ten Bf 110 groups (400 aircraft), of which 200 aircraft (Bf 110 D-0) fly 10 sorties per month. This equates to a maximum monthly consumption of 4000

The Bf 110 D-0 had removable fuel tanks and covers. (Petrick)

tanks (the Bf 110 has two outer wing tanks). A three-month reserve (= 12000 tanks) is adequate. More reserve supply is not necessary, for if the need arises due to heavy operations the industry can begin producing 4000 tanks per month. Bf 110 and Ju 88 tanks are identical, and the total reserve stockpile is set at 20000 for the time being.

The General Staff rejects the idea of retrofitting those Bf 110 aircraft already serving with front-line units. The production lines should immediately switch to the bomber configuration, and the acquisition of equipment should be directed so that all aircraft in front-line service capable of dropping bombs (3/5 of total procurement, 2/5 *Dackelbauch* without bombing systems) are operational. This is ten groups, or 400 aircraft, which must constantly be available with two ETC 500 racks. The procurement of equipment for these 400 aircraft is to be directed toward the production of the currently running Bf 110 series, including those aircraft coming off of repair status and, additionally, availability of parts for these 400 systems is to be guaranteed.

6/40

The Messerschmitt company delivers the first 13 production Bf 110 D-0/B aircraft with ETC 500 racks. The first and second squadrons of *Erprobungsgruppe 210* are given this bomber version of the Bf 110 for the purpose of developing fighter-bomber tactics. The group's third squadron receives at the same time the Bf 109 E fighter-bomber version. Over the coming weeks the group makes successful attacks on shipping in the English Channel. ZG 1 receives two Bf 110 C-6s fitted with the MK 101 for evaluation, focusing on low-level strikes.

Allowing for normal design work and manufacturing preparations, it must have been in mid-1939 or earlier (roughly corresponding to the introduction of the C variant) that production of the ETC version was approved. This is borne out by the fact that the first Bf 110 with ETC racks was finished as early as April 1940, and that the first production Bf 110s were fitted with these by June; and from July onward virtually all manufacturers had switched over to building the Bf 110 with ETC racks. The use of the Bf 110 as a high-speed bomber or dive bomber was therefore not, as claimed by many publications, a reaction to the experiences in the Battle of Britain. More likely, it was the same planning which stressed the Me 210 as a Stukazerstörer *that also led to the newly defined role for the Bf 110. As early as 1938, it was abundantly clear to the majority of leaders within the* Luftwaffe *and the* RLM *that the Bf 110 heavy fighter was unable to hold its own against lighter interceptors. Its main role was to engage the enemy's air force and other targets on the ground. For this purpose, heavy rear-firing defensive armament was considered essential, something the Bf 110 lacked. Thus the contract for a new development known as the Me 210, at a time when the Bf 110 C had not yet rolled off the production line. However, the ETC configured variant was ordered to cover the mission spectrum until the arrival of the Me 210. The Bf 110's use as an escort fighter flew in the face of conventional wisdom and is evidence of the ruthlessness of the Nazis (read: Göring), even against their own people.*

7/1/40 (GL)

The *C-Amt's* program from 7/1/40 calls for Bf 110 B-0s with factory serial numbers of 918 and 941 to serve as testbed prototypes for the installation of the *Gerät 3302*. The date of the first flight is to be determined by the delivery date of the *Gerät 3302*. (The *Gerät 3302* was the BMW P 3302 jet engine with a rating of 600 kp/6000 kN thrust.)

1./Erprobungsgruppe 210 *received its first Bf 110 C-6 in the summer of 1940. (Mankau)*

Bf 110 C-1 (*W.Nr.* 3080) is in the process of being converted as the prototype for the Bf 110 E and is expected to be cleared for its first flight in August. At the same time, a Bf 110 C (*W.Nr.* 2143) is serving as the prototype for the installation of the DB 601 N and should also be ready to fly by August.

648 *Zerstörer* and 21 reconnaissance sub-variants of the Bf 110 C have been produced. By production's end in October 1940 an additional 94 *Zerstörer* will also be built. Of the Bf 110 D, 103 have been produced and a further 160 are to follow. End of production is also October 1940. The Bf 110 E-1 has not yet entered production, and by the planned end of its production in August 1941 it is expected that 795 are to be built. An additional 270 C- and E-series reconnaissance platforms are planned for delivery up to August 1941.

7/9/40
III./ZG 26 loses the first Bf 110 over England. Over the coming two months it becomes apparent that the Bf 110 is ill-suited as a long-range fighter. In combat with Hurricanes and Spitfires its maneuverability is inadequate, so that on the one hand the *Zerstörer* pilots are unable to get into a firing position, and on the other they are unable to shake off an attack from the rear. The *Zerstörers* need their own fighter protection.

This I./ZG 52 Bf 110 C-2 (or C-4) shows off the camouflage pattern introduced in mid- 1940 along with the new position of the aft machine gun. The cover over the gun trough has been left unpainted. (Mankau)

7/12/40 (GL)
The 900 liter tanks for the Ju 88 and Bf 110 are the same, except for the support braces that only the Bf 110 utilizes. In order to provide the option of using the tank on either aircraft type, a stockpile of 13000 to 15000 pieces is to be delivered with the support braces included in the packing.

The 100 Bf 110 300 liter outer tanks for I./ZG 76 have not yet been delivered. As of yet, only the *Ob.d.L. Fritzlar* reconnaissance group has been supplied with 18 tanks.

The *Generalluftzeugmeister* has decided that the 601 N engines on hand are to be installed exclusively in the Bf 110. This means that installation in the Bf 109 is to be dropped mid-production. A decision has not been made as to whether the engine will be fitted in the Bf 109 at a later date.

7/19/40 (GL)
The 601 N engines in stock are to be used for converting those Bf 110s currently in front-line service. This action halts any further conversion of the Bf 109 E groups (one group converted so far). The Bf 109 F series retains the 601 N powerplant. The next new series Bf 110 will retain the DB 601 A as originally planned.

At this time the Bf 110 D-0 aircraft are being delivered either with *Dackelbauch*, or bomb hardpoints. As these aircraft must be employed at different sites, the General Staff requests that these aircraft be given separate designations as soon as possible. It is important that designations be selected which cannot be garbled in telex messages.

7/20/40 (Mtt)
During trials with two 1000 kg bombs at Rechlin, a Bf 110 D-0's tires are completely worn after seven takeoffs. Tests using a standard D-0 show that only approx. 2 mm of tread is worn after 7 takeoffs. This problem has only cropped up with the D-0 series, which has a takeoff weight approximately 1000 kg greater than its predecessors. The C-series also has this problem in field units when flown with a heavy load. It is believed that the cause is the angle of the landing gear struts, which is too forward. As an interim solution, the angle is to be set at 0% in relation to the wheels. The effect on taxi stability is expected to be minimal.

7/26/40 (GL)
For the time being, the General Staff refuses any further refitting of Bf 110 aircraft with the 601 N engines, other than those *Zerstörer* groups currently undergoing the conversion. A decision as to whether refitting can occur at a later date is not expected before the end of August.

The following designations are established in order to differentiate between those Bf 110s with and without *Dackelbauch* and with and without bombs:

D-0 2 external tanks, 1 *Dackelbauch*
D-2 2 external tanks, either bombs or *Dackelbauch*, only produced by Mtt Augsburg
D-3 2 external tanks, only fitted for bombs; produced by Focke-Wulf, Miag, Gotha

8/9/40 (GL)
LC 3 is to allocate 70 engines for a monthly production of 30 replacement Bf 110s and 10 Bf 109s. This is in conjunction with the mandated refitting of a total of three Bf 110 groups and the one Bf 109 group already re-engined. In addition, a rotating stock of 30 engines is to be held in reserve, equating to 10% of the 280 engines currently installed in operational aircraft. LE is requested to provide an opinion on whether the number of DB 601 N engines in reserve should be increased over the coming months.

LC 2 states it has come to its attention that the field units are fitting a single centerline external tank to Bf 110s in place of the two outer wing tanks. This is of concern for two reasons; firstly, that it is an entirely new methodology, and secondly, that this prevents the ability to carry bombs. Neither the General Staff nor LC 2 believe this is a good thing.

8/10/40
The *Luftwaffe* reports a *Zerstörer* strength of 444 aircraft.

8/15 to 8/19/40
On 15 August the *Luftwaffe* loses 26 *Zerstörer* planes over England, 8 more on 16 August and 14 on 18 August. Among the losses suffered on 16 August is a Bf 110 C-6 (S9+TH). Although this makes it obvious that the Bf 110 is unable to fulfill its role as a heavy fighter, in an operations conference on 19 August Göring nevertheless orders its continued use as such, but with fighter escort.

The centerline 900-liter tank was a field modification. (Petrick)

The experiences over England accelerated the employment of the Bf 110 as a bomber, to be sure, but this switching of roles had begun in June, i.e. before the first Bf 110 loss over England. During the Battle of Brit-

ain, E.Gr. 210 operated the Bf 110 bomber either singly or in small formations, increasing their success by putting the element of surprise and terrain following tactics to good use.

8/20/40 (GL)
The General Staff calls for the Ju 52, Ju 88, He 111, Bf 110, Fi 156 and BV 138 to be fitted for operations in tropical conditions.

8/30/40 (GL)
LC 3 is asked to provide 45 DB 601 N engines in reserve for the month of September, 35 in October, and then a constant 30 until a total of 180 reserve engines are on hand (to supplement 280 'active' engines). This will meet the requirement issued by L E "601 N Resupply Situation," in accordance with the position paper LE 2 Az 90 c (A II D) dated 8/19/40.

9/1/40 (GL)
According to the *C-Amt* program, Bf 110 V5 has been assigned to Arado to be fitted as a testbed for an Arado gunsight mockup. The actual prototype sight is to be fitted in Bf 110 (*W.Nr.* 2106). Bf 110 V8 (*W.Nr.* 913) with Jumo 210 G engines is to be built by Messerschmitt for the installation of *Gerät* 3302 by 11/50. *W.Nr.* 918 and 941 (Bf110 B-0s) are also to be modified to accept the *Gerät* 3302. The DB 601 N and jettisonable wing tips are now fitted to the Bf 110 C (*W.Nr.* 2143). Bf 110 C-1 (*W.Nr.* 3387) is at Rechlin for testing the ETC 1000 and bombsight.

9/6/40 (GL)
Bf 110 bomber load configuration: Both LC 2 and the General Staff have rejected refitting those aircraft assigned to field units for the time being. The modification will shortly be introduced on the production line.

9/13/40 (GL)
Installation of a contact altimeter in 8 Bf 110s within the night fighter division is currently underway. Request a completion date. The General Staff requests that the contact altimeter procurement situation be explored in anticipation of an upcoming requirement that Bf 110 bombers also be fitted with the instrument.

Production of the Bf 110 E 1 continues based on previous agreements at a ration of 2/5 to 3/5 with and without *Dackelbauch*, respectively. Some of the Bf 110s supplied with *Dackelbauch* have had the tanks removed by field units. The question is put forth whether this ratio should be maintained in production.

Currently, a further six Bf 110 aircraft have been armed with the MK 101. Additional crew training for these six planes is not required. The aircraft are being operated from the same site where previous deliveries have been made.

A total of 75 MK 101 mounts for the Bf 110 have been contracted for. The contract for the MK 101 gun itself totals 220.

In addition to the cannons already fitted into the Bf 110, trial installations are also being made in the He 115 and Do 217. As no orders have been given with regard to further installation in the Bf 110, a decision is requested as to whether acquisition of the MK 101 and its mounts can be reduced.

9/14/40 (Ob.d.L.)
According to a strength report, the *Luftwaffe* has the following Bf 110s (nominal strength, serviceable in parentheses):

Zerstörer/fighter bombers:
Bf 110 C: 151 (85)
Bf 110 D: 103 (71)
Night fighters:
Bf 110 C and D: 41 (22)
Tactical reconnaissance:
Bf 110 C-5: 5 (-)
Strategic reconnaissance:
Bf 110 C-5: 32 (17)

This Bf 110 C-5 (5F+MM) of 4./(F)/14 *was based in Normandy during the autumn of 1940. (Ries)*

9/17/40 (GL)
(Notes for the meeting with the *Reichsfeldmarschall*) Trial fitting of two Hispano Suiza 404 cannons in the Bf 110.

9/27/40 (GL)
Chief of the General Staff has decided to outfit and perpetually maintain four Bf 110 *Zerstörer* groups with the 601 N. The resupply quantities required by these *Zerstörer* groups equals the production of the Messerschmitt Company, Augsburg. Of the remaining 601 N engines currently on hand, 40 are to be set aside as rotating inventory for the Bf 110 *Zerstörer* groups. The remaining 601 N engines are to be distributed as follows: 1/3 for rotating stock and 2/3 for fitting into Bf 109 airframes.

The General Staff wants to continue with the Bf 110 E-1 at a ration of 2/5 to 3/5 with and without *Dackelbauch*. Until further notice, the General Staff orders the continued production tempo for the Bf 110 C-6 with MK 101 at a rate of 10 per month. Feedback desired. The General Staff requests establishment of the variant designations for the Bf 110 E.

10/9/40 (GL)
Eight Bf 110s have now been fitted with the contact altimeter. No reports are yet available. Nevertheless, it is planned to install the contact altimeter along with the new instrument panel on production aircraft starting no later than November 1.

Although no accurate field reports are available regarding the use of the MK 101

Aeroplane *magazine released this photo showing the cockpit of a captured Bf 110 on 11 October 1940.*

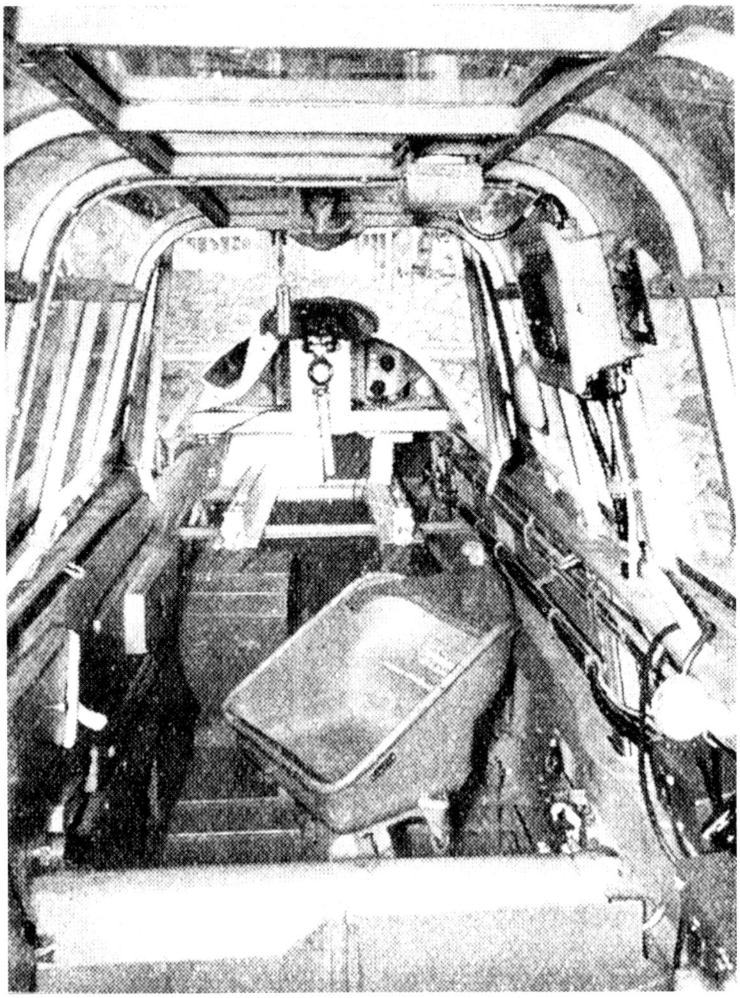

This is another photo published by Aeroplane *on 11 October 1940, with another view of the Bf 110[s interior.*

armed Bf 110, the General Staff wishes production to continue. It is possible to fit a further six aircraft with the cannon in the immediate future. LC 6 is asked to provide evaluation reports.

10/18/40 (GL)
Other than the existing group, it is not possible to refit any more Bf 109 E aircraft with the 601 N at the present time. As is now reported, deliveries of the necessary engine conversion parts is not expected before 12/1/40. The current production run of 601 N engines is allocated for:

1.) installation in all newly built Bf 109 F-1, -2
2.) installation in all newly built Bf 110 (Mtt AG is to maintain stock levels for the existing four groups)
3.) installation in 40 replacement Bf 109 Es (these are conversions) to maintain the existing Bf 109 E group strength
4.) rotating reserve supplies of engines in 1.) through 3.) above

The General Staff asks that production of the Bf 110 with MK 101 continues at the proposed rate of six per month.

10/26/40 (GL)
The General Staff requests preparations for tropical use be expanded for the following types: Ju 52 - 180 aircraft (instead of 100), Do 17 P - 30 aircraft (instead of 12), He 111 H-5 - 12 aircraft (instead of 12 He 115), and Bf 110 - 80 (addition)

By the end of October, 1100-1200 601 N engines will have been delivered. These have been installed in the four converted Bf 110 groups and the one Bf 109 group, plus in the replacement aircraft for these five groups, as well as in various aircraft belonging to the *Aufklärungsgruppe der Ob.d.L.* Approximately 130 engines have been supplied to LE as rotating reserves. The remainder of the engines are being utilized for installation in the Bf 109 F 1 and F 2, with a lead time of 5-6 weeks, and for the Messerschmitt-produced Bf 110, with a lead time of 7-8 weeks.

Continued production of the Bf 110 with MK 101 cannot be carried out.

The General Staff states that an inventory of 120 Bf 110 night fighters is to be maintained constantly. This means that the entire production, with the exception of the Messerschmitt (601 N) *Zerstörer* output, is to be used in the night fighter role.

11/1/40 (GL)
According to the C-Amt's program, Bf 110 B-0 (*W.Nr.* 918) has been cleared for the Junkers Company and *W.Nr.* 941 for the Rechlin Test Center.

According to the program, the following numbers of Bf 110 C and D aircraft have been delivered: 195 C-1, 358 C-2, 1 C-2/B, no C-3, 155 C-4, 12 C-6, 39 C-7, 83 D-0, 21 D-1, 72 D-2, 124 D-3, and 6 D-4. A further 64 D-3 variants are to be built by January 1941. 66 Bf 110 E-1s have been built, and a further 254 are to be completed by July 1941.

Of the 475 Bf 110 E-2s projected for completion by November 1941, 11 have been built.

11/6/40 (GL)
Projected deliveries for November, December: Bf 110s including reconnaissance versions: Nov: 115; Dec: 100.

The General Staff reemphasized its position requiring six Bf 110s with the MK 101 per month. At the present time, production has not yet been initiated.

The General Staff requests that the 601 N engine series be primarily fitted in the Bf 109 E. In order to free up sufficient quantities of the engine, the General Staff has agreed to have two months' worth (November and December) of Bf 110s (Mtt) be equipped with the 601 A instead of the 601 N, as long as this will guarantee that the Bf 109 aircraft can then be powered by the 601 N. The N-engines must be allocated to the following: 1) Bf 109 E production, and 2) replacement engines for III./ZG 26 and *Erprobungsgruppe 210*. If insufficient quantities of the engine are available, then the following groups are not required to be equipped with the engine or can have their N-engines swapped out for A-engines: II./ZG 26 and II./ZG 76. Since 601 N production is expected to pick up significantly beginning in January, the Bf 110 will be switched over to the N at that time. Conversion will end around April. Deadlines will be established in the new program.

11/21/40 (GL)
Russia requests delivery of a Bf 110 complete with armor, bulletproof glazing, variable pitch propellers, and rubber dinghy. Request views on the matter.

The General Staff effectively dispenses with the idea of installing further MK 101s in the Bf 110.

12/1/40 (GL)
According to the *C-Amt's* program, Bf 110 E-1 (*W.Nr.* 3445) with MK 404 is undergoing trials at Tarnewitz. Bf 110 E-1 (*W.Nr.* 3480) is at Messerschmitt and is to serve as the prototype for production aircraft fitted with the MK 404 once the results of the tests are made available.

1/10/41 (GL)
The General Staff concurs with the idea of rearming new aircraft for use in the night fighting role at Werl, instead of having suppliers produce this variant directly.

1/22/41 (GL)
Neither the ETC 50 hardpoint of the Bf 109 nor the SBO rack can be fitted to the Bf 110 for carrying 50 kg bombs. Therefore, 100 racks (specially designed for the Bf 110) for carrying 50 kg bombs are to be acquired. A minimum of four practice bombs is to be carried by a Bf 110 (either C or D). Request deadline.

LC 2 announces that both the Bf 110 C/D as well as the He 110 H-4/H-5 are suitable for *Warschau* (Me 321). A decision by the General Staff on the number of each type is urgently needed. LC 2 announces delivery deadlines for resupply.

A message on the C 3 fuel situation has been sent by the senior engineer that proposes to reinstall 601 A engines in the Bf 110 again. The General Staff expresses its view with regard to the number of engines in operation as follows: On 1/1/41 front line units responded with the following operational engine counts:

Bf 109 E-1 – 16; Bf 109 E-3 – 1; Bf 109 E-4 – 59; Bf 109 E-6 – 1; Bf 109 E-7 – 34; Bf 109 E-8 – 2; Bf 109 F-1 – 5; Bf 110 C-1 – 4; Bf 110 C-4 – 40; Bf 110 C-5 – 12; Bf 110 C-7 – 14; Bf 110 D-0 – 18; Bf 110 D-2 – 20; Bf 110 D-3 – 8; Bf 110 E-1 – 176; Bf 110 E-2 – 14; He 111 P – 8; Do 215 – 68

Plans call for the following distribution of DB 601 N engines among units by 4/1/41: 6 groups of Bf 110s = 480; 5 groups of Bf 109 E-7 Ns = 200; 12 groups of Bf 109 Fs = 480; and Rowehl = 70, for a total of 1230. It is expected that 70% of these aircraft/engines will be operational. Meaning that on 4/1/41 there are approximately 850 DB 601 N engines in active operations that will need fuel allocated.

1/30/41
III./ZG 26 arrives in Africa with its Bf 110s

1/30/41 (GL)
With minor changes, the *Rost 24 SD 2* bomb rack can be fitted to the Bf 110 E.

With regard to the Bf 110 C and D carrying 50 kg bombs, LC 2 states that with industrial capacity currently stretched to its limits, it would be extremely difficult to meet this requirement and asks that it be dropped. This equipment would not be available for delivery any sooner than the end of the year.

Warschau (Me 321): LC 2 will immediately provide the General Staff with delivery dates for the refitted aircraft. Once the deadline schedule is received, the General Staff will establish the number of Bf 110 and He 111 aircraft planned for this purpose. The next new production Bf 110 E aircraft are to be delivered to *XI Korps* for testing. LC 2 provides the factory serial numbers. The aircraft are to be special-purpose built. GL proposes that, for security reasons, a test site be made available well away from the front (e.g. Faßberg). Needed are two large hangars and associated personnel, plus a starter cart.

The General Staff requests information on the modified production of 601 N and A engines resulting from the new situation with the C 3 fuel. Also requested is information regarding the changes in the delivery plans for production of the Bf 110 fitted with 601 N and 601 A engines.

2/6/41 (GL)
Regarding carrying 50 kg bombs with the Bf 110 C and D: the General Staff again stresses that the reasons are critical enough to keep the requirement in place. Again requests position, particularly in regard to the deadline situation.

Warschau: In addition to the six Bf 110s for *XI Korps*, a further six He 111 H-5 aircraft are to be immediately pulled from production for this purpose. The chief of the General Staff cannot make a decision on the intended units or specific aircraft types until the test report from *XI Korps*. GL will contact *XI Korps* directly on the matter of selecting the airfield to be used for the tests.

C 3 fuel situation: Aircraft manufacturers have begun converting Bf 110s from the N to the A engines. Precise production figures can be found in Program 19, which will be published this week.

2/13/41 (GL)
Documentation for the GM 1/Bf 110 operations has been prepared and will be submitted to the managing chief engineer of GL.

2/20/41 (GL)
It is planned that the Bf 110 C-7, D-2, and D-3 series will be capable of carrying the 50 kg cement bombs (four per aircraft). 100 sets of bomb racks will be obtained for training purposes. Deadlines are as follows: 20 racks by 15 March, and the remaining 80 by 30 April.

3/14/1941 (GL)
Bf 110 GM 1 system: Viewpoint of the GL's managing chief engineer is requested. The General Staff orders increased production of the Bf 109 at the expense of *Zerstörer* production. In light of this increased demand, it is requested that the Bf 110's program be changed (more reconnaissance types instead of heavy fighters).

3/20/1941 (GL)
For the upcoming program, the GL anticipates an increase in fighters at the expense of *Zerstörer* types.

3/27/1941 (GL)
GM 1 system: Experiments are underway for all relevant front-line types. Status of these experiments is forthcoming. Final status depends on the matter of the tank (protection against damage from enemy fire). Bf 110: with 30 minutes' performance at 6000 m, the system provides a speed of 620 km/h and a maximum altitude of 12.5 km.

4/10/41 (GL)
The General Staff requests position on complaints by the front line units regarding tail wheel flutter and asks for information on intended short-term fixes.

This "pilot's memorial" supposedly occurred on 31 March 1941 at Schaffen-Diest in Belgium. It is a Bf 110 C-1 (or C-3) with FuG III and gun trough aft of the canopy. (Ries)

4/17/41 (GL)
Despite the conversion requirement given to the aviation industry to only supply Bf 110s with A engines, aircraft are still being delivered with N engines. Request status regarding how long and how extensive this will continue to be.

Tropicalized aircraft will be delivered in the following numbers: April – 20; May – 20; June 22; July –49; August – 20; September – 14; October – 8; November – 5. Of these, 10 per month will be delivered with N engines.

4/6/41 – 4/26/41
During the conquests of Yugoslavia and Greece, I. and II./ZG 26 and II./ZG 76 were primarily used in the ground support role in light of the fact that there was little in the way of enemy air defense.

5/1/41 (GL)
Bf 110 – tail wheel flutter eliminated by using friction brakes on the fixed section of the shock cylinder and inserting a control lever connected with the moving part of the tailwheel. 300 modified components are expected to be available by 5/741 and delivered to Stavanger-Forus. More will be delivered on a regular basis. *Luftflotte 5* has been informed.

Warschau: the General Staff orders 400 sets of modified components for the Bf 110 (including radiators). Deadlines are requested. LE 2 has ceased conversion work. All further work will be done by Hansen & Co., Schneidemühl. In order to have 80 Bf 110s converted by 6/1, 40 aircraft per week must be delivered for conversion starting immediately.

The Bf 110 with MK 404 is in Tarnewitz and can be turned over to a front-line unit. It is requested that the recipient of this aircraft be *SKG 210*. An additional aircraft will follow at a later date. The General Staff will make the unit assignment.

Since the tropical kits could not be supplied quickly enough, the heavy fighter units deployed to North Africa with their Bf 110 Es initially lacking the protective equipment. This photo shows two such aircraft from 9./ZG 26. (Petrick)

Five operational Bf 110s with MK 101 are currently at SKG 210 and are rarely, if ever, used. In order to acquire experience, it is recommended that some of these aircraft be assigned to *X Korps*, possibly after being tropicalized. The General Staff will pull one aircraft and assign it to *X Korps*. Plans for an accelerated conversion for tropical suitability are to be made.

Starting in May, Bf 110s will only be delivered with A engines. Tropicalized Bf 110: There are no DB 601 Ns available for the 118 Bf 110 E-2s to be produced by Miag. In order to avoid the manufacturer having to switch out engines on the production line, it is proposed that LE carry out the monthly conversion of 10 aircraft to N engines.

The requirements for weapons systems recently submitted by the night fighter divisions and the space needed for the *Lichtenstein* system makes the use of Bf 110s and Me 210s problematic, due to the limited available space. The General Staff requests fundamental views on the suitability of these types for the night fighter role.

According to the *C-Amt* program, Arado now has completed the installation of a mockup of the remotely controlled Arado gun system in the Bf 110 B-0. 2106 is undergoing ground tests with the weapon system and 3664 is in flight testing. The system is also being installed in 3685 and 3708.

The Bf 110 Es of II./ZG 76 *took part in operations against Crete in May of 1941. (Petrick)*

5/5/41 (GL)
Due to lack of space, LC 2 rules out both the Bf 110 and the Me 210 as being suitable for night fighters using the equipment/systems required by the night fighter divisions.

5/15/41 (GL)
Bf 110 tail wheel flutter: 20 sets (not the 300 noted in previous minutes) have been delivered to *Luftflotte 5*. Production continues.

Warschau: At the present time, 24 of the 80 Bf 110s projected for this role have been converted. With regard to the requested 400 conversion sets, these will be available on time for any further conversions that may be needed.

Bf 110/Me 210 night fighter: LC 2/III has contacted the night fighter division on this matter. Beginning in December 1941 with five aircraft and increasing to twelve per month, the Do 217 will be produced as a night fighter.

The General Staff concurs with equipping 50 Bf 110s with fixed aft-firing MG 17s. A decision on additional aircraft being fitted will be made after combat experience data has been collected.

5/41
I. and II./ZG 26 and II./ZG 76 fly escort missions and ground attack missions in the conquest of Crete.

5/23/41 (GL)
Warschau: Based on the latest test results, the He 111 H-3 through H-6 can be used as tow aircraft in addition to the Bf 110. Performance is better than the Bf 110. The General Staff is requested to provide clarification as to whether the He 111 is to be incorporated into plans in place of the Bf 110 in the event of operational deployment. GL cautiously issues a contract for 200 sets of towing components.

The Me 210 will begin production as a *Zerstörer* starting in May 1942, with a reconnaissance version following in September. It is not possible to extend production of the Bf 110 series due to the situation with the engines.

Counter to previous planning, the General Staff calls for the numbers of He 111 *trop* and Bf 110 *trop* to be doubled.

5/30/41 (GL)
Warschau Süd (Warsaw South): So far, it has only been possible to complete 250 aircraft, of which 100 are four-engined, 40 six-engined, and 110 gliders. Timetables can only be established once engines have been delivered. It is planned to complete the last 50 *Warschau Süd* aircraft as gliders. The General Staff urgently requests that the largest number of gliders and engine-powered aircraft be produced for June. The General Staff asks for data on how the Bf 110 and He 111 are equipped for making problem-free take-offs while ensuring the necessary range (data requested on the equipment to be removed and the remaining fuel quantities). The General Staff calls for the tow planes to be configured using field equipment in the shortest time possible.

For the Bf 110, it will be impossible to double the output of the tropicalized aircraft since production is ceasing.

6/12/1941 (GL)
Warschau tow planes: Once the factory conversion is complete for Bf 110 (approx. 8 days) and He 111 (approx. 1 day) towplanes, the field units can configure the aircraft for towing or combat as needed. It takes approximately 1/2 day. For towing, the following items are removed: armor; PVC; additional fuel tanks; and some of the armament. Currently, the range is set at 450 km, with a radius of approximately 280 km (reduced power return leg). Efforts will be made to increase the range to 500 km.

6/23/41
The invasion of the Soviet Union begins. Only *Schnellkampfgeschwader 210* and II./ZG 26 are involved with their Bf 110s in the attack. The other Bf 110s are in Africa or being used in the night fighting role.

6/271941 (GL)
The General Staff has passed the tropicalized requirement on to LC 2. Among other requirements, by 10/1 there must be: 1 *Zerstörer* Wing of Bf 110 E-2 *trop* and D *trop*, totaling 120 aircraft; 10 squadrons, of which approximately 1/3 are Bf 110 E-3 *trop* and 2/3 Fw 189 *trop*, for a total of 80 aircraft.

Summer 1941 (Mtt)
Prof. Messerschmitt proposes that the DB 605 be installed in the Bf 110. No follow-up on the suggestion, since the Bf 110 is expected to be replaced by the Me 210.

7/3/1941 (GL)
Bf 110 D *trop* thru E-2 *trop*: The aviation industry will be producing 85 more aircraft, comprising the make-up quantity plus a further 75. To offset the difference, all Bf 110 D through E-2 variants under repair will be converted to *trop* (15 aircraft monthly = 45 aircraft total). It has not been determined where the remaining 30 aircraft will come from. Independent of this, conversion kits are to be made available.

Bf 110 E-3 *trop*: Since there are neither sufficient quantities of aircraft under repair, nor are aircraft available for conversion, *Zerstörer* variants will most likely need to be utilized. In the event of this happening, the requirement for Bf 110 E-2 *trop* would increase by 40 aircraft. The *trop* conversion parts are the same for the E-2 and E-3.

7/17/41 (GL)
The General Staff calls for Bf 110 night fighters to be armed with four fixed forward-firing cannons. Research is underway to determine the feasibility of switching MG FFs out for MG 151s and MG 131s in place of the MG 17s.

In general, the Bf 110 tow planes for the Me 321 Warschau *flew in their original unit markings. (Mankau)*

7/24/41 (GL)
Combat experience has shown that 50% of aircraft put out of commission were done so by hits in the cooling system. New developments are therefore planned to include partial armor plating.

There are presently two MK 101-armed Bf 110s at *SKG 210* (Wing T.O. Kabisch). An additional four aircraft are planned for deployment to Africa. LB is asked to accelerate the transfer of these to Africa. LC 6 is to set up a line of communication with the two organizations for the purpose of acquiring operational reports.

The General Staff calls for the greatest amount of firepower possible for the Bf 110, Me 210, and Do 217 night fighters. At the very least this should include four cannons.

8/7/41 (GL)
The General Staff dispenses with the need for Bf 110 reconnaissance aircraft for the months of August and September and calls for *Zerstörer* aircraft in their place. This means that the 2 MG FF (fixed) must be refitted, and 40 MG FFs must therefore be made available for both the month of August and the month of September.

A contract is issued for 50 sets of two fixed aft-firing MG 17s with RF 1 for the Bf 110. The General Staff reports on the effectiveness of the aft-firing armament. A decision is needed, since sets must be planned for.

8/21/41 (GL)
The Bf 110 reconnaissance version, delivered as scheduled, is now to be converted over to the Bf 110 *Zerstörer* configuration.

The General Staff rejects restarting Bf 110 production with one MG 15. Request proposals regarding heavier firepower (such as two fixed MG 17s, MG 81 Z, etc.).

"Restarting production" in this case refers to the Bf 110 F, which was supposed to bridge the waiting period until the Me 210 appeared.

9/25/41 (GL)
The General Staff has decided that bombers, *Zerstörer,* and night fighters will not be fitted with two fixed aft-firing MG 17s and the RF 1. This will only be available for the Bf 110 reconnaissance version. The 50 fuselage modification components on order will be passed on to the repair sites. Some aircraft operating in reconnaissance units can be retrofitted. The MG 81 Z has been prioritized mainly for *Zerstörer* aircraft.

The General Staff has decided that of the 30 Bf 110s being produced each month, 22 are to be delivered as night fighters and 8 as *Zerstörers*. No more reconnaissance versions are to be built. Of the 8 *Zerstörer* aircraft, two can be non-tropicalized, if this expedites production. In the event that more than 30 aircraft are produced, the extras are to be delivered as night fighters. The night fighters are to be equipped with two additional MG 151s. It is planned that starting around May 1942 all Bf 110s will be fitted with MG 151s as fixed weapons in place of the current MG FFs. The General Staff asks that opening and closing movement of the hatch be researched with an eye toward expanding the field of fire for the MG 81 Z. Procurement situation for the MG 81 Z, as well as mounting configuration and timetable for prototype installation are discussed.

The General Staff is asked about combat reports following operations by the two MK 101-equipped Bf 110s currently serving with *XII. Korps*.

This Bf 110 E-3(8H+OK) of 2./Aufkl. Gruppe 33 *is fitted with the fixed aft-firing gun. (Petrick)*

10/1/41 (GL)
According to the *C-Amt* program, Bf 110 E-1 (*W.Nr.* 4110, PN+CX) with DB 601 F is undergoing tests in Rechlin as the prototype

for the Bf 110 F, and Bf 110 E-1 (*W.Nr.* 3914, TE+SJ) is being prepared at Messerschmitt as the second prototype for the Bf 110 F. According to the program, Bf 110 E-1 (*W.Nr.* 4116, SJ+KD) is to serve as the prototype for the Bf 110 G with installation of the DB 605, and is expected to be ready for flight testing in November 1941. (In the program from 2/1/42 this same aircraft has the DB 601 F engine and serves as the prototype for testing the DB 601 F.)

10/16/41 (GL)

In order not to hold up new Bf 110 production (i.e. the Bf 110 F), the required eight *Zerstörer* are being delivered as tropicalized versions. For the two *Zerstörer* being employed in the north, the sand filters can easily be removed in the field. The General Staff nevertheless asks for a detailed study of how sand filters act in extremely cold weather.

According to the program, from December 1941 through March 1942 Miag will supply 50 *Zerstörer*, meeting demands up to June '42. In the event that additional requirements are issued, these must be made by no later than April in order to separate them from night fighter production (Gotha).

The movement of the hatch when opening and closing it must be improved upon to provide the MG 81 Z with a better firing arc. The prototype fitting corresponds to proposals from *E-Stelle* Tarnewitz.

40 MK 101s are now available. The General Staff is requested to explore the possibility of fitting a portion of the eight *Zerstörer* aircraft with this cannon.

12/13/41

The *Luftwaffe* has 44 Bf 110s remaining in their original role as *Zerstörer*, of which 28 are operational.

Initially, the rate of production for the Bf 110 F-2 was just eight per month. This aircraft flew with 1./ZG 1 during the winter of 1941/42. (Petrick)

12/15/41 (GL)
In a letter to the Messerschmitt AG, GL/C-E complains that when test flying the first Bf 110 F-4s produced by the GWF the minimum permissible oil pressure was not achieved in most cases. Immediate fixes are discussed. GL notes that these problems could have been avoided if Messerschmitt had communicated with DB. In order to prevent similar problems with the DB 605, Messerschmitt should get in contact with Daimler-Benz at once and send a prototype engine to DB. Furthermore, the test flights in Rechlin provided entirely unacceptable maximum pressure altitudes, particularly with the port engine. Every effort must be made to attain a maximum pressure altitude of 5.7 km.

12/23/41 (GL)
The 601 F engine for the Bf 110, just introduced, has problems with the oil foaming. These have not yet been eliminated, and for this reason there have already been considerable delays in Bf 110 deliveries. The airframes, however, have been completed on time. The secretary of state calls for the DVL's involvement in the basic matter of oil foam buildup in engines and possible solutions. In the long term, it may be necessary to develop new types of oil. *Professor* Kamm of the *Kraftfahrttechnisches Institut* is also to be involved. The current problems with the Bf 110/601 F can only be surmounted through technological and/or design methodology for the oil feed, as in similar cases previously.

1/1/42 (RLM)
The GL/C-B2 department publishes a leaflet for the Bf 110 E which also makes mention of the F-2, F-3, F-4, G-2, G-3, and G-4 variants. The F only differs from the E in its type of engine, while the G is also expected to make use of improved fixed and flexible armament.

1/5/42 (Mtt)
The Messerschmitt AG replies to the letter from GL on 12/15/41 and draws attention to the fact that it was not Messerschmitt, but the RLM, which insisted that the prototype be sent to Gotha most expeditiously without the Messerschmitt AG having the opportunity to test the aircraft itself or have Daimler-Benz test it. The same applies to the maximum pressure altitude. Without extensive testing the altitude set by the RLM will never be attained. For future developments, it is requested that enough time be given to allow new systems to be tested together with Daimler-Benz.

1/30/41
III./ZG 26 arrives in Africa with its Bf 110s.

2/1/42 (GL)
In the aircraft program the Bf 110 (*W.Nr.* 4116) has the DB 601 F and serves as the prototype for the series with the new powerplant. It is expected to be ready to fly in April 1942. Currently, the only thing lacking are the oil coolers. (This is probably a typographical error, since at this point the Bf 110 F with DB 601 F engines is already being supplied to field units.)

3/6/42 (Conference at Carinhall)
Minutes No. 46/42, Top Secret, Carinhall
Generalfeldmarschall Milch: As an alternative solution in the event the Me 210 is abandoned, it is presently being clarified what increase can be expected for the Bf 109 and Bf 110. The six Me 210 groups planned for the spring would then need to be equipped with Bf 109s and Bf 110s. The necessary armor plating must be carried out according to schedule.

General Jeschonnek: It will be necessary to comb the Chief of AW for Ju 87s and Bf 109s yet again in order to ensure these groups are operational, since it will take some time before production of the Bf 109 and Bf 110 can be increased.

Reichsfeldmarschall: The matter of increasing Bf 109s and Bf 110s needs to be clarified. A decision can only be reached after *Prof.* Messerschmitt and *Hauptmann* Diesing have made their presentation.

3/10/42 (GL)
On 3/9/42, in a conference including all interested parties and representatives from the

The Bf 110 was pressed into service as a strike fighter to fill the vacancy left by the Me 210. This Bf 110 D-3 of Erg.ZG has been retrofitted with additional armor and dust filters on the turbocharger intakes. It carries two 250 kg concrete bombs. (Petrick)

Messerschmitt company, the *Reichsmarschall* decided to stop production of the Me 210 immediately…ZG 1 and ZG 2, which were to have been equipped with the Me 210, are to comprise other aircraft types. The resources freed up at Messerschmitt should be immediately devoted to production of the Bf 110 and Bf 109.

3/12/42
Report on the conference regarding the Me 210 in the *Reichsmarschall's* special train on 9/3/42 (see also Me 210).

The *Reichsmarschall* condemns in the sharpest terms the RLM's premature stoppage of the Bf 110, Ju 87, and Ju 88 in favor of the Me 210. As a result, he will bring three men from the GL division up on charges before a military tribunal. Since the Me 210, without conversion to the S configuration, is not able to cover its originally intended role (due to danger of spinning), he asks how this failure could have appeared in spite of the fact that the Bf 110 had, to a great extent, served as its inspiration.

Flugbaumeister Malz: The assumption that the Bf 110 was a full-blown inspiration was a false one, as the example of the rudder illustrates: entirely unsatisfactory handling of the twin rudder concept carried over from the Bf 110 contrasted with the satisfactory handling of the single rudder design not found on the original.

The *Reichsmarschall* responded by heatedly saying that *Gen. Oberst* Udet and Messerschmitt had repeatedly given him the opposite explanation, the last time being in the autumn of 1941. Any claim along the lines that the Me 210 is a completely new aircraft is nonsense.

3/12/42 (Memorandum GL/C-B 2)
On the orders of the *Reichsmarschall*, further construction of the Me 210 has been immediately halted. As a result of this order, the following measures are to be implemented immediately and with greatest priority through the use of night shifts and Sunday work days (excerpts): Bf 109s, Bf 110s,

and Ju 87s will be utilized to fill out the two *Zerstörer* wings of ZG 1 and ZG 2. For this purpose, an undetermined number of workers will be reassigned for repairing Bf 109s and Bf 110s. The companies affected by this decision are yet to be determined. Likewise, in order to accelerate production of new aircraft, an as yet undetermined number will be transferred to 109 and 110 factories (final assembly and flight operations). For fitting the Bf 110 with armor, Mtt is to prepare a mockup fit immediately and get in touch with the senior director of the armor plate network in order to ensure that this plating is fitted to previously produced Bf 110s. To this end, production of 210 S plating can be halted immediately. The Henschel Company is to remain involved in the manufacture of Bf 110 plating and will receive technicians from Mtt for the purpose of accelerating the increase in production.

In the event that continuance of the Me 210 is not possible in spite of the changes, special measures must be agreed upon immediately. Proposals regarding renewed production of the Bf 110 and an increase in Bf 109 output at the expense of Me 210 production will be prepared by GL/C-B 2 and at the same time submitted to the senior network director in a special meeting.

In light of the close formation flying and the poor weight distribution, it comes as no shock to learn that the majority of tow formation operations ended in failure.

3/17/42 (GL)

Oberst Vorwald reports on the measures introduced after agreement was reached with the General Staff, the various departments, and the aviation industry. These include: equipping ZG 1 and ZG 2 with Bf 109s and Bf 110s, which will be fitted with armor plating for their role as strike aircraft. 160 Bf 109 E7s are to be converted, along with 80 Bf 110 Es. Replacement aircraft are in addition to this number.

Direktor Frydag reports on the result of a meeting at Henschel regarding how the armor plating is to be fitted. By 5/5/42 all armor plating for the Bf 110 is to be delivered, and the same applies to the Bf 109 by 5/20/42.

3/21/42 (Conference at Rominten)

Minutes No. 58/42, Top Secret, Rominten

Generaloberst Jeschonnek: "How are the two *Zerstörer* wings that are not getting the Me 210 supposed to look?"

Reichsfeldmarschall: "The two wings are to be used in the strike role and therefore need to be allocated Bf 110s and Bf 109s with SD racks and Hs 129s."

Generaloberst Jeschonnek: "The required six groups can't be equipped from scratch with Bf 110s by June, due to a lack of sufficient numbers of the type. On hand are: two Bf 110 groups from new production and two Bf 109 groups from new production. The need for the remaining two groups can't be filled by Bf 110s."

Feldmarschall Milch expresses his opinion that the Me 321 is a fraud. Already, 36 people have been killed testing the machine. The aircraft is poorly built, trimming is impossible, and the control forces are too strong. Göring asks what the transport glider has accomplished by way of operations thus far. According to *Generaloberst* Jeschonnek, two sorties have been flown with *Flotte 4* and *2* at Ösel. But the expense is in no way comparable to the results. Towing with three aircraft is too difficult, and 50-80% of all takeoffs end in failure.

3/21/1942 (GL)

Oberst Vorwald reports on the directions of the General Staff regarding the stocking of ZG 1 and 2. Meeting the requirement of 80 Bf 110s by 5/15/42, plus 40 replacements per month is proving difficult, since there are only 70 Bf 110 aircraft under repair at this time. C and D series aircraft cannot be readily used, since these versions lack the bomb racks. It would therefore be more advantageous to cover replacement aircraft numbers using new production aircraft. A problem with this is the order of the *Reichsmarschall* directing that new production Bf 110s are to be used in the night fighter role. GL/C is looking into whether it is possible to utilize converted Bf 110 C and D types with simplified equipment as night fighters. Once the technological potential has been clarified, St/GL will present the matter to the *Reichsmarschall* for a decision.

4/14/42 (GL)
Fl.Oberstabsing: Alpers reports on the results of the network director's research into the matter of increasing Bf 110 production. The *Generalfeldmarschall* determines that the desired number of aircraft produced each

The GL/C chief and the General Staff are continuing to review the matter of fitting the Bf 110 C and D variants and the Bf 109 E-7 with additional armor.

4/19/42 (Conference at Rominten)
Minutes No. 58/42, Top Secret, Rominten
Generalfeldmarschall Milch: "By the end of 1942 Bf 110 production should be running at 65 aircraft per month, with efforts made to increase this to 125."

Reichsmarschall: "Focus on increasing production as quickly as possible."

According to *General* Fink, the blind search system has proven effective. Delivery of larger quantities would be good. *Reichsmarschall* Göring wants a deadline set with the companies of Lorenz, Gema, and Telefunken in order to prod them along.

Once the Bf 110 C-4/U1 (here W.Nr. *2132, KD+TB) no longer served a useful purpose as a tow plane, it was assigned to* I./NJS 1 *in Schleißheim as a trainer.*

month be increased to 125, and agrees in general to the idea of transferring the Siebel 204 from the Luther Works. A prerequisite for any final decision is clarification on further construction of the Me 210.

As the Ju 88 has also proven itself to be an effective *Zerstörer*, this raises the question of whether the Me 210 is necessary at all. Also under consideration is the cheaper Ar 240, which would be used to replace the Bf 110 and Me 210.

4/21/42 (GL)
From a meeting with the *Reichsmarschall*, the *Generalfeldmarschall* announces the following: The Me 210 is to be dropped from the program on the orders of the *Reichsmarschall*. The Gotha and Luther companies are to be pulled from the Me 210 manufacturing program, with all jigs, etc. now available for other purposes. The Me 210 work force now freed up is to be used for producing the Bf 110 and Go 244. The *Reichsmarschall* desires that the monthly

German radar-guided night fighter operations really got underway with the all-black Bf 110 F-4 using the FuG 202. Here are three aircraft from 5./NJG 1. (Petrick)

output of Bf 110s be increased to 150. The planning necessary for this is to be undertaken immediately. The Bf 110 remains in the wartime priority category.

4/26/42 (Meeting at the Staff Office)
Minutes No. 74/42, Top Secret, Staff Office Villa
Generaloberst Jeschonnek proposes that the idea of forming a high-speed bomber group (*Schnellkampfgruppe*) be prioritized again. This would involve establishing a group in the West using an Me 210 squadron and two Bf 109 G fighter squadrons. This would not have a negative impact on Bf 110 and Bf 109 production. The Bf 109 and 110 will have priority.

5/5/42 (GL)
Bf 109 G production is interrupted due to additional technical difficulties with the DB 605. For the time being, the DB 605 engine should only be operated at the same performance level as the DB 601 E and is only authorized 100 hours between overhauls.

There is a gap in Bf 110 production resulting from the shortages known from the previous year. GL/C-B2 is tasked with closely monitoring deliveries from the companies producing subassemblies.

Oberst Vorwald suggests that the Gotha Company be absolved of responsibility for the Go 244 so that it can concentrate exclusively on the manufacture of the Bf 110. In order to meet the *Reichsmarschall's* demands of 150 Bf 110 aircraft per month, Gotha will have to be saddled with a monthly production rate of 75 aircraft.

For the remainder of the war, *Prof.* Messerschmitt's responsibilities will be limited to actual developmental work.

5/12/42 (GL)
Approval is given for development of a high altitude night fighter. For a night fighter covering the intermediate altitudes, consideration is being given to an adaptation of the Bf 110 and Ju 88. The L In 3 is to advise on which of the two types is preferred for development.

5/19/42 (GL)
Assuming that the operations director at Gotha is freed of responsibility for producing the Go 244 and that production of the Siebel 204 at Luther is halted, the network manager can offer a monthly output of 75 Bf 110s for the two factories. An additional precondition is the availability of the necessary work force and materials. Wing production by Erla must be transferred to Sindelfingen. Orders are given to increase Bf 110 production to 150 aircraft per month.

5/26 and 5/27/42 (GL)
A review of the tactical requirements for ongoing and upcoming new developments is needed. The General Staff is asked to provide the requirements for the Bf 110's replacement in advance. Intentions are to present these requirements to the best aircraft designers by the end of July 1942 and include them in the work on achieving the design goals.

These requirements are documented in the "Technische Richtlinien für den Kampfzerstörer" (Technical Guidelines for the Heavy Fighter) dated 8/7/42.

Work on the Argus pipes (Argusrohr) continues. Every means at hand should be used to accelerate the introduction of the Argus pipe for the Ju 88 and Bf 110. The research departments are to be involved.

Reputedly, the Argus pipe was to offer a boost in speed and was even tested on a Bf 110. The loss in efficiency at higher speeds and the reduction in range prevented its operational deployment.

6/1/42 (GL)
Despite the *Führer's* orders, it will take time to meet the requirements for bomb rack kits for the Bf 109 and Bf 110. For the Bf 110 F-4, both types of racks will be supplied via

6/9/42 (GL)
The *Generalfeldmarschall* asks *Major* Storp to submit the specific requirements for the Bf 110's replacement by no later than 6/30/42. These should also take into account the possible use of the type in the night fighting and high speed bomber roles. Once the General Staff submits its requirements, research is to be made as to how closely the He 219 meets them and what modifications would need to be made. Attempts must be made to significantly reduce the timetable for the He 219. Development of a competing aircraft design is approved as long as there is sufficient developmental resources available and the deadlines are adequate.

Other than this photo and a mention by GL, *nothing more is known about this variant and the attempts to increase speed.* (Deutsches Museum, *Munich)*

LZA Liegnitz. Bf 110 F-2s were produced with the complete kits already fitted. The connections have not been guaranteed.

The forecast for the month of June calls for 20 Bf 110 aircraft. The reason, according to Gotha, is that the company is suffering from a shortage in materials. The *Generalfeldmarschall* expects that everything be done to significantly boost production figures during June and July.

6/19/42 (GL)
Study 1011 calls for an increase in *Zerstörer* aircraft to 200 per month.

Because of the engine situation, the Me 210 can only be produced at the expense of the Bf 109 and Bf 110. The *Generalfeldmarschall* informs the Chief of the General Staff that Bf 109 and Bf 110 production is to take priority over the Me 210 in all situations. At the Augsburg plant, once Me 210 production is completed they will build wing sections for the Bf 110.

6/30/42 (GL)
Stabsing. Burgsmüller reports on the trials using the 3.7 cm cannon installation at Rechlin. The cannons have been sent to the companies so that they can study the best ways of fitting the weapon. No serious problems are expected. *Generalfeldmarschall* Milch is in agreement with concentrating on the 3.7 cm *Flak*. However, requirements for later installation of the 5 cm, 7.5 cm, and 8.8 cm *Flak* must also be taken into account.

Summer 1942 (Mtt)
The DB 605 is tested in Bf 110 *W.Nr.* 4622 (TF+UU) and *W.Nr.* 4623 (TF+UV). Areas explored are installation and flight handling. Servo-tabs, blower intakes, radiators, fuel pumps, and spark plugs are not working properly.

7/1/42 (GL)
According to Delivery Program 222 184 Bf 110 Fs have been supplied, with a further 316 expected before production ends in January 1943. Six Bf 110 Gs have been delivered so far. The number of Bf 110 Gs expected by 9/30/44 is projected at 2646, with no production end date established as of yet.

7/7/42 (GL)
Gotha's Bf 110 production is unsatisfactory. The *Generalfeldmarschall* assigns *Oberstabsing*. Alpers the task of dealing with the plant manager in an "energetic" manner. Gotha must be part of the program by 15 September. Any shortages in the work force will be filled by GL/A. The company must deal with the matter of housing quickly.

7/14/42 (GL)
Seven Bf 110 *trop* have crashed on their transfer flights. Probable cause is due to engine problems. GL/C-B is to review production at the Luther Company. The *Dobbas* transport system has not proven effective with the Bf 110, as it causes the engine to overheat.

7/21/42 (GL)
The companies of Messerschmitt, Erla, Luther, and others have reduced output by as much as 25% in comparison with the figures provided in the preview. *Generalfeldmarschall* Milch asks that the senior managers of these companies be informed that the delivery numbers specified in the preview must be adhered to at all cost.

7/21/42 (Mtt)
The repair companies of Bachmann von Blumenthal & Co. and Hansen Schneidemühl have reported problems with the oil temperature for the Bf 110's DB 601 engines. In order to rectify the situation, Messerschmitt AG and Daimler-Benz want to work out a detailed evaluation program.

8/4/42 (GL)
Bf 110 Recovery Plan: The Luther Company will be involved in the program starting in November 1942, while the Gotha Company will not be able to begin until at least mid-1943. Gotha is stretched to capacity with the Go 244, which is also to be part of a recovery plan. The *Generalfeldmarschall* orders that the Go 244 is to be de-prioritized in favor of the Bf 110. Gotha must then move up the date considerably for Bf 110 recovery.

The Gotha Company asks for 250 female and 50 male Russian workers for Bf 110 production.

8/12/42 (Mtt)
According to information from the *E-Stelle* Rechlin dated 8/11/42, in Africa two Bf 110 Fs caught fire while taxiing and a third on landing. Immediate measures (moving the ventilation lines) have been decided upon.

8/17/42 (GL)
Bf 110 Fires from the OBS Perspective: Since neither the Bf 110 nor the DB 601 has a tendency to catch fire, the large numbers of these fires cannot be easily explained. According to a report from *Stabsing.* Ulsmann, non-standard seals have been used and fuel lines have become unsealed through rubbing. It is expected that a stopgap solution can be found.

Program Study 1012: An increase in Bf 110 production is not possible due to the situation with the DB 605 engine. As will be mentioned later under "Fighters," Bf 110 production can only be increased once production of 800 fighters has been assured. The extra engines will then be divided equally among the 110 and the 109.

If testing the Me 210 using the DB 603 shows the feasibility of this new engine type, this may possibly be a way to increase *Zerstörer* output.

8/18/42 (GL)
The He 219 production model has been discussed in a development meeting. It is worth considering at this point which combat *Zerstörer* will eventually be dropped. To this end, performance data of the Bf 110, Ar 240, Fw 187, Me 210, and Me 210 with DB 603 G will be compared. The Fw 187 offers no advantages whatsoever as a *Zerstörer*. The Fw 187 and Ar 240 would have to be rebuilt from the ground up. Bf 110 production has ceased. Due to their performance, consideration of these three types can be set aside.

8/20/42 (GL)
The recovery plan for the Bf 110 has been approved by the *Reichsmarschall*. The Go 244 is to be dropped. Arrangements have already been made to have the workforce for the Go 244 shifted over to help with increased production of the Bf 110.

There is a bottleneck with propellers, with the Bf 109 and Bf 110 awaiting back orders. This can be offset by using the propellers already manufactured for the Me 210.

8/26/42 (GL)
Report on the dealings with Gotha on the matter of whether a commissioner needs to be involved. The *Generalfeldmarschall* asks that the matter be looked into and recommendations made. The *Reichsmarschall* is in agreement that the Go 244 should cease production with 450 aircraft. The *Generalfeldmarschall* agrees that the Bf 110 should be given priority at the expense of the Go 244.

9/1/42 (GL)
Go 244 production should cease as soon as possible so that the aviation industry can be freed from the burden of manufacturing this aircraft. Recognition for exceptional performance is to be given by GL/C-B to the Luther Company for its production of the Bf 110. It must be stressed to the Luther Company the importance of getting ahead, particularly since Bf 110 production at Gotha is not yet running satisfactorily. A copy of this document is to be given to the Gotha Company.

9/9/42 (GL)
A proposal is made to dispense with the idea of appointing a commissioner for Gotha. Gotha's main problem is that it suffered from poor equipment supervision. *Direktor* Frydag recommended placing material requirements, purchasing, and warehouse management under a materials controller.

9/14/42 (GL)
The ratio of Bf 110 day *Zerstörer* and night fighters will be reviewed by the General Staff. The Rf 2 b rearview telescope is planned for

large-scale trials in the following aircraft (in order of importance): all Bf 110 F-3s and Bf 110 F-2s, and as far as possible for Bf 109 Gs and Me 210/410s. A follow-on contract will be forthcoming once the test results are in.

9/15/42 (GL)
Bf 110 production is part of September's program. Luther has an average of 9, and Gotha is in arrears by 12 aircraft. The *Generalfeldmarschall* calls for an increase in airframe production, even if the engine situation means that the airframes must be temporarily set aside without engines.

9/16/42 (GL)
Oersting. Mahnke asks that a decision be reached regarding the number of DB 628 high altitude engines planned for production. The engine will be on the test bench by late 1942. 150 engines are planned for the testing stage. Production is expected to begin by mid-1944. Plans for series production must begin immediately. In view of this information, the *Generalfeldmarschall* decides that production plans call for 250 DB 628 engines. It is planned to equip 100 Bf 109s and 30 Bf 110s. The *Generalfeldmarschall* orders that the Bf 110 continue in the program with a production run of 150 aircraft.

9/30/42 (GL)
According to Aircraft Program No. 22 E, Top Secret 2102/42, as of this time 377 Bf 110 F aircraft have been delivered from the Miag and Gotha companies. Messerschmitt Augsburg and Gotha have also delivered a further six Bf 110 Gs. Maximum monthly output of Bf 110 Fs is planned at 55. The Bf 110 G is expected to reach its peak monthly output of 150.

10/6/42 (GL)
NJG 2 has found the Do 217 to be unsuited for the night fighting role. *Oberstlt.* von Loßberg takes the view that the Bf 110's gross weight is already pushing the limit for a close support night fighter. Even the He 219 might possibly be too heavy.

The flame suppressor system on the Bf 110 F-4 is not safe enough. Engines are lasting only 20 to 50 hours. The premature outages of engines can be traced back to the current valve seating arrangement. Whether and to what extent the *Fla V* system is involved cannot be determined without a detailed investigation.

Up to this point there are six known cases of the DB 605 catching fire. It is believed that the primary reason has to do with the bearings.

10/20/42 (GL)
In order to halt the breakthrough of enemy tank units, *Generalfeldmarschall* Milch's view is that the Ju 188 or Bf 110 with twin 3.7 cm guns should be considered. Allocation of the 3.7 cm guns will be clarified by *6. Abteilung*. Prototype installation is already underway. The *Generalfeldmarschall* orders that emphasis be placed on accelerating installation of the MG 131 in the Bf 109. Similarly, the 3.7 cm, 5 cm, and 7.5 cm installations in bomber and heavy fighter aircraft should be pursued with great urgency.

11/1/42 (GL)
The Bf 110 (*W.Nr.* 2656) is at Tarnewitz for testing the RZ 65, according to the aircraft program. Bf 110 G-2 (*W.Nr.* 4622) is at Messerschmitt, undergoing various tests with performance enhancing equipment. 4624 has been fitted with the prototype flame suppressor. (During the summer of 1942, 4623 also served as a testbed for evaluating the DB 605 installation.)

11/2/42 (GL)
In addition to the installation of 10 3.7 cm cannons per month in Hs 129s, there are also plans for approximately 10 Bf 110s for OBS. The General Staff *6./Abt.* is requested to provide any final requirements. Installation must be done in the field, since there are no more resources available for factory conversion.

11/3/42 (GL)
The use of Bf 109 Gs against American Liberator bomber formations has proven to be rather ineffective, since the Bf 109's armament is too weak. It is recommended that the Bf 110 be fitted with the MK 101. *Oberst* Vorwald points out that the MK 101 is needed for the Hs 129. The only weapon available for the Bf 110 is the 3.7 cm *Flak*. Up to now, the General Staff has only authorized 10 cannons per month for installation in aircraft. This number must be increased.

11/17/42 (GL)
3.7 cm installation in the Hs 129 and Bf 110 must be accomplished by the aviation industry, since it cannot be done in the field.

12/1/42 (GL)
There are two problems remaining with the DB 605: the main- and large end bearings and the idler wheel for the starter motor. The reasons for the inadequate lubrication remain a mystery for DB, but it appears that the problem can be minimized by increasing the pressure in the oil reservoir. The matter of the bearings is expected to be looked into by specialists. In some cases, the large drive wheel for the starter is broken. Rigidity should be improved by attaching a flange.

12/19/42 (Mtt)
In Messerschmitt Report 389 information on a projected Bf 110 is given which would be armed with two MK 108s in the nose, two MG 151s in the fuselage, two MG 151s under the fuselage, an aft-firing MG 151 using the RF 4 periscope, and an MG 81 Z in the aft gunner's position.

12/22/42 (GL)
Program Study 1013: A decision must be reached in August 1943 as to whether the Bf 110 should continue in production up to early 1945. By that time the production at Focke-Wulf should be 250 aircraft; in addition there are 280 Me 410s. (Focke-Wulf even quotes an output of 500 aircraft). *This is in reference to the Ta 154.*

Increasing the oil pressure of the DB 605 is not sufficient to provide it with the necessary takeoff performance. The prerequisite for this is the introduction of an oil slinger.

1/8/43 (GL)
The He 219 can in no way meet the needs of the night fighter service over the next two years. *Generalfeldmarschall* Milch considers it very fortunate that, in addition to the Bf 110 G, the Ta 154 will also be available to supplement the inventory.

Galland points out that the increased allocation of Bf 110s for the night fighters has caused a critical situation for the *Zerstörer* units. At the present time, these shortages make establishment of new *Zerstörer* units impossible.

1/16/43 (GL)
Study 1014: The Me 410 with two DB 603s will total 300 aircraft by May 1945, with the Bf 110/DB 605 production ceasing by then, earlier if it is used as a bridge to cover the Me 210/DB 605 conversion.

1/21/43 (GL)
The DB 605's takeoff rating authorization is discussed. The present state of the DB 605 makes it a borderline case. As a result, the takeoff rating has been limited by reducing the manifold pressure. A new, follow-on engine development with improved bearing races is expected to be produced starting in April, and this should eliminate the need for reducing manifold pressure. Recently, 20 newly built aircraft were forced to land at Erla's field due to piston damage. The pilots are even refusing to get into the cockpit. Field units have had significantly better experience. Once the aircraft reaches altitude the engine becomes much more reliable.

The DB 605 was extremely unreliable in 1943, with a tendency to chew up pistons and catch fire. Many Bf 109, Bf 110 and He 177 crews lost their lives because of engine problems. (Ries)

1/26/43 (GL)

Testing of the Bf 110 With Flak 18 has not yet concluded. However, the GL/C-B has no intentions of approving the aircraft yet. *Oberstlt. i. G.* von Loßberg reports that the weapon itself is functioning well, and the cannon cover will be finished by Messerschmitt in short order. Arrangements have been made to have the next Bf 110s manufactured armed with the 3.7 cm gun. Despite the fact that the cannon will probably not work at temperatures below 30 degrees, *Oberstlt.* von Loßberg nevertheless feels it is ok to ship the aircraft after the covers have been manufactured. The airplanes will be finished in three days.

During the winter of 1943 the Bf 110 G-2/R1 (here S9+AN) flew anti-tank missions in the area of Poltava. This aircraft is fitted with tropical equipment. (Petrick)

accompanied by another aircraft carrying its ammunition. *Oberstlt. i. G.* von Loßberg states that the Hs 129 is extremely uneconomical. It carries twelve rounds of ammunition, but cannot be reloaded, whereas the Bf 110 with 72 rounds and reloadable is much more viable. In addition, the Hs 129 is uneconomical from a flying standpoint. *Oberstlt. i. G.* Vorwald explains that the Hs 120 with 3.7 cm has been stopped based on the verdict of the KdE; the focus is now on the Bf 110 with 3.7. Responding to a question from *Dir.* Frydag, *Oberstlt. i. G.* Vorwald states that the 3.7 cm gun is to be installed in the five Hs 129s still projected for February, provided there is sufficient work force.

Oberstlt. Pelz has already received orders from the chief of the General Staff to set up the squadrons. The crews will be formed within Germany and fly to the front in their aircraft. The airplanes will be operated as part of *Luftflotte 4*.

The one Hs 129 with 3.7 cm which *Oberstlt.* von Loßberg reported as certified is being sent immediately to the Eastern Front

1/43

I./ZG 1 and III./ZG 26 are assigned the first Bf 110 G-2s.

2/3/43 (GL)

A total of 60 Flak 18 have been released by the General Staff for installation in aircraft, of which 48 have already been allocated, with 12 more following. The General Staff's *6.Abt.* asks for the following distribution: 40 weapons for Bf 110 = 40 aircraft; 20 weapons for Ju 87 = 10 aircraft. At the present time, work is being done to fulfill the *Generalfeldmarschall's* orders calling for 25 Ju 87s to be armed with Flak 18 guns. The General Staff will make a final decision regarding the release of additional 3.7 cm guns and 20 more *Pak 40s*.

The General Staff's *6.Abt.* requests that a study be made into the possibility of converting Bf 110 Fs into 110 Gs by swapping the DB 601 engine out for the 605. Furthermore, the possibility of making 20 reinforced engine support arms available for this purpose should be explored.

2/9/43 (GL)
Procurement situation: The Bf 110 is in the program. Projected for March: 82; quota met, ahead of schedule by 52. Another increase in advance deliveries.

2/12/43 (GL)
The DB 605's problems still have not been cleared up. This applies particularly to fighters, where the lubrication system is a tight fit and is frequently the cause of malfunctions. Reserve engine supplies are quite low at the present time.

2/26/43 (GL)
Prof Nallinger from Daimler-Benz reports on the problems with the DB 605. During the initial flights, the connecting rod bearing would seize up. At first, the engines had no oil on initial startup and ran dry. The situation was remedied somewhat starting in the latter half of November by using better filling methods, ventilation, and by using a cold-start mixture during the colder part of the year. Pistons and bearings are still being ruined, though. The DB 605's oil content is limited and cannot be increased to the quantity desired. Good results have been achieved by slowly applying the throttle during engine run-up. This approach was decided upon in Wiener Neustadt on 2/15/43 and is to be passed on to the other production facilities. Aeroshell medium weight oil will continue to be used during the engine break-in period. Another chief complaint is the shaking, which

The useful combat life of the Bf 110 F-2 was increased in part due to the fitting of an MG 81Z in the aft position, as seen here on a machine from III./ZG 26 in Italy in 1943. (Petrick)

has been traced back to poor quality Bosch spark plugs. Resources are not yet available to produce better quality spark plugs.

From a design perspective, it has been noted that when using cold oil the diameter of the oil lines is not adequate and should be enlarged. Nallinger wants a one-hour engine run-up under low-load conditions but with high rpm. The pistons should be given a bit more play, and the cylinder surfaces should also be of better quality.

A further problem is that of foam buildup with the oil, which is particularly notable in the Bf 109 and can be traced back to the oil reservoirs, which are too small. Working together with Messerschmitt, efforts will be made to increase the container capacity by six to ten liters. DB's authorized oil pressure of a minimum of 2.6 ata within the airframe cannot be met by the Bf 109 with its 2.3 ata, but was accepted due to the pressure of getting sufficient numbers to the front. The people at Messerschmitt have as yet been unable to modify the Bf 109 so that the minimum acceptable standard of 2.6 ata can be achieved.

DB still has plans for testing a two-hole lubrication system, and the introduction of an oil slinger is also planned for a later date. This removes the oil foam, and in doing so increases the pressure. Oil pressure can also be increased significantly by pressurizing the oil tank, since this causes the foam bubbles to compress and the oil pump can therefore draw more oil. DB would welcome efforts to retroactively increase oil tank pressure on all airframes already produced, as well as all new Bf 109 deliveries.

The device for increasing oil pressure in the tanks, which was tested in Rechlin, can be fitted into the Bf 109. The same should also go for the Bf 110, since Gotha has also been having the same problem.

Cuno believes that installation of the oil slinger, which would be an immediate stopgap solution, would be difficult for the Bf 109. He is of the opinion that overpressurizing the oil tank will provide a marked improvement, as will a low-strain initial break-in period for the engines.

The participants in the meeting are in agreement that an engine should be run 20 hours before it can be pushed to its limit. Currently, by the time an engine is sent to the field, it has only been run for about six hours. In the view of DB, a four-hour electrical run-up would offer some relief, but there is neither sufficient electricity nor run-up stands available for this. *Herr* Mahnke of Junkers states that they do not need the electrical run-up, since there are no problems with oil content in the Jumo 211.

Generalfeldmarschall Milch would like to acquire 40 to 50 more metric tons of fuel per month for DB so that the engines can be broken in around an hour longer than is presently the case.

On the matter of establishing the takeoff performance rating, *Prof.* Nallinger proposes sending 25 engines with twin hole lubrication to the front and, after the low-load run-up period, testing these for 20 hours using takeoff and emergency power. Prerequisite is the increased oil pressure within the oil tank. For the aircraft already off the assembly line, once the pressure release valves have been fitted the authorized takeoff rpm (not the takeoff rating) can then be set.

3/10/43 (GL)

Bachmann, von Blumenthal & Co., and Fürth are carrying out conversion of the Bf 110 F-2 to G-0 standards by strengthening the engine supports and installing DB 605 engines in ten aircraft. Designation of these modified aircraft: Bf 110 G-0.

3/18 and 3/19/43 (Mtt)

Messerschmitt has ended interim firing tests with the MK 109 (nos. 0504 and 0505) in a Bf 110 nose section.

3/19/43 (GL)

The developmental meeting discusses armament configuration of fighters and *Zerstörer* aircraft. The prototype model for the Bf 110 night fighter, the Bf 110 G-6, should be finished by April. Galland calls for all Bf 110 G *Zerstörer* operating as heavy fighters against four-engined bombers in the Mediterranean and in the West to have the same field conversion kit as the night fighters, i.e. two additional MG 151/20s with 200 rounds each, fitted beneath the fuselage. It has been determined that this kit reduces the speed by 20 to 25 km/h, but Galland maintains that this is irrelevant. The only things allowed to fly are so called "fire engines," which are not effective. *Generalfeldmarschall* Milch makes the following decision: This only simplifies things. The G-2 is stricken, and there will only be the G-4. The G-2 should be replaced by the G-4 as quickly as possible.

It is apparent that when the participants in this meeting mention the Bf 110 G-4, they are referring to a G-2 with two additional MG 151s under the fuselage. The night fighter is designated as the Bf 110 G-6. These designations were later not accepted as official.

4/13/1943 (GL)

Procurement situation for aircraft: Bf 110 – 105 airframes (quota 94, ahead by 27); Me 210 – 4 airframes (quota 12, ahead by 6); Me 410 – 25 airframes (quota 30, in arrears by 40).

4/30/43 (Göring's Country Manor, Obersalzberg)

The radar program has gotten off to a good start, but there are still no requirements submitted from the tactical side. Therefore, *Feldmarschall* Milch has set up a commission under *Oberst i.G.* von Loßberg to come up with a clear-cut plan.

Three He 219s are in the factory test stage, with three more being sent to Rechlin in April and May. Flight handling is good. At 514 km/h, the speed at ground level is approximately 10 km faster than the company

Having a standard armament configuration of four MG 17s and two MG 151/20s, the Bf 110 G-2 was poorly equipped for attacking four-engined bombers. (Petrick)

claims. Due to the move to Schwechat and other reasons there are not enough resources available to build both the He 219 and the He 111 bomber transport. Göring wants the He 219 series to be produced at a minimum rate of 50 per month and decides that, for the time being, production can go ahead at the expense of the bomber transport.

5/18/1943 (GL)
Procurement situation for aircraft: 105 Bf 110s have been delivered (quota 100, ahead by 79).

5/20/1943 (GL)
Prof. Dr. Bock presents the status of switching over from alloys to steel and other materials: airframes: the Bf 110 aluminum requirements are dropping more slowly than planned.

5/21/43 (GWF)
GWF has completed work on the Bf 110 G-4 prototype, *W.Nr.* 5429, with two MK 108 cannons in the nose.

6/1/43 (GL)
Procurement situation for aircraft: Bf 110 – 125 aircraft (quota 100, ahead of schedule by 79); Me 210 – 1 airframe (quota 3, behind by 6); Me 410 – 40 aircraft (quota 42, behind by 54)

6/4/43 (GL)
A report on the experiences of *10. Nachtjagdstaffel* ZG 1 is given, with their Bf 110 G-2 aircraft being used to protect the harbor at Kerch and the surrounding airfields. Due to outstanding cooperation with searchlight batteries, 28 kills have been recorded within the space of just two months. One crew brought down four aircraft in a single night. The prerequisite for such successes is that the searchlights can acquire the aircraft in time and keep them in their beams long enough. These Bf 110s have no radar, and the anti-aircraft batteries are not directed by *Würzburg-Riesen* radars. Attacks begin with several Bf 110s already in the air. When enemy aircraft are detected approaching, the fighter direction officer contacts individual aircraft. The anti-aircraft guns continue to fire until the fighter has acquired the enemy plane. The fighter pilot then announces he has made contact, and the anti-aircraft guns immediately stop firing. Each battery has a loudspeaker system and listens in on the traffic between the pilot and control officer. This ensures flawless cooperation. A proposal is made to use similar methods at other sites, as well as in Berlin. The Bf 110 G-2 with two MG 1512 and four MG 17s is felt to be both effective and adequate for operations in Russia.

Jumo 211 and DB 605 production is being held up due to the lack of crankshafts. Production should nevertheless continue, with a surplus of engines being built until the crankshaft resources can catch up. Up to now, crankshaft production has been in the Rhineland. The transfer of resources, particularly machine shops, has been held up due to the matter of electrical power supply.

12 Bf 110 G-4s with oil slingers are to be sent to Rechlin for a broad-based testing program. The oil slinger is necessary since oil pressure alone is inadequate and the pressure release valve does not fit on the Bf 110.

6/15/43 (GL)
The *General der Aufklärer* reports that the Me 410 has proven to be a most effective reconnaissance aircraft. The bulk of tactical reconnaissance, however, is still provided by the Bf 110, and is in urgent need of replacement by the Me 410.

This Bf 110 F-3, from 1./(F)/124, was already outmoded by the time it began operations at Kirkenes in the winter of 1943. (via Horst)

The *General der Jagdflieger* reports that, at the present time, six Bf 110s with Flak 18 are being produced per month. This rate will continue with the GM 1 system fitted. A portion of these are being used to engage enemy armor. Now the last group from the Eastern Front is being used in this capacity. Currently, 20 Flak 18 guns are available each month, and some of these are being fitted to Ju 87s as well. Combat reports have been mixed. In some instances, the *Flak 18* has been removed from Ju 87s and the aircraft have reverted to dropping bombs. The allocation for the Bf 110 could be increased. According to Galland, the Flak 18 is fundamentally flawed when operating at altitude. Galland proposes that the Bf 110 production rate continue at six per month. Vorwald suggests looking into whether the more modern and lighter *Flak 36* can be acquired; it is so new that it is not yet available. Milch would like to have three to four prototypes converted, and if it is better, then production should switch to the new gun. Eschenhauer informs the group that the Flak 18 production will be ceasing. In order to make up for losses, Galland will take a further 20 Bf 110s with Flak 18.

According to Galland, the Bf 110 with Flak 18 and GM 1 has been flown. Results were most satisfactory. At an altitude of 9.5 km it still had a climb rate of 5 to 10 m.

General der Aufklärer Berlin reports that the most problematic aircraft on the front are the 126, 189, 110, and 88. Presently the Bf 110 is being used for tactical reconnaissance, with an eventual shift to the Me 410 and later the Ta 154 and Do 335.

Fighter production should be increased. Bottlenecks are being caused by the shortage of crankshafts for the DB 605. The crankshaft problem is slowly turning into a catastrophe. This is neither due to the machining resources nor to the work quality, but due to steel, which is only being made available in inadequate quantities and only in certain dimensions.

During the discussion of the He 219, which has just scored five kills on its first operational sortie, *Generalfeldmarschall* Milch determines that the Bf 110 will not be suitable for the night fighter role in the future. Night fighting units, however, would prefer to get as many Bf 110s as possible throughout this year and for the first half of 1944, when the replacement becomes available. Their interest in the Bf 110 ceases for the second half of 1944. That is the situation.

Geschwader Streib would like to have six Bf 110s with GM 1 to be used for hunting Mosquitoes. According to Pasewald, there will be no problem in fulfilling this request. A prototype has already been fitted. According to Vorwald there are 10 aircraft with GM 1 being produced for the night fighters. Delivery of the six aircraft can probably take place in June. However, with the increased manifold pressure the oil slinger matter becomes critical.

6/18/43 (GL)

In the event of some type of Allied landing, the Bf 110 should also be employed with cluster bombs. For this, though, there is nowhere to carry them, since the *Zerstörer* planes are being produced without ETCs. It is requested that the ETCs be sent separately to field units, where they can later be fitted when and if the need arises.

The *Generalfeldmarschall* explains that a large number of accidents and deaths can be traced back to the fact that the DB 605 engine is still not functioning properly. There is, therefore, serious lack of trust in the engine, both in reference to its installation in the Bf 109 as well as in the Bf 110. Field units have a very negative opinion of the DB 605. Furthermore, it is felt that the He 177's DB 610 engines will embody all the mistakes of the DB 605 when it appears in front-line units starting in August.

Using the two-hole lubrication system has not proven effective in increasing oil pressure, and it is decided to revert back to the standard three-hole system. It is not possible to increase pressure with the Bf 110. If something needs to be done with regard to the Bf 110's night fighter role, then the oil slinger should be installed. For fighters, increased pressure can be achieved, but the slinger cannot be fitted.

Report by *Generaling*. Eisenlohr: *The DB 605 is still giving us lots of problems, even though it's been in production for 1 1/2 years: bearings, connecting rods, pistons, oil seals. The bearings will have to be designed anew, since the crankshaft does not rest on every point but jumps around here and there. This leads to dry spots and the formation of grooves and pits in the bearings. Major improvements are expected with the introduction of the oil slinger, something of a necessity for the Bf 110. The oil slinger reduces the foam and throw out the impurities. Implementation has been agreed upon, but it's still not clear what results it will give us, where it's needed, or where it can be used. In addition, there is the question of whether and when it will be ready from a production standpoint. The sealing material currently in use is of poor quality and is effectively worthless. The oil quality, too, seems to change constantly and is sometimes unusable. In spite of that, other engines that do not have nearly the problems of the DB 605 run with it.*

The reports on problems from night fighter units that you have in front of you date from the period of 1 February through 1 March, a time when the measures of low-load burn-ins, etc. have not yet been applied. The situation must get better."

It is decided to use a Junkers slinger for the Bf 110 and He 177, and a smaller DB slinger for the Bf 110. The slingers should be installed by platoons in field repair units. Regarding the matter of ball bearings, trials are underway using cambered bearings. In addition, the DB proposes strengthening the crankshafts, something the DB will need the support of the *Amt* and the *Industrierat* for so that production of the new dies can begin as soon as possible.

6/22/43 (GL)
Bf 110 G-4 production is ongoing with two ETC 50s under each wing and a fitted 2 x ETC 500 kit. The 2 x MG 151 weapons pack will be introduced around July and is applicable to 100 per cent of all aircraft. For the purpose of making separate deliveries, *Genst. 6. Abt.* will release these kits to the depots.

The *Genst. 6. Abt's* requirement for equipping two Ju 87s per month is being fulfilled by an improved conversion program, which projects a rate of five aircraft per month and at an earlier completion date. The requirement for six Bf 110s per month will not be affected by this. In case of a shortage of weapons, *Genst. 6. Abt* will make further allocations and/or release *Flak 36* and later Flak 43 cannons.

6/29/43 (GL)
Genst. 2. Abt. is asked to provide the sites for equipping 50% of the night fighting units with the GM 1.

The *Generalfeldmarschall* establishes the following prioritization order for aircraft: Fighters (Bf 109, Fw 190), Bf 110, Me 410, Ju 188, Ju 87, Ju 52, and Ju 290.

200 sets of twin-barreled and 800 sets of single-barreled 21 cm *Wurfgranate* have been ordered. All are in agreement that these are adequate numbers.

The number of He 219s being produced have been kept to a minimum, and will peak at 10 per month. The 50 per month rate called for in the program can only be achieved if the He 177 repair facilities are transferred from Eger to Rostock. Another possibility is moving production to Milec. The *Generalfeldmarschall* orders that the plans of GL/C-B for an initial batch of 150 (100 Milec, 50 Eger) be carried out.

7/13/43 (GL)
In preparing for a meeting at Göring's HQ, *Generalfeldmarschall* Milch mentions that the wide angle antenna has been certified. There are three aircraft waiting to be fitted, and Hermann will get all of these.

7/16/43 (GL)
Topic of the meeting: Aircraft for the *General der Nachtjagd*: delivery of the V-series He 219s is underway (maximum of 10 aircraft per month, in December 1943, end: mid-1944). From January 1944 onward the type enters full scale production, which based on previous requirements will reach a maximum output of 50 per month by March 1945. Research is being undertaken on increasing production to 150. The *Generalfeldmarschall* orders that the He 210 be manufactured in

Polish territory (Milec and Buczin). (As ordered earlier, He 111 production is to remain at Rostock.) The *Generalfeldmarschall* is to be given a plan. In the opinion of *Obersting.* Alpers, it is potentially feasible to produce the 150 aircraft in the second half of 1945. The *Generalfeldmarschall* points out that efforts must be made to achieve 150 aircraft as soon as possible. In conclusion, *Stabsing.* Friebel emphasizes that, based on information obtained jointly from GL/C-B and GL/C-E, the Heinkel Company is behind by a million man hours on the V-series as a result of never having been allocated a labor force.

The *General der Nachtjagd* is confronted with a shortage in inventory brought on by demands being made from all sides. Currently, he has been tasked with establishing three night fighter groups; in addition to this the current deficiencies also need to be made up (170 aircraft as of 4/1/43). *General* Kammhuber asks that these aircraft be made available immediately through an emergency measure; either C or E models would be adequate. *Oberstleutnant i.G.* Eschenauer points out that the current allocation of Bf 110s for day fighters be maintained at all costs; any drop in favor of the night fighters is unthinkable. The *Generalfeldmarschall* emphasizes that the defense of German territory is what is driving the fighting in Sicily in the first place. Therefore, it is absolutely necessary to turn all available Bf 110s over to the night fighting units. Other missions will have to be dropped, and at the same time strive to ensure that the massive outages already caused by enemy bombing raids on the German industry do not become even worse.

On the recommendation of *Oberstlt.* Eschenhauer, 40 aircraft will be allocated to the day fighters instead of the original 30. The remaining 30 aircraft are to be made available for night fighter units.

Obersting. Alpers provides details of plans to increase Bf 110 production by the end of 1943. A precondition is that personnel be assigned to the project. The shortage in personnel is currently leading to a slump in the manufacture of components. The scope of the program remains as originally planned, with the present run lasting only through September. After that, it should continue at the same level. The *Generalfeldmarschall* underlines the importance of producing precisely this aircraft, and calls for preferential support in producing the Bf 110 through the allocation of personnel.

As far as the *General der Nachtjagd* is concerned, the Bf 110 can dispense with the armor for the rear gunner, but should retain the armament. Of utmost necessity is armored glass for the side windows and armored skirting for the Bf 110. (The left armored glass plate must not be fitted with all-weather glass, as this diminishes visibility considerably). According to *Stabsing.* Friebel and *Oberstabsing.* Alpers, work is already underway.

In order to train new night fighter pilots, some Bf 110s were fitted with dual controls and instrumentation along with blind flying shrouds. (Bundesarchiv *Koblenz*)

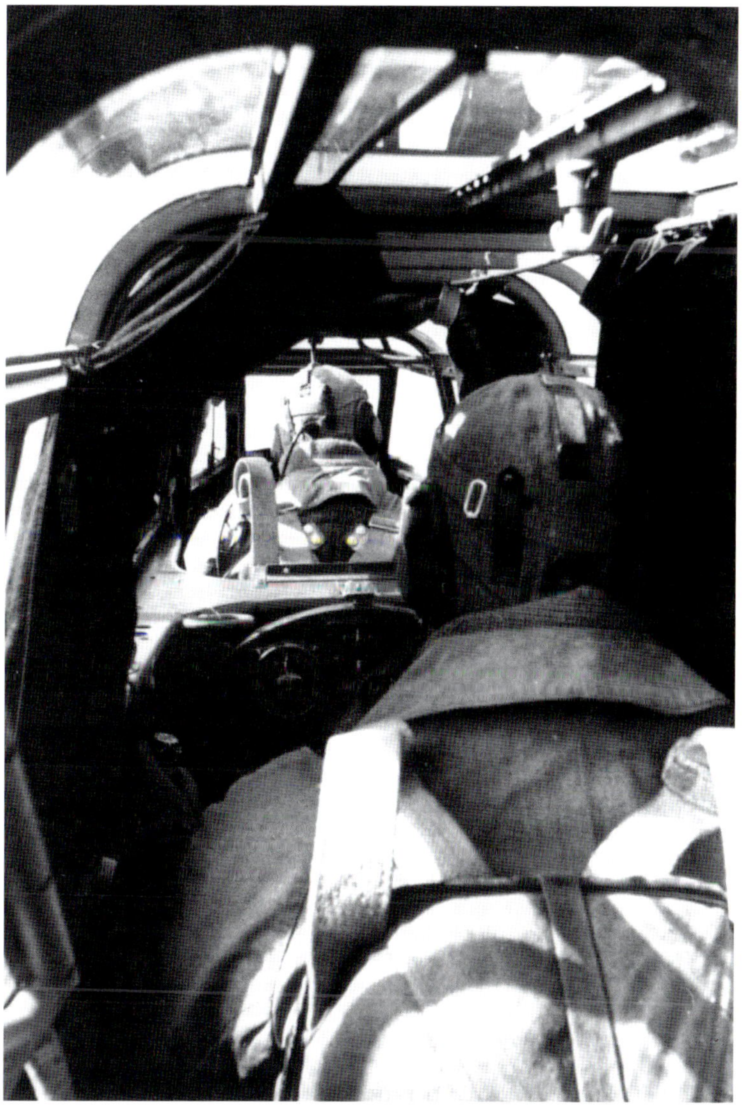

The *General der Nachtjagd* calls for a greater allocation of Ju 88 C-6 aircraft. *Oberstlt. i.G.* Eschenauer points out that some of these aircraft are needed for escort duties in the Mediterranean. Only after much effort was it possible to make 20 aircraft available to the night fighter units over the last few months. If it is not possible to get more airplanes allocated, then an increase in production must be considered with the caveat that the Ju 88 C-6 is not particularly suited to the night fighter role; it would be more advisable to switch straight to the Ju 88 G.

Since the *General der Nachtjagd* places more value on the Bf 110 than the Ju 88 C-6, the *Generalfeldmarschall* considers it advisable that the *General der Nachtjagd* relies on the Bf 110 and lets the *Genst. 6. Abt.* have the Ju 88 C-6 for other purposes. The *Technisches Amt* will work to ensure that the Ju 88 G enters production without any problems.

The Ju 188 will be produced as a night fighter starting in December 1944, with 20 of the type planned for production starting in January 1945. It is hoped that by this time at least 40 He 219s will have already been delivered. *Stabsing.* Friebel points out that the Ju 88 R, which was developed from the C-6 and G, is of the same quality as the Ju 188 J, so there is no point in moving up a deadline. Both have the BMW 801. Thus, this aircraft is indeed suited for night fighting operations, provided that it is available in sufficient numbers.

Oberst Peterson draws attention to the fact that, aside from the *FlaV* equipment, the *Lichtenstein* antenna causes the greatest drop in performance. *Oberstabsing.* Günther reports that serious efforts are already underway to change the way the antenna is mounted to the aircraft, namely by using ceramic rods. The new ceramic antenna would be mounted as a rod on the fuselage skin and would be covered by a plexiglass bubble, so that it would not be exposed. The *Generalfeldmarschall* calls for work to proceed at an accelerated pace so that the night fighter forces can be equipped with the system before the year is out.

The *General der Nachtjagd* mentions that the need for 3 cm guns is becoming more urgent for operations against the enemy's four-engined bombers. The ultimate would be for each night fighter type—He 219, Ta 154, Ju 88 G, and Ju 188 (also desired for the Bf 110)—to be armed with six guns, ideally with two MG 151s, two MK 108s, and two MK 103s. *Obersting.* Mix reports that the Bf 110 will shortly be produced with two MK 108s in place of the MG 17s. The prototype is just being completed. The He 219 initially began with four MK 108s and two MG 151s, but the two MK 108s will eventually be swapped out for MK 103s.

Obersting. Mix reports that just this week the MK 108 was fired for the first time with live ammunition while in flight. Several sorties were made with fair success, and it is hoped that by next week 10 aircraft can be handed over to Jever. Work on the MK 103 is slightly behind schedule. Company tests have so far gone well.

Oberst i.G. Pasewald poses a fundamental question hitting at the heart of the developmental program. The question concerns the fact that the MK 108 can only carry 60 rounds of ammunition, since the converted airplanes do not have sufficient room remaining to carry any more rounds. This means that with the high rate of fire the ammunition will run out quite quickly. The night fighter units must therefore decide what their ultimate goal should be: lots of guns with little ammunition and selectable rate of fire, or few weapons and lots of ammunition.

General der Nachtjagd Kammhuber reports that *Hauptmann* Frank was able to score six kills in a single mission with the Bf 110. He attacked a seventh, but ran out of ammunition before he could bring it down. This would seem to be the optimum for the Bf 110. He had been fortunate and effectively chewed up the targets from back to front. Flying an He 210, Streib brought down five aircraft before he, too, was finished.

General der Nachtjagd asks that the white camouflage used currently by *1./I*__* be put into general use, since it has proven to be quite effective. The *Generalfeldmarschall* orders:

(*Original incomplete, hence the gap)

a. Those aircraft now being manufactured as night fighters will have a white coating over their fighter camouflage, like the pattern that proved effective in *Hauptmann* Meurer's mission.
b. The *Nachtjagd-Korps* will carry out trials using light blue and will report on the results of same.
c. A white color will be developed that has roughly the same color tone as that of *Hptm.* Meurer's aircraft, but with the difference that it will be used as a base color.

The DB 605 is still alive. Measures introduced have not been studied as to their effectiveness. The oil slinger is to be installed in the Bf 110 as a matter of course and should, as soon as it is available, be retrofitted to the night fighters already delivered. Those engines with modified bearings will be tested in ten Bf 109Gs and four Bf 110s. DB hopes to build 1000 oil slingers in September, which will initially be installed in the night fighters. The night fighters should be handled carefully, since the loads and the running time are greater. In addition, the pilots are unable to read the engine monitoring gauges located outside on the nacelles.

General Kammhuber addresses the altitude requirements. The Bf 110 is useless if the enemy approaches at heights of 10000 m. He calls for exhaust turbines or GM 1. GM 1 is useful for 1/2 hrs' flight time and is already in production as the U7. The first aircraft have just been delivered. The Bf 110 is, according to Kammhuber, ideally suited for altitudes of 4000 to 6000 m, but more than 6500 to 8000 m its performance drops off considerably and becomes an extraordinarily weak and sluggish gun platform. Friedel claims the exhaust turbine has been researched. It offers no advantages over GM 1, since the additional weight and the air cooler for the supercharger both have an impact on the aircraft's performance. The reasons for the sluggishness will be looked into, but it is believed that the cause lies with the large "chimneys" (flame dampers) and the wing loading. A new version of the *FlaV* system is currently undergoing trials. This should improve the elevator response. New wing end caps designed to reduce wing loading will also be tested with the new *FlaV* system.

At the present time, 10 aircraft with GM 1 are being produced each month. Kammhuber calls for 50% of the output.

The *Lichtenstein* wide angle radar is discussed. Range is about 2 km. As of now, there are one or two available, which will equip Ju 88s with *SN 2*. According to Kammhuber the Ju 88 plays a relatively minor role; he wants to have the *Lichtenstein* wide angle radar system without the *SN 2* installed in a Bf 110 G-4 and offers to make an aircraft available for this purpose. At the same time there will be a Bf 110 with *SN 2*. Telefunken is working on making the normal *Lichtenstein BC* capable of switching over to wide angle. Kammhuber would like to make acquisition of the wide angle radar dependent upon test results. According to a statement by a Messerschmitt technical expert, the 1 m^2 span of the *Lichtenstein BC* causes a speed loss of 10 km/h and the *SN 2* a loss of 20 km/h. Focus in the immediate future will be on the *SN 2*.

It is proposed that current night fighting methods be expanded by employing 30 high-speed, long-range aircraft (BMW 801 powered Ju 88s) and *SN 2* radars with a range of 8 km. The Bf 110 is ruled out because of its 1 hr 20-30 min loiter time.

7/27/43 (GL)
Generalfeldmarschall Milch claims that Germany has been on the defensive for the last 1 1/2 to 2 years. The *Luftwaffe* now apparently recognize the serious importance of this fact. To this end, many more fighters as well as Bf 110s and Me 410s are needed. A lack of workers is the main thing preventing an increase in production for both airframes and engines. He arranges for the requisite number of workers to be made available for the fighter and engine programs.

A minimum of 20 Bf 110s with 3.7 cm cannon are to be allocated to Galland for air-to-air combat vice antitank missions. These are the same aircraft, but with GM 1. At the moment, it appears that tank kills have taken a back seat. All Bf 110s will now have mainly night fighting or heavy fighter roles. The general consensus is that the major problems with aircraft production have now been brought to heel, but *Generalfeldmarschall* Milch is nevertheless closely watching both companies producing the Bf 110. Both seem to have everything in order.

7/30/43 (GL)
Discussion is about which aircraft will be used as a shadow plane with *SN 2* in the night fighting role. According to Kammhuber, the most suitable is the Ju 188. The Ju 88 C-6 is too small. It is a sick bird and has too short a range. Since the Ju 188 will not be produced for a while yet, he would like to see the Ju 88 R-1 (later G-1) with *SN 2* and wide angle radar. As these cannot be delivered in sufficient quantities, it is proposed that the remaining *SN 2*s be fitted in the Ju 88 C-6. Kammhuber states that his people do not fly the Ju 88 C-6 because they have not been trained on it. What can be put into immediate use is the Bf 110. He would need the *SN 2* with wide angle radar for the Bf 110. At present, Kammhuber has 10 Bf 110 G-4s kitted out with the equipment as shadow planes. He poses the additional question of whether these shadow aircraft should be deployed with flame dampers. These eat up about 30 km/h of speed. Since the Ju 88 R 1 is also not immediately available, Milch wants to give Kammhuber more Ju 88 C 6s with *SN 2* and crews.

Galland wants to bring down 60 to 80 aircraft in an enemy bombing raid. In order to accomplish this, everything in the *Westgruppe* and the groups of *Befehlshaber Mitte* will be needed. He is losing 30 to 50 aircraft per day. He wants to take three *Zerstörer* groups and another bomber group used in the *Zerstörer* role and combine them into a central wing. With these 100 to 120 *Zerstörer* airplanes, he hopes to be able to engage the enemy formation in one long running sustained attack. These groups would include two groups each of Bf 110s and 410s. The Me 410s must have the KWK 5 cm and the Bf 110s the Flak 18 or the conversion kit with the two MG 151s, or at least *Nebelwerfer*. Using factory-fresh Bf 110s would have no value. Successes with the Flak 18 have been made, and he just needs 80 to 100 of them. At the present time, it is unknown whether or not the Bf 110 and the Me 410 can carry the *Nebelwerfer* due to its recoil.

7/43
In Parchim, *Oberfeldwebel* Paul Mahle equips the first Bf 110 G-4 with two oblique upward-firing MG FF/M.

The RAF begins jamming the night fighters' *Himmelbett* system using aluminum strips (Window, or *Düppel*). This ultimately results in new attack tactics that, because of its inadequate range, leave the Bf 110 behind compared to the more modern He 219 and Ju 88 G.

8/2/43 (RLM)
In Special Directive 110/865/055 "Special Measures for Defending the *Reich*," the RLM orders that Bf 110s be fitted with the 21 cm *WGr. 42* based on the specifications of *Erprobungskommando 25*.

8/3/43 (GL)
Under the order of the day "Increasing Homeland Defense," *Oberstingr.* Alpers discusses the matter of airframes: the program structure calls for an increase in fighters, heavy fighters, and night fighters; focus on the Bf 109. Bf 109 production will amount to 1000

This Bf 110 G-2 is only fitted with a pair of MG 151/20s, but makes up for this by carrying no less than six Nebelgerät air-to-air mortars. (Petrick)

aircraft as early as December 1943 (compared to May 1944 in the program). For the Fw 190, an increase in the rate of production will not be possible until early 1944 due to the effects of the bombing. It will not be until August 1944 that we will see 1056 aircraft, in March/April 1944 2000 (1460 under the old program).

Due to resource constraints, the Bf 110 *Zerstörer* and night fighter will only achieve a peak production rate of 200 aircraft per month (March 1944). The Me 210 has expired. The Me 410 has a limited potential for increased production (from 50 to 70 around the end of 1943/beginning of 1944), since Mtt Augsburg has production of the Me 262 at the same time. For the *Zerstörer* aircraft, total increase amounts to an average of 50 aircraft, starting immediately.

For the Do 217, the only version staying in the program is the night fighter. For the Ju 88 C-6 *Zerstörer* and night fighter, it is proposed that output be increased to 60 instead of 40.

The He 219 is presently entering production in Rostock. *General* Kammhuber asks that every effort be made to increase the output to 50 aircraft as quickly as possible. According to *Generalfeldmarschall* Milch, the matter must be decided whether it is worth it to continue with the previously established increase of 150 aircraft, or if it is better to switch to the Ju 188, which will most likely be produced in large numbers anyhow.

Subject: Better Firepower/Altitude for Fighters - Heavy Fighters

General Galland explains that it is important to shift over to the KWK 5 faster than is being done. It needs to be clarified whether the Me 410 alone can cover the requirements, or whether attempts need to be made to switch the Bf 110 over to the KWK 5 as well. In

General Galland's view, in the future there will most likely be a shortage of fighters or heavy fighters with heavy weapons.

The *Generalfeldmarschall* explains that an increase in Bf 110 production to 200 aircraft is not possible given the current resources. Converting another factory over to production of this older aircraft type is not acceptable. Me 410 production will increase markedly during the second half of 1944 (250 aircraft in December 1944) and could now possibly be increased to 280 to 290 airframes. *Generalfeldmarschall* Milch would like to use the Me 410 in the day fighter role, leaving the Bf 110 for the night and thereby relieving the situation somewhat in that arena.

It is expected that the Americans will soon be coming over at altitudes above 10000 m. In that event, neither the Me 410 nor the Me 209 would be of any use. 10000 m to 10500 m is considered the Me 410's limit. The Ju 188 with BMW 801 I is the only aircraft up to this task. In this light, the entire production program as it has been planned would be built on a false premise. Also up for discussion is operations using the GM 1. With Flak 18 and radioman, the Bf 110's service ceiling without the GM 1 is 8000 m in formation and 8500 m when operating alone. This is too low. Therefore, the Bf 110 with GM 1 as a stopgap measure must become available soon so that 9000 m in formation can be attained.

Subject: Bf 110 Day - Night

The night fighter arm must be beefed up. To do this, a further 100 to 200 aircraft for *Wilde Sau* missions need to be employed in addition to the standard night fighter operations using the Bf 110. In addition, there's the pursuit night fighting method, which needs high speed machines with long range. With current aircraft, which are approximately 20% faster than the enemy, the enemy planes are not intercepted until they are already over the target. Furthermore, the range of the primary aircraft used, the Bf 110, is so limited that it is not possible to have the formations concentrate on the attack. The He 219, in contrast, scores four to five kills per sortie thanks to its speed and four-hour endurance. *Oberst i.G.* von Loßberg points out that in the summer months night fighter operations over the *Reich* are concentrated in certain areas. As the nights become longer, the night fighter forces will be spread out over more areas. But then coverage will become too thin. *General d. Fl.* Kammhuber also draws attention to the great importance of aircraft for the night fighting role. With a quota of 700 aircraft, the current inventory is at 400, with 260 operationally ready.

The *Generalfeldmarschall* supports the wishes of *General* Galland, ordering 60 Bf 110 assigned to the day fighters, with some of these being equipped with 3.7 cm and GM 1. For the 3.7 cm weapon, clarification must be made immediately as to whether the GM 1 and the second crewman needed for reloading can be combined into the same area while still attaining the required altitude. The remaining 90 Bf 110s will be passed via *Genst. 6. Abt.* on to the night fighters. The *Generalfeldmarschall* instructs GL/C-B to make every effort to increase Bf 110 output by 10 aircraft per month (to be assigned to the night fighters as well), and for this task gives his approval for pulling workers from the Ju 88 C-6 program, with the express approval of subcommittee chairman *Dir.* Frydag.

General Galland feels it is absolutely vital that all Bf 110s be accounted for so that they will no longer be used as private touring planes.

Oberstltn. i.G. Eschenauer asks GL/C-B to speed up production of the GM-1 conversion kits.

General Galland requests that kits for the Bf 110 be drawn from the night fighters; they are needed for conversion of 150 aircraft. The *Generalfeldmarschall* authorizes this.

8/10/43 (GL)

Von Loßberg reports that there are currently four night fighting methods in use that, depending on the weather, are either combined or standalone: 1. The standard method of patrolling an airspace; 2. *Zahme Sau* pursuit method of seeking out and entering bomber streams—method still in the training stage; 3. Use of *Wilde Sau* techniques using massed forces are planned when the weather is favorable; and 4. Overwater pursuit. Using the *Rotterdam* radar system, this will prove to be quite effective.

The preconditions for *Zahme Sau* and overwater pursuit techniques are the availability of the *Lichtenstein SN 2* and the wide angle antenna. The nose antenna for the Bf 110, which is the main airframe planned for this role, has still not been clarified, unlike the wing antenna for the Ju 88. Ten aircraft are currently being kitted out with the system, of which 8 have the wing antenna. The fuselage antenna has not been clarified, either. Telefunken has promised approximately 200 *SN 2* systems for the months of August and September. In October, when conversion should be in full swing, the greatest number of these is expected. The wide angle antenna is promised for August in the amount of 160, and in September 340. Due to flight handling, the Bf 110 will not be fitted with the wing antenna. However, the Bf 110 is the most important type, since all units along the coast operate this aircraft. Telefunken is able to continue producing the antenna in Werneuchen. Telefunken must therefore be transferred to Werneuchen.

Discussions on *Düppel* (aluminum strips) countermeasures continue. *Dr.* Schultze has developed a portable transmitter that holds promise. It is able to distinguish stationary objects (*Düppel*) from fast moving ones (aircraft).

There are serious difficulties with equipping the aircraft with FuG 16, FuG 16 Z, and FuG 16 ZE. Within *XII. Korps* there are 450 aircraft without the FuG 16, i.e. without the capability of being controlled and without radio communication capability. The two-seat night fighters also lack 100 systems. An increase in output for the systems for August and September would be possible, but it hangs on 1500 men being allocated.

8/4 through 9/4/43

Five Bf 110 with MK 108s have been built and are being tested.

8/13/43 (GL)

Tank hunting on the Eastern Front is the topic of discussion. The Ju 87 G-1 with two 3.7 cm Flak 18s has proven effective, and production should continue. Everything possible should also be done for the Bf 110 and the Hs 129 as well.

8/15/43

The first Bf 110 G-2 with the M 5 conversion kit (2 x 2 *WGr.*) is delivered.

8/17/43 (GL)

According to the program, Tank should theoretically get the Luther and Gotha *Werken* for production of the Fw 190. In *Generalfeldmarschall* Milch's opinion, this will not happen—the plan was flawed. According to the procurement plans the Bf 110 is shortly expected to reach 200 per month by September 1944 as *Zerstörer* and night fighter variants, then continue at 100 per month as a night fighter only. The Ta 154 is expected to later be produced in larger numbers, but still has to prove its suitability for the role. Milch estimates a need for 350 to 450 night fighters per month for the latter half of 1944 and 1945. He is unable to say exactly whether the Bf 110's performance will be up to the task of 1945, but he does believe that it will indeed be suited, since the British cannot convert their night aircraft (Lancasters) that quickly. By 1946, however, the Bf 110 will most likely be of little value. In his opinion, the Ju 188 will continue to nudge ahead of the Bf 110, since it has more internal space, more range, and can carry more armament. But Junkers is currently operating at maximum capacity and will not be getting a new factory in the near future, meaning that Gotha and Luther would then have to switch over to Ju 188 production and would not be available for the Fw 190. The He 219 would only be produced in small numbers.

8/20/43

Von Loßberg reports that during the night of 17/18 August the night fighter's *Wilde Saus* were active in large numbers. 148 night fighters and 5 day fighters were in operation over Berlin. Too late, it was discovered that the main target was Peenemünde. 30 night fighters were flying over Peenemünde and scored 24 kills in short order, and a further 18 on the bombers' egress from the target. The twin-engined free-ranging method therefore has great potential. On the 18th night fighters were also employed during the day, and using the Bf 110 brought down 17 or 18 enemy aircraft. During the night mission 9 machines were lost, with considerably more during the day, with a combined total for the two days amounting to 32 total losses and 35 aircraft damaged. Most of the crews were able to bail out safely. *Hauptmann* Frank's group flew into a swarm of British fighters over Lille and lost 5 aircraft without ever breaking through to the four-engined bombers. This indicates that there is no purpose in having Bf 110s engage bombers that have fighter escort.

It was impossible to get the *Flak* to cooperate with the night fighters over Berlin; the *Flak* kept up a steady rate of fire the entire time, even though there were 200 German night fighters in the air and only a few enemy intruders at the time. In a telegram to *Reichsmarschall* Göring, Milch asks that the *Flak* only be allowed to shoot up to 3000 m when night fighters are over the site.

Concerns about replacements for the night fighters are discussed. In the raid mentioned above, within the space of 24 hours *12. Fliegerkorps* lost its entire replacement complement for a month. 35 machines had previously been promised, but this will now need to be increased to 55. This, according to *Oberst* von Loßberg, does not serve the night fighters' best interests. It is brought out that the recent production increase has led to a surplus of 65 night fighters and 75 day *Zerstörer* aircraft. *Generalfeldmarschall* Milch wants to see the Bf 110's production for all of next year exceed the rate of 140, with 200 being the target. The increased demand for the Bf 110 also means an increased demand for the DB 605 with the *B-Getriebe* for twin-engined aircraft, but this has not been taken into account. Milch believes that the Me 410 will become the day *Zerstörer*, and the Bf 110 will eventually be used exclusively in the night fighting role. With enough Me 410s available, the Bf 110 will need to take over the night completely, and the Ta 154 will supplement both roles. Von Loßberg states that he has spoken with individual experts within the night fighter program. They believe the Ta 154 in its original concept with Jumo 211 engines is a feasible design, even if the radioman can't see out. The Bf 110 has been revamped to the point where the radioman can't see out either.

8/43 (*Erprobungskommando 25* Action Report)

Bf 110 with 3.7 cm *Flak* fitted with 21 cm standard barrels. Finished installation of semi-fixed MK 101 in Bf 110 G at Tarnewitz.

9/7/43 (GL)

The developmental state of the GM 1 system is discussed. This system has not yet been cleared for production. Up to this point, systems have been delivered for the Bf 109, the Bf 110, and the Ju 88, but these are constantly being subjected to modifications, particularly with the tanks. No data is available for the other types planning to utilize this system (including the Me 410). The night fighter units stationed in Belgium are removing the GM 1 systems from their Bf 110s since the British and Americans are not coming over at altitudes above 7000 m and they do not want to be carrying any unnecessary ballast. In spite of this, *Generalfeldmarschall* Milch would still like to have GM 1 systems made for these aircraft and stored in clean facilities, since they might one day be needed. First, though, the system is required for day Bf 110s, the Bf 109, the Fw 190, and the Me 410.

Direktor Nallinger from Daimler-Benz complains about Messerschmitt. All of Messerschmitt's airframes, i.e. Bf 109, Bf 110, Me 210, and Me 410, do not meet the conditions outlined in the engine installation portfolio. The oil back pressure and the water back pressure have been too high from the outset and had to be approved under protest—made together with officials in the face of delivery quotas. Messerschmitt has accepted markedly poorer operational safety in favor of minor theoretical aerodynamic benefits. (Compare Me 210/410 on 9/7/43). With or without oil slinger, the Bf 110 is still not cleared for operations at altitude.

The DB 605 is causing considerable problems. The Junkers and Daimler Benz companies report on causes and measures being taken to increase the life of the bearing seats. *Prof.* Nallinger of DB reports on efforts the companies that produce the DB 605 are introducing or have already made to cure the DB 605's problems. Some of the measures used to improve its reliability include increasing the oil flow quantity and installing an oil slinger, which will separate impurities from the poor grade oil currently being used.

Reichsmarschall *Göring asks whether the DB 605 is even necessary given that the DB 603 is coming soon. Milch responds by saying that it is needed as long as the Bf 109 and Bf 110 continue, and they will be produced in large numbers over the next year.*

It is learned that the DB 605 could be put into production starting in April 1944 using the DB 603 blower. First flight of a Bf 109 powered by a DB 605/603 supercharger is planned for 9/8/43. The DB 628-powered Bf 109 was not successful. The Bf 109 with DB 605 plus 603 supercharger and GM 1 is better than the 109 with the DB 628.

9/13/43 (GL)
In principle, the fact is that the number of anti-armor aircraft available on the front is entirely dependent upon the number of weapons reconfigured for use by aircraft.

The current status of Bf 110 G-2 R with 3.7 cm armament: 20 aircraft are operational, and are presently being employed in homeland defense. The General Staff's instructions:

a) From production: 1943, six in July, six in August, 15 each from September through November. Deliveries in accordance with these instructions will be according to plan through the end of September 1943.
b) Conversion kits. In addition to the planned deliveries in a), by the end of September a further 60 kits consisting of the weapon and the airframe components are to be available for retrofitting; conversion will be carried out by the *General der Jagdflieger* at the Ansbach airbase. A total of 14 kits have been delivered as of 9/18. The remainder of the quota could not be filled because the work force allocated by the *General der Jagdflieger* did not arrive until mid-September.

9/14/43 (GL)
The situation with the *Lichtenstein SN 2* is discussed. An He 219, a Bf 110, and a Ju 88 are operating on the front. Two more Ju 88s and an He 219 are ready for pickup, while two Ju 88s are in Gütersloh and three in Diepensee, along with a Bf 110, but these are not yet ready. There are seven Ju 88s being readied in Werneuchen and six in Stendal. The main problem is with the Bf 110. Work started in Werl, but from the outset there were problems with fitting the equipment. Attempts are being made to finalize the layout this month. The original distance between antennas and the antenna switch was too great. A machine gun will need to be removed

so that the switch can fit into the cockpit. In addition, Messerschmitt is searching for a suitable way to fit the MK 108, which is now in development. Another sticking point is the expected numbers. Using Telefunken's best engineers, a completion time of one week per aircraft was achieved in the testing area at Diepensee. Five aircraft can be worked on side by side, but that is the limit, since the two systems interfere with each other. Based on this experience, Werl cannot be expected to produce more than five or ten Bf 110s in September. In order to remove these obstacles by October, Telefunken's testing area will need to be restocked and 100 men, trained exclusively on airborne radar acquisition, will have to be made available through a radio equipment special allocation directive. Furthermore, a fully equipped Ju 88 and Bf 110 must be provided for training.

Von Loßberg sees dark times ahead for the long-range and ultra long-range night fighters, because during a recent operation over the North Sea three of the five Bf 110 night fighters deployed were shot down. With their flame dampers and all the extra equipment, they are slower than the He 111 from 1939.

Trials and test squadrons have been initiated, since without them the *SN 2* will never get out the gate. These could not be afforded up until now.

For operational reasons, the Bf 110 in Diepensee is regularly flown with a three man crew, even though the third crewman has no opportunity to buckle himself in. This is causing problems with the chief of flight safety. Milch sanctions this approach, but only for test purposes.

Attempts will be made to increase the range of the wide angle *Lichtenstein* BC on three Bf 110s to two kilometers, in order to dispense with the need for the *SN 2*. To this end, the aircraft will be in Werneuchen 8 to 10 days and then ferried to a specialist in Oberpfaffenhofen. A report is expected in 14 days. The *Lichtenstein* BC and C1 are ready for production and stable, and not even the wide angle antenna is expected to cause delays.

The improved Jumo 211 will first be installed in the Ju 88 C-6. With the *SN 2*, this aircraft is so slow that it can't even catch up to the bombers. The climb rate is also unacceptable.

Procurement situation, totals for August: Bf 110 – 150, Me 210 – 7, Me 410 – 40.

Prognosis for September: Bf 110 – 150 aircraft according to the program. 102 night fighters are expected to be delivered in September (actual requirement 90).

Prototype installation of the Flak 18 in the Bf 110 has been cleared. In antitank sorties on the Eastern Front the weapon functioned well. *Erprobungskommando 25* noted problems when firing the gun between altitudes of 7000 and 8000 m, however. The same parts are always breaking. The Flak 18 is also not very popular with anti-aircraft units; since its introduction it has required the most careful attention. Galland has made the suggestion of installing the Flak 43. According to Milch, though, this gun is not yet ready and will not be expected in the field until at least January 1944. Those entering production in September can only be used for installation and firing trials.

Generalfeldmarschall Milch claims that the requirements of the field often do not correspond with the industry's deliveries. For example, armor is fitted to aircraft in the factories. When they get to the field, however, the first thing the troops do is pull the armor off. Such unnecessary work needs to stop at the source.

9/17/43 (Night Fighter Conference)

The *Reichspost* and AEG have jointly developed the *Spanner 2* device. 15 to 18 of these can be expected by early October. A pre-production run of 50 has started. Prototype fitting into the Bf 110 is underway, and when completed then testing can begin. *Spanner* systems are to be installed in six each of Bf 110s and Ju 88s. Additional allocations are possible, since Kammhuber rejects having them fitted into the Ju 88 C-6. For *Major* Hermann, nine *Spanner* are to be installed in Bf 109s. Hermann has already tested the system operationally, but the aircraft was shot down by friendly anti aircraft fire.

Kammhuber complains that he is not getting enough aircraft, and that some are going to Galland. Standard strength is dropping at an extraordinary rate. In places, group strength amounts to no more than 11 to 15 aircraft. On the other hand, there are 18 machines at the factory waiting to be picked up.

Kammhuber addresses the topic of fuselage tanks: "We have asked to get fuselage tanks for the 110 as quickly as possible. But that has not happened yet."

Genfeldm. Milch: "Why fuselage tanks?"

Kammhuber: "We've now got wing drop tanks fitted, but these cause a serious loss in speed. Fuselage tanks are better suited for long flights."

Kammhuber: "The GM 1 system has not proven satisfactory. We had one machine in the air; its performance wa not up to par; it became particularly bad in its flight handling. Landing qualities were also quite bad."

Von Loßberg: "The moment the pilot extends the landing flaps the machine becomes so tail heavy that it takes one hand to hold it steady. This puts the pilot's life directly at risk."

Vorwald: "On Monday I had a big meeting on the 110 G-4 U7. This was first designed as a tank with three bulkheads, so that it's not so prone to sloshing around except at certain times. This may not be the best solution, but it's going to be put into general use immediately, because it's the quickest way. The ultimate solution will be a triple compartmentalized container with internal expansion. The matter is being handed over to the E-Stelle, next week actually. The E-Stelle representative was there."

Hoffmann: "I broached the matter with Mtt yesterday. They will try to develop a new gear system for trimming the elevators so that there's not as much elevator travel when the flaps are extended as there is now. This should reduce the extreme case of tailheaviness in the aircraft."

Petersen: "In general, we can say that the Bf 110 is at the end of its useful life. There's the FlaV system, then the SN 2 and its huge Christmas tree. Add the GM 1 and possibly external tanks! That's not possible—it's inconceivable. In short, the plane's performance and flight handling are at an end. We have got to be absolutely clear on this point."

Genfeldm. Milch: "How long does the GM 1 last?"

Vorwald: "About an hour."

Genfeldm. Milch: "Well, there's nothing else available. Do you really need it now?"

Kammhuber: "At the moment, not yet."

Genfeldm. Milch: "But later, for getting up to altitude."

Kammhuber: "We've got nothing for altitude. We'd have absolutely nothing if the enemy were to come over tomorrow at high altitude."

Vorwald: "We can feasibly get up to altitude."

Von Loßberg: "I think, though, that the SN 2 can't get up to altitude with the reduction in performance; in particular, its climb rate is almost as bad as that of the Ju 88: maximum permissible cruising speed of 240 and a 3 m/s rate of climb. It gets a little better above 2000 m."

Genfeldm. Milch: "I'll ask that it be tested at Rechlin. Then Kammhuber can be kept informed so that he is involved."

Hertel: "I can provide some information on the tanks. A contract has been issued for 200 kits, but only 40 will be delivered by the end of this month. It will be put into full scale production starting in November."

Hauptmann Meurer reports that he has had good success with the two oblique firing MG FFs he had fitted in his Bf 110. The MG 151 will not work because the gunner can get hung up on it. Von Loßberg proposes to simply copy the idea; there are a lot of people who think highly of it. Kammhuber is of the opinion to let the field units install it themselves. It is simpler that way, since you can't make it applicable across the board. One will want it and the other one won't.

9/18/43 (Mtt)
GL/C-E tasks the Messerschmitt AG with exploring the possibility of fitting the Jumo 211 F, developed by Focke-Wulf for the Ta 154, into the Bf 110. Since the engine weight is more than that of the DB 605 already installed in the Bf 110, the research is to be carried out in conjunction with the planned lengthening of the fuselage. Engine blueprints and documentation are to be requested from Focke-Wulf, Bad Eilsen.

9/21/1943 (GL)
Subject: High altitude Aircraft. It is anticipated that American Flying Fortress bombing raids will be made at higher altitudes. Countermeasures are discussed. The Bf 110 is planned for both day and night operations. However, as a night fighter with flame dampers and the Christmas tree antenna, it requires the GM 1. An alternative might be the DB 605 fitted with the 603 blower. In *General* Galland's view, there is another option in addition to the Bf 110 with GM 1: the Bf 110 with extended wing tips and GM 1, with the next step then being the 603 supercharger. *Oberst* Petersen explains that such an aircraft reached an altitude of 11 km in Rechlin. Without the oil slinger the engines cannot withstand the altitudes needed for day and night time operations. Installation can proceed, the prototype is finished, oil slingers are being built, and full-scale production can begin. The GM 1 has been tested, and the triple compartmentalized tanks are being shipped this week. Because of all its additional equipment, the night fighter version is in much poorer shape. *General* Galland stresses that the Bf 110 (G 2, rear guns, two man crew, armor, without GM 1 and with 4 air-to-air mortars and 4 cannons, standard, without wing tip extensions) has a ceiling of 9.5 km in formation. From this information, it seems that the Bf 110 is the better basis for high altitude operations.

For wing tip extensions, the wing strength is already at its limit, and therefore the extensions must be jettisonable for dogfighting. The Bf 110 has a wing load factor of 2.9. The wing will break as soon as 3 is reached, and for a *Zerstörer* with wingtip extensions, 3 is an exceptionally low figure. The extensions increase the span of each wing by 1.25 meters. Increasing the span-chord ratio has a positive impact at higher altitudes, boosting the ceiling by 1000 m. Galland wants to see a lengthened wingspan as standard. The Bf 110s used in *Wilde Sau* operations should not be fitted with flame dampers as they interfere with the airflow over the wing. Instead, shield plates can be attached that prevent the pilot from becoming blinded. The night fighters want to retain the flame dampers, since every formation hides five to six Beaufighters.

Galland is getting three Bf 110 G-2/U7s with GM 1 each month. He would like to have more. In the first meeting on the GM 1's criticality, the GM 1 was distributed as follows: Initially the Bf 109 G-5, then 20% for the Bf 110 G-2/U7 and 10% for the night fighters. Galland says there are not anymore *Zerstörer* G-2s, unless they are part of the homeland defense. The 20% should be armed with the 3.7 cm *Flak*. According to Milch, this should be changed; with Galland's concurrence, 100% should be fitted with the GM 1.

9/27/43 (GL)
Regarding the extended wing tip modification for the Bf 110, once developmental work has concluded a report is to be given to the

Genst. 6. Abt. outlining the possible start dates for implementation.

9/28/43 (GL)
Milch and his colleagues have not only pushed *Zerstörer* production over the 100 per month mark, they have now reached 200. Approximately 1000 is now the plan. Fighter output is now five times what it was 1 1/2 years ago, and is expected to increase by another 3.5 times to 3500.

Generalfeldmarschall Milch asks that studies be made as to whether the 603 blower can be fitted into the Bf 110 as soon as possible, i.e. doing for the Bf 110 what is already being done for the Bf 109. He calls the Bf 109 and Bf 110 "old ravens."

9/43
A Bf 110 G-4 nose is in development with two MK 108s, an FuG 220, and an FuG 212.

9/43 (*Erprobungskommando 25* Action Report)
Initial studies using 30 cm air-to-air mortars on the Bf 110 – as well as the Flak 43 (3.7 cm).

10/12/43 (GL)
Generalfeldmarschall Milch estimates that there are currently not much more than a thousand active fighters and 600 Bf 110s.

10/15/43 (GL)
The *General der Jagdflieger* asks that installation of the MG 81 Z guns alongside the GM 1 system in Bf 110s be explored.

10/19/43 (GL)
The wide angle antennas have been tested in the Ju 88 and Bf 110, with negative results. Ruggedness and design configuration were unfit. The installation is more a bricolage than anything. The *Generalfeldmarschall* had ordered that an He 219, a Ju 88, and a Bf 110 were to be thoroughly tested with wide angle antennas over a 14-day period. Using the *Rotterdam Halbe* system, the copy of the British system, ranges of 50 km have been test flown.

In three months the *Luftwaffe* has lost 2877 aircraft.

10/26/43 (GL)
Galland mentions that further improvements for the Bf 110 have come from the field units, where two MG 151s have been installed in place of the four MGs, now giving the type four MG 151s as its basic armament. Night fighters also hang two more under the belly, giving a total of six. This needs to be put into production quickly. Mix makes the proposal that the troops be given orders to fit the MK 108 instead, since the department's efforts are now focusing on the 108.

Galland continues by saying that, if the marriage of the Jumo 213 with the Bf 110 is successful, then it would be too early to drop the type. Milch's opinion: if we bring in the 213, it will probably beat the 410. According to Knemeyer, the final data should be available in a few days. People still have faith in the DB 628 high altitude engine, which would give the plane with longer wings respectable high altitude performance. Hoffmann, however, points out that aircraft would then have a strength factor of 2.66, meaning that it would fly apart the first time it was put into a sharp turn. A new wing needs to be built.

A further aspect is that the factories now building Bf 110s are supposed to be producing the Fw 190 by the end of 1944, at which point the Me 410 is expected to replace the 110. *Generalfeldmarschall* Milch thinks that

Replacement of the four MG 17s with two MG 151/20s, as seen here on this aircraft from 8./ 26, was a field modification. Industry-wide, the official plans called for the utilization of the MK 108. (Petrick)

if one saw what a useful aircraft one was getting then Bf 110 production could continue, at first with wingtip attachments and then later with the new wings. Production should not exceed 200 per month, and Fw 190 production can be shifted to the countryside. This is not yet ripe for a decision, though.

Production potential for the Jumo 213 looks good for 1944, much better than for the DB and BMW, and in the event that it is decided to be used in the Bf 110 could even be increased. In the event the Jumo 213 E is a hit, Milch thinks that you would have a true standard powerplant and would not need the others anymore. Air-cooled engines would only be needed for those aircraft operating at low altitudes.

10/29/43 (GL)
According to Petersen, Prince Wittgenstein has racked up 22 kills in the East with an oblique firing weapons system installed in the field. Aircraft are being modified at Tarnewitz night and day. Von Loßberg reports on *Hauptmann* Meurer, who with an oblique-fitted MG FF has also scored 22 kills in his group. The weapons sets for the Bf 110 are being used. Petersen calls for this weapon to be introduced in series production. According to Hoffmann, prototype installation work is underway for the Bf 110 and the Me 410.

Galland reports that in his area of operations Me 410s are being fitted with Flak 43 guns. The installation is quite good and will most likely be approved for the Bf 110. The Bf 110 is increasingly being delivered with the Flak 18. He asks that armament be switched over to the Flak 43 as soon as possible. On the same topic, the ZFR 4 gunsight has proven to be exceptionally effective. 80 of these have been ordered for delivery as soon as possible, followed by another 20 per month.

In a discussion on strategy, Knemeyer reports on fighter development, and that the Me 262 has first priority for Messerschmitt. As of yet, there has been no kind of agreement as to whether the Me 209 will replace the Bf 109. Messerschmitt is also responsible for the 410, the 110, and monitoring the Bf 109. With the DB 605, the Bf 110 is too slow. Messerschmitt cannot fulfill all this tasking (compare Me 210).

Performance boosts for the Bf 110 by the Jumo 213 and DB 605 D engines and the associated modifications are discussed. By fitting the Jumo 213 the weight ahead of the main spar increases by 1000 kg. This necessitates the firewall being moved aft, a new torque nose box to take the engine, new fuselage attachment points, new undercarriage wells since the landing gear has to be moved forward by 150 mm, and a new wing. In order to offset the shift in the center of gravity, the fuselage would have to be lengthened by 700 mm. On the other hand, the DB 605 with 603 G blower, the DB 605 D, would require far fewer modifications. The wing cutout in the torque box, the rocker arms for the engine, the intake system, covers, and the landing gear struts all need to be modified.

For the DB 605 D the maximum pressure altitude is 7.5 km compared to the B version's 5.8 km. Speed increases from 580 to 620 km/h. In comparison with the DB 605 D, the Jumo 213 is faster by 20 km/h but the maximum pressure altitude is 1.5 km less. Milch points out that the Jumo 213 A is of no interest, since it will only be built for a short time before production is switched over to the E. Hoffmann states that the Jumo 213 has enormous potential, but as of yet no research has been initiated.

With regard to the Bf 110 with Jumo 213, Von Loßberg asks about the endurance, something that would be of particular interest for the night fighters. The Bf 110 G-4 with *SN 2* and external tanks is at its limit with regard to speed. Therefore, for any improvement in Bf 110 performance the focus will need to be on internal tanks. 3 1/2 to 4 hrs at minimum cruise power is necessary. This will probably work by lengthening the fuselage, shifting the center of gravity, and because the canopy is quite long.

Milch's opinion is that this is practically a new machine, with the scope of changes comparable to the Me 410 as a follow-on development of the 210. The comparison needs to extend to the Ta 154, the Ju 388, and the He 219 in order to determine whether the effort is worth it. In any event, it seems that it is worth the effort to fit the Bf 110 with the DB 605 D, since this can be made faster. Installation of the DB 628s laying around should also be explored. There were no advantages noted when the engine was installed in the Bf 109, since the performance increase was offset by the enormous frontal drag generated by the second blower stage; the whole thing was very roughly done. Because of its basic design and its wing loading, the Bf 110 is an airplane well suited for flying at altitude, and its possible the installation might be beneficial.

10/43 (*Erprobungskommando 25* Action Report*)*
5 cm KWK installation in the Me 410 at *E-Stelle* Tarnewitz. Installation of Flak 43 (3.7 cm) in the 410 postponed in favor of the Bf 110.

11/43
The first Bf 110 G-4/U9 with two MK 108s (*W.Nr.* 480092) leaves the production line, but without FuG 212 and flame dampers.

11/5/43 (Night Fighter Conference)
Von Loßberg reports on the situation with the SN-2 System: "There have been 42 machines built and delivered to the night fighters. At present, the He 219 has been grounded. At Venlo there are two Ju 88 Rs and four Bf 110s in operation. In Twenthe three Bf 110s are operational. In Gütersloh, NJG 2 has 10 Ju 88 C-6s and 3 Ju 88 Rs, of which three are operational due to a lack of specialists. In the documentation here you will see that the Lichtenstein wide angle and C1 systems fail after takeoff in 50% of the cases. Something goes wrong with the SN-2 in one out of three takeoffs. The equipment is still in its developmental stage. In operation are an estimated 12 out of 49 SN-2 machines; the others are out of action due to avionics or other reasons. The British are using a new tactic. They are flying more widely spaced apart and are using warning systems. When attacked, the airplanes form a long line."

Von Loßberg reports on the Bf 110: "There were fears that the MK 108, which is fitted in the forward fuselage, would blind and cover the glass with soot. To prevent this, we have planned for a) flame suppressor, and b) window sprayer like the ones that are being used successfully with the fighters.

The Meurer Group has installed two oblique firing FFs in its 110s and has been using them with considerable success. This installation will not work when the extra fuselage tanks are fitted. On the other hand, these tanks are needed most urgently, since the external wing tanks cost too much speed, particularly when used in conjunction with the SN2. (**Schmidt:** Are the tanks armored?) They are protected just like the other tanks, and this is naturally a more critical area."

Schmidt: "It is best if we do this 50/50: 50% with extra tanks and 50% with the oblique armament."

Von Loßberg: "Another possibility would be to mount the guns behind the extra tank. It does not increase the weight by much. (**Zuruf:** We need clarification: a third crewman or a fuselage tank or the GM 1! If the fuselage tank is put in, then the GM 1 and the third crewman are gone."

Zuruf: "The night fighters have a requirement for increasing the aircraft's performance at altitude, and this means using the fuselage tank."

Hoffmann: "The operational requirement will be met in the future in the fact that we are getting the 605 D. Additionally, the option of using available 628 engines is being explored. On another point, I might just add that for the 110 there is such a limited amount of leeway with regard to the center of gravity that we can do relatively little. We have got to be careful that we do not completely cock up the Bf 110 by adding equipment, but at least keep the aircraft of use to us to some extent. We have got to more or less throw out everything we can in order to at least keep it usable for high altitude operations at night."

Schmidt: "That's the most important thing: the altitude. Otherwise you will find yourself out there at night with 40 Mosquitoes."

Von Loßberg: "I believe that the best suggestion is the 605 D."

Hoffmann: "Research into installation is ongoing, and a prototype plane has been set aside."

Mann: "Production was expected to begin in February."

Schmidt: "We have got to have the GM 1 by then."

Von Loßberg: "As near as I can figure, it will be long after February before the GM 1 is working."

Schmidt: "Cross bulkheads are being incorporated into the design. Cross bulkheads also need to be put into the fuselage."

Hoffmann: "I am not convinced that the cross bulkheads in the GM 1 tank will eliminate the problems with the flight handling. The main reason that the aircraft has such a limited play in its center of gravity will still be there. (**Vorwald:** Just because of its weight?) "People are looking into ways of eliminating the problem."

Von Loßberg: "I would suggest that we carry out the recommendation of the General that we have a limited number of kits built with the oblique guns, that we say: either oblique weapons and external tanks, or internal tanks and no oblique guns. The question is, what percentage should be oblique guns?"

Vorwald: **"50%"**

Alpers: "The factories are already so overtaxed. They have got to increase their output to 200. This makes it difficult to allocate production. (**Vorwald:** Can't Luther and Gotha be allocated?) That would work."

Vorwald: "So that Gotha would make the fuselage tank and Luther the oblique armament."

Von Loßberg: "The oblique armament means that the factory would operate as it does now. The oblique guns are easy to install. It would be a conversion kit that would fit into the machines as they are now, without any problem."

Alpers: "I would suggest not breaking it down 50/50, but 65% (Zuruf: Closer to 50%). Half extra fuel tanks, half oblique guns. Which ones? 131 or 151? (**von Loßberg:** Two FFs.) Installation of four MG 131s or four 151s is currently being looked into."

Von Loßberg: "Two FFs should be fitted, not 151s, because a pilot can get caught in them when trying to bail out."

Alpers: "I have received documents on the installation of the oblique guns. They say that four MG 131s or 151s are being looked into. Now I am told that they should be two FFs. We have not checked to see if there are enough FFs in the numbers we would need."

Von Loßberg: "A check has shown that there are about 1200 to 1600 FF weapons left."

Schmidt: "We've still got one matter remaining: how to get to higher altitudes."

Vorwald: "At present, research is being done with the 628. There are 150 of them. Currently, it will not be going into the Bf 109. Knemeyer thinks there's potential in putting the 628 into the 110. That would be a jump in altitude. We have got to push this 628 issue."

Von Loßberg: "The Ju 88 C-6 is at Venlo. It is proposed that an oblique armament be fitted, consisting of two MG 151s. The parts will be taken from the Bf 110's bathtub armament. Question: Can the Bf 110 do without its bathtub armament? It is often removed because it is so unwieldy. I would then recommend that we have these 110 kits removed and the weapons used for the 88 C-6 and R 2's oblique armament. For the most part, the field units can do this themselves. Some components, such as the ammunition belt feed, will need to be supplied by the aviation industry."

Zuruf: "The troops are all for taking the four machine guns out of the Bf 110 and dropping in the two 151s in exchange."

Von Loßberg: "The 108 is being fitted on the production line. Shame about the work." (Comment: field units do not want to fly with two 151s.)

11/9/43 (GL)
The oil slinger has not yet been fitted into the Bf 110 because the oil cooler is inadequate. Up to now Messerschmitt has always ordered the old one, even though the new one has been technologically feasible for over a year. Messerschmitt has been vague when it comes to installation of the new coolers in production plans. Messerschmitt's contract called for taking care of all issues for incorporating components into the engines of the Bf 109, 110, and 410. He himself confessed that by taking on new tasks he has not pushed basic issues for old matters as much as he perhaps should be doing. *Generalfeldmarschall* Milch recommends getting that in writing.

11/12/43 (GL)
On the subject of daylight air defense at altitudes above 10 km, discussion centers around a Bf 110 with extended fuselage, lengthened wingtips, DB 628, Flak 43, and ZFR 4, which would be produced at a rate of 50 per month. According to information provided by *Erprobungskommando 25*, since the Me 410 is going to the bomber sector, this seems to be the only way for any kind of aircraft to be able to cover the higher altitudes for the months of February, March, and April. Replacement aircraft might be the Ju 188 and the 399 with the Jumo 213 E. The reason for the urgency is that it is believed that B-29s are already in England and will soon be appearing over Germany. 50 airplanes can be built using the available stockpile of DB 628s, but production of the DB 628 would then need to be resumed. Currently a Bf 110 is being modified to take the DB 628, and should not take much effort. The airframe would need to have its fuselage lengthened by 60 cm, but this modification would not be overly difficult.

Milch had decided on building a high altitude version of the Bf 110 roughly eight weeks ago. This is the short fuselage G-4/U 7 with DB 605 B and GM 1. From a flight handling standpoint, the plane is flawed, i.e. it is tricky to land and at altitudes of around 8000 m is unstable in its yaw axis.

The first short fuselage Bf 110 with DB 628 is being built in Rechlin and is expected to take to the air during the second half of November. It carries 70 kg of ballast in the aft fuselage section. Von Loßberg suggests removing the forward firing machine guns and installing heavy oblique firing armament. This should not affect the center of gravity. Following a long argument over why the DB 628 was abandoned, Schilo points out that it will take four to five months until the final form prototype engines will be complete. According to Mann, it will be about seven to eight months before the DB 628 is produced. Assuming that, Milch believes the high altitudes could best be covered by the Jumo 213 E in the Ta 152 and Fw 190, but he wants to make good use of the available 150DB 628s. There is also discussion of installing the temporary DB 605 AS and the definitive 605 D in the Bf 110.

As soon as possible, Milch would like a comparison study between the DB 628 and DB 605 D in the Bf 110. To this end, two short fuselage Bf 110s should each have DB

628s and DB 605 AS fitted and evaluated by *Erprobungskommando 25*. Working in cooperation with DB, Gotha should build additional machines using the DB 605 D, making use of the longer fuselage design. The DB 605 D seems to have more potential than the DB 628, since it does not require a supercharger air cooler. Gotha has already built three longer fuselage Bf 110s.

11/15/43 (GL)
Plans are for 50% of the Bf 110 G-4s to be constructed with the oblique firing guns and 50% with extra internal tank or GM 1. Completion dates have yet to be set for this version and the other versions with oblique firing armament.

11/16/43 (GL)
For the Bf 110, there will be a delay with the MK 108 – the barrel sleeve armor sheaths were ordered from the Procurement Office too late.

Production of the Flak 18 guns converted for the Bf 110 began at the start of the month. Based on the experience of *Erprobungskommando 25*, it looks as though it will be necessary to switch over to the Flak 43. The *General der Flakartillerie* will ensure that the Flak 43 is available for installation in aircraft. Prototypes are currently being fitted into 110s at Messerschmitt. As of yet, no prototype layout drawings from the test unit have been sent to Messerschmitt; copies are still being made.

11/30/43 (GL)
In the planning for high speed bombers, night fighters, and heavy fighters it is projected that the current figure of 332 aircraft per month will increase to 1140—to include the Do 335 and the Ar 234—by late 1945/early 1946. The *Zerstörer* and night fighters this year are the Bf 110, Me 210, Me 410, and Ju 88. This series will expand when the Do 335 and Ar 234 go into production, as well as the Ta 154 and He 219 pure night fighters. The *Reichsmarschall* has set the numbers of Ta 154s at 350 per month, and those of the He 219 from 150 to 100. Added on are 150 Ar 234s per month. Killing the He 219 in favor of the Ju 388 is discussed, since both have virtually the same performance and there are too many types. This, however, would lead to an unacceptable drop in total output.

11/30/43
Bf 110 G-4 (*W.Nr.* 6309), with a field-mounted oblique armament consisting of 2 MG FF/M has been delivered to the Gothaer Waggonfabrik so that the kit can be designed for series production. The only thing the GWF considers to be in order is the installation position and wants to redesign the whole arrangement.

12/43
The U9 conversion with two MK 108s is renamed the R3, and production begins.

12/1/43 (GL)
According to Aircraft Program 225-1, monthly production of the Bf 110 G is to be raised to 150. Furthermore, in the heavy fighter class by the second half of 1945 the monthly output is projected as 500 Ta 154s, 200 Me 410s, and 90 Do 335s. An additional 490 JU 88 Gs, 100 He 219s, and 40 Ju 388J-1s are also to be built.

12/3/43 (GL)
Bf 110 landing gear production has been impacted by bombing raids on Berlin. Both plants that produce undercarriage parts for the Bf 110 are in Berlin, BMW in Reinickendorf and Deutsche Industriewerke in Spandau. BMW was hit particularly hard, but the number of melted machinery is low. BMW production is being moved to the former Pieron Works at present. All production tools, particularly the templates, have survived. Finished landing gear components were carefully stored in the basement. Production should resume again in a few days. Milch orders that production be shifted out of Berlin immediately.

The Bf 110 is considered an old machine on its last legs. However, it must be retained as long as it can continue to fulfill its tasks. The Bf 110 is better than no airplane at all. Production of the Bf 110 will end when the He 219 reaches 100 machines.

The Tank plane was only built to have a design that made use of wood alongside the duraluminum aircraft. If it turns out to be good, all the better, but it has got to be built even if it is only used in the East. The matter of penetration for the wooden cockpit has, in the meantime, been resolved for 2 cm, but not yet for 3 cm. With regard to the variants, Galland, Vorwald, Knemeyer, Diesing, and KdE are in agreement that the B-series be abandoned. According to a submission by Focke-Wulf, the C-variant is expected to enter production in August 1944, beginning with 10 units in the Posen District, with the second district coming online with 20 in September and reaching 50 by October. There will not be a startup period when switching from the Jumo 211 powered A-model to the C with metal cockpit and Jumo 213, and some of the 800 aircraft in arrears will be made up. Milch is curious whether this will actually result in an increase in output.

Bf 110 follow-on developments using the DB 605 D or DB 628 are discussed. CE 2 has initiated work in the aviation industry which has resulted in the following. The Bf 110's wings will be enlarged by 41 m^2 with a load factor of about 5 instead of the 2.5 using the jettisonable wing tips. The engine to be installed is the DB 605 D or AS. Armament will consist of two MK 108s and an MK 103, or a Flak 43 for special roles. General aerodynamic improvements to the airframe are also being worked on, as is a new engine installation that will make better use of exhaust thrust energy. In addition, there is a new intake system designed to better ensure the maximum pressure altitude, a retractable tailwheel, a new front cockpit, and improved water radiators. The fuselage will probably be lengthened by 600 mm. With such modifications, performance has been calculated as follows: 6000 m altitude – 580 km/h; 8000 m – 620 km/h with GM 1; 10000 m as maximum pressure altitude – 650 km/h; and absolute ceiling using GM 1 is 12500 m. With this design, it would be possible to attack B-29s. A prototype will be ready by the end of January. Installation of the DB 605 D will be completed by the end of December and will then go into testing. Construction of additional testbeds has been arranged with Gotha. Messerschmitt believes it possible that the new wing will be ready by February or March. Milch is amazed at the performance figures. The data comes from the company and are corroborated by results from ZG 26, where 450 km/h at 11000 m was flown with a Bf 110 equipped with Flak 18 and GM 1 and powered by DB 605 B engines. Milch nevertheless expresses doubts about the figures, and Knemeyer agrees with him.

The DB 628 has not given the performance expected of it. It has no output with maximum throttle at altitude. Given the data at hand, Milch has no interest in the DB 628 and only wants to use the existing small quantity. The improved performance Bf 110 is only of interest to Milch if it can be made available in 1944, unless it could continue through 1945/1946. He would like to know the projected deadlines for the modified fuselage and the new wings, and asks that this be accurately reviewed and the results submitted. Too much pressure can't be put on Messerschmitt, otherwise the Me 262 will suffer.

12/13/43 (Night Fighter Conference)

Von Loßberg: "The Bf 110 oblique armament kit was resolved in the last meeting: 50% of production without extra internal tanks. They will have to fly with external tanks with the two FF oblique firing guns patterned after the Parchim model. For the last six months or more the group has used this armament to make successful kills. Now CE 2 has decided that this configuration is amateurish and not suited for the task. The company has found a better way. Yet they have been shooting with it for more than six months. No disadvantages have cropped up. Kills have successfully been made as far away as 600 m, even by day. The Parchim installation is quite simple."

Scheibe: "For production purposes, some changes need to be made prior to installation. Gotha will start this beginning on 20 December. If installation in large quantities is to be done, then it is not quite suitable in its present form. Production can be started up very quickly. Installation is quite simple."

Genfeldm. Milch: "Who was the first one to make the oblique guns for the 110?"

Von Loßberg: "Hauptmann Meurer – Parchim!"

The armament for the Ju 388 J that the night fighters want is discussed. *General* Kammhuber had asked for two MK 103s, two MK 108s, and 2 MG 152s. Von Loßberg does not see the sense in the MK 103, since the engagement distance for the night fighters is less than 400 m. When installed in an oblique configuration the MG 151 would offer advantages over the MK 108. The weapons still stick out and cause problems when trying to bail out. This does not matter for the He 219, the Bf 110 is getting the MG FF, and the Ta 154 can't because of center of gravity issues. On the Ju 88 the MG 151 could be fitted in either the forward or aft bay.

Junkers has promised 130 improved performance Jumo 211s for December 1943, and this should increase in subsequent months. These should be installed in the Ju 88 C-6, but the production is expected to run out in January with 17 produced, so the startup of engine production will probably come too late. However, as many aircraft as possible are going to get the new engines when they go in for repair, particularly the SN-2 equipped planes since their performance has dropped considerably with the fitting of the antenna system. All Ta 154s are also expected to get the improved performance Jumo 211s.

Problems arising from installation of radar systems are discussed. For example, 850 *Lichtenstein SN 2* systems have been shipped from the factory, 500 tested, 121 checked out in aircraft, and 34 in operation. Testing the system in an airframe takes more than a day. In contrast, *Hauptmann* Schuster in Venlo made a one-off installation in a Bf 110 where all the equipment was freely accessible, and calibration took a total of one hour and ten minutes. The machines coming from Gotha have the equipment installed in such a fashion that it takes the technicians days to get to it and calibrate it. Approximately 20 personnel from Telefunken and the RLM were responsible for determining the Gotha installation configuration. The field personnel are not trained well enough to rid the equipment of its teething troubles. So more technicians are needed at the airfields who, even though they may not be officers, must have the authority vis-à-vis the crews.

12/14/43 (GL)

A report is made on the experience with the *Lichtenstein SN 2*, a system which is still quite sensitive. All damage reports are to be sent to Telefunken so that they can find solutions as quickly as possible.

The *Lichtenstein SN 2* will certainly be unable to acquire targets at ranges less than 600 m, meaning that an *SN 2* and C 1 combination will have to be used as before. The C 1, however, is subject to jamming. Von Loßberg says that jamming the *Lichtenstein* BC system means that no targets can be acquired at ranges of around 2000 m. If the *SN 2* can be extended out to 500 or 600 meters, then something can possibly be done with it.

The *SN 2*, whose weaknesses are known, is in production. It was the shortest developmental period in the history of radio technology, from March 1943 to production in September 1943. The *SN 2* will be replaced by the SN 3, expected to enter full scale production in the autumn. This makes the *Lichtenstein* BC system superfluous and the BZB designation obvious.

As of yet there is no method to counter jamming. The most suitable seems to be switching over to waves in the 10 cm range. Two Ju 88 Rs and a Bf 110 are in operation with the *Naxos Z*. A total of 10 Ju 88 Rs and Bf 110s are expected to be built with the system, but now Ju 88 C-6s are also going to be converted over. The machines do not have the *SN 2* and, according to von Loßberg, don't need it either, since the *Naxos Z* can get within a few hundred meters of the target (bombers equipped with *Rotterdam*). Other attendees at the meeting recommend that the *SN 2* be additionally fitted so that bombers not equipped with *Rotterdam* can also be acquired. As there are sufficient quantities of *SN 2* systems available for both initial installation and refitting, it is proposed that all aircraft be fitted with the system. Hermann suggests that two planes be equipped in order to get some hands-on experience.

The *Freya-Halbe* system appears to be suited for acquiring targets. It was installed in an airframe that was later fired upon and had to crash land. One Bf 110 is being modified, and a further 20 systems are on hand.

The *Rosenthal-Halbe* system is in operation with a Ju 88 and a Bf 110, with three other aircraft also being equipped. There are 7 systems available, but no operational data yet. The system is tuned to the strongest frequency of the enemy's radar systems (*Monica* radar warning system), and the pilot then flies toward the enemy aircraft. The *General der Jagdflieger* wants three additional machines fitted with the system. Von Loßberg does not see the point in taking Bf 110s with the *SN 2* system. Since the new planes all have the SN 2, the *General der Jagdflieger* should have two Bf 110s sent to Werneuchen for installation with BC. Fitting will take about 10 days.

The *Spanner* systems suffered a serious blow in that they were originally designed for armor and now had to be built to withstand higher altitude operations. Bomb damage has delayed the delivery of *Spanner* systems from AEG (10 systems). The *Spanner* systems designed by *Oberpostrat* Heimann were not without their problems and had to be reworked. As of now, three altitude-safe systems are available and are being used in *Wilde Sau* operations. The range of the *Spanner* depends upon the exhaust of the aircraft being attacked. The device seems to be best suited for hunting Mosquitoes, since these have a clearly visible exhaust flame. Using the *Spanner*, a pilot can see about three times farther than with the naked eye. The question is therefore raised whether it is of any use in view of the new night vision goggles. *Generalfeldmarschall* Milch would like developmental work to continue with the *Spanner*.

A viable search radar system has been developed by taking the Neptun J rear warning radar system and pointing it forward. The same results have now been achieved with the *Neptun V*. Both are to be compared at Werneuchen. *Neptun J* causes less of a loss in speed.

Several defective MK 108 guns have been discovered installed in the Bf 110. After the tenth or eleventh shot they simply break down. Gotha has Bf 110s, but without weapons. The MK 108 V 5, the final version, will not be available until March of next year. The delivery situation for the MK 108 seems to be in such order that it looks as though the procurement plans will be met. 443 of the 1000 weapons to be delivered this month have already been supplied. It actually looks as though the goal will be met.

12/15/43 (GWF)
Design data for the Bf 110 H is laid down during a meeting at the Gothaer Waggonfabrik.

12/28/43 (GWF)
A timetable is established at a Bf 110 H conference at Gotha outlining the deadlines for the modifications established on 12/15.

1/3/44
Start of work on the Bf 110 G-4/R6. The GM 1 tank is to be moved forward and reshaped. The gunner's seat can be folded off to the side, thereby giving the gunner the ability to operate the MG 81 Z from a kneeling position.

1/14/44 (GL)
Gotha has 42 Bf 110s ready for pickup, and another 79 are complete and undergoing initial flight trials. Milch demands that these be picked up as soon as possible. It is possible that a hailstorm of bombs could appear and then 121 aircraft would be lost. Galland will have them picked up.

The Do 335 was addressed in the developmental meeting (approximately 30 pages of steno minutes). The V1 and V2 are flying, and the V3 will be flying in a few days. With regard to production planning, it has not yet been established in what numbers the Do 335 will be built nor, other than Dornier-Süd, where production will occur.

According to *Generalfeldmarschall* Milch, this could be a replacement for the Bf 110 and a considerable improvement on the Me 410.

MK 103 production startup has also been delayed due to bomb damage.

During a discussion on introducing the Bf 109 with the DB 605 AS engine, talk yet again revolved around the sluggish work of the Messerschmitt Company. It has been determined that *Prof.* Messerschmitt appears to be the driving force in his company and has many ideas that then lead to too many projects. On the other hand, his staff is significantly smaller than those of other companies. For example, Junkers has approximately 1000 engineers employed for two ongoing types compared with Messerschmitt's 250 for four ongoing types and four to five more in the wings. Vorwald points out that Wiener Neustadt is responsible for production of the Bf 109, Gotha has it for the 110, and Zeppelin for the 323. Milch states that no one should offer more than he can build. And when someone builds something that is constantly breaking, he must also have the support service to build it again.

As a result of the planning for the new procurement program 225, the matter of what to do with the Luther and Gotha companies has become most urgent. According to current planning, Gotha is projected to switch over to the Fw 190 and Luther to the Do 335. But if the improved Bf 110 with DB 605 AS and increased wingspan is to continue in production then a decision needs to be made soon, because preparations for the switch need to start now. If orders are given calling for the Bf 110 to be done away with, then it would no longer be possible to resume production.

New features would be the DB 605 AS engine with the 603 blower, then the engine support mounts, the intake system, the engine nacelles above, behind, and below, with the instruments being moved into the cockpit, and later the oil and lubricant coolers. Changes to the fuselage involve only a new forward cockpit, which would have minor modifications to improve aerodynamics. The attached armored plating causes significant drag. The wing would be increased in area to 41 m^2, and in addition there would be a new upper undercarriage to better brace the engine. With regard to the empennage, the tailplane would be reinforced with a new rudder made out of wood. The design is complete, and production data is presently available. A new rudder is being built in order to finally compensate for the various characteristics of the night fighter's equipment. The undercarriage would have a retractable tailwheel, which is also complete. A strengthening of the struts has already been implemented. A new standardized instrument panel is expected, and the engine gauges are to be moved into the cockpit.

The design papers for these comprehensive changes will be available on 15 March, with those for the engine installation accessible on 15 February. A test prototype will be available on 15 January, with six more coming in the following month. These aircraft will have only the 605 D installed. In all probability, some of these could be handed over to the field quite soon. Based on previous planning, the Bf 110 with DB 605 D will enter production slowly, with 20 no earlier than June and 30 in July, but again these will only be the ones fitted with DB 605 D engines. This engine installation offers the greatest advantages with regard to performance. Full-scale series production will not begin any time before the end of the year.

By modifying the airframe and engines, the performance with the GM 1 jumps from 590 km/h to 650 km/h at 10 km altitude. Service ceiling increased from 11.5 to 12.5 km, with speeds at that altitude going from 480 to 550 km/h. The GM 1 offers no advantages up to an altitude of 8 km, but below that performance can be boosted significantly by using water alcohol injection (MW 50).

Peterson points out that even in its new form the airplane is an old crate that can no longer be counted on if the enemy comes in with escort fighters. If it is possible to cover this altitude region with a more modern airplane, then the Bf 110 is no longer necessary, since this is the only positive thing about the Bf 110.

The participants in the discussion are in agreement that the new engine should be procured, but that the new wings can't be afforded. New jigs would be necessary for the new wings, and these could not be built, since there are not even enough resources for the more modern types. Seats for the new undercarriage are also not possible. If the Bf 110 continues in production, then more modern types would have to be abandoned due to the situation with aluminum. The Bf 110 is to continue as a night fighter until July 1945 and as a heavy fighter until January 1945. Production will peak in October 1944 at 200 per month. Aircraft that can cover the higher altitudes (Bf 110, Ta 154, Ju 388, and the Ju 188 with Jumo 213 E) are discussed.

The decision is made to terminate Bf 110 production in mid-1945 as planned. The modified fuselage is dropped, but the DB 605 D will be introduced for the entire series starting in mid-1944. In the event that the required altitude causes problems for the daytime heavy fighters, then the Bf 110 could be given priority for them, and the Ta 154 would be used to beef up the night fighters. In any event, the GM 1 can't be incorporated into the Ta 154 design. In addition, single engined fighters will also be available for covering the higher altitudes. Starting in mid-1945 the Do 335 should replace the Bf 110.

1/18/44 (GL)
Upcoming projects are discussed. For Bf 110 night fighters, this means SN 2 systems being installed across the board, something that requires 350 to 400 man-hours per airframe. The aviation industry only has pre-built installation kits and antennas. It was brought out that the *General der Jagdflieger* prefers the SN 2 be fitted into the Ju 88, since the focus is now on *Zahme Sau* operations and the Bf 110's endurance is too limited for such missions.

The production of high-speed bombers, heavy fighters, and night fighters continues unimpeded, and numbers are above the program.

1/25/44 (GL)
Only 12 *Flak 3.7* guns were produced in December. Production has resumed, meaning that 10 can be delivered in January and at least 20 in the following months.

The MK 103 still has problems due to the lack of individual components. The Hs 129, Bf 110, and Me 410 aircraft currently available can still be fitted with the gun, but the missing parts will have to be supplied later. At the present time, 500 rounds can safely be put through the cannon, which equates to about 10 missions.

2/1/44 (GL)
Galland has taken delivery of 40 unfinished Bf 110s. The field accepted them prematurely without checking them out thoroughly beforehand, but that should now be corrected. Galland is happy that they were not still at Braunschweig/Waggum, otherwise they too would have been wiped out. Thus, only 25 were destroyed at Waggum. According to Galland, these machines are simply standing around, since some parts are missing, and the ground crews are installing the guns themselves.

2/5/44 (GL)
Currently there are about 50 Ju 87s and 20 Bf 110s grounded due to the absence of the Flak 18 gun. Bomb damage precluded the delivery of any more than 8 weapons ready for installation in the month of January; 80 guns are projected for the month of February. Assuming that no further interruptions occur, production should catch up starting in March. Given this information, there are no plans to use these aircraft for other purposes.

2/15/44 (GL)
Gotha is in the clear. The shift of production resources is in progress. The loss of Luther will be picked up by Gotha. Luther is shifting the final assembly of the fuselage to Helmstedt. Wiring will be moved to near Braunschweig. The new production facilities are expected to be up and running in about two months.

2/22/44 (GL)
The destruction caused by an air raid on the Luther facilities in Braunschweig is discussed. Final assembly has been hit the hardest, with the assembly plant almost completely destroyed. There are no plans to rebuild it. A hangar was found at the Waggum airbase, and half of the fuselage and wing assemblies have been placed there. Final assembly has been moved to one of the hangars used for initial flight testing. Material for 50 aircraft has been turned over to Gotha; it is hoped that 30 will be built at the temporary factory itself. The Helmstedt temporary factory had been planned for some time, but now there is greater pressure. 40 complete fuselage units are planned for assembly at Helmstedt. A point of concern is the main plant, which will have to be moved. This is where components and the forward fuselage are built. Three factories in the area around Braunschweig are needed, each with 4000 square meters of space. Sugar and canning factories are options. Some wing assembly can be moved to the Protectorate, particularly to Bohemia-Moravia.

It would be quite hard to hit the storage areas. Most of the equipment is stored in the basements in the surrounding villages, 10 meters underground. Almost all the people working there are Russians.

The Bf 110 is planned for production at Luther up until early 1945, when it will be replaced by the Do 335. Milch says that, with the DB 605 D, a new age has dawned for the Bf 110: 2000 m more maximum pressure altitude and a speed increase of 60 km/h. If the Bf 110 can be made so "fresh" again, then it could easily serve alongside the Do 335. From a developmental standpoint, this should be resolved shortly; we will have to wait for the airplane's first flight. Alpers says he has contracted with Gotha and Luther for an additional 500 aircraft each (approx. 5 months' production time). The companies should report the latest date for which they would need to be informed of what type to build. Diesing cautions that the DB 605 D is not yet available. According to Milch, the companies should still know that such a possibility exists.

2/23/44 (GL)
Generalfeldmarschall Milch reports on the destruction caused by bombing, which has had a major impact on production. The British are conducting pure terror raids by night, while during the day the Americans are hitting the centers of production. A Fighter Staff (*Jägerstab*) needs to be established in response.

Among other things, *Generalfeldmarschall* Milch says that they are ready to see if the Bf 110 with the DB 605 D will offer such performance that it will not need to be replaced by another type at the beginning of the New Year. The other type then would not need to be produced in such great numbers, and they could achieve some sort of commonality. When he took over, there were more than 50 different types, compared to the 20 now extant. Everything is now based on the Bf 109 and Fw 190 and their modifications.

2/24/44
An air raid on GWF has hit production and the testing division hard. Among other things, three prototypes with the DB 605 D installation were destroyed.

2/25/44 (Developmental Meeting)
Diesing: "The prioritization of fighter production has compelled the Armament Office to order that the entire fighter, heavy fighter, and night fighter production, engines, and supplier industry be given top priority in all areas, starting with transportation, etc."

Milch: "There is a real urgency to have something happen with regard to night fighters, since 110 production is being hit hard from both sides. There has been somewhat of a branching out already; Gotha does not just build in Gotha. It has got to be established where we can do it. I do not put much stock in doing in Gotha what we had talked about doing with Luther in Braunschweig. We still need the resources. I have given the company notice that there might be another production batch of 110s, even though production is supposed to end at the beginning of next year. This all depends on the question of whether the 605 D, if it is good, can give us what we need. It is possible that even the 110 will continue as an important night fighter.

As far as the weapons go, it appears that 100 MK 103s will be built. MK 108: 1500 in February; 1750 in March; and 2000 in April. These are official figures from the Reichsminister RuK."

2/29/44 (GL)
C-B 2 reports that during the attack of 2/27 on Gotha, 18 of the 147 Bf 110s at the site were destroyed and about 56 damaged. GI/C will investigate to what extent this jam was due to problems with calibrating the SN 2, something which will also involve the Telefunken Company. Due to the danger from bombing raids, production needs to be shifted away from Braunschweig and Gotha. Vorwald proposes that the Bf 110 only be used as a night fighter and the Me 410 replace it in the day *Zerstörer* role. The *Reichsmarschall* must agree to this first.

Milch would like to have the performance of the DB 605 D reviewed, particularly with a view toward making the Bf 110 a superior aircraft. Mr. Haspel from Daimler-Benz states that more modern engines (i.e. DB 603) would be delayed by the design work still to be undertaken for the DB 605 D.

The required number of DB 605 AS engines, the interim design to the DB 605 D now planned for the Bf 110 as well, is addressed. There are currently 400 on order, of which 290 are to be installed and 110 held in reserve. Planning for a further 200 had been contracted for, but since the initial production facility for the DB 605 D (Steyr) has been struck, the AS may have to continue in production. Galland suggests keeping the AS in production until the D is available. The AS situation is tense; Gotha had built a couple machines, but these are now destroyed.

Galland complains about the slow deliveries of the Bf 109 with DB 605 AS. According to Vorwald, this is due to the absolutely rotten work at Messerschmitt. The AS engine's painful path through Messerschmitt has led to a field investigation of Messerschmitt. At the moment it is being built by Erla in Antwerp.

3/2/44 (Developmental Conference)
Vorwald: "In one of the last meetings with 6. Abteilung, we considered how we could somehow assist the fighter-heavy fighter program in its current crisis by slashing the types...It was also suggested, assuming the command staff was in agreement, to produce the 110 exclusively as a night fighter if the 410 could be only used as a heavy fighter instead of a high speed bomber. However, this is undoubtedly only one of the points that would require the approval of the Reichsmarschall. I must emphasize this."

Milch: "We only wanted to come up with a common vision. I can say that we are seriously considering whether we can't keep producing the Bf 110 with the aid of the improved D engine as a night fighter beyond the current program. It runs out at the beginning of 1945. However, we believe that we can move this machine into a much higher performance class with its improved engine, in terms of altitude as well as speed. It should not be sold off as long as we do not actually have a better night fighter. I see the real night fighter in the 88, 188, 388 size category, where three crewmen are on board. But we are not able to meet all our needs with this type.... We will keep the recommendations on the 410 going for now; in order to avoid being caught with our pants down somewhere, we have pushed for 1000 more machines than are currently in the program and allocated more to the 110 so that we can have a breathing space of several months to see what we will do with it. We need this breather, for one thing so that we can thoroughly test Tank's 154 to find out if it really makes the 110 completely superfluous. With the new equipment, the 110's performance should increase by 2 km maximum pressure altitude and a speed improvement of about 60 km… In any case, the D engine has much better performance."

Knemeyer hands over a comparison table for the 110 and the 154.

Milch: "Well, the Ta machine is far better in this area, and here too. Above 11 km the 110 is somewhat better due to its lower wing loading, etc. But for night fighting this is not that important."

Diesing: "The planes will not be in the field before October of this year."

Milch: "Since this whole thing isn't clear, I have said: we'll continue a little bit longer with the 110. We can still decide if we want to go even further."

Petersen: "The 110 is currently being produced with the SN 2, with quite a large antenna, with a receiver with 15 tubes and BC 1 a."

Koller: "From a tactical side, we have tried to determine what we should support, what we need to meet the airspace needs on the one hand, and on the other, to meet the Luftwaffe's requirements—purely from a tactical standpoint without regard for weapons potential. We have worked it out in such a manner that we have said: what's necessary, not what's wanted. I have figured it out for the fighters, first for the single-engined types, as follows. As of 1 February there are currently 54 fighter groups available with 1810 aircraft. Our requirements would be—let's see here, it will take a second: 82 fighter groups with 5656 aircraft, which would need to be restocked at a monthly rate of 2660…Zerstörer unit: currently 10 2/3 groups with 623 aircraft. Our requirement: 24 heavy fighter units with 1280 machines. Monthly resupply without taking into account losses, 484." Milch: "Our planning is higher." Koller: "Resupply for night fighters: 590…When I look at the total numbers, they seem to be relatively high in view of the current state. When I compare them with the enemy, they are downright modest. The fighters are opposed by 12000 enemy fighters from England, America, Italy, and Russia…. The total resupply is 5000 monthly. This number can and must be reached, assuming the Luftwaffe is given the support needed."

Beginning in the spring of 1944, the Bf 110 G-2 flew against the American bombers armed with two MK 108s and four MG 151s. (Petrick)

3/11/44 (GWF)
A memorandum from the GWF shows that the raid on 2/24/44 has set development of the Bf 110 back by at least six months. Based on previous data, production problems can be expected to intensify if production begins without sufficient evaluation.

3/16/44
43 Bf 110s from ZG 76 attack an American bomber formation approaching Augsburg. Although the Bf 110s are able to shoot down 18 B-17s, they themselves lose 26 of their number at the hands of the fighter escort.

3/44 (*Erprobungskommando 25* Action Report)
Three Bf 110s with Flak 43 have been assigned to ZG 1 (Königsberg-Neumark) for operational testing.

5/4/44 (GWF)
Based on the RLM decision to build the Bf 110 H exclusively as a night fighter, GWF determines to drop the GM 1 system, keep the old radiators, and modify the coolant lines.

5/5/44 (GWF)
The first prototype of the Bf 110 G-4/R8 is completed at Gotha.

This belly landing occurred on 16 April 1944 during a training flight with Erg.Staffel *261. The aircraft is equipped with the FuG 111 (evidenced by the two antennae), but has the newer pitot tube, meaning that it's probably a Bf 110 C-3. (Petrick)*

5/13/44 (GWF)
The prototype for the Bf 110 G-4/R6 (*W.Nr.* 730059) and the second Bf 110 G-4/R8 (*W.Nr.* 140030) are completed.

5/44
The *Luftwaffe* accepted 158 Bf 110 night fighters in May.

6/44 (*Erprobungskommando 25* Action Report)
21 cm aft-firing gun (*Krebs* System): one Me 410 from ZG 26 for functional firing. Installation in 20 Fw 190 A-8s and provided to the *Sturmstaffeln. Schräge Musik* with optical resolution: From 5.44 installation of two oblique firing 120 mm barrels in Fw 190 A-8s and Bf 110s. Firing trials with the Bf 110 have begun. Flak 43: Bf 110 and two Me 410s in operation. Two Bf 110s shot down on the first mission, the third Bf 110 (*W.Nr.* 170067) returned to Parchim. Me 410 (*W.Nr.* 120253) returned to Parchim due to malfunction. Me 410 (*W.Nr.* 10241) shot down on its first mission, 5/17/44, at Parchim!

6/3/44 (GL)
In addition to the heavy *Zerstörer* and night fighters (Ju 88, Ju 388, He 219, and Do 217), according to the disposition for the reduced "Fighter Staff Aircraft Program" the following types are either in operation or planned: Bf 110 G-2; Me 210 A/C; Me 410 A/B/C; Ta 154 A 1-2 and Ta 154 C-2 as heavy fighters; and the Bf 110 G-4, Ta 154 A-4, and Ta 154 C-1 as night fighters in the *Luftwaffe*.

The belt feed for the Flak 43 *was a major improvement on the clip magazines of the* Flak 18. *(Mankau)*

6/9/44 (GL)
Von Loßberg states that it would be better if some of the effort currently being put into the He 177 could be struck off and diverted to keep the Ju 188 alive. The Ju 88 can be dropped as a second-class night fighter and instead let Heinkel build the He 219. With a truly first class machine such as the He 219, he can't understand how this bird in the hand could be lost for two in the bush, namely the Ta 154 (which is worse in every respect) and the Ju 88 G, which is slower than the He 219 by some 40 km/h and also has relatively poor visibility from the cockpit.

Another item on the agenda was Program 226. There is a need to save 4000 metric tons of aluminum, the amount by which the program exceeds the output potential. Another problem stems from the *Reichsmarschall*'s orders for increasing He 177 output from 100 to 200 per month, something that most certainly cannot be accomplished. Some program figures will need to be lowered accordingly. Production of the Me 410 and possibly the Bf 110 are expected to terminate sooner than planned.

6/10/44
The test center at Tarnewitz ends its evaluation of the Bf 110 G-4/R6 and sends it back to Gothaer Waggonfabrik on 6/12.

6/16/44 (GL)
The RLM issues a report: "MK 108 armed Bf 110s in Operation." It is determined that *IV./NGJ 1* at St. Trond is equipped with Bf 110s, of which only a portion are fitted with two forward firing MK 108s. The others have four MG 151s and two MG FFs firing upward at an angle of less than 70 degrees.

Oberltn. Schnaufer permits each pilot to individually select the type of armament. He himself has four MG 151s and two MG FFs. Because of increasing successes, more and more pilots are choosing the MK 108.

Geschwader Kommodore Maj. Jabs has little love for the MK 108 due to its unusual properties. In nighttime combat the limit of visibility is little more than 150 m. Almost all kills are made at a range of less than 100m. Kills using the MK 108 nearly always result in damage to the attacking aircraft, which is struck by pieces from the stricken aircraft, even with one hit.

Oblt. Thun observes that most of the experienced crews do not care much for the MK 108, first of all due to the muzzle flash, which blinds too much, and secondly that there is not enough protection against barrels bursting.

6/44
The only unit still operational with the Bf 110 is II./ZG 1; all others are operating in the night fighting capacity. The last missions flown by integral Bf 110 G-2 heavy fighter groups are flown over Hungary around the end of the month. The *Zerstörer* units flying the Bf 110s are converted over to the Bf 109.

6/26/44
Hitler calls for fighter production to be increased to 1000 per month. In exchange, the current requirement for 200 He 177s per month will be dropped.

6/19/44 (GL)
Study 1033 (top secret 2039/44) calls for increasing Bf 110 G production from 140 per month in July to 220 in September and October 1944. Output should drop after then. End of production is projected for November 1945 with a final output that month of 10. Starting in February 1945 the He 219 is expected to be produced at a constant rate of 50 per month, while the Ju 88/388 will rise from 280 in September 1944 to 420 beginning in the autumn of 1945.

6/29/44
Göring orders the production of bombers, torpedo bombers, and training aircraft to stop.

6/30/44 (GL)
Fuel shortages have forced several test programs to be shortened or canceled. With regard to the *Jägergerät X*, von Loßberg asks about what type of aircraft is to tow it. Can the fighters get to the enemy with it? Nowadays the *Zerstörers* generally have a hard time getting through to the bombers even with fighter protection.

7/30/44
The *Führer* gives highest priority to fighter production in order to protect the *Reich*. The total number of fighters, night fighters, and heavy fighters is expected to rise to 10000. Of the 5000 more airframes, 400 *Zerstörer*, and 500 night fighter planes are to be built.

7/1/44 (GL)
The Lightning Program, which is based on the *Führerbefehl* from 6/30/44, strikes 20 types from the program, including the Ta 154 and the Me 210/410. The Bf 110 G-4, Ju 88 G, and the He 219 remain in the program, but in reduced numbers. In their places come the Do 335 and the Ju 388, of which 550 per month each is to be built, and the Me 262 and Ar 234 jets (each at 500 per month). At the top of the list is the Fw 190 at 2600 per month, compared to the monthly 500 output for the Bf 109.

8/8/44
The first production Bf 110 G-4/R8 is accepted

9/44
The RLM reduces the number of developmental and construction contracts for the Bf 110.

9/28/44
A memorandum of the Gothaer Waggonfabrik lists the remaining developmental work for the Bf 110. According to the memo, work will end on the windscreen and a wooden version of the extended wing tips. Development of the engine shroud for the DB 605 E and the MW 50 system is expected to continue.

By the end of 1944, most night fighters looked like this example of a Bf 110 G-4 at Werneuchen. (Petrick)

After the war the British put this Bf 110 G-4 on display. Formerly 3C+BA of Geschwaderstab/NJG 4, *it is kitted out with the FuG 218 V2* Neptun, *the FuG 101 radar altimeter, new flame dampers, and increased armor protection. (Newark Air Museum)*

9/44
The *Luftwaffe* acquires 187 Bf 110 G-4s, 27 He 219s, and 305 Ju 88 G night fighters. For *Zerstörer* types, the last 40 Me 410s are accepted.

11/44
The Emergency Fighter Program is initiated. Development of the Bf 110 is halted and production reduced.

12/15/44
Aircraft Construction Program 227-1—the last construction program of the RLM—calls for a monthly production of 550 Do 335s, 750 Ju 88 Gs, 150 Ju 388 Js, and 50 He 219s in the heavy fighter/night fighter class. The Bf 110 is no longer mentioned.

1/20/45
In the *Führer* Emergency Program, even the Do 335 and other piston-powered night fighters no longer take priority. The Ta 152 is the last significant piston-engined aircraft.

2/45
The last 17 Bf 110 G-4s roll off the production line.

Spring 1945
British troops find brand new, blown up Bf 110 G-4/R3s in the Luther Works at Braunschweig Waggum.

Ar 240 Chronicle

1933/34 (Ar)
At Arado, Walter Blume works on the concept of ball-shaped turrets armed with two 2 cm cannons. Development broke off in 1934 once it becomes obvious that such weapons systems using two turrets each armed with one gun, ammunition, and crewman would weigh 1000 kg and would require approximately 620 hp to turn them at a speed of 450 km/h.

1934/35 (Ar)
Continued studies lead to a weapons system consisting of a turret with two cannons located on both the upper and lower fuselage, which results in the E 500 bomber design from 1935. The required unrestricted aft field of fire produces a twin boom configuration with two rudders and outward protruding horizontal stabilizers. Initially, the RLM called for a mockup, but the program was abandoned in 1935 when the RLM opts for the lightly armed high speed bombers (Ju 88, Bf 162).

1937/38 (RLM)
The *Luftwaffe's* goals are pushed even further. The early destruction of the enemy's air power and industry in enemy territory is at the top of the list. A review of the aircraft types necessary for such roles calls for a heavy fighter/*Zerstörer* in addition to the fighters and heavy bombers. By exploiting its effective penetration range, such a plane would destroy important individual targets by dive bombing, while at the same time its performance, flight characteristics, and combat potential would also ensure air superiority in the areas the bombers were operating in.

10/15/38 (RLM)
The *Amt* issues guidelines for the second generation of heavy fighters.

10/30/38 (Ar)
Generaling. Reidenbach, Chief of LC II Division within the Air Ministry, visits Arado and initiates development of the Ar 240 (see Me 210, same date). Speed is to be as high as possible with a potential range of 2000 km. Dive bombing capability is a requirement, but there is no problem with high altitude performance requirements. Defensive armament, sighting, and observation options are discussed.

1938 (Ar)
Arado assumes that the engines available for installation in the *Zerstörer* aircraft will not be any more powerful than those of the enemy at any given point in time. Thus, compared to the single engined fighter, the twin engined *Zerstörer* type is at a disadvantage from the outset with regard to its power loading per engine due to the load incurred by having to fly much greater distances. The air resistance caused by a greater number of drag inducing protrusions can't be offset either. Thus, at any given time, it has to be assumed that the aircraft will suffer in performance, particularly in regard to climb rate. A heavy fighter with inadequate defensive firepower is, therefore, effectively the same as an inferior fighter. It must be assumed that a *Zerstörer* with poor defensive armament either won't be able to penetrate to its full range or will suffer inordinately heavy losses. For the *Zerstörer* armament, Arado calls for the heavy fighter to have defensive armament

safely providing a 45 degree coverage above and to the sides, with a gunner and the use of a highly accurate sighting system for the sake of effectiveness. To cover the highly vulnerable area of the upper fuselage, the twin rudders and upper/lower fuselage turret systems are carried over from the E 500 design. Since a rotating turret with a gunner inside is too large and heavy, the gunner is placed in a nonswiveling seat inside the cockpit. The gun mounts are located at the aft cockpit/fuselage transition point to reduce drag. The gunner is expected to cover the lower area as well, and is provided a periscope sight for this purpose. For various reasons, Arado rejects the use of a retractable sighting mechanism or the use of multiple reflective gunsights.

1939 through 1942 (Ar)
Working together with Siemens Apparate und Maschinen G.m.b.H., LGW, Deutsche Versuchsanstalt für Luftfahrt, and Askania, Arado develops the gun turret system and remote power drive, and with the Optisch Anstalt C.P. Goerz designs the periscope sight. Following unsatisfactory tests with the electro mechanical FA 4 remote drive unit and the hydraulic FA 9, the FA 12 eventually provides acceptable results using components from the HD 151 and tested in the Bf 110. The final product is the FA 13.

3/31/39 (Ar)
The mockup of the Ar 240 is put on display.

5/16/39 (RLM, Ar)
Arado is given preliminary approval to develop and supply six Ar 240 prototypes (*Zerstörer*).

6/25/40 (Ar)
The Ar 240 V1 takes to the air for the first time. Pilot is *Flugbaumeister* Kröger.

9/15/40 (Ar)
Flugbaumeister Kröger pilots the Ar 240 V2 on its maiden flight.

2/12/41 (Ar, RLM)
Since the initial order for six prototypes is insufficient for follow-on developmental work and field unit trials at the same time, Arado proposes building a further six null-series aircraft which would then be delivered in the time period between September 1941 and April 1942. Two would supplement the V4 through V6 in field unit testing, two would remain with the company for follow-on development, and two would act as testbeds for the DB 605.

5/9/41 (Ar)
First flight of the Ar 240 V3.

6/7/41 (Ar)
According to a memo addressed to *Generaling.* Lucht, V3 testing is almost at an end. The deficiencies of the V1 and V2 have been rectified and handling is now easy, particularly on takeoff and landing. *E-Stelle* Rechlin will conduct follow-on checks on 6/10. Performance trials have been postponed since the aircraft has not yet been fitted with its planned dual spinner propellers. The program should be concluded by mid June.

8/3/41 (Rechlin)
Hptm. Knemeyer test flies the V3, finds the flight handling along the vertical axis to be fully acceptable, and considers the type to be well suited for instrument flying.

2/6/42 (*Akademie der Luftfahrtforschung*, Berlin)
At the academy, Arado presents the status and the developmental history of the rotating weapons system. Its task is considered fundamentally completed.

3/6 and 3/25/42 (*Versuchsstelle für Höhenflüge*)
The Arado 240 V6 and V5 are transferred to the VfH for testing.

3/16/42 (RLM)
Arado is given a contract to develop the Ar 240 C with DB 603 engine, building four prototypes (V9 through V12) and 36 pre-production null-series machines.

4/14/42 (GL)
Since the Ju 88 has proven effective as a heavy fighter, the question is raised as to whether the Me 210 can be done away with.

The Ar 240, being a cheaper aircraft to build, is also a possible option as a replacement for the Me 110 and Me 210. By 1943 there must be at least a small production batch (one wing) of a lightweight, high speed combat aircraft that can be used for daylight raids against the British Isles.

5/12/42 (GL)
For the short term, *Flugbaumeister* Friebel proposes using the Me 109 *Jabo* and the Me 210 as a high speed bomber. There is no question of using the Ar 240 temporarily in operations as a high speed bomber.

According to *Generaloberst* Jeschonnek, there are intentions to reestablish a *Zerstörergruppe* in the West. Options for equipping this group include the long-range Me 109 *Jabo* and the Me 210, or possibly a later development of the Ar 240.

Generalfeldmarschall Milch's verdict is that the Ar 240 will not be used as a high speed bomber in its current version. Further developmental work will continue with the Ar 240. Still to be cleared up is the improved performance brought on by the DB 603's installation and other measures.

6/9/42 (GL)
Stabsing. Friebel reports on the Ar 240: tests have shown that the Ar 240 falls below the desired speed performance by some 45 km/h. The unusually high wing loading is causing major problems with flight handling, particularly in the night fighting role. The aircraft currently in use with *Oberst* Rowehl's unit cannot be converted to high speed bombers since the airframe will not support the DB 603 without extensive modifications. Following a detailed technical review, it is recommended that the type no longer be considered for the bomber role.

Oberst Rowehl reports that the first airplanes they received were lemons. The flight handling of the Ar 240 have now become so bad that they can't even beat the speed of the Ju 88 C and B. Furthermore, the defensive armament and performance of the Ju 88 is better than the Ar 240. Nor can the field units recommend adoption of the type as a reconnaissance platform. The *Generalfeldmarschall* decides that the Ar 240 is to be canceled as a bomber altogether. The 20 reconnaissance prototypes contracted for *Oberst* Rowehl will go ahead and be built.

The He 219 seems to be the best replacement for the Ar 240. In the He 219, the *Generalfeldmarschall* sees the potential of combining the *Zerstörer* and night fighter and, possibly, the high speed bomber into one major aircraft type. The projected performance figures are probably adequate for all three roles. Current planning calls for production to start in December 1944, with the possibility of an earlier startup. The weapons issue must be reviewed again with regard to the remote control operation. The *Generalfeldmarschall* assumes that remote controlled armament will only be of limited use. In any event, other options will need to be planned for this time period. Of late, reports from the field and the *General der Jagdflieger* assess the fixed weapon with rear sight to be quite effective, indicating that this is a potential consideration as an easy solution for remotely controlled weapons.

Oberst Vorwald emphasizes that the He 219 is called into question for the night fighter role due to its center of gravity issue. *Oberst* von Loßberg points out that the defensive armament is a poor compromise because of the poor downward visibility.

8/7/42 (RLM)
The RLM publishes the "Technical Guidelines for the Bomber *Zerstörer*." From the cover letter to Arado it emerges that full-scale production of a bomber/heavy fighter based on these guidelines could not be initiated prior to 1946. The company is therefore asked to continue developmental work on the Ar 240 in accordance with the guidelines in order to obtain an aircraft as close as possible to the concept of a bomber/heavy fighter in the interim.

8/18/42 (RLM Developmental Conference)
Theme: heavy fighter/high-speed bomber/night fighter from a single type. Models discussed include the Me 110, Me 210 with DB 601 or DB 603, Ar 240, Fw 187, He 219, and Ju 188. The Ar 240 is abandoned for unknown reasons.

8/26/42 (Ar)
Evaluation of the Ar 240 A-03/U1, the first Ar 240 with DB 603 engines.

11/6/42 (GL)
The Ar 240 is dropped from the developmental program, as it is not possible to obtain the type in large numbers in the foreseeable future. Also canceled is the contract for building 20 Ar 240 B-0 at Ago (Apparatebau GmbH Oschersleben).

12/42 (E-Stelle Rechlin)
The test center evaluates an Ar 240 with DB 603 engines and a 16.6 m wingspan. *Oberstleutnant* Thierfelder offers a very positive assessment. Test reports designate the machine as the Ar 440, but at this time there is only the Ar 240 A-04/U2 that has these characteristics.

1/19/43 (E-Stelle Rechlin)
The test center publishes a comparison between the Ar 440, Me 410, Ju 88 S, and the He 219. At 661 km/h—47 km/h faster than the Me 410—the Ar 440 (flown as the Ar 240 A-04/U2) is clearly superior in terms of speed and also offers the greatest range.

2/16/43 (GL)
Chief of C-E: Although the Ar 440 prototype is superior to the Me 410 by more than 30 km/h, initiation of production cannot be justified alongside the Me 410's production, which has already started. The aircraft would not be available until much later and would then be a contemporary of the much superior Do 335. On the other hand, the Me 410 would benefit considerably in terms of speed by fine tuning the Ar 440's excellent engine into a standard powerplant. The *Generalfeldmarschall* decides to cancel the Ar 440. However, in order to recognize *Dr.* Blume for his outstanding work involved in the creation of this aircraft—which only failed to reach operational status due to external reasons caused by the present wartime situation—*Admiral* Lahs is asked to prepare a writ for awarding Blume the title of professor.

2/28/43 (Ar)
Evaluation of the Ar 240 V9, the first prototype of the Ar 240 C/Ar 440.

3/16/43 (GL)
Within the scope of the developmental meeting, the fighter/heavy fighter engine is explored for use in the Me 209, Me 410, He 219, Fw 190, Ta 154, and the Do 335 forward powerplant. Work on this engine has already started. The DB 603 G is planned for the Me 209, Me 410, He 219, and the Do 335. The engine also has potential for the Ta 154, Fw 190, and the Ar 440.

3/19/43 (GL)
Generalfeldmarschall Milch emphasizes that the Ar 440, which was actually quite good and superior to all others, possibly even the Me 410, had to be abandoned because it was too costly.

5/13/43 (Versuchsstelle für Höhenflüge)
According to a report by the VfH, the Ar 240 has proven itself across the board.

5/43 through 6/43 (E-Stelle Rechlin)
The Ar 240 A-03/U1 is flown at Rechlin with the GM 1 system.

8/43 (*Fernaufklärungsgruppe 100*)
The Group reports that in operations using the Ar 240 the best possible results have been achieved with the periscope sight.

9/9/43 (Ar)
The Ar 240 V10 is completed, the last of this type.

2/4/44 (GL)
Compare Me 410, same date. Knemeyer mentions the Ar 440, which was faster than the Me 410. *Generalfeldmarschall* Milch thinks that the Ar 440 only came to grief be-

cause it was too late. Had it appeared earlier, then the Ar 440 would have been accepted, but the jigs for the 410 were already done. In addition, there was a considerable delay due to lack of desire for the type; Messerschmitt should never have made it through.

2/25/44 (GL)

Rowehl reports: "Yesterday morning at 8:30 A.M. an Arado 240 flew over London and had 20 minutes of good photo time. Speed was 650 km/h, engines were 603s with blowers and GM 1 systems. I am unfortunately unable to provide any further details. Altitude was 10500 m. I do not know if there were any fighters in the area. In any case, it was a nighttime photography platform that was able to take very high quality photos over a period of two nights."

Genfeldm. Milch: "It is a shame we don't have any more Arados."

Summer 1944 (Ar)

The Ar 240 V10 crash lands when its landing gear malfunctions and is not repaired. This is the last machine of this type with the DB 603.

10/44 (E-Stelle Rechlin)

The test center reports on visibility comparisons using various sighting mechanisms: "With the Lotfe 7 E roughly the same results were achieved in all visibility conditions as with the naked eye, and the periscope was at least as good. In comparison with the periscope, the Revi with the armored glass offered reduced visibility by about 10% during the day, 20% at dusk, and 35% at night."

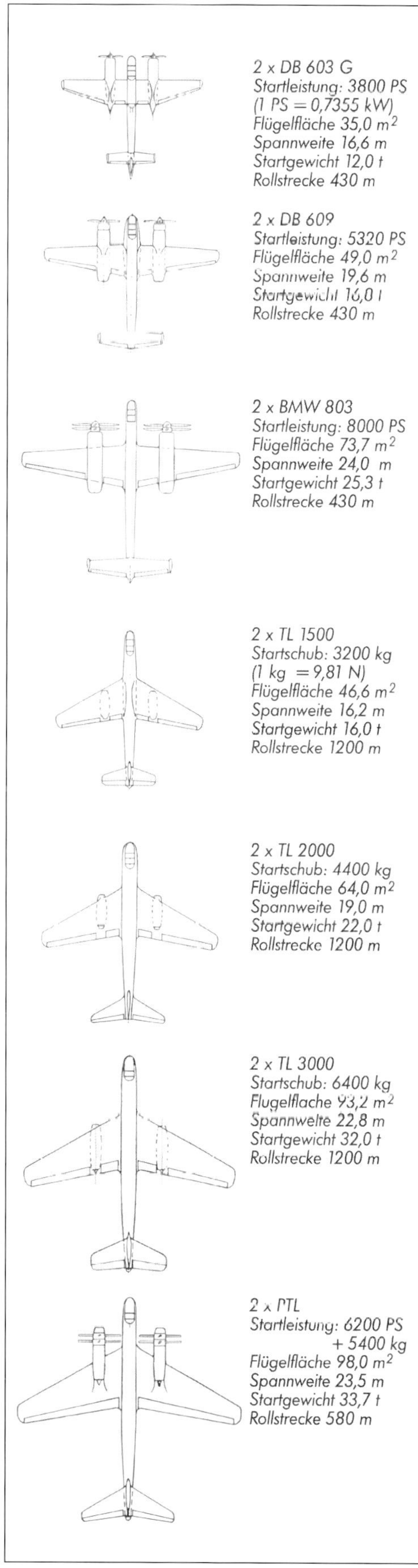

After the cancellation of the Ar 440 in 1943, the Arado company began working on a successor to the two-seat heavy fighter/high-speed bomber and explored several concept studies.

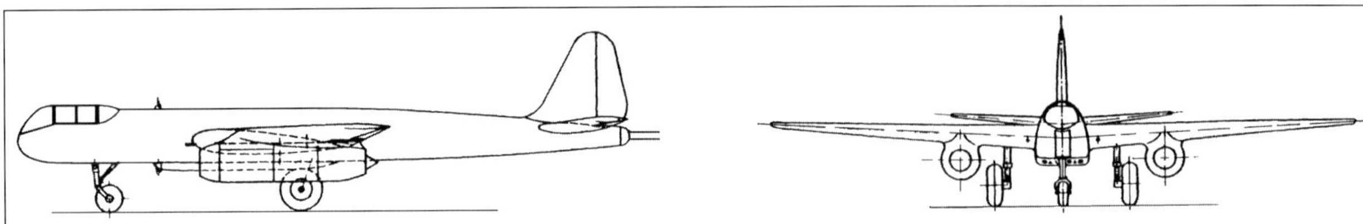

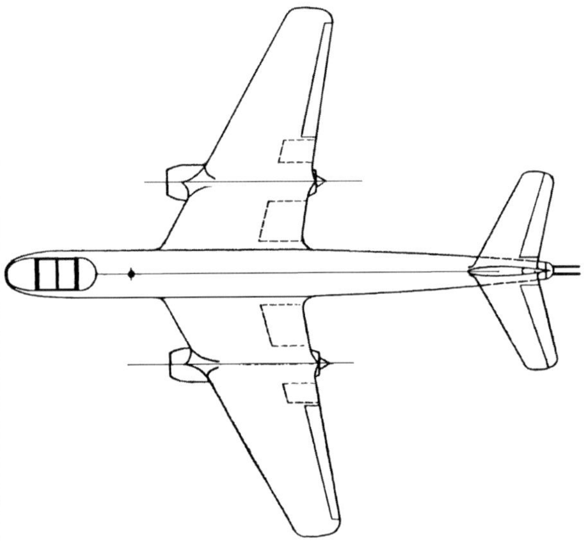

Flügelfläche	46,6 m^2
Spannweite	16,2 m
Länge	18,0 m
Höhe	3,0 m
Haupträder	1320 x 480
Bugrad	935 x 345
Startgewicht	18,3 t
Triebwerke	2 x TL 109-012

Schnell-bomber	Zerstörer	Nachtjäger	Schlecht-wetterjäger	Zwangs-aufklärer
Ferngesteuerte Abwehrbewaffnung mit Periskopvisier				
2 MK 213	2 MK 213		2 MK 213	2 MK 213
Starre Angriffsbewaffnung				
	3 MK 103 4 MK 213	2 MK 108 3 MK 213 2 MK 108 schräg 3 MK 213 schräg	3 MK 103 4 MK 213	
Bombenlast 1 x 2500 kg 2 x 1000 kg 4 x 500 kg	Bombenlast 2 x 500 kg 2 x 250 kg	Ausrüstung Nachtjäger Leitanlage	Ausrüstung Schlecht- wetter Leitanlage	Ausrüstung 2 Reihen- bildner

above: To Arado's engineers the best variant appeared to be a design utilizing swept wings, two 1500 kp class jet engines, and the dimensions of the Ar 440.

below: The crash of the Ar 240 A-04/U2 in the fall of 1944 brought to a halt the type's military operations. (Kranzhoff)

Me 210/410 Chronicle

Late 1936 (RLM)
The tactical-technical requirements are drawn up anew. This results in the Bf 110 no longer being considered fully suited for these roles, and a successor is under consideration. Significant new requirements include the ability to carry a bomb payload of 1000 kg and increased defensive firepower.

9/4/36 (RLM)
The Daimler-Benz Company offers the RLM development of a 40 liter engine (DB 603) for the first time. A developmental contract is issued a few weeks later.

2/37-3/37
Udet stops the development of the 40 liter engine (DB 603).

1937/38 (Mtt)
Based on the new requirements, Messerschmitt's project bureau draws up about 70 optimal figures—some in parallel working groups—and these result in the P 1060 Project in late 1938. It emerges from later statements that a twin fuselage aircraft was among the alternatives explored. Messerschmitt and Lusser's project bureau come to the conclusion that the requirements can best be met by a new design, not a follow-on development of the Bf 110.

The issuer of the contract must certainly have been informed of this, but assumed that the new aircraft would not differ considerably from the Bf 110.

Autumn 1938 (RLM)
The exact time and contents of the contract issued to Messerschmitt are not known. From the following statement by Reidenbach and the procurement plans, and later statements by Göring, it can be concluded that the RLM expected an uncritical solution from Messerschmitt that would be similar to the Bf 110, and therefore, without waiting for the prototypes, immediately issued a contract for approximately 2000 aircraft.

In the fall of 1938 the Me 210, as it had now been designated, goes into design. The short timespan between the contract and introduction causes the participants to design and build the jigs alongside the airplane. By the time the first prototypes are flying, the construction jigs are therefore also virtually complete.

10/30/38 (Arado)
Generalingenieur Reidenbach, Chief of the RLM's LC II Division, visits the Arado Company. He is assuming that within a year the "Tommies" will be coming. With the 109, Germany is well equipped for a good while in the fighter sector, but the 110 is not what it should be. It isn't fast enough, and its defensive armament is too weak, primarily when firing downward. A new *Zerstörer* is needed, one each from both Messerschmitt and Arado. Messerschmitt should remain conservative, and Arado can press into new territory. The aircraft need to be ready in a year.

11/1/38 (RLM)
The acquisition plan (for 4/1/42) calls for 16 heavy fighter wings, of which at least seven or eight would be equipped with Me 210s. Additionally, there are plans for 8 dive bomber wings that will initially be stocked with Ju 87 Bs, but these would be replaced as soon as possible with the Me 210.

One wing (*Geschwader*) has three groups (*Gruppen*); one group comprises three squadrons (*Staffeln*), and one squadron has 12 aircraft. In addition to this there are the staff planes.

12/13/38 (GL)
The C-Amt's program through 4/1/42 projects 3200 heavy fighters (this is about 300 below the requirements due to the aviation industry's conversion from the Me 110 to the Me 210).

9/2/39 (Mtt)
H. Wurster carries out the first flight in the Me 210 V-1. He is reputed to have said upon landing that the aircraft needs to be made at least one meter longer. Messerschmitt supposedly responded that three million jigs would have to be thrown away to do so.

10/17/39 (Mtt)
The Me 210 V1 is flown by Neidhart, a pilot from the test center. He rates the stall characteristics as very good, the rudder forces very high, and the motion around the vertical axis to be unsatisfactory. It is very difficult to hold the aircraft in all three axes. He believes, however, that these criticisms can be rectified through simple measures.

right: This was probably the appearance of the Me 210 V1 when it was test flown by Neudhart at the E-Stelle *(Radinger)*

below: On its first flight the Me 210 V1 most likely lacked the registration code, but otherwise appeared as it does in the photo, i.e. without paint. (Radinger)

2/3/40 (GL)
Approval is given for resumption of the DB 603's development.

July 1940 (Mtt, E-Stelle)
The E-Stelle criticizes the despicable handling of the Me 210 on takeoff. Measurements taken during flight testing show that minimal application of throttle produces incredible rolling acceleration. The problem is believed to be due to an outline flaw in the wing profile.

7/15/40 (Mtt)
Prof. Willy Messerschmitt states in a report that the flight handling characteristics are in order. Forces and effects are generally the same as or somewhat less than those in the Me 110 C. Stall handling is acceptable both with and without leading edge slats, meaning that it is up to the E-Stelle to determine if they should be abandoned. There is very little design work left to be done before full scale production can begin, with only the dive brakes and automatic dive recovery system yet to be worked out. To improve the rearward arc of fire, production models should have the single rudder provisionally fitted to the V2 and standard from the V5 onward. Procurement status for internal systems,

right: When this photo of Dr. Würster posing in front of the Me 210 was taken, research on the type's unusual flight handling characteristics was already being undertaken using attached strips of cloth.

semi-finished components, etc. has not yet been clarified with the subcontractors, something which could endanger the startup of full scale production. Only four of the sixteen prototypes ordered are currently in the test flight stage. Evaluation of flight handling and air-to-air weapons firing tests have not yet been completed.

Here the only argument given for the single rudder is the rear field of fire. As is admitted later (3/12/42), the flight handling of the twin rudder configuration was completely unsatisfactory. The cause may have been the same as for the Ar 240, i.e. that the vertical stabilizers were affected by the airflow from the engine nacelles due to the short fuselage.

9/5/40 (Mtt)
Fritz Wendel is forced to bail out of the Me 210 V2. Recovering from a dive at a speed of 650 km/h, the aft fuselage began porpoising, which in turn set up a vibration in the horizontal stabilizers and subsequently led to their disintegration.

This accident shows that the fuselage was not only too short for stability, but also was too weak.

9/27/40 (GL)
The General Staff calls for the Me 210 to be able to carry as many flares as possible with the capability of dropping them singly.

11/6/40 (GL)
The *Generalluftzeugmeister* rejects rumors that the Me 210 was running into problems both in production and in terms of performance. He admits that the empty weight has risen to 1.4 metric tons due to subsequent requirements. To this end, certain roles will call for the fitting and/or removal of specific conversion kits.

12/19/40 (E-Stelle Rechlin)
The Me 210 V-9, prototype for series production versions, is test flown. Pilots Neidhart and Malz discover that the machine stalls out when flown in a steep bank in a "dirty" configuration. It is difficult to achieve stability around the pitch axis. In a fly-off with a Bf 110 E/N, the 110 enjoyed a clear superiority in the fact that it recovered more quickly following a separation of the airflow.

Stalling, i.e. separation of airflow over an airfoil, most often occurs when sliding. It is particularly dangerous when occurring during the landing phase, since there is no altitude available for recovering the aircraft. To the observer, it is amazing that this characteristic was not followed up on. This deficiency later became the cause for the failure of the first Me 210 version.

2/19/41 (E-Stelle Rechlin)
The director of the test center urges that, instead of a counterbalance, inherently balanced elevators be developed as quickly as possible with simultaneous amplification so that the landing characteristics of the Me 210 can be fixed.

2/20/41 (GL)
The General Staff wants the Me 210 to be produced as a tropicalized version, although this cannot delay initiation of production. The General Staff asks for an investigation into the possibility of fitting the GM 1 system into part of the bomb bay.

As production of the Me 210 got underway, no one could have foreseen the scale of the problems looming on the horizon. (Moor)

3/14/41 (GL)
Prototype fitting of tropicalized equipment on the Me 210 is initiated. The General Staff is asked how many aircraft are to be fitted. Prototype installation and investigation of the GM-1 system in the Me 210 is initiated. A statement is forthcoming.

3/20/41 (GL)
The General Staff requests 200 tropicalization sets for the Me 210.

3/27/41 (GL)
The General Staff points out that the 200 tropicalized sets for the Me 210 is only a temporary figure and will most likely need to be increased.

4/3/41 (GL)
The General Staff calls for three groups (120 aircraft) to be equipped with Me 210s having balloon deflectors. The final version of the deflector (fitted to the wings) should be of an acceptable weight and be fitted to all new bomber and heavy fighter aircraft types.

4/17/41 (GL)
180 sets of balloon deflectors for 120 aircraft are contracted out. Starting in December the balloon cable cutters will be supplied as part of the series production.

5/1/41 (GL)
Weapons needs of the night fighter units and space requirements for the Lichtenstein system make its use in the Bf 110 and Me 210 problematic. The General Staff asks for a final opinion on the suitability of these aircraft for the night fighting role.

5/15/41 (GL)
LC 2 states that, for lack of sufficient space, both the Bf 110 as well as the Me 210 are out of the question for use in the night fighting role in view of the equipment and systems needed by the night fighter divisions. Starting in December 1941 the Do 217 will be produced as a night fighter, beginning with five, then rising to twelve per month. The General Staff asks that the date for production startup of the Me 210 reconnaissance version be announced, and calls for the Me 210 to be equipped with the BZ A 10 bombsight as standard, plus the installation of two MG 151/20s in place of the MG 151s.

5/23/41 (GL)
Production of the Me 210 as a *Zerstörer* is to begin in May 1942, with the reconnaissance version following in September. The Bf 110 series can't be extended due to the engines. According to LC 7, the BZ A 10 can only be fitted starting with the 50th aircraft, and is projected for 1/3 of the total production due to limited resources. The Revi 12 c sight will be fitted up to the 50th aircraft. The second MG 151 will also be fitted with a 20 mm barrel.

5/30/41 (GL)
BZ A 10 sights can be retrofitted starting with the first airframe, but as was stated on 5/23, it is only available for 1/3 of the production run and not before the 51st airframe. The General Staff finds this decision unacceptable.

6/5/41 (Mtt)
Several problems are causing a delay in production startup. *Generalluftzeugmeister* Ernst Udet calls in an industry advisory council at Messerschmitt's Augsburg facility, and all parties involved in the Me 210's development are to submit their problems and have neutral observers give advice on how to overcome the crisis. Messerschmitt is given the task of eliminating the following problems immediately:

1. The Me 210 oscillates in its vertical axis, making accurate sighting when firing difficult.
2. The power driven elevators are not the best solution; an internally balanced elevator system needs to be fitted.
3. The tendency to veer during takeoff and landing must be eliminated by lengthening the fuselage.
4. The recent engine fires with the DB 601 on the Bf 110 and Me 210 need to be clarified and eliminated with the help of the Daimler-Benz Company.

5. The supercharger intake protective screen proposed by DB must be modified for aerodynamic reasons.
6. The instability in the vertical axis caused by extending the dive brakes must be eliminated.
7. The automatic dive recovery system does not meet expectations.

6/12/41 (GL)
A detachment for evaluating the Me 210 will not be needed at Rechlin until 1 July. The matter of resource availability for the BZ A 10 must still be clarified; still needed are 20 precision engineers and electricians.

6/27/41 (GL)
At present, it is unclear whether a 20 mm barrel for the port MG 151 will be required. If necessary, a decision by the chief engineer is requested. Installation in the Me 210 is estimated for sometime after 8/1/41.

6/27/41 (Letter from the *Generalflugzeugmeister* to *Prof.* Messerschmitt)

"Dear Messerschmitt!

The problems recently encountered with your 109/110/210 and Warschau Süd designs prompt me to speak to you plainly on the matter.

As much as I acknowledge the performance of your designs, which have made such a decisive impact in front-line operations, I feel compelled to impress upon you in the strongest terms that I believe you are going down the wrong path. With military aircraft one must—particularly in war—design with safety in mind and not be forced to constantly add time consuming reinforcing measures after the fact. This then makes for more harmonious cooperation between development and production. I am reminded of the wing reinforcements to the 109, the undercarriage problems with the 109 and 210, and the delays in rectifying problems with the control surfaces on the 110.

I consider it my duty, not only as Generalluftzeugmeister—one who is responsible for ensuring that new types are produced on time and that their performance is up to par but also as your friend, to unequivocally express to you that this path you've taken is dangerous and can lead to no end of problems for us all. It is because of your favored position as a designer, which up until now has brought you unlimited trust and high recognition, that you must have a particularly keen sense of your responsibility and should give you cause to view yourself and your performance in a more critical light.

I ask you to take all measures necessary to avoid such setbacks with the 210, the engine-powered *Warschau Süd*, and the Me 264, as well as other projects you are working on. If I may give you some good advice: use the experience and the recommendations coming from the field and from my colleagues so that the Messerschmitt Company can preserve its good name.

Heil Hitler! Udet"

7/3/41 (GL)
The *Generalflugzeugmeister* would like to submit recommendations for the possibility of fitting the Me 210 out as a night fighter. In light of the latest experiences there is an increased interest in a two-man rubber dinghy for the Me 210.

7/17/41 (GL)
Dimensions for the night fighting systems have not yet been established. Space will be made for the two-man boat. The General Staff accepts the recommendation to have just 1/3 of all Me 210s, preferably the non-tropicalized ones, be fitted with the *Kutonasen* (balloon cable cutters).

7/24/41 (GL)
Experience has shown that 50% of losses are attributable to hits in the radiator systems. Consequently, partial armor plating is planned for all new aircraft types. The General Staff calls for as much firepower as possible, at least four cannons, for the night fighter versions of the Bf 110, Me 210, and Do 217.

7/25/41 (Letter from the *Generalflugzeugmeister* to *Prof.* Messerschmitt)

"Dear Messerschmitt"

The meeting with Hentzen on 7/22 has once again caused me serious concerns. This month we're still not getting any Me 210s for front-line testing, meaning that yet again the type's introduction is going to be delayed by another month. The latest accident with the Me 210 could most certainly have been prevented if, as outlined in the minutes from 7/4/41—of which four copies were given to your representative for immediate action—strengthened landing gear had been fitted. I therefore consider it a serious oversight that your company did not learn anything from this and that, as a consequence, yet another valuable aircraft has been lost, not to mention the fact that the trials so urgently needed have suffered another setback. I'm still considering the repercussions of this case.

I've studied the blueprints for making the undercarriage lighter and was amazed to find that you weakened the landing gear to save 3.5 kg. As I have been told, the undercarriage currently has an outward cant of 1 degree. If this is true, then it seems clear to me the reason behind aircraft's tendency to ground loop. I consider it absolutely necessary that the undercarriage be forward angled at a 1-degree angle and would be grateful if you could tell me the method used to measure this forward angle on the Me 210.

The Me 210 V 12 was broken up after this belly landing. Such incidents caused Generalluftzeugmeister *Udet no end of concern. (Moor)*

Furthermore, I have the impression that you are making far too many changes after the first blueprints were completed. V-types and production versions are so different that the test and evaluation results are of no use for field units. I don't need to dwell further on this avoidable dual work and the other company-driven costs and problems.

One thing, dear Messerschmitt, needs to be absolutely clear between us: no longer can aircraft be lost due to weak undercarriage units at normal airfields, for landing gear systems have no place when it comes to breaking new technological ground in aircraft construction. Nor can belated changes and tinkering be allowed to unacceptably delay the introduction of a war-critical aircraft type.

All these unnecessary annoyances and unacceptable time delays of late compel me once again to apply a tougher scale for reviewing your new types and to instruct my offices accordingly. In the future, I ask that you keep them fully informed so that close cooperation will avoid any further situations of a similar nature.

Most sincerely, and Heil Hitler!
I remain your Udet"

7/26/41 (letter from *Dr.* Maier, FKFS at the University of Stuttgart, to Mr. Caroli of Messerschmitt AG)

Dr. Maier writes that the forward angle of 1 degree as well as the current camber will improve the Me 210's tendency to ground loop. However, it won't be significant at lower taxi speeds if air damping does not play a role.

7/31/41 (GL)

The General Staff calls for the 20 mm barrel on the Me 210's port side as well. No armor sleeve barrels are needed.

July 41 (RLM)
The BAL production oversight committee takes the first two Me 210 A-1s. Over the next few months the committee will take even greater numbers of aircraft.

9/25/41 (GL)
Development of the oblique cameras in the Me 210 is broken off.

10/16/41 (GL)
The General Staff asks that research be done into fitting SD 2 racks into the Me 210's bomb bay.

11/6/41 (Mtt)
According to a telephone conversation with B1B-TU, the *Kutonase* is only to be installed on one third of the aircraft. Since de-icer boots aren't expected to be fitted to production versions before late 1942 at the earliest, the *Kutonase* won't have de-icers for the time being. Final inspection of the *Kutonase's* test fitting on *W.Nr.* 123 will take place on 10/4/41 by the RLM and DLV.

November 1941
Erprobungskommando 210 receives the first 16 Me 210 A-1s. Initial flights show that experienced pilots have no problems whatsoever coming to grips with the airframe's unique features. However, particular caution is needed when dealing with the aircraft's tendency to veer on takeoff. Flight handling and performance are considered as good as or better than those of the Bf 110. New pilots, however, are having considerably more difficulties.

12/12/41 (GL)
Following an investigation at the Messerschmitt Company on 11/17/41, *Dipl. Ing.* Frydag, *Major* Storp, and *Major* Peterson are in agreement that the Me 210 will be a viable aircraft.

The C-E *Amt* establishes which changes are to be made based on timeliness and technological potential. In May 1942 400 Me 210s will be produced by Messerschmitt and authorized licensed manufacturers. Of those, 300 will have the established modifications and 100 will be set aside for training purposes and not be certified as front-line ready. To carry out modifications after the fact starting in May 1942, by 1/15/42 the company is to be provided an airbase with hangar facilities and 300 qualified field personnel. The Messerschmitt Company is to provide the management personnel, and is also responsible for ensuring the work is carried out.

Starting with the 401st aircraft, the established changes are to be introduced on the production line. Any other necessary modifications that have not yet been taken into account will have to be implemented on a second version which is projected to begin production in August 1942.

The Command Staff is informed that the Me 210 will primarily be used as a close-support aircraft in 1942. In general, the requirements for dive bombing and automatic dive recovery system are still in place. The Command Staff's requirements are based on its use as a light bomber. Some of the modifications can probably be put off until the introduction of the planned version two. However, for the close-support role additional armor plating will be needed. The GL/C-E and the Command Staff will draw up the necessary modifications as soon as possible.

The steel required for armor protection will need to be determined and allocated.

Reconfiguring the aircraft as a close-support plane cannot interfere with its planned production as a light bomber. The aircraft are to be procured from the Messerschmitt Company, and it is expected that they will need to be specially modified with extra armor plating.

Major Peterson points out the need for an extended fuselage due to the type's spin characteristics and the need for greater reliability of the remotely controlled weapons system. The aircraft has a tendency to suddenly stall out. The airflow separates without giving any prior warning, and losses in the field must be taken into account. Field units are to be instructed on this matter when the type is introduced. Research is to be undertaken as to whether the radiator flaps on the upper wing are the cause of the sudden separation of airflow.

The Command Staff intends to have three wings established for close-support operations by May 1942. Plans call for these to be equipped as follows: two wings with Me 210s; one group with HS 129s; and the remainder with Me 109s, if possible the Me 109 E.

For conversion the field will be expected to provide an airbase with hangar facilities and personnel.

12/16/41 (GL)
Based on the General Staff's desire for close-support aircraft, it is decided to tailor the Me 210 for the close-support role. Dive bombing capability is therefore dropped. The first 100 Me 210 aircraft won't be changed, the next 300 will have the changes introduced by work teams, and starting with the 401st aircraft all modifications will be part of the production line. The scale of armor protection for the Me 210 is currently being worked out by the Messerschmitt Company in conjunction with departments within the GL. For the close-support mission, a group of Me 109 Es and a group of Hs 129s are to be set up also. The Ju 87 will not be used as a close-support aircraft due to manufacturing constraints.

12/16/41 (*I./SKG 210*, Landsberg)
Three training aircraft are damaged, either due to faulty landing gear or by crash landing (10- 20%).

12/23/41 (GL)
A final meeting with the *Genst.Fü-St./Gruppe T* and the GL/C took place regarding the construction of close-support aircraft. The 101st through 400th Me 210 will be retrofitted for the close-support role, and in so doing, the dive brakes and other changes called for by the General Staff for the Me 210 light bomber will be dispensed with. The General Staff's modifications can be carried out from the 401st production plane onward and will be incorporated into the new production run as standard. GL/C-B is determining with *Genst. 6.Abt.* the number of Me 210 high-speed bombers and the deadline for initiation of production. For the first 300 close-support aircraft, there are serious difficulties in getting conversion airfields. The final deadline schedule will be set up by 1/5/42. The two Me 210 wings for close-support are to be ready by 1 May.

1/13/42 (GL)
The General Staff calls for the two Me 210 wings with armor protection for the close-support role to be ready by 1 April 1942. The Messerschmitt Company begins conversion work at Landsberg starting on 1/15/42 and asks for the armor plates to be delivered starting on 2/10/42. The deadlines for the armor plates, which are drop forged and then heat treated, are unacceptable. The swages will take an estimated 6-8 weeks to make. As the General Staff's deadline must be adhered to at all costs, the armor will initially be needed to be welded together from straight or simply curved plates. This welded construction should be roughly the same quality as that of the final production version. On 1/15/42 the best approach for this welded construction will be determined at Schönefeld. LC will arrange to have an Me 210 transferred from Rechlin to Schönefeld for this purpose.

1/15 - 1/31/42 (I./ZG 1, Lechfeld and Landsberg)
Within the space of just two weeks, eight aircraft have crashed while undergoing training flights, two of which are total losses. Three crewmen die. Causes are crash landings, operator errors, and undercarriage flaws.

1/20/42 (GL)
The straight armor plates are to be supplied by the steel works and the shaped ones by Henschel. According to data from Mr. Frydag, 160 airframes can be delivered with armor plating by the end of April at best, whereas the Messerschmitt Company offers less favorable dates. By the time the dead-

line is finally resolved, research needs to be undertaken to determine the possibility of delivering the remaining aircraft to the two wings without armor protection.

1/27/42 (GL)
240 aircraft are expected to be delivered with armor by 5/15/42. Prerequisite for this is the allocation of the Lechfeld airbase to Messerschmitt, including hangar space, which can probably be returned to the General Staff sometime after July 1942. Landsberg must remain the conversion base, as the demand of 900 aircraft is expected for 1942.

2/10/42 (GL)
The Me 210 comes under harsh criticism from the front lines. The Me 210 program will probably have to be changed. GL/C will submit proposals to St/GL on 2/14/42.

2/24/42 (GL)
By 2/24/42 the Henschel Company has delivered 80 sets of armor plating for the Me 210 S. In addition, Henschel will supply another 240 sets. Henschel will assume production assuming electricity and 25 additional workers can be made available.

3/3 - 3/9/42 (I./ZG 1, Tours Airfield)
Within a week, the first group of *Zerstörergeschwader 1* report that one aircraft is damaged while taxiing, eight have crash landed, and three have crashed while on training flights. As a rule, the accidents are attributed to young, inexperienced pilots who find themselves in a flat spin.

3/6/42 (Memorandum No. 46/42, Top Secret, Carinhall)
Milch: "A key issue here is, that the matter with the high-speed bomber has not been cleared up."

Jeschonnek: "The Me 210 in its current configuration can't be imposed on the crews. It goes into a flat spin quite easily, and the reason has not yet been found. Then there are serious problems with the engine installation. Twice now, engines have broken free in flight. Crews have died when the plane noses over on the ground. It is extremely questionable whether the Me 210 can enter operations this spring. For its intended role the plane is entirely unsuited in its current configuration."

Milch: "Prof. Messerschmitt wants to try lengthening the type's fuselage to make it operationally ready."

Herr Reichsfeldmarschall: "Prof. Messerschmitt, a representative from GL, Major Storp and Hauptmann Diesing, are to report on Monday 3/8/1942 to discuss the 210."

Milch: "As an alternative, in the event that the Me 210 is abandoned, we are examining to what extent Me 109 and Me 110 production can be increased. The six groups planned with the Me 210 for the spring will then have to be equipped with the Me 109 and the Me 110. The necessary armor plating will have to be carried out on time."

Jeschonnek: "It will be necessary to comb the Chief of AW once again for Ju 87s and Me 109s to ensure that these groups are operational on time, since an increase in Me 109 and Me 110 production will be slow at first."

Reichsfeldmarschall: "The matter of increasing Me 109 and Me 110 production needs to be cleared up. A decision can only be made once Prof. Messerschmitt and Hauptmann Diesing present their findings."

Milch: "In order to fulfill the Führer's wish of fielding a high-speed bomber in any form, we've thought of taking the Me 109, which can carry a 250 kg or maximum 500 kg bomb. By using drop tanks its range can be increased to 1300 km." **Herr Reichsmarschall:** "Agreed."

Milch: "The Arado 240 is a potential replacement for the Me 210 from 1943 onward. This would be the first aircraft assigned to the Gruppe Rowehl for reconnaissance purposes. Its bomb load would still have to be determined. The plane has quite good performance. With the Db 601 E installed it has a maximum speed of 645 km/h at maximum pressure altitude, with two DB 614s it's 775 km/h, and with two DB 605 engines it is 685 km/h. As a heavy fighter, planned armament is two MG 151s, 2 MG 17s, and 2 MG 81 Zs. As of now, there are no plans for a bomb bay; research will have to be undertaken to see how bombs can be carried."

Reichsfeldmarschall: "Research is to begin immediately on the feasibility of using the Arado as a replacement for the Me 210. At the same time, possible increase in production needs to be looked into. I expect a report on any decision made."

3/10/42 (GL)

On 3/9/42, at a meeting attended by all interested offices and representatives of the Messerschmitt Company, the *Reichsmarschall* orders the cancellation of the Me 210 effective immediately. The 240 Me 210 S aircraft currently under construction are to be finished. The Me 210s planned for ZG 1 and 2 are to be replaced with other aircraft types. The resources freed up at Messerschmitt by this action are to be immediately applied to the Me 110 and Me 109. Developmental work on the Me 210 is to continue at an accelerated pace. GL/C is to work with GL/A and KDE and come up with a work program based around the situation resulting from the *Reichsmarschall's* decision. This is to be submitted to St/GL as soon as possible.

3/10/42 (Mtt)

Willy Messerschmitt and Theo Croneiß receive a telegram from GL/C informing them of the cancellation of any further Me 210s. A decision on resuming production will be made by the GL and the field after evaluation of a new type with lengthened fuselage, inherently balanced elevators, and slats, as well as elimination of all criticisms. As a replacement, a rise in production rates for the Bf 109 and Bf 110 is planned. The *Reichsmarschall* expects that the gap caused by the Me 210's cancellation will be bridged by increased production of the Bf 110 and Bf 109 using every conceivable means.

3/12/42

Report on the meeting regarding the Me 210 which took place in the *Reichsmarschall's* special train on 3/9/42

Notes

Prof. Messerschmitt, ordered to appear at the meeting alone, brought along Messrs. Hentzen, Caroli, and Hederer. The *Reichsmarschall* approved the participation of Mr. Hentzen and later that of Mr. Caroli (Test Director at Mtt) for matters pertaining to flight handling. The meeting lasted approximately two hours.

The *Reichsmarschall* opened the meeting by first listing all the main criticisms of the Me 210. Up to now, he'd only received favorable reports on the Me 210, which makes the blow all the harder to learn of the type's failure; indeed, it is the hardest blow since the founding of the *Luftwaffe*. If he were to envy *Gen. Oberst* Udet anything, it would be that he does not have to deal with this failure any more.

Hauptmann Diesing reports on the experience with the Me 210 up to this point. Operations and accident statistics: one outage for every 50 flight hours with very limited live-fire and bombing flights. Inadequate operational readiness prevents sufficient flight training (18 hours before the first operational mission). Main criticisms: tendency to ground loop; difficult takeoffs and landings; danger of spinning; problems with the hydraulic and electrical systems; only cleared for 50 kg bomb payload at a dive angle of just 30 degrees; Me 210 S prototype not yet available; weapons system only works in one test airframe; and lack of evidence on its effectiveness from wide-scale testing. He cannot recognize the results from the long-term evaluation conducted at Lärz, since field personnel are not participating. To the question of whether he, as a *Geschwaderkommodore*, could be responsible for the springtime deployment of the Me 210, he must answer in the negative.

Prof. Messerschmitt differentiates between defects in equipment and defects in the airframe and acknowledges responsibility for equipment defects only insofar as these are a result of being fitted to the airframe. He recognizes that the flight handling criticisms are very serious, but sees no possibility of ensuring these defects are eliminated by the time the aircraft is due to enter service. He explains that the spin dangers in particular were recognized too late.

The *Reichsmarschall* says that the tests were a failure; they were carried out by pilots who were either too good or "lauric"(*sic*). He announces impending changes in the way evaluations will be done in the future. His question on the dates for implementing critical changes on the airframe was answered entirely unsatisfactorily by *Prof.* Messerschmitt.

Main points of the ensuing debate:

Major Storp: As late as October 1941 he took the view with the *Staatssekretär* that the aircraft's problems could be corrected in time so that it would be flying by its service entry deadline. Today, because of this failure, on the orders of *Gen. Oberst* Jeschonnek, he must ask the *Reichsmarschall* on a decision regarding the springtime deployment of the Me 210 S.

The *Reichsmarschall* condemns in the sharpest terms the RLM's premature stoppage of the Bf 110, Ju 87, and Ju 88 in favor of the Me 210. As a result, he will bring three men from the GL division up on charges before a military tribunal. Since the Me 210, without conversion to the S configuration, is not able to cover its originally intended role (due to danger of spinning), he asks how this failure could have appeared in spite of the fact that the Bf 110 had, to a great extent, served as its inspiration.

Flugbaumeister Malz: The assumption that the Bf 110 was a full-blown inspiration was a false one, as the example of the rudder illustrates: entirely unsatisfactory handling of the twin rudder concept carried over from the Bf 110 contrasted with the satisfactory handling of the single rudder design not found on the original.

The *Reichsmarschall* responded heatedly by saying that *Gen. Oberst* Udet and Messerschmitt had repeatedly given him the opposite explanation, the last time being in the autumn of 1941. Any claim along the lines that the Me 210 is a completely new aircraft is nonsense.

Prof. Messerschmitt complained about the following: late arrival of the field requirements, and the field generally involved too late in the program. Direct cooperation between the field and the industry is nonexistent, e.g. front-line visits by Mtt engineers are forbidden by the RLM (response to query: *Gen-Ing.* Reidenbach). Personnel such as Ziegler at Rechlin can't be had, despite the promise of *Gen. Oberst* Udet. Foreign war prizes are not made available.

Quite upset, the *Reichsmarschall* stated that he is already deeply concerned about field contact with the industry. Comment on the prohibition of front-line visits: "These conceited executives! I'll hold Reidenbach accountable for this." Comment on the Ziegler matter: "Another of those cases in which the executives simply failed to carry out the instructions of *Gen. Oberst* Udet."

Malz pointed out that the field units' needs would have been known sooner if Messerschmitt AG had delivered the aircraft earlier. The matter of providing examples of captured aircraft is also corrected (e.g. Spitfire, IL-2). An attempt to offer an explanation regarding the prohibition of front-line visits by Mtt engineers did not occur in view of the *Reichsmarschall's* anger.

The *Reichsmarschall* then made the decision on the Me 210 already known through the telegram and admonished the Mtt AG to make every effort to at least partially fill the resulting gap.

Malz drew attention to the dragging work at Mtt AG on all matters dealing with development. On behalf of the *Staatssekretär*, the following comparison figures were presented:
Designers at the drafting table:
Junkers 450, Messerschmitt AG 190
Additional design engineers:
Junkers 125, Messerschmitt AG 120

With this pool of personnel, work is exclusively focused on the following types:

Junkers:	Ju 87 D, Ju 88, Ju 288
Messerschmitt AG:	Bf 109, Bf 110, Me 264, Me 210, Me 309, Me 321, Me 323, Me 163

The *Staatssekretär* hopes to shortly recommend that either Mtt AG be allocated design engineers (something he personally thinks is not organizationally sound and therefore considers a mistake), or that the Mtt AG's scope of tasking be reduced.

The *Reichsmarschall* sees in these comparison numbers, which for him were entirely new, the key as to why the Me 210 was such a total failure. He intends to make more design engineers available to the Mtt AG, as he expects *Prof.* Messerschmitt to produce a design whose performance is on par with the Bf 109, the absolute best fighter in the world (following comment: "I'll shortly be releasing some engineers from within GL!")

Following the meeting there was a private discussion between the *Reichsmarschall* and *Prof.* Messerschmitt lasting approximately 1/2 hour. *Prof.* Messerschmitt later provided unsolicited details on its contents to Malz. The only significant thing appears to be the comment that *Prof.* Messerschmitt has access to the *Reichsmarschall* in the event serious problems arise.

3/12/42 (Memorandum GL/C-B 2)
Based on the orders of the *Reichsmarschall*, further construction of the Me 210 is halted effective immediately. To carry out this order, the following measures are to be undertaken with utmost urgency using night shifts and Sunday work crews:

I.
Efforts will be made to have a decision rendered by 5/1 on whether continued construction of the type can be undertaken by focused improvements.

1a) Six aircraft are to be modified using the most expeditive means possible by 4/1 (lengthening of fuselage, leading edge slats fitted, and horizontal stabilizers internally balanced) and made ready for a quick series of trials. Autopilot must be installed. Configuration of the aircraft: *Zerstörer* without armor. Regensburg will provide the final deadline by Monday, 3/16.

1b) A further ten aircraft will be provided with armor, of which four will go to Rechlin for extended testing. For these trials, the Test Center Command will compile a test detachment consisting of members from test centers and field units for Augsburg.

1c) Ten aircraft from existing stock (i.e. with short fuselage) are to be sent to Tarnewitz immediately for weapons trials. For the transfer flight and the evaluation Mtt is to provide three pilots and the KdE an additional two pilots (ferry flights to be undertaken only in good weather).

II.
Before the possible production continuation of the type goes into effect on 5/1, in cooperation with GL/C-B there will be a shift in Mtt AG personnel using the following guidelines:

1. Effective immediately, the special modification facilities at Landsberg and Gablingen will fall under the direction of Messerschmitt Company associates. The personnel pulled from the aviation industry will return to their respective companies.

2. For Obertraubling and Leipheim Mtt will provide approximately 2000 personnel for accelerating the work on the Me 323 and the Me 163 B.
3. Bf 109s, Bf 110s, and Ju 87s are to be used to strengthen the two heavy fighter wings, ZG 1 and ZG 2. To this end an as yet undetermined number of workers will be detached for repairing Bf 109s and Bf 110s. The facilities involved have yet to be established. Equally, an as yet un determined number will be reassigned to 109 and 110 plants (final assembly and flight operations) in order to accelerate the output of new built aircraft.

4. For the Me 109, production of armor plating is to begin immediately (so called "*Bismarckhütte*") in order to make as many aircraft as possible from repaired stocks available for setting up ZG 1 and ZG 2 above and beyond the number already being produced. Exactly how many aircraft can be made available from repairs to Me 109 Es or F-2s will be determined in a special meeting.

5. For fitting the Me 110 with armor Mtt will immediately build a mockup with fittings and will liaise with the network management for armor plating for the purpose of assuring these plates can be fitted to previously produced 110s. To this end, production of armor plating for the 210 S can cease immediately. The Henschel Company will remain involved in the manufacture of Me 110 plating and will receive skilled technicians from Mtt to accelerate the increased output.
6. Mtt will introduce the necessary changes to the jigs for the modified Me 210 version, effective immediately.
7. It is determined that all subcontractors for the Me 210 will continue working so that the resources are not lost.
8. GL/C-B 1 instructs the GL Liaison Office Budapest to inform the Hungarians of imminent major changes to the type, and that the Mtt Company will immediately institute all measures necessary. Since as a result there will be a temporary lag in work at Augsburg, the Hungarians should pull out the 70 workers located there until further notice.

In general, it is also noted that all potentially necessary materials can be drawn from the Me 210 stockpile. Any modifications not specifically addressed in protocols 201 and 212 may not be carried out, with one exception: a reinforced bulkhead for protecting the crew in the event the machine flips onto its back (i.e. a roll bar).

III.

In the event that the Me 210 will not be continued despite these changes, special measures will be agreed upon at once. Corresponding recommendations re: renewing Bf 110 production and increasing the output of the Bf 109 at the expense of the Me 210 will be drawn up by GL/C-B 2 and simultaneously presented by the network management at a special meeting.

3/17/42 (GL)

Oberst Vorwald reports on the measures that have been initiated following coordination with the General Staff, the various departments involved, and the aviation industry. Efforts are being made to have a decision made on the Me 210's future by 5/1/42. By 4/5/42 Messerschmitt will supply six modified aircraft to Regensburg for flight trials. A further ten aircraft with armor are to be built. Of these, four are planned for extended flight testing in Rechlin, and the remaining six are to go to ZG 1 and ZG 2's personnel for trials under the direction of KdE in Augsburg or Lechfeld.

ZG 1 and ZG 2 are to be stocked with Me 109s and Me 110s, which will be armor plated for the close-support role. 160 Me 109 E7s and 80 Me 110 Es are to be converted, in addition to the replacement aircraft.

Oberst Vorwald reports on the results of his Hungary trip: The Hungarian aviation industry has, within the guidelines of the German-Hungarian Treaty, done a commendable effort in carrying out the necessary expansion work. Start of the German-Hungarian Cooperative Program (Me 210, Me 109, DB 605) is dependent upon the timely delivery of the promised tooling machinery. German deliveries are backlogging.

3/21/1942 (Memorandum for Record No. 58/42 Top Secret, Rominten)
***Generaloberst* Jeschonnek:** "How will the two heavy fighter wings look, since the Me 210 won't be coming?"

Reichsfeldmarschall: "The two wings will be used as strike wings, and therefore need to get Me 110s, Me 109s with bomb racks, and Hs 129s."

***Feldmarschall* Milch:** "The 321 (Gigant) transport glider from Messerschmitt is a fraud. *Feldmarschall* Milch ordered a detailed review by Oberstleutnant Dinort. Already 36 people have been killed testing the plane. The machine is poorly built, trim is impossible, and control pressure is too high. Messerschmitt even had a movie using mockups made for the Führer's birthday. Director Tank, Focke-Wulf, has been given a contract to develop a transport glider capable of carrying the new 32 ton tank Messerschmitt—Adolphine has run aground, as it is unusable for long range flights."

3/24/42 (GL)
The Opel Company takes over sponsorship of the Messerschmitt Concern. The *Generalfeldmarschall* orders this to be carried out and stresses that Messerschmitt is expected to render utmost cooperation.

3/25/42 (Letter from Willy Messerschmitt to Test Center Director Franke)
" Dear Mr. Franke!"

You are certainly aware that the field is having problems with the Me 210 and that, contrary to all expectations these are mainly attributable to stalling. As there is a large number of these aircraft already produced and it is still under construction, it is urgent that the aircraft be brought in order. The defects already known (ground looping on landing, unpleasant handling of the elevators) have been taken into consideration by lengthening the fuselage and fitting a counterbalanced elevator, both of which were approved by the test center and, after just a few flights, were considered satisfactory by both the field and the test center. The remaining criticisms of the landing gear (hydraulics, weapons, etc.) are fundamentally engineering issues and can be remedied in the near future. The most critical point is one that we have all been the least concerned about. The problem basically lies in the fact that there's no established minimum operating speed set for the aircraft. Naturally, we can't set the requirement today and implement it in short order so that the airframe, when in a spin, is able to smoothly recover when controls are neutralized at any given rpm."

4/8/42 (Letter from Willy Messerschmitt to Test Center Director Franke)
"It will be of interest to you to know that, according to information from everyone who has flown the aircraft, the improved slat makes it more forgiving than the Me 110. I am not yet certain how it was possible that none of the pilots, not even our factory test pilots, noticed the unpleasant stall characteristics."

Although over three hundred Me 210 A-1s had been built, during the spring of 1942 the type continued to suffer from hydraulic problems with the landing gear, as evidenced by the damage inflicted upon W.Nr. *153 (VC+SQ). (Petrick)*

4/14/42 (GL)
Continued construction of the Me 210 is still not finally resolved. *Oberst* Vorwald reports that the six Me 210 test examples won't be finished by Messerschmitt until 4/20/42 at the earliest. The delay is based on the increase in the number of changes, from 4 to 40. Renewed series production of the Me 210 can't begin before 10/1/42.

As the Ju 88 has proven itself to be an effective *Zerstörer*, the question arises as to whether the Me 210 can't be dispensed with. Another possible option is the less expensive Ar 240, which would then replace the Me 110 and the Me 210. There has to be at least one small batch of high-speed light bombers available (one wing) by 1943, which can then be used to attack the British Isles in daylight.

4/19/1942 (Memorandum for Record No. 58/42 Top Secret, Rominten)
***Generalfeldmarschall* Milch gives a presentation on the situation with aircraft deliveries:**

"The Me 210 will no longer be a significant player in 1942, and whether or not it will be produced at all depends on the evaluation. Series production can't begin until four months after that is completed. For 1943 its performance won't particularly stand out. After queries and assessment on the Me 210's potential, which Generaloberst Jeschonnek and Major Storp among others have completely rejected, the Reichsmarschall has directed the Me 210 be dropped from the program. The engines and other usable components are to be utilized for other products, and the rest is to be sent to the scrapyard. Nevertheless, the planned evaluation is to continue in order to gather general technical experience."

Generalfeldmarschall Milch: "A potential high speed bomber candidate is the Arado 240, of which two samples are being flown by the Gruppe Rowehl as reconnaissance platforms. Unfortunately, the aircraft have not met the speed figures quoted by the company. Production is contingent upon this."

4/21/42 (GL)
The *Generalfeldmarschall* relays the following from a meeting with the *Reichsmarschall*: The Me 210 is dropped from the program on the express orders of the *Reichsmarschall*.

The six Me 210s and ten Me 210 S aircraft planned for evaluation are to be completed and tested. All further work on the Me 210 is to cease immediately.

The Gotha and Luther companies are to be withdrawn from the Me 210 license building program for good; all jigs etc. can be utilized for other purposes. At the parent factory semifinished components and jigs, as well as type-associated equipment is to remain where it is. Completed airframes are to be put into storage. Further use and/or scrapping will be ultimately decided following completion of trials.

Engines and components not type-associated can be utilized for other purposes immediately.

The air attaché at the Hungarian consulate is to be officially informed that the Me 210 aircraft is frozen due to technical problems. Once modifications have been carried out a final verdict will be rendered in a few weeks.

The work force freed up from Me 210 production is to be put to work on the Me 110 and Go 244 assembly lines. GL/C will report on the transfer on 4/27/42.

Mtt AG CEOs Seiler and Croneiß are scheduled for the *Generalfeldmarschall* on 4/23/42. Chiefs of GL/A and GL/C will also attend the meeting.

4/26/42 (Memorandum for Record No. 74/42 Top Secret, Villa Stabsamt)
***Generaloberst* Jeschonnek:** "After the test results are in, a decision must be made for the Me 210 on whether it is suited in the first place and if so, for what roles. Initially the Me 210 will be produced with the DB 601 F, then later with the DB 605."

Generaloberst Jeschonnek recommends reemphasizing a high-speed bomber group. To this end, a group would be set up in the West, consisting of an Me 210 squadron and two Me 109 G *Jabo* squadrons. There can be no negative consequences impacting series production of the Me 110 and Me 109 as a result of this.

Generalfeldmarschall Milch reports that the Me 210 is being built at the Augsburg plant. There are about 500 airframes completed and a further 200 half finished.

The Me 109 and 110 have priority. If the Me 210 is agreed upon, 100 airframes are to be delivered over the course of this year, beginning with 30 in July at the earliest.

4/27/42 (GL)

Oberstlt. Petersen reports on the test flight results of the modified aircraft conducted by the test detachment. The airplane's handling on takeoff and landing, as well as the flight and stability characteristics are markedly improved, with no complaints whatsoever. The maximum speed at low levels was, on average, 475 km/h. Still expected are the results of the extended testing of the landing gear. In addition, the matter of armament has yet to be resolved fully. *Oberstlt.* Petersen recommends not scrapping the airframes already built or in various stages of assembly. Instead, these should be completed insofar as the extended testing is showing positive results.

The *Generalfeldmarschall* emphasizes that the Me 210's production was first halted because of the field units' demands. The *Reichsmarschall* later ordered the full cancellation of the Me 210 based on the negative assessment of the Chief of the General Staff and *Major* Storp. The decision therefore remains to cease all work on the Me 210 and divert the subcontractors to other projects. Testing will continue.

Oberst Galland will keep the crews at Lechfeld for testing the Me 210. KdE should wrap up the technical evaluation during the second half of May, by which time recommendations on the Me 210's use as a strike plane, heavy fighter, light bomber, or possibly a trainer can be made.

Oberstabsing. Alpers reports that all work on the Me 210 has been stopped. 80% of the subcontractors have been switched over to the Me 109. The Regensburg Works will be diverted to Me 109 production. At the Augsburg Works there were approximately 1800 workers employed on the Me 210. GL/C-B calls for 1200 men to be transferred to the He 177, Go 244, and propeller production.

5/5/42 (GL)

Oberstlt. Petersen reports that the five Me 210s have so far completed 140 takeoffs. The landing gear is in order. The matter of armament has not yet been fully resolved. Otherwise, the results presented on 4/27/42 have been confirmed. The Me 210 appears to be well suited for operations as a high-speed bomber. Technical evaluation will be finished by the end of May. There are no valid reasons for not continuing with preparations to manufacture the Me 210 in Hungary.

For the remainder of the war, *Prof.* Messerschmitt's responsibilities will be limited to actual developmental work. *Direktors* Croneiß and Seiler will jointly be accountable to the GL for carrying out assigned responsibilities.

5/12/42 (GL)

Flugbaumeister Friebel proposes using the Me 109 fighter-bomber and the Me 210 as high-speed bombers in the short term. There is no question of using the Ar 240 as a high-speed bomber in the foreseeable future.

5/25/42 (GL)

A meeting took place at Lechfeld on 5/24/42 addressing the use of the Me 210 as a night fighter. *Hptm.* Streib considers the Me 210 suitable for the night fighting role and receives three machines for combat trials. The *Generalfeldmarschall* decides that the Me 210 can only be considered for the night fighter role if the necessary modifications are tenable.

Otherwise, the type's application is established as follows: one squadron is to be maintained on the Channel for attacking heavy fighter targets and shipping, plus one group in Norway for convoy protection duties, i.e. 12-20 aircraft will be needed to maintain stocks within these units. The remaining production can then be made available for the night fighting units. *XII Korps* will render a decision on the type's suitability as a night fighter within 14 days. With the exception of night fighter trials, the evaluation program will be terminated; the General Staff will give its opinion whether the Me 210 should be used as a strike aircraft, in which case testing will resume. Events at GL must proceed in such a manner that the Me 210 replacement type is in full scale production by 1944.

6/1/42 (GL)
Presently 52 Me 210s are on order with a resupply rate of 20 per month. The General Staff will follow this up with possible further options.

6/9/42 (GL)
Full scale production of the DB 603 at Pomo is delayed by possibly two to three months. This jeopardizes supplies of the Do 217 in the autumn of 1942, since there won't be sufficient output of DB 603s for the planned startup of Do 217 M production at Marienfelde (60 engines needed per month). The necessity of ensuring the Ostmarkwerke begins production of the DB 603 as planned is stressed. The *Generalfeldmarschall* provides informational data from a developmental report provided by the Daimler-Benz Company. The DB 603 was first offered to the RLM on 9/4/36. A developmental contract was issued a few weeks later. Development was halted in February/March 1937 and then was permitted to resume on 2/3/1940. In the case of the DB 603, developmental supervision on the part of the RLM failed utterly. *Oberstlt.* Petersen fears that there won't be any test results for the Do 217 this year, as the aircraft with different powerplants can't be expected for delivery before August.

Oberst Vorwald asks for a decision on Me 210 production in Hungary. It is proposed that the Hungarians continue building the Me 210, since there would be major gaps in production if they switched over to the Me 109 or Me 110. The General Staff agrees.

The General Staff has not yet rendered a final verdict on the Me 210's role. The Chief of the General Staff sees its main function as a heavy fighter in the East. According to the Messerschmitt Company, there will be 95 airframes completed by the end of 1942.

6/19/42 (GL)
Oberstabsing. Alpers reports: up to now, the Messerschmitt Company has been contracted to modify 95 aircraft that are to be delivered by the end of 1942. Currently, there are a total of 354 completed airframes, 108 unassembled aircraft, and a further 98 in the initial stages of production (540 aircraft in total). According to a recommendation by the Messerschmitt Company, the aircraft can be completed in lots of 10, 30, or 40 airframes each. The *Generalfeldmarschall*, in cooperation with the General Staff, decides that efforts are to be made to have Messerschmitt complete all the aircraft called for by the General Staff as soon as possible, i.e. by September 1943.

The Chief of the General Staff's *Führungsstab T* has approved the Me 210 to be built exclusively as a heavy fighter. Due to the engine situation, the Me 210's production would affect the output of Me 109s and Me 110s. The *Generalfeldmarschall* informs the Chief of the General Staff that Me 109 and Me 110 production takes precedence in

For the most part, the 354 Me 210 A-1s that had been produced found themselves in open storage by June of 1942. (Radinger)

every instance over that of the Me 210. At the Augsburg Works, wings for the Me 110 are to be built once Me 210 production ceases.

7/7/42 (GL)
Although there are enough engines for testing the DB 603, there are insufficient testbeds. The *Generalfeldmarschall* calls for the DB 603 to undergo thorough trials as it is one of the most critical engines.

7/14/42 (GL)
There are concerns of problems with mounting the DB 603 (switching over to glide bearings) and the Jumo 213 (high rpms). Research institutes should work together to work out these matters.

7/21/42 (GL)
The German percentage of Me 210s built in Hungary are to be produced as *Zerstörer* airframes. Reconnaissance aircraft are not needed.

8/4/42 (GL)
According to the current airframe program, the Me 210 is to be powered by the DB 601 until May 1943. Following this, the DB 605 is planned as in Hungary. All Me 210 airframes are expected to be delivered by Messerschmitt by the autumn of 1943.

8/7/42 (RLM)
The RLM issues the "Technical Guidelines for the Bomber-Destroyer."

8/17/42 (GL)
The *Reichsmarschall* is in agreement with the plans for modifying the Me 210.

A field report on the combat trials of the twelve Me 210s used on the Western Front states:

1. Operational readiness is good with minimal maintenance personnel (65-70%)
2. Flight handling at night is adequate.
3. The remote MG 131 barbettes have proven effective for the time being; no jams have occurred.
4. Only marginally inferior to the Spitfire in terms of speed.

Requirements:

1. Replacement parts
2. PC 500 in streamlined form, enabling two to be carried in the bomb bay
3. BZA system for anti-shipping operations and *Kutonase*

The *Generalfeldmarschall* asks that these bombs be sent to the squadrons. *Oberst* Kleinrath mentions that the Me 210 is planned for ZG 2 with two groups and, in addition, for convoy escort missions. The *Generalfeldmarschall* welcomes the news that field data is being collected so that the value of this type can be established once and for all.

If trials with the DB 603 in the Me 210 show the suitability of this new type, this can potentially lead to an increase in *Zerstörer* production.

8/18/42 (RLM Developmental Meeting)
Topic of heavy fighter/high-speed bomber/night fighter using one standard type. The Me 110, Me 210 with DB 601 and/or DB 603, Ar 240, Fw 187, He 219, and Ju 188 are discussed. The Ar 240 is dropped (probably because it has the same performance as the current Me 210); in its current form the Fw 187 does not have sufficient range and payload and, due to its cockpit design, is ruled out as a night fighter. The He 219 is the ideal night fighter to be sure, with its massive firepower, as well as excellent range and speed, but is too luxurious for a *Zerstörer*. With the DB 603, the Me 210 is considerably faster than the Ju 188 and also has the range for a night fighter, but would need a completely new canopy for the night fighter role, something the *Generalfeldmarschall* has already re-

jected. Furthermore, its development potential is in question, and in the comparison it lacks night fighting equipment, meaning that its weight would increase. Friebel therefore recommends the Me 210 as a *Zerstörer* and the He 219 as a night fighter. Milch tosses the Ju 188 into the ring, since its speed is only 20 km/h less than the He 219. Unlike the He 219, which would require new production, the Ju 188 could be built using existing facilities. A decision is not reached.

9/9/42 (GL)
Oberstlt. Petersen reports that Messerschmitt will deliver 210 Me 410s with the DB 603 by 12/1/42. The *Generalfeldmarschall* calls for the Me 410 to be as simple a design as possible. Production planning is to be undertaken. The 410 is primarily being considered as a day bomber against England. Major airframe modifications for its use as a heavy fighter are unacceptable in view of a sensible approach to full scale production. Initial Me 410 production is expected to be a run of 125 aircraft, with an increase to 200 airframes, including deliveries from Hungary.

9/14/42 (GL)
The Rf 2 b rear-aiming gunsight is planned for all Bf 110 F-2s and F-3s and, as much as possible, is to be tested with the Me 109 G and Me 210/410 on a large scale.

9/16/42 (GL)
Do 217 production is dropped from 100 aircraft to 70 in favor of Me 410 production. According to Study 1012 the Me 410's initial production run is expected to total 125 aircraft, increasing to 200 with deliveries from Hungary included.

10/6/42 (GL)
Oberstlt. Petersen reports that the Do 217 with DB 603 is not expected to offer any type of performance which would warrant the continued production of this aircraft type. Of consideration is an increase in Me 410s at the expense of the Do 217. *Oberstlt.* Petersen assesses the Me 410 as being quite good from a technical standpoint. The *Generalfeldmarschall* orders GL/C-B to terminate the Do 217 soon and look into increasing Me 410 production.

10/12/42 (GL)
The Command Staff relates that the Me 410 has potential as a high-speed bomber and, in addition to this type, the Me 610 is to be called for as a *Zerstörer*. The Command Staff therefore recommends that the Do 217's production be stopped in September 1943 and using the engines made available for the Me 610, which is expected to go into production in early 1944. The General Staff agrees with this proposal. The GL/C-B, however, considers this proposal to be impractical from a time standpoint. C-B 2 will work out a plan for the earliest possible production date of the Me 610, as well as a quicker termination of the Do 217.

10/20/42 (GL)
C-B 2 informs the *6.Abteilung* of the General Staff on production initiation of the Me 410. 60 airframes will be complete by April 1943, so that the first group can go to the front on 5/1/43. Field crews can begin familiarizing themselves with the type beginning in February 1943. The *Generalfeldmarschall* orders that maximum effort be undertaken to get the MG 131 installed in the Bf 109 and, if necessary, will intervene personally. By the same token, urgency is to be given to installing the 3.7, 5, and 7.5 cm guns in bombers and heavy fighters.

11/42 (Mediterranean Theater)
III. Gruppe of ZG 1 is transferred from Russia to the Mediterranean in August 1942 and begins operating Bf 110 fighter-bomber missions in the area of El Alamein in September/October. It converts to the Me 210 A-1 in late October/early November, and primarily operates out of Sicily over the North African theater. This is the first combat theater in which the Me 210 operates in large numbers.

above: III./ZG 1 *with their new Me 210 A-1s at the Trapani airfield. (Petrick)*

right: This Me 210 A-1 (W.Nr. *039, DU+II) was among the modified aircraft operating from Trapani. (Petrick)*

11/2/42 (GL)

The GL/C-B is unable to take a position on production initiation of the Me 610, since there have not been any more details of the type forthcoming. Making replacement parts immediately available for the Me 210s operating in Africa would mean a corresponding delay in production deliveries. The General Staff's *6. Abteilung* is in agreement.

"Bombing up" an Me 210 (here W.Nr. 2290, BN+CO at Trapani) by hand required took the efforts of more men than a football team, despite the use of a block and tackle. (Petrick)

11/10/42 (GL)
200 examples of the MK 103 in an interim design are to be produced by the end of July 1943. Continued production is possible at a rate of 50 per month. Full-scale production with a sheet metal nacelle is expected to begin in early 1944 at a rate of 300 per month. An additional increase to 1000 per month by the end of 1944 is dependent upon Rheinmetall-Borsig getting machine tooling and 700 workers for production, plus a further 70 for the construction of a hangar at Guben.

11/17/42 (GL)
The final plan for terminating the Do 217 and initiating the Me 410 at Dornier is not yet available. The *Generalfeldmarschall* expects that, in view of the Messerschmitt Company's new managerial situation, the matter outlined by the KdE regarding the problems with the Me 410's initiation of production at Messerschmitt can be resolved in a positive manner. It is possible that there will be delays in production of the modified aircraft in light of the Me 210 being sent to Africa, but as of now these are not anticipated.

11/23/42 (GL)
The General Staff's *6. Abteilung* poses the question of whether the increase in fighter-bomber or high-speed bomber (Me 410) production for tactical reasons is still feasible. GL/C-B considers an increase possible, but a decision must be made now, since the manufacture of jigs for the new Ju 188 bomber are already well underway.

11/26/42 (Mtt)
Representatives from the RLM, DB, and Mtt discuss the installation of the standard powerplant (DB 603 G) in the Me 410. It is assumed that the weight will increase by 500 kg as a result of the front radiator and engine armor, as well as the 300 kg ballast. Mtt has fundamental concerns regarding the size of the standard powerplant (1310 mm diameter) and the forward shift of the center of gravity. In order to resolve the flight handling characteristics, the department asks that a test airframe be built using the standard powerplant and ballast. The use of the Me 309/Ju 287 engine is to be explored using as many common components as possible. To this end, Mtt and Junkers are to provide five personnel

each to work at Augsburg under the direction of Mtt. Work can begin on 1/1/43 and should be completed by 5/1/43. It is hoped that the prototype engine is available by 7/1/43. Production of the standard powerplant can begin in early 1944 at the earliest.

12/8/42 (GL)
Deliveries of the Me 410 began according to plan with five aircraft.

12/9/42 (GL)
Production of the Me 410 is to be increased at the expense of the Ju 188 and other aircraft types as soon as the K.d.E.'s investigation has certified the airframe as being free of problems. However, increased production is not possible until after the end of 1943, but 1944 should see a significant number roll off the assembly lines.

12/15/42 (GL)
A detailed report on fighter-bombers and the Me 410 is expected on 12/22/42. The *Generalfeldmarschall* instructs an investigation into whether the Do 217 can be switched over to the Me 410 even earlier, taking into account a certain loss of airframes. Detailed investigation is to be made whether the Norddeutsche Dornier-Werke, formerly slated to produce the Ju 188, can be switched over to the Me 410. A prerequisite, however, is that fighter-bomber and fighter potential can be increased at other sites so that the requirement of 3000 can be attained as quickly as engine production will allow. Switching the Norddeutsche Dornier-Werke over to the Me 410 will free up the Jumo 213 which, in the view of the *General der Jagdflieger* and the K.d.E., should be utilized for the Fw 190 and not the Me 410; the Me 410 should be produced with the DB 603 as originally planned. *General* Galland asks that additional planning for fighters be included. On the matter of production initiation of the Do 217 M 3, a detailed report is needed with particular emphasis on performance figures of the Me 410.

12/22/42(GL)
According to Study 1013 monthly output of Me 410s should reach 280 by early 1945.

12/29/42 (GL)
Chief of C-E draws attention to the altitude dangers for medium bombers incurred by striking the Do 217 in favor of the Me 410. The *J-Projekt* (Do 217 with DB 603 and TK 9 exhaust supercharger) would ensure a 10 km operating altitude for the Do 217, which is critical for the Fritz X. The *Generalfeldmarschall* realizes the decisive significance of a bomber operating at higher altitudes over heavily defended targets (England, etc.). The *General der Kampfflieger* also welcomes this potential, but the Me 410 cannot be permitted to suffer under an extension of Do 217 production. Among other things, the *Generalfeldmarschall* decides to look into extending the Do 217 through to mid-1944, having the TK 9 installed in the Do 217 series as soon as possible, i.e. from September 1943, that the Me 410's production is not handicapped, and that the number of losses caused by the delay in the Wismar production startup must be made up elsewhere. The switch from the Do 217 to the Ju 188 for high altitude operations should take place in mid-1944.

1/8/43 (GL)
In a developmental meeting, it is determined that the Me 410 has roughly the same performance as the Me 109 G, i.e. speed at sea level and at maximum pressure altitude and its time to climb rate. *Generalfeldmarschall* Milch calls this performance data "heartwarming." Takeoff handling, in comparison with the Me 210 with lengthened fuselage, is worse due to the more powerful engines, but it is manageable. Counterrotating propellers must be introduced as soon as possible, especially if the quality of flying personnel deteriorates or remains as poor as it is currently. The remotely operated defensive armament is a dud and cannot be maintained as well as manually operated guns. According to *General* Galland, it has proven relatively effective with the Me 210, certainly better than expected. The *Generalfeldmarschall* considers it important that the plane become a success. The number of complaints is felt to be remarkably low.

1/16/43
The Me 410 with two DB 603s will be produced at a rate of 300 per month beginning in May 1945 (according to Study 1014), by which time the Bf 110 with two DB 605s will have ceased production (earlier if the Me 210 with DB 605 is introduced as a bridge between the two types).

1/19/43 (GL)
During the developmental meeting, high-speed bomber projects from the different companies are presented. According to the request for tender, these must be able to carry a 500 kg bomb load over a range of 2000 km at a speed of at least 750 km/h. Dornier submits Project 231, later to become the Do 335. Messerschmitt presents the Me 109 Z, which can be realized in short order, but also hints at the Me 262 as being able to carry a bomb load and can already fly at 850 km/h. Heinkel prefers the turbojet (particularly since this aircraft will not be operational for at least another three years), and in the event that the piston engine must be used, the twin plane is preferred. Junkers submits a project with two engines in tandem or a single 4000 hp engine driving two tractor propellers. This project, however, would require more developmental time than that of the Dornier. Like Heinkel, Junkers sees the best potential in turbojet engines. In the subsequent discussion, Messerschmitt points out that he does not have the resources for developing such an aircraft, and that the counterrotating propellers planned for the Me 410 would be desirable for the Me 109 Z as well.

1/21/43 (GL)
Messerschmitt has dropped the twin design and put the Me 309 on ice in order to devote all its design resources to the Me 209. Manufacture of the jigs for increased Me 410 production is in no way assured.

1/26/43 (GL)
According to Study 1015 the Me 410 *Zerstörer* production has been increased from 300 to 400 at the expense of the Ju 188.

2/5/43 (GL)
Discussion in this developmental meeting focuses on alternatives in the aviation industry in the event of destruction by bombing raids. One scenario is having the Me 210 and 410 produced by Messerschmitt at Augsburg exclusively. *Oberst i.G.* Vorwald explains that Dornier-Munich could be switched to the Me 410, and the Do 218 would then be built only at Wismar. *Obersting.* Alpers reports that the Messerschmitt Company is unable to maintain the current pace of Me 410 conversion work, i.e. insofar as this consists of 210 parts, as a result of not being assigned the number of workers it had requested. The company promises the following deliveries: 35 by March; 15 in April; 20 in May; 26 in June; and remaining at 26 for the time being until the matter of workers is resolved. The use of 3000 Dachau concentration camp inmates, prisoners of war, and foreign workers is dis-

below: With the RLM already giving consideration to the Me 410, this Me 210 A-1 (W.Nr. 025) was being flown by Stab III./ZG 1 in Chinisia. This particular machine survived until October 1943, when it crashed during Reich defense operations. (Petrick)

bottom: In the Mediterranean theater the Me 210 continued flying with 50 kg bombs carried beneath the center wing sections. The racks were later removed. (Spenser)

cussed. According to Frydag, on 2/4 Dornier Nord was assigned the Me 410 and can be dropped from Ju 88 planning.

2/9/43 (GL)
Regarding the procurement situation for the Me 410, it is reported: poor output due to design changes and poor supplies of propellers and components. This involves 20 prioritized aircraft. *Oberstlt.* Petersen reports that a fly-off with fighters has shown that the Me 410 is clearly superior to the Fw 190 at low levels. The GL/A has taken steps to remedy the serious personnel problems at Messerschmitt.

2/11/43 (GL)
Generalfeldmarschall Milch is of the opinion that the use of the Me 410 in the East should be considered and included in future planning. Construction capacity at Messerschmitt is stretched to its limits by the ongoing projects: Me 209, 328, 163, 262, and 410. The *Generalfeldmarschall* feels that this work load must be divided up and proposes that Messerschmitt should concentrate on the Me 209 and 410. The jets could possibly be shifted to a special plant under the direction of Lippisch and Horten. *Dir.* Frydag recommends Siebel for this. In the same vein, an industrial divide between design and manufacture of turbojet and piston engines is considered essential. Research into this is to be undertaken and discussed in future meetings.

2/16/43 (GL)
Chief of C-E: Although the Ar 440 prototype is more than 30 km/h faster than the Me 410, production initiation cannot be justified in view of the Me 410's production already begun. The aircraft would not be available until much later, and would then be a contemporary of the superior Do 335. On the other hand, by refining the Ar 440's excellent powerplant into a standardized engine, the Me 410 would also profit from a boost in speed. The *Generalfeldmarschall* decides to cancel the Ar 440.

2/26/43 (GL)
According to the Messerschmitt Company, there was a two month delay in testing the Me 410 due to the fact that a larger water radiator needed to be fitted. The Me 410 is currently flying with the old radiator. With the new larger one it will be faster, since the flaps had to be extended well aft to clear the smaller one. The only other point is that testing revealed that the louvers have a tendency to crack along their leading edge, but otherwise everything went smoothly.

A lack of sufficient personnel will most likely result in a minus of 67 airframes in comparison with procurement plan 222. *Generalfeldmarschall* Milch considers the delay disgraceful and demands that someone from the RLM review production at Messerschmitt. He suspects that Messerschmitt will submit a new proposal in July in which the minus won't be 14, but 18 machines. An increase in personnel is proposed for the Augsburg Works. This will not be possible for 1943, since engines for a planned 100 airframes are on hand. This will be clarified within the scope of the study and the entire company management. Due to the initiation of full-scale production, orders for materials covering 1000 aircraft are authorized. It will be necessary to classify the Me 410 in prioritization category 2 in order to acquire additional personnel for the main plant and the subcontractors. Adherence to the program is dependent upon continued favorable progress of the Lechfeld trials. The *Zerstörer* version will be a subtype of the series (possibly using conversion kit 221/103) and falls chronologically behind the high-speed bomber.

3/5/43 (GL)
Discussion centers on transferring design responsibilities for various Messerschmitt aircraft to other companies. The Me 109 was transferred from Messerschmitt to Wiener Neustadt. Based on talks, Siebel would be glad to take over the Me 262, but is more reserved when it comes to the Me 410 due to the remotely operated weapons. Messerschmitt would like to keep the 262 and give up the 410. The RLM believes keeping the 262 at Messerschmitt is sensible and comments on the Me 410 proposal as follows: "It is typical to hand the matter off when they

start walking on crutches." A decision is not made.

3/9/43 (GL)
Discussion on production of the Ju 88, Ju 188, and Me 410. According to *Obersting.* Alpers there have been problems with reallocating Me 410 production within the aviation industry. C-B had planned to get the Henschel Company involved in the Me 410 production network. But since the Henschel Company is already well advanced, with preparations for beginning production of the Ju 188 in accordance with supply plan 222, a decision must be made on whether these preparations can be abandoned in favor of the intended startup of the Me 410. In accordance with a recommendation by the Henschel Company, if Henschel could hold off on building the Me 410 by six months it could produce 500 Ju 188 aircraft, but overall output of the Me 410 would drop by 640 airframes. According to *Dir.* Frydag, restarting large-scale production of the Ju 188 is no longer viable if we are now switching over to the Me 410, since the companies still involved in producing the Ju 88 are operating at their limit. *Gen.* Vorwald expresses his opinion that it seems necessary to shift to the Me 410 immediately. Particular problems have arisen in that the Henschel jigs for the 188 can't be used at sites like ATG or Junkers because in building them Henschel went over to a new system. They are effectively unusable. *Dir.* Frydag points out that terminating work on this project at Henschel could have a negative impact on the morale of those workers involved in the program. KdE *Oberstlt.* Petersen responds to a query by the *Feldmarschall* by saying that it is indefensible from an evaluative standpoint to forego producing the Me 410 in greater numbers. *Dir.* Frydag's proposal to have the Me 410 built with the involvement of the Volkswagenwerk is rejected by the *Generalfeldmarschall* as impractical.

The biggest threat to production of the Me 410 was the lack of adequate labor. (Bundesarchiv *Koblenz)*

Conclusions:
The *Generalfeldmarschall* concludes that, in view of the favorable test results, as many Me 410s are to be manufactured as possible. A production loss of 640 aircraft is unacceptable. These aircraft are more valuable than 500 Ju 188s. For this reason Henschel must switch over to producing the Me 410. The matter of using the jigs needs to be cleared up. Attempts must be made to build the questionable 500 Ju 188s by increasing production at other companies. The *Generalfeldmarschall*, after listening to KdE, determines that those crews intended for the Me 410 will have specialized training so that this high performance aircraft can achieve the greatest success.

3/16/43 (GL)
In a discussion on the fighter bomber it is mentioned that the number of Ju 88 S aircraft is small, and the Me 410's numbers for 1943 will not be particularly large. Of the intended 420 aircraft, the bulk will not be available until the second half of the year. As this is a new aircraft, technical difficulties can be expected.

The fighter/heavy fighter engine is discussed within the scope of the developmental meeting. This engine is intended for use in the Me 209, Me 410, He 219, Fw 190, Ta 154, and the Do 335 (forward). Work on this engine has been initiated. For the Me 209, Me 410, He 219, and Do 335 the planned engine is the DB 603 G. This engine is also a possibility for the Ta 154, Fw 190, and Ar 440. The Jumo 213 will also be a fighter/heavy fighter engine, planned for the Ta 154 and a bomber/transport engine (Ju 188).

3/19/43 (GL)
Generalfeldmarschall Milch sees the Me 209 and the Me 410 as Messerschmitt's biggest tasks. The 209 is to be finished as a design concept, and the Me 410 is to be put into production.

Armament for various aircraft is a topic of discussion. The Me 210's weaponry includes two MG 17s with 1000 rounds per barrel and two MG 151/20s with 350 rounds. The Me 410 is to have two MG 131s with 600 rounds each, and in its *Zerstörer* version four MG 151/20s. Galland considers the Me 210's armament unsatisfactory and calls for the 210 group in the Mediterranean to be fitted with four MG 151/20s as well. Furthermore, he hopes that the two MK 108 with 120 rounds each or the four MK 108 with 100 rounds each conversion kits will be made available for the Me 410, but this is not possible for the first lot. For all versions, Galland wants to see the MG 17 replaced by the MG 131. The bomber crews also prefer the MG 131.

The Me 210 is not planned as a night fighter. It will only be used in the heavy fighter role and, on occasion, as a high-speed bomber. The Me 410 is a heavy fighter with a fundamental secondary role of high-speed bomber.

Generalfeldmarschall Milch emphasizes that the Ar 440, which was actually quite good and superior to all others, possibly even the Me 410, had to be dropped because it was too costly.

3/23/43 (GL)
As a result of the drop in delivery figures in February and the poor forecast for March the C-B has arranged a review of the Messerschmitt Company's production status. Independent of this, following a visit by the F.d.E. to Augsburg the Chief of GL/C was told that, on the surface, it seemed as though production was not making the advances necessary for large-scale manufacturing. The Messerschmitt Company puts the blame for the current deficiencies on the lack of an adequate work force. In the view of *Obersting.* Alpers, the personnel shortage has had such a telling effect because other measures were never taken in adequate measure to make up the loss in a timely manner. In addition, the concentration camp prisoners that have been assigned are still in need of training.

On the 17 March it was determined that Messerschmitt would be given several design engineers from Siebel, some of which were on loan from Focke-Wulf. *General* Vorwald has arranged for a conference on 3/24 in which a decision will be made on all measures yet to be taken. The *Generalfeldmarschall* recommends getting *Dir.* von Mitterwallner and the Henschel Company involved in order to put pressure on Messerschmitt for a timely handover of the blueprints and documents needed for license production.

4/6/43 (GL)

The following decisions have been made in reference to the Me 410:

Investigation into fitting an SC 1000 with reduced fins or a Madelung parabrake in the bomb bay.

Y-Installation: *Oberst Dr.* Wölbling: prototype fitting is underway. Deadlines for testing have not yet been established.

Installation of Lotfe C 7 D: Rechlin has determined that installation is possible, but it will be necessary to modify the seat and move the autopilot, as it makes operation extremely awkward. It offers the advantage of allowing an Me 410 formation to attack from altitude. *Oberstlt.* Petersen points out that the actual fitting of the system will be quite difficult. The autopilot will have to be taken out and the rudder controls repositioned.

The *Generalfeldmarschall* emphasizes that the use of the Lotfe C 7 D will compel the enemy to restructure his defenses. He will have to fly combat air patrols at high altitudes and will squander fuel needlessly. Installation of this system is therefore of critical importance. Nevertheless, the schedule for installation will have to be pushed back, as it would otherwise interrupt production startup at Messerschmitt.

*This Me 210 A-1 (*W.Nr. 281, *SO+MU) crashed on 23 March 1943 while flying with the* Technische Akademie der Luftwaffe *in Augsburg. This series of photos shows the recovery operation. (Radinger)*

4/13/43 (GL)
Four Me 210s and 25 Me 410s have so far been delivered out of a quota of 30 and a deficit of 40. *Generalmajor* Vorwald demands that efforts be made to ensure the theoretical program quota of 30 aircraft can at least be produced.

4/30/1943 (Memorandum for Record No. 74/42 Top Secret, Göring's Country Manor, Obersalzberg)
Feldmarschall Milch presents the aircraft procurement figures for 1943 and 1944 based on Program 223/1 dated 4/15/43 and provides data on the introduction of new aircraft types.

Me 410—430 in 1943—began production with 25 airframes in April. Presently the bomb bay has capacity for only one SD 1000 or smaller equivalent bombs. The bomb bay and/or the SC 1000 is to be modified so that the SC 1000 can also be carried by the Me 410 internally. Speed, firepower, and armor protection are, in *Generalfeldmarschall* Milch's view, adequate for conducting daylight missions against England. *Oberst* Pelz is urgently pushing for the Me 410 to be capable of night fighting operations. Large numbers of Me 410s are expected to be produced in 1944.

5/18/43 (GL)
Five Me 210s and 42 Me 410 airframes have been delivered.

5/20/43 (GL)
Prof. Dr. Bock reports on the state of converting from alloys to steel and other materials. The *Generalfeldmarschall* stresses that this cannot cause any delays with the Me 410 and the Ta 154. Conversion can therefore only be of such scope and apply to full-scale production insofar as it does not impact deadlines or threaten numbers.

6/1/43 (GL)
One Me 210 and 40 Me 410s are delivered.

6/18/43 (GL)
Me 410 production has been reviewed. There are no concerns at present.

5/25/43 (GL)
The *Angriffsführer England* criticizes the lack of DB 603 engines in reserve. He points out that all Do 217s and Me 410s were shipped out without equipment or special tools for the DB 603, so that even the most simple maintenance work can't be carried out.

6/3/43 (GL)
In June Daimler-Benz is expected to deliver 100 DB 603s to Messerschmitt. Discussion centers on when the DB 603 A/D will be replaced by the E/F, and then by the G/K for the Me 410. The DB 603 E/F and G/K have a 70 mm longer propeller shaft necessary for the urgently needed rapid-change variable pitch propeller. The rapid-change variable pitch propeller, however, is still in its testing stages at Messerschmitt and VDM. Messerschmitt has also not taken any precautions with regard to the airframe and intends to introduce the Me P6 propeller at the same time the DB 603 G/K engine is installed. *General* Vorwald confirms the weeks-old decision to initially power the Me 410 with the DB 603 A, followed by the DB 603 A and D. Starting on 1 January 1945 the Me 410 will convert to the standard fighter/heavy fighter engine in the form of the DB 603 G/K and rapid-change variable pitch propeller. The DB 603 E/F has been ruled out for both the Me 410 and the He 219.

DB reports that the DB 603 engine is being tested both on the test bench and in the air. It was discovered that the oil pressure is too low, and all engines already installed in the Me 410 are at risk. Testing at DB is dragging due to the fact that Messerschmitt is supplied evaluation components (water radiators and oil reservoirs) quite late. *General* Vorwald determines that cooperation between Messerschmitt and Daimler-Benz is very bad. By installing an oil slinger the oil pressure in the aircraft can be brought under control. The oil slinger is to be introduced on the production line starting in mid-July, and a refitting program is being drawn up for those aircraft already delivered. The Messerschmitt Company is instructed not to send any more bare engines to the field, but instead to supply quick-change engines.

Currently DB is using Me 410 *W.Nr.* 2300 as a test bed. Once testing is finished with the oil cooler, the current engine, and the wing radiators, the aircraft will then be evaluated with the fighter/heavy fighter engine with the 1200 mm radiator head. Another test bed will be provided for the 1100 mm radiator head. The first bomber engine with a 1310 mm diameter was completed on 31 March at Backnang and is presently undergoing trials on the test bench. Two radiator heads with 1200 mm diameter will be finished by the end of June, and two with 1100 mm diameter by the end of July. Messerschmitt has not provided data on how the wing will change with the water radiators de-installed.

6/4/43 (GL)
Generalfeldmarschall Milch announces that the Me 410 is in full-scale production, and that he expects it to play a decisive role next year. The Me 410 is expected, as much as possible, to be used in the long-range night fighter role, i.e. as a bomber striking the bases of those British night bombers just returning from their missions. *KG 2* is not to fully convert to the Me 410, as it would be senseless; instead only one group will be employed in long-range night fighter operations. The Me 410 appears well suited for submarine protection operations in the Mediterranean and the Bay of Biscay, as well as acting as a torpedo bomber, a role which is presently being filled only by the He 111. However, changes will have to be made, as its speed is still too high for such a role.

6/11/43 (GL)
The suitability of the Me 410 (as well as that of other aircraft) for submarine protection is discussed in view of range, speed, and safety. As few changes as possible should be carried out on the airframe, i.e. basic weaponry with two MG 17s or MG 131s starting in late 1943, two MG 151s and, if ready, a conversion kit with two MG 151s in the bomb bay. This would be option no. 1. Fuel capacity can be increased by adding two 900 liter drop tanks. This option no. 2 is possible beginning in the autumn of 1943. Other variations (option no. 3) would include 650 liters of fuel in the bomb bay, or 650 liters of fuel in place of the remote controlled weapons. The removal of the FDSL barbettes and replacement with fuel is being drawn up at present. The auxiliary fuel tank in the bomb bay has been designed, but it has not yet been built. Compared with fighters, the Me 410 is more practical, insofar as there is the freedom to install electronic surface search radars and the like so that contact could be maintained with the vessels to be escorted even at night. In addition, the requirement for single-engine flight overwater at mid-range would be met, and there would be the possibility for navigational systems to be fitted. The Me 410 *Zerstörer* variant is considered superior to the Beaufighter in terms of speed and is able to hold its own against the Mosquito.

Disadvantages include the non-armored engines and the radiators, which are quite susceptible to enemy fire in their location beneath the wings. With engine armor the Me 410 would suffer qualitatively, as the center of gravity would shift markedly forward. Development of the standardized engine had taken so long because the shift in the center of gravity caused no end of problems and resulted in many changes to the airframe. Development of the Me 410 with standardized engines is complete, and it only remains for it to be introduced on the production line, but this would incur serious difficulties if standard powerplants were required to be armored. The entire developmental process would have to be repeated.

The MK 103 can be expected starting in the spring of 1944. It is proposed to forcefully engage in the development of semi-fixed barbettes as have already been tested on the Me 410.

6/15/43 (GL)
In a discussion on the use of the Ta 154 as a bomber, *Generalfeldmarschall* Milch points out that the Me 410 will be built in large numbers and can carry a 1000 kg bomb internally.

In the area of the *Angriffsführer England*, an Me 410 is said to have increased its speed by 40 km/h through the use of filler paste, something which possibly indicates the potential of this measure or the poor build quality. It is pointed out that an earlier application of semi-gloss paint on an He 111 boosted its speed by 25 km/h. This measure should be recommended to the *General der Kampfflieger*. Application of filler is quite time consuming and only stays on for a limited amount of time. It is determined to have the field remove the four ETC 50s.

Development of bombing methodology is discussed. Initial results from Greifswald in 1936/37 revealed shortcomings using the level bombing sights, which resulted in a shift to dive bombing. In the meantime, bombsights for level bombing (Lotfe 7 D) have improved to the point that level bombing now enjoys a greater accuracy than can be achieved with dive bombing. Consequently, 100% of the bomber force should be fitted with Lotfes. For attacking moving targets—primarily shipping—high-speed level bombing looks promising. It is therefore proposed that dive brakes no longer be fitted on the assembly line, and that the field be instructed to remove them.

In this vein and with regard to the planned high altitude harassment operations by the Me 410, installation of the Lotfe 7 D in the Me 410 is discussed. It has been researched and, if necessary, is technically possible. Since the autopilot would have to be relocated, the effort would be great and its operation would be awkward. The matter was set aside eight weeks ago, but it was never fully abandoned, as Messerschmitt would have been overtaxed with such a modification. The modification is extensive and affects the design of the airframe, something only Messerschmitt can do. Most problematic is the fact that the bombardier, who takes over flying the approach to the target using the Lotfe 7 D in conjunction with the autopilot, does not have enough time to acquire the target visually and have the Lotfe acquire it before bomb release. Several options are being explored as to how the Lotfe can be incorporated, then a decision will be made to examine a plane in Rechlin with the goal of finding a way to fit the Lotfe.

Among other items, the *General der Aufklärerflieger* reports that the Me 410 has fully proven itself as a reconnaissance platform, as long as it is utilized properly. It is suited for the tactical reconnaissance role (range up to 1200 km), but not as a long-range reconnaissance platform (range 2400 km) or for battlefield reconnaissance (range 600 km). However, the Me 110 makes up the bulk of tactical reconnaissance aircraft, and these are in urgent need of replacement by the Me 410.

In expressing the desires of the night fighters with regard to fitting several Me 110s with GM 1, *General* Galland goes on record as saying that he is quite satisfied with the Me 410/GM 1/3.7 cm cannon combination.

6/18/43 (GL)

The Lechfeld airbase is expected to be home for the Me 262 once the Me 410 squadron leaves (in approximately two months). The manufacturing process of the Me 410 has been reviewed, and there are no concerns at the present. The Me 410 is part of the finalized program. Regarding the Me 410 with Lotfe 7 D, it is said that only one aircraft per squadron should be fitted, assuming that it even comes to that.

6/22/43 (GL)

The *Heereswaffenamt* will make available 200 5 cm antitank cannons to equip the Me 410 with this weapon. GL/C-B 6 is responsible for providing the ammunition.

The approximately 400 Me 410s projected through the end of 1943 are to be broken down as follows: 220 bombers, 80 reconnaissance aircraft, and 100 heavy fighters. Until such time as the heavy fighter series is produced, these are to be manufactured using conversion kits. Starting in June 10 per month are expected to be built.

The *General der Kampfflieger* dispenses with the fitting of ETC 50s beneath the wings.

Genst. 6. Abt. is not in agreement. In the event that these are removed in individual theaters, *Genst. 6. Abt.* will arrange to have the parts shipped back for fitting on the assembly line. *Genst. 6. Abt.* is to issue a directive shortly on outfitting the auxiliary reconnaissance version and the *Zerstörer* with the BZA 1; *Genst. 6. Abt.* calls for a wing for torpedo operations as soon as possible, as well as 20 aircraft per month resupply. The procurement situation is to be reviewed as early as today.

6/26/43 (Memorandum for Record No. 74/42 Top Secret, Göring's Country Manor)
General Meister presents plans for the prosecution of the war in the Atlantic and against England through the summer of 1944: one heavy fighter wing is planned for the war in the Atlantic, equipped with Me 410s and Ju 88 G 1s. One Me 410 bomber wing is planned for the war against England.

6/29/43 (GL)
Among other things, the *Generalfeldmarschall* states in his latest trip report from the West that there are no suitable auxiliary tanks for the Me 410. *JG 26* calls for the MK 103 in order to be able to engage from a distance of 800 m. The *Generalfeldmarschall* presents the following order of precedence for the prioritization of production: fighters (Me 109, Fw 190), Me 110, Me 410, Ju 188, Ju 87, Ju 52, and Ju 290. In a meeting with the *Führer*, the subject of using the Me 410 as a submarine escort came up. *Generalfeldmarschall* Milch calls for documentation on this. With regard to the 21 cm *Wurfgranate*, 200 sets of double tubes and 800 sets of single tubes are on order. All are convinced that this is best. *Erprobungskommando 25* complains that the Flak 18 on the Me 410 can't be reloaded by the radio operator. It is limited to its twelve rounds. A recommendation is made to push for the 21 cm *Wurfgranate* and the RZ 65. Comment: the RZ 65 has not proven effective.

7/6/43 (GL)
Bomb developments are discussed. The SD 500 is important, as it is expected to be carried by the ME 410, the Ta 154, and the Do 232, since it has a smaller diameter than the SC 500. The Me 410's bomb bay is felt to be cramped. Two SD 500s or SE 500s can fit inside. Crews have flown with two SC 500s (50% charge/weight ratio), but this left a 10 cm wide gap between the bomb bay doors. A wooden cover is being worked on. The best bomb for the Me 410 is currently the SD 500, but production is due to end and this is reserved for the Me 410. The SD 500 with a 30% explosive charge/weight ratio is due to be replaced for the Me 410 with the SE 500 with a 15-20% ratio, but this is not yet ready.

7/9/43 (GL)
According to *Oberst* Pelz, the Me 410 has a remarkably poor range, particularly at night. For all practical purposes, in its current configuration it offers very little in the way of a bomber. The range is the cardinal problem. Compared to the Ju 188, the Me 410 has the characteristics of a heavy fighter. *Oberst i.G.* Pelz's proposal to shift part of the Me 410 production over to the Ju 188 S (comment: this is the later Ju 388 K) is not possible in the view of *Obersting.* Alpers, since it involves two different factories and engine types. The *Generalfeldmarschall* points out that the Me 410 was only given to the *General der Kampfflieger* due to a shortage in aircraft; it is most urgently needed for fighter operations. The *General der Kampfflieger* will continue to have to take the Me 410 since he will not be able to get enough of the desired Ju 188s. Furthermore, the Me 410 is fast (620 km/h); the Mosquito is the only plane that can touch it. The Ju 188 S will be even better, being 10 km/h faster and with a three-man crew and greater range. As an alternative, the Ta 154 is virtually out of the question. The first machine with Jumo 211s is currently flying. With the Jumo 213 it is expected to reach speeds of 700 km/h, but since it has no internal bomb bay it will probably be slower than the Me 410. The *Generalfeldmarschall* assumes that the Me 410 will still be needed in large quantities over the next two years. The Do 335 will be the replacement for the standard twin-engined aircraft. The Me 410 can only carry the SD 1000 as its 1000 kg bomb.

Follow-on development of the high-speed bomber and *Zerstörer* is discussed with regard to turbojet options. *Generalfeldmarschall* Milch introduces a version of the Me 109 Z into the discussion, which would have two jet engines in place of its piston engines and would be built using on-hand components. A problem is the very limited range. In addition, this option is lacking merit because the Ar 234, a design which has made an excellent impression, will already be available. On a wide scale, the aviation industry is working on projects which will make current types, e.g. the Ju 88 H and Do 335, faster by using turbojet engines (BMW 003). With a supplemental turbojet, the Ju 88 H would be 100 km/h faster. However, this would result in a serious reduction in range.

7/13/43 (GL)
Blueprints for the GM 1 system for the Me 410 and other aircraft are not yet ready. This is the sole reason why these systems cannot be delivered. Documentation is also lacking for the exhaust systems for the Me 410. It is proposed that production startup for the Hs 128 C 1 with more powerful engines be delayed by three months. For its part, GL/C-B 2 has no concerns, since the numbers will remain the same. Reason: simultaneous switch over to the Me 410.

7/16/43 (GL)
As a night strike fighter, the Me 410 will be used to attack British night bombers using SD 1 bombs on their still illuminated airfields.

7/19/43 (GL)
The Henschel Company has limited capabilities for producing the Ju 88 S 2, since Henschel is currently switching over to the Me 410. The situation between Junkers and Henschel needs to be cleared up. In the future, the Ju 188 S is expected to fly bombing missions against England as the Me 410, Ta 154, and the turbojet bombers, although fast, do not have the necessary range.

Based on experience, new developments take anywhere between 4 1/2 and 5 years before entering production, i.e. a new development just underway now will not be in the field before 1947/48. The Do 335 is expected to enter production in April 1945 at a rate of two per month and be in full-scale production by the end of the year. This means that it would only take three years, a feat unique in the annals of the aviation industry. It takes 1 1/2 years just for a canopy to enter production. *Generalfeldmarschall* Milch believes that medium bombers (Ju 188) will be needed over the next three years as well, since there will not be enough larger aircraft and the faster ones (Do 335) won't have the range or the payload. The technological leap with the Do 335 will not be as great as it first appeared. A decent jet bomber with a range of about 2400 km and a bomb load of 1000 kg is not expected before 1948/49, possibly in early 1948. Numbers for the Do 335 have not yet been worked out in detail. At the present time 34 are planned for September 1945, with possibly 60 by December. By 1946 the monthly rate could reach 150 or 200 units.

The developmental resources of the aircraft companies are expected to concentrate on the more important tasks. Messerschmitt is to continue working on the Me 410; other types will be turned over to different companies.

3/27/43 (GL)
Generalfeldmarschall Milch determines that Germany has been on the defensive for the last 1 1/2 to 2 years. Now this fact seems to be having a major influence in the thinking at the highest levels of the *Luftwaffe*. It means that many more fighters, as well as Me 110s and Me 410s, are needed. Increasing production of both airframes and engines is hindered primarily because of the lack of laborers. He arranges to have the requisite number of workers provided for the fighter and engine programs.

Large numbers of Me 410s are expected to be delivered with the KWK 5. *Prof.*

Messerschmitt states that he is only aware of this variant from a model he has seen exhibited. Petersen answers that this is a Staaken installation, and they supplied the installation blueprints. Messerschmitt: "That could also be fitted into the Me 262."

The requirement for jig technicians and workers needed at Dornier, Messerschmitt, and Henschel to meet program deadlines, has partially been fulfilled at the beginning of July. Now these personnel should be entered under the Me 262 contingent, something which would lead to a collapse of the Me 410. *Generalfeldmarschall* Milch answers: "Where should we get them if we don't have them?" Dornier-Munich is currently in the process of switching over to the Me 410, and quite soon will see its operations and its volume tripled. Personnel from Dornier-Munich are to be sent to Messerschmitt-Augsburg to work on the Me 410. After three months these people, now trained with hands-on experience, are to be returned to Dornier. During that time Messerschmitt's people can work on the Me 262. The transferred personnel should be well treated and feel at home. If need be, the *Reichsbahn* can assist in transporting personnel from Munich to Augsburg. Dornier and Messerschmitt sit next to each other, and each has a specific stake in the Me 410 that needs to be changed.

7/30/43 (GL)

Galland hopes to achieve 60 to 80 kills for every attack on the enemy. To achieve this, all groups in the West and from *Befehlshaber Mitte* must be involved. He has 30 to 50 losses per day. He wants to combine three *Zerstörer* groups and a bomber group used in the *Zerstörer* role, and with these 100 to 120 *Zerstörer* planes attack the enemy formations in one long stream. This would involve two groups each of Me 110s and 410s. The Me 410 would have to have the KWK 5 and the Me 110 the Flak 18, or the weapons pack with two MG 151s, or the *Nebelwerfer* at the very least. Galland asks that the deal with the KWK 5 be resolved. The prototype has been built in Staaken; an aircraft is being sent for test firing. At present it is not clear whether the Me 110 and the Me 410 can withstand the recoil of the barrel.

8/3/43 (GL)

Production of various aircraft must be increased for boosting homeland defenses. The Me 210 production is winding down. For the Me 410, increased production potential is limited (from 50 to 70 in late 1943/early 1944), since Messerschmitt is beginning production of the Me 262 at the same time. 100 aircraft are expected to be built in the first quarter of 1944. Dornier-Munich and Henschel can't help with increasing *Zerstörer* production, as they are currently involved in wrapping up current types (Do 217 and Ju 88) and will not be starting production of the Me 410 until early/mid next year. The planned numbers for the Me 410 are: September 1943 - 65; December 1943 - 70; March 1944 - 82; and June 1944 - 108. The Me 410 is expected to be increased to 107 in March, and in June to 128. Petersen considers the Me 410's numbers to be too low, as the heavy *Zerstörer* with extra firepower has an impact, and hopes that there will be an increase in production from January onward. As of now there are three Me 410 groups, two with Galland and the third with Peltz, but these are not fully stocked. Milch does not want to see the old Me 110 production increased as originally planned, since the Me 410's production will increase markedly during the second half of 1944. Up to now, plans call for 250 aircraft per month to be built by the end of 1944, but this could now possibly be raised to 280 or 290. *Generalfeldmarschall* Milch wants the Me 410 for daylight operations, leaving the Me 110 available for the night and able to relieve the situation there. According to von Loßberg, operating the Me 410 at night would be disastrous.

Thanks to its better range and high altitude performance, *Oberst* Peltz considers the Ju 188 much more suited for the bomber role than either the Me 410 or the Ta 154, and would gladly dispense with the Me 410 if he could get the Ju 188 instead. He would further welcome it if there was only the Ju 188 instead of the He 219, Me 410, Ta 154, and Ju 188. Presently the Me 410 is being used for nighttime raids on British airfields (long range night fighting operations). In view of the engine bottleneck with the DB 603, it seems more important to build the Me 410 for this purpose than use the Do 217 for night fighting.

The airframe's potential of coping with weapons more powerful than the 5 cm gun is discussed. There appears to be little hope. According to Milch, the 3 cm gun is planned for use with the Me 410. Galland doesn't feel this is altogether too tragic a state, since he believes that the MK 103 can cover the situation.

It is expected that the Americans will soon be coming over at altitudes above 10000 m. In that event, neither the Me 410 nor the Me 209 would be of any use. 10000 m to 10500 m is considered the Me 410's limit. The Ju 188 with BMW 801 I is the only aircraft up to this task. In this light, the entire production program as it has been planned would be built on a false premise. Also up for discussion is operations using the GM 1. With Flak 18 and radioman, the Bf 110's service ceiling without the GM 1 is 8000 m in formation and 8500 m when operating alone. This is too low. Therefore, the Bf 110 with GM 1 as a stopgap measure must become available soon so that 9000 m in formation can be attained. Right now the Me 410 is the only plane capable of reaching 10500 m. With the GM 1 it could get as high as 11500 m, and at 660 km/h would be a very fast aircraft. The whole barbette system, radio equipment and radio operator (i.e. 380 kg) could be left off to get even more altitude. The DB 603 G will be fitted, making the Me 410 a very good high altitude platform. During the discussion on night fighting the Me 410 is brought up for daytime operations with Galland and nighttime operations with Hermann. There is, however, a lack of crews, and with the ongoing conversion to the 3.7 cm, GM 1, and *Nebelwerfer*, this action does not seem practical at the moment. In this context Milch points out that more losses are being suffered over the homeland than on the front lines.

The *Generalfeldmarschall* gives orders that *Prof.* Messerschmitt is to compile documentation on the Me 410's performance with a pilot and with the barbettes and radio equipment de-installed, allowing the second crewman to be dispensed with, and submit these by 8/10/43. For armament, Galland calls for two MK 103s and two MG 151s, with the MG 17s being removed. Calculations for the Me 410 with KWK as a special variant are also to be made. GL/C-E will report on the installation of the new 3.7 cm *Flak*, which no longer requires a loader, on 8/10/43. Research is to be undertaken on the viability of attaching a small shaft to the Me 410's skin without having to make any further changes.

It was in this context that tests using the extended wings of the Me 310 on Me 210 W.Nr. 179 (VN+AQ) took place in August and September 1943. See the Me 310 overview.

Convoy patrols along the German coast will be carried out by the Me 410, Ju 188, etc.

8/13/43 (GL)

Aircraft types suitable for the anti-tank role are discussed. For the Me 410, installation of the KWK 5 is currently being evaluated, but according to *Generalfeldmarschall* Milch this will not be available until next autumn or winter at the earliest, since it will be needed for homeland defense at least until then.

Based on a requirement by the *Angriffsführer England*, a Ju 88 S 2 is to be built with a large bomb gondola capable of carrying large numbers of flares with the same range as the S 1. This could only be done at Henschel and at considerable cost, as they are now building the Ju 88 A 4. Henschel will be winding down production of the Ju 88 at the start of 1944 and will then switch over to the Me 410, meaning that the Ju 88 S 2 could have an impact on its production startup. The necessity of the Ju 88 S 2 should be discussed again with the *General der Kampfflieger*.

8/20/43 (GL)

Gen.Dir. Frydag at Henschel laments the fact that they ever went over to the Me 410. Had they stayed with the Ju 88 it would now have been easier to switch over to the Ju 388. If necessary, they can still switch back to the Ju 88 (as unpleasant as this may be). For Henschel, 170 Me 410s per month are planned for the final stage of 1945, with the company working to achieve a rate of 250 internally. The ultimate goal for the Me 410 is 400. *Oberst* Rowehl considers the Ju 188 to be superior from a flying standpoint at the same range and speed. Baumbach also feels that the Ju 188 in its faster version is the better aircraft. Milch considers whether the Me 410 planned for the bomber force can be replaced by the Ju 188. According to von. Loßberg, the night fighters would also like the Ju 188 over the Me 410, but would ultimately prefer the He 219. Henschel is presently manufacturing the jigs for the Me 410, but has done practically nothing yet with the airframe itself. Production should begin in June 1944, but not using the standardized engine initially as it will not be ready by then. Therefore, the engine planned for the Me 410—the DB 603—can't be allocated to the Ju 388 without causing problems. For the Ju 188, less than 100 of the planned 450 per month have been taken on charge. If Henschel were to build them then the 170 Me 410s they were to produce would be lost. Blohm & Voss has been diverted to the Messerschmitt Corporation and is currently involved in manufacturing trainer aircraft. There is currently great demand for dual controls, etc. The matter will be reexamined and, if possible, a decision will be made next week.

8/24/43 (GL)

Gen.Dir. Frydag presents information on the Me 410/Ju 188: Contrary to earlier reports the Ju 188 E 2 will cease production. If the Henschel Company switches from the pro duction startup of the Me 410 to the Ju 388 (the subject of debate a few days ago), not only will this mean abandoning the Me 410 jigs, which are virtually complete, but the jigs they earlier made for the Ju 188 would also be useless. Both jigs—the Me 410 and the Ju 188—would have been created for nothing. Furthermore, the Ju 388 won't be available until later (September at the earliest), whereas whatever happens the Me 410 will appear in May, and in a lot of 170 at that. This would mean that Henschel would lose 850 aircraft. Given the circumstances outlined, a switch in production would be irresponsible. Production of the Me 410 could be increased to 250 without any problems. Together with the output of Dornier-Süd a total monthly production would amount to 400 (but not until mid-1945).

Oberst Pelz once again addresses the matter of altitude. Although the Me 410 has the DB 603, which in its G variant gives a maximum pressure altitude of 13 km, it does not have a pressurized cockpit and does have high wing loading. Currently the Me 410 can reach 10.5 km and might be able to attain 11.5 km. The *Generalfeldmarschall* determines that the Me 410 is designed for speed and that the altitude issue will not reveal too much more. However, it should be considered that the enemy won't be operating at higher altitudes in all the theaters. To a great extent, the Me 410 was pushed through at the urging of the *General der Jagdflieger*, who considered the Me 410 to be an outstanding fighter and one that needs to be produced at any cost. The number of Me 410s will be put to good use, even if it is higher, but it is hoped that the number of bombers would also increase. Milch and Kleinrath are of the opinion that the *Luftwaffe*, in light of the overall critical situation, will play a deciding role in determining the outcome of the war, and that the senior leadership must come to grips with this fact. On the other hand, setbacks have to be expected in areas that today can't even be imagined. Milch points out that he is using every means necessary to persuade the *Oberkommando der Luftwaffe* and the highest authorities within the *Reich* to come to a *Wehrmacht* planning conference and increase involvement in the area of the *Luftwaffe*. Entirely different approaches have now become necessary. He hopes that tomorrow's discussion with Speer will bear fruit in this sense. The *Generalfeldmarschall* orders

Henschel to build the Me 410. An expansion at Junkers will be attempted, but this is primarily dependent on personnel.

It is reported that a Marauder with extended wings has been found. Milch feels it is appropriate to undertake investigation of the Me 410 along these lines. *Herr* Hoffmann says that there is research being done on high altitude variants of the Me 410.

8/27/43 (GL)
Speed boosts for the Ju 88 and Me 410 using two additional turbojet engines are discussed. The Me 410, because of its high landing speed, would not be able to carry the weight of the engine (BMW with about 540 kg per engine) and would drop like a brick on landing. The power barbettes, the armor, and possibly the second crewman would have to be thrown overboard. Range is also a consideration. Right now the Me 410 has an average duration of two hours twenty minutes and would return to base at about the two hour point. By utilizing the supplemental engines the range and normal cruising speed would drop. Performance must be calculated precisely. The *General der Jagdflieger* should be asked if, in view of these circumstances, he still is interested in the Me 410 with auxiliary turbojet engines. In *Generalfeldmarschall* Milch's view, the *General der Jagdflieger* will not be interested at all due to the range. The Ju 88, with increased wingspan and the longer fuselage carrying 3600 kg of fuel, is better suited to the task and would have a speed in excess of 700 km/h with the turbojet. However, its undercarriage is at its load limit as it is, so problems can be expected. The takeoff weight of the Ju 188 is restricted at the moment, due to the fact that it is well over the landing gear's load limit.

8/31/43 (Mtt)
According to the latest planning the entire de-icing system won't be applied until late March 1944 with the B-1 series due to issues with acquiring the steel wing leading edge.

8/43 (*Erprobungskommando 25* Field Report)
Flak 18 installed in the Me 410 at the Vechta airfield.

9/7/43
The DB 605 is causing major problems. To improve its operational reliability, one of the measures will be to fit an oil slinger to remove contaminants present in the poor grade oil currently being used. An oil slinger is also planned sometime in the future for the DB 603 in the Me 410, something which is not necessary at present (the aircraft is ok at all altitudes it can currently reach without the slinger) and has not been fully tested at altitude.

Direktor Nallinger from Daimler-Benz complains about Messerschmitt. All of Messerschmitt's airframes, i.e. Bf 109, Bf 110, Me 210, and Me 410, do not meet the conditions outlined in the engine installation portfolio. The oil back pressure and the water back pressure have been too high from the outset and had to be approved under protest—made together with officials in the face of delivery quotas. Messerschmitt and his people are extremely talented theoreticians who trouble themselves with every little millimeter. The relationship with operations is always bad. A large percentage of powerplant operational reliability is sacrificed for a minute aerodynamic advantage for the whole airplane—on paper. A DB modification to the blower intake that perhaps was not as aero-

Hauptmann *Horst Grayer of* Erprobungskommando 25 *at Achmer examines the ammunition feed for the* Flak 18 *gun. (Petrick)*

dynamically refined could have improved both performance and maximum pressure altitude to the point that it would have eclipsed any apparent disadvantage. The cooling and oil systems have led to mountains of files being generated in the battle being fought together with the Ministry. It is impossible to get a proper oil or water system put in, even though other companies are able to. One cannot claim that the conditions of the installation portfolio can't be met. The other airframes all have it. This is the ultimate proof of the necessity for allowing the engine factories to build the powerplants themselves so that such nonsense can be put to rest. Messerschmitt currently builds its own (fighter/heavy fighter) engine (for the Me 209 or Me 410). *Generalfeldmarschall* Milch says that if this is the case, people will be pulled from Messerschmitt and transferred to Daimler Benz. He wants to see a wrap-up report on the matter. He wants to hit Messerschmitt at the spot where they think they don't need to follow the orders of the Ministry. In the past, engines were built by airframe companies. Engine companies are responsible for all new engines. It goes without saying that airframe companies can be critical and should also be involved.

Because of the oil and water temperatures, Daimler Benz calls for the diameter of the new fighter/heavy fighter engine to be 1100/1200 mm and does not want to be responsible for what Messerschmitt is doing: an engine with a diameter of 1030 mm. Even the other aircraft manufacturers are against Messerschmitt. Milch allows that the engine should be developed first, followed by the fighter, otherwise—as experience has shown—the best engine for the airframe will not be available when needed.

According to Nallinger, Daimler Benz and the other airframe producers are in agreement that the smallest possible diameter is 1100 mm. Messerschmitt was of the opinion that it could be bettered and went about building a smaller engine. But it won't work, because the radiator in this engine is too small.

Production has not yet been approved for the GM 1 systems. Up to now systems have been delivered for the Bf 109, Bf 110, and the Ju 88, but they are subject to constant modifications. No documentation is yet available for the other types (Me 410) planned for the system.

The DB 627 is also to be explored for the Me 410. It would take it well. The DB 627 is a follow-on development of the DB 603 with a supercharger on both sides and new components for operating at higher altitudes. Since DB is overloaded with developing the DB 605 with the 603 supercharger, the DB 603 G is to be built first, then the DB 627 (which will be suspended until that time) as well as the DB 603 radial engine, which can potentially enter production in 1947.

9/13/43 (GL)

The Me 410 is to be built according to the following formula: the required number of reconnaissance aircraft (currently 10 per month), the remainder to be equally divided between *Zerstörers* and bombers. No dive brakes are to be fitted to the *Zerstörer* and reconnaissance versions, and the *General der Kampfflieger* will make a decision regarding the bombers.

On 9/10/43 the General der Nahkampfflieger stated that dive bomber units can no longer be employed anywhere.

The conversion kit for ordnance has been abandoned, with the exception of fitting the cables for four ETC 50s. The day *Zerstörers* no longer require the *Kutonase*, but 100% of the bombers need to be fitted with it. Starting in September 1943 there will be the requirement for drop tanks to be carried. Dornier is to build its first 20 aircraft as bomber-destroyers. According to *Genst. 6.Abt.* single groups of Me 410s can be expected to be operating in the East by this winter. Appropriate winter preparations need to be made.

The *General der Jagdflieger* calls for 50 Me 410s with KWK 39/I 5 cm for attacking airborne targets. The prototype has been built and trials will begin shortly. Assuming that there are no unexpected difficulties encountered during the evaluation, starting in November 1943 the monthly production rate of converted aircraft is expected to be 10.

9/14/43 (GL)

Seven Me 210s and 40 Me 410s were delivered in August. As a result of startup problems, the Donauwerke in Hungary has not yet been able to fill its monthly production quota.

Firing trials have begun with the MK 103. There are currently 82 MK 103s that can't be fitted; there is no production line installation at present. For the Me 410, work on the design of the installation has been concluded. Messerschmitt is to undertake installation. This solution seems ill-advised. Personnel at Messerschmitt work at a pedantic pace, and Messerschmitt has a full plate with other matters as well. Messerschmitt did quick work with the KWK 5, but unfortunately it was provided with the wrong cannon. Prototype installation of the MK 103 is expected to take place at Travemünde, if necessary under the direction of Lufthansa. They did the prototype fitting of the KWK at Staaken in a very professional manner.

The final verdict is not yet in on the Me 410's frontline operational effectiveness. The *Zerstörer* needs to be lightened by about 1800 kg. Rechlin has a machine ready for modification, but it's lacking engines. The supplemental GM 1 system is to be installed at a weight of 500 kg. The aircraft must then be flown with these weight saving measures. It is expected that it will be able to fly for one hour with the GM 1 at an altitude of 10.5 to 11 km. A follow-up GM 1 meeting is to take place in four weeks, by which time testing results should be ready.

There is a discussion on whether the Do 217 *Kehl* with DB 603 for attacking warships is more important than the Me 410 attacking bombers. Presently there are Do 217 *Kehl* aircraft already built awaiting engines, but the situation with deliveries of the DB 603 is improving dramatically. Pomo and Marienfelde are keeping true to their word. Once production is well underway the situation will improve from October onward. Then *Kehl* equipped aircraft are expected to receive the engines as quickly as possible. In this month 20 DB 603 engines are still to be delivered to Rechlin for testing in the Me 410 and He 219, and for follow-up testing of the Ostmark engines.

Manufacture of the MK 108 did not go according to plan last month. Production of the planned 300 weapons fell quite wide of the mark. 300 weapons are expected to be built this month. Production of the MK 103 has also fallen somewhat behind as a result of manufacturing resources being finally transferred from Berlin to Guben.

The RLM must learn by experience that the first thing the field units remove when the aircraft arrive at the front is the armor installed on the assembly line. Such unnecessary double labor needs to stop as soon as possible.

9/15/43 (GL)

Generalfeldmarschall Milch thinks about using the Me 410 with 5 cm KWK in the winter as a tank buster and in the spring for air-to-air missions. To the complaint that the machine is too vulnerable for the anti-tank role because of its liquid-cooled engines and general design, he responds by stating that if there is nothing else available it will be used. Furthermore, over a ton of weight is expected to be taken out of the plane. Petersen adds that the discussion on 9/13/43 brought out the belief that about 1800 kg could be dropped from the single-seater high-speed *Zerstörer*.

9/21/43 (GL)

Oberst Petersen claims that the Me 410 without the four *Nebelwerfer* but with bombs can reach an altitude of 10 km; the lighter Me 410 is expected to reach 11.5 km and will also then have an hour's worth of GM 1. There is no doubt that the high wing loading of the Me 410 brought on by fitting four *Nebelwerfer* led to a significant deterioration in the plane's aerodynamics.

In view of the high wing loading, *Generalfeldmarschall* Milch's opinion is that the aircraft needs to be configured as follows: all weapons in the fuselage (minimum armament is two MK 103s plus two MG 151s or four MG 151s—insufficient according to *General* Galland and maximum of four MG 151s plus *Nebelwerfer*), dispensing with all additional weight such as the aft-firing barbettes that were originally planned for the bomber version, installation of the GM 1, and no *Nebelwerfer*. Aside from this, the matter of increasing wingspan by using a stronger wingtip is to be explored. *General* Galland expresses reservations about the suitability of the Me 410.

As the bulk of Me 410s are to be delivered as *Zerstörers*, an attempt must be made to design these so that they can also be operated during daylight against bombers at an altitude of 10.5 km. This initially appears possible by simply lightening the airframe. (Prototype late September); in extreme emergency the earlier planned use of the type as a high-speed bomber can be abandoned. However, it is much more important to field aircraft in such a configuration that they can engage the enemy approaching at high altitudes. This Me 410 is considered to be stage 1 and is to receive the whole lightening treatment; stage two involves GM 1 and weapons refitting. The lighter aircraft is to be evaluated quickly. KdE and the *General der Jagdflieger* need to work most closely on this issue.

Research into the Me 410's operating altitude is ongoing at C-E 2. The *Generalfeldmarschall* was informed of a remarkably high altitude achieved by an Me 410 operated by a reconnaissance replacement group in Posen (fully tanked, with weapons, without GM 1 or bombs - 11.5 km). *Oberst* Peltz wants to investigate this claim further. *Oberst* Petersen reports a very good grouping with the Me 410/KWK 5 narrow version. C-B is already anticipating startup of production. The matter of using cast HE bombs for the Me 410 is to be explored further. For this, the *General der Kampfflieger* calls for ballistic drops to be carried out at a later date.

Oberst i.G. Dr. Pasewald points out that the *General der Kampfflieger* has asked that, when new high-speed bombers are delivered, they be refitted and even retrofitted with the dive brakes that were removed a month earlier. The *Generalfeldmarschall* stresses that the lightening steps are not to be applied across the board for all Me 410s, but only to those aircraft assigned to the *General der Jagdflieger* as heavy fighters.

Details of the Hungarian program: Production of the Me 210 will be extended by a few months. The Me 410 B, originally planned for 75 aircraft, can't be produced in these numbers, since the difference between the B and C models is so great that the B version must run longer than the last recommendations called for; beyond this, the effort that would go into producing the jigs would not be worth it. The B-series is now expected to run with a total of 450 airframes; the C version will later be introduced with a new canopy. The Messerschmitt Company, Augsburg's delay in switching over is also to be taken into account in this matter. Compared with the old program there will be a minus of 125 aircraft by the end of 1945. Introducing special measures for those German suppliers will make it possible to recoup these losses.

9/27/43 (GL)
GL/C-E 21 Memorandum No. 9919/43 outlines the developmental state and application potential of turbojet engines. According to this document, series production of the BMW turbojet engine can begin in early 1944. The *Genst. 6.Abt.* demands these be prioritized for aircraft defending the *Reich* and in the following precedence: a) Me 410; b) Ju 188 R and *Zerstörer* G; and c) Ju 388 J. Available capacity is to be utilized to the extreme as soon as definitive test results are on hand. Plans should be made for manufacturing 1000 engines per month. Work in this area is to be undertaken with utmost urgency given the importance of these engines.

In addition to the previous requirement of 50 Me 410s and 150 Ju 88s with KWK 5 cm guns, the *Genst. 6.Abt.* calls for production to continue at a rate of 20 aircraft per month of each type.

9/28/43 (GL)
Next month approximately 20 Me 410s will have to be stockpiled without their propellers, because for months VDM has lacked the personnel.

The large-wing Do 217 with *Kehl* is ending production. October will see the last 40 delivered. The *General der Kampfflieger* would like to have them continue, but this would lead to a drop in Me 410s. A decision has to be made at the top; the *Generalluftzeugmeister* is unable to do anything.

Generalfeldmarschall Milch wants to focus all efforts on fighters and *Zerstörer* aircraft until well into next year. Fighter production is expected to increase from its present level of around 1000 per month to 3500. He had not expected *Zerstörer* production to exceed 100 for a while yet, but now it is at 200. It must be brought up to 1000.

Milch expects that in the long term the *General der Kampfflieger* will hand over his Fw 190s, Me 410s, and Ta 154s to the *General der Schlachtflieger* and receive bombers in exchange, such as the Ju 188, Ju 388, and Ju 288, as well as the He 177.

In Milch's opinion—and he has Galland to back him up on this—the 21 cm rocket is a stopgap solution that will be dropped the moment the 5 cm is on board. The 5 cm weapon is the only one that really provides any results. The 5 cm weapon is still a long way off, and Galland urgently needs the *Nebelwerfer* until then.

10/5/43 (GL)
The DB 603 E is discussed. The DB 603 is the DB 603 A engine with the 603 G single-stage blower, and is expected to have nearly the same performance as the 603 G from the outset. Originally it was to enter production in January 1944, but Daimler Benz is now saying April. The DB 603 E is of interest primarily for the Me 410, then for the He 219. It will require certain changes to the airframe, e.g. larger oil reservoirs and possibly larger radiators. An investigation needs to be made into what time the airframe will be able to take this engine, and after that engine production should tailor itself to meeting aircraft requirements in switching engines over to the DB 603 E. Switchover can possibly take place in February/March 1944. The DB 603 G is dependent upon the standard engine, expected to enter production sometime around October 1944. Radiator version (ar-

Before the Me 410 was armed with cannons, III./ZG 1 filled the gap by fitting its aircraft with the 21 cm Wurfgranate air-to-air mortar. (Petrick)

mored or non-armored) for the standard powerplant has not yet been resolved; this still needs to be addressed with regard to the airframe. Introduction of the MP-8 Messerschmitt propeller in conjunction with the standard powerplant will most likely cause major problems. In addition, there is discussion on the performance and possible production sites for the Messerschmitt propeller. The propeller is supposed to be for the Me 410, since dive brakes can now be dispensed with and because the landing distance can be shortened by at least 50%. It is believed that the VDM personnel don't want the MP propeller and are sabotaging it. Dörnemann and Ebert from VDM are to report to Milch and present their reasons. Another problem lies in the fact that VDM is already overtaxed with other propeller designs, and as a result will have more problems making room than with the developmental series. Relocation also plays a role. At present there are airframes being stockpiled due to lack of propellers (eight Me 410s and 33 Ju 188s). It is hoped that VDM will be close to catching up with the Ju 188 and Me 410 by the end of October, but replacements will be in short supply.

The KWK 5 cm is installed in the Ju 88 P 4 and the Me 410. Auto-Union is making the modifications to the cannons. The 39.1 began production as early as September with a batch of 20 guns, meaning that there will be enough weaponry in October to meet demand. Development has concluded, and the installation is currently undergoing trials. Messerschmitt is supplying the documentation/blueprints for the series based on the prototype built at Staaken and is expected to carry out installation at its Augsburg facility. During ground firing tests it was reputedly discovered that the installation was rather weak and in need of strengthening. As a result, the Me 410 aircraft have not yet been flown to Tarnewitz. *Generalfeldmarschall* Milch is confusing this with the MK 103, which was discovered to have too weak an installation.

10/12/43 (GL)
The decision to increase Me 410 production and deflect other companies for this will put pressure on bomber production, but now there is no going back. The decision whether to build bombers or Me 410s must come from above. Discussion focuses on where Ju 188 production can be increased. Henschel comes up again, and then the loss of 840 Me 410s. All other companies would need twelve months from the time the decision is made to build the Ju 188 until the first one rolls off the assembly line.

A special cast iron bomb without a steel jacket for the Me 410 is discussed. This would not fall ballistically and would tumble. It could only be used for area targets. 50 have been contracted for.

The Me 410 can be converted from a *Zerstörer* to a bomber in one day. This means that in order to fulfill the *Reichsmarschall's* orders expected today, calling for bombers and *Zerstörers* to be made available in equal numbers, it will initially be necessary to convert the *Zerstörer* planes already on hand. Production bombers are expected starting in January. At that point the *Zerstörers* and reconnaissance units will get 10 each and the bomber units the remainder. Me 410 production using the final version of the heavy fighter canopy is not expected to be affected by this; this means that only the auxiliary *Zerstörer* will be abandoned as a result. Thierfelder points out that 10 aircraft per month is too little to sustain a group.

Conversion from a high speed bomber to an auxiliary heavy fighter was accomplished mainly through the fitting of a Waffenbehälter 151 A *gun pod. (Petrick)*

Generalfeldmarschall Milch points out to Thierfelder and Peltz that there is a reconnaissance group in Posen that can easily reach altitudes of 11.5 km with their Me 410s without using GM 1, and can even climb higher at will. This is in direct contradiction to the claims of Galland, Peltz, and Thierfelder, who talk of the bomber reaching 8 km without bombs. He won't be able to believe them anymore. The claims must be checked out with armament, full tanks, without GM 1 and without bombs.

The Me 410 has provided excellent groupings using the KWK narrow version. It is planned to give the go ahead for starting full scale production.

10/15/43 (GL)
A bottleneck has occurred with propellers as a result of the VDM's move from Hamburg, Frankfurt, Marburg, etc. with a backlog of now 13000 propellers. By the month's end, it is expected there will be 300 to 400 Me 410s and Ju 188s that won't be able to fly. Currently there is a shortage of nine propellers for the Me 410. (Note: the contradiction that hundreds of aircraft will be grounded and that in fact there is currently only a shortage of nine propellers cannot be explained by the meeting minutes. Even the number of 13000 propellers in comparison to 400 airframes seems too high.)

Development of the Messerschmitt propeller at VDM is discussed. Frankfurt and Rechlin each have an Me 410 for testing. Dornier has acquired two new 410s for this purpose.

Oberst Petersen reports that the Messerschmitt/Prause MP 8 propeller has thus far proved reliable in 20 hours of testing with the DB 603 in a Do 217. Although naturally this narrow basis can't be used to certify the propeller as ready for production, the propeller is indeed a solid candidate for the fighter/heavy fighter standard powerplant, especially for the Me 410 and He 219 (landing brakes, nosewheel!).

10/19/43 (GL)
The aircraft stockpiled last month because of the shortage of propellers have now been shipped, but this month three Me 410s will be stockpiled again out of 28 completed, due to the shortage of propellers.

10/26/43 (GL)
Vorwald reports a "Salto" in Me 410 production. The Me 410 was planned in large quantities as a *Zerstörer*, and all material was allocated to the heavy fighter division. Dornier began production as a heavy fighter. The *Reichsmarschall* order requires the wheels be turned back to the high speed bomber. This machine has an entirely different canopy than the *Zerstörer*. The switchover, however, is not to proceed jerkily; the material manufactured for the heavy fighter can't simply be scrapped. The transition needs to proceed in a smooth and soft manner.

This statement indicates that Dornier is expected to begin production of the single-seat Zerstörer *with GM 1 system.*

Based on an investigation into the hit probabilities, *Oberst* Galland does not believe the effectiveness of the 5 cm gun. To hit a four-engined aircraft from a distance of 1000 m requires a series of shots. He therefore puts much more stock into the effectiveness of a rapid-fire weapon such as the MK 103. The KWK 5 cm with automatic reload can be expected to hit a maximum of two out of 20 shots at a distance of 1000 m, assuming the desired 60 rounds per minute rate of fire is achieved. The KWK is viewed as a stopgap measure, as it was built originally as a single-loader.

Generalfeldmarschall Milch estimates that in 1944 a minimum of 1000 Me 410s

Galland's fears were realized, and the Me 410 A-1/U4 proved to be an ineffective weapon. It saw action in relatively few numbers through the end of 1944. (Petrick)

will be delivered, possibly even 1600. According to the current program, 400 per month are expected for production in 1945.

10/29/43 (GL)
According to Milch, the *Reichsmarschall* ordered a court martial investigation of Messerschmitt on 10/28/43 for the purpose of resolving the several months' delay in the Me 262 program. Messerschmitt claims that this is a result of not being allocated sufficient numbers of workers, etc. by the RLM. The RLM has never experienced a delay in such magnitude. In addition, people can only be allocated when they are available. Furthermore, according to Milch the delay occurred because the Me 209 is now being prioritized. Milch relays an order from the *Reichsmarschall* stating that meetings with Messerschmitt can only take place with a witness present, and in certain cases with a stenographer.

The possibility of using 800 to 900 kg terror bombs with the Me 410 is discussed, something which would have more effect on a city than two 500 kg bombs. The options explored thus far have been unsatisfactory.

Galland reports that in his area of responsibility Me 410s have been fitted out with Flak 43s. Installation is quite good and will most likely be approved for the Me 110. The Me 110 is increasingly being delivered with the Flak 18. He asks that production be switched over to the Flak 43 as quickly as possible. In this context the ZFR 4 gunsight has proven outstanding. 80 units are on order for delivery as soon as possible, with a further 20 per month.

In September 1943 Galland and a few other high-ranking fighter pilots paid a visit to Erprobungskommando 25 *at Achmer, where they inspected the two Me 410 A-1s fitted with* Flak 43 *cannon and telescopic gunsights. (Petrick)*

In a strategy discussion regarding fighter development, Knemeyer reports that the Me 262 has top priority at Messerschmitt. Not a finger is being lifted to make the Me 209 the replacement for the Me 109 at the present time. In addition, Messerschmitt is tasked with the 410, the 110, and oversight of the 109. In its current form the Me 410 is not suited for the high-speed bomber role, nor as a proper *Zerstörer*, i.e. if it is to be sensibly mobilized for the field, an enormous amount of extras needs to be stuck on. With the DB 605 the Me 110 is too slow. Messerschmitt can't fulfill all tasking, so that consideration should be given to prioritizing Me 262 development, doing a lot more with the Me 410 (multi-load equipment, oblique guns, etc.), and activating real improvements to the performance of the modern single-seat fighter in the 2000 hp class based on the Fw 190 instead of the Me 109, which won't be operationally effective in any of its forms by next year. The Me 209 would then be dropped altogether. This old junk would then be modernized by the freed up plant capacity, as planes do not appear in any large numbers until they are already outmoded. The Jumo 213 could help modernize the Me 109.

Milch has the death of the Me 209 at the top of his list, but expects lobbying and increased partisan activity. Knemeyer claims that the only one who would fight against nixing the Me 209 would be Messerschmitt.

All his people are aware that he would do everything in his power to block such a move. Petersen believes that Messerschmitt fiddled around with the Me 309, and that it would have gone into production had not the RLM hollered in time. Milch retorts that he also fiddled around with the Me 210, causing the Me 410 to then be finished too late. The Me 410 is not to Messerschmitt's credit, either. He would never have had the Me 410 built if there had not been so much already invested in the Me 210. Messerschmitt has had some great successes and some total misses, both side by side, and it was unfortunately very difficult to say in advance whether his next design was a hit or a miss.

10/43 (*Erprobungskommando 25* Field Report)

Completion of Flak 43 first installed in the Me 410.

11/12/43 (GL)

Two prototypes of the lightened Me 410 with GM 1, Flak 43, and ZFR gunsight: one in Rechlin and another with *Erprobungskommando 25*. According to flight testing data the operating altitude is 10 to 10.5 km. From an airframe perspective, a decision can be made on potential production; from a weapons perspective, the tactical units would still need to levy the requirements.

Due to the demands of Hitler and Göring's orders, at the present time only 10 to 15 Me 410s per month can be delivered as *Zerstörer* aircraft. The rest go to *Oberst* Peltz in order to meet Hitler's orders for attacking England. Milch wants to petition the *Reichsmarschall* again, asking that something be shifted from the bombers to the heavy fighters in order to get a larger production batch underway. Once again it is stated that the *General der Kampfflieger* places no value in the Me 410 and would prefer to have the Ju 88 S. The Me 410 is expected to leave the assembly line as a true *Zerstörer* by mid-1944; the numerical equipment has not yet been resolved. Everything that's produced as a heavy fighter is to be supplied in the lightened form and with the armament Galland has called for. The Dornier-Werke Munich have reverted from the *Zerstörer* back to the bomber. The heavy fighters have a different canopy. It is not clear how long the decision of the *Reichsmarschall* calling for only small numbers of the Me 410 to be built as a heavy fighter is valid for. *Generalfeldmarschall* Milch is of the opinion that emphasis should be laid on the *Zerstörer* version now so that there will be something on hand in the event the boys start coming over at higher altitudes next year that our fighters can just barely reach now.

11/15/43 (GL)

The delivery forecast for the Me 410 calls for the following over the next three to five months: 10 reconnaissance aircraft; 10 heavy fighters, and the rest of the monthly production as high speed bombers. Then reverting again to Program 223. For the heavy fighter the following program numbers are planned: Nov, Dec 1943 - 10 each; Jan through Mar 44 - 15 each; Apr through Jun 44 - 20 each; Jul through Sep 44 - 30 each; Oct through Dec 44 - 50 each, then continuing with a maximum of 100. The final tally amounts to 240 bombers, 100 heavy fighters, and 60 reconnaissance aircraft for a total of 400. 50% of the *Zerstörers* are to be armed with the KWK 39, and 50% with two MK 103s. The entire production run is single-seaters with GM 1 and new cockpit.

In late 1943 only a small number of Me 410s were delivered as auxiliary heavy fighters; the overwhelming majority went to the bomber units instead. (Petrick)

11/15/43 (*Amtsgruppe Recht*)
During a meeting between the *Reichsmarschall* and *Prof.* Messerschmitt, the *Reichsmarschall* asked why Messerschmitt did not come to him directly with the matter of delayed deliveries for the Me 262. Messerschmitt claimed that he was forbidden to do so by *Generalfeldmarschall* Milch.

In a sworn affidavit, the financier Seiler states: during a discussion sometime in early 1942 between the *Generalfeldmarschall* Croneiß, the managing director and him, the failure of the Me 210 prompted a shakeup in Messerschmitt's management, in which he and Croneiß would assume management of the company. During the course of this discussion, *Generalfeldmarschall* Milch explained that Messerschmitt must be led carefully; for example, it is unacceptable when Messerschmitt uses his direct contacts with the *Führer* and the *Reichsmarschall* as a threat against the men in the *Amt* at every opportunity whenever he feels that he is unable to get his point across. He and Croneiß both assured the *Generalfeldmarschall* that they would work to ensure Willy Messerschmitt finally understood he had to march in step. In view of the unpleasant situation with the Me 210 catastrophe and the involvement of the *Führer* and the *Reichsmarschall*

he and Croneiß did not see the need for Messerschmitt to visit the *Führer* or *Reichsmarschall* directly. On the trip home, Croneiß therefore suggested he would tell Messerschmitt that the *Generalfeldmarschall* had forbidden such visits. He (Seiler) pointedly stressed that *Generalfeldmarschall* Milch had not forbidden direct contact with the *Führer* or the *Reichsmarschall*. With the tension between Messerschmitt on the one hand and Croneiß and him on the other, a directive from both of them at the time probably would not have been followed. More now than ever, he is of the opinion that it would serve no useful purpose for Messerschmitt to petition the *Führer* or the *Reichsmarschall* by himself; his truly artistic style quite often prevents him from presenting and seeing how things need to be reasonably approached from a purely industrial standpoint. Furthermore, it is inexcusable that Messerschmitt at least did not give a personal report to the *Generalfeldmarschall* immediately following such meetings. He (Seiler) cannot fulfill the tasking he is given by the *Feldmarschall* when Messerschmitt does not adhere to company discipline.

(The results of this investigation were provided by the *Reichsmarschall* to *Prof.* Messerschmitt on12/7/43.)

11/16/43 (GL)
Deliveries of the KWK 5 cm are going according to plan. The order to Junkers for the Ju 88 has been filled, and the weapons for the ME 410 were sent out at the beginning of the month.

Based on the experience of *Erprobungskommando 25*, there needs to be a switch from the Flak 18 to the *Flak 25*. The weapons are available, the prototype installation is complete, but there is as of yet no documentation on hand, as Messerschmitt is still having it drawn up. Documentation should be available in November. The blueprints were to have been prepared in an office in Travemünde, but after six weeks it still hasn't been possible to get a man to work on this.

11/30/43 (GL)
The third quarter of 1945 calls for the Me 410 to be manufactured using wooden wings. Every effort is being devoted to getting as much use as possible from the aluminum. For reasons of materials, the *Reichsmarschall* has set the final production totals for the Me 410 at 150 instead of 400. A reminder is given on whether a decision on the use of the Me 410 with MK 103, GM 1, and heavy nose and tail armament will still be forthcoming. Galland demands 100 per month. British press reports are quoted that attribute 610 km/h to the Me 410, although in fact it isn't flying faster than 460 km/h over England.

Galland thinks that, if the heavy armament (KWK 39) is adopted, there shouldn't be talk of anything less than 150 per month for the fighter sector.

According to Galland, on 11/29/43 the Me 410 first launched mortar rounds with two-second time delay fuses head-on into an enemy formation. Ten bombers were shot out of the formation in the first go. Because of fighter escort they were unable to approach the formations from behind; they then attempted to make a head-on pass, and in so doing were able to force a wave of 30 bombers to jettison their payload well before the target and abort the attack. During another recent raid, all but one of a wave of 13 bombers were shot down.

11/43 (*Erprobungskommando 25* Action Report)
Generalfeldmarschall Milch believes that if the Do 335 is as good as people believe, it will make the Me 410 and many other types of much less interest. It is proposed that the pre-production series of the Do 335 be built in Friedrichshafen and the Dornierwerk in Munich be responsible for full scale production. Since the number of Me 410s is to be reduced in any case, it seems possible to have Munich, due to begin production in two months (i.e. two months before the program), build a sensible number of the Me 410 straight through and then replace it with the Do 335. The number of Me 410s to be built by Dornier is still open. The Do 335 will probably be the high-speed bomber, heavy day fighter, and long-range reconnaissance platform. For future planning, there are still the Ta 152 exclusively for the fighters, the turbojet-driven Me 262, the Do 335 as a fighter, *Zerstörer*, and high-speed bomber, the Ju 388 as a bomber, and the He 177 for strategic bombardment, plus a proper jet bomber from Junkers. In case some resources are freed up through the cancellation of the He 219, these are to be channeled to the Do 335. The Do 335 is also expected to assume the role of the high-speed night fighter, since the Me 262's range is inadequate.

Milch reports that at the recent Insterburg exhibit, the *Führer* stated that the Me 262 and the KWK 5 cm in the Me 410 are of utmost priority. Efforts are now being made with every means possible to finish these.

Milch views the Me 410 as an induced labor birth. It was unusable when the *Amt* accepted it. It has been fixed, sometimes by doing things which ran counter to the company itself. However, from a technical standpoint, it is a type already on its way out.

With regard to the light version of the Me 410, it is confirmed that Galland wants all *Zerstörer* production to be with the streamlined canopy and G-supercharger. There is a need for this aircraft. Now that the *Führer* has seen the 5 cm gun, a wing should be established or, at the very least, the second group. Peltz does not want the Me 410, but since a requirement for a high-speed bomber is ever present and the Ju 88 S is not available in sufficient quantities, the Me 410 is being foisted upon him. He would much prefer to let Galland have them all. To set up a group with 5 cm armament, Galland needs 30 instead of 10 Me 410s over the next few months. Peltz reports that the Me 410 has adequate performance, but the problems arise when trying to utilize that performance. The machine is quite sensitive. Up to now, the bomber units have lost about 80 Me 410s, of which 30 were during training, 30 on take-off, landing, ferrying, etc., and only 20 at the hands of the enemy. Of these 20, some crash landed, etc. From radio intercepts it is known that enemy night fighters have flown at speeds in excess of 620 km/h without even getting close. On the other hand, the Me 410's military impact is limited. How much effort goes up in smoke just to get one 500 kg bomb over the target? *Generalfeldmarschall* Milch considers the Me 410 fantastic as a heavy day fighter.

Delivery quotas projected for the month of April are 10 reconnaissance variants, 10 *Zerstörer* planes, and 52 bombers; in May 10 reconnaissance planes, 20 *Zerstörer*, and 53 bombers. The bombers will continue at 50 per month, but *Zerstörer* numbers will increase. Reconnaissance variants will settle at 20, the bombers at 50, and the *Zerstörer* planes at 80. The ultimate goal is to have a wing at constant readiness, one that can, for example, function as a counter invasion wing or be used as a *Zerstörer* wing against England. The Me 410 will most certainly be flown as a bomber *Zerstörer* in the event of a landing or during heavy daylight raids.

12/14/43 (GL)
Problems with the MK 108 have been resolved to the point that the industrial plan can be fulfilled. Due to damage from a bombing raid on Rhein-Metall, the MG 131 will have delays in December and January. Not all components of the MK 103 have the required strength, and as a result there won't be any of these weapons in December, either.

12/16/43 (*Erprobungskommando 25* Action Report)
Installation of 5 cm KWK in three Me 410s, which will be operationally ready on 12/24/43. During operations *Erprobungskommando 25's* fighter squadron will provide cover.

12/17/43 (GL)
The *Reichsmarschall* has decided to distribute the Me 410 in accordance with Galland's recommendations.

1/14/44 (GL)
The MK 103 has not yet been tested and had problems. Eight or nine small parts were not durable on the production version and broke prematurely. The MK 103 won't be functional until these problems are rectified shortly. In spite of this, it has already been supplied to the antitank units in the field as armament on the Hs 129.

The Do 335 is discussed in the developmental meeting (approximately 30 pages of steno minutes). The V1 and V2 are flying, with the V3 following in a few days. The prototype has been flown by *General* Peltz, *Oberstlt.* Diesing, *Oberst* Petersen, and others (totaling about 60 hours). The flight handling is quite good. Stability is ok or can be made acceptable through minor tweaking. The original Messerschmitt standardized forward engine had, as expected, thermal problems. A standard powerplant built by Dornier functioned problem-free. Messerschmitt totally ruined his airflow and had no way for the air to escape. The Do 335 will most likely be 10 km/h faster with the Dornier engine. By the end of 1944 it is expected that 82 Do 335s will have been delivered, including prototypes. The fighter version will be delayed for the time being since the night fighter has not yet been resolved. The Do 335 A-0 (total of 270 aircraft) is expected to enter production in August and will be built at the Dornier-Süd plant, i.e. at Dornier-Munich, the repair facilities at Oberpfaffenhofen and in Friedrichshafen. The *Zerstörer* version, the Do 335 E, will follow in production starting in February 1945.

The production planning does not yet clarify the quantity of Do 335s to be built, nor the manufacturing sites (other than Dornier-Süd). According to *Generalfeldmarschall* Milch, it could be a replacement for the Me 110 and a considerable improvement on the Me 410.

Regarding the state of the KWK 5 cm, it is determined that installation will be made based on a proposal by the *Amt*. Lufthansa converted three aircraft at Staaken, making use of the so-called wide version. Once initial teething troubles had been overcome, the weapon is now functioning fairly reliably after a four to six week evaluation period. In the meantime, various levels of consultation have resulted in the KWK 39/narrow version being introduced. The narrow version is 80 kg lighter and is just now being delivered by the *Heereswaffenamt*. This necessitates Messerschmitt having to come up with a new approach to installation. The first aircraft won't be delivered until December. The delay is due to Messerschmitt, to the prototype fitting of the narrow version, and the fact that the drawings were not done up in time. Trials have begun in Tarnewitz. After 1000 rounds had been fired both in the air and on the ground it was discovered that the belt links come apart, sometimes causing the shells to be fed crossways and become jammed. The changes are on record as having been made and are being introduced on the assembly line. At present, there are no concerns with the operation of the weapon itself. The 5 cm shell is not ok, however, and assuming there are no further setbacks, should be finished in six to eight weeks.

As of 1/10/44 Dornier-Munich has delivered two aircraft; the next eight will be finished by 1/15/44 and a further twenty by 1/31/44. Plans call for twenty in February and fifteen each for the months of March through May. Further production is seen as 20, 25, 30, 35, 38, 40, and a maximum of 45 through to March 45.

A bombing raid against Leipzig burned up the heating documentation at Rheinmetall Borsig. Heating is necessary at altitude, however. Initially the series will have to be produced without heating, but this should come into being as soon as possible. Galland says the guns will not fire. His people recently went up against the enemy, but not a one got anything. The guns fired at lower altitudes. The reasons will be investigated by experts at the *Amt* and the test center.

MK 103 production startup is also delayed due to bomb damage. Startup of the MK 103 in the Me 410 is now expected in March 1944.

During a discussion on introducing the Bf 109 with the DB 605 AS engine, talk yet again revolved around the sluggish work of the Messerschmitt Company. It has been determined that *Prof.* Messerschmitt appears to be the driving force in his company and has many ideas that then lead to too many projects. On the other hand, his staff is significantly smaller than those of other companies. For example, Junkers has approximately 1000 engineers employed for two ongoing types compared with Messerschmitt's 250 for four ongoing types and four to five more in the wings. Vorwald points out that Wiener Neustadt is responsible for production of the Bf 109, Gotha has it for the 110, and Zeppelin for the 323. Milch states that no one should offer more than he can build. And when someone builds something that is constantly breaking, he must also have the support service to build it again.

1/18/44 (GL)

The *Generalfeldmarschall*, in a discussion on field depots, asks why dive brakes are still being fitted on the production line. There is unanimous agreement that the He 188, Do 218, and the entire Ju 88 family no longer need dive brakes. The *General der Kampfflieger* calls for the Me 410 bomber version to continue being fitted with dive brakes until the variable-pitch propellers are available. At present they are being delivered with the brakes.

The Me 410 currently is spending rather a long time in the field shops. They have got to carry out an enormous amount of modifications brought on by the conversion from *Zerstörer* to bomber. Eschenauer describes the to and fro as follows: "It happened like this: first we had switched back from *Zerstörer* to bomber and in December/November had to make the *Zerstörers* into bombers. Starting in January they began coming in as bombers; now in January we've got to make bombers into *Zerstörer* planes because the *Reichsmarschall* ordered that there needs to be more *Zerstörer* types, 30 per month to be exact. And from February on we might have everything right, in my estimation." Milch directs that when it comes to current Me 410 production no changes can be made without his express orders. The production of high-speed bombers, heavy fighters, and night fighters is ahead of schedule and remains uninterrupted. An attack against Friedrichshafen, where forward fuselage and center sections are built for the Me 410, had no additional effect.

1/25/44 (GL)

Oberstlt. Bohlan reports on the 5 cm cannon for the Me 410; serious complaints were made as early as November 1943. The problems are 1) in electrical problems, with small switches breaking easily and 2) with the ammunition belts, which come apart between the third and thirtieth shell. The problem with the switches breaking can, with a high degree of probability, be fixed by making up new parts. The belt problems are more difficult; new belts will have to be made. An optimistic estimate has these taking at least 8-10 days, meaning that the 30 aircraft planned for delivery by 1/31 will not be finished. It will probably be sometime in the first third of February before they will be available in an up-to-date form. A decision needs to be made as to whether the aircraft should be delivered with the old belts by 1/31, or if the delay caused by fitting the new belts is acceptable. The belt separations are due to *Material St.37*, which was done right in the first version, but subsequent manufacturing was not up to the standards specified. *Oberst* Petersen: "The material was changed when the belts went into production." *Oberstabsing.* Hauser: "There was no approval given for this change. Apparently there was a problem in passing the manufacturing directives from the company responsible for development to the manufacturer. The first belt using the correct heat-treated material will be finished on 1/25, when a courier will take it directly to Tarnewitz for firing trials. Production will continue independent of the results, so that belts will continue to be supplied over the course of the week. This would mean that the belts can be swapped out in the aircraft starting some time after 2/1." *Oberstlt.* Bohlan: "The swap out is difficult, as it necessitates a laborious procedure to remove each cannon. Another problem lies in the fact that the weapons can't be fired at Auto-Union, Chemnitz, but need to be transported to Oberpfaffenhofen for firing trials."

The *Generalfeldmarschall*: The planes must be delivered, as there is no way the field can do without them. 30 airplanes are to be delivered this month, regardless of whether they can fire 100 or 3 rounds. If a plane breaks down in the field, then a team will be sent out to fix it in the field, and indeed a second team will be put together so as not to interfere with the output in Oberpfaffenhofen. I would ask that the *Gen.d.Jagdfl.* form such a team from master weapons craftsmen to focus exclusively on this task.

A bombing raid on Rheinmetall Borsig has caused delays with delivery of the MG 131. The fighters are not as affected by this, but the situation with the Me 410 is more critical, as it uses a special version of the MG 131 for its defensive armament. The guns needed for January won't be delivered until the last week in January. Some machines have been supplied without the guns. These will be fitted in the field. Starting in March production is expected to be back at normal levels.

The MK 103 still has problems due to failure of some components. The Hs 129, Me 110, and Me 410 aircraft already built can still be fitted with the weapon, but the delicate parts will need to be sent with the aircraft separately. At present, they are good for 500 rounds, which is about ten sorties.

1/28/44 (GL)
For the discussion item of Ju 290/390 defensive armament it has been mentioned that evaluation of combat camera film shows the bulk of shots being fired with no hope of hitting the target, due to the fact that the sighting is not correct. A gunsight to counter this tendency is in the works. It is first expected to be installed in the Me 410 with MK 103. The semi-fixed mounting of the weapon is of great importance in order to compensate for the aircraft's movement.

2/1/44 (GL)
More than 1000 rounds on the ground and 700 in the air have been fired through the 5 cm aircraft cannon (KWK 39/1). On seven operational sorties just one round could be loosed off each time. The failure has been traced to ammunition belt links, which are too weak. Using the new links, 400 rounds (22 each) were fired on the ground at Tarnewitz without any trouble. It can be assumed that 80% of the airplanes currently armed with the 5 cm BK will misfire. Four sets of the new links have been delivered,

with 106 sets expected to be produced by 2/14. The *Generalfeldmarschall* is to be kept up to date on the status of deliveries.

Up to now, these have been manufactured by DWM in Berlin. Production continues at the Auerwald Company in Grünheide near Chemnitz. Auto-Union will swap 30 units of the 5 cm BK in February and deliver 20 aircraft with this weapon. The first eight will be ready by 2/10. A few more alterations are needed on the weapon before it can be considered frontline ready.

28 aircraft have been taken on charge by 1/31 and four are ready for acceptance flight testing. 13 are ready for pickup at Oberpfaffenhofen and 8 at Augsburg. All have the old-style belts. *Genst.6.Abt.* refuses collection and calls for the new version of weapons and belts.

All aircraft with the 5 cm BK are to be tested by II./ZG 26 at Oberpfaffenhofen, together with the *Erprobungskommando*, the KdE, and specialists from Borsig. Efforts are to be made to get this operational as quickly as possible. The *Generalfeldmarschall* determines that the field prematurely acquired a piece of equipment that was not yet finished. More problems can be expected. In order to discover these soon, the field must conduct firing trials immediately, preferably in the mountains. The field can't expect 100% satisfaction with such new technology; it must work hand in hand with development. GL must protest against the fact that the field abuses and casually overstresses newly tested equipment and then turns around and accuses GL of supplying poor quality equipment.

The test center proposes deploying the Ju 188 and the Me 410 with the small air-to-air X 4 missile. The single-seat Fw 190 fighter is also expected to be tested.

The DB 603 E is to go into production in June. The initial lot is only sufficient to cover Do 335 and He 177 aircraft. This means that the Me 410 and He 219 will have to continue using the DB 603 A. A decision is put off for now. 30% reserve stockpile seems too low a number for the He 219, but at the present time it can't be increased. There are plenty of reserves of the DB 603 A.

2/4/44 (GL)

The KWK is being test fired at Oberpfaffenhofen. The second version of belt links built by the Sasse Company has also been found to stretch. It is assumed that the belt will work once necessary improvements have been made. At Tarnewitz a belt has had 384 rounds through it without a hitch. The new terminal quick break switches are being supplied. The piston buffers are failing at a temperature of just minus 30 degrees. Heating needs to be installed since enemy formations are coming over at altitudes above 8000 m. Messerschmitt was given a contract more than eight weeks ago. Construction supervisor Oberpfaffenhofen has now brought in a company in Munich that put up a heating unit in one day. Whether it is functional remains to be seen. All Me 410s are keeping low, and the squadron is conducting extensive firing tests once the changes have been made. Start of these tests is determined by when Auto-Union supplies the belt clips. Nine aircraft were erroneously shipped off. A test on 2/3 revealed that two aircraft were able to fire five rounds and three got off a single round each. The planes are to remain at Leipheim until the conversion parts have arrived from Chemnitz.

It is assumed that the Auerwald Company in Grünheim will be manufacturing 1000 belt links daily starting on 2/10. Petersen mentions that the prototype belt was fired without any problems. The copy was made by prisoners of war, who were much more casual in adhering to tolerances.

During a performance review of German and foreign aircraft, Petersen points out that the Me 410 is a well designed aircraft from an aerodynamic standpoint, but the pair of 1.4 m wide "pianos" (radiators) slung beneath the engines cause performance to drop.

Knemeyer mentions the Ar 440, which didn't have all that, and as a result was faster. *Generalfeldmarschall* Milch opines that the Ar 440 only failed because it appeared on the scene too late. Had it been available earlier, the Ar 440 would have been selected, but the jigs for the 410 were already at hand. Furthermore, there was considerable delay due to a lack of desire; one would have never gotten it through with Messerschmitt. With the Me 410, such changes to the cooling system are possible thanks to the introduction of the standardized engine.

The MK 103 is now functioning to the point where it can be installed in the wing and/or fuselage. Its life expectancy, which at the end of the previous year was around 500 to 600 rounds, has now climbed to 3000 rounds. Full-scale production of the MK 103 can be expected starting in March 1944. For those weapons already delivered, the weak parts must be swapped out at 500 rounds. In order to do this, personnel from Rheinmetall Borsig need to travel to the Eastern Front, since the only plane flying with the MK 103 is the Hs 129. At present, 328 MK 103s have been delivered, and 100 per month are being built. Production is expected to increase to 125 in March, in April to160 of the new version, in May to 200 and then to 250. The intended goal of 800 per month by the end of the year (these include the engine cannon for the Ta 152 and Do 335) is not yet confirmed, but is not sufficient to meet demands in any case.

In a planning point on toss bombing using the TSA steep-angle bombsight it was established that the Me 410 is probably capable of making torpedo attacks at wavetop altitudes if we have electronic range-finding equipment available to us. Tests with reducing the trajectory have been carried out with very positive results. It depends on using the fins presently found on air dropped torpedoes and finding a way to attach the body. It seems that this can be accomplished in short order.

In the planning point on attack tactics against bomber formations it is mentioned that whole salvos can be fired from the launcher into the formation; the seven-barreled weapon is now available.

2/5/44 (GL)

According to FS Füst IA 15043/44, Top Secret, sent to GL/C-E, 10 improved performance Me 410s are being called for as reconnaissance platforms. GL/C-B 2 and GL/C-B 3 will jointly work out the deadline for equipping the type with the DB 603 and G-supercharger.

Research is to be undertaken into whether and when the Me 410's two MG 17s can be replaced by two MG 131s.

2/15/1944 (GL)

The Hungarians are lagging rather far behind with the Me 210. This is the result of the absence of consolidated deliveries from Germany. Consolidated deliveries, which were to have begun in the fall of last year, never happened. Emergency measures are in place. Deliveries will be made easier now that the Me 410 has been abandoned. From a manufacturing standpoint the situation is thus: production is backlogged, especially in the building of the tail units. We started empennage construction in Hungary ourselves, because they would never be shipped from Germany, but we never got it properly going. Other production has now settled down and in fact, this should be rectified by next month.

More Me 410s are being delivered. It seems to be dependent. From a production standpoint Dornier is well ahead of schedule.

2/18/44 (Developmental Meeting at the General Staff)

Milch: *"How are things looking with the 5 cm gun in the Me 410?"*

Petersen: *"I can't say just yet. Given how far along the airframes are, it looks like we should go ahead with it."*

Mix: *"Böhler told me yesterday that four aircraft had been completed by 2/16. By 2/18 there will be eight, and by the 19th we'll have twelve. Stipulation for this is that there won't be any unforeseen problems with shipping the guns from Chemnitz to Oberpfaffenhofen."*

Petersen: *"Upper Bavaria had poor weather and as a result the transports had to lay over in Chemnitz three days."*

Mix: *"A further twelve aircraft will be finished by 2/26. These are the planes for the second squadron. The next twelve for the third squadron will be done by 3/4. Again assuming uninterrupted transport. It must be said that the overall picture has improved vastly with the latest guns on 2/14. The belt link problems seem to have been corrected. The new spring steel belt fired off 700 rounds at Tarnewitz ...antitank shells! An opinion will be made as soon as we get the ammunition. At present, the transport planes can't get through because of the weather."*

Petersen: *"The new shell from Bruxmüller shoots true. The only thing they're still working on is the fuse. The shell will probably also be ready in two to three weeks."*

Generalfeldmarschall Milch reports that the Generals of the Fighters and Bombers inspected a Do 335 and drew up a lengthy list of requirements for the machine. If these were to be fulfilled, the Do 335's sense and purpose would be overturned - frittered away - and serious delays would be incurred. He sees the Do 335 as a long-range *Zerstörer*, actually, that would only be able to carry out harassment raids over long distances with a single bomb. It seems entirely possible that, if the turbojet version is successful this version would be pushed through quite quickly and the interest for a Do 335 bomber version would drop, especially if it turns out that these machines are suitable for the night fighting role, something which appears entirely possible. He sees in this an airplane that can hunt Mosquitoes, a heavy escort fighter able to cover the Ju 290 overwater. The numbers are small at first, but these will improve considerably over the next year. Perhaps by this time there will also be a *Strabo* (Ar 234) for it to fly cover for. Consideration needs to be given, however, that this will be the only O-plane having an effective speed at the necessary combat altitudes.

2/23/44 (GL)

Generalfeldmarschall Milch reports on destruction caused by bombing, which has set production timetables back considerably. The British are flying pure terror missions at night, while the Americans attack production centers during the day. A Fighter Staff is to be established in reaction.

Milch reports that on 2/22/44 several Me 410s with 5 cm cannons were used in combat for the first time. Ten Me 410s on a training flight shot down three confirmed and another probable four-engined bombers approaching Regensburg. Seven aircraft fired off all their ammunition without a single problem being encountered.

2/25/44 (Developmental Meeting in the General Staff)

Mix Report on the 5 cm cannon for the Me 410:

"The commissariat representative told me yesterday that the multi-loader system is ok. Problems have been rectified. On the 23rd modifications were carried out on all weapons already delivered. Twelve aircraft have been produced by the 20th of February. Before delivery, each of the guns has been fired on the test stand 21 times and sighted in with three or four rounds (?). Four more planes were completed on 2/23. These firings have shown that there has been a gradual improvement in the functioning of the weapon. Recently there have been other problems, this time with the live Sprenggranate 38 shells supplied by the Heeres-Munitions-Anstalt's

Lochstadt warehouse. A large percentage of them can't be loaded. The shells are too long, some by up to 8 mm. This ammunition is now being pulled so the damage is minimal. The Rechlin Test Center immediately sent a representative to the ammunition factory, who will hopefully fix the situation in short order."

"On 2/22/44 the planes on a training flight made contact with the enemy, and of the ten which took off, four scored kills—three with cannons. During this mission three 5 cm PK guns suffered outages, one after two rounds, a second after ten rounds, and a third after one round when the ammunition could not be loaded. During training flights on 2/23/44 the six aircraft taking off had the following results: three aircraft fired all their ammunition—21 rounds; one made 12 shots, another 14, and a third 2. With the last aircraft, the screw on the locking strap came loose as it had not been tightened properly, so this can be considered an operator error. The airplane was flown again and functioned absolutely normally. An automatic switch failed on the aircraft firing 14 rounds, and a gun jammed on the one firing just 12 rounds. Yesterday I heard that two more planes with the 5 cm PK have been shot down."

Petersen: "Two planes crash landed. It is still unclear as to why. An investigation needs to be carried out. Already five aircraft have had to make forced landings. This is drawing attention. An investigation needs to be made to see if the crews are not being properly trained."

Von Loßberg: "The hydraulics didn't have enough pressure. This has now been increased. I will follow up on the matter."

Mix: "The tests at Oberpfaffenhofen were carried out at altitudes of up to 8000 m, where temperatures of minus 50 degrees were registered. No problems with weapons because of this cold were noted. It must be stressed, however, that the weather over the last few days has been very favorable: dry. Notwithstanding this, all efforts are being made to get heating. Yesterday the first squadron should have taken delivery of the provisional heating elements and barrel heaters. Installation time for one man is two to three hours. Beyond this, work is being done on a monitoring and bay heating system, as a result of a discussion that took place on Monday. The recommendation that the Messerschmitt Company initially made was rejected in the meeting on the 21st as not being practical. The new proposal is being pushed through. With regard to combat operations, Müller has told me some things which I'll pass on with reservations. Experience from enemy encounter on the 22nd, based on information provided by Oberleutnant

Scheel: Opened fire with the cannon at a range of 800 m and pressed home the attack to within minimum range. No hits were noted at longer ranges. The absence of tracer rounds is sorely felt. I would like to comment on this—the 5 cm HE rounds are not equipped with tracers. We can stick tracers to our shells. We have already planned for this. But I do not think it's right to use tracers with these larger rounds, for the rate of fire is only 40 per minute after all. I went to the General der Jagdflieger again about this. We have got to make a recommendation that with the Me 410, which by the is being built with the 151, we utilize the 15 mm barrel instead of the 2 cm one. Then we have both ballistics."

Milch: "I don't think tracers are of any value for an extremely short trajectory. The shell drops off at just 500 m. There is also the possibility that these would just be compounding errors. If a fighter unit asks for tracers, it is evident that it knows nothing about shooting. Maybe he was shooting at the ground and as the separation changed he then made one mistake after another. As a result, it serves no purpose. If we can help him by providing the 151, then that should be more than enough for him out to 800 m. In emergencies, it can also shoot as far as 1000 m. It's 1.5 meters off then, but still within the scatter box. But I reject the idea that the 5 cm gets the tracers."

Mix: "We can plan for tracers with rounds, but I have my doubts."

Milch: "No, that would just cause mistakes. Let's drop it."

Mix: "I would still ask that we use the 15 mm barrels." (The speaker hands over a sketch with explanations.)

Diesing: "The prioritization of fighter production has compelled the Armament Office to order that the entire fighter, heavy fighter and night fighter production, engines and supplier industry be given top priority in all areas, starting with transportation, etc."

Eschenauer: "I see a need emerging, not today perhaps, but certainly by the day after tomorrow. We're still building the Me 410 as a heavy fighter and a bomber. There are efforts underway at Luftflotte 3 to fit the bombers with oblique firing armament in order to carry out night fighting operations. My point is this: if the Me 410 can fly as a night fighter over England, then it can do the same here as well. If the whole night fighter issue has gotten to this point, I would suggest going ahead with laying down the Me 410 as a heavy fighter, but in a sensible way, so that the bombers aren't shut out. Instead, planning should incorporate the idea that, from a given point on, the plane is to be built as a heavy fighter only. They don't all need the 5 cm; the 151 and 103 work as well. That way we can have some breathing room."

GenFeldm. Milch: "I'm of the same opinion. You need to tell the Chief of the General Staff so that he can issue the requirements, since he will have to bring it up with the Reichsmarschall."

v. Loßberg: "I think it will be difficult using the 410 as a night fighter because of its landing characteristics; better as a heavy day fighter."

Genfeldm. Milch: "We have it as a heavy day fighter. I've given the company advance warning that there's a possibility of the 410, whose production will be winding down early next year, being produced in an additional batch.

With regard to the weaponry, it looks as though we'll be getting 100 MK 103s. Is it ok?"

Mix: "They have a limited lifespan. We won't get the lifespan we want until March."

Genfeldm. Milch: "That doesn't help. It is important that we get these weapons. Only when we fire it can we get experience. Evaluations can never provide the ultimate experience. Things are constantly being changed and improved. Naturally, you can't put in a weapon that doesn't fire. When the weapon has a certain percentage of being potentially effective, then you've got to go with it. An engine isn't complete until we've got no more use for it—the same goes for armament. 125 in March, then 160, 250, 300—these are confirmed for production, barring any bomb damage. 108: February 1500, March 1750, April 2000. These are official numbers from the armaments minister."

2/29/44 (GL)

Discussion revolves around Me 510 production at Messerschmitt-Augsburg and Dornier Munich. Both plants have reduced the number of planned deliveries (projected). *Generalfeldmarschall* Milch demands an explanation. It is mentioned that the Dornier airplanes all have nothing to do with the KWK.

For the February Me 410 projections, 71 aircraft undergoing acceptance flights and cleared for their first flights have been struck off. C-B 2 reports that snow drifts have prevented flight operations at Augsburg. *Gen.-Ing.* Hertel will look into the reasons why the airfield was not cleared like at Lechfeld and Oberpfaffenhofen. The aircraft are to be ferried out to other airfields at once.

The *Generalfeldmarschall* calls for Messerschmitt's dispersal into the Leonberg Tunnel to move faster. Any special installation/de-installation work is to stop.

Oberst Petersen reports that the caliber problems with the Heeresmunition ammunition for the BK 5 have been corrected. Shells and fuses are ready. The ammunition has been certified after no problems were encountered when firing 1000 rounds. The shells can be expected in the field as early as March 1944.

Alpers reports that Eschenhauer has proposed concentrating the manufacture of the Me 410 as a heavy day fighter, dropping the reconnaissance version and dispensing with the idea of the Me 410 C-3 canopy (instead continuing with the B-3). It is considered important to design production so that when a factory is bombed out, work can continue without interruption at the next plant, thereby minimizing losses in output. The dispersal of production resources is discussed further.

This signifies the end of the ME 410 C and the shift of the Me 410 B-3 reconnaissance version to the B-7 and B-8.

3/2/44 (Developmental Meeting in the General Staff)

Vorwald: "In one of the last meetings with 6. Abteilung, we considered how we could somehow assist the fighter-heavy fighter program in its current crisis by slashing the types…It was also suggested, assuming the command staff was in agreement, to produce the 110 exclusively as a night fighter if the 410 could be only used as a heavy fighter instead of a high speed bomber. Another suggestion involved dropping the Me 410 C in favor of the 410 B-3..."

Koller: "The next item would be the proposal to have the 110 fully incorporated into the night fighting forces and balance out the heavy day fighters by having all 410 bombers built as heavy fighters. This would mean no more 410s for bombers against England. The command staff is in agreement. We recognize the crisis. For this reason we've got to scrap the idea of using the 410 as a bomber against England. Up to now, it's only succeeded making harassment raids there anyway. Successes not exactly playing a decisive role. It was a good means to compensate for the weather and a good transition. I believe that our present situation makes it necessary to agree with the recommendation. However, this is undoubtedly only one of the points that would require the approval of the Reichsmarschall. I must emphasize this."

Milch: "We only wanted to come up with a common vision.... We'll keep the recommendations on the 410 going for now...."

Koller: "From a tactical side, we have tried to determine what we should support, what we need to meet the airspace needs on the one hand, and on the other, to meet the Luftwaffe's requirements—purely from a tactical standpoint without regard for weapons potential. We've worked it out in such a manner that we've said: what's necessary, not what's wanted. I have figured it out for the fighters, first for the single-engined types, as follows. As of 1 February there are currently 54 fighter groups available with 1810 aircraft. Our requirements would be—let's see here, it will take a second: 82 fighter groups with 5656 aircraft, which would need to be restocked at a monthly rate of 2660…Zerstörer unit: currently 10 2/3 groups with 623 aircraft. Our requirement: 24 heavy fighter units with 1280 machines. Monthly resupply without taking into account losses, 484."

Milch: "Our planning is higher."

Koller: "Resupply for night fighters: 590…When I look at the total numbers, they seem to be relatively high in view of the current state. When I compare them with the enemy, they are downright modest. The fighters are opposed by 12000 enemy fighters from England, America, Italy, Russia…. The total resupply is 5000 monthly. This number can and must be reached, assuming the Luftwaffe is given the support needed."

3/24/44 (GL)

A streamlining commission was set up which is to determine what is genuinely needed in terms of aircraft types and what should be dropped. In this context, Petersen draws attention to the dive brakes that are still on the Me 410, even though the *Amt* called for their removal nine months ago. Peltz reintroduced them.

3/31/44 (GL)

Generalfeldmarschall Milch gives a speech on the occasion of the establishment of the Fighter Staff. Among other things, he points out that Germany is losing approximately 1300 aircraft per month—not at the hands of the enemy—and only a portion of these can be patched up again. Of these, 50 to 60% are unnecessary and do not have anything to do with technical problems; they can be traced back to recklessness, operator error, and similar things. The lifespan of an airplane is two to three years, then it's either worn out, shot down, or outmoded.

We agreed to make a single seat Me 410 with the GM 1. 30 were built, and now it is said that we don't want them any more. They are blocking the production hangars and need to be modified. The workers are scratching their heads.

3/44 (*Erprobungskommando 25* Action Report)

The two *Flak*-armed Me 410s have been assigned to ZG 1 (Königsberg-Neumark) for operational trials. Operational testing of the Me 410 with 500 kg RS assigned to the *Zerstörergeschwader*.

4/7/44 (GL)

Heavy armament in aircraft is discussed. *Generalfeldmarschall* Milch says that, at the time of Stalingrad, people wondered what could be done to attack tanks. The 3.7 cm gun was fitted to the Ju 87, but this is no longer adequate, and tests were done using the heavy calibers—8.8, 7.5, and 5 cm. The 5 cm is now being used mainly in the Me 410 for engaging four-engined bombers, so that quantitively it has met its purpose.

On the topic of the standardized engine it has been established that, after initial resistance from every side with the exception of Heinkel and Dornier, all companies have now agreed on siting the radiator forward of the engine. This offers several advantages, such as protecting the engine in the front, short piping for the coolant system, arrangement of many components right in the immediate area of the engine (which reduces

The single-seat Me 410, with GM 1 boost system but still retaining the WB 151 A mortars, proved to be of little combat value. II./ZG 26 *only used this type for a short period of time in early 1944. (Petrick)*

diversity), and better access, as there is no longer this tight squeeze. Other approaches should not be ignored, however, and at present there is an Me 410 being converted to the radiator configuration of the Mosquito in order to see what can be done with this.

5/8/44 (*Luftwaffe* High Command, quoted in Green, Warplanes)

The *Luftwaffe* High Command orders that all Me 410 A-1s and B-1s be converted to Me 410 A- 1/U2 and B-1/U2 *Zerstörer* versions.

5/8/44 (letter from the Messerschmitt Company to Ludwig Hansen & Co., Schneidemühl)

The Me 410 is to be simplified. To this end, all high speed bombers (A-1 and B-1) are to be converted to Me 410 A-1/U-2s (= *Zerstörer*). For the heavy fighters (= 410 A-1/U-2, A-1/U-4, B-2, B-1/U-4, and B-6) and reconnaissance types (= 410 A-3 and B-3) the dive brakes and associated fittings are to be left off. Both measures are to be implemented immediately. Those airframes and center sections already being worked on are subject to this measure so far as possible.

5/12/44 (GL)

In June it is expected that 200 DB 603 As with G-supercharger will be available, in July 450, in August 295, in September 65, and in October 10. Then the switch to the DB 603 E, which has the same blower. Of these 820, 225 are planned for reserves. Due to the increased deliveries of superchargers, we can expect retrofit modifications. 140 are planned for the Me 410 and 64 for the He 219 for the month of June, and 240 for the Me 410 and 60 for the He 219 next month. Starting in September, the Me 410 is to begin rolling off the assembly line as a *Zerstörer* with the DB 603 E as a direct replacement for the A engines. According to *Professor* Messerschmitt, the DB 603 E can be fitted to the Me 410 with only minor changes, but there's got to be a mockup available beforehand. *Generalmajor* Galland says that they will be produced in reasonable numbers beginning in August. Galland calls for the G-supercharger on the DB 603 for a group of He 219s with support, as well as for all Me 410s. *Oberstingr.* Alpers draws up a new program for the Me 410 taking into account the installation of the DB 603 E and DB 603 A with G-supercharger.

5/28/44 (GL)

Discussed are operations using steel spars in different aircraft types, such as the Me 262. With regard to the Me 410, it is stated that the type is winding down production, and it would probably serve no purpose to make a big deal out of increasing the wingspan and having wooden wings with steel spars. Nevertheless, it should continue to progress developmentally in order to see through the matter with the wood/steel spar combination. The Me 410 design work can be carried over to the Me 262, and that could some day be important. It is decided to keep the matter of steel spars for the Me 410 open for the time being and continue development.

6/2/44 (GL)

Topic of discussion is wooden wings. With production of the Ju 352 coming to a close, necessary resources will be freed up. With regard to Messerschmitt, it is stated: the Me 410 test wings made of wood with steel spars are expected for static trials in August or September. It will be the first type to be fitted with the new wing. When work first began on the wooden wing, there were no plans to cease production of the Me 410. It was expected that there would be large numbers produced with the larger wings. That matter has been closed in the interim. The Me 262 wooden wing must now be produced parallel to the 410, since the 410 wooden wing is out of the question for the 262 due to the sections. A lot of work has already gone into the Me 410 wing, as there was still the expectation that it would be converted over. Messerschmitt is still working on the wing. As a result, the 410 wing should be built in any case for test purposes.

6/9/44 (GL)

Up for discussion is the 5 cm KWK 39 in the Me 410 and the three-week old suggestion regarding 4/151/20. The group now has 53 aircraft, of which 16 are of the latest configuration. The others are in the process of being checked out and retrofitted by an industry team. Over the last few days there have been problems with the electrical system that are not connected with the weapons. The guns break down for unknown reasons after just a few shots at altitudes of 3000 to 4000 m. The problem is not known to occur on the ground.

The quad gun configuration is keeping the test center busy in two versions; one is relatively heavy and borrows a lot from the unit's own field design, and the other is a lighter version. It is hoped that the lighter one can be used. It is apparently easier to build. It would be advantageous if Auto-Union, who would be the most likely candidate to take over production, would make a builder available so that some preparations can be made parallel to the design work.

The 5 cm KWK 39 will no longer be required in its former numbers, instead needing an output rate of just 15 per month. This equates to maintaining a single group with this fat weapon; all remaining aircraft are to be initially fitted out with two MK 103s and two 151s. Now there is the test center's suggestion of using the 151/20 quad gun pack. This was suggested once before in a meeting

This armament configuration, consisting of two chin-mounted MG 151/20s, was probably a front-line modification. (Petrick)

This particular aircraft had its 5 cm BK cannons replaced by a quad of MG 151/20s. (Petrick)

at the *Reichsmarschall's*, but the quad pack was not yet available (the suggestion hearkens back to 1941). At the time, Göring said that he wasn't interested in it since they had the MK 103. Orders were given to keep one group with the 5 cm and convert all others with the 410 to two 103s, two 151s, and two 131s. Within the *Generalluftzeugmeister's* staff, a proposal was made to have a quad gun pack conversion kit made and, if it were successful, to have a few of these built and offer them to the *General der Jagdflieger.*

The Me 410 armament was ordered to go to ZG 26; the first group with KWK 5 cm, the second group with the 151 twin pack. For ZG 76, the first group had two MK 103s, while the second and third group got 151s. Now all are to be armed with 103s; the 151 twin pack is an interim solution that will slowly be phased out with the advent of the 103. Bohlan is convinced that the quad pack will be introduced. This should be considered purely an action of the *Technisches Amt* for the time being, and the quad needs to be built, tested, and implemented at Auto-Union in a small batch of 10, 20, or 30 units. The company will have some of the strain relieved, as the 5 cm will not be produced in such large numbers as originally planned. He has no doubt that by then the 5 cm will have ended its useful life in the air and we will be grateful to be able to have this quad to hang in the airplane. Vorwald says that in a few weeks the KWK output will drop to 15 per month; this could possibly be used against ships taking part in the landings so that we aren't just standing around waiting for units to attack that have to fly without fighter protection. It doesn't happen like that any more, but we've seen it in Posen and Silesia. Waiting for a mission without fighter protection is relatively senseless.

It is clear to Vorwald that the KWK 5 cm will drop to 15 per month and there will be an accelerated effort to have the MK 103 fitted in the Me 410. To Vorwald's question on the state of the MK 103, Hauser explains that it has passed muster from a testing standpoint and there are 36 more guns than can be fitted at the moment. On the other hand, Messerschmitt and Oberpfaffenhofen are going very slowly with the startup of manufacturing the pod. This is critical. The first five machines were expected any day now. However, they have hung up on the pod, which is undergoing fundamental changes. The first plane with two MK 103s is expected to roll out in June.

Vorwald would like to have a timetable overview that includes items affecting the MK 103 over the next month, what is confirmed for next month, and what difficulties still exist. *Oberst* Bohlan's recommendation with regard to the 151/20 quad pack is accepted, i.e. several test prototypes will be made by within the purview of the KdE, *Technisches Amt*, evaluated, and shown to the *General der Jagdflieger*, so that he can then decide how much of the production run should be armed with the guns.

Bohlan continues by stating that the quad conversion kits should fit. The 5 cm cannon-armed gunships were only fitted on the lower fuselage with a remarkably simple, flat covered gondola. This would mean that the quad pod could be hung from the same mounts, and then the other gondola could be removed.

Petersen feels that with the two MK 103s and two 151s the 151 quad conversion kit won't offer much. The only advantage would be that it would offer a spray effect and could fire incendiaries. If the 103 is successful this will be scooped up before all else. Vorwald replies that the 103 will be in the field sooner, and it is a good thing that they'll be able to make a comparison.

Additionally, mention is made of the ability to increase the KWK 5 cm's rate of fire to around 140. The prototype cannons are expected to be accepted on 8/15. At the present time Mauser is test firing them. The increased rate of fire would be three or four times greater. As far as effectiveness goes, its 400 gram warhead next year will be adequate for engaging four-engined machines.

Mix suggests that, if the Me 410 with the 5 cm cannon is only able to operate under fighter protection, the 5 cm should be immediately removed and the twin MG 151 gun pack be installed in its place. This the *General der Jagdflieger* would consider appropriate, while from a developmental standpoint as well as from Tarnewitz there are efforts to produce six of these packs. Bohlan responds that this would involve a fundamentally new decision on the part of the *Reichsmarschall* who, at the meeting in Berchtesgaden, was only persuaded with great difficulty to drop the numbers of groups with the 5 cm gun from several to one.

Oberst Bohlan reports on ZG 26's operations over the last few weeks in Posen. A total of 13 Me 410s were in use, one of which was an aircraft modified with six MG 151s. Four aircraft were shot down by the remaining 12 Me 410s with 5 cm KWK, of which probably only one was hit with the 5 cm gun. The remaining three were brought down with the MG 151/20 incendiary rounds after the 5 cm's ammunition had been fully expended. *Leutnant* Daso scored a kill with the 151. He reported that after only a short burst he saw a sea of flames in front of him. This shows that the KWK 5 cm can't score even when the weapon functions as it should. The one hit made with the cannon was from a shell through the wing, where it tore a huge hole. The airplane continued to fly, and *Leutnant* Daso fired another burst with the MG 151, whereupon it caught fire. The others were clearly brought down with the MG 151/20 after the 5 cm had fired all its ammunition.

Vorwald believes that it will have a better success rate with a more rapid rate of fire. In contrast, Bohlan does not hold out much hope for this. He is of the opinion that the best effect is achieved using rounds between 20 and 30 mm, for bombers are virtually always brought down as a result of fire. This can be accomplished without difficulty by using 20 to 30 mm caliber rounds, which also offer the excellent advantage of not requiring the gunner to be quite as accurate as with larger caliber guns and their limited quantity of ammunition.

Vorwald assumes that the 5 cm gun will most likely be used against the landing fleet. Von Loßberg believes that the difference between two 151s and two 103s or six 151s will hardly be noticeable. He therefore believes that the expense of making two at a time is not justified. Furthermore, he does not think much of using heavy fighters in daylight in any case. It's not economical to send a fighter for protection and a *Zerstörer*, i.e. three engines in total, against the enemy so that only one does the shooting. This is better accomplished with the single-seaters.

Mix agrees with the opinion of von Loßberg. Priority must be given to producing 45 Me 410s with MK 103s this month, while the prototype installation of four MG 151s will probably take one to one and a half months at the *E-Stelle* Travemünde. Then it will have to be tested and sent to the manufacturer. He expects the plane no earlier than nine months hence.

Bohlan responds by saying that it is only temporarily at Tarnewitz. When *Dr.* Wacke at Auto Union sends a production representative to Tarnewitz, then the time span cited by Mix will become significantly shorter.

Another item on the agenda is Program 226. There is a need to save 4000 metric tons of aluminum, the amount by which the program exceeds the output potential. Another problem stems from the *Reichsmarschall*'s orders for increasing the He 177 output from 100 to 200 per month, something that most certainly cannot be accomplished. Some program figures will need to be lowered accordingly. Production of the Me 410 and possibly the Bf 110 are expected to terminate sooner than planned.

6/9/44 (GL)
The Me 410 is not mentioned.

6/44 (*Erprobungskommando 25* Action Report)
21 cm aft – firing gun (*Krebs* System): one Me 410 from ZG 26 for functional firing. Installation in 20 Fw 190 A-8s and provided to the *Sturmstaffeln*. *Schräge Musik* with optical resolution: From 5.44 installation of two oblique firing 120 mm barrels in Fw 190 A-8s and Bf 110s. Firing trials with the Bf 110 have begun. Flak 43: Bf 110 and two Me 410s in operation. Two Bf 110s shot down on the first mission, the third Bf 110 (*W.Nr.* 170067) returned to Parchim. Me 410 (*W.Nr.* 120253) returned to Parchim due to malfunction. Me 410 (*W.Nr.* 10241) shot down on its first mission, 5/17/44, at Parchim!

6/30/44
Hitler orders increased production of fighters (see Bf 110).

7/1/44 (GL)
In the *Blitzprogramm*, derived from the *Führerbefehl* of 6/30/44, 20 types are redlined, including the Me 210 and the Me 410.

9/44
The *Luftwaffe* takes on the last 40 Me 410s.

On 18 July 1944 Me 410 A-1/U2 3U+KN from 5./ZG 26 *crash-landed at Königsberg. No longer in production, such events ensured that the Me 410 vanished from the* Luftwaffe's *inventory at a fairly rapid rate. (Petrick)*

left: By the autumn of 1944 the Me 410 A-1/ U4 was only able to operate in defense of the Reich from airfields far removed from the front lines and in areas without enemy fighter protection. These aircraft of 5 Staffel, Zerstörergesch-wader 26, *are seen at rest at the airfield in Königsberg, Neumark. The sub-type is derived from the factory number of 3U+BN, which begins with 420.... (Petrick)*

below: Four ME 410 A-1/U4s of 6./ZG 26 *are captured preparing to take off for an autumn combat mission.*

right: This Hungarian modification began only after Me 410 production in Germany had ceased. (Schmitt)

below left: II./ZG 76 *flew this Me 410 B-2 from Seerappen in November of 1944. (Petrick)*

below right: These reconnaissance variants from 2./(F)/122 *were photographed at Kastrup in April of 1945.*

below: These Me 410s are lined up ready for the scrapyard in the autumn of 1945. The aircraft closest to the camera belonged to an air-sea rescue unit. (Imperial War Museum)

Overview of the Types

Designation of aircraft, series variants, etc. followed a system established by the *Reichsluftfahrtministerium* (RLM, Air Ministry), which also was responsible for issuing these designations. The aircraft name stemmed from a sequential number added to an abbreviation of the manufacturer responsible for the initial design of the airframe. Based on this, the *Zerstörer* designed by the Bayerische Flugzeugwerke was given the designation "Bf 110." New designs received the appellation "Me" (e.g. Me 210) when the Bayerische Flugzeugwerke was reorganized under the name Messerschmitt. In official documentation the Bf 110 designation was retained up until the end of the war. Accordingly, it is also used here, even though postwar literature commonly refers to the type as the Me 110. At RLM office meetings it was often simply called the "110," whereas at Messerschmitt AG and in contemporary press reports the designation Me 110 came into use from early on.

Single letters were initially used to differentiate between the various subtypes of a particular airframe, e.g. Bf 110 B or Bf 110 C. Later, around 1940, it became necessary to break these subtypes down even further in order to distinguish lesser modifications, and to do this numbers were again appended to the designation, such as Bf 110 C-1.

During the course of the war, many basic aircraft types were dropped and their roles taken over by specialized variants of existing models, necessitating an even more refined classification yet again. This resulted in the addition of an "R" in combination with a number, e.g. Bf 110 G-4/R3. It must be pointed out that these aircraft came from the assembly line as such and were not, for example, the result of a field modification. Having said that, these factory conversions often made up a relatively large percentage of the production. The characteristic components were permanently attached to the airframe and could only be removed at considerable expense of time and effort. In theory, the factory conversion designations could be issued to each series individually, but in most cases were the same for all variants when the scope of conversion was identical; compare the Bf 110 G-2/R3, G-3/R3, G-4/R3. However, they were often used in conjunction with a single specific variant. Due to the large numbers involved, these factory conversions are quite well documented in type sheets, manuals, etc.

In the manuals, e.g. that of the Bf 110, "R" stood for "special sub-variants deviating from the standard series." These manuals used both "R1" and "R-1" as designators. In aviation literature the abbreviation "R1" and "R-1" were interpreted to mean "*Rüstsatz*," or factory modification pack. This has led to some problems in discussion, since company data and the manuals understood *Rüstsatz* to mean something different. Thus, you have *Rüstsatz 1* for the Me 410, a weapons pod with two MG 151s that made the Me 410 A-1 into an Me 410 A-1/U2 and not, as might be supposed, an Me 410 A-1/R1. The *Rüstsatz 2*, two MK 103s, was standard equipment on the Me 410 B-2. For the Bf 110 G there were *Rüstsatz B1*, *B2*, and *M1* through *M51*, which were sometimes also fitted to the Bf 110 G-2/R3 as an addition. As a result, the authors have used the letter "R" as an abbreviation for "*Rüstzustand*" (armament status).

Follow-on field conversions were different from factory conversions in that the former were carried out on completed airframes and were designated with a "U." Field conversions often applied only to individual aircraft, but could also (particularly with Messerschmitt) be carried out on a relatively large scale. It was often the case that the same supplemental designator applied to the same modification for different variants, e.g. Bf 110 C-1/U4, D-2/U4, and E-2/U4. This, however, did not apply across the board. To be sure, the conversion designation was only relevant for a specific aircraft type. If a conversion proved effective it could be adopted on the production line, where it would lead to either a new series or a factory conversion designation. For example, the field converted Bf 110 G-4/U7 was subsequently produced in series as the Bf 110 G-4/R6. Since follow-on conversions sometimes had the nature of prototypes, and if they proved unsuccessful were not pursued further, they were often only mentioned in company reports. Consequently, the information on them can be somewhat sketchy today.

Factory modification packs in their real sense were also different from R-type status designations. On the one hand, these were components that were not permanent and could be swapped out in the field in relatively short order to tailor an aircraft for a particular role. As an example, for the Bf 110 there were the B-1 and B-2 hardpoint sets and the M-1 through M-5 weapons sets. These packs, however, were indicated in the aircraft's designation only on a limited basis. Modification kits also embraced components that were not part of the basic airframe type and were installed in the airframe while still at the factory, based on the type's intended role.

In the following descriptions, the authors have provided the data to reflect the aircraft's state as new, fresh off the assembly line. The *Luftwaffe* would then often modify these. Improvements, aftermarket application of armor, additional armament or bomb hardpoints, as well as one-off modifications carried out by the user led to the fact that the data for the aircraft portrayed would no longer hold true. This makes it difficult, if not impossible, to classify photographed airplanes as a particular sub-variant. In some cases the differences are not discernable to the naked eye. For example, the Bf 110 E-1 differed from the Bf 110 E-2 only in the fact that the E-1 could be flown both with and without the *Dackelbauch*, whereas as a rule the E-1 did not use the *Dackelbauch*. An E-1 without *Dackelbauch*, therefore, was externally indistinguishable from an E-2.

The *Luftwaffe's* Tactical Guidelines for the *Rüstungsflugzeug II* (1932)

Role:	a) two-seat fighter
	b) reconnaissance
	c) light bomber
No. of engines:	1
Crew:	2 men
Armament:	
for a)	2 fixed machine guns
	1 flexible machine gun
for b)	1 fixed machine gun
	1 flexible machine gun
Ordnance:	
for a)	12 x 10 kg bombs
for b)	50 kg bomb load, either 5 x 10 kg or 1 x 50 kg
Speed:	
cruise at 6 km altitude:	280 km/h
max. at 6 km altitude:	310 km/h
Endurance:	
for a)	2 hrs at max. throttle
for b) and c)	1000 km
Climb rate:	6 km in 12 min
Operating altitude:	6 to 9 km

No aircraft based on these tactical guidelines was ever built. However, these show that the *Reichswehr* was already involved in developing aircraft in the heavy fighter class even before the days of the Third Reich.

The *Luftwaffe's* Tactical Guidelines for the *Rüstungsflugzeug III* (1934)

Role:	heavy fighter
No. of engines:	1-2
Crew:	3-4 men
Armament:	2 x 2 cm cannons/ 1 twin-barreled machine gun
Equipment:	automatic pilot automatic controls IFR instrumentation high altitude oxygen system heating
Speed:	
cruise at 6 km altitude:	330 km/h
max. at 6 km altitude:	400 km/h
landing:	Less than 100 km/h
Endurance:	2000 km at cruising speed
Climb rate:	6 km in 15 min
Operating altitude:	up to 9 km
Airfield size taxiway:	500 x 500 m
Key points:	a) speed b) range c) climb performance d) maneuverability

Emphasis is on the heavy fighter *Zerstörer*. The same aircraft type should be able to function as a high altitude strategic reconnaissance platform through the use of different armament and equipment. Night operations must be taken into account for both aircraft variants. For night operations, use of sound damping in addition to reduced exhaust illumination is expected. The aircraft must be able to be operated by pilots of average flying skill. Maximum speed at operating altitude must be maintained for up to 20 minutes at multiple points throughout the mission. When in a spin, the aircraft must be easily recoverable. Turns must be able to be flown at operating altitude without any loss of altitude.

The mandated radius of operation is understood to include: attaining an operating altitude of 7 km before overflying the front lines; flying at this operating altitude at cruise speed above enemy territory up to the front lines and back; and descending to the landing point. Distance from the takeoff/landing point to the front lines: 50 km.

These guidelines revealed those performance features desired by the *Luftwaffe*; they were not requirements *per se*, as this type of aircraft had not yet been clearly defined. Even though it was not clearly stated, it can be assumed that the two 2 cm machine guns were to have been located in turrets, as the difference in speed between the reconnaissance version and the heavy fighter was expected to be 50 km/h. Furthermore, such a turret was under development at the time by the Mauser Company.

The desired high altitude performance assumed the use of a turbocharged engine, which was just entering its developmental stage at the time the guidelines were issued. At first, liquid cooled inline engines with a capacity of about 20 liters (later 30 liters) were envisioned for the fighters and heavy fighters. 20 liter carbureted engines were then in development at BMW, Junkers, and Daimler-Benz, but an industrial streamlining action only left the Jumo 210 remaining. According to the wishes of the RLM the 30 liter engine was to have been developed by Daimler-Benz, where it was indeed produced as the DB 600 carbureted engine.

Unrealized First Generation *Zerstörer* Projects

Ago Ao 255

Type:	All-metal cantilever twin-engined low-wing monoplane
Engines:	2 x Jumo 210
Armament:	4 x 2 cm machine guns

No further details are known. B. Lange indicates the Ao 225 was a heavy fighter project with DB 606 dual engine buried in the fuselage driving two tractor propellers via extended shafts. Apparently it was a counterproposal to the Me 210 and Ar 240.

Dornier Project

No details are known about Dornier's project for a heavy fighter.

Gotha's Project 3001/3002

Type: All-metal cantilever twin-engined high-wing monoplane, engines in fuselage driving propellers via extended shafts running through lengthened booms.

Engines:	2 x DB 600
Armament:	4 x 2 cm machine guns, of which two were housed in a turret at the aft end of the fuselage.
Wingspan:	16 m (Project 3001)
Wingspan:	17 m (Project 3002)
Length:	11.1 m (Project 3001)
Length:	12.8 m (Project 3002)
Undercarriage:	inward retracting
Tailwheel:	non-retracting, swiveling

The unconventional power arrangement did not sit well with the conservative *Luftwaffe*, and was a contributing factor in its rejection of the project.

Heinkel Project

No details are known about Heinkel's project for a heavy fighter.

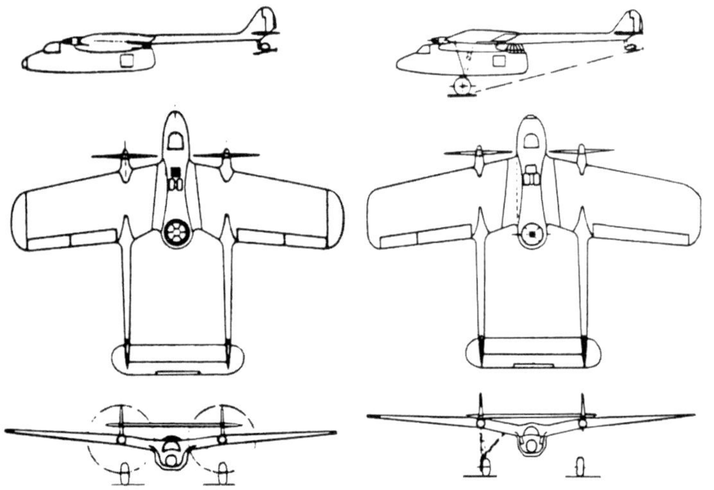

Gotha-Projekt P. 3001 Gotha-Projekt P. 3002

FW 57

The aircraft development program from 11/1/35 called for the FW 57 V1 to be powered by Rolls-Royce Buzzard engines in June 1936. The V2 and V3 were to follow in July and August 1936, respectively, and be powered by the DB 600. This meant that the FW 57 lagged some four months behind the Bf 110. More telling, however, was the fact that even at this early date, i.e. well before the first flight of any of the heavy fighter designs, a notation in the program stated that there would be no question of acquiring the type. A small pre-production batch of five aircraft was formally left in the program as a matter of routine, to be built between January and April 1937. On 1/1/36 the aircraft development program carried the memo that, based on a determination from 11/35, the FW 57 V1 would be powered by the DB 600 as well. Production deadlines remained unchanged. Thus, the RR engine was never installed. According to delivery plan no. 4 from 11/1/36, there was amazingly a call for a total of 13 machines to be built between June and December 1937. This intent had, however, disappeared by the time delivery plan no. 5 was issued on 4/1/37.

This all indicated that the RLM was having its doubts about the concept of the FW 57 even in its design phase. With a wingspan of 25 m, this machine was significantly larger than the Do 17 medium bomber at 18 m and the He 111 with approximately 23 m, and its weight was close to that of the He 111 with bombs. As its gun turret would have given it more drag than the bombers, the FW 57 would have lagged well behind them in view of the fact that it would have been powered by the same engine as the He 111. Due to its slower speed pursuit of single-seat fighters was out of the question, and in fact quite the opposite would have been the case—these could easily have flown rings around the FW 57 and gotten through to the bombers. Due to its early rejection by the RLM, the aircraft was never intensively tested, nor was any effort made on the part of Focke-Wulf to eliminate the type's teething troubles.

According to Schliephake's "*Flugzeugbewaffnungen*," Rheinmetall-Borsig proposed the 3 cm MK 101 as a project design for the FW 57 heavy fighter's nose armament.

The permissible fitted weight of the heavy fighter was what determined the caliber. This weapon corresponded to the idea of targeted single rounds fired over longer ranges, while the MG FF had a higher rate of fire at shorter combat ranges. Since the FW 57 never went into full-scale production, the gun was first installed in the Bf 110 B in 1938.

As a result of the type's limited significance, only a small amount of information has survived.

FW 57 V1, 1936 *Zerstörer*, 1937 Multi-Role Aircraft

Type: Twin-engined all-metal cantilever low-wing monoplane
Fuselage: All-metal monococque construction, glazed canopy and cockpit. Aft machine gun position (turret) and radio compartment located behind the wings.
Wings: Three-piece, triple-spar, all-metal monococque design
Flaps: Planned
Empennage: Cantilever, aerodynamically and statically balanced
Undercarriage: Two forked-type struts, hydraulically retracting rearward into bays in the engine nacelles, hydraulic brakes
Tail: Tailwheel, non-retracting
Engine: 2 x DB 600 D, maximum pressure altitude 4 km
Propeller: VDM, three-bladed
Flexible armament: Turret for 2 cm MG fitted as a mockup
Fixed armament: Not fitted, probably two fixed 2 cm MG planned
Ordnance: Not carried
Fuel: 1000 liters
Crew: 3 men
Wingspan: 25 m
Length: 16.4 m
Height: 4.1 m
Weight (on takeoff): 8.3 tons
Weight (empty): 6.8 tons
Payload: 1.5 tons
Wing loading: 113 kg/m²
Max. speed: 365 km/h at sea level
Cruise speed: 300 km/h at sea level
Landing speed: 110/km/h
Service ceiling: 9100 m
Range: 1550 km at sea level with 990 kg fuel

The FW 57 V1 flew for the first time in mid-1936 with Kurt Tank at the controls, and Tank assessed its flight handling characteristics to be average. It was later forced to make an emergency landing in swampy ground and was wrecked. It cannot be confirmed whether it was ever rebuilt or whether the V2 and V3 were finished. In 1937 there was an FW 57 at the edge of Focke-Wulf's factory airfield, to be flown by *Flugzeugbaumeister* Hans Sander to an unnamed military base. He rated the FW 57 as a heavy, cumbersome plane that was anything but a pleasure to fly.

The Fw 57 was rebuilt following its crash landing. (Focke-Wulf)

Hs 124, 1936 *Zerstörer*, 1937 Multi-role Aircraft

According to the Aircraft Development Program from 1/1/1936, three prototypes and five pre-production examples of the Hs 124 were to be built, all with the Jumo 210 engine. Construction of the two prototypes for the heavy fighter (V1 and V2) was planned for June and July 1936. The Hs 124 V3 high altitude long-range reconnaissance platform was to then follow in August of that year. These dates corresponded to those of the FW 57 and were four months behind the deadlines for the Bf 110. Acceptance of the pre-production versions was anticipated sometime during the period between June and August 1936, with field testing taking place between August '36 and January '37. Delivery Plan 4 from 11/1/36 called for delivery of a total of 13 Hs 124s between July 1937 and March 1938. On 3/21/37 the Hs 124 could no longer be found in Delivery Plan 5.

Photos reveal the existence of three different Hs 124s, all of which carried no registration markings. Of these, the one with the turret is generally classed as the Hs 124 V1, while the Hs 124 V2 has the glazed nose and BMW engines and the Hs 124 V3 lacks the clear nose section. As of this writing, however, the authors have been unable to find any official confirmation of these designations as they relate to the above-mentioned features.

The V1 was listed in the Manual of Aviation (*Handbuch der Luftfahrt*) as early as mid-1937 as the multi-role Hs 124. In 1939 the Aircraft Type Listing (*Flugzeug-Typenbuch*) showed the airplane with BMW 132 engines and corresponding to the proposal made by the Henschel Company (see below). It is conceivable that postwar writers drew their conclusions about the V1 and V2 from this and, when a photo later appeared showing an Hs 124 with solid nose and fixed weapons, turned it into the V3. It is entirely possible that these photographs show the same machine, but at different periods of time and with different nose sections.

The Hs 124 V1's canopy had an enclosed/unglazed center section and was open to the rear.

Hs 124 V1, 1936 *Zerstörer*, General Assessment

Tail:	retracting (based on contemporary literature)
Engine:	2 x Jumo 210 C
Fixed armament:	Turret planned for the nose (*A-Stand*) with two 2 cm MGs, none actually fitted. One MG 15 in the
Additional data:	see Hs 124 proposal

The Hs 124 V1 was flight ready some time in June 1936. As no photos of the airplane show it with registration or armament, it is assumed that these were applied immediately after construction. The authors have found no documental evidence on the plane's flight testing or on any potential weapons installation.

For reasons of flutter safety the tailplanes were set in a fixed position on the fuselage for all prototypes. The necessary adjustment of the elevators was achieved by "tipping" the aft section of the fuselage, which was attached at a pivot point. This feature is identified by a bubble on the aft fuselage directly ahead of the empennage.

With its turret, the Hs 124 V1 went a long way toward meeting the original ideas of the RLM. However, since production-ready turrets still required considerable developmental time, and their weight and drag significantly reduced an aircraft's performance, development broke off in 1936.

Hs 124 V2, 1936 *Zerstörer*, 1937 Multi-role Aircraft

Engine:	2 x BMW 132 Dc, NACA shrouds with split cowl flaps
Performance:	see Hs 124 proposal

According to the Aircraft Development Program of 1/1/36 the Hs 124 V2 was also to have been powered by the Jumo 210 and completed in July 1936. All known photos captioned as the Hs 124 V2, however, show it with BMW 132 engines. It is unknown whether the Jumo 210 was ever fitted. The first flight with BMW 132s is believed to have taken place in April 1937. Modification of the V1 to this configuration would have been possible at this time. The prototype shown in the photo is unarmed, but the vertical slit in the nose anticipates two pivoting 2 cm machine guns, one above the other, as armament. According to statements in the "*Luftfahrt Geschichte*," there were plans for fitting two semi-fixed machine guns in a split mount, with the pilot using the aircraft to roughly sight and fire the weapons and the gunner taking care of fine adjustments and making range calculations. There is no evidence that any weapon was fitted, however. In a later version offered by Henschel, an almost identical Hs 124 with an MG 15 in the *A-Stand* was seen (see Hs 124 proposal).

The canopy shape indicates that Henschel emphasized the bomber and reconnaissance roles with this prototype. The airframe was designed to carry an external payload.

Hs 124 V3, 1936 *Zerstörer* and High-Altitude Strategic Reconnaissance Aircraft, 1937 Probable Strike Aircraft

Engine: 2 x Jumo 210 C
Fixed armament: 4 x 7.9 mm MG or 2 x 7.9 mm and 2 x 20 mm MG in metal covered nose
Flexible armament: 1 x MG 15 in *B-Stand* planned, not fitted

According to the developmental program from 1/1/36 the Hs 124 V3 was to be built as a high altitude reconnaissance platform with completion in August 1936. Only one photo exists that can be attributed to the Hs 124 V3. This shows a two seat Hs 124 with Jumo 210, smooth-skinned metal nose, and what appears to be fixed armament. Some authors speculate that Henschel was attempting to shift over to the Bf 110's choice of armament. However, it is also possible that, since the *Luftwaffe* had already decided on the Bf 110 by this point, this was simply a show of the standard armament for the strike version. Ultimately it has not been proven that this is in fact the Hs 124 V3. As the nose section in this case is bolted on, it could also be the V1 with a swapped out nose section.

Hs 124, Bomber, Strike Fighter, Strategic Recce (1937 Proposal)

Type: Twin-engined all-metal cantilever low-wing monoplane
Fuselage: Three-section riveted monocoque construction using metal alloys, forward section with armament removable, glazed canopy and cockpit. Aft machine gun position (turret) and radio compartment located behind the wings.
Wings: Three-piece, smooth-metal skinned, box center section, triple-spar, tapered outer sections bolted to center section, monocoque design
Flaps: Hydraulically activated, fabric-covered, located between fuselage and ailerons
Empennage: Cantilever, with two end caps. Fabric-covered control surfaces, aerodynamically and statically balanced. Trim tabs adjustable in flight.
Undercarriage: Two forked-type struts, hydraulically retracting rearward into bays in the engine nacelles, fitted with "Ördinger" ring shocks,

One of the prototypes, possibly V2, was converted as the prototype for the multi-role version. (Heumann, Henschel)

One example of the low-level strike fighter was also built, possibly based on the V3. (Flieger, *Henschel)*

hydraulic brakes

Tail: Tailwheel pivoting, capable of being locked for landing, non-retracting

Equipment: Heating

Engine: 2 x BMW 132 Dc, NACA shrouds with split cowl flaps, maximum pressure altitude 2.6 km

Propeller: VDM, three-bladed, 3.3 m diameter, electric variable pitch

Flexible armament for bomber and reconnaissance: 1 x MG 15 on special mount in nose, 1 x MG 15 in aft dorsal position

Flexible armament for strike version:
1 x MG 15 in aft dorsal position

Fixed armament for strike version:
4 x MG 17 or
2 x MG 17 and 2 x MG FF

Ordnance for bomber version:
2 x 250 kg under the wing center section or 12 x 50 kg under fuselage and the wing center section or
2 x 250 kg under the wing center section and 6 x 50 kg under the fuselage with reduced fuel load

Ordnance for strike version:
42 x 10 kg under the fuselage
40 x 10 kg under the wing

Camera system for reconnaissance version: Zeiss RMK S 1818 with 50 mm focal length

Electronic systems: Long and short wave transmitters, receivers

Fuel: 1750 liters in three tanks in the wing center section, 800 liters in add'l tank in the fuselage spine

Oil: 2 x 55 liters aft of the engines

Crew: 3 men for bomber and reconnaissance versions, 2 men for strike version

Wingspan: 18.2 m

Length: 14.5 m

Height: 3.75 m

Wheel base: 5.2 m

Tailplane span: 5.24 m

Weights (Bomber/Strike/Recce)

Weight (on takeoff): 7.23 t/6.95 t/6.55 t)

Weight (empty): 4.25 t/4.2 t/4.25 t

Payload: 0.62 t/0.63 t/0.54 t

Bomb load: 0.6-0.9 t beneath the fuselage and wing for the bomber
0.42-0.82 t for strike version

Wing loading: 132.5 kg/m^2

Performance: Bomber, Strike (Reconnaissance)

Max. speed: 363 (380) km/h at sea level
410 (435) km/h at 3000 m
385 (410) km/h at 6000 m

Cruise speed: 320 km/h at sea level
370 km/h at 3000 m

Authorized Dive speed: 550 km/h

Landing speed: 100/km/h

Takeoff speed: 110 - 120 km/h

Climb rate: 4.4 (3.6) min to 2000 m

Climb rate: 9.3 (7.3) min to 4000 m

Climb rate: 17.1 (12.7) min to 6000 m

Service ceiling: 7900 (8500) m

Range: 1820 (1950) km at sea level with 1340 kg fuel
1860 (2000) km at 3000 m with 1340 kg fuel
2450 (2700) km at sea level with 1340 kg fuel
4200 km with extra tanks for recce version

Ranges given at 60% engine power

After the *Luftwaffe* decided in favor of the Bf 110 *Zerstörer*, Henschel offered the Hs 124 as a multi-role aircraft with the above data and features in type descriptions from 8/27/1937 and 8/27/1939 (the data is mainly derived from data sheet no. 71: Hs 124 from 8/7/1939). This, however, did not result in a contract for full-scale production.

The three variants were fundamentally the same. They differed only in the bomb arrangement and the nose. Bomber and recce versions had the Hs 124 V2's typical nose, which housed one MG 15. The bomber version carried a bombsight in its nose as well, whereas the reconnaissance version had instead a camera. The strike version had a metal-skinned nose with fixed guns, which was probably to have carried over to the Hs 124 V3. It was also possible that the bomber canopy was to have been used for the strike version, too. All three versions had a window in the floorboard ahead of the pilot to allow for ground observation. It cannot be determined from the descriptions whether the aft fuselage was to pivot as on the prototypes.

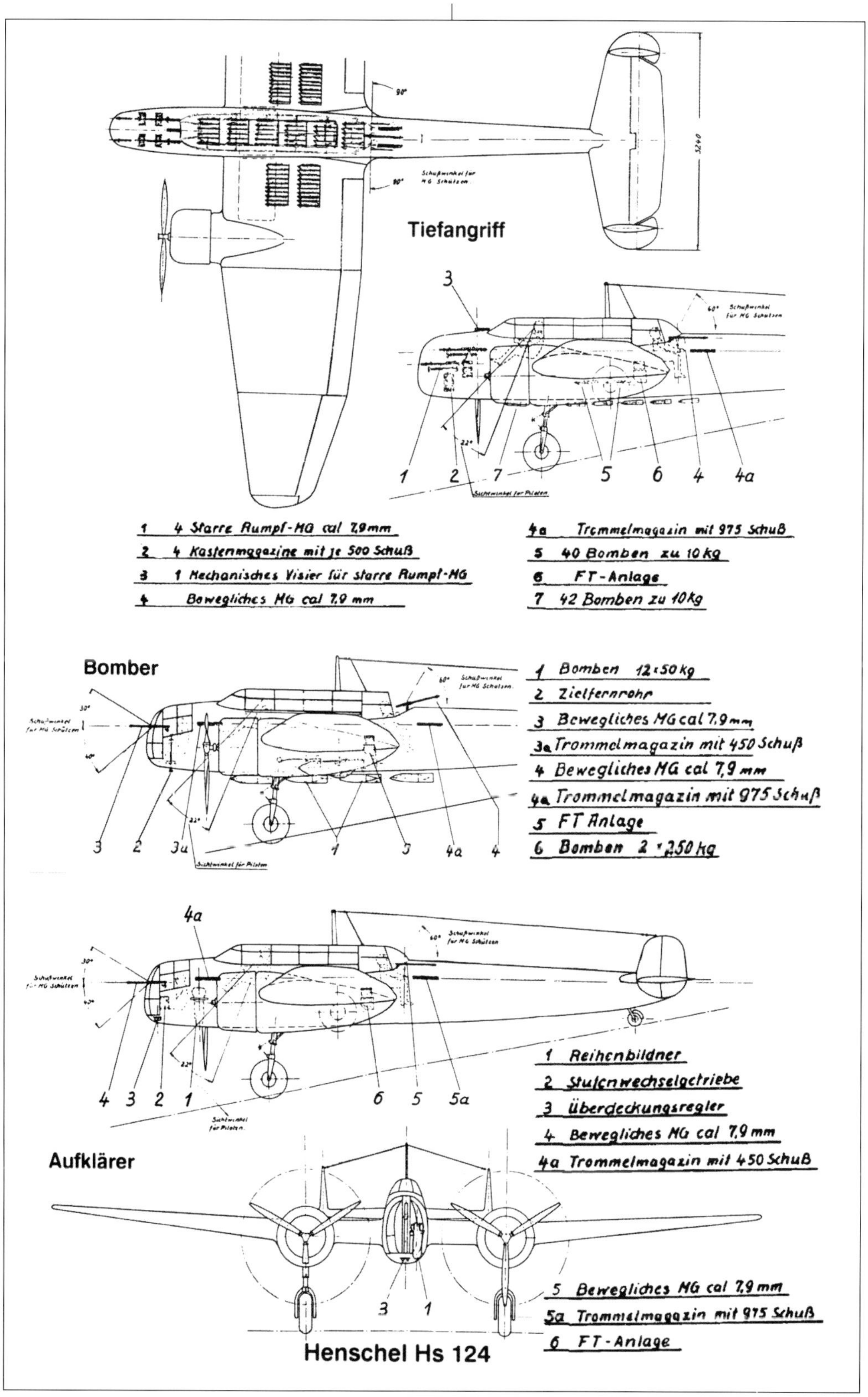

Drawings showing the Hs 124 as a multi-role fighter-bomber.

below: Drawings for a wind tunnel model of the Bf 109 done to provide an estimate of the increased drag caused by two engine nacelles.

opposite page, top: the Bf 110 V1 still with horizontal stabilizers braced, rectangular radiators and the round oil coolers beneath the wings. (Radinger)

Bf 110

After looking at different layouts in early 1934, the Bayerische Flugzeugwerke was awarded a contract in July of that year to develop a fighter destroyer and build three prototypes and five pre-production versions. It was planned to use the Jumo 210 for the powerplant, and first delivery was scheduled for 1936. In 1935 the 30 liter DB 600 engine also came under consideration and was initially to be installed in the Bf 110 V3.

Bf 110 V1

as Bf 110 B, but:

Vertical stabilizers:	More rectangular than on production models
Undercarriage:	Semi-retractable (main wheels not fully covered when raised)
Engine:	2 x Jumo 210s (probably B-models)
Radiators:	Beneath engines, rectangular type (not rounded as on Bf 110 B)
Propeller:	Two-bladed type
Fixed armament:	None
Flexible armament:	None

The Bf 110 V1 flew for the first time on 12 May 1936 with Dr. Hermann Wurster at the controls. It had a different nose profile than later series versions, as well as a deflective glazing over the aft crew position and rectangular rudders. When retracted, the main wheels protruded from the bay by about a tire width. The V1 was used for general flight and engine testing and went to the Travemünde test center in October 1937 with the registration D-AHOA.

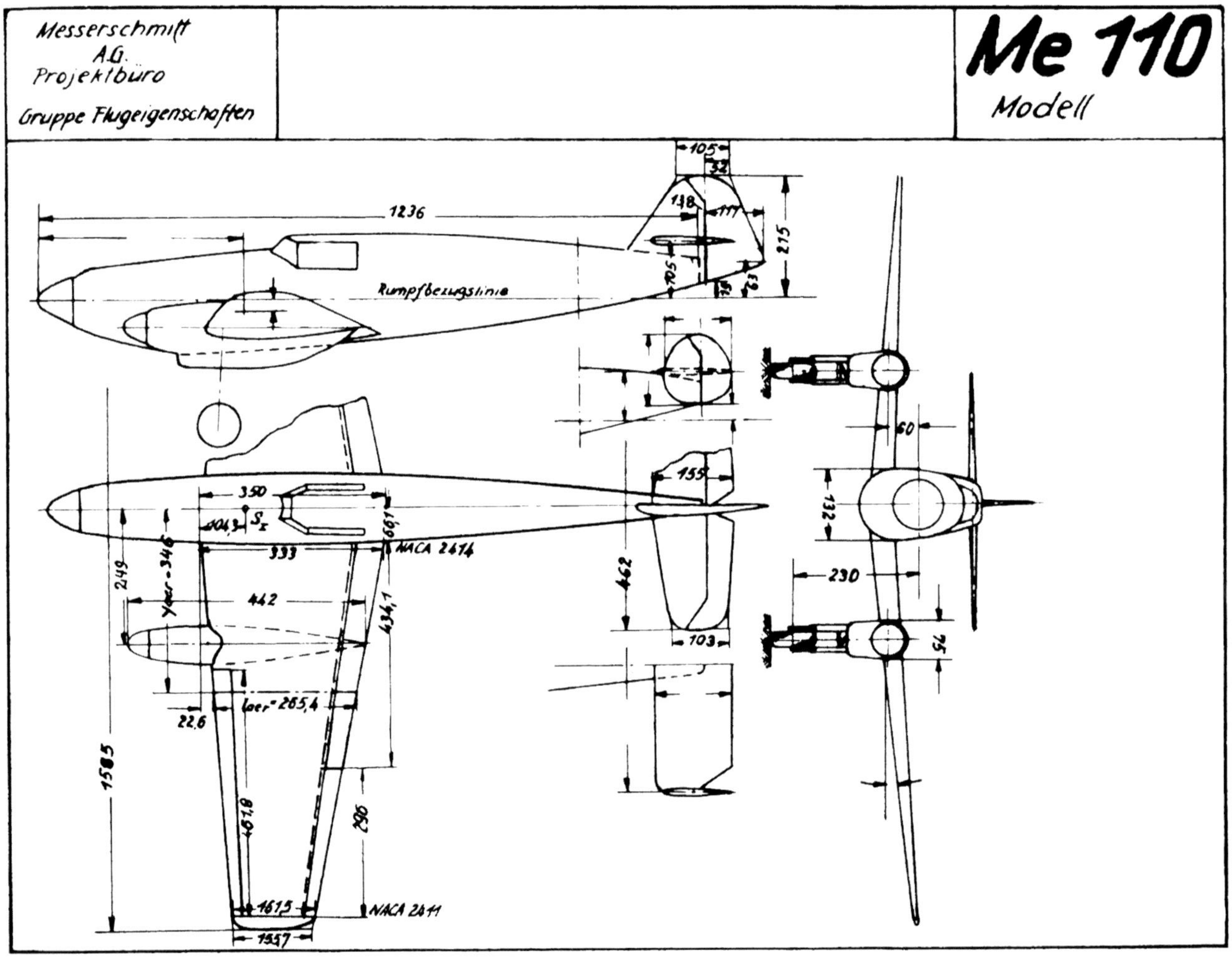

opposite page, bottom: The rectangular rudders are unique to this prototype. Notice the absence of undercarriage doors. (Radinger)

top: In this picture, the V2's rudders seem to have their final form.

below left: As with many other prototypes, the Bf 110 V2 initially flew without any type of registration codes.

below right: This V3 flight ended at the perimeter fence. The observer's hatch is similar to that of the Bf 110 G.

bottom: The nose was similar to both predecessors, but the engine nacelles have the design of the C-series. It was in this configuration that the evaluation of the DB 601 engine took place. (all photos, Radinger)

Bf 110 V2

The Bf 110 V2's maiden flight took place on 10/24/36. Initially tested at Augsburg, it was also demonstrated (on 1/23/37) at Rechlin. The trials spectrum was the same as for the V1. The rudders were different from those on the V1. No further details are known.

Bf 110 V3

Engine:	2 x DB 600s, later 2 x DB 601s
Propeller:	Three-bladed type
Fixed armament:	None
Flexible armament:	None

The Bf 110 V3 first took to the air on 24 December 1936. It was later given the registration code D-ATII and served as an engine testbed for the DB 600. Like those machines fitted with the Jumo 210, and unlike the subsequent Bf 110 C series with DB 601s, the radiators were fitted beneath the engines and only the oil cooler was underneath the wings (See also the Bf 162). The radiators initially had a rectangular shape analogous to the V1.

For years a photo has appeared in aviation publications purporting to show the Bf 110 V1 (see p. 20). The aircraft in the picture has the early nose and no registration code, to be sure, meaning that it is undoubtedly one of the early prototypes. However, the three-bladed propellers and the air intakes on the port side of the engine nacelles reveal the airplane in the photo to be powered by the DB 600, while according to data published in the aircraft developmental program the Bf 110 V1 was fitted with the Jumo 210. In addition, the undercarriage is fully retracted into the wheel bays. These details are appropriate for the Bf 110 V3.

The V3 flew as a test platform with Messerschmitt in 1940, powered by the DB 601. It was in this state that the machine was modified with the radiators later to be found on the Bf 110 C.

Bf 110 A *Zerstörer*, Heavy Fighter

The aircraft development program from 1/1/36 called for a pre-production series of seven aircraft in addition to the construction of the three prototypes. In July 1936 Messerschmitt was given a preliminary order for building nine Bf 110 A-0s. The seven aircraft, with factory numbers 910 (D-AISY), 911 (D-AAHI), 912 (D-AEDO), 913 (D-AISO), 914 (D-AOMY), 915 (D-AUDU), and 916 (D-AYGE) were built as Bf 110 A-0s and were identified in flight logs from August 1938 through February 1939. The two remaining ones (918 and 919) were built as Bf 110 Bs.

It is presently not known what type of armament was intended for the A-series. This was apparently never really established in the first place, since the matter of armament was not firmly established until just before the Bf 110 B-0 was delivered (July 1938). As testbeds, the Bf 110 A-0s were generally flown without armament. Aviation publications often show pictures of the Bf 110 A with a nose similar to that of the first prototypes. The Bf 110 V4 (A-0) D-AISY looks just like the Bf 110 B in photos.

Since the RLM had ordered the Bf 110 V3 with the DB 600 engine as early as August 1935 and prototype testing was expected to have concluded by March 1937, it can be assumed that the A-0 series was also to have been fitted with this engine type. The Jumo 210 was a stopgap solution necessitated by the fact that the DB 600 had technical problems, the RLM did not intend to acquire the carburetor for the Bf 110, and a seamless shift to the DB 601 was out of the question at the time.

The authors have been unable to determine which engine was ultimately planned for the Bf 110 A and why this series did not go into production. One aviation publication once claimed that the Bf 110 A was to have been fitted with the DB 600 and was abandoned when the engine did not materialize. Another theory is that it was to have been powered by the Jumo 210 B carbureted engine and was forced to give way to the Bf 110 B with the Jumo 210 G fuel-injected engine.

Those aircraft of the A-0 series actually built were given the Jumo 210 engines and spent their lives carrying out various tests. In delivery plans from 1938 onward the Bf 110 As were included with the Bf 110 Bs. This leads to the conclusion that the Bf 110 A differed only minimally from the Bf 110 B.

The fourth 110 (D-AISY) in a lineup with other A-series models. The aircraft closest to the camera has a retractable tailwheel. (Nowarra)

top: fixed guns of the Bf 110 B and C variants.

above: The initial use of the MG-FF can be identified by this "bump", a feature of the B-1 through C-3 variants.

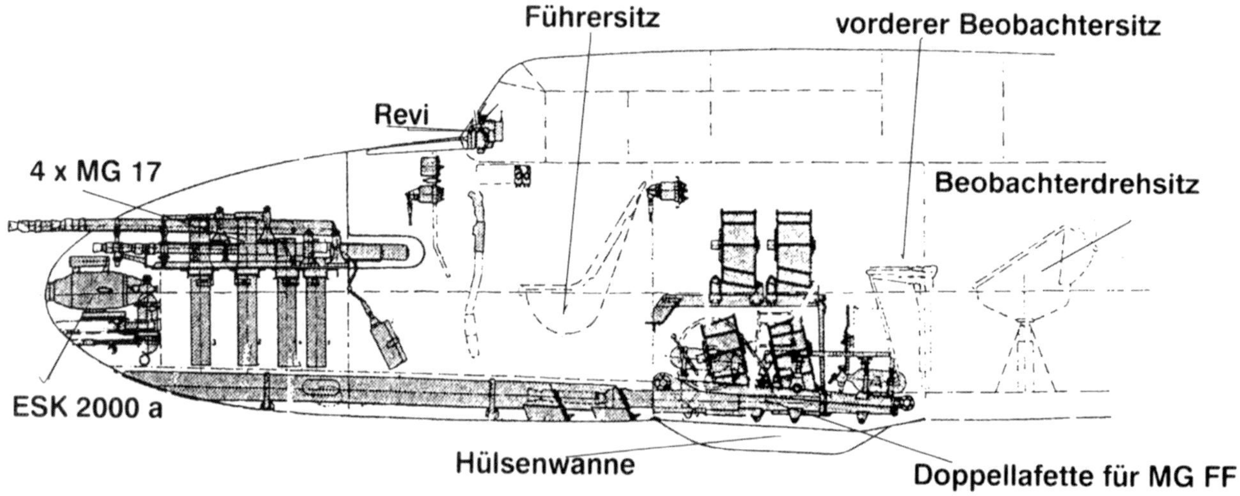

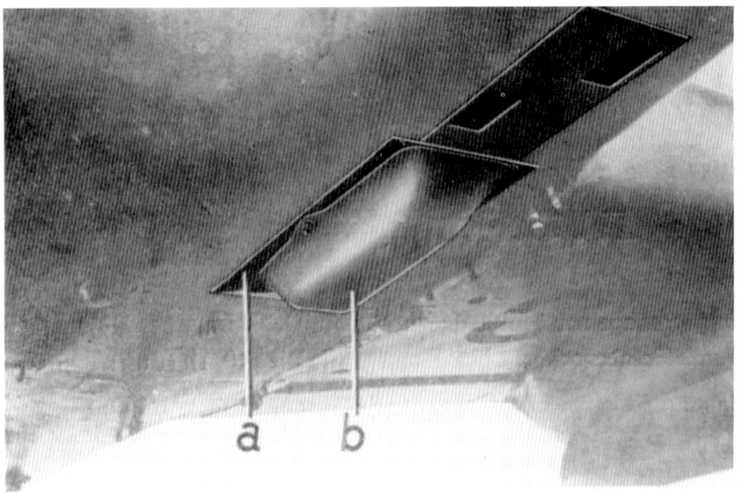

Abb. 13: Rüstzustand als Zerstörer

FuG III a U in the forward section of the observer's compartment.

Bf 110 B *Zerstörer*, Heavy Fighter

Description is basically derived from acceptance papers from the Jüterbog flight training school from November 1938:

Type: Twin-engined all-metal canti lever low-wing monoplane

Wings: Two-piece, attached to the port and starboard fuselage sides, duraluminum-metal skinned, box center section, single-spa with duraluminum I beam, duraluminum ribs, flush riveted, fully cantilever external skinning, connection points made of steel.

Fuselage: Monococque construction without bulkheads or longerons using a fully cantilever external skin, duraluminum metal skinned, flush riveted.

Canopy: Steel frame with plexiglass panels, 5-sectioned, sections 2 and 4+5 removable in emergency.

Pilot's compartment: Spacious with good visibility, fitted with an instrument panel forward and control levers port and starboard.

Gunner's compartment: Aft, swiveling seat, with fixed seat in center section for operating the radio equipment and MG FF.

Undercarriage: Two single-strut VDM type retracting rearward into bays beneath the engine nacelles, and a non-retracting tailwheel.

Horizontal control system: Cantilever, attached to the aft fuselage section

Horizontal stabilizer: All-metal, attached with three bolts and adjustable with the landing flaps.

Elevators: Three-section, fabric-covered and Flettner (trim) tabs and counterbalance.

Vertical control system: Two-piece, located at each end of the horizontal stabilizer

Vertical stabilizer: All-metal construction

Rudder: Fabric-covered with aerodynamic counterbalances, weighted, and Flettner (trim) tabs

Landing aids: Automatic slotted wing ahead of ailerons, landing flaps inside next to the ailerons

Engine: 2 x Jumo 210 G

Performance: 2 x 730 hp

Oil cooler: Located under wings

Radiator:	Located under engines
Propeller:	VDM-VS, 3.1 m diameter
Fixed armament:	4 x MG 17 2 x MG FF
Flexible armament:	1 x MG 15 on pivot arm mount
Electronic systems:	FuG III a U, Peil G V, FuBl 1, Ei V 4
Autopilot:	K 4 ü 1
Fuel:	2 x 360 + 2 x 250 = 1220 liters in wings
Oil:	2 x 35 liters aft of the engines
Crew:	2 men
Wingspan:	16.9 m
Length:	12.07m
Height:	3.9 m

Wheel base:	4.6 m
Tailplane span:	4.5 m
Main wheel:	815 x 290
Tail wheel:	350 x 135
Tail wheel:	Retractable
Weight (on takeoff):	5.65 t)
Weight (empty):	4.1 t
Wing loading:	147 kg/m^2
Max. speed:	480 km/h at 3900 m
Cruise speed:	432 km/h at 3900 m
Landing speed:	140/km/h
Takeoff speed:	110 - 120 km/h
Dive speed:	600 km/h
Climb rate:	1000 m/min
Service ceiling:	approx. 8000 m
Endurance:	3 - 3.5 hrs
Range:	1200 - 1400 km

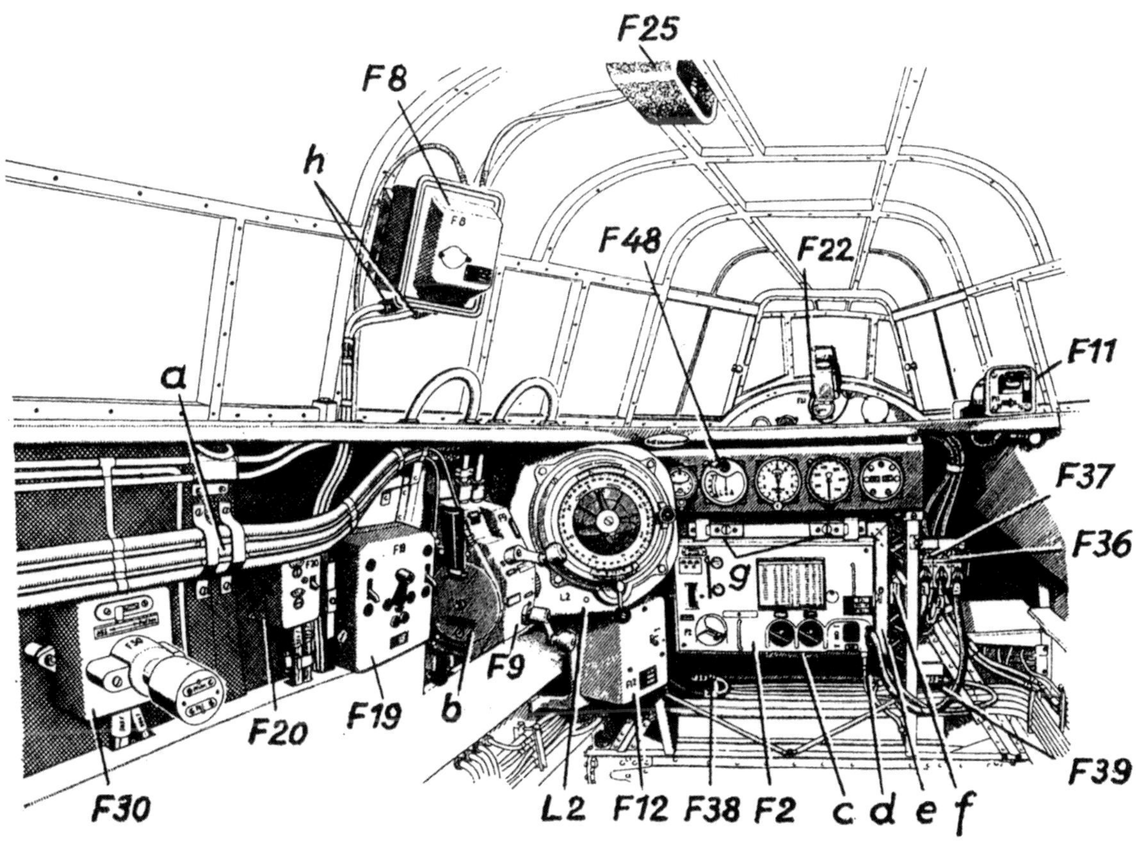

vorderer Beobachterraum

FuG III a U in the aft section of the observer's compartment.

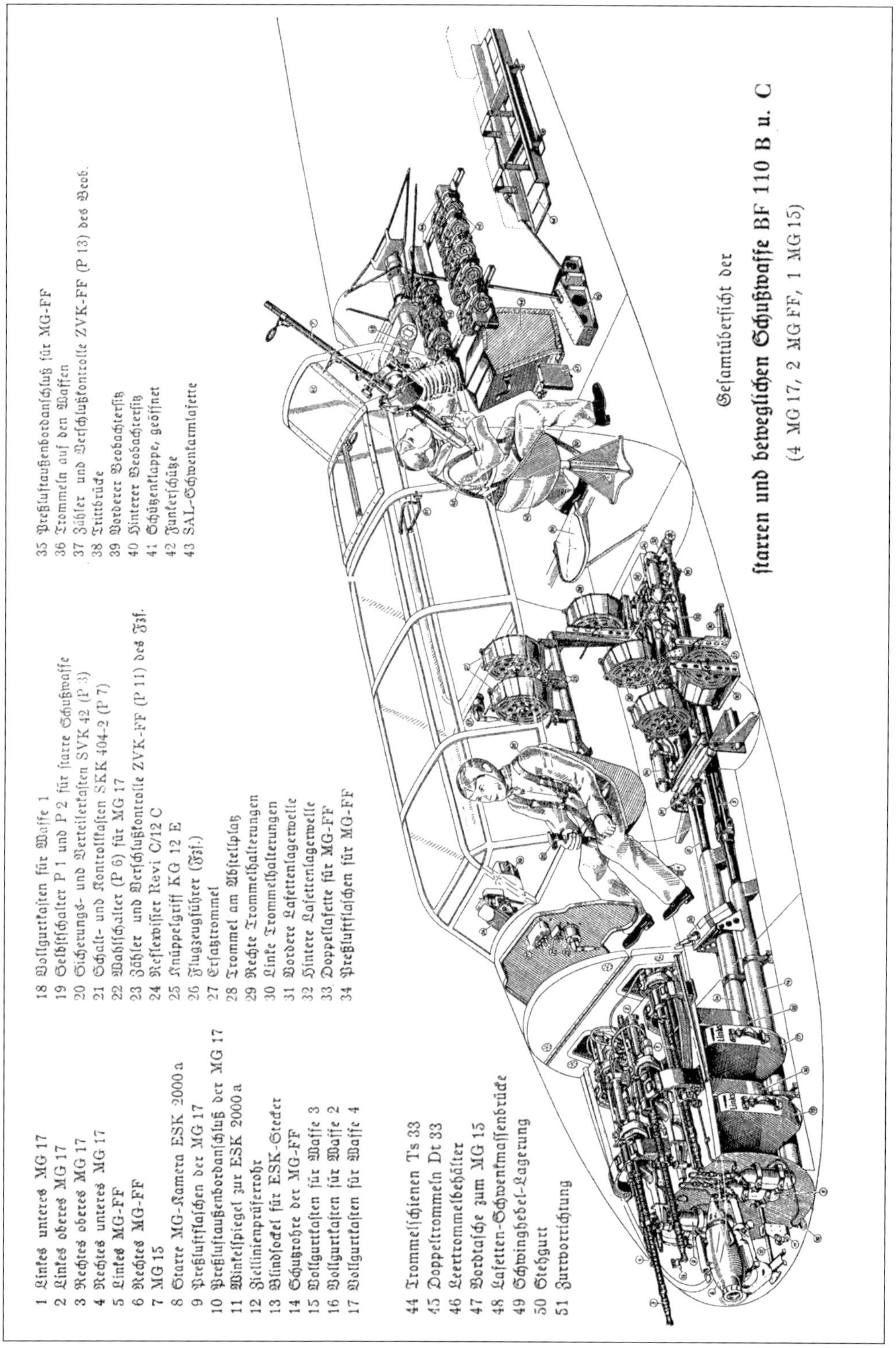

Note: The K 4 ü automatic pilot was, according to L.Dv.T 241/1, only installed on a production basis beginning with the Bf 110 E and was a distinguishing characteristic compared to the C-series. The type sheet that covers versions up to the Bf 110 E-3, however, mentions the Bf 110 B-1 having a K 4 ü 1. It is possible that by this time the B-1 had been equipped with the device for training purposes.

As the early DB 601 was still quite prone to problems, it was decided to begin production of the Bf 110 with the Jumo 210 G using the designation Bf 110 B.

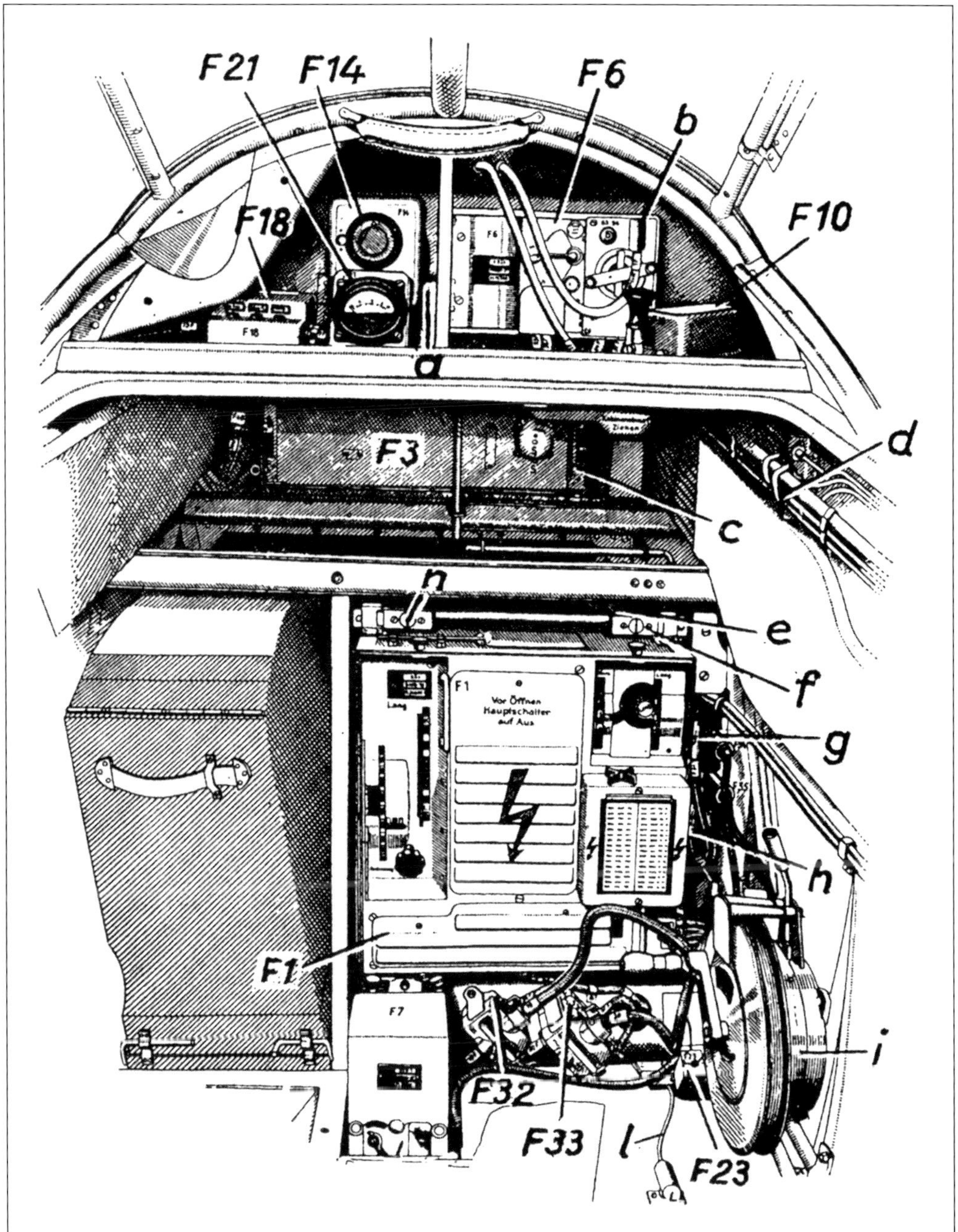

hinterer Beobachterraum

FuG III a U im hinteren Beobachterraum

This less powerful engine appeared sufficient for training purposes and as a higher risk business venture. Due to the anticipated startup of DB 601 production the planned number of Bf 110 Bs was intentionally kept low.

Unlike the FuG X used later, the FuG made use of two fixed antennas, which ran from the antenna mast to the two rudders on the Bf 110 B and C-1.

Bf 110 B-0 *Zerstörer*, Heavy Fighter

As the Bf 110 B.

In official documentation from 1938/39 the only differences noted were between the Bf 110 B and C. Some time around 1940 a further delineation of the type took place. In accordance with delivery plan no. 7 from 1/1/38 deliveries of the Bf 110 B were to begin in April 1938 with two aircraft, and would end following the construction of 86 aircraft of this type in February 1939.

below: Bf 110 B and C instrument panel. (Radinger)

bottom: Notice the two antenna wires associated with the FuG III of the Bf 110 B. (Petrick)

In the flight logbook of Dr. Hermann Wurster, the Bf 110 B V7 (*W.Nr.* 917) is mentioned for the first time on 4/19/38 which, like 918, was part of the batch of nine pre-production aircraft ordered in July 1936 and was the prototype for the B series. At around the same time the pre-production versions 918 through 920 were completed and designated Bf 110 B-0.

Bf 110 B-1 *Zerstörer*, Heavy Fighter

As Bf 110 B, Production version.

The Bf 110 B-1s built by the Gotha Company were, with few exceptions, used predominantly at heavy fighter training schools. Those aircraft made by BFW (Mtt Augsburg) were utilized as testbeds, as well as in the training role.

Aircraft Procurement Program No. 11, flight logs, and loss reports show that Messerschmitt Augsburg built seven Bf 110 As, a single Bf 110 B V7 prototype, three pre-production B-0s, and 22 Bf 110 B-1s. In addition, Gotha produced 62 Bf 110 B-1s.

Aircraft Procurement Program No. 11 listed the total number of Bf 110 Bs with Jumo 210 as 95, not including the prototypes V1 through V3. Other documentation reveals that the number 95 also includes the seven Bf 110s, which may possibly have been rebuilt to Bf 110 B standards.

above: This Bf 110 B was probably built by GWF and was still flying in its original identification coding after the camouflage change in 1940. (Petrick)

left: Colors and the central MG 15 on this Bf 110 B reveal post-delivery wartime modifications. (Mankau)

Bf 110 B-2

The Bf 110 B-2 and Bf 110 B-3 designations also pop up occasionally in aviation-related publications, claiming that these are Bf 110 B-1s modified after the fact for the flight training role. The authors have found no basis in fact for these claims.

Bf 110 C *Zerstörer*, Heavy Fighter

Description is basically derived from acceptance papers from the Jüterbog flight training school from November 1939:

As Bf 110 B, but

Engine:	2 x DB 601 A
Performance:	2 x 1000 hp
Oil cooler:	Located under nacelles
Radiator:	Located under wings
Propeller:	VDM-VS, 3.1 m diameter
Fixed armament:	4 x MG 17 2 x MG FF
Flexible armament:	1 x MG 15 on pivot arm mount
Electronic systems:	FuG III a U, Peil G V, FuBl 1, Ei V 4
Life raft:	Possible, but not carried as a rule
Fuel:	2 x 375 + 2 x 260 = 1270 liters in wings
Oil:	2 x 35 liters aft of the engines
Crew:	2 men
Wingspan:	16.276 m
Length:	12.07m
Height:	4.1 m
Wheel base:	4.6 m
Tailplane span:	4.5 m
Main wheel:	875 x 320
Tail wheel:	350 x 135
Tail wheel:	Non-retractable
Weight (on takeoff):	6.75 t 6.95 t overloaded
Weight (airborne):	6.04 t
Weight (empty):	4.57 t
Wing loading:	153 kg/m^2
Max. speed:	530 km/h at 3900 m
Cruise speed:	465 km/h at 3900 m
Landing speed:	140/km/h
Takeoff speed:	110 - 120 km/h
Dive speed:	700 km/h
Climb rate:	15 m/sec
Service ceiling:	approx. 8500 m
Endurance:	2 - 2.25 hrs
Range:	750 - 800 km

The Bf 110 C was the first production version with the 30 liter engine the RLM had been asking for since the summer of 1935. In order to increase maximum speed even more the wingtips were clipped in comparison with those of the Bf 110 B series. However, the very first C-series still had the long wings, and it wasn't until series production was underway that the variant was delivered with the shorter wings. The intake on the right engine was also modified shortly after production began in order to increase the maximum pressure altitude. Moving the radiators from under the engine to a point beneath the wings helped to offset the heavier weight of the DB engines, and was probably better from an aerodynamic standpoint as well. The higher speed in comparison with the Bf 110 B caused a significant drop in the range since the larger engines had a greater fuel consumption rate. This trend continued throughout the war; aircraft were fitted with more powerful engines and their ranges shrank. More equipment and additional armor plating tempered increases in speed somewhat, but in the main it was the range that suffered.

Discounting minor modifications to the gunner's hatch, the fuselage designs of the B and C series were identical.

Bf 110 C-1, *Zerstörer*, Heavy Fighter

Documentation from 1938/39 only differentiated between the Bf 110 B and C ver-

The dark greens, the two antennae, and the old MG 15 configuration betray this aircraft as a C-1. (Petrick)

sions. Sometime around the end of 1939 there occurred an additional classification category of the series to reflect differences in electronic equipment and armament. The C-1 corresponded to the original C. Delivery Program No. 10 from 1/1/39 showed that Messerschmitt in February 1939, Miag and Gotha in April 1939, and Focke-Wulf in May 1939 were to have begun production of the Bf 110 C. In actual fact, however, Focke-Wulf for example did not initiate deliveries of the type until August 1939.

Bf 110 C-1/B, Dive Bomber

As Bf 110 C-1, but
Ordnance: 1 x SC 1000 or
2 x SD 1000 or
2 x SD 500 kg or
2x SC 250 kg carried on
2 ETC 500/IX b underneath the fuselage
Revi C 12/D

In October 1940 (as manufacturers were already beginning production of the Bf 110 E), D. (Luft) T. 579/6 was published, which contained the description and installation/removal guidelines for ordnance. According to this document, the Bf 110 C-1, C-2, and D-0 variants could be converted into dive bombers in short order by simply fitting ordnance and racks. Conversion required the skills of a four-man team. The designation of these aircraft then became Bf 110 C-1/B, C-2/B, and D-0/B.

With two 500 kg bombs, the Bf 110 C-1/B was designed to fly at altitudes between 300 and 5000 m, ranges of 255 to 350 km, and speeds of 445 and 320 km/h, taking into account 1/2 hr of combat.

The number of modified aircraft must have been small, since on 25 June 1940 the General Staff had rejected the idea of converting airplanes in the field, instead opting for conversion at the repair facilities. As the

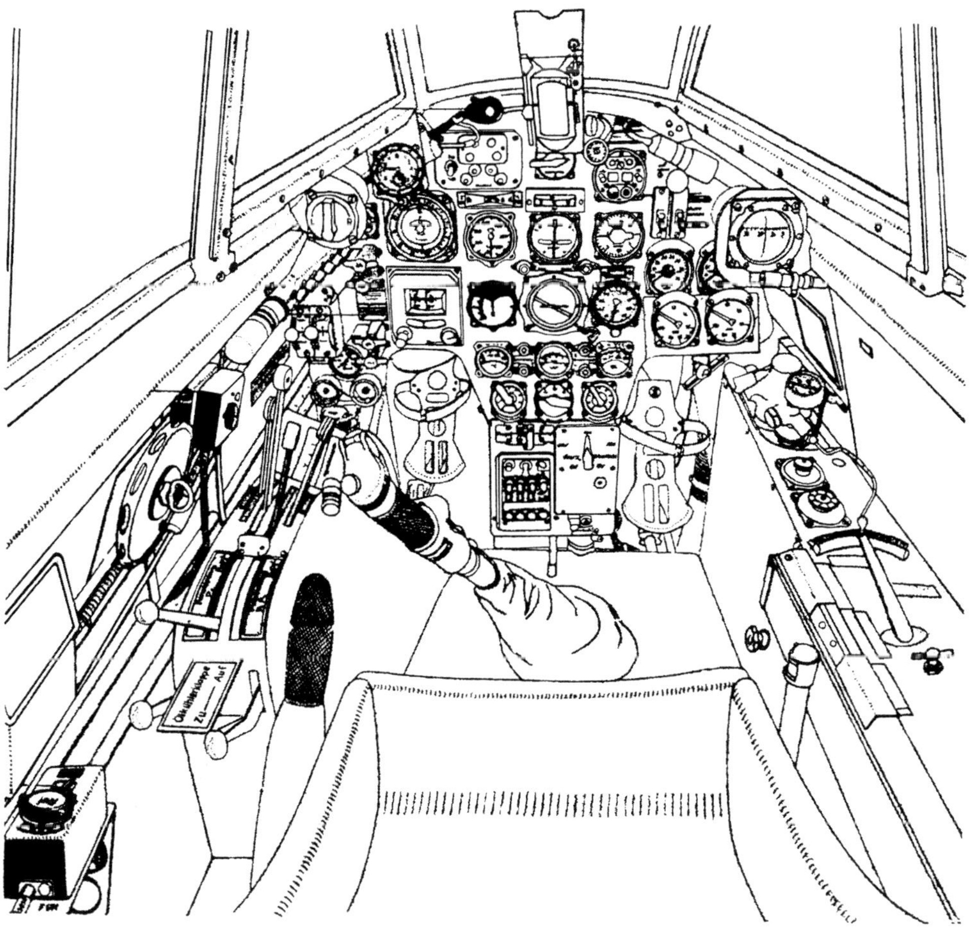

Instrument panel of the bomber version.

undercarriage was too weak to support the increased load in the long run, the C-7 series appeared in place of these conversions and went a long way toward fulfilling the General Staff's desires for the converted Bf 110 C-1 through C-4.

Bf 110 C-1/U1

See Bf 110 C through E, tow plane for the Me 321.

Bf 110 C-2, *Zerstörer*

As C-1, but
Electronic systems: FuG X in place of FuG III a U.

According to the C-Amt's program from 10 January 1940, the four manufacturers built 359 Bf 110 C-2s from October 1939 through July 1940. Orders for Focke-Wulf, Miag, and Gotha were originally higher, but according to a Messerschmitt AG memorandum dated 22 June 1940, effective 1 May 1940 all unbuilt aircraft of this series were to have been delivered as C-4s.

For the Bf 110 C-2 as well as all subsequent variants, the FuG X fixed antenna ran from the antenna mast on the canopy to the right rudder. The antenna to the left rudder was dropped. Some aviation publications suggest that the aft gun compartment was modified in comparison with the Bf 110 C-1. Some photos, however, show a single antenna in conjunction with the offset mounted MG 15. From this, it can be concluded that on delivery the Bf 110 C-2 had the same layout as the old model and was only modified at a later date (see Bf 110 C-4)

The gunner's compartment is now a little bit roomier.

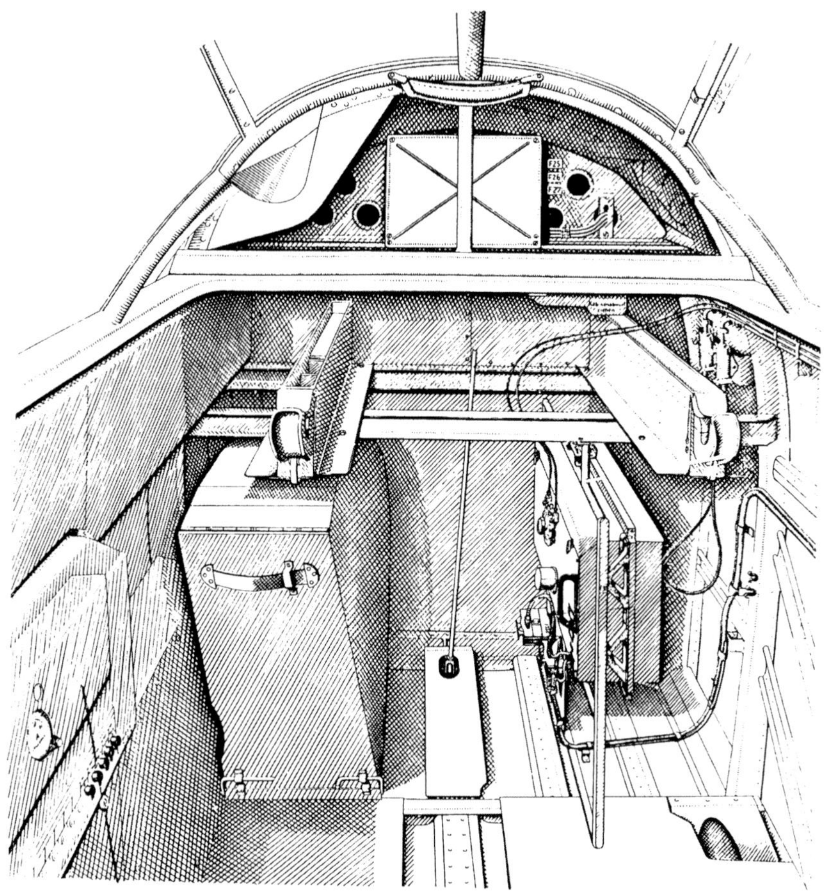

hinterer Beobachterraum

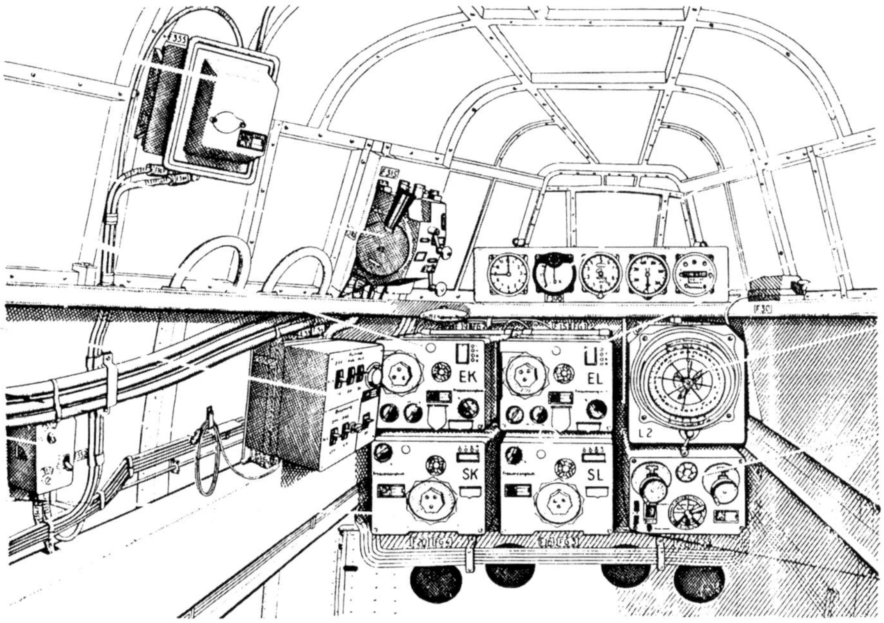

Diese FuG X Geräte sah der Funker ab der Baureihe C-2

Bf 110 C-2/B, Bomber

As C-2, but
Ordnance

According to the C-Amt program, from 10 January 1940 a single Bf 110 C-2/B was built by Miag in July 1940 immediately prior to the production line switching from the C-2 over to the C-4.

Bf 110 C-2/U1
See Bf 110 D-3/U1

Bf 110 C-3, *Zerstörer*

As C-1, but
Armament: MG FF "M" in place of MG FF

According to the C-Amt programs, the Bf 110 C-3s were not new builds. This seems logical, since the FuG X radio system was available before the MG FF "M." However, in the RLM variant listing the type was mentioned, and in loss reports there appear about 20 Bf 110 C-3s. These include factory numbers, which lie between those of the C-1 and, in some cases, are identified with those of the C-1. It is therefore likely that Bf 110 C-1s were, for example, retrofitted with the MG FF "M" when in the shop for major repairs, where they were awarded the designation Bf 110 C-3.

Those aircraft fitted with the MG FF had a pronounced bulge on the underside of the center fuselage, typical of the Bf 110 C-1 and C-2. This was lacking with the MG FF "M."

The MG-FF "bump" and a single antenna indicate that this aircraft is a Bf 110 C-2. (Petrick)

right: MG 15 on a pivoting arm mount and the gun trough were features of the original defensive armament configuration. (Fleuret)

below: That this is a C-4 is indicated by the lack of the MG-FF "bump"

Bf 110 C-4, *Zerstörer*

As C-2, but

Armament:	MG FF "M" in place of MG FF
Flexible armament:	1 x MG 15 on cross-member mount

Originally the C-4 series was not planned, as production at all four manufacturers was expected to shift from the Bf 110 C-2 directly to the Bf 110 D-0. Several events occurred in the spring of 1940, however, that necessitated continued production of the C version. First, an improved version of the MG FF (the MG FF M) appeared on the scene. Second, fuel pumps for the auxiliary tanks on the Bf 110 D-0 could not be had in sufficient numbers, and third, a requirement was issued for the Bf 110 to be able to carry bombs on two ETC 500 racks underneath the fuselage. The General Staff therefore ordered continued production of the Bf 110 C at a 3/5 ratio of the total output capacity. According to a Messerschmitt memorandum dated 22 June 1940, approximately 120 aircraft originally planned as Bf 110 C-2s were to be delivered as C-4s due to the new machine guns. A further 80 were to have been built as "C-4s with bombs" in place of Bf 110 D-0s between July and August 1940. These, however, were later designated as Bf 110 C-7s. Since the RLM delivery figures are lower than those contained in loss reports, and the loss reports the aircraft are called Bf 110 C-4s built as C-2s, the Bf 110 C-2s must have been brought up to C-4 standard after the fact.

Some aviation publications assert that the Bf 110 C-4 was the first variant to have armor reinforcement. This was not the case with new-built machines (see Bf 110 C through E, strike aircraft).

Initial deliveries of the Bf 110 C-4 began at the same time a new camouflage pattern was introduced. Up until the spring of 1940 both fighters and *Zerstörer* planes were supplied in the colors of *Schwarzgrün 70*, *Dunkelgrün 71*, and *Hellblau 65*, with the green shades completely covering the fuselage sides. Sometime around May 1940 the fuselage sides were sprayed in *Hellblau 65*, and one of the two green colors was replaced by *Grau 02*. Splotches of *RLM 02* were often applied to break up the light blue fuselage sides. Since available paint was often used up and aircraft in the field were not always immediately repainted, it was common to find both camouflage schemes side by side in the different *Geschwader* throughout the summer of 1940. However, it can be assumed that as a rule those aircraft up to the Bf 110 C-2 variant were painted in the 70/71/65 pattern, and the C-4 and subsequent versions had the light blue fuselage sides.

According to a manual (L.Dv. 578/1, supp. 1, Feb 1941), the defensive armament was modified for the Bf 110 E. The manual fails to mention whether previous variants had this modification, which involved moving the MG 15 from one side to a center mounted configuration. Nevertheless, photographs show that the Bf 110 C-4 and earlier versions (even the Bf 110 B) flew with the new layout. Originally the MG 15 was mounted on a pivot arm. In order to provide the greatest possible field of fire the gun could be swiveled on the arm to the right and left. The gunner sat on a special rotating seat and could stand up if he wanted to fire downward. For this he had a free standing belt attached

The new MG 15 configuration was also retrofitted to older aircraft. (Petrick)

to the floorboard. Operating the weapon required him to raise the gunner's canopy section, which then acted as a wind break. During normal flight the gun was stored in a trough located on the starboard fuselage side. This arrangement did not prove especially effective and, beginning in the spring of 1940, airplanes started appearing with the canopy section missing altogether and the gun locked in the center. Starting some time around the summer of 1940 the gun was mounted in the center and the aft canopy section had a rounded cutout, enabling the gunner to fire even with the canopy closed (albeit with an extremely limited field of fire). The new configuration could be found on virtually every Bf 110 by mid-1940; probably, it was fitted both at the factory as well as in the field units. Part of the reconfiguration included a cover plate for the gun trough, which was fitted to some aircraft unpainted. As a rule, the old camouflage pattern and the old weapons arrangement went hand in hand, but there were also combinations of old pattern and new gun configuration as well. The new camouflage scheme was normally paired with the new gun configuration, yet some photographs show the new pattern in conjunction with the retrofitted trough cover plate. It can safely be assumed that minor modifications such as these were not exclusively reserved for changes in variants, but depended more on what was available at the time.

Bf 110 C-4/B Bomber

As C-7.

Gotha supplied four machines under the designation Bf 110 C-4/B. These were later carried on the books as Bf 110 C-7s, however (q.v.).

above: Aufklärungs-gruppe 10 *flew this Bf 110 C-5. This aircraft shows a cover plate fitted in front of the turbocharger intake on the right engine nacelle. (Petrick)*

below: In individual cases, the Bf 110 C-5 was also fitted with the aft-firing armament typical of the E-3. (Ries)

below right: Only 12 Bf-110 C-6s were built. (Petrick)

Bf 110 C-5, Reconnaissance

As C-2, but
Camera: Rb 50/30 in place of MG FF "M"

The Gothaer Waggonfabrik, according to the C-Amt program dated 1 November 1940, built 90 Bf 110 C-5s from May to October 1940, with a further 10 reputedly following by December. These numbers are borne out by a modifications directive (Bf 110 No. 174 from 10 January 1942, calling for the cameras to be fitted with electrical heating), which also states that 100 were built. BAL, however, only took on 75.

The Bf 110 C-5 chronologically followed the Bf 110 D-1 (D-4) reconnaissance version. Apparently the Bf 110 C-5's range suited the recce pilots for operations in the tactical reconnaissance role. The Do 17 P and Ju 88 D could be employed for strategic long-range reconnaissance missions.

Bf 110 C-6, *Zerstörer*

As C-4, but
Armament: 1 x MK 101 in place of 2 x MG FF "M"

In mid-1939 an MK 101 was installed in Bf 110 B-1 *W.Nr.* 928 (D-AAPY) and demonstrated at Rechlin on 7/3/39. Despite Hitler's orders, the type did not go into production in any great numbers. To be sure, on 22 June 1940 a Messerschmitt memorandum addressing a switch in Bf 110 production mentioned the idea of 99 Bf 110 C-6 aircraft being built at Gotha from May through October. According to C-Amt minutes from 10 January 1940, the Gothaer Waggonfabrik had built six examples using the Bf 110 C-5 reconnaissance version as a basis during the July/August time frame of that year. This document also claims that a further six had been built earlier, for a total of just twelve Bf 110 C-6s completed. The Bf 110 C-6 failed in part because the Bf 110 was, as a whole, ineffective in the *Zerstörer* role. By the time the Bf 110 C-6 was ready for production, production was switched over to the bomber as a direct consequence of the type's lack of success as a *Zerstörer*. In addition, the Bf 110 was increasingly finding use in the night fighter role. Although on 27 September 1940 the General Staff—without having combat reports available—called for production to continue at a rate of ten per month and on 18 October at a rate of six per month, on the 26th of that month the *Generalluftzeugmeister* decided that continued production was no longer feasible. The field did not quite know what to do with their machines, so the Gen-

above: The cover of the Bf 110 G-2/R1's MK 101 was significantly smaller than that of the Flak 18. *(Petrick)*

left: MK 101 with the cover removed. (Mankau)

eral Staff rejected any further production of the type on 21 November 1940. On 1 May 1941 there were five operational Bf 110 C-6s in the inventory of SKG 210, but these saw little or no combat use.

On 12 March 1942 thoughts again turned to using the MK 101 in the Bf 110 G for the purpose of engaging four-engined heavy bombers. By this time the entire inventory of MK 101 was fully committed to the Hs 129, and only the Flak 18 was available for this purpose.

Bf 110 C-7, Bomber

As C-4, but

Ordnance:	1 x SC 1000 or 2 x SD 1000 or 2 x SD 500 kg or 2 x SC 250 kg on 2 ETC 500/IX b under fuselage
Undercarriage:	Strengthened wheels and tailwheel, conversion carried out only at repair facilities

According to the C-Amt program from 10 January 1940 the Bf 110 C-7 was only built at the factory in small numbers beginning in July 1940, and overlapped production of the Bf 110 C-4 and D-1 through D-3. However, it too was converted at repair facilities from older versions of available planes, as evidenced by loss reports and comments found in type overviews. In a C-Amt program drawn up by the Mtt AG on 14 October 1940, it was designated as the "C-4 with bombs." The Bf 110 C-7 designation replaced the original designation of Bf 110 C-4/B in order to avoid confusion, just as with the Bf 110 D-0/B. It appears that all Bf 110 Cs with ETC hardpoints were ultimately lumped together collectively under the designation of Bf 110 C-7.

The Bf 110 C-7 was drawn up because on 25 June 1940 the General Staff had rejected the idea of refitting Bf 110s in the field with bomb racks, and instead called for production versions (including the expiring C-series) to be modified for bombing. The role of the Bf 110 C-7 was assumed by the Bf 110 D-3, which could carry external auxiliary tanks, as soon as sufficient numbers of fuel pumps became available.

Drawings from the Bf 110D manual. The dual antennae were carried over from an earlier basic drawing.

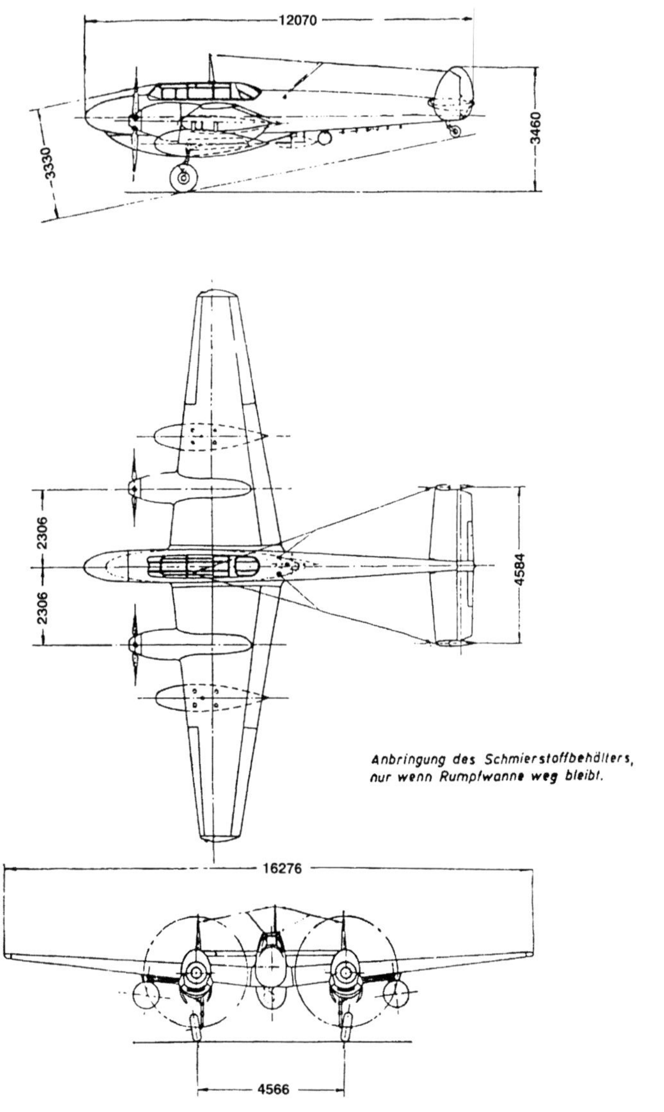

Bf 110 D

According to L.Dv.T. 2413/1 (Design) from November 1940, the Bf 110 D series had the following additional features compared with the Bf 110 C: extra fuel and oil tanks, life boat, 110% engine power output, reinforced main gear tires and enlarged tail gear with a larger tailwheel.

Differentiation was made between *Rüstzustand I* with underfuselage fuel tank (*Dackelbauch*, 1050 liter capacity fuel tank plus 106 liter oil reservoir) and external wing tanks (2 x 900 liter) and the *Rüstzustand II* without the belly tank, but having external wing tanks and an oil reservoir (75 liter) underneath the fuselage.

For a time, the D series was produced alongside the C. In mid 1940 the ratio was 2:5 D versions to 3:5 C models. The reason for parallel production was a temporary shortage of fuel pumps that prevented the exclusive manufacture of the D series. Once this shortage was rectified, production of the Bf 110 C-4 and C-7 was terminated in favor of the Bf 110 D-3.

The *Dackelbauch* has been cited in publications as being dangerous, as remaining gas fumes could supposedly cause an explosion. This allegedly was the reason behind its replacement. The authors do not concur with this argument. Firstly, no RLM discussions made mention of this potential, whereas such discussions were common for other problems encountered in the field. Secondly, the *Dackelbauch* was also used with the Bf 110 E-1. Thirdly, the fumes could have been eliminated by blowing in nitrogen. This would have necessitated the development and construction of a system, something which would have been possible had there been a need. In the authors' opinion, the *Dackelbauch* - like the 900 liter tank - disappeared once there was no longer a need for the Bf 110 in the long range heavy fighter role. Sometime around June of 1940 the General Staff increasingly saw the Bf 110 in the role of a fighter bomber, obviating the need for the use of the *Dackelbauch*.

With regard to the 900 liter fuel tanks, it must be said that it could be used with all Bf 110 D and E series airframes and, in principle, with the F and G as well. Publications almost always, and erroneously, associate the tanks with the Bf 110 D-3 variant.

Bf 110 D-0, *Zerstörer* with Extended Range

As C-4, but	
Engine:	2 x DB 601 A
Performance:	2 x 110 hp
Fuel:	additional *Dackelbauch* and external wing tanks
Oil:	106 liters in *Dackelbauch*
Tires:	875 x 320, reinforced
Tailwheel:	465 x 165
Takeoff weight:	7.1 tons 9.3 tons in overloaded configuration
Gross weight:	7.65 tons (w/o external wing tanks)

This series had been planned as early as the spring of 1939 and was carried under the designation Bf 110 D/R1 and D-0/R1. Plans called for a total production run of 260 Bf 110 D-0s through June of 1940 (Mtt: 138, FW: 66 and Miag: 66). Messerschmitt built the Bf 110 D-0 starting in March 1940, where it replaced the Bf 110 C-2. On 3/26/40 the first Bf 110 D-0 (*W.Nr.* 3134 / SE+ZR) was shipped to Rechlin for testing.

On 6/22/40 Messerschmitt assigned the license producing firms the responsibility of supplying Bf 110 C-4/B and Bf 110 D-0/B airframes in place of the Bf 110 D 0 version. For its own part, Messerschmitt intended to switch over to the Bf 110 D-0/B starting in July.

Focke-Wulf handed over its first Bf 110 D-0, which had immediately followed the Bf 110 C-4, to the *Luftwaffe* on 7/28/1940. According to Focke-Wulf documentation, during the period from 7/28 through 8/31/1940 33 Bf 110 D-0s were delivered to the *Luftwaffe*. FW subsequently began supplying the Bf 110 D-3.

Messerschmitt AG wrote to Miag on 6/12/40 instructing the company to supply 24 Bf 110 D-0s as early as July in accordance with the RLM program. In September of that year Miag was expected to deliver the last 16 out of a total of 66 Bf 110 D-0s as well as start production of the Bf 110 D-1 with the first ten airframes. Miag, however, wouldn't have been able to initiate production of the D-0 until September due to a lack of parts. As a result, production of the Bf 110 D-0 never got underway at that site.

According to Delivery Plan 17c from 7/3/40, Messerschmitt was only expected to build 103 Bf 110 D-0s. However, six of these were converted to Bf 110 D-1s (reconnaissance) and another into a Bf 110 D-0/B bomber in April 1940. A further 14 machines were modified as Bf 110 D-0/Bs in May.

In the *C-Amt* program of 10/14/40 the six reconnaissance aircraft appeared as Bf 110 D-4s and the Bf 110 D-0/Bs of Messerschmitt as Bf 110 D-2s. According to *C-Amt* Program No. 18 from 11/1/40, by this date 83 Bf 110 D-0s had been built exclusively by Messerschmitt, with no further production anticipated. The D-0s supplied by Focke-Wulf were, in the main, carried under the designation Bf 110 D-1.

The auxiliary tanks were hidden beneath the fabric covering. The Bf 110 D-0 was originally fitted with the older pivoting arm gun mount and carried green camouflage upper surfaces.

Bf 110 D-0/B, Bomber with Increased Range

As D-0, but

Ordnance:	Up to 2 x SD 1000 under fuselage
Fuel:	External auxiliary tanks only (no *Dackelbauch*)
Oil:	75 liters in drop tanks

The first Bf 110 D-0/B, which could swap out its belly tank for two ETC 500 racks (*W.Nr.* 3167), was built at Messerschmitt in April 1940 and sent to the Rechlin Test Center. Another example (*W.Nr.* 3175) followed in May. In June 1940 the General Staff ordered that a portion of the new Bf 110s rolling off the assembly lines were to be equipped with the ETC 500. As an emergency measure Messerschmitt consequently fitted 13 Bf 110 D-0s (*W.Nr.* 3321-3324, 3336-3344) with ETC 500s, removing the belly tanks in the process. These machines were designated as Bf 110 D-0/Bs. According to Delivery Plan 17c from 7/3/40, Messerschmitt was to have followed with an additional 75 D-0/Bs until replacing them on the assembly line with the Bf 110 E-1. These, however, were delivered under the designation Bf 110 D-2.

Based on an FW note from 9/26/40, FW also supplied Bf 110 D-0/Bs, which differentiated from those then being delivered from Messerschmitt (probably Bf 110 E-1s) in three key areas: they had no performance-boosted engines; only two armored plates on the forward fuselage; and the smaller oxygen system with eight instead of twelve bottles. The FW machines later carried the designation Bf 110 D-3.

In the C-Amt program from 14 October 1940 the Bf 110 D-0/B did not appear as its own version, meaning that its numbers were carried under those of the D-0, D-2, and D-3.

Bf 110 D-1, Reconnaissance with Increased Range, renamed D-4

A quota/actual comparison study of those Bf 110 aircraft delivered by Messerschmitt drawn up in April 1940 listed three BF 110 D-1 reconnaissance aircraft without fuselage gondola (*W.Nr.* 3149, 3150, and 3151) and three Bf 110 D-1 reconnaissance aircraft with gondola (*W.Nr.* 3161, 3162, and 3163), all of which were delivered in April 1940. In later loss reports these factory numbers popped up under the designation Bf 110 D-4 (q.v.). A letter from the Messerschmitt AG to Miag dated 6/12/40 (see Bf 110 D-0) reveals that the reconnaissance variant was originally to have been delivered as the D-1 based on the Bf 110 D-0. As the fuel pumps could not be obtained, the program change of 6/14/40 saw the Bf 110 C-5 reconnaissance version substituted in place of the Bf 110 D-1. On 6/20/40 the Rechlin Test Center published a flight route leaflet of a Bf 110 D-1 with drop tanks but lacking the belly tank and external ordnance. In the minutes from the RLM meeting of 7/26/40, which established the variant designations, the D-1 is not listed.

Bf 110 D-1, *Zerstörer* with Increased Range

As D-0, but

Fuel:	External auxiliary tanks only (no *Dackelbauch*), (also with 2 x 300 liter wing tanks)
Oil:	75 liters in drop tanks

According to a type overview the Bf 110 D-1 was a heavy fighter with increased range, like the D-0, but lacked the belly tank. Based on the C-Amt program of 10 January 1940 Focke-Wulf built 17 Bf 110 D-1s in July 1940 and four in August. According to Focke-Wulf's monthly reports there were 16 built in July 1940, and a further 17 Bf 110 D-0s were reported as supplied in August. Those factory numbers listed in FW documents as being assigned to Bf 110 D-0s for the most part appear in loss reports as Bf 110 D-1s, with some of the later ones as D-3s even. This is the result of the reclassification, which saw the Bf 110 D-0s produced by Focke-Wulf redesignated to D-1s, while the original D-1s were renamed as D-4s. The difference between the C-Amt's data and the delivery reports can be traced back to the fact that the August 1940 Focke-Wulf monthly report available to the authors listed all Bf 110s supplied as D-0s, of which the last were built as D-0/Bs and then later assigned the designation D-3.

Bf 110 D-1/U1

This variant was, according to information provided by Gerd W. Heumann and subsequent authors, a night fighter with the "*Spanner*" infra red system. These authors, however, have not found any evidence for this designation. Nevertheless, *Spanner* systems were installed in Bf 110 Cs or Ds, as several photographs bear out.

Bf 110 D-2, *Zerstörer* or Bomber with Increased Range

As D-0/B, but

Ordnance:	(without *Dackelbauch*) up to 2 x SD 1000 under fuselage
Fuel:	External auxiliary tanks only, or *Dackelbauch* in place of bombs
Oil:	75 liters in drop tanks or 106 liters in *Dackelbauch*

The Bf 110 D-2 was originally to have been produced under the designation Bf 110 D-0/B, but at the request of the General Staff was renamed on 7/26/40 and built at Messerschmitt. Unlike the Bf 110 D-3, the belly tank had the option of being fitted or left off. According to the C-Amt, between July and September 1940 there were 73 aircraft built, of which 21 were D-2/Ns. There was no clear demarcation between the Bf 10 D-0 and the D-2 based on factory numbers.

Field units, many on their own initiative, sometimes replaced the two extra tanks beneath the wings with a single fuel tank underneath the fuselage. This measure was rejected by the General Staff, as it meant that bombs could no longer be carried. There was no special designation for this modification. It was applicable to both the D-1 and the D-3.

Bf 110 D-3, Bomber with Increased Range

As D-0/B, but

Ordnance:	Up to 2 x SD 1000 under fuselage
Fuel:	External auxiliary tanks only (no *Dackelbauch*)
Oil:	75 liters in drop tanks

Since on 6/25/40 the General Staff called for 3/5 of the Bf 110 Ds to be fitted with ETC 500s and only 2/5 with the *Dackelbauch* belly tank, a variant was created that from the outset would not be fitted with the *Dackelbauch*. This was designated the Bf 110 D-3 on 7/26/40. From documentation available to the authors it was not clear at what factory number FW actually switched over to the Bf 110 E-2. Loss reports, in conjunction with the factory numbers the RLM assigned to FW, indicate that the D-3 remained in production at FW three months longer than originally planned and, instead of the planned 107 aircraft, FW ultimately built 180 Bf 110 D-3s.

Due to the parallel production of the D-3 and the E-1 some of the measures introduced for the E series were also applied to the Bf 110 D-3. One example is Focke-Wulf's application of two armored plates in the nose on some Bf 110 D-3s. The extended pitot tube, not introduced until the E series, also occasionally cropped up on the Bf 110 D-3.

Without cockpit heating, the Bf 110 D-3 was not a pleasant machine to fly for the pilots of ZG 1 *during the winter of 1942/43. Armor plating and sand filters have been retrofitted. This airplane also exhibits the large pitot tube typical of the E-series model. (Petrick)*

above: It was unusual to find an experimental plane at a competing aircraft manufacturer with the sub-designation of /U1. (Mankau)

below: The periscope sight proved to be a superior solution for remotely operated weapons.

Bf 110 D-3/U1, Testbed

As D-3, but

Flexible armament: Remote controlled Arado FA 13 weapons system with 2 x MG 81 Z.

In the log books of H. Beauvais (Rechlin Test Center) and Kröger (Arado), the Bf 110 D/U1 was mentioned with the factory serial number 3708 (RB+GL) and served as a testbed for the remote controlled Arado weapons system. This factory number came from a batch of Bf 110 D-3s. The authors are unaware of any other identification of the Bf 110 D-3/U1 or Bf 110 D/U1 in conjunction with the Arado weapons system, but Arado did make use of two additional Bf 110 D-3s (*W.Nr.* 3364 and 3685) and a Bf 110 C-1 or C-2 (*W.Nr.* 2105). Nowarra categorizes the latter as a Bf 110 C-2/U1. The authors have no proof of this. This designation would also overlap that applied to the tow aircraft for the Me 321. As official listings from the C-Amt show 3708 without the U1 suffix, this may possibly simply be an unofficial Arado designation.

Bf 110 D-4, Reconnaissance with Increased Range

As C-5, but

Fuel: External auxiliary tanks and belly tank

Oil: 75 liters in drop tanks

According to Delivery Plan 17 c from 3 July 1940 the Bf 110 D-0s with factory numbers 3149 (NO+DN), 3150 (NO+DO), 3151 (NO+DQ), 3163 (KE+UG), 3164 (KE+UH),

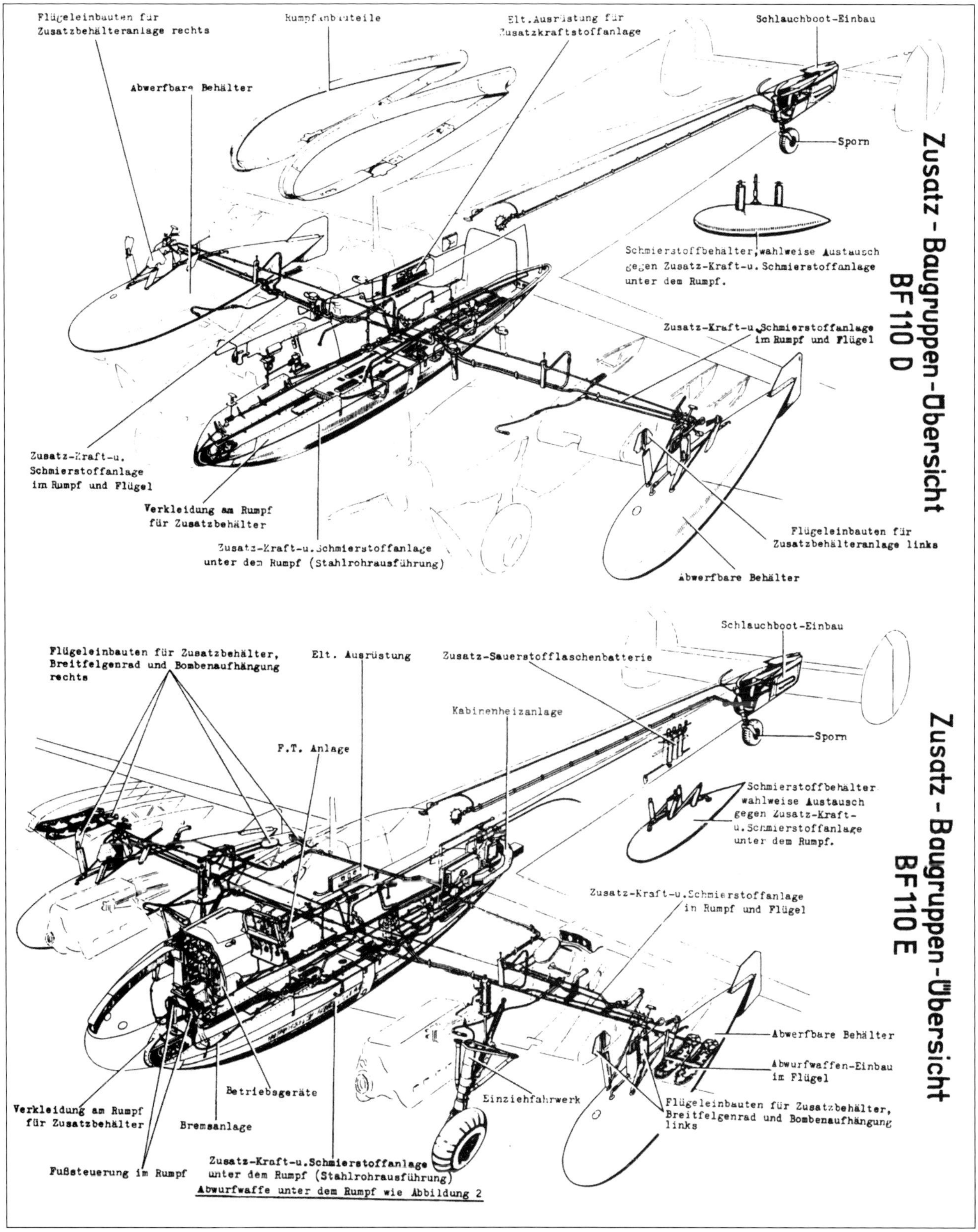

and 3165 (KE+UI) were modified to Bf 110 D-1s at Messerschmitt in April 1940. The first three were reconnaissance aircraft without belly tanks, and the remaining three were fitted with the *Dackelbauch*. The six serial numbers also showed up in the modification instructions (Bf 110 No. 174 from 10 January 1942, according to which the cameras were to be fitted with electric heating). Based on several loss reports, the *Luftwaffe* carried these as Bf 110 D-4s, and they were not used in reconnaissance units. The C-Amt's program from 14 October 1940 also designates these six recce planes as Bf 110 D-4. The background behind this reclassification may be that on 26 July 1940 the *Generalluftzeugmeister* assigned new designations for the Bf 110 D-0 and D-0/B at the request of the General Staff.

Bf 110 E

The Bf 110 E-1 was conceived in early 1940 as a follow-on development of the Bf 110 D-9 and was to be built by all four manufacturers starting in August/September 1940. When in mid-1940 a part of the production switched over to bombers and the consequent redesignation, there emerged two different sub-variants: the Bf 110 E-1 and the Bf 110 E-2. Unlike the Bf 110 D, these had hardpoints for four bombs beneath the wings only, as well as improved equipment in the form of automatic pilot, heating, and increased oxygen capacity. The new heating system could be recognized by the rectangular air intakes on the upper part of the forward nose and on the right side of the fuselage. These intakes enabled one to differentiate between the Bf 110 E and previous models. The Bf 110 E had the Revi C/12 D sight, which unlike the C/12 C could simultaneously function as a bombsight and was installed in all Bf 110 bombers. The cross member mount for the MG 15 fitted into the Bf 110 E was much lighter than the pivot arm mount and permitted use of the defensive armament with the gunner's canopy closed, but it did reduce the arc of fire. Along with the rear-firing gun, the observer's layout was also altered. Whereas before there had been two separate seats available for the functions of radio operator and gunner, this was now replaced by an oblong lightweight seat. A removable strap acted as a backrest for take-offs and landings.

During the production run of the Bf 110 a flutter brake on the tailwheel was introduced, but this was also fitted to those aircraft already delivered, to include earlier models. The flutter brake can be recognized as a triangular scissors attached to the strut. The pitot tube also changed during production, from a small hook-shaped version affixed beneath the wing to a larger one at about the same position along the wingspan, but jutting well forward of the leading edge. The new pitot tube also saw use on some Bf 110 D-3s being built under license by other manufacturers at the same time. Once production of the Bf 110 E was underway its armor was increased. Externally the most notable change

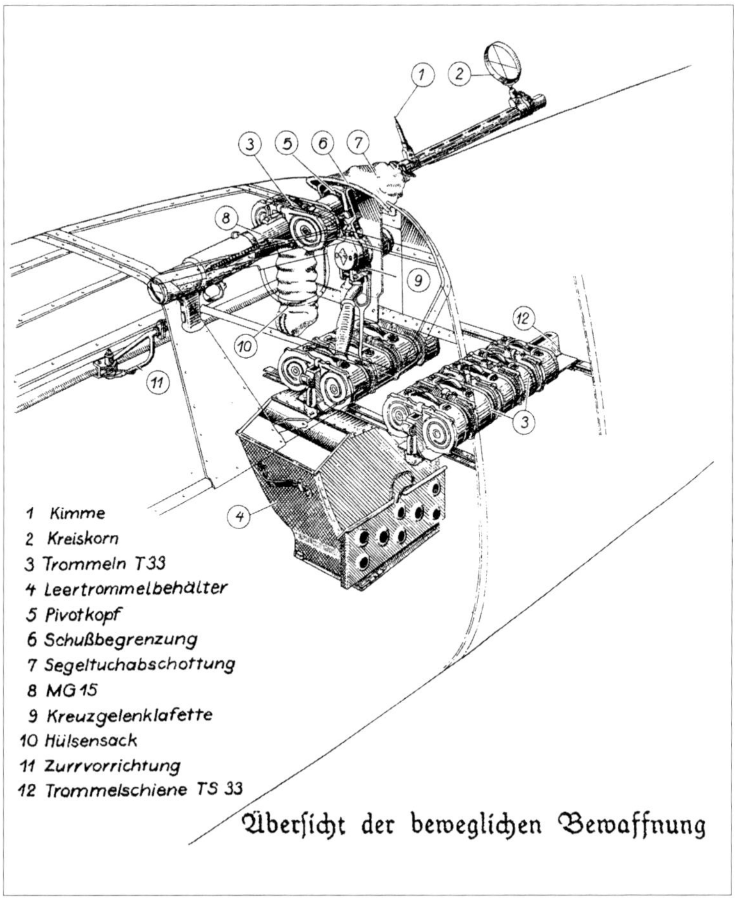

below: This defensive armament configuration was, according to the manual, applicable to the E-series, but it also appeared on earlier models.

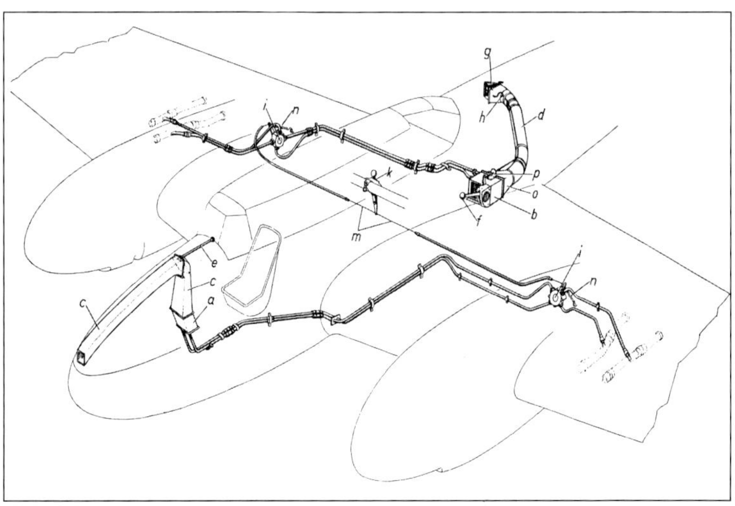

bottom: Heating was reintroduced on the E-series version.

left: Air intake for the heating system, deflector plate in front of the engine air intake, and two ETC 50 racks beneath the outer wings were all characteristics of the E-series Bf 110s. This particular aircraft is lacking the additional armor plating. (Petrick)

below left: Even on aircraft already delivered, with the introduction of armor plating the compressed air bottles were transferred from their unprotected location to the armored area beneath the floorboard of the observer. The observer was also given a longer seat.

below: Shortly after initiation of production, the stubby pitot tube of the Bf 110 E was replaced by one protruding well ahead of the wing leading edge. Unusually, this Messerschmitt-built Bf 110 E-2/N (W.Nr. *3996, DJ+MN) was fitted with both. (Mankau)*

was the armored windscreen. The armor was also retrofitted to earlier models already delivered. As the starboard engine apparently sometimes drew in exhaust gases, a deflector plate was fitted ahead of the air intake some time during the E's production time frame. During the Bf 110 E's production, the Bf 109 E versions with the MG FF as engine cannon were dropped, and the open spinner was replaced by a closed one. The spinners for the Bf 109 E and the Bf 110 E were the same, so that those on the Bf 110 E initially had the openings for the MG FF and were later capped off.

right: On the bomber version of the Bf 110 E, the bomb control panel box was located beneath the instrument panel.

Abb 3: ASK R ZSK 244 A und Wahlschalter für „Rumpf-" und „Flügel-Bomben" unter dem Instrumentenbrett des Führers

below: This Bf 110 E-1 "Dackelbauch" *operated with 5./NJG 1 at Deelen in February 1941. (Petrick)*

Bf 110 E-1, *Zerstörer* or Bomber with Increased Range

As D-2, but

Fixed armament: Revi C/12 D reflective sight
Flexible armament: 1 x MG 15 on cross member mount
Ordnance: (minus *Dackelbauch)*
2 x SC 250 or
2 x SB 500 or
1 x SD 1000 or
2 x SC 1000 + 1 x SC 250 on 2 ETC 500/IX b under fuselage additional 2 x 250 kg bombs under outer wings
Autopilot: K 4 ü
Equipment: Cockpit heating
Increased oxygen (12 bottles vice 8)
Longer observer's seat compared to the two separate ones in the Bf 110 C and D
Fuel: Auxiliary wing tanks only, or *Dackelbauch* in place of bombs
Oil: 75 liters in drop tanks, or also *Dackelbauch*
Main wheel: 935 x 343
Tail wheel: 465 x 165
Weight (on takeoff): 7.5 t
9.3 t overloaded

Like the D model, the Bf 110 E-1 series was delivered initially in the 2/5 with *Dackelbauch* and 3/5 without. Due to its limited effectiveness, but primarily because the *Dackelbauch* variant was unable to carry the bombs demanded by Hitler, the *Dackelbauch* was abandoned. The capability of being fitted with this *Dackelbauch* was the most prominent feature of the Bf 110 E-1 series. According to the C-Amt program dated 1 November 1940 (corrected edition from 1/7/40), in the period from September 1940 to July 1941 a total of 320 airframes of this variant were to have been produced at Messerschmitt, with 305 of these being the Bf 110 E-1/N. Loss reports show roughly the same totals, but with the number of Bf 110 E-1/Ns being much lower, as the high octane fuel could not be obtained in sufficient quantity.

Bf 110 E-1/U1, Night fighter

was, according to information provided by Gerd W. Heumann and subsequent authors, a night fighter with the "*Spanner*" system; the authors have been unable to find any evidence of this (See Bf 110 D-1/U1). As the Bf 110 E-1/U1 designation would most certainly have not been applied twice, and there is documentation showing that it was used for another sub-variant, these claims must be considered false (See Bf 110 C through E, tow plane for the Me 321)!

Bf 110 E-1/U2

was, according to information provided by Gerd W. Heumann and subsequent authors, a fighter bomber with increased payload, or a command and control aircraft with a three-man crew (additional control officer); the authors have been unable to find any evidence of this. The lightweight seat in the radio compartment would have permitted carrying a third crewman without the need for any type of modification.

Bf 110 E-2, Bomber with increased range

As E-1 bomber, but
Fuel: Auxiliary wing tanks only, (no *Dackelbauch*)
Oil: 75 liters in drop tanks

The only difference between the E-1 and the E-2 was the optional fitting of the *Dackelbauch* on the E-1, whereas the E-2 as a rule could not carry it. Thus, a Bf 110 E-1 without *Dackelbauch* looked no different from a Bf 110 E-2. *Zerstörer* and night fighter units used them side by side.

According to the C-Amt program from 1 November 1940, numbers of Bf 110 E-2s built totaled 212 at Miag's Braunschweig plant, 122 at the Gothaer Waggonfabrik, and

*left: This Miag-built Bf 110 E-2 (*W.Nr. *4008, DJ+MZ) on its factory transfer flight, still carrying the factory coding and a 300 l drop tank beneath the fuselage. The machine has already been fitted with supplemental armor and has the tailwheel flatter damper. (Petrick)*

*below: Seen behind this Miag-built Bf 110 E-2 (*W.Nr. *4495, CD+MO) is its intended successor, the Me 210. (Nowarra)*

Two 300 l fuel tanks could also be carried on the fuselage ETC racks for ferry flights. (Petrick)

94 at Focke-Wulf. Messerschmitt was to have completed just 47 Bf 110 E-2s, as the Bf 110 E-1s were rolling off the assembly lines at the time. Deliveries of the 475 Bf 110 E-2s were expected from November 1940 through November 1941. Loss reports show about 73 of these factory serial numbers assigned to Focke-Wulf for the D-3 version. Apparently Focke-Wulf produced the D-3 series three months longer than was intended in November 1940 and ended up delivering only 21 Bf 110 E-2s. About 60 of the E-2s Gotha had planned to produce are at present unaccounted for according to factory serial numbers. Production figures adjusted accordingly, it seems that only 401 Bf 110 E-2s were actually built.

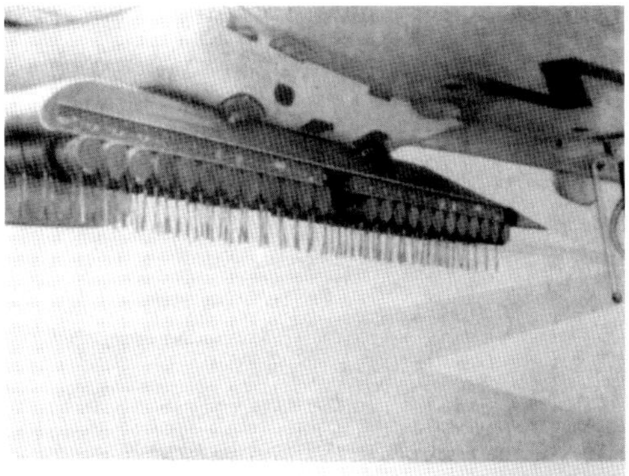

Abb. 4: Einhangroste ER 4 ETC 50 (unter dem Rumpf der Bf 110 E) mit je 96 SD 2 am Rost 24 beladen

far left: The Luftwaffe *used SD 2 bomblets for attacking soft-skinned targets.*

left: The M1 conversion kit, although introduced for the F-series model, could also be used on the Bf 110 E. (Griehl)

Abb. 5: Einhangroste ER 4 ETC 50 mit je 4 SC 50 beladen

below left: The SC 50 was dropped singly or in salvos against armored targets.

Bf 110 E-3, Reconnaissance with increased range

As E-2, but

Camera:	Rb 50/30 in place of MG FF "M" and ETC 500
Ordnance:	Only 2 x 50 kg under wings

From November 1940 through August 1941 the C-Amt program (1 November 1940) shows that 179 Bf 110 E-3s were to have been supplied by Gothaer Waggonfabrik. The actual total, according to loss reports and Modification Instruction 174 (electrical camera heating), was in fact 200.

According to the manual there was a weapons system for the Bf 110 E-3 and F-3 with two fixed aft-firing MG 17s and an RF 1 A periscope sight. This was not given any additional designation. Approximately 50 sets were fitted to aircraft as they cycled through the repair facilities. The authors have not yet seen this system in a photo of any F-3, but have come across a picture of a C-5 with this armament configuration.

below: This is a Bf 110 E-3 of 5./Aufkl.Gr *in 1940 on the island of Guernsey. (Petrick)*

above: This Bf 110 E-3 trop *of* 2.(H)/14 *over Africa. (Petrick)*

below: As this 1942 photo of a Bf 110 from 1./SKG 210 *in Russia shows, rear-firing armament wasn't only installed in reconnaissance aircraft. Registration coding, the SD 2 bombs suspended beneath wing-mounted racks, and the 250 kg bombs ready for loading onto fuselage racks all indicate this machine to be a bomber variant. (Petrick)*

left: About fifty reconnaissance aircraft were retrofitted with fixed aft-firing guns.

below: The rear-facing sighting periscope was unusually tall.

Abb. 7: Einlegen der Vollgurte in den Gurtkasten

Abb. 13: Rückblickfernrohr RF 1 A und Stirnstütze, auf dem Haubendach befestigt

below: To reduce blinding, some night fighters had their MG 17s fitted with the shrouds typical of tropicalized versions. (Selinger)

Bf 110 C through E, Night Fighter

Up to the Bf 110 E series the night fighting forces were not given any specialized subvariants, instead only reluctantly being assigned aircraft from the production runs. For training purposes, the night fighters also had to make due with older airframes from other units. It was not until the introduction of radar systems that specialized night fighter variants (Bf 110 F-4 and G-4) were designed. The first radar system (the FuG 202) wasn't available until the Bf 110 F-4 entered production, but it was also retrofitted in the Bf 110 D and E series. It seems as though the idea of building a Bf 110 E-4 alongside the

right: C9+FM of 4./NJG 1 has been kitted out with an infrared illuminator and gunsight (spanner gear). As this aircraft lacks the heating system, it is probably one of the D-3 series. (Petrick)

left: When available, E-series aircraft were also retrofitted with the FuG 202. New aircraft were delivered to the field without the radar. Note the non-standard camouflage pattern. (Modell Magazin)

Bf 110 F-4 existed, or to designate as such those airframes retrofitted with the FuG 202, for this variant was mentioned in the Bf 110 variant overview and in the manual for airborne radio systems. Yet this variant does not appear in any loss reports, etc.

As a rule these night fighters were painted black. But since night fighter crews sometimes operated during daylight hours and made use of older *Zerstörer* airframes, it was possible to find aircraft in the standard *Zerstörer* camouflage pattern operating with the night fighters. The common light blue camouflage scheme typical from mid-1943 onward was most certainly carried by several leftover old crates.

above: This black Bf 110 E-1 with "Dackelbauch" *and light colored undersides flew with 6./* NJG 1 *at Deelen in 1941. (van Heijkop)*

left: On many C to E night fighter models there was a type of bracing stub located between the MG-FF gun ports, the purpose of which remains unknown. (Modell Magazin)

Bf 110 C through E, DB 601N Powered Aircraft

Bf 110 airplanes with the DB 601 N motors were given the N suffix following their variant designation, e.g. Bf 110 E-2/N. Since the N engines required high octane fuel, the engines were marked on their nacelles with the letter "N" as well.

The N motors were sometimes retrofitted into Bf 110s in the field in addition to being installed at the factory. The urgency given to equipping the Bf 109 and Bf 110 with these engines fluctuated over time. On 1/1/41 there were 2 Bf 110 C-1s, 20 Bf 110 C-4s, 6 Bf 110 C-5s, 7 Bf 110 C-7s, 9 Bf 110 D-0s, 10 Bf 110 D-2s, 4 Bf 110 D-3s, 68 Bf

above: N-series engines were marked by a large letter "N" on the engine nacelles. This night fighter is unique, in that it was an older Bf 110 D-3 without heating but with the FuG 202 set. The black paint and the radar system hint that this photo was taken during operations in the spring of 1943. (Ries)

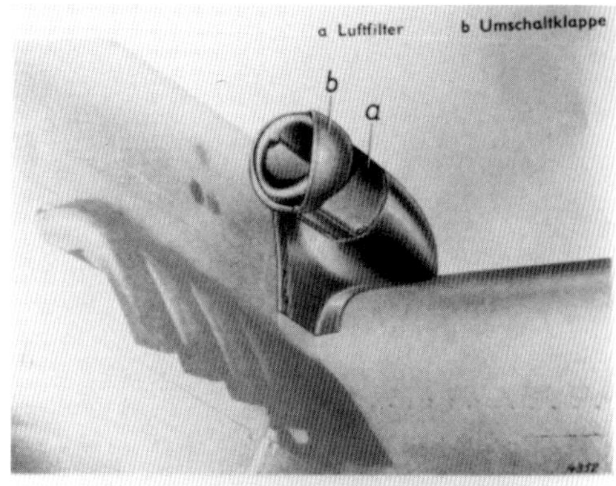

Abb. 5: Sandabscheider des rechten Motors (Klappe geöffnet)

110 E-1s, and 7 Bf 110 E-2s fitted with the engine.

Bf 110 C through E, Tropical Equipment Fitted Aircraft

Tropicalized aircraft were designated with the suffix "trop," for example Bf 110 E-2 trop. As the demand could not be met by new-built E-series, earlier versions were upgraded to the trop standard. Equipment included sand filters fitted in front of the engine air intakes, dust filters over the six gun barrels, sun shades in the canopy, additional rescue gear, and enlarged radiators. The large radiators are often cited erroneously in aviation literature as indicative of the Bf 110 F. Many authors also misidentify the dust filter barrels for the MG 17 as MK 108s.

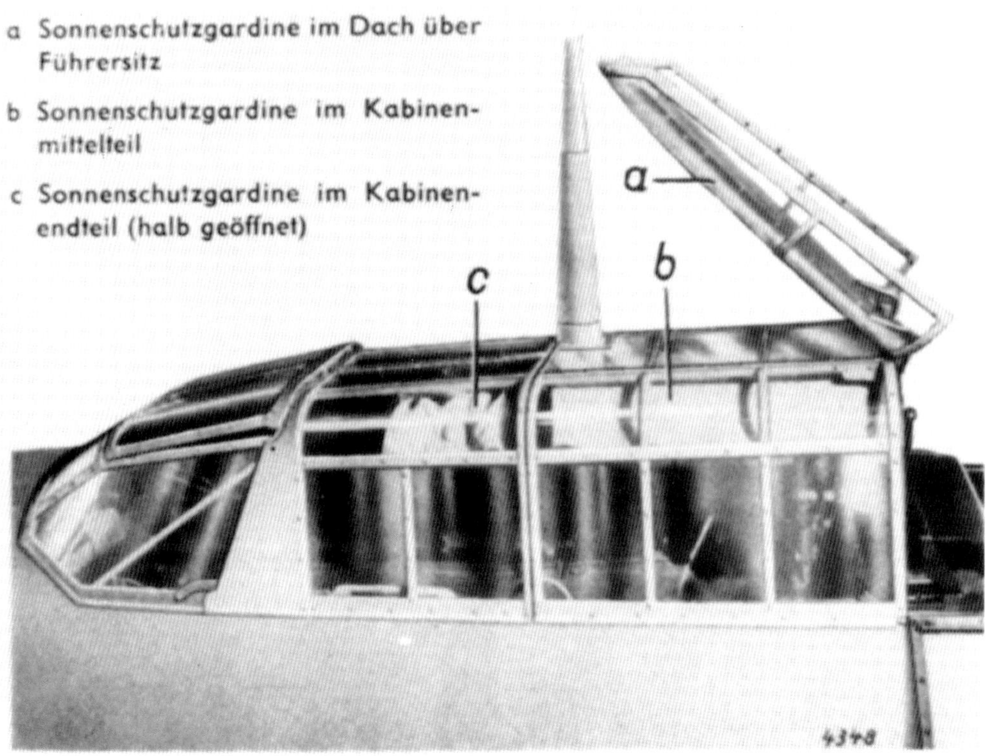

Abb. 1: Sonnenschutz

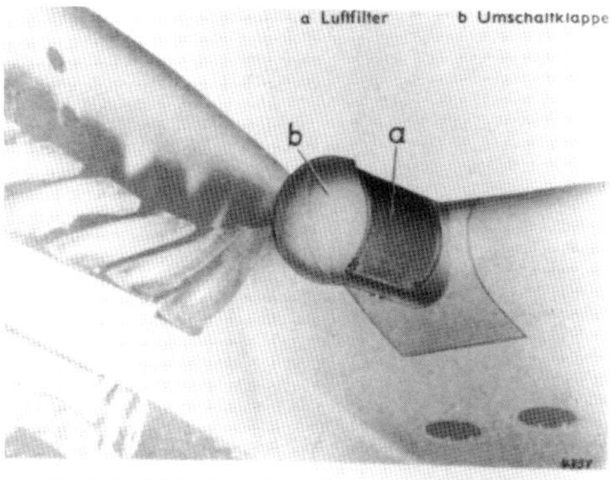

Abb 4 Sandabscheider des linken Motors (Klappe geschlossen)

Abb. 6: Untere Triebwerksverkleidung des linken Motors

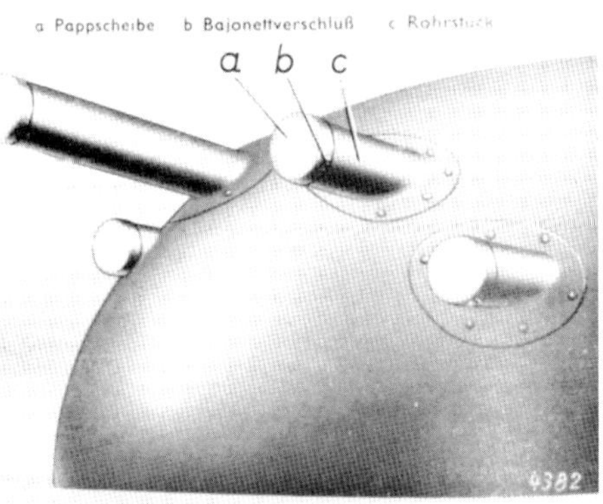

Abb. 13: Laufabdichtung für MG 17

Bf 110 C through E, Me 321 Tow Aircraft

According to Gerd W. Heumann and subsequent authors, the conversion to tow aircraft for the Me 321 (*Troika* teams) in 1941 was made exclusively using Bf 110 C-1/U1s with the following features: no armament; tow gear mounted in the aft gunner's position; and a cable brace over the empennage. This claim is false on the one hand because the Bf 110 lifted into the air before the glider, and would have been unable to get the tail section off the runway if the cable ran over the top of the empennage. It is also false because the first conversions were made using the Bf 110 E-1/U1.

On 1/30/41 the *Generalluftzeugmeister* decided to provide *XI Korps* with six new Bf 110 Es for testing purposes as tow aircraft for the Me 321 *Warschau*. The first flight of the Me 321 V1 behind a three-plane team of Bf 110s with N motors took place on 3/8/41. On 5/1/41 the General Staff called for the Hansen Company in Schneidemühl to convert 80 Bf 110s for towing by no later than 6/1/41. To this end, they were to be supplied with 40 airframes per week, effective immediately. On 5/15/41 there were 24 machines undergoing modification. For towing the following items were removed: armor; PVC; auxiliary tanks; and some of the weaponry. At least on one side the wing/fuselage fillet was also removed in order to fit the tow cable as closely as possible to the fuselage axis. The cable ran back along the fuselage underneath the empennage. This cable was anchored to the Bf 110 and ended at a coupling behind the tailwheel. To accommodate this coupling the lower section of the extreme aft fuselage was removed. The authors have been unable to ascertain whether cables ran along both sides of the fuselage and were joined together at the coupling, as they have been unable to find either a drawing or photographs showing an airplane from both sides. This can be assumed, however, since the cable can be seen regardless of which side the airplane was photographed from. According to test reports the port tow plane had an outrigger to ensure the traction force went through the centerline and thereby reduced the chance of the plane ground looping. As the airplanes were expected to operate for long periods at high rpms and slow airspeeds they were fitted with the tropicalized radiators to improve cooling efficiency. Additionally, they were fitted with two mirrors in front of the windscreen to enable the pilot to observe the glider. Range was approximately 450 km. On 5/23/41 it was decided that the He 111 H-6 was more suited to the task of towing, and on 3/21/42 the towing concept's flaws were revealed to the RLM in a report showing that 50 to 80% of takeoffs ended in mishap. The heavy gliders were later towed exclusively by the He 111 Z and the Me 110s

above: Bf 110 E-1s mostly served as the basis for conversion to tow planes. This is W.Nr. *4100 (PN+CN) with a white "S" on the nose, assigned to* SoSt (GS) (Sonderstaffel Großsegler - *Special Heavy Glider Squadron). The machine lacks armor plating, has a rear-view mirror, large radiators, and towing gear terminating at the end of the shortened fuselage. (Petrick)*

right: This old Bf 110 C with green splinter camouflage flew glider towing missions with the rear-view mirrors, towing gear and minus rear-firing defensive armament. (Petrick)

As the wolf's head was the symbol of a replacement heavy fighter training group, these two tow aircraft were most likely assigned to Lehrgeschwader 1 *following their service in the* Troika *teams. (Petrick)*

were handed over to other units, although they did retain some of their components.

Bf 110 .../U1

At least some of the tow planes were constructed on the basis of the Bf 110 E-1 and were given the designation Bf 110 E-1/U1. Evidence from flight logs shows the existence of factory numbers 3858 (VJ+OF), 3861 (VJ+OI), and 3862 (VJ+OJ), which were flown by II./GS-Gr. Bf 110 E-1/U1 (3955, TF+CY) was also used for towing transport gliders according to photographs. There was another Bf 110 E-1 (3971, DE+WO) at *Sonderkommando* Leipheim, the site where the Me 321 was developed and tested. On 5/19/51 Bf 110 E-1 3932 (TF+CC) and Bf 110 E-1 3974 (DE+WR) crashed while towing a Ju 52 at *Sonderkommando* Merseburg. Merseburg was the field where the Ju 322 was developed and tested. Two additional Bf 110 E-1s (4030 (BC+FV) and 4031 (BC+FW)) were also working with this special detachment in September 1941. Also in that month Bf 110 E-1 4100 (PN+CN) and 4101 (PN+CO) were operating with SoSt (GS) at Winniza-Süd. 4099 (PN+CM) also seems to have operated as a tow plane, according to a photo.

In addition to the Bf 110 E-1/U1s, a Bf 110 C-1 (1794, SD+AN) was also used at *Sonderkommando* Leipheim for towing purposes. At Winniza-Süd, Bf 110 C-2 2101 (BA+CL) suffered 80% damage on 9/23/41 while operating with the SoSt (GS), and in October 1941 Bf 110 C-2 2638 was lost at Orsha while in service with the SoSt (GS) 22. Bf 110 C-2 2132 (KD+TB) also served as a tug. At Merseburg, Bf 110 C-4 216 (KD+UH), 2169 (KD+UM), and 2281 (GL+ZC) were also used for towing. Additional aircraft flown at *Sonderkommando* Merseburg were Bf 110 E-2 3729 (KB+UI) and 3732 (KB+UL).

As far as can be determined from photos, the tow planes retained their original identification codes. It wasn't until they were passed on to other units that different codes were applied.

Since the tow tugs are identified in aviation publications as Me 110 C-1/U1s and, as will shortly be shown, the U3 through U6 designations were used for aircraft in the C through E series, one would not be far off the mark in assuming that a similar method applied to tow aircraft for the Me 321, i.e. the U1 designation refers to the conversion to tow plane undertaken on the C-1 through E-2 series. The authors, however, only have documentary evidence for the Bf 110 E-1/U1. Yet it should be pointed out that the Bf 110 D-3/U1 was clearly not a tow plane, according to flight log entries.

Bf 110 C through E, Strike Aircraft

The Bf 110 E series was initially produced without armor protection for the crew. During the production run, however, cockpit armor to include an armored windscreen made its way onto the assembly line. This was in accordance with Modification Instructions Bf 110 No. 98, No. 104, and No. 144 that mandated these measures were to be retroactively applied to all Bf 110 Es and could be installed in aircraft of the C and D series as well. For the Bf 110 E-1 there was a difference between armor configuration I, with plating in the nose, behind the pilot, and behind the observer/gunner, and armor configuration III, with additional plating under the seats. For the Bf 110 E-2 the corresponding configurations were II and IV.

L.Dv. T. 2513/1, Addendum 6 described the retroactive modifications to the Bf 110 C-1, C-2, C-3, C-7, D-2, D-3, E-1, and E-2 strike planes. These modifications to strike aircraft were necessary, as the Me 210 S, originally intended for this role, was abandoned. There were also conversion sets U3, U4, and U6, which differed in the location of the armor. All these aircraft were given full cockpit armor protection in accordance with armor configurations III and IV of the Bf 110 E and were fitted with two ETC 500s under the fuselage and two double ETC 50s or two double 24 SD 2s under the wings. There is no accurate information on the actual number of modified aircraft, but it was probably limited mostly to aircraft of the E series, as the older variants generally went to the night fighters.

The armored windscreen could be fitted to any C- through F-series machine. (Petrick)

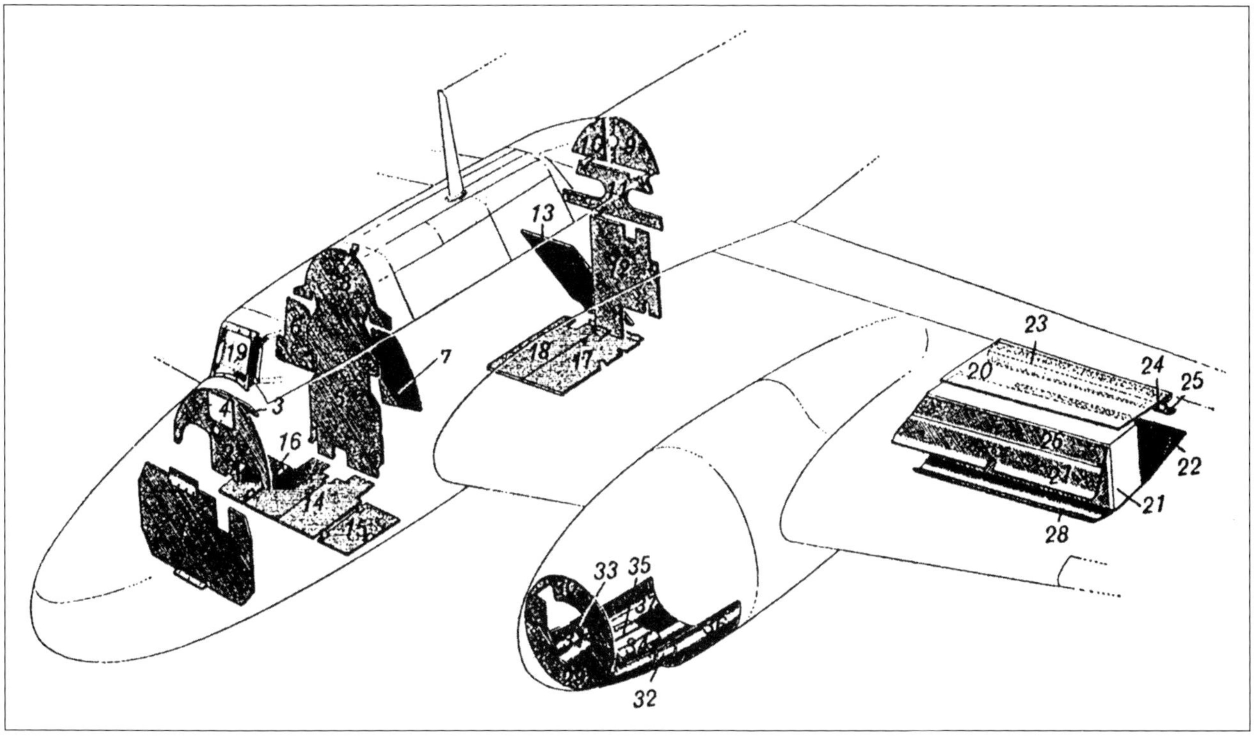

above: The plentiful armor plating of the U4 conversion variant.

left: With its wing-mounted ETC racks, extra armor, and sand deflectors, this Bf 110 D-3 has been converted to a U4 or U6 sub-variant. (Petrick)

Bf 110.../U3, Strike aircraft

Armor: On the canopy and in front of the radiators

Bf 110.../U4, Strike aircraft

As Bf 110.../U3, but

Armor: Additional engine armor in front and underneath
Engine: Additional sand deflectors

Bf 110.../U6, Strike aircraft

As Bf 110.../U4, but

Armor: Engines with frontal armor only

Bf 110 C through E, With Dobbas cargo container

With the frequent redeployment of bomber units, there arose the problem of how to quickly move ground equipment along with the aircraft. Since the transports were needed in the field for resupplying the front, in 1942 the RLM had a "Dobbas" cargo container developed that could be hung underneath *Zerstörer* and bombers. A maximum load of 900 kg was planned for the Bf 110. Airspeed with the container dropped by about 70 km/h, i.e. the cruising speed was now somewhere around 300 km/h. Endurance was estimated at 2 hours, providing a range of approximately 600 km. Flight handling was not seriously affected by the container, although rudder forces were found to be increased somewhat and rudder effectiveness reduced. The takeoff run was rather long. Takeoff and landing took place at around 170 km/h. Single engine flight with the Dobbas was not possible, and if an engine did go out the container had to be jettisoned. On 7/14/42 the RLM determined that the Dobbas cargo system was not viable with the Me 110, as the engines tended to overheat. In principle, the Dobbas could be hung on any Bf 110 with ETC 500 hardpoints, but during its life, if it was ever carried it was mainly used with the Bf 110 E.

This Bf 110 E, here fitted with the Dobbas *fuel tank, has the new nose typical of the G- series, indicating that this is a testbed aircraft. (Nowarra)*

Bf 110 C through E, High Altitude Oxygen System

According to an operating instruction from 10/31/41 the bottles for the oxygen system were moved from the aft fuselage of the Bf 110 C, D, and E variants and relocated to the armored floor plate in the observer's/gunner's compartment. This measure was taken to prevent the massive and sudden increase in pressure when the bottles stored in the aft section were hit from blowing out the fuselage tail. The Bf 110 C variant retained, as before, four bottles each for the pilot and the gunner. The D and E variants had six each.

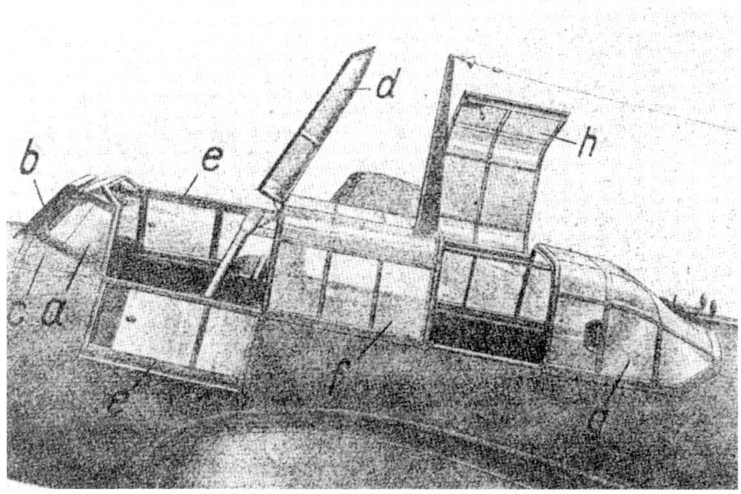

According to the manual there were two types of canopies standard for the Bf 110 F.

Bf 110 F

According to the C-Amt program, from 10 January 1940 Bf 110 production was to have ceased in the autumn of 1941 with the E-2/3 series. In September 1942 the last two Bf 110 E-3s were to be built, and in November the last 8 Bf 110 E-2s were planned. Starting in May 1941 production of the Bf 110 E would taper off, while at the same time Me 210 production would be initiated, with full production in December. Simultaneous production of both types was ruled out, as engine production would not have been sufficient to meet demand.

When Me 210 production failed to materialize as planned in the autumn of 1941, the General Staff began thinking about renewing production of the Bf 110, with a call for replacing the MG 15 with the MG 81 Z. On 9/25/41 the General Staff decided that, of the 30 Bf 110s per month that would be produced, Gotha would build 22 as night fighters with two MG 151s under the fuselage, and 8 would be manufactured by Miag as *Zerstörer* planes (at the time Miag was also building the Si 204 and Gotha the Go 244). A reconnaissance version would be dispensed with. Deliveries of the *Zerstörer* would begin in December 1941. Sometime around May 1942 the MG FF would be replaced with the MG 151/20. In December 41 the RLM first began receiving reports of oil foam buildup in the DB 601 F engines of the Bf 110. From this, it can be deduced that the new aircraft being produced in the winter of 1941 belonged to the F-series. On 12/23/41 the *Generalluftzeugmeister* announced that, because of the problems with the oil there would be a delay in deliveries of the Bf 110 F. As far as the airframe went the aircraft were finished, but could not be supplied due to the engine problems. The *Luftwaffe* took the first four Bf 110 Fs on charge in February 1942. According to a C-Amt report dated 6/1/42 there were plans to produce a total of 500 Bf 110 Fs, of which 184 had already been delivered. The remainder would follow within the year. If one adds up the factory serial numbers in the loss reports for the F-series, these total 518 aircraft. It is possible that supply problems with the DB 605 led to the F model, which in its later sub-variants differed from the G only in its engines, being produced approximately two weeks longer than originally planned. On the other hand, during the spring of 1943 there were ten Bf 110 F-2s converted to Bf 110 G-0s.

left: The Bf 110 F instrument panel (Deutsches Museum, *Munich)*

below: Left cockpit controls

bottom: Right cockpit controls

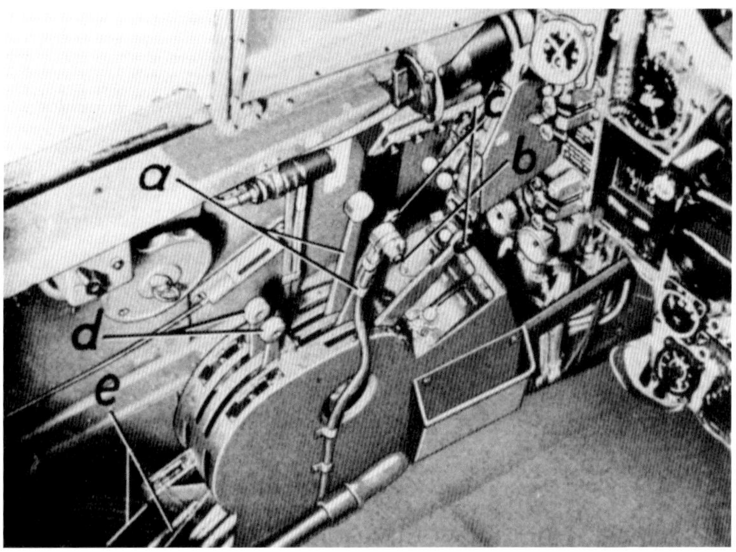

Compared to the E, the F's engines had a new nacelle design and new spinners—similar to the shift from the Bf 109 E to the Bf 109 F—and externally looked very much like the Bf 110 G. The only differences were—like on the Bf 109 F/G—small openings that, on the Bf 110 G, were located slightly ahead of and above the exhaust stubs and directed the flow of air to the spark plugs. The Bf 110 F, like the Bf 110 E, was initially fitted with the MG 15 in the observer's compartment. According to the manual from November 1942 (effective June 1942), the F-series would "shortly" be reequipped with the MG 81 Z with modified canopy glazing.

Unlike the Bf 110 E the F model had a roll bar behind the pilot.

Delays with the Me 210 freed up supplies of engines for the Bf 110, and at the same time required its continued development and production as the Bf 110 F. The Me 210's production was finally terminated on 3/9/42. Out of the gap-filling Bf 110 F a long term solution was found that led to the Bf 110 G. Production was concentrated at Miag and Gotha, which were freed up from all other types in order to fully focus on the Bf 110.

Bf 110 F-1

According to the manual there were originally no plans to build the Bf 110 F-1. It can be surmised that the limited use of the *Dackelbauch* Bf 110 E-1 version led to the

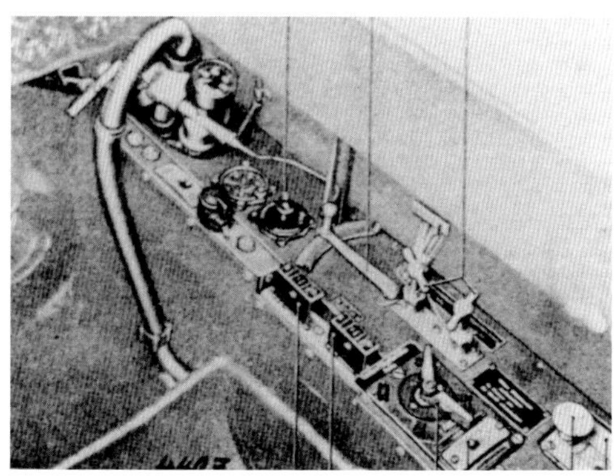

similar F-1's production not being considered—at least for the time being.

Bf 110 F-2, *Zerstörer* or Bomber with Increased Range

As E-2, but

Engine: 2 x DB 601 F
Performance: 2 x 1350 hp
Equipment: Precision altimeter installed
Precision and standard altimeter locations switched
Elt attitude indicator
Modifications to pilot instrument panel, installation of two UV lights above panel
Tropical equipment can be fitted
Fitting of outer wing points for pressurized oil system
Roll bar
Propeller: VDM, three-bladed, 3.4 m diameter
Fixed armament: 4 x MG 17
2 x MG FF "M"
Flexible armament: 1 x MG 15 (MG 81 Z)
Electronic systems: FuG X, FuG 25, Peil G V, FuBl 1
Life raft: not standard
Fuel: 2 x 375 + 2 x 260 = 1270 liters in wing
2 x 300 liters in drop tanks or
2 x 800 liters in drop tanks
Oil: 2 x355 liters aft of the engines
1 x 75 liters in drop tank
Crew: 2 men
Wingspan: 16.276 m
Length: 12.07 m
Height: 4.0 m
Wheel base: 4.6 m
Tailplane span: 4.584 m
Main wheel: 935 x 345
Tailwheel: 465 x 165
Tailwheel non-retracting
Weight (on takeoff): 6.75 t as *Zerstörer*
9.34 t as *Zerstörer* with bombs
Weight (empty): 6.03 t as *Zerstörer*
7 t as *Zerstörer* with bombs
Wing loading: 243 kg/m^2 max.
Max. speed: 530 km/h at 5100 m
570 km/h at 5400 m
Landing speed: 140/km/h

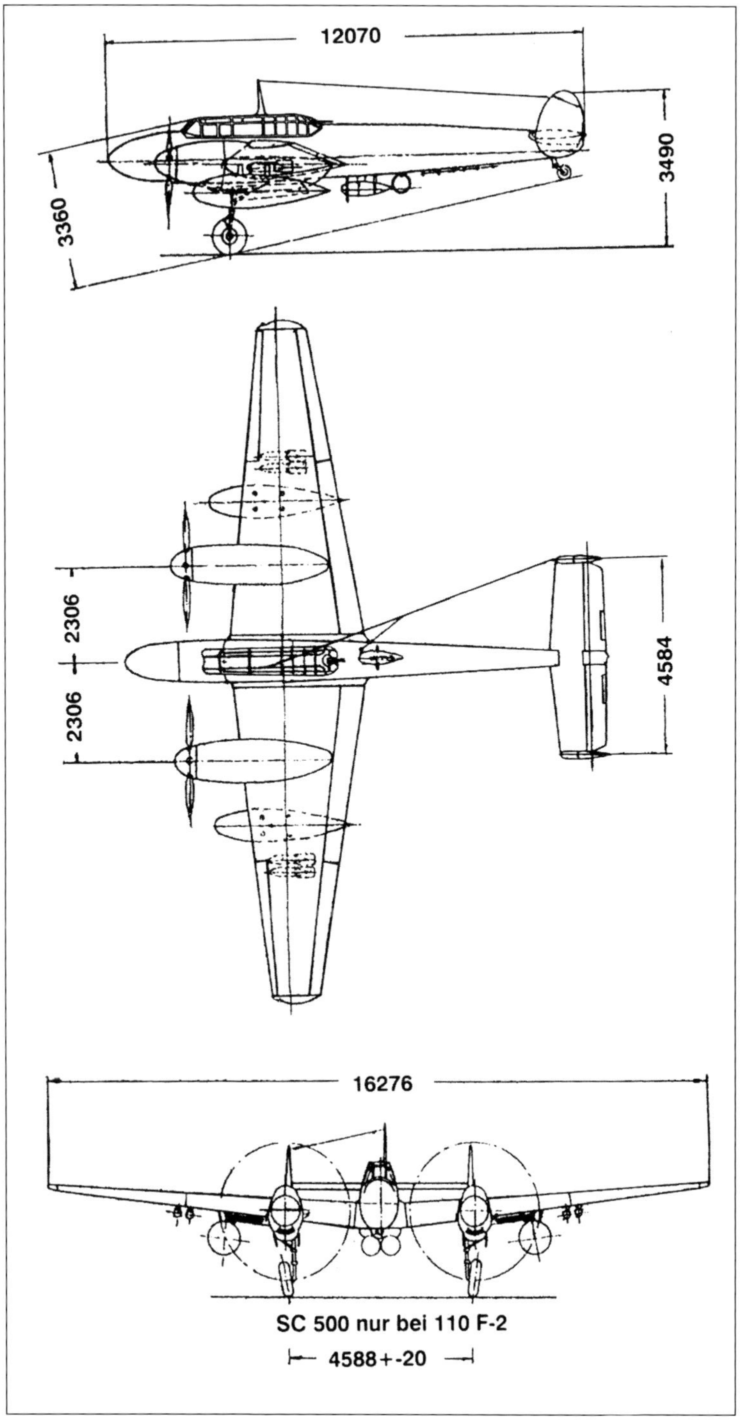

Three-view from the manual for the Bf 110 F-2 and G-2.

Takeoff speed: 110 - 120 km/h
Dive speed: 700 km/h max
Climb rate: 6000 m in 9 min

The Bf 110 F-2 began production in December 1941, with Gotha (now the new controlling facility for Bf 110 manufacture) building a pre-production batch of approximately five airframes that were tested in Rechlin. The first machines, however, were not turned over to the *Luftwaffe* until Febru-

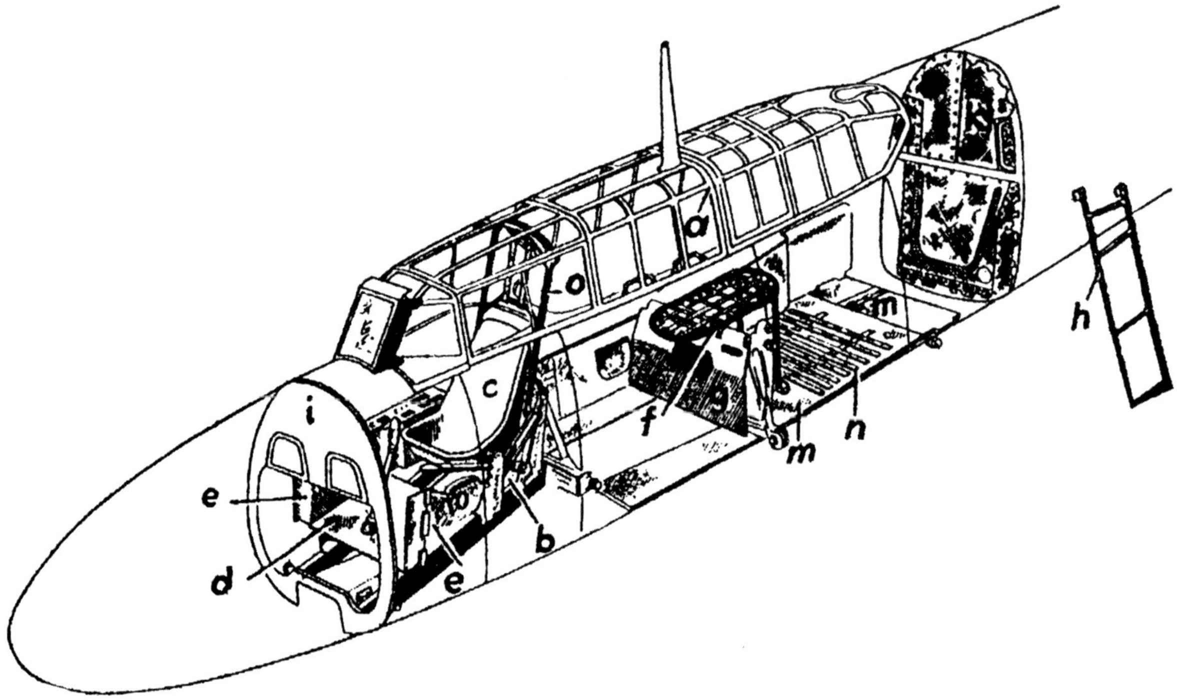

a Windschutzaufbau
b Sitzbrücke
c Führersitz
d Bodenbleche im Führerraum
e Verkleidungsbleche im Führerraum
f Beobachtersitz
g Verkleidung des Hauptholm trägers
h Einsteigleiter
i Abdeckung
k Segeltuchschottwand
m Bodenbleche im Beobachterraum
n Lattenrost
o Überschlagschutz

Anordnung der Rumpfeinrichtung

ary 1942 because of the aforementioned engine problems. Minutes from a GL meeting on 10/16/41 indicate that Miag was to build Bf 110 F-2s at a rate of eight per month. When the Me 210 dropped out and the Bf 110 was forced to assume the role of armored strike fighter in Russia, the ratio was altered in favor of the F-2. According to loss reports about 195 F-2s were built.

Starting on 6/1/42 the Bf 110 F-2 was to be fitted with the M 2 factory conversion kit (2 x ETC 500) at the point of manufacture, as Hitler had ordered that as many aircraft as possible be able to carry a bomb load.

left: The older style aft-firing gun position and the lack of air scoops on the engines were features of the Bf 110 F. (Petrick)

right: Oblt. *Schenck, commander of* I.ZG 1, *was the only one to fly the Bf 110 F-2 with a 1000 kg and a 250 kg bomb. (Petrick)*

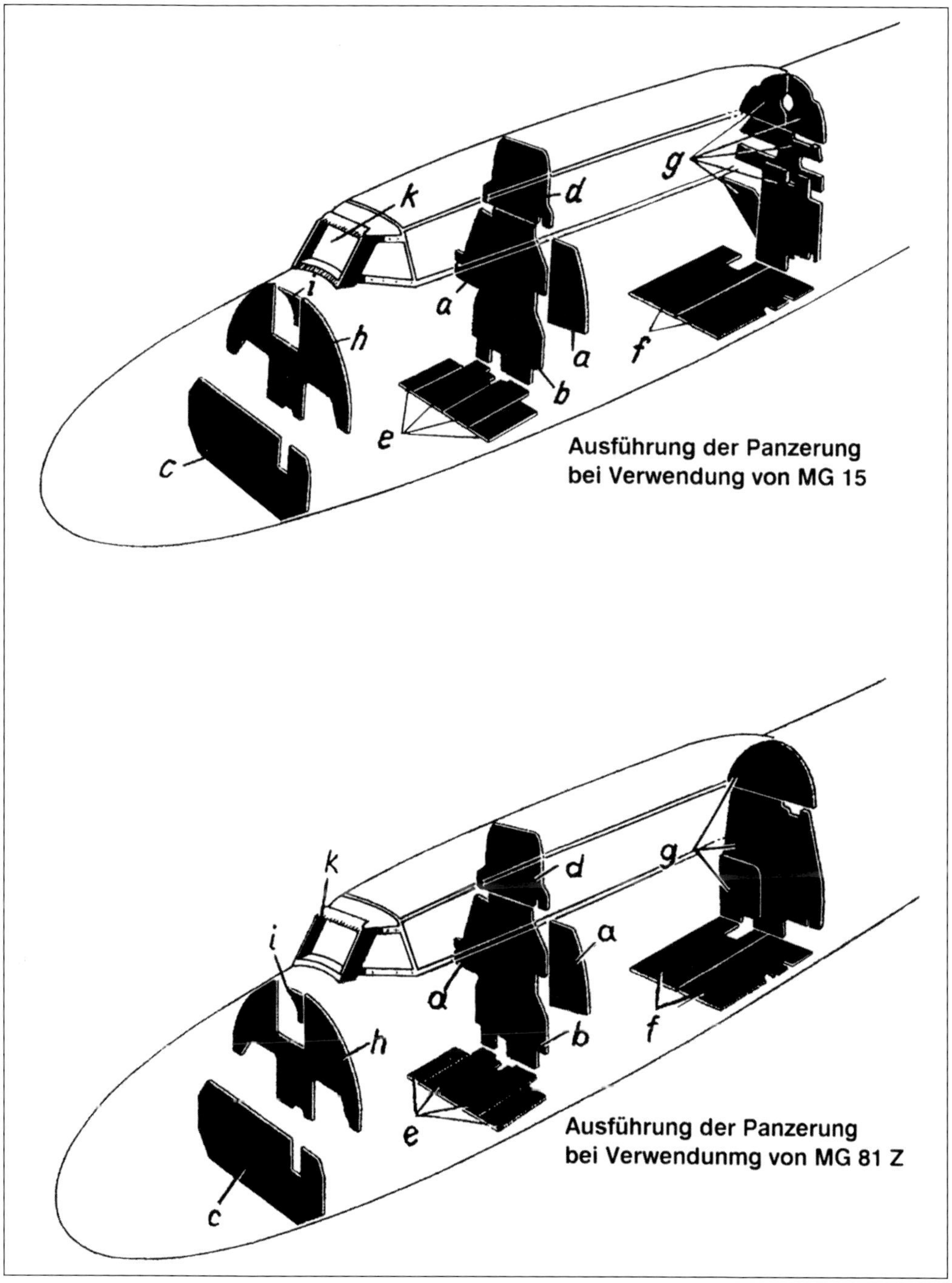

Abb. 2: Anordnung des Rüstsatzes unter dem Rumpf

left: A few Bf 110 F models were fitted with a twin-barreled machine gun in the old-style canopy. (Petrick)

Bf 110 F-3, Strategic reconnaissance with increased range

As Bf 110 F-2, but

Camera: 1 RB 50/30 and motorized 7 x 9 hand-held camera

Armament: minus MG FF and factory conversion kits M 1 and M 2

Ordnance: Only 2 x 50 kg underneath wings

The Bf 110 F-3 corresponded to the Bf 110 E-3 with the improvements of the F-2.

right: Final assembly for this F-3 is taking place at the Luther Works in Braunschweig. (Deutsches Museum, *Munich)*

below: Camera installation on the Bf 110 F-3 and G-3

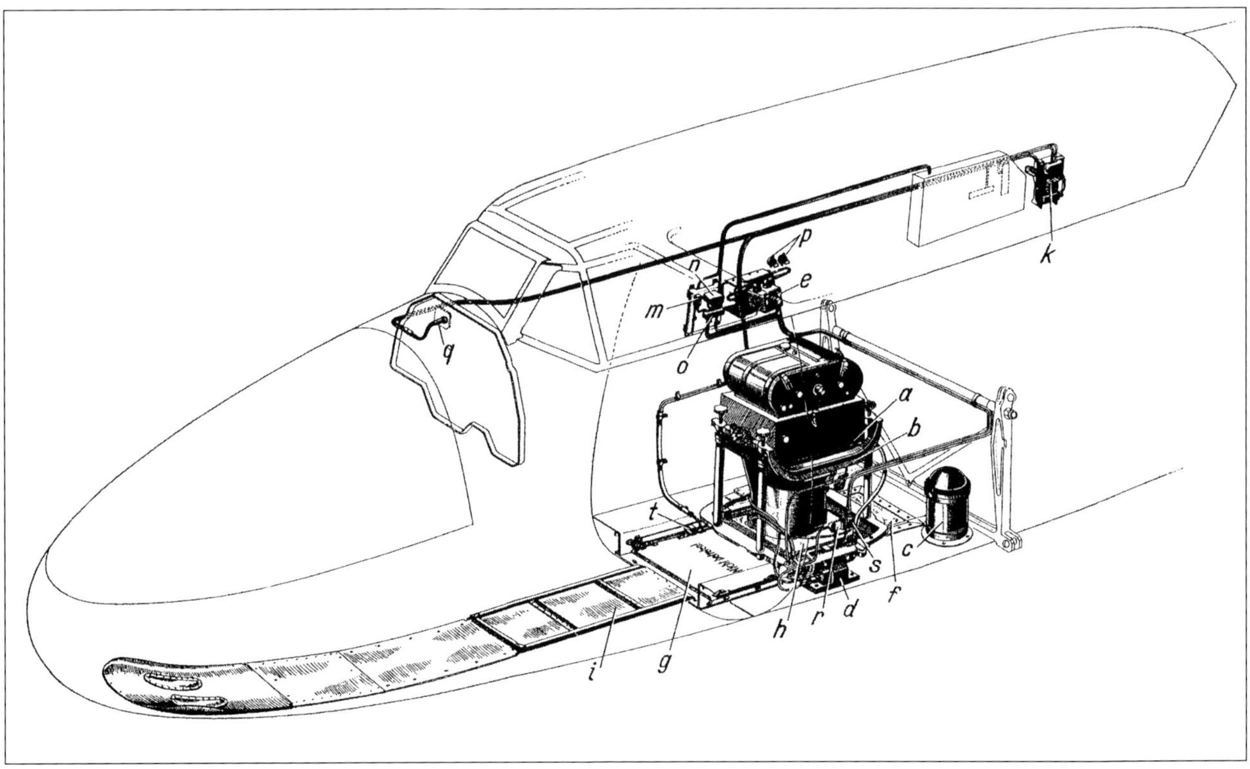

At the end of September 1941, when the decision was made to restart Bf 110 production, the General Staff rejected the idea of building more Bf 110 reconnaissance versions. But when the Me 210 never appeared, reconnaissance versions started to be built beginning in mid-1942. Based on known factory serial numbers, it appears that 38 Bf 110 F-3s were built at Miag.

Bf 110 F-4, Night fighter

As Bf 110 F-2, but

Fixed armament:	4 x MG 17 2 x MG FF
Electronic systems:	FuG X P, FuG 25, Peil G V, APZ 5 A, FuSG 202, FuBl 1
Equipment:	Night fighting equipment and systems APZ 5 DF system to supplement Peil 5 Blinking mechanism for searchlight Tropical equipment cannot be fitted
Length:	12.91 m (with FuG 202 radar antenna)
Max speed:	470 km/h at 5100 m

According to RLM claims and the manual the Bf 110 F-4 was always fitted with the M 1 factory modification set comprising two MG 151/20s. Some propaganda photos show this night fighter without the barrels for the MG 151s due to security reasons. The absence of MG barrels gave rise to some authors attributing an MK 108 weapon in the gondola to the F-4 series. However, production of the MK 108 did not begin until the Bf 110 had ceased being built.

A *Führer* directive ordered all aircraft to be capable of carrying bombs. On 6/1/42 the RLM accordingly decided that the Bf 110 F-2 would be delivered with the two M 1 and M 2 modification packages. The authors do not know where the night fighter units kept the ETC 500s or whether, as claimed in the manual, all Bf 110 F-4s really left the production line with the M 1 kit fitted. The F 4 was flown both with and without the extra weaponry.

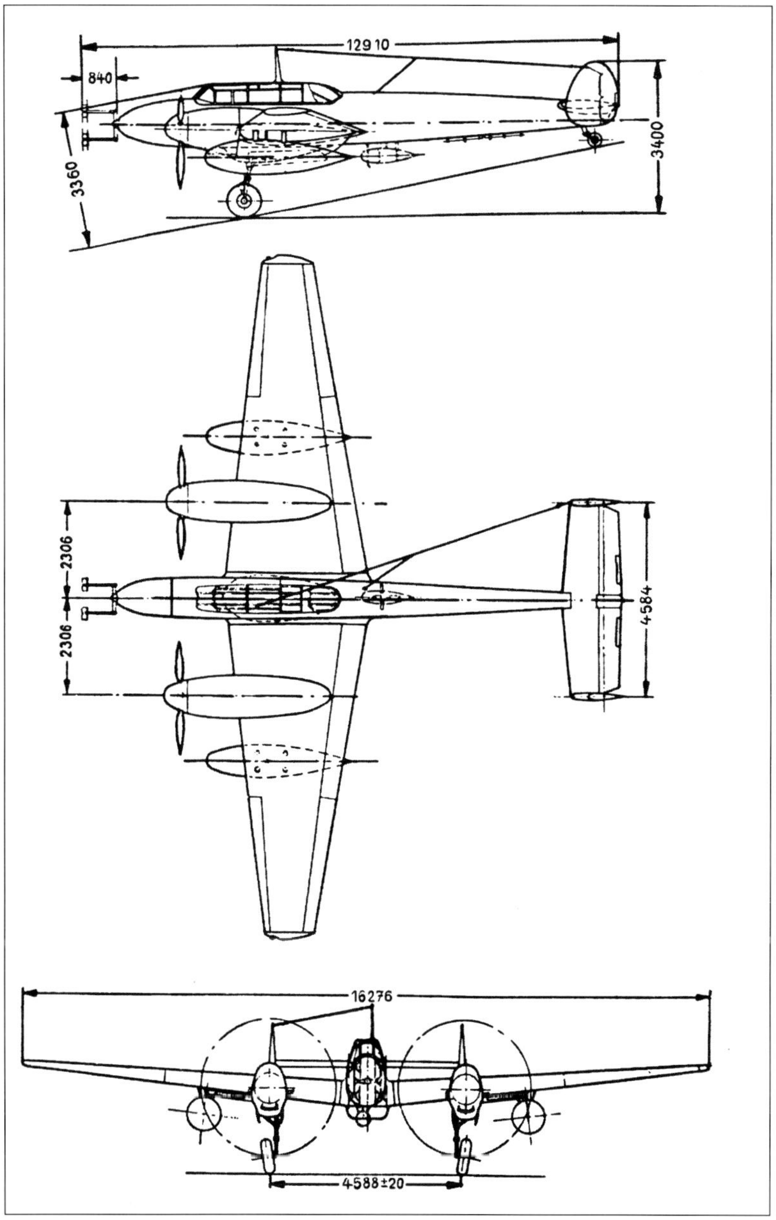

above: Three-view of the Bf 110 F-4 and G-4, from the manual

From the spring of 1942 onward, the field depots became increasingly responsible for fitting the night fighting radar systems and the antenna array for the FuG 202. Prior to that time, the night fighters were directed by radio into the bomber stream and had to then acquire their targets by sight. They differed from the day fighters only in their black paint and some equipment modifications. The

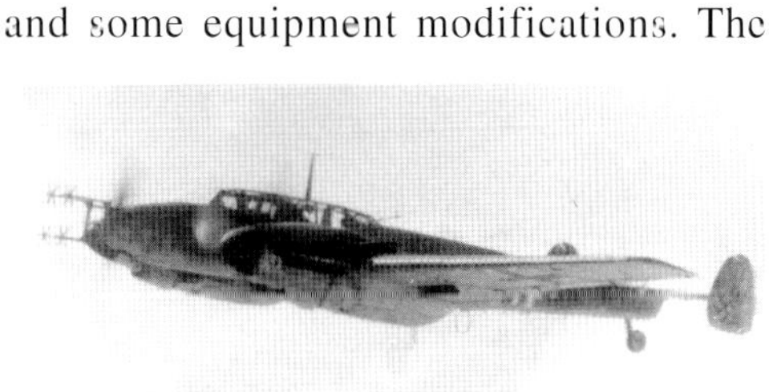

left: This photo shows a Bf 110 F-4 flying with the camouflage pattern standard from 1943 onward. It is assigned to Nachtjagdraum-staffel 7 *in Belgium. The M 1 conversion kit has been removed. (Petrick)*

above: The box beneath the fuselage of this Bf 110 F-4 of I./NJG 1 *looks similar to the "bump" for the guns of the C-1. Its purpose is unknown. (Petrick)*

white/light blue paint scheme was not used until some time around mid-1943, by which time the majority of night fighters had most likely been fitted with radar antennas (FuG 202).

The FuG 202 antenna caused a speed loss of about 10 km/h. The M 1 modification package nibbled an additional 20 km/h, and the flame dampers were responsible for another 30 km/h, meaning that the Bf 110 F-4 was some 60 km/h slower than an F-2 without the attachments.

The new Bf 110s were, according to original planning, to be produced at a ratio of 3/4 Bf 110 F-4s for the night fighters, to be built at Gotha. However, the increased demand for strike fighters caused the General Staff to give the night fighters older airframes without bomb equipment, and to beef up the *Zerstörer* units with new planes equipped with ETC hardpoints. This meant that the percentage of F-2s was increased, and the Bf 110 F-4 was also used in *Zerstörer* wings without its night fighting equipment. From March through December 1942 about 285 Bf 110 F-4s were built, probably all at the Gothaer Waggonfabrik.

Bf 110 F-4/U1, Night Fighter

Heumann has identified a Bf 110 F-4/U1 with the factory serial number 5197 and the registration code D5+LT of 9./NJG 3. This machine was supposed to have had the large vertical stabilizers, 2 x MK 108 oblique firing guns, and 2 x MK 108s in the weapons bay. He indicates a small production run having taken place in the years 1942/43. Other authors repeat this claim. However, it is a false one. The serial number belonged to a Bf 110 G-2, and the MK 108 was neither fitted into the weapons gondola nor used as an oblique firing gun in the Bf 110 F-4. And in any event, it would not have been available in 1942/43. The large vertical stabilizers were also not introduced until 1944. The authors have found no further evidence supporting the existence of a Bf 110 F-4/U1.

Bf 110 F-2/F-3/F-4, Modification Packs

The following modification kits were available for the Bf 110 F series:

***Rüstsatz* B 1:**	75 liter underbelly oil container
***Rüstsatz* B 2:**	two 300 liter (900 liter) underwing fuel tanks
***Rüstsatz* M 1:**	two MG 151s with 200 rounds each under the fuselage
***Rüstsatz* M 2:**	two ETC 500 under the fuselage
***Rüstsatz* M 3:**	two ETC 50 under each wing
***Rüstsatz* M 4:**	two 24 SD 2/XII racks under each wing

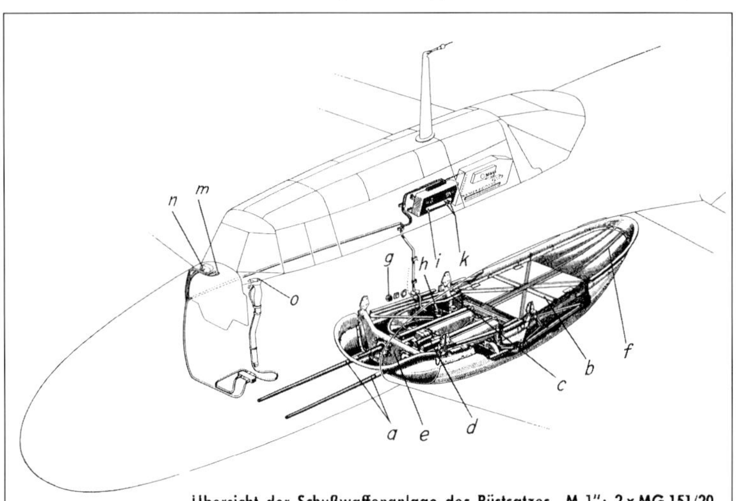

Übersicht der Schußwaffenanlage des Rüstsatzes „M 1": 2 x MG 151/20

below right: This Bf 110 F-2 is fitted with the M 2 and M 3 conversion kits and flew with I./SKG 210 *in Russia during the summer of 1942. (Petrick)*

The B 1 and B 2 kits could be fitted at will, and the M 3 and M 4 were optional kits for the three variants. The M 1 kit was standard for the Bf 110 F-4, an option for the F-2, and not generally fitted to the F-3. The M 2 could be installed on the Bf 110 F-2, but then without the option for the M 1, and was an option for the Bf 110 F-4 as well.

Bf 110 G

The most prominent difference between the F and G series was the shift from the DB 601 E engine to the DB 605 B. The DB 605 B was a follow-on development of the DB 601 E with nearly identical installation dimensions, but with a larger cylinder volume, larger turbocharger, and greater rpms (maximum of 2800). Compared to the DB 601 E it had a crossed spark plug configuration, which supposedly gave it better power and fuel consumption.

A significant change was the switch from ball to sleeve bearings. This change, together with an increasingly poor grade of oil being used, led to serious problems that not infrequently caused engine fires, plane crashes, and fatalities. Until a lasting solution could be found, the use of emergency power was forbidden, so that the DB 605 offered no better performance than the DB 601 during this period. These problems were aggravated all the more by the Messerschmitt Company's unorthodox incorporation of the engine block into the overall powerplant. The RLM considered the DB 605 a sick engine, and by the war's end the problems still had not fully been resolved. An important interim measure taken for the Bf 110 was the introduction of oil slingers, while at the same time DB set about redesigning the bearings. The Messerschmitt Company, however, delayed the fitting of these oil slingers and their associated oil coolers for months because (according to RLM claims) they tended to concentrate more on new aircraft instead of getting the old ones working properly.

Like with the DB 605 in the Bf 109 G, there were also problems in the Bf 110 G with spark plug temperatures. Both machines therefore were fitted with inlets angled slightly upward and located just above the exhaust pipes, the purpose of which was to direct air onto the plugs.

The prototype installation of the DB 605 in Bf 110 *W.Nr.* 4116 was to be undertaken in November 1941 according to the C-Amt's program of 10/1/41, and it was planned that the type would serve as the prototype for the Bf 110 G at the same time. The aircraft type sheet published by the RLM GL/C from 1/1/42 already referenced the F-2, F-3, F-4, G-2, G-3, and G-4. During the first half of 1942 Gotha built six Bf 110 G-0 pre-production aircraft with DB 605s that were subsequently company tested and evaluated at Rechlin.

Trials with the Bf 110 G-0 *W.Nr.* 4623 TF+UV showed that the Flettner rudders were too small for single engine flight. Furthermore, they revealed that the layout of the supercharger intake, radiators, fuel pumps, and ignition system needed improving. Despite these unresolved problems production of the Bf 110 G series began in December 1942.

Bf 110 G-0, *Zerstörer* or Bomber

As F-2, but

Engine: 2 x DB 605 B
Fixed armament: 4 x MG 17
2 x MG FF "M"
Flexible armament: 1 x MG 15
Ordnance: 2 x SC 250 or
2 x SD 500 or
1 x SD 1000 or
1 x SC 1000 + 1 x SC 250 on 2 ETC 500/IX b hardpoints beneath the fuselage, plus an additional two 50 kg bombs under each wing
Electronic systems: FuG X, Peil G V, FuBl 2F

8./ZG 26 *operated this Bf 110 G-2* trop *in Africa. The G-series could be identified by the small scoops in front of the exhaust stubs. This is an early machine, evidenced by the pitot tube location. (Petrick)*

Max speed:	595 km/h at 6100 m

The first six Bf 110 G-0s (*W.Nr.* 4621-4625, TF+UT through UX and 4627, TF+ZU) were inserted among the F-4s at Gotha and tested between about July and December 1942 at Rechlin and Augsburg. According to Delivery Program 222 from 6/1/42 six Bf 110 Gs had been delivered by this time, and a further 2646 were to follow by 9/30/44. In Aircraft Program 22 E from 9/30/42 the number of Bf 110s delivered had not yet risen.

The conversion of 10 Bf 110 F-2 aircraft to G-0s, which involved only installing the DB 605 and its support cradle, was to be undertaken by Bachmann, von Blumenthal & Co. in Fürth, according to a decision by the *Generalluftzeugmeister* made on 3/10/43. Since at this time the G-series was already being produced—and a few G-2s, G-3s, and G-4s had already been lost—this group of G-0s was not a pre-production batch for the G, but an improved F variant. According to the aircraft type sheet from 11/1/44 the G-0 was fitted with the M 2 mod pack. The description above refers to this group, but is an approximate overview for the pre-production series as well.

Bf 110 G-1

According to the manual the Bf 110 G-1 was not planned.

Bf 110 G-2, *Zerstörer* or Bomber

As F-2, but

Engine:	2 x DB 605 B
Performance:	2 x 1475 hp
Propeller:	VDM-0-12078A/B, 3.426 m diameter
Fixed armament:	4 x MG 17 2 x MG 151/20
Flexible armament:	1 x MG 81 Z
Electronic systems:	FuG 10 P, Peil G VI (according to Bf 110 G service manual from 4/28/43)
Electronic systems:	FuG 10 P, APZ 6, FuG 25 (according to aircraft type sheet from 11/1/44)
Weight (on takeoff):	7.79 t as *Zerstörer* 9.3 t as *Zerstörer* with bombs
Weight (empty):	5.56 t as *Zerstörer* 7 t as *Zerstörer* with bombs
Wing loading:	243 kg/m² max.
Max. speed:	595 km/h at 6100 m
Landing speed:	140/km/h
Takeoff speed:	110 - 120 km/h
Dive speed:	700 km/h max
Climb rate:	6000 m in 8 min
Ceiling:	approx. 11000 m
Range:	900 km (1300 km with drop tanks)
Modification Packs:	as F-2, supplemental
M 5 mod pack:	four *Nebelwerfer 21* in place of M 3 or M 4 pack

According to data in the manual and the aircraft type sheet from 11/1/44, the Bf 110 G-2 had as standard armament two fixed MG 151/20s in the fuselage and an MG 81 Z in a modified aft compartment for defense. But Monogram Close Up 18 indicates that the G-2 was initially kitted out with the armament of the F-2 (MG FF and MG 15) and delivered with the old style gunner's configuration. This may have been a result of a mixup with the Bf 110 G-0. What is certain is that at least the F-2 was, for a time, like the E-2 equipped with the MG 15 and had two fixed MG FF "M" guns. As a rule, the Bf 110 G-2 had the MG 151/20 and MG 81 Z combination. The authors have been unable to establish whether or not intermediate types were built, nor in what numbers. Normally it can be assumed that the large spinner and old style aft position are features of the Bf 110 F, and the newer style aft position is an identifying mark of the G series. The Bf 110 F had the extended pitot tube common to the Bf 110 E. For the most part, the G-series had the pitot tube protruding directly from the wing leading edge. In between there were also variations on this theme with the new gunner's position and the F type pitot tube. It is currently unknown whether these were late F models, early G models, or a combination of both.

The first Bf 110 G-2s were handed over to the units in mid-January 1943. The first loss of a G-2 was registered on 1/21/43.

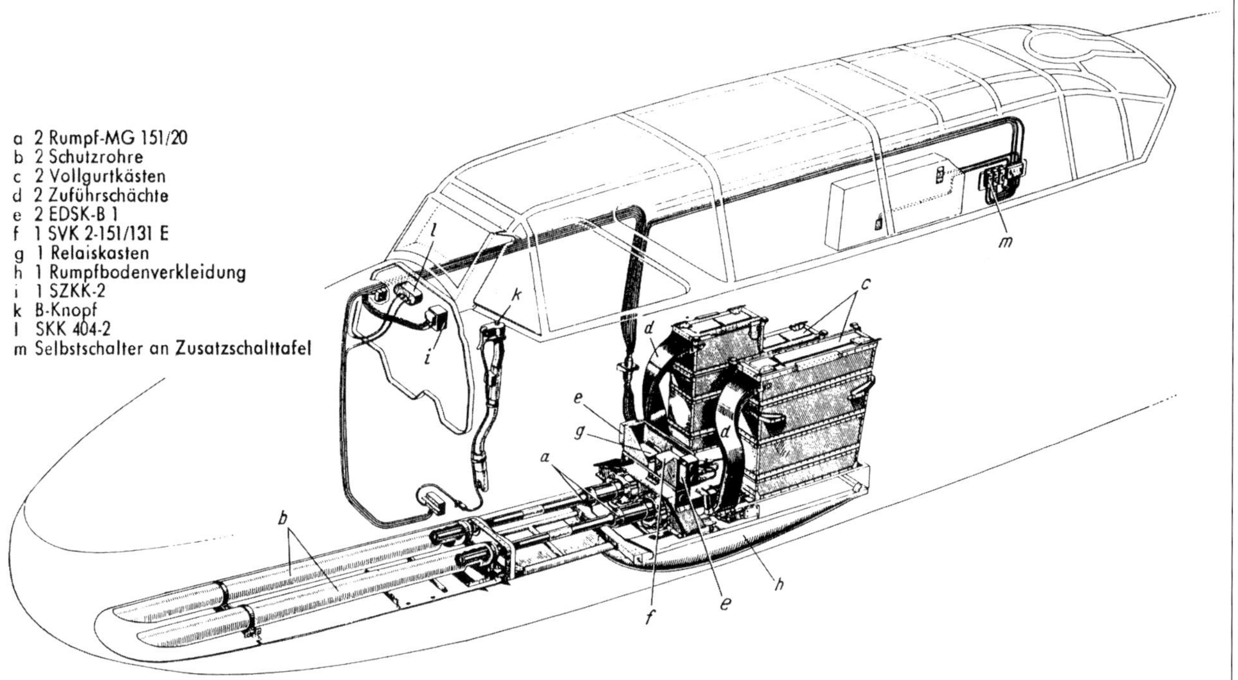

Übersicht der Schußwaffenanlage Rumpf-MG 151/20

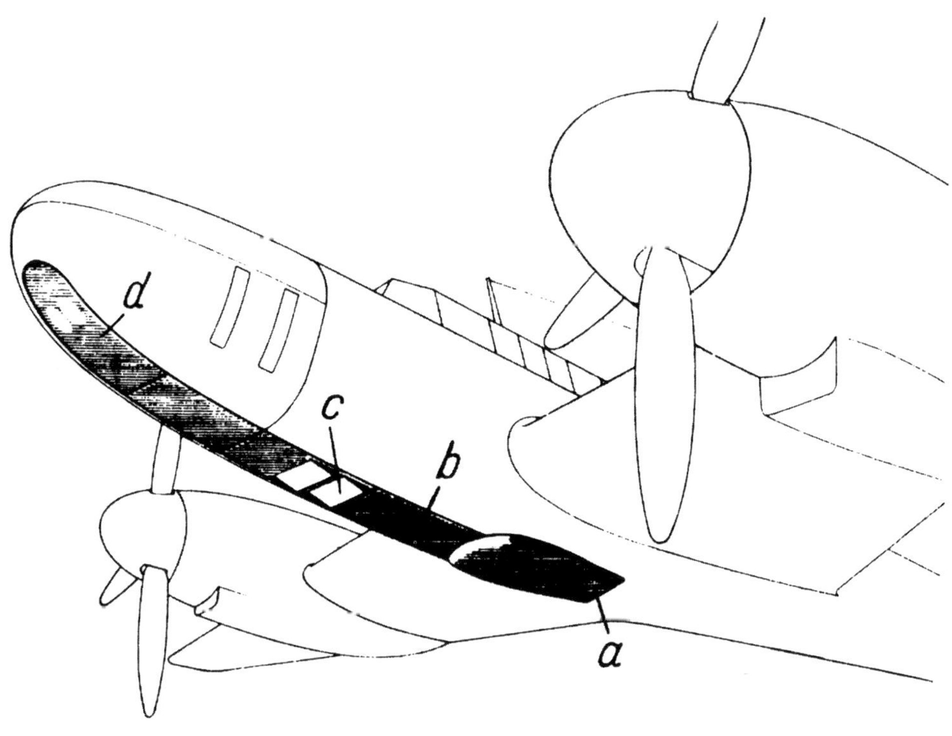

a Rumpfbodenverkleidung
b Vorderer kleiner Deckel
c Deckel mit Entlüftungskiemen
d Schußöffnungen der MG 151 20

Rumpfbodenverkleidung für Rumpf-MG 151/20

below right: The new canopy made climbing in and out of the cockpit easier and also sported defensive armament with increased firepower. (Petrick)

On 3/19/43 Galland, in a meeting with the RLM, claimed that there was no point in using the Bf 110 G-2 to attack bombers with its standard armament configuration (4 x MG 17 and 2 MG 151/20 guns). Instead, he called for all *Zerstörer* aircraft to be fitted with the M 1 modification pack (2 x MG 151/20s) underneath the fuselage, as was the case with the night fighters. He considered the 20 to 25 km/h loss in speed an acceptable trade off. Their combat effectiveness against bombers was further increased by using the M5 kit, which caused an even further loss in speed. Two hundred sets of double-barreled M 5 modification kits were ordered on 6/29/43.

On 6/4/43 the standard armament was determined to be adequate for operations in Russia. There the G-2 was also being used successfully by ZG 1 in the night fighting role, in which searchlights would pick out enemy aircraft for the night fighters.

Abb. 9: Rechter Vollgurtkasten für MG 151/20, geöffnet

As a rule, the Bf 110 G-2 had the old style rudders. Individual cases of larger rudders can sometimes be seen in photographs, however.

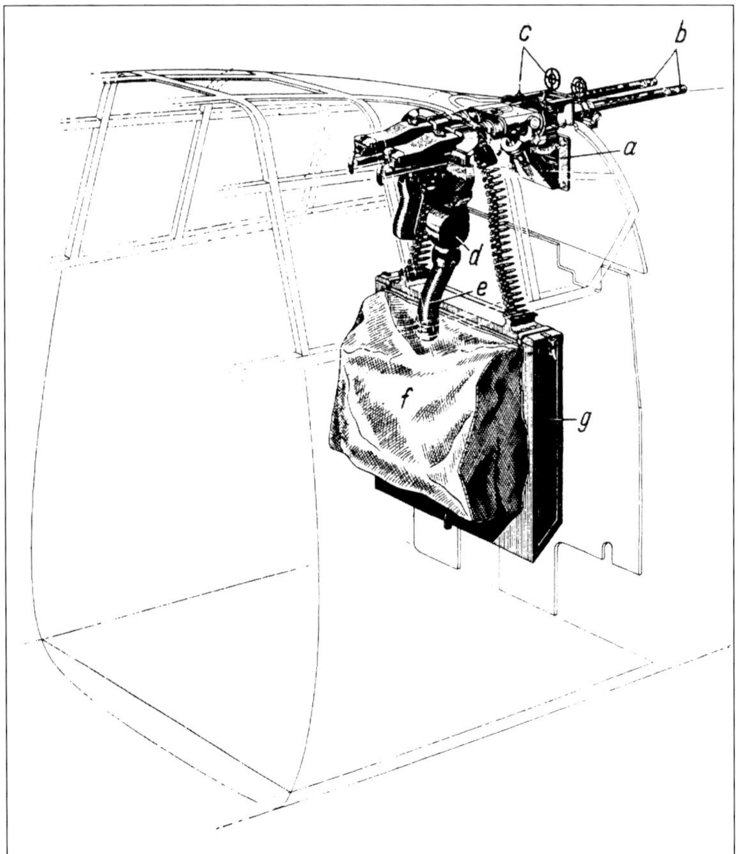

a Schwenkarmlafette LG 81 Z/3
b MG 81 Z
c Ve 46
d Gemeinsamer Leerbehälter
e Metallschlauch
f Hülsensack
g Vollgurtkasten

Ubersicht der Schußwaffenanlage MG 81 Z

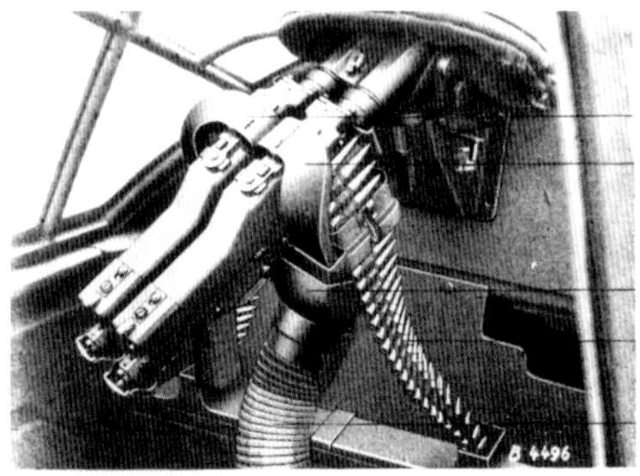

a Abführschacht
b Gemeinsame Leerbehälter
c Metallschlauch
d Vollgurt 17 81

Abb. 14: Munitionszuführung des MG 81 Z

left: On a ferry flight, the crew of this Bf 110 G-2 stuffed the cockpit full as well as carrying a luggage pack beneath the fuselage. The aircraft is fitted with the older inboard pitot tube. (Petrick)

below: Taken in the spring of 1944, this photo of a G-2 (1E+TE) of Ergänzungsstaffel ZG 1 *shows the outboard pitot tube. (Petrick)*

bottom left: The Bf 110 G-2 also carried rocket-boosted armor piercing bombs, here a PC 500 RS. (Petrick)

bottom right: The Bf 110 G-2 was factory fitted with the M 1 conversion kit at the Luther Works. (Ewald)

Manual illustration of the M 5 conversion kit.

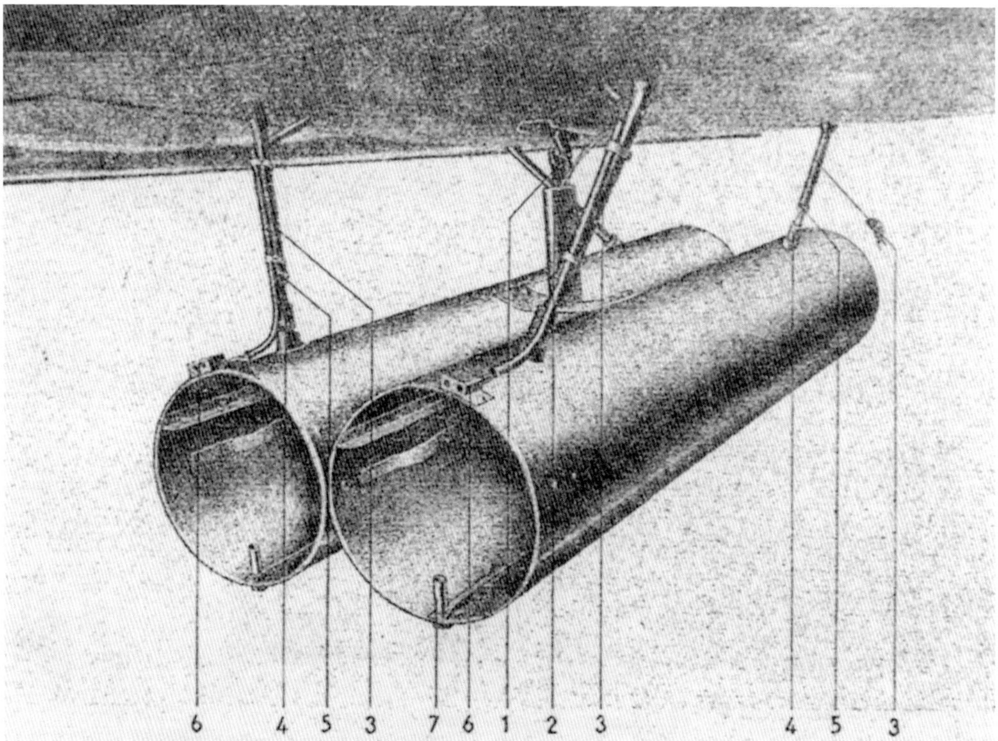

Instrumentation for the M 5 conversion kit.

Bf 110 G-2/U1, *Zerstörer* or Bomber

As G-2, but

Fixed armament:	MG 151/20 in place of MG FF "M"

According to Monogram Close Up 18, this was a conversion to the MG 151/20 carried out on those Bf 110 G-2s originally fitted with the MG FF "M." The authors have been unable to confirm the existence of this variant. In the aircraft type sheet from 11/1/44 it is not shown, but it did identify the Bf 110 G-0 as the only variant of the Bf 110 G with forward firing MG FF guns. The authors assume, then, that the U1 kit was only valid for the Bf 110 G-3 (q.v.)

Bf 110 G-2/U?, *Zerstörer*

As G-2, but

Fixed armament:	1 x Flak 18 under the fuselage, no MG 151/20

In June 1942 the 3.7 cm BK (Flak 18) was sent to several companies for them to look at ways of installing the cannon. In October 1942 *Generalfeldmarschall* Milch believed that the Bf 110 with Flak 18 could be used to destroy tanks, and in November the RLM called for the Bf 110 conversion to proceed at a rate of ten per month. At the same time a desire was expressed for using the Bf 110 with MK 101 against Liberator formations, as the use of the Bf 109 was relatively ineffective due to the latter's weak armament. Since the limited numbers of available MK 101s were needed for the Hs 129, the only possible gun for the Bf 110 was the Flak 18. The guns were to be installed in the field. It was later discovered that field units did not have the means to carry this out, and the aviation industry was needed to come up with a solution. As was the habit, the RLM gave this conversion type its own designation, but the exact number is unknown to these authors. The armament went into production with the Bf 110 G-2/R1.

Bf 110 G-2/U7, *Zerstörer*

As G-2, but

Fuel:	additional 440 kg GM 1 for 45 min
Flexible armament:	minus MG 81 Z
Armor:	no armor in aft position
Maximum speed:	590 km/h at 10000 m
Maximum speed:	480 km/h at 11500 m
Ceiling:	approx. 11500 m

On 13 February 1941 the documentation for the GM 1 systems in the Bf 110 had progressed to the point where they could be shown to the *Generalluftzeugmeister's* chief engineer. Design work on the system continued over the next several months. By the summer of 1943 the RLM feared that enemy high altitude bombers would be appearing (e.g. the B-29) over Reich territory. In order to successfully bring countermeasures to bear by the spring of 1944, specialized high altitude fighters (Bf 109 G-5) and *Zerstörers* (Bf 110 G-2) were kitted out with GM 1 systems that, at this point, were not yet fully developed. The systems consisted of a tank and an injection system, which sprayed nitrous oxide (N_2O; GM 1 = *Göring Mischung*, Göring Mixture) into the engine air intake in front of the supercharger. With the additional oxygen boost the performance could be increased by about 300 hp per engine above the maximum pressure altitude, i.e. the ceiling and speed above 8000 m. Up to the point of the maximum pressure altitude the GM 1 system was only just so much ballast weight. Since the GM 1 only provided the performance that was otherwise lost by the lack of oxygen at higher altitude, in principle this injection boost placed no additional load on the engine; thus it could, within the scope of normal restrictions for takeoff and combat boost, be used as long as the GM 1 fuel held out.

The nitrous oxide was carried in supercooled liquid form in an insulated cylindrical tank (length about 1600 mm, diameter about 650 mm) and stored in the aft section of the observer's area. It prevented the MG 81 from being operated and the gun was removed, as was the aft armor for reasons of weight. The second crewman remained in the aircraft in order to operate the radio system. The GM 1's additional weight caused a shift in the Bf 110's center of gravity, so that the flight handling with a filled GM 1 tank was unpleasant, if not downright dangerous. The MG 17 in the nose was sometimes removed to provide added high altitude performance by reducing the weight even further.

The Bf 110 G-2/U7 was delivered in small numbers (10% of G-2 production) during the summer of 1943. Galland, however, called for the GM 1 system only in combination with the Flak 18. On 9/21/43 Milch decided to acquiesce to these demands. At the same time, series production was just beginning of an improved, although not finalized, form for the GM 1 tank, see Bf 110 G-2/R2

Bf 110 G-2 with DB 628, *Zerstörer*

As G-2, but

Engine:	2 x DB 628
Fixed armament:	1 x Flak 43 under the fuselage, no MG 151/20s ZFR 4 gunsight
Fuselage:	lengthened by 60 cm
Wingspan:	extended tips

On 11/12/43 the RLM, concerned about high altitude defenses, engaged in a discussion of a modified Bf 110, of which 50 would be produced by the spring of 1944. However, the Bf 110 G-2/U7 was adopted for this role. The DB 628 was fitted to a normal Bf 110 G-2 for evaluation purposes during the winter of 1943. It was, however, already apparent that the DB 605 D with DB 603 supercharger (or the DB 605 AS) offered much more potential. This version also never really took off due to the Bf 110 G-2's poor showing with the DB 628 powerplant. Fuselage and wingspan increases were further explored with the Bf 110 H-2 project.

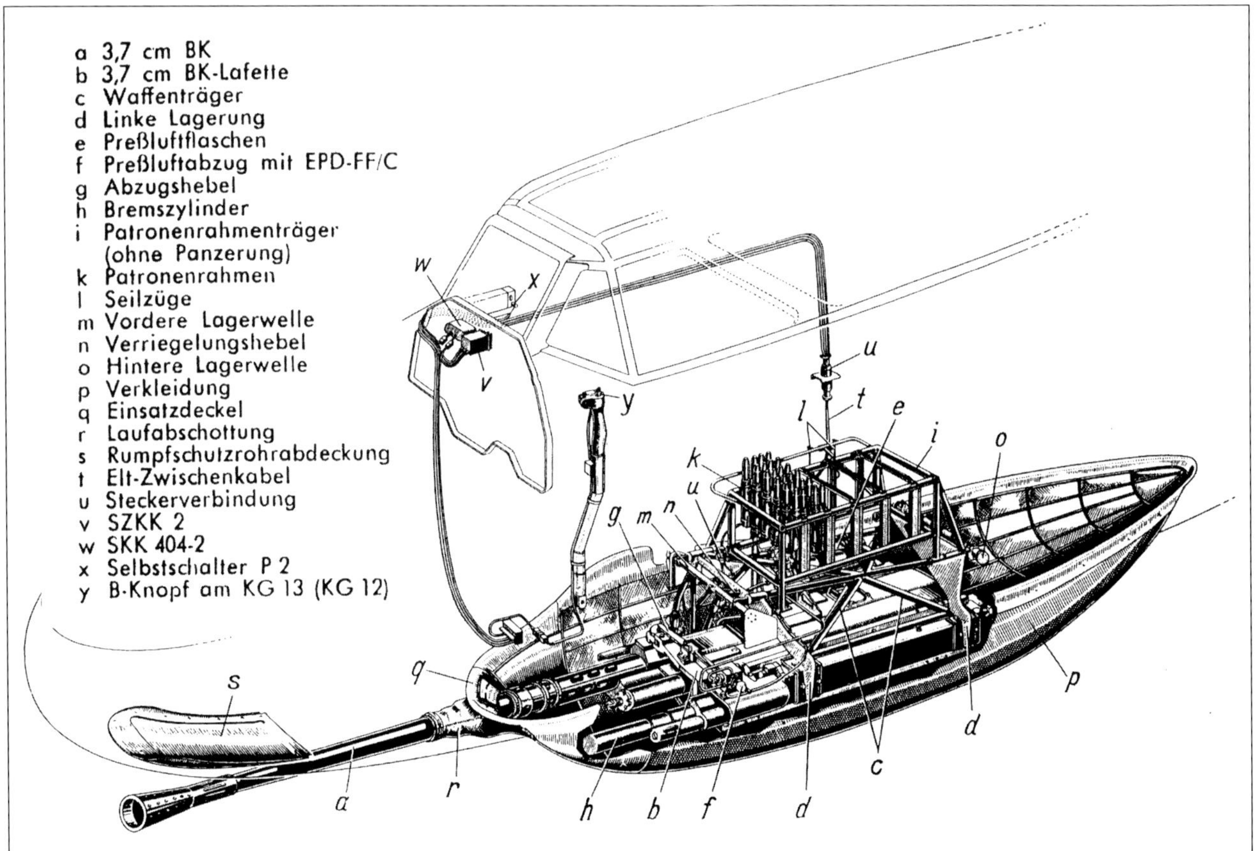

Bf 110 G-2/R1 mit Rüstsatz R1: 3,7 cm BK, Einbau-Gesamtübersicht

Abb. 1: Gesamtansicht 3,7 cm BK mit Verkleidung

Bf 110 G-2/R1, *Zerstörer*

As Bf 110 G-2, but

Fixed armament: 1 x Flak 18, no MG 151/20s

In late January 1943 the first Bf 110s with BK 3.7 were delivered and an order issued to establish a squadron with *Luftflotte 4*. The Bf 110 G-2/R1 was the first variant used against tanks, as were identically armed Hs 129s, Ju 87s, and Ju 88s. By April 1943, however, it became obvious that the Bf 110 was ill-suited for the role and, starting in August 1943, was used by *Erprobungskommando 25* for daylight attacks against bombers, with ZG 76 following suit in early 1944. The gun's installation in a large underbelly gondola reduced the Bf 110's speed by about 30 km/hr. This negatively affected the lateral stability, so much so that, as before, the pilots were compelled to close to within about 300 m of the bombers if they wanted any chance of scoring a kill. In order to alleviate the problem somewhat, several aircraft were later fitted with larger vertical stabilizers.

The 3.7 cm Bordkanone (Flak 18) was installed in the Bf 110 on its side and carried 66 rounds in 11 frames. It was reloaded by the radioman/gunner and was a temperamental and unloved gun. There were efforts to have it replaced with the Flak 43. These, however, were only installed in prototypes, if only to keep the concept of the *Zerstörer* attack against bombers with such weapons alive in the face of increased fighter protection in the spring of 1944.

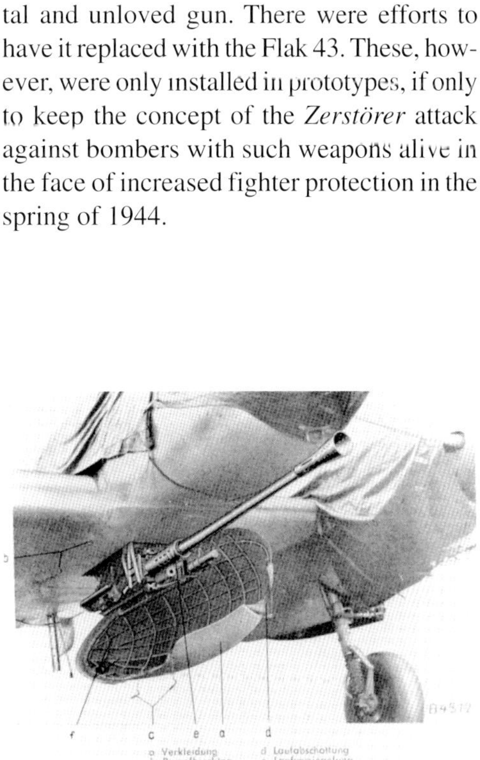

Abb. 11: Verkleidung abgeklappt

right: Over the course of time, the underfuselage gondola underwent minor changes. (Petrick)

a Patronenrahmenträger
b Verschlußbügel
c Führungsschiene
d Patronenrahmen
e Ladetisch
f Seilzug „Vorlauf"
g Seilzug „Patronenrahmen"
h Löffel
i Seilzug „Hülsenklappe"

Abb. 5: Patronenrahmenträger

a SKK 404-2
b SZKK 2
c Rechter Schußzähler und Schauzeichen
d Linker Schußzähler (blockiert)
e B-Knopf
f Handgriff der Heizanlage

Abb. 10: Bedienanlage im Führerraum

far right: This Bf 110 G-2/R1 operated from Poltava with 5./ZG 1 in March of 1943. Used in the anti-tank role, the Bf 110 G-2/R1 retained the four MG 17s. (Petrick)

Bf 110 G-2/R2, *Zerstörer*

As Bf 110 G-2/R1, but

Fuel:	additional 440 kg GM 1 for 45 min
Flexible armament:	minus MG 81 Z

left: During Reich defense operations, the G-2/R2 often flew without the MG 17s in order to get better high altitude performance. This machine was photographed in the summer of 1944 while operating with I./ZG 1. (Petrick)

Armor:	no armor in aft position
Maximum speed:	450km/h at 11000 m

The first Bf 110 G-2 fitted out with Flak 18 and GM 1 flew sometime around June 1943 and, according to Galland, had an exceptional rate of climb (5-10 m at 9500 m). The designation for this aircraft is unknown. It is possible that it, too, was identified with a U number. It was equivalent to the Bf 110 G-2/R2

The RLM, ever fearful of high altitude bomber strikes, initiated the concept of a heavy, twin-engined, but single-seat high altitude fighter based on the Bf 110 and Me 410. Because specialized high altitude engines such as the DB 628 could not yet be had, it was decided to fit GM 1 systems. Weight was to be reduced by as much as possible in order to ensure the needed altitudes were reached. Accordingly, plans called for the second crewman, his armor, and some of the radio equipment and defensive armament to be removed. A heavy caliber fixed gun was considered essential to survive against the heavily armored and armed bombers. The Bf 110 G-2/R2, built some time after July 1943, followed the concept, although for the time being the second crewman was necessary in order to load the Flak 18. With the introduction of the Flak 43 he could be dispensed with.

In 1944 this concept was replaced by the heavily armed single engine fighter (e.g. Fw 190 with two MG 151/20s, two MK 108s and GM 1 system), as these were less obvious to enemy fighters.

Bf 110 G-2/R3, *Zerstörer*

As Bf 110 G-2, but

Fixed armament:	2 MK 108 with 135 rounds each in place of four MG 17s

The R3 was the full-scale production variant of the conversion tested in the Bf 110 G-4/U9.

In order to increase weapons effectiveness the field installed two MG 151s or 151/20s in place of the four MG 17s. There was no modification designation for this change. The RLM did not support this measure, as it preferred the MK 108 solution instead.

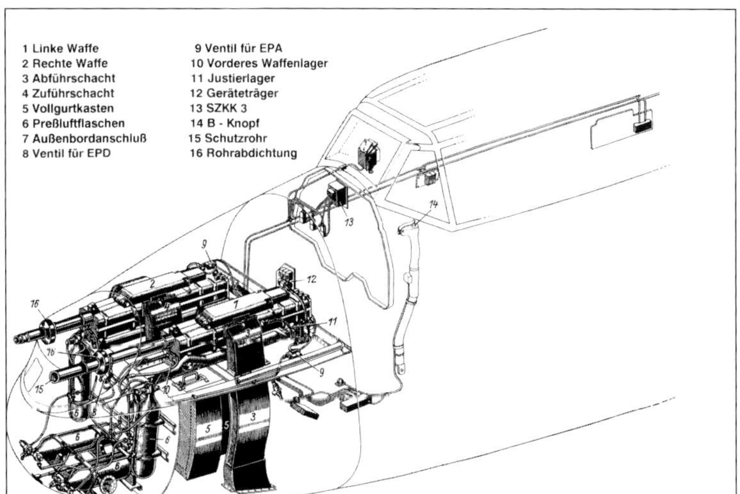

Bf 110 G-2/U 9 Schusswaffenanlage, Übersicht der MK 108

below: With four MG 151/20s, two MK 108s and four Nebelgerät *air-to-air mortars, the Bf 110 G-2/R3 was a dangerous opponent for the bombers (although it needed its own fighter protection). (Smithsonian Institution)*

above: The large rudders were rarely seen on the G-2, but were clearly advantageous for this aircraft carrying the Flak 18 *and* Dödel. *Due to the picture's fuzziness, it can only be speculated that the plane is armed with the MG 81Z and the MK 108, indicating a G-2/R4.* (Bundesarchiv *Koblenz)*

above right: The gun ports for the MG 151s have been painted on this Bf 110 G-3. (Ries)

Bf 110 G-2/R4, *Zerstörer*

As Bf 110 G-2/R1, but

Fixed armament: 2 MK 108s with 135 rounds each in place of 4 MG 17s

Bf 110 G-2/R5, *Zerstörer*

As Bf 110 G-2/R2, but

Fixed armament: 2 MK 108s with 135 rounds each in place of 4 MG 17s

Bf 110 G-3, Strategic Reconnaissance with Increased Range (or Bomber)

As Bf 110 G-2, but

Camera:	1 RB 50/30 or 1 RB 75/30
Armament:	without MG 151 *Rüstsatz* M1 (according to bomber manual)
Ordnance:	only 2 x 50 kg under each wing *Rüstsatz* M2 (according to bomber manual)
Equipment:	high altitude oxygen system moved behind the cockpit due to camera installation
Electronic systems:	add'l FuG XVII
Weight (empty):	5.97 t
Weight (airborne):	7.46 t
Weight (airborne):	9.16 t with auxiliary tanks and bombs

According to the Bf 110 G-3 operations manual from 4/28/43 the G-3 was exclusively a reconnaissance version, and the M1 and M2 mod packs could not be installed. In the manual from 8/27/43 the use of these kits was listed as an option when the G-3 operated as a bomber.

Production of the Bf 110 G-3 began in January 1943. On 6/15/43 the *General der Aufklärer* briefed the RLM that, among other things, the Me 410 had fully proven itself in the tactical reconnaissance role. The bulk of tactical reconnaissance, however, still rested with the Me 110, which was in urgent need of replacement by the Me 410.

Bf 110 G-3/U1, *Zerstörer* or Bomber

As G-3, but

Fixed armament: 2 MG 151/20s in place of camera equipment

According to loss reports, in the late summer of 1943 there were at least two Bf 110 G-3/U1s (*W.Nr.* 5684 and 5691) active with I./ZG 76. The statements in Monogram Close Up 18 that the U1 conversion included retrofitting with the MG 151, and the manual's claim that the Bf 110 G-3 could also be kitted out with the M1 weapons pack led the authors to believe that the Bf 110 G-3/U1 was a reconnaissance aircraft converted to a *Zerstörer* configuration. It differed from the Bf 110 G-2 by the high altitude breather system.

Bf 110 G-3/R3, Strategic Reconnaissance with Increased Range

As Bf 110 G-3, but

Fixed armament: 2 MK 108s with 135 rounds each in place of 4 MG 17s

Bf 110 G-4, Night Fighter (or Bomber)

As Bf 110 G-2, but

Empennage: enlarged vertical stabilizer, wooden construction (medium, late production batches)
Electronic systems: FuBl 2F, FuG 202, APZA 6, Peil G VI, FuG 10 P, FuG 25 (4/28/43)
Electronic systems: FuBl 2F, FuG 220, APZA 6,FuG 16 ZE, FuG 10 P, FuG 25 (11/1/44)
Armor: armor plating in forward cockpit area (late production batches)
armor skirting in the nose section (late production batches)
Weight (empty): 6.09 t as night fighter
Weight (empty): 6.18 t as bomber with 1.7 t bombs
Weight (airborne): 7.92 t as night fighter with M1 kit without auxiliary tanks
Weight (airborne): 9.37 t as bomber with 1.7 t bombs

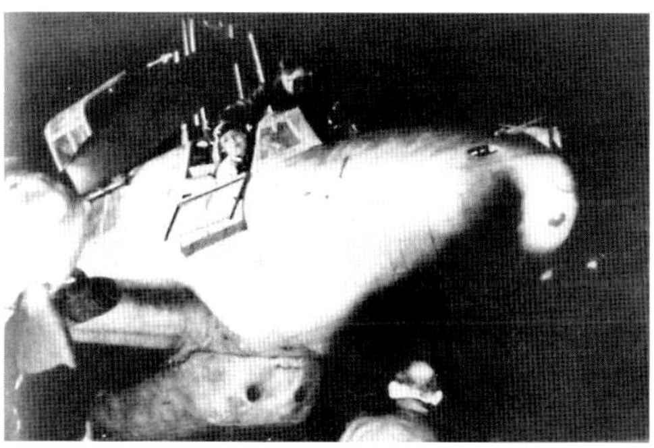

Ballast: 55 kg at the tailwheel to balance the center of gravity
Max. speed: 510 km/h at 5800 m
Landing speed: 140/km/h
Takeoff speed: 110 - 120 km/h
Dive speed: 700 km/h
Climb rate: 6000 m in 9.1 min
Range: 880 km (1270 with auxiliary tanks)
Endurance: 1 hr 20 min

According to the manual, from October 1943 the G-4 was also used as a bomber, but without the night fighting gear. A report from 6/22/43 states that the G-4 was fitted at the factory with the M 2 (two ETC 500 racks) and M 3 (two ETC 50s under each wing) in June 1943. However, it was expected that 100% of production would be equipped with the M 1 modification pack (two MG 151/20s beginning in July.

The original flame dampers reduced its speed by about 30 km/h and negatively affected the flight handling at high altitudes. The M 1 kit cost 20 km/h. The use of the Lichtenstein SN 2 radar with its massive antenna lowered the speed by a further 20 km/h, so that the Bf 110 G-4 in September 1943 was no faster than the He 111 of 1939. In addition, the antennas had a destabilizing effect. As a result, new reduced drag flame dampers were developed and fitted in the final months of production. To improve performance the M1 kit was often removed by

above: Compare this photo of a C-series canopy to the following pictures.

left: This propaganda photo shows the Bf 110 G-4 minus radar antennae and without the MG 151 barrels. Some authors claim that the guns are MK 108s. Initially, the G-4 carried the same armament as the F-4, i.e. four MG 151s and the FuG 202 system.

below: Roll bar, radio and radar equipment, and the schräge Musik *gun configuration all made the G-4 cockpit a much more cramped affair than that of the C-series. (all photos, Mankau)*

the field units and was later abandoned altogether. In its place came the MG 151/20 or MK 108 in the nose, and the MG FF oblique firing guns. The FuG 202's antenna array switched from the heavily braced initial version to a later, single braced type.

For reasons of stability, larger wooden rudders were introduced parallel to the introduction of the SN 2 radar system in order to bring the night fighter's flight handling in line. Individual cases of the old style SN 2 in combination with the small rudders have also been noted. These measures, however, did not lead to a new designation for the aircraft. Later versions of the SN 2 antenna array have the antenna pointed at an angle. This version occurred with both types of bracing.

above: The large antennae destabilized the aircraft and made single-engined flight difficult with the smaller rudder. As a result, this combination was seldom seen. (Griehl)

right: The Bf 110 G's armor was increased in the spring of 1944.

below: To improve flight handling, the enlarged wooden vertical stabilizer was introduced at about the same time as the SN 2 radar system.

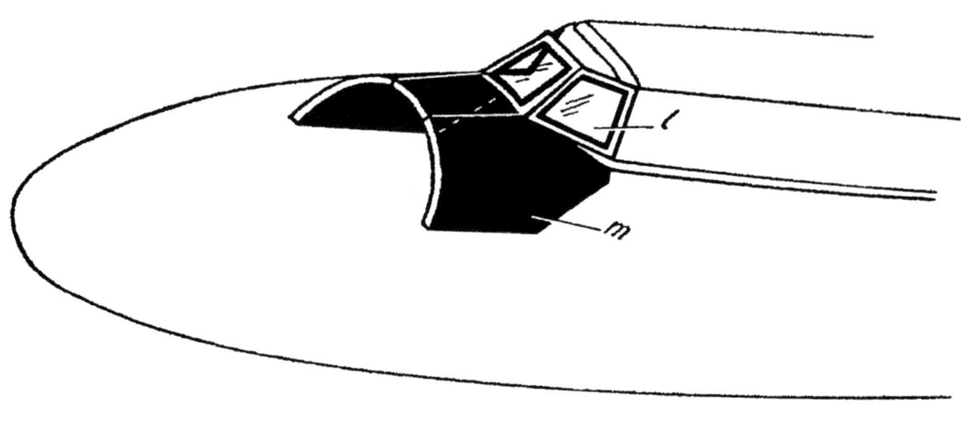

Sämtliche neu ausgelieferten Flugzeuge der Baureihe Bf 110 G sind mit Panzerscheiben (7 l) ausgerüstet. Beim Baumuster Bf 110 G-4 ist zusätzlich die Panzerschürze (7 m) eingebaut.

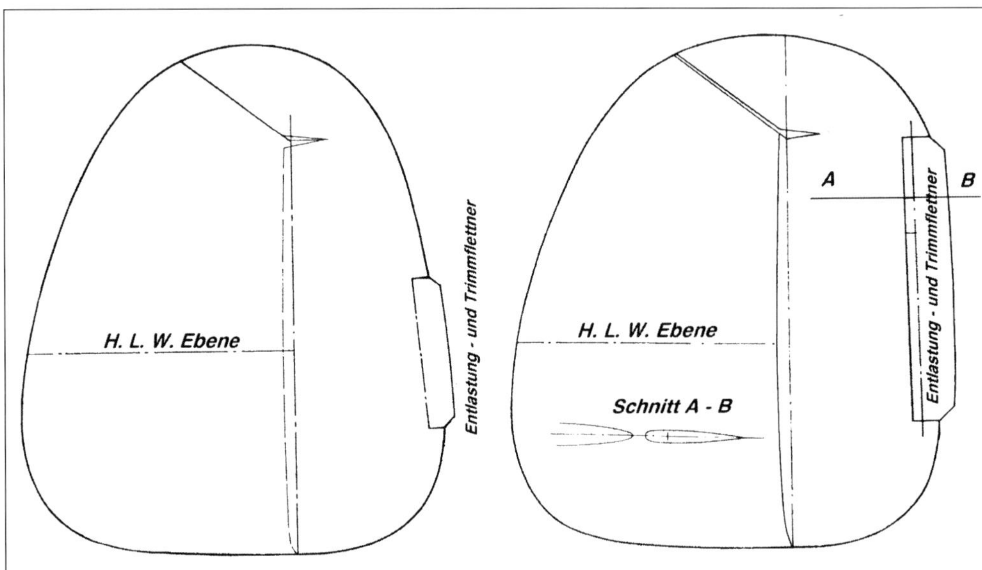

The increasing number of radio systems, as well as the growing threat from enemy night fighters prompted the desire in 1944 for a three man crew. After having to monitor the radar systems for hours on end, the radioman became night-blind and was useless as a gunner and observer. To get around this a gunner—usually the crew chief—flew on board, sitting behind the radioman on the long seat. Due to the cramped space the gunner had a belly parachute, and the radio operator wore a back 'chute. For reasons of weight and space, however, the Bf 110 was limited to three crewmen, or two crewmen and a GM 1 tank (Bf 110 G-4/U7), or two crewmen and an auxiliary fuel tank (Bf 110 G-4/U8). Only in the variant without tanks in the cockpit could the two MG FF oblique firing guns be carried (Bf 110 G-4/R8). In the night fighter conference of 11/5/43 it was established that approximately 50% of the night fighters would be built with oblique guns and 50% with auxiliary tanks.

above: The radar equipment severely hampered the radio operator's view. Since he was virtually blind at night from staring at his radar screen, the operator was of no help in locating enemy aircraft at close range. (Lutz)

left: Other than the updated radar system, one of the final alterations was the improved flame dampers for the exhaust. (Nowarra)

The poor short-range search capability of the SN 2 radar system (large antennae) necessitated the additional installation of the wide-angle radar (small antennae). (Petrick)

Bf 110 G-4a through G-4e, Night Fighter (or Bomber)

These designations infrequently appear in loss reports, with the "d" letter appearing as early as the end of 1943 and the "e" letter appearing in May 1945. Heumann and others interpret this designation as indicators of differences in radar systems installed. The authors have found no evidence to support this claim. This interpretation is not convincing in light of the fact that airframes underwent other modifications (oil slinger, larger rudder, etc.) with different radar systems.

Bf 110 G-4/U1, Night Fighter

As Bf 110 G-4, but

Flexible armament: without MG 81 Z

There is a Bf 110 G-4/U1 also listed in the weapons operations guideline and the weapons manual for the G-2. These documents, however, indicate that the flexible guns were not installed. The fixed armament was the same as for the G-4. This may possibly be a case of mixup with the Bf 110 G-4/U7.

Bf 110 G-4/U7, Night Fighter

As Bf 110 G-4, but

Fuel:	additional 440 kg GM 1 for 45 min
Flexible armament:	without MG 81 Z
Armor:	none in aft compartment

Compare with Bf 110 G-2/U7. The first ten Bf 110 G-4/U7 high altitude night fighters for combating Mosquitos were delivered in June 1943, and were in fact converted Bf 110 G-4s. The General Staff ordered that 50% of the aircraft be so equipped on 6/29/43. According to a report in the RLM, the field considered the GM 1 systems to be useless and potentially dangerous ballast in some cases and, since the British never flew at altitudes above 8000 m, these were largely removed. At this time the systems had not yet been fully developed. Trials with Bf 110 G-4/U7 *W.Nr.* 5457, NM+SE at Messerschmitt's Augsburg facility showed that the aircraft with full GM 1 tank and without ammunition was tail-heavy and unstable at higher altitudes. This effect was exaggerated with extended landing flaps, making any second pass after an aborted approach nearly impossible.

Bf 110 G-4/U8, Night Fighter

As Bf 110 G-4/U7, but

Fuel:	additional 540 liters fuel in the aft crew compartment in place of GM 1
Oil:	additional 35 liters in a tank behind the cockpit
Flexible armament:	without MG 81 Z
Armor:	none in aft compartment
Range:	additional 350 km

Considering its speed and firepower the Bf 110 was a good night fighter. The kill successes were comparable to those of the He

219 and Ju 88. Its biggest shortcoming was its limited endurance (approx. 80 to 90 minutes loiter time) which, among other things, made it impossible to form up larger formations from different areas. In the relatively constricted space of the *Himmelbett* method (ground-controlled night fighters) the Bf 110's range was adequate. When operations switched to pursuit engagements (*zahme Sau*) it no longer proved up to the task, and even mod packs and factory conversions were insufficient to increase its range. This led in 1944 to the gradual phase-out of the Bf 110 in favor of the Ju 88 and He 219.

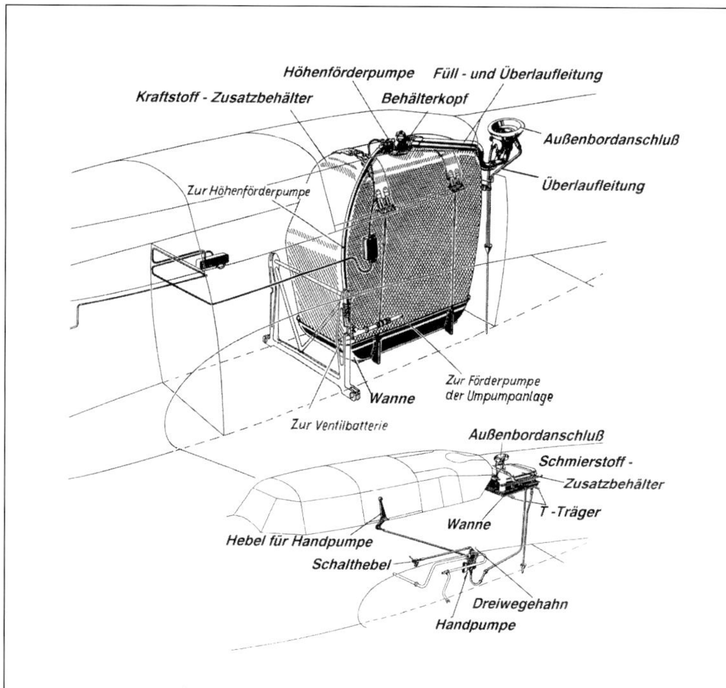

Übersicht Betriebsstoff Zusatzanlagen für Bf 110 G-4/U8

Bf 110 G-4/U9, Night Fighter

As Bf 110 G-2, but

Fixed armament: 2 MK 108s with 135 rounds each in place of 4 MG 17s

The first known mention of the MK 108 in the Bf 110 is dated 12/19/42. Messerschmitt Report No. 389 references a Bf 110 version that included: two MK 108s; the M 1 mod pack; one MG 151/20 with Rf 1 periscope sight fixed to the rear; and the MG 81 Z. In March 1943 the first test installation took place in a nose section of a Bf 110. The first prototype fitting occurred at Gotha in May 1943 with the installation in Bf 110 G-4/U9, *W.Nr.* 5429, which was then tested at Gotha and, in September 1943, at Messerschmitt's Augsburg plant. Firing trials showed problems with the shell ejection port; the shells bounced against the MG 151 gondola. The gas pressure damaged the FuG 202 antenna, soot dirtied the windscreen, and smoke powder found its way into the cockpit. A flash suppressor for the muzzle appeared indispensable for night operations.

Five machines are believed to have been built in August 1943. In September 1943 the MK 108, FuG 220, and FuG 212 were integrated into the aircraft's nose, and the Bf 110 G-4/U9, 480092, was completed, although it still lacked the FuG 212 antenna and flash suppressors.

When production began in December 1943 the designation was changed to Bf 110 G-4/R3, as it was for the other sub-variants.

Bf 110 G-4/R3, Night Fighter

As Bf 110 G-4, but

Fixed armament: 2 MK 108s with 135 rounds each in place of 4 MG 17s

No modification, but a production version. The standard engagement distance for night combat was about 100 m in 1944. At

below: A Bf 110 G-4/R3 typical for the spring of 1945, with angled SN 2 antennae. (Petrick)

above: Muzzle flash suppressors were seldom fitted to the MK 108. (Petrick)

right: Although the MG 151 armament wasn't a conversion package, at the wing level field units converted to the weapon relatively frequently. The guns seen here on this Bf 110 G-4 with early-style SN 2 antennae have been fitted with flash suppressors. (Ries)

this range, many night fighter pilots felt that the MK 108 was too effective, since their own planes regularly suffered damage from parts flying off the stricken—even with just one hit. The goal of the night fighter was to catch the bomber on fire. The 2 cm guns were adequate for this task. Additional problems with the MK 108 included covering the windscreen with sooty residue and the blinding flash from the muzzle. To counter these problems, designers developed a windscreen wiper system and a flash suppressor.

Bf 110 G-4/R6, Night Fighter

As Bf 110 G-4/U7, but

Fixed armament:	2 MK 108s with 135 rounds each in place of 4 MG 17s
Flexible armament:	1 x MG 81 Z

No modification, but a planned production version. Work on this variant began on 1/3/44. The GM 1 tank was to be shifted forward and reshaped, so that it would be possible to carry a rear gunner. Although this version was mentioned in the aircraft type sheet from 11/1/44, it is doubtful if it was ever realized since it was never used (see Bf 110 G-4/U7)

Bf 110 G-4/R7, Night Fighter

As Bf 110 G-4/U8, but

According to the aircraft type sheet form 11/1/44 this was the production version of the G-4/U8

Bf 110 G-4/R8, Night Fighter

As Bf 110 G-4/R3, but

Fixed armament:	additional 2 MG FF/M with 120 rounds each as oblique firing guns in the aft cockpit

The first installation in the Bf 110 G was reputed to have taken place in July 1943 by weapons crewman *Ofw.* Paul Mahle with the assistance of *Hptm.* Rudolf Schönert of II./NJG 5. The guns were taken from Bf 110 Fs. Because of the limited headroom the sights were situated behind the pilot, and only the reflective plate was located above him. The installation proved to be so popular that soon other aircraft at Parchim were being fitted with the system. In September 1943 the RLM received a report on *Hauptmann* Meurer's

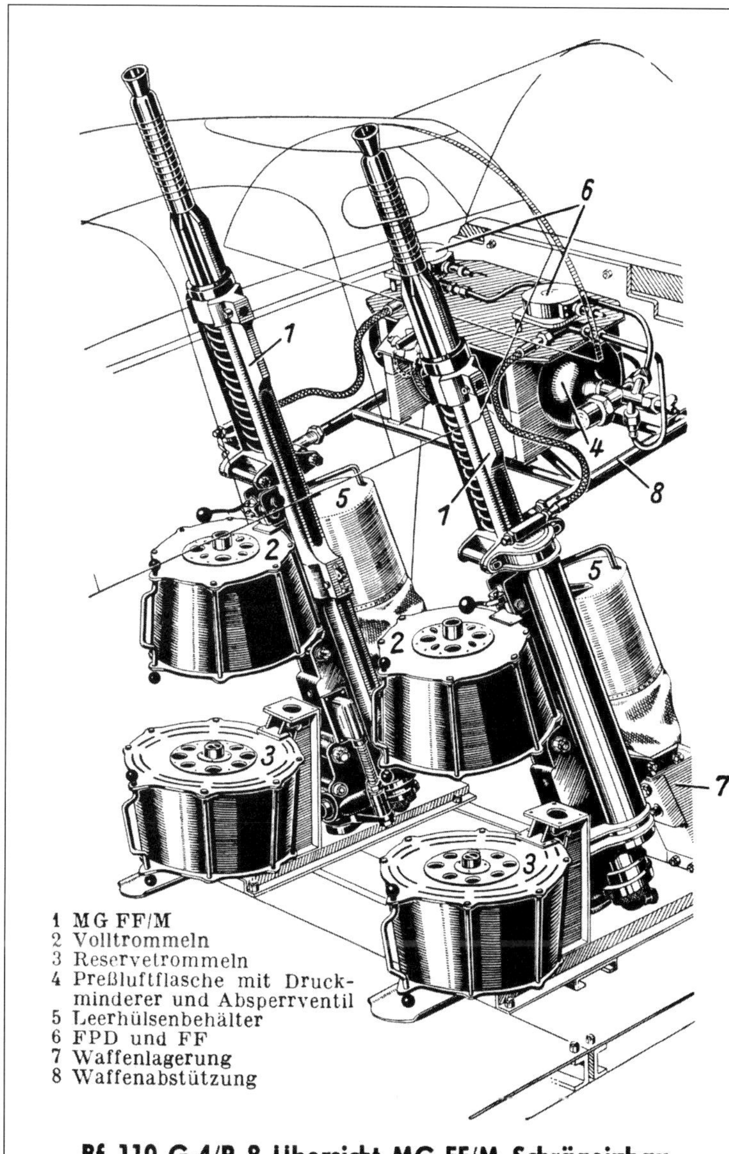

Bf 110 G-4/R 8 Übersicht MG-FF/M Schrägeinbau

successes he had achieved using two upward firing MG FFs. The MG 151/20 was ill-suited for use in the Bf 110 G-4, as the crews could become caught on the gun's long barrel if they needed to bail out. In October it was decided to go into full scale production. In November the GWF was given an example of a "*schräge Musik*" (jazz music) configured plane in order to come up with a design for series production. The prototype was completed on 5/13/44. Series production of the Bf 110 G-4/R8 began in July 1944, with the first production machine rolling off the assembly line on 8/8/44. The authors do not know if those aircraft modified in the year prior to the production version appearing had a special designation. However, as these were conversions undertaken in the field, it is doubtful that they were given any unique designation.

Since the Revi 16 N was difficult to sight using the MG FF—and there were also problems with fitting the head armor—in March 1945 a Bf 110 G-4/R8 (*W.Nr.* 140655, G9+AA) was experimentally kitted out with the Revi located beneath a plexiglass cover on the panel above the pilot.

top left: Thanks to their compact size, the two schräge Musik *MG FF posed no danger to crewmembers attempting to bail out. The bump in the canopy provided increased head clearance for the gunner.*

above left: This photo of a Bf 110 G-4/R8 shows the schräge Musik *MG FF and the flash suppressors of the MK 108 to good effect. (Petrick)*

Bf 110 G-4/R9, Night Fighter

As Bf 110 G-4/R3, but

Fixed armament: two additional MK 108s, with 100 rounds each, firing obliquely in aft fuselage section

Since the R8 modification kit only utilized existing stock for installation of the MG FF, once these were used up the MK 108, just as short, would then be used. Due to its explosive firepower, the gun was not without its problems, since there was real danger of being struck by the victim's wreckage at the close ranges typical for engagement. The MK 108 was first proposed for installation in the Bf 110 on 5/9/44. In September 1944 the prototype was nearing completion and delivery to the test center at Tarnewitz. It is questionable whether the variant ever went into production, and mention of the gun's installation in the Bf 110 F-4 in other aviation-related publications (Heumann and others) is nonsense.

Bf 110 G-6, Night Fighter

As Bf 110 G-4, but

In an RLM meeting on 3/19/43 the night fighter version of the Bf 110 G was designated G-6, while the G-4 was a G-2 with additional armament. This designation, however, was never accepted.

Bf 110 H

The H-series and H-2 through H-5 subvariants were defined in a meeting at Gotha on 12/15/43. According to meeting reports (GL) from 12/3/43 and 1/14/44, a sample installation of the DB 605 D was to be completed by December, with a sample aircraft finished by the end of January 1944. Construction of further examples using the DB 605 D was initiated. Design blueprints for the Bf 110 H were expected to be ready by 3/15/44. The DB 605 D, which offered major improvements over the previous version, was not expected to be available before the end of 1944. Since even with these changes the Bf 110 was still an "old crate"—the continued production of which adversely affected the manufacturing of more modern types—production of the night fighters was still expected to end in July 1945. It was anticipated that Bf 110 production would peak in October 1944 with 200 per month. Engines and a few other minor modifications were to be introduced into production in mid-1944; modifications to the airframe (fuselage and wings) would be abandoned, however. Work over the next few months concentrated on implementing the DB 605 D (E) with the MW 50 system, but suffered a six-month setback

The compact, close set barrels of the armament on this Bf 110 G-4/R9 indicate the presence of MK 108s. (Petrick)

with the destruction of the GWF research department. Prototype for the DB 605 E installation was Bf 110 G-4 *W.Nr.* 730040. In November 1944 Bf 110 development ceased altogether, with the emergency fighter program measures, at which time it was determined to let production run out. The Bf 110 H remained a concept only.

The DB 605 D was originally a DB 605 A with takeoff performance improved by some 75 hp through higher compression and C 3 special fuel. The DB 605 E was similar to the D, but had the reduction ratio of the DB 605 B. On the ultimate DB 605 D/E, which was expected to offer better performance at higher altitudes, the turbocharger would also be replaced by one similar to that used on the DB 605 G. Although these measures meant a drop in performance at sea level by about 50 hp, at 10,000 m the larger supercharger boosted performance from 790 to 930 hp. In addition, plans called for the use of water methanol injection (MW 50), enabling an increase in takeoff performance by 325 hp. A precursor to the DB 605 D would be the DB 605 AS, which only made use of the modified turbocharger (no MW 50 fuel injection) and, at altitude, was only marginally inferior to the DB 605 D in terms of performance. The larger turbocharger necessitated a change to the engine mounts and the nacelles, meaning that the DB 605 could not simply slide into the production run.

Bf 110 H-2, *Zerstörer* or Bomber for High Altitudes

As Bf 110 G-2, but

Engine:	2 x DB 605 E with new mounts new air intake new cowling new lubrication system new cooling system larger radiators new starter
Performance:	2 x 1435 hp
Equipment:	new instrument panel with standard IFR panel engine gauges (formerly in the nacelles) new interior lighting new hydraulic system for retractable tailwheel new electrical system new oxygen system
Propeller:	new, dependent on test results
Fixed armament:	2 x MK 108, each with 135 rounds 1 x MK 103 with 140 rounds Revi C 16 D ZFR 4 gunsight
Flexible armament:	1 x MG 81 Z
Ordnance:	same as Bf 110 G-2
Mod pack:	M 5 with 21 cm air-to-air mortars
Armor:	for cannon ammunition armored glass in forward crew compartment
Fuel:	2 x 300 liters in drop tanks, new mounts
Oil:	increased capacity container
Fuselage:	section 18 lengthened by 600 mm reinforced
Length:	12.67 m
Wings:	fitted with 1.25 m wingtip extensions increasing the load factor from 2.5 to 5 by strengthened main spar new undercarriage base, new firewall around engine
Wingspan:	18.576 m
Empennage:	reinforced elevators enlarged rudder made of wood
Main undercarriage:	reinforced
Tailwheel:	retractable
Weight (gross):	9.4 t
Weight (landing):	8.6 t
Max. speed w/ GM 1:	580 km/h at 6000 m 620 km/h at 8000 m 650 km/h at 10000 m
Ceiling w/GM 1:	12.5 km

Bf 110 H-4, Night Fighter for High Altitudes

As Bf 110 H-2, but

Engine:	new Ebersbacher flame dampers

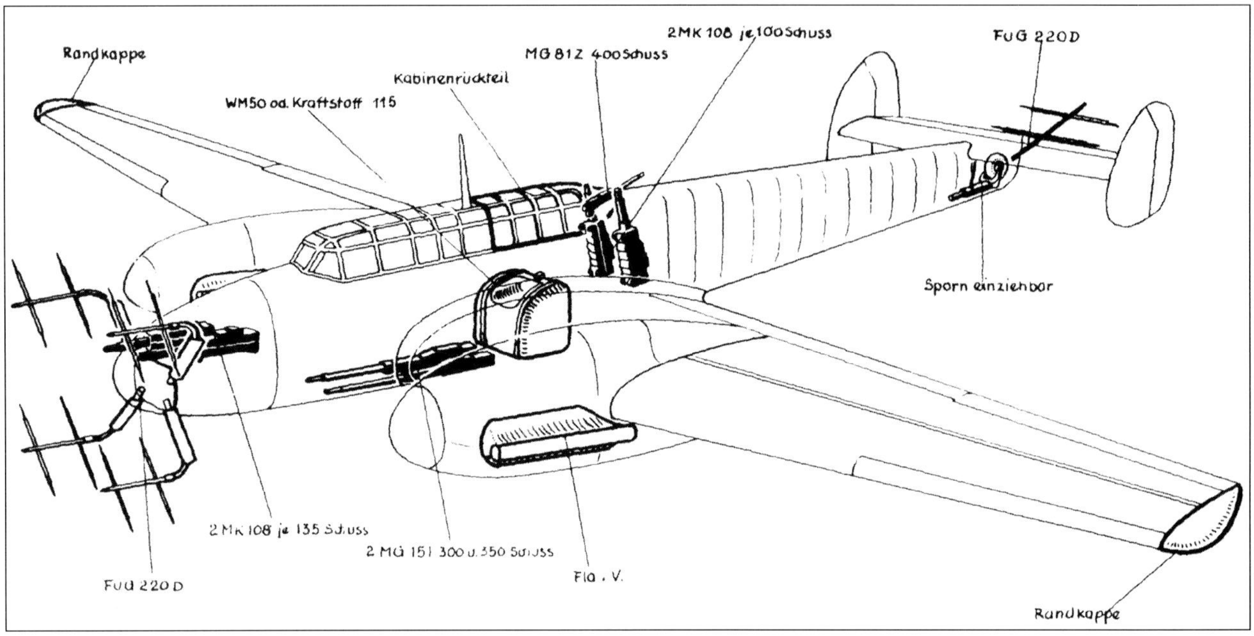

Sketch showing the planned modifications inherent to the Bf 110 H-6. Note that there is no mention of the new DB 605 engines.

Electronic systems: FuG 220 (Li SN 2), FuG 16 ZY, Uhu II FuG 135, FuG 101
Fixed armament: 2 x MG FF or 1 MK 108 *schräge Musik*
Armor: armored skirting in nose
Crew: 2/3 men

Bf 110 H-5, Single-Seat Heavy Fighter

As Bf 110 H-2, but

Fuselage: removal of gunner's seat including equipment and armor
Electronic systems: FuG 16, FuG 25 in place of FuG 10 P with APZ 6
Ordnance: none
Armor: none in aft section

Bf 110 H-6, Night Fighter

As Bf 110 G-4/R9, but

Engine: 2 x DB 605 E
Electronic systems: FuBl 2 F, FuG 220, APZA 6, FuG 16 ZY, FuG 10 P, FuG25, Peil G VI
Fixed armament: 2 x MG FF or 1 MK 108 *schräge Musik*
Armor: armored plating in forward cockpit armored skirting in nose
Crew: 3 men

This description of the H-6 is derived from the aircraft type sheet for the Bf 110 from 11/1/44. Compared to the H-4 description from 12/15/43 the fuselage and wing extensions have been abandoned.

Work done at the Gothaer Waggonfabrik reveals that the Bf 110 H-6 was to also have included the following additional changes:

Engine: MW 50 system for improved performance below maximum pressure altitude
Fuel: new lines in the fuselage 135 liter MW 50 tank beneath the third crewman's seat
Equipment: new oxygen system in the aft fuselage adequate for three crewmen
Fuselage: sections 17 and 18 rein forced, built of duraluminum

The authors have found no evidence that the H-6 series actually ever went into production. However, with the exception of the engines, the features noted above were implemented on the G-4 series.

Heavy Fighter Tactical Technical Requirements (1936/37)

Role: anti-bomber escort and strategic reconnaissance attack from behind, above and behind, and below and behind
day/night capable
takeoff and landing often at night
secondary role: strike attacks against enemy ground defenses

Type: enclosed canopy, multi-seat

Special features: valence, speed, range, climb rate
fully instrumented for IFR and long range navigation
fully equipped for night operations (searchlights)
radio crewman's seat immediately behind the pilot

Speed: cruise at 6 km altitude: 400km/h
max at 6 km altitude: 550-600 km/h

Endurance: 3 hrs at max. throttle at 6 km altitude

Climb rate: 5 km in 8 min

Service ceiling: 10 km without bombs

Takeoff/Landing features: four at a time, field airstrip, 600 m takeoff run

Fixed armament: 2 heavy rapid fire guns, at least 2 cm caliber with 300 rounds each

Flexible armament: Dual MG 15 in upper deck, aft

Field of fire: vertical 0 - 30° upward, horizontal 20° either side

Bombs: 10 x 10 kg, simple air-to-air gunsight

Communications systems: radio transmitter and receiver
extendable DF antenna
autopilot
air-to-air radio system (50 km range)
ground to air receiver (200 km range)
capable of firing five signal flares

Rescue and emergency equipment:
high altitude oxygen system, 2 hrs at 6000 m altitude
anti-icing system for canopy
anti-icing system for airframe
opening side windows

At the time these requirements were issued, aerodynamics and currently available engines did not allow the mandated flight performance (v_{max} = 600 km/h at 6000 m altitude) to be reached. O 9/4/36 the Daimler-Benz Company offered the RLM development of a 40 liter engine for the first time. A developmental contract was issued shortly thereafter. However, the RLM stopped development in February/March '37 on the instructions of Udet.

This meant that the required flight performance would have to be achieved in part by improving the efficiency of 30 liter engines, but also by reducing drag through aerodynamic refinement and a relatively low weight. Low weight meant less lift was needed, enabling smaller wings with less drag. As a result, by using a smaller, shorter fuselage to save weight, smaller wings could be employed that would themselves be lighter and consequently be able to be designed even smaller. This would in turn result in lower drag and higher airspeeds.

In 1937/38 Messerschmitt and Heinkel were in heated competition for the fastest airplane in the world. The two record-breaking planes (the He 100 and the Me 209) were characterized by their extremely small dimensions, in addition to their outstanding surface finish. As a consequence of these developments, over the next couple of years less ambitious aircraft were designed to be as small as possible, i.e. both fuselage and wings had the smallest dimensions permitted by their intended roles. The result was a relatively high speed at low altitudes. There were, however, serious disadvantages associated with this approach: the stubby fuselages meant that these planes suffered from lateral instability, something which, for example, made it difficult for the He 100 to sight in its version as a fighter. The small wings required a high landing speed. This limited usefulness as a night fighter and also required a higher caliber pilot. High altitude performance suffered considerably as a result of the small wings, and in later years, weight increase brought on by the need for ever more equipment and armament was also affected by the small wings.

The two aircraft based on these tactical-technical requirements (the Me 210 and the Ar 240) were, on the one hand, optimized for maximum speed at lower altitudes. Ultimately, though, the resulting disadvantages led to the failure of both types. Dimensions had to be increased for their follow-ons (the Me 410 and Ar 440) in order to achieve flying qualities that would be acceptable. Flight performance was then achieved with the help of the larger DB 603, which was not cleared for development until 3/4/40. Milch's later verdict on this decision by Udet: "The RLM's developmental leadership clearly failed in the case of the DB 603."

Kampfzerstörer Technical Guidelines from 7 Aug 1942

Role: *Kampfzerstörer* (bomber/heavy fighter) against both ground and air targets day/all-weather capable close support night fighting aerial reconnaissance in primary combat zone

Engine: 2 x DB 603 G, or DB 627 or DB 628 or Jumo 213

Crew: a) 1 pilot and 1 radioman/gunner close together in communal area
b) for pilot, free forward field of view to 25° below horizon, for sighting up to 70°
c) instruments below 25° field of view
d) cockpit heating
e) roll bar
f) emergency exit
g) pressurized cockpit

Forward armament: 2 x MG 151 with 500 rounds each
2 x MK 103 with 100 rounds each

Aft armament: 1 x MG 131 in LLG with 750 rounds, manually operated
2 x MG 151 fixed with 300 rounds each, operated by pilot with periscope sight

Bombs: 2 x 500 kg or
1 x 1000 kg cleared for dropping at 90 deg. Or 8 x 50 kg max bomb load or aerial torpedo as special load

Sight: BZA

Electronic systems: FuG 15 with targeting feature, FuG X, FuG 101 or 103, FuG 25 a

Armor: Canopy and engines protected against rounds of 2 cm caliber from the front, and as dive bomber from below

Speed: approaching that of a fighter

Range: 1200 km (2100 with drop tanks)

Climb rate: good

Dive speed: 600 km/h (propeller brake and ribbon 'chute)

Takeoff run: 700 m to an altitude of 20 m

Landing speed: 165 km/h

Flight handling: good takeoff and landing qualities (use of a nose wheel is to be considered as a basis, otherwise controllable tailwheel), problem-free stability, excellent IFR qualities, problem-free stall handling

Ar 240

On 30 October 1938 Arado was given initial information on a *Zerstörer* the *Luftwaffe* wanted based on the technical guidelines from 15 October that was also capable of dive bombing and had better defensive firepower than the Bf 110. For Arado there was a greater risk in building, as the company would most likely not expect to be awarded the contract for a production version; *Luftwaffe* planning from 7 November 1938 called for about 3000 Me 210s to be built by 1942, yet no Ar 240s. Arado received the preliminary contract for development and construction of six prototypes on 16 May 1939. Based on available research, Arado envisioned remote controlled barbettes for the defensive armament both above and below behind the cockpit, with a periscope to be used as a sighting mechanism.

The performance data listed below and on the following pages in large part stems from Arado calculations and not from that derived from test flights. The information differs in various reports and is dependent upon the time the calculations were made.

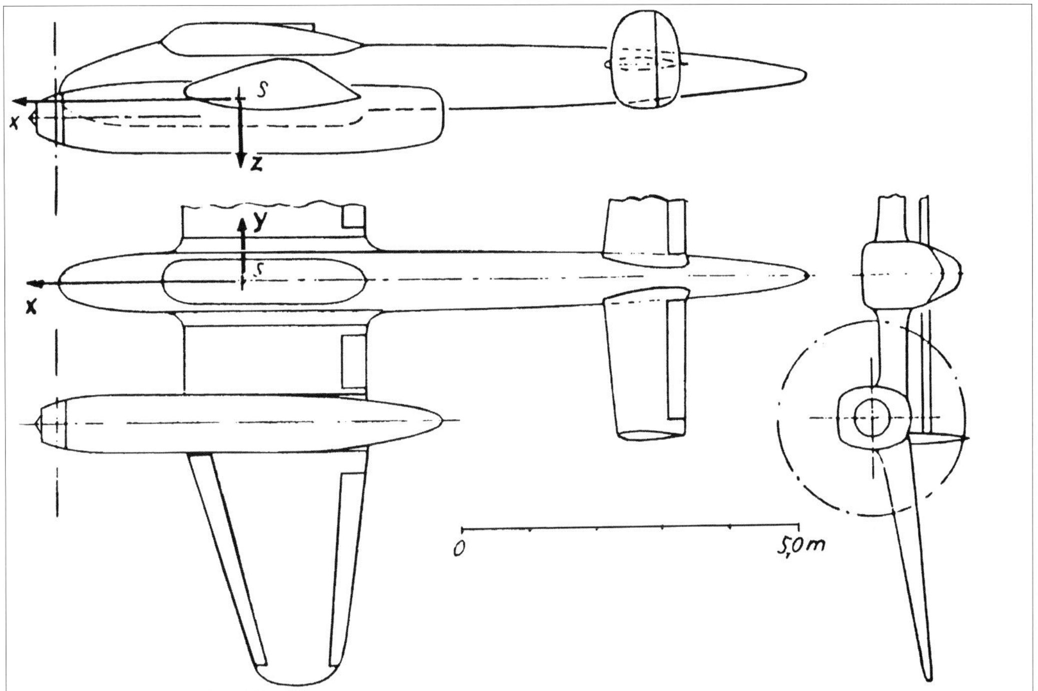

Projektentwurf E-240

Ar 240 V-1 and V-2

Engine: DB 601
Wing: outer section with 17.5° sweep
Wingspan: 12.16 m
Length: 11.80 m

Arado began development by drawing from the Bf 110, but chose instead much smaller dimensions. This would have the effect of reducing weight and drag. The small wings, however, required considerable lifting aids, which were planned as extendable slats. Arado double-slotted traveling ailerons outside the engine nacelles and Fowler flaps between the engines and fuselage. To allow the pilot the capability of dive bombing the fuselage nose was partially glazed. Bombs were planned to be carried externally, which simplified the choice of bombs, but reduced approach speeds when carrying ordnance. The Ar 240 V1 flew for the first time on 6/25/1940, to the disappointment of its creators: it was unstable, had unpleasant flight handling, and the radiators located ahead of the engines proved to be inadequate. Neither bomb racks nor defensive armament had been fitted.

One cause of the poor flight handling was, as with the Me 210, a poorly designed wing profile. With the short fuselage, the vertical stabilizers found themselves in the slipstream of the engine nacelles and had minimal effectiveness in the neutral position as a result. The extremely small wings, selected in order to achieve higher airspeeds, led to unacceptable takeoff and landing qualities in spite of the lifting aids. Finally, in all probability the nose did not meet the idea the contracting party had in mind for the Ju 87's replacement. Ar 240 V1 underwent general flight testing until it was lost in a crash on 4/18/1941.

The Ar 240 V2 first flew on 9/15/1940 and was basically the same as the V1. For a time (summer 1941) it carried MG 17s in the wing roots, but lacked any defensive armament. New leg coolers were fitted after 8/11/41, and these seemed to solve cooling problems during takeoff, i.e. flying slowly at high engine rpms. Along with these, Dornier dive brakes and new ailerons (from November 1941) were tested. Ar 240 V2 flights were documented in flight logs until 11/5/1942, at which time it was put into storage and most likely eventually scrapped some time in 1944.

The first two prototypes had a central cockpit and an extended forward fuselage similar to that of the Bf 110. (Koos)

Ar 240 A

The A series was planned around the DB 601 E engine. In two instances, however, the DB 603 A was also fitted.

Ar 240 V3 through V6

Fuselage:	Full-vision canopy ahead of the wings, pressurized cockpit, lengthened
Wings:	lengthened, unswept outer sections, no leading edge slats
Engines:	DB 601 E
Fixed armament:	2 MG 17s in the wing root (only applicable to V5 and V6)
Flexible armament:	2 x MG 81 Z (only applicable to V5 and V6)
Wingspan:	14.30 m
Length:	V3=12.60 m, V4=?, V5/V6=12.81 m
Wheel track:	4.25 m

The RLM intended the Me 210 to enter full scale production and the Ar 240 to be built in small numbers as an experimental design for testing new technology. Initially, plans called for the *Luftwaffe* to only operate single examples of the Ar 240 operationally in order to conduct trials. New features, such as pressurized cockpit and remotely operated defensive armament, were to be tested using the V3 through V6. The contractor also wanted a full-vision canopy with 60 to 65 degree downward forward field of view. Unlike the old specification requirements, which called for operations as a dive bomber, the desired goal was now high altitude operations. For a low flying dive bomber a pressurized cockpit was unnecessary ballast. Accordingly, it was planned to use the Ar 240 V3 for testing at the factory, while the V4 through V6 were to be turned over to the *Versuchsstelle für Höhenflüge* for trials. The high altitude requirement not only necessitated a pressurized cockpit, which was moved to the nose to meet the visibility requirements and keep the dimensions to a minimum, but also led to the need for larger span wings. As can be seen from the type sheet of 1/1/1942, the aft fuselage was initially the same as that of the first two prototypes. However, anticipated problems with stability in the yaw axis prompted the designers to lengthen the fuselage. The V3 initially flew without the defensive armament, as it was not yet ready.

The V3 first took to the air on 5/9/1941. On 6/7/41, according to a letter to *Generaling.* Lucht, flight testing at Arado had almost finished. The shortcomings of the V1 and V2 had been corrected, and handling—especially on takeoff and landing—was now easy. *E-Stelle* Rechlin took over follow-on testing on 10 June. Performance measurements were suspended for a time, as the machine had not yet been fitted with its final propeller design with dual spinners. It was estimated that this program would terminate around the middle of July. In order to fully correct the faults in the vertical axis the V3 was initially fitted with small, then larger, fins on the tailcone. On 8/3/41 *Hptm.* Knemeyer test flew the V3 at Rechlin and found the flight handling in the vertical axis to be flawless, meaning that blind instrument flights were entirely within the realm of possibility.

As photos show, the V3 was first flown without coolers on the undercarriage struts. These were not tested until three months after the V3's maiden flight, and then initially on the V2. Construction of the Ar 240 V4 began at almost the same time as the V3. It

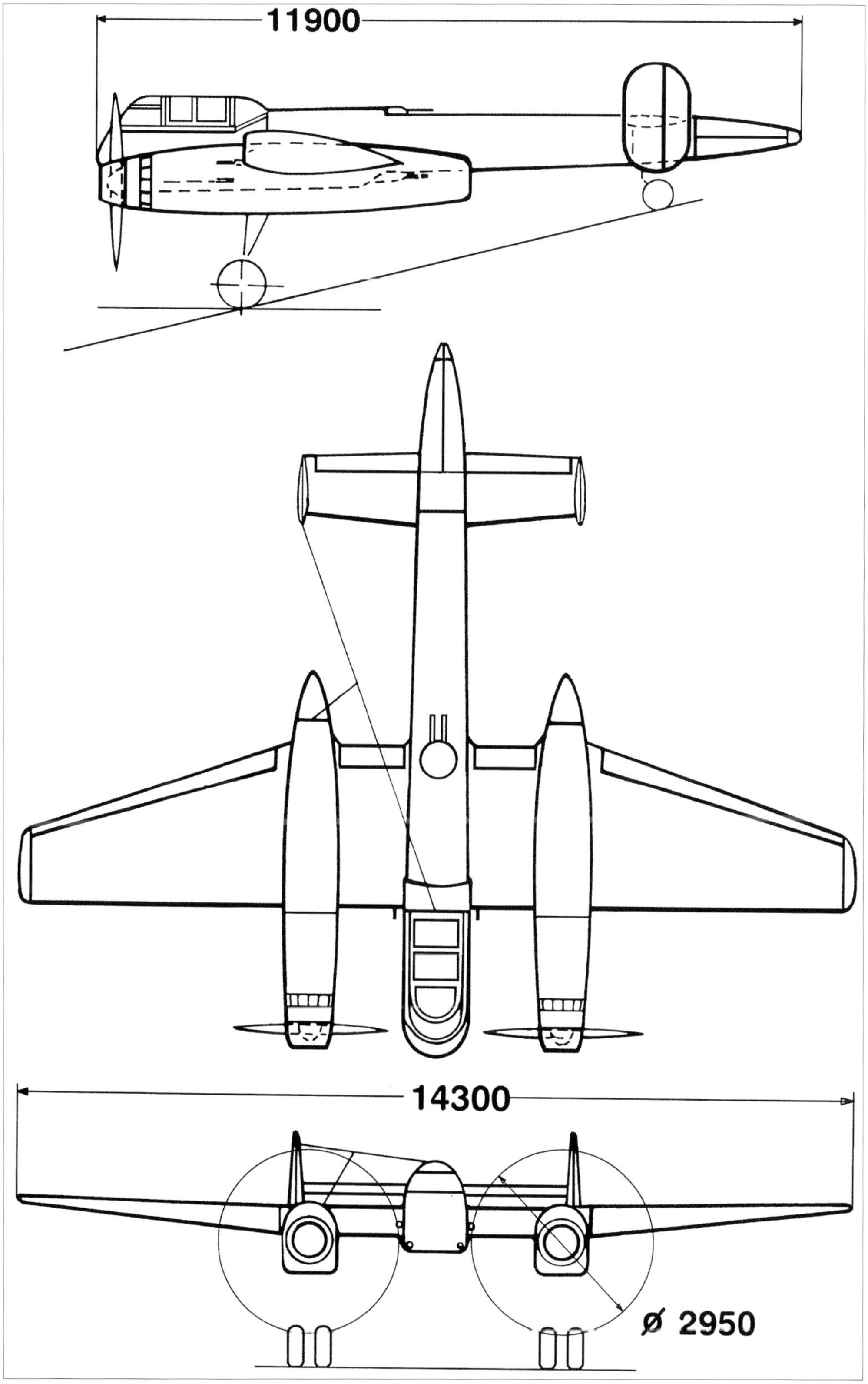

In the RLM's initial identification sheet, the fuselage length of the Ar 240 A was shown as being too short. This was due to the fact that the data was derived from the first design drawings.

flew for the first time on 6/19/1941 and, as a result of an engine malfunction, was destroyed on 8/7/41. It was originally planned as a testbed for the pressurized cockpit, after which it would then have been turned over to the *Luftwaffe*. Because of the V4's loss, the V3 was employed for testing the pressurized cockpit from 8/19/41 until at least November of that year. The V3 remained at the manufacturer as a testbed, and was used for

The Ar 240 V3 was very similar to its successors, lacking only the strut radiators, the auxiliary tailfins and the armament. Initial test flights were carried out without the propeller spinners. (Petrick)

basic trials with the aerodynamics technical division there. In 1944 it was used for testing components for the Ar 234's pressurized cockpit system.

The V5 and V6 were built between July and September 1941 and made their first flights on 9/11/41 and 1/18/42, respectively. The V5 carried out its performance flights under the control of the BAL in the winter of 1941, and on 25 March 1942 went to the *Versuchsstelle für Höhenflüge*. The V6 had already been turned over to the VfH shortly before then, on 6 March. Evaluation was twofold. *Stabsing.* Friebel, commenting on the Ar 240, reported on 6/9/42 that testing had shown the Ar 240 to fall short of the desired airspeed by 45 km/h. The extremely high wing loading caused the most serious flying problems, particularly for night flying. Following a detailed technical explanation, it was recommended that the type not be further considered for the bomber role. *Oberst* Rowehl reported that the first airplanes had been "souped up." The Ar 240's flight handling had deteriorated to the point where it could no longer even beat the speeds for the Ju 88 C and B. Furthermore, the Ju 88's defensive armament and performance was better than those of the Ar 240. He could not even recommend it as a reconnaissance platform for the field. This verdict was the beginning of the end for the Ar 240 B, which for a time had been discussed as a replacement for the Me 210. Probably as a result of its poor performance the Ar 240 was sent back to Arado, and on 10/20/42 was turned over to the VfH for a second time. With the exception of a few minor details, the Ar 240 V5 and V6 were identical to the Ar 240 A-01 and A-02. A later, better assessment of the Ar 240 made in 1943 leads one to believe that the engines had not been "souped up," but suffered a loss in performance due to other factors. This realization, however, no longer carried any weight when it came to the Ar 240's fate.

Ar 240 A-0

Since the six prototypes initially ordered were inadequate for follow-on development, as well as simultaneous field evaluations (not the least of which was due to the fact that the V1 and V2 had significant differences in design), on 2/12/1941 Arado proposed building a second lot of six pre-production aircraft that would be delivered between September 1941 and April 1942. Of this lot, two (Ar 240 A-01 and A-02) would supplement the V4 through V6 in field trials. Two others (A-03 and A-04) would be kept at the company for follow-on developments, and two would be testbeds for the DB 605.

The Ar 240 A-01 and A-02 were built in accordance with the proposal. However, construction of the A-01 did not begin until June

Except for minor modifications, the Ar 240 A-0 with DB 601 was virtually identical to the V 3 through V 6 prototypes. (Lang)

1941, and its first flight took place on 6/5/1942. Work on the Ar 240 A-02 was initiated in July 1941, with it being cleared for its maiden flight on 9/20/1942. Both had MG 17s in the wing roots and MG 81 Zs in the barbettes. Following a brief period of evaluation at the factory and test centers they were assigned to the Eastern Front. A-01 flew with *Erprobungsgruppe Ob.d.L.* from 10/20/42 onward before being lost on 2/14/43 while in service with 3./(F)/100. The A-02 operated on the Eastern Front from October 1942 until at least 1/21/1944. According to a report from the VfH on 5/13/43, both machines gave a good accounting for themselves. This is in contradiction to the assessment of the V5 and V6 on 6/9/42. The end of the Ar 240's developmental life in early 1943 made any front-line experience moot.

The Ar 240 A-03 and A-04 were refitted with the DB 603 while still under construction, and were subsequently designated Ar 240 A-03/U1 and Ar 240 A-04/U2. Assembly of the A-03 began in August 1941. A venture with four-bladed propellers was made with the finished A-03/U1 on 8/26/42. It served as the testbed for the DB 603, which was to be used in the Ar 240 C ordered on 3/16/42. Flight testing showed that the elevators were too small, a problem which led to changes in the Ar 240 C's design. A-03/U1 was sent to Rechlin in late 1942 and flew there from May until at least June with the GM 1 system. At the conclusion of the trials it went to Brandenburg in June, and from there to Italy in July, where it was lost on 7/14/43 while flying with 2.(F)/122.

The Ar 240 A-04/U2 was initially built with the empennage and outer wings of the A series, but in September 1942 converted over to the empennage and wings of the Ar 240 C. In December 1942 it was at Rechlin, where it was given an outstanding assessment following evaluations by *Oberstleutnant* Theirfelder. A fly-off with the Ju 88 S, He 219, and Me 410 showed the Ar 240 to be markedly superior. It was these results that prompted *Generalfeldmarschall* Milch's positive appraisal of the Ar 240 C and Ar 440, even if they did not lead to the success Arado had been hoping for. Once Ar 240 development had been stopped for good, the *Reich* took over the Ar 240 A-04/U2, using it in Italy in 1943 and over England in early 1944. Sometime between its flights at the test center and those over England it was fitted with DB 603 engines with G-turbochargers and the GM 1 system. In March 1944 it operated over Corsica. Following this period, Arado claimed it back again for testing purposes, where it was destroyed in a crash landing in June 1944.

The two machines with DB 605s were later carried under the designations Ar 240 V7 and V8.

Ar 240 A with DB 601 E

According to an Arado type description from 9/26/1942: *Zerstörer*, horizontal and dive bomber, strike fighter, night fighter, high altitude strategic reconnaissance.

Type: twin-engined all-metal cantilever mid-wing monoplane
Fuselage: three-piece, center section with wing center section, tail fitted with Dornier dive brakes
Canopy: pressurized cockpit, two man crew sitting back-to-back
Wings: three-piece, center section attached to fuselage and engine mounts
Arado traveling ailerons and Fowler flaps
Undercarriage: twin-wheeled single-strut hydraulically retractable
Vertical stabilizer: Dual
Engine: 2 x DB 601 E
Performance: 2 x 1350 hp
Oil coolers: Located under engines
Radiators: ahead of engines and struts
Propeller: VDM-VS, three-bladed, 2.96 m diameter
Fixed armament: 2 x MG 151/20 in lower fuselage
2 x MG 151/20 in wing roots
2 x MG 151/20 in removable belly gondola, optional
Flexible armament: 2 x MG 131 Z in remotely operated dorsal and ventral barbettes
Sight: periscope as part of the FA 13 weapons system
Ordnance: 1 x 1000 kg or 1 x 1800 kg on Rack I or
2 x 500 kg or 2 x 250 kg or
2 x AB 250 or
8 x SC 50 kg on multiple racks on Racks I and II
Armor: cockpit and radiator engines
Electronic systems: FuG X, FuG 15, FuG 25 a
Fuel: 2275 liters in wings, 2 x 300 liters possible under fuselage

The Ar 240 A-04/U2 was fitted with DB 603s, longer wings and larger rudders in an effort to obtain early test data for the projected Ar 240 C. (Petrick)

Oil: 2 x 55 liters aft of the engines
Crew: 2 men
Wing area: 31 m^2
Wingspan: 14.34 m
Length: 12.81 m
Height: 3.96 m
Wheel base: 4.25 m
Tailplane span: 4.7 m
Main wheel: 840 x 300
Tail wheel: 560 x 200
Tail wheel: retractable
Weights:
(gross, w/o bombs) 8.69 t
(empty): 6.8 t
Wing loading: 280 kg/m^2
Max. speed (w/o bombs): 500 km/h at sea level
605 km/h at 6000 m
Landing speed: 148 km/h
Climb rate (w/o bombs): 6000 m in 10.5 min
Service ceiling (w/o bombs): 9300 m
Range (w/o bombs): 1870 km with 2275 liters
Endurance: 3.6 hrs

When this type sheet was made the Ar 240 A with D 601 had not been current for some time. The improved version of the Me 210 was already in production, and the Me 410 was on the brink of entering full scale production. The type sheet generally reflects the performance of the Ar 240 V4 through V5 and the two pre-production Ar 240 A-01 and A-02, but with regard to the armament and ordnance it shows only what was being offered.

Ar 240 A with DB 603 A

According to an Arado type description from 12/12/1942:

Engine: 2 x DB 603 A
Performance: 2 x 1750 hp
Maximum pressure altitude: 5700 m
Radiators: ahead of engines and struts
Propeller: VDM-VS, four-bladed, 3.4 m diam.

Weights:	
(gross, *Zerstörer*):	8.98 t
(gross, bomber):	10.5 t max.
Weight (empty):	6.77 t
Wing loading:	322 kg/m^2
Max. speed:	530 km/h at sea level 668 km/h at 6400 m
Landing speed:	140/km/h
Climb rate (w/o bombs):	6000 m in 9.7min
Service ceiling (w/ bombs):	9500 m
Service ceiling (w/o bombs):	10200 m
Range (*Zerstörer*):	1800 km with 2275 liters
Endurance:	3.3 hrs

This data sheet reflects the performance figures for the Ar 240 A-03 and was possibly an offer for this multi-role aircraft. At the time it was prepared the RLM had already stopped development of the Ar 240. It is possible that this offer was a more basic alternative to the Ar 240 C and Ar 440, which by this time had already been developed.

Ar 240 B

The planned B-series differed from the A only in its use of the DB 605 engine.

Ar 240 V7 through V8

Prototypes for the Ar 240 B-0, as Ar 240 V5 through V6, but:

Engine: 2 x DB 605 A/1

According to Arado's proposal from 2/12/41 the last two aircraft from the Arado 0-series were to be powered by the DB 605. The Ar 240 V7 and V8 with DB 605 appeared for the first time in the aircraft program of 1 February 1942. Initially, these two airframes served as engine testbeds. The V8 was also to have been fitted with a fixed, aft firing MG 151/20 in the port engine nacelle. The V7 was handed over for testing on 10/15/42 and the V8 on 12/10/42. They were prototypes for the small production run of 20 Ar 240 B-0s to have been built by Ago. Following weapons trials and other tests the machines most likely went to Russia in early 1943. It is known that the V8 suffered a crash landing on 8/3/43 while in service with 1.(F)/100. According to statements by Captain E.M. Brown, who test flew a number of German airplanes after the war for the Royal Aircraft Establishment, there was an Ar 240 with DB 605s in France in the autumn of 1945 and, according to his assessment, had extremely poor, potentially dangerous flight characteristics.

Ar 240 B-0

As Ar 240 V7 through V8.

Arado (probably in early 1942, at the same time the V7 and V8 were ordered) was awarded a contract for 20 Ar 240 B-0s. The Ar 240 B-0 was conceived as a high speed reconnaissance platform and had two fixed MG 17s as armament. It is unclear whether the type was to have the MG 81 Z guns for defensive armament like the prototypes or, like in the type description, it was to be armed with the MG 131 Z. According to RLM Plan 222 (still valid as of 9/21/42) the Ar 240 B-0 was to be built and supplied by Ago from February to October 1943. With the failure of the Me 210 the RLM for a time considered building the Ar 240 in its place. This might have been the Ar 240 B version. In meetings on 12 May and 9 June 1942, however, the RLM determined that using the Ar 240 as a temporary high speed bomber was out of the question. *Oberst* Rowehl also rejected its use as a reconnaissance platform. Milch, however, continued to allow construction of the Ar 240 B to proceed at this time, as well as developmental work on the Ar 240 with DB 603. Nevertheless, on 11/6/42 the entire contract for the Ar 240, in particular the 20 Ar 240 B-0s, was suspended. By this time there was no longer a demand for an Ar 240 with DB 605 due to its performance, and in any event there were questions about the availability of the DB 605. Initial production of the Me 410 with DB 603 was imminent and, as evaluation results were showing, there was no longer any anticipation of major problems.

Ar 240 B Type Description

Based on Arado type description from 9/28/1942:

Engine:	2 x DB 605 A
Performance:	2 x 1475 hp
Maximum pressure altitude:	5800 m
Weights (gross, w/o bombs):	9.09 t
(empty):	7.16 t
Wing loading:	293 kg/m^2
Max. speed (w/o bombs):	523 km/h at sea level 614 km/h at 6000 m
Landing speed:	149 km/h
Climb rate (w/o bombs):	6000 m in 10.5 min
Service ceiling (w/o bombs):	10200 m
Range (w/o bombs):	1800 km with 2275 liters
Endurance:	3.3 hrs

Ar 240 C

The Ar 240 C was a version with DB 603 and additional airframe modifications when compared with the A-series.

Ar 240 V9 through V12

The construction contract for the Ar 240 V9 through V12—the prototypes for the C-series—dates from 16 March 1942. The V9 and V10 were intended for evaluation of flight handling and engines. The final version with new canopy was to have been achieved by the V 11 and V12. The halt in developmental work resulted in a delay in finishing the prototypes V9 and V10 and cancellation of the V11 and V12 altogether. The V9 ventured into the air for the first time on 2/28/43, with the V10 following on 9/9/43. Both were kitted out as reconnaissance aircraft. The V9 is reputed to have been lost on takeoff in the summer of 1943. The V10 remained with Arado for testing purposes. In the summer of 1944 it crash landed when the landing gear failed to function and was not rebuilt. The V9 and V10 exhibited the older style cockpit arrangement, had no armament, and had the engines of the Ar 240 A-04/U2, but otherwise had the features of the Ar 440 listed later.

Ar 240 C, *Zerstörer*, Level Bomber, Night Fighter, Reconnaissance

According to Arado's design description from 11/6/1941:

Wings:	new, with greater engine nacelle separation and new profile
Vertical stabilizer:	strengthened
Horizontal stabilizer:	enlarged
Engine:	2 x DB 603 A
Performance:	2 x 1750 hp
Max. pressure altitude:	5100 m
Oil coolers:	ahead of engines
Radiators:	ahead of engines and struts
Propeller:	VDM-VS, four-bladed, 3.4 m diameter

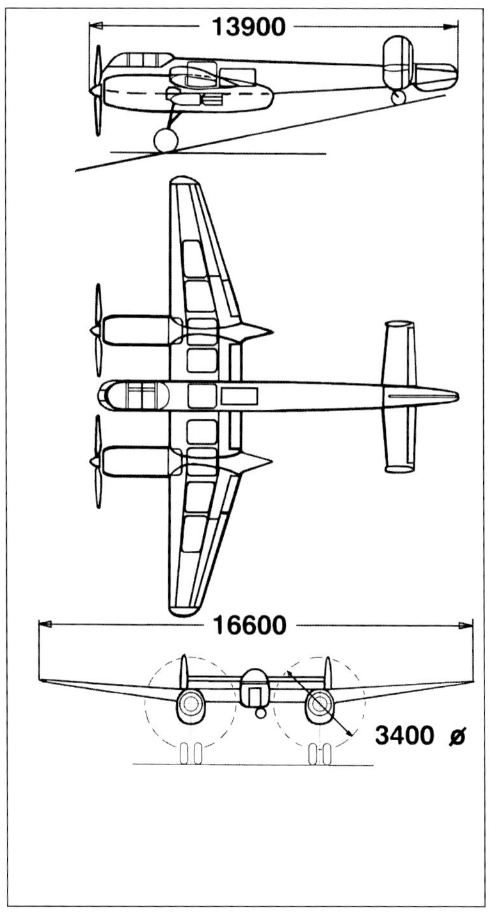

No photos of an Ar 240 V 9 or V 10 exist, but this Arado drawing for the Ar 440 gives a good idea of the general layout of the two prototypes.

Fixed armament as *Zerstörer*: 2 x MG 151/20 in lower fuselage
2 x MG 151/20 in wing roots
2 x MG 151/20 in removable belly gondola, optional
Fixed armament as bomber: 2 x MG 151/20
Flexible armament: 2 x MG 131 Z in remotely operated dorsal and ventral barbettes
Sight: periscope as part of the FA 13 weapons system, plus BZA
Ordnance: 1 x 1000 kg or 1 x 1800 kg on Rack I or
2 x 500 kg or 2 x 250 kg or 2 x AB 250 or
8 x SC 50 kg on multiple racks on Racks I and II
Armor: cockpit, radiator and engines
Electronic systems: FuG X, FuG 15, FuG 25a
Fuel: 295 kg in fuselage, 2 x 230 + 2 x 260 + 2 x 235 + 2 x 160 in wings (= 2065 kg), 2 x 243 possible in gondola tanks
Oil: 2 x 70 liters aft of the engines
Crew: 2 men
Wing area: 35m^2
Wingspan: 16.6 m
Length: 13.45m
Height: 3.96 m
Wheel base: 4.9 m
Tailplane span: 5.45 m
Main wheel: 840 x 300
Tail wheel: 560 x 200
Tail wheel: retractable
Weights
(gross, as *Zerstörer*): 10.7 t
(gross, as bomber): 11.82 t
(empty, as *Zerstörer*): 8.48 t
(empty, as bomber): 8.28 t
Wing loading: 280 kg/m^2
Max. speed (w/o bombs): 537 km/h at sea level
674 km/h at 6450 m
Landing speed: 143 km/h
Climb rate (w/o bombs): 6000 m in 9.4 min
Service ceiling (w/o bombs): 9750 m
Range (w/o bombs): 2330 km with 2065 liters
Range (w/ 1000 kg bombs): 2020 km with 1800 liters
Endurance: 2.9 hrs

Starting in early 1941 Arado began working on a follow-on development of the Ar 240 A with an eye toward using the DB 603. As a result of the larger engines the propeller spinners jutted out ahead of the canopy, but there were no initial plans to extend the aft fuse-

This three-view shadow drawing shows the shorter design of the projected Ar 240 C, a design which never came to fruition.

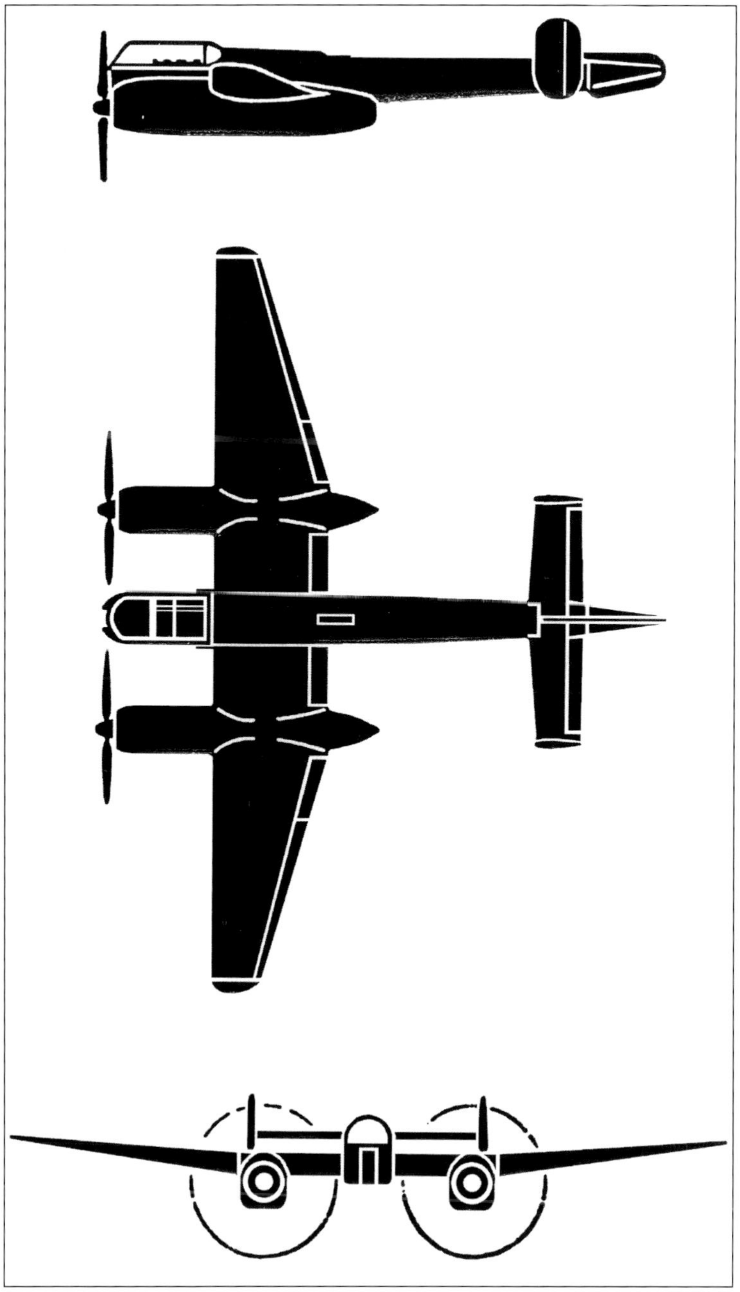

lage in order to compensate for the shift in weight. More powerful engines called for larger propellers, which in turn necessitated a greater distance between the engine axes and the fuselage. Since this resulted in a new inner wing section, it was also redesigned to accommodate an MG 151/20 and was given a new profile. The experience with the Ar 240 A led the designers to also incorporate larger outer wings, rudders, and elevators into the design at the same time. At first the canopy was of the same design as the newly built Ar 240 A, but over the course of development it underwent modifications and would have a different shape on the third and fourth prototypes. On 3/16/42 the RLM awarded a contract for construction of prototypes V9 through V12 and 36 production Ar 240 C-0s, which would be used in the reconnaissance role, but withdrew the contract just a few months later on 7/27/42. It is no coincidence that the award of the contract coincided with the halt to the Me 210 and its withdrawal with the subsequent rebirth and continuation as the Me 410. *Dir.* Blume tried to get this decision revoked on 9/21/42 and proposed having Ago build the 36 Ar 240 C-0s in conjunction with the 20 Ar 240 B-0s already contracted for, i.e. starting in October 1943. The bulk of material was already available at the time. But on 11/6/1942 the RLM canceled the entire AR 240 program. Nevertheless, Arado continued work on the project, albeit now under the designation Ar 440.

Ar 240 D

According to Arado's design description from 11/6/1941:

Engine:	2 x DB 614
Performance:	2 x 2020 hp
Max. pressure altitude:	8700 m
Length:	13.27m
Weights	
(gross, as *Zerstörer*):	11.05 t
(gross, as bomber):	12.17 t
(empty, as *Zerstörer*):	8.83 t
(empty, as bomber):	8.63 t
Max. speed (as *Zerstörer*):	561 km/h at sea level 755 km/h at 6450 m
Landing speed:	145 km/h
Climb rate (w/o bombs):	6000 m in 8.7 min
Service ceiling (w/o bombs):	12000 m
Range (w/o bombs):	2380 km with 2065 liters
Range (w/ 1000 kg bombs):	2040 km with 1800 liters
Endurance:	2.65 hrs

The Ar 240 D was conceived parallel to the Ar 240 C and differed only in its powerplant. Little is currently known about the DB 614. It is not mentioned in the book "*Flugmotoren und Triebwerke*" from the series "*die deutsche Luftfahrt*." Lange's "*Buch der deutschen Luftfahrttechnik*" describes it as a DB 603 G for HZ systems, something which is undoubtedly untrue. Nowarra claims (*die deutschen Flugzeuge 1933 - 1945*) that it was a simplified version of the DB 604. The DB 604 is a known engine and was a 24 cylinder X-block with a 48.5 liter capacity and 2350 hp. It weighed 130 kg more than the DB 603. In the book "Warplanes of the Third Reich" the DB 614 is cited as a DB 603 G with three-stage turbocharger. In view of its takeoff rating and additional weight, the variant was probably based on the DB 604. A further clue is found in the fact that the DB 604 was canceled by the RLM in 1942. Shortly thereafter the Ar 240 D also disappeared, and there were no further projects using the DB 614.

Ar 240 E, Special Bomber

According to Arado's type sheet from 6 March and minutes from 10 and 17 March 1942:

As Ar 240 C, but

Fuselage:	same
Wings:	lengthened outer sections and dive brakes between the engine nacelles and ailerons
Vertical stabilizer:	same
Horizontal stabilizer:	enlarged

Fixed armament:	2 x MG 151/20 forward 1 x MG 151/20 aft
Ordnance:	2 *Schloss* 1000 racks under fuselage and 2 *Schloss* 500 racks under wings 1 x 1000 kg or 1 x 1800 kg on Rack I or
Ordnance:	2 x 1000 kg under fuselage or 4 x 500 kg under fuselage and wings
Wing area:	41 m^2
Wingspan:	19.0 m
Tailplane span:	larger, not yet defined
Weight (gross):	14 t
Weight (empty):	9.76 t
Wing loading:	340 kg/m^2
Max. speed (w/o bombs):	660 km/h at 7000 m
Max. speed (w/ bombs):	610 km/h at 7000 m
Landing speed:	140 km/h
Climb rate (w/o bombs):	6000 m in 9.4 min
Service ceiling (w/o bombs):	10700 m
Service ceiling (w/ bombs):	9000 m
Range:	3000 km with 2500 liters

The special bomber version of the Ar 240 C was to have been fitted with extended outer wings and additional hardpoints for bombs beneath the wings. The dive brakes were to have been moved from the tail cone to underneath the outer wings. This series was renamed the Ar 240 E on 17 March 1942. The new components were to have been tested on the V9 through V12. As with the Ar 240 C, the intended powerplant was the DB 603 G, with the DB 627 and BMW 801 J also considered as potential candidates. Along with the C-series, this project was canceled as well.

Ar 240 F *Kampfzerstörer*

Based on Arado conference minutes from 3/17/1942:

As Ar 240 E, but

Fixed armament as *Zerstörer*:	2 x MG 151/20 in lower fuselage 2 x MK 108 or MK 103 in wing roots
Ordnance:	2 x *Schloss* 1000 under the fuselage
Weight (gross):	11.18 t
Weight (empty):	9/16 t

Ar 440 A

Based on Arado's project description:

As Ar 240 C, but

Fuselage:	lengthened, no dive brakes, new tank
Cockpit:	nose glazing altered
Wings:	with new fuel tank system
Vertical stabilizer:	taller
Engine:	2 x DB 603 A
Performance:	2 x 1750 hp
Propeller:	VDM-VS, four-bladed, 3.4 m diameter
Fixed armament as *Zerstörer*:	2 x MG 151/20 in lower fuselage 2 x MK 108 or MK 103 in wing roots 2 x MG 151/20 in removable belly gondola, optional
Flexible armament:	2 x MG 131 Z in remotely operated dorsal and ventral barbettes
Sight:	periscope as part of the FA 13 weapons system, plus BZA
Ordnance:	1 x 1000 kg or 1 x 1800 kg on Rack I or 2 x 500 kg or 2 x 250 kg or 2 x AB 250 or 8 x SC 50 kg on multiple racks on Racks I and II

Armor: cockpit, radiator and engines
Electronic systems: FuG X, FuG 15, FuG 25 a (FuNG 101 as night fighter)
Fuel: 533 kg in fuselage, 2 x 213 + 2 x 194 kg in wings (= 1347 kg), 2 x 450 liters possible in external tanks
Oil: 2 x 60 liters aft of the engines
Wing area: 35m^2
Wingspan: 16.6 m
Wing chord
(inner): 2.65 m
(outer): 1.00 m

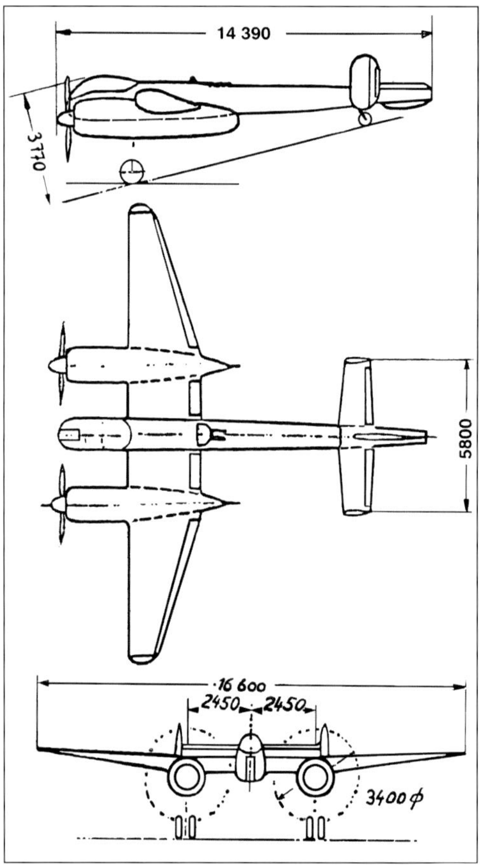

Sketch from Arado's submission for the Ar 440.

Length: 14.30 m
Height: 3.97 m
Wheel base: 4.9 m
Tailplane span: 5.80 m
Main wheel: 840 x 300
Tail wheel: 560 x 200
Tail wheel: retractable
Weights
(gross, as *Zerstörer*): 11.26 t
(gross, as bomber): 12.26 t
(empty): 9.24 t

Flight performance based on an Arado design comparison between the Ar 440 and the E 530 project:

Engine: 2 x DB 603 G
Performance: 2 x 1900 hp
Weight (gross): 12.427 t
Max. sustained speed: 603/km/h
Max. speed w/ emergency boost and GM 1: 740 km/h
Climb rate (w/o bombs): 7.9 m/s
Range: 2070 km

The Ar 240 C was renamed the Ar 440 in early November 1942. It was fundamentally not a new aircraft. The designs were different due to the follow-on development drawn up in the interval, which in part stemmed from experience with the Ar 240 A-03/U1, A-04/U2, and Ar 240 V9 and V10, but in the main was a result of tailoring the design to the RLM's "technical guidelines for the *Kampfzerstörer*" on 8/7/42. Yet the Ar 440 was not fundamentally a new aircraft. The main differences were a new canopy glazing offering better view forward and downward, increased length (ahead of and behind the wings), enlarged elevators and built up rudders, as well as the use of the DB 603 G standardized engine. It should be noted, however, that at the time the Ar 440's development had been stopped the specifications for this standardized engine had not been formally set. The good performance of the powerplant Arado developed using the DB 603 A as its engine, however, led to the standardized engine based on the DB 603 G leaning heavily on that developed by Arado. Trials using testbeds and prototypes revealed the Ar 440's great potential. Flight performance was outstanding and could not be touched by any other contemporary aircraft (including the Mosquito), and flight handling was good as well.

Compared to the Me 410, the Ar 440 clearly had better performance. What must be taken into account, however, is the fact that the Arado had changed considerably in the years 1941/42. Fuselage, wings, and control surfaces had grown, and the wing design and profile were completely new. These follow-on developments could not be undertaken on the Me 210/410 due its production startup. *Generalluftzeugmeister* Milch's sentiments could lead one to conclude that he would gladly have replaced the Me 410 with the Ar 440. Since, though, the Me 410 already had production facilities, semi-finished assemblies, jigs, etc. available, a large number of these could be built in the foreseeable future. For the Ar 440 there were neither manufacturing resources nor jigs on hand. In order to create these, production of another type would have to be shortened at the expense of losing several hundred aircraft. In addition, the RLM felt that the Ar 440 would not be available that much sooner than the superior Do 335, something which would have unnecessarily increased the number of *Zerstörer* types. Milch knew that some of the Ar 440's superiority came from the good Arado engines. He hoped that some of this superiority could be offset by adopting the similar standardized engine for the Me 410 C. The view often found in aviation publications that the jigs had been completed and that the Ar 440 was only a victim of the RLM's ignorance is clearly a false one. Ago's peak output capacity for the Ar 240 B was planned at a rate of four per month during August and September 1943. On 12/2/42 Milch informed *Direktor* Blume of the Arado Works that the Ar 240 (Ar 440) was being canceled. In so doing, Milch stressed that he was fully aware of the type's performance capability, and it was only the lack of production resources and the need to reduce the number of duplicate types that led to his decision. Blume accepted the decision with much difficulty, and over the coming months made several, albeit unsuccessful, attempts to get the Ar 440 into production again. On 2/16/43 the RLM yet again confirmed that the Ar 440 was superior to the Me 410, but Milch could not justify starting production alongside the Me 410.

The unwelcome decision for Arado led shortly thereafter to enough resources being available for development and construction of the Ar 234. The Ar 234 was markedly superior to both the Ar 440 and the Me 410 in several key areas, and took over the roles of reconnaissance and high speed bomber. As the development of the Ar 234 into a night fighter shows, with minor modifications it could also have taken on the role of *Zerstörer*. Since the Ar 234 entered production much sooner than the Do 335 and proved to be an outstanding design, had the war lasted longer sooner or later it would certainly have nudged the Do 335 aside.

Me 210

Me 210, Drafting the Project

Based on Messerschmitt project layout design description from May 1939 and wind tunnel model drawings:

Wingspan:	15.56 m
Wing area:	33.6 m^2
Length:	11.05 m
Flexible armament:	remotely controlled barbettes with MG 131
Weight (empty):	5.607 t
Weight (gross):	8.133 t
Fuel weight:	1865 kg, of which 258 kg in fuselage

According to Messerschmitt's project design engineers, the Me 210's intended roles of dive bomber and medium range heavy fighter called for greater defensive firepower than that found on the Bf 110, although for weight saving reasons the radio operator would continue to function as gunner. As the RLM was particularly dissatisfied with the Bf 110's ventral defensive armament, this area would be covered by an FDSL remotely operated weapons system. Messerschmitt handed development of this weapons system to Rheinmetall-Borsig, which transferred the electrical portion over to AEG. In order to better detect the enemy a free field of vision was considered absolutely necessary, and the gunner was only afforded a single sighting device (consisting of three individual sights). The desired ventral defensive potential led to a canopy bulged at the sides, enabling the gunner to see over the side of the narrow fuselage. On the final version, the area below

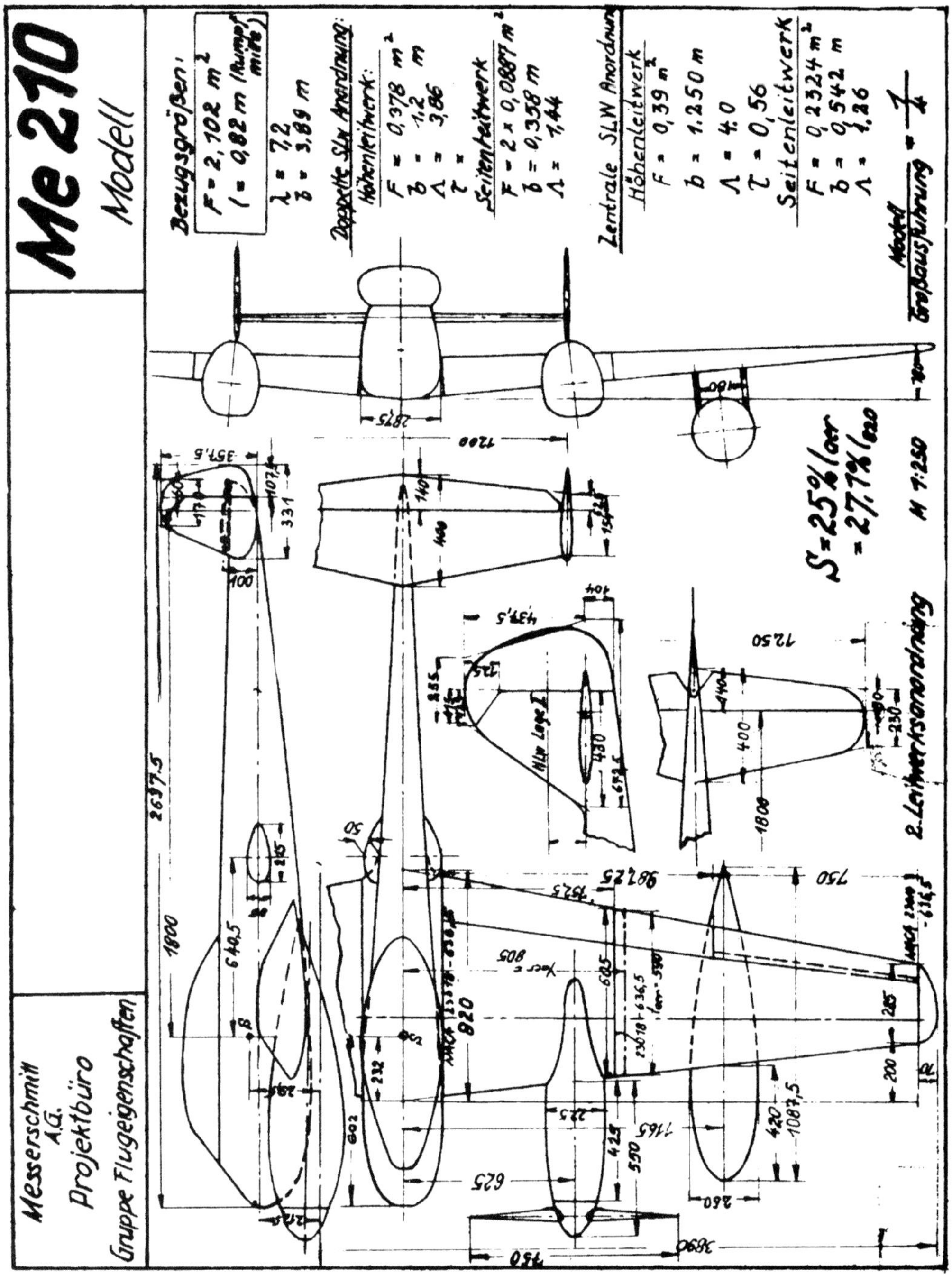

Research into two different rudder configurations took place as early as wind tunnel testing on models.

the fuselage visible to the gunner was from 4 m outward. The guns were controlled so that they both pivoted simultaneously along the y-axis. For movement along the x-axis, the gun being operated could swivel up to 45 degrees outward, while the other unneeded gun would move 7 degrees in the same direction and then remain locked.

The twin rudders of the Bf 110 had proven reliable, so that was also the first choice for the Me 210. However, since the fuselage tapered off sharply the guns had to be mounted laterally, and in these circumstances a single, central rudder had its advantages. Therefore, for purposes of wind tunnel testing a single rudder model was built alongside the twin ruddered version.

Its intended role as high speed dive bomber and the payload specified by the contractor (at the time the contract was issued the *Luftwaffe* only had 50 kg and 250 kg bombs) prompted the designers to locate the bomb bay directly beneath the cockpit. This resulted in the Me 210's wedge-shaped appearance, with a relatively fat looking forward fuselage section and a very narrow aft fuselage. There was a bend in the fuselage just ahead of the barbettes. The dive bombing requirement was also the reason why the designers dispensed with a nose. This offered good visibility when dropping bombs.

As on the Bf 110, the Me 210's wings also had a constant sweep. The wind tunnel model even took into account the use of 900 liter external tanks like those found on the Bf 110 D.

Subsequent requirements levied by the RLM led to modifications to the original design, and by April 1939, for example, the third iteration of an Me 210 design description had been drawn up. The authors do not know exactly what all was changed. At least one change apparent from available documentation involved the tank capacity and location. The new requirements initially led to a change in the weight distribution, resulting in the outer wings being given a greater sweep. And finally, the empty weight was increased.

From the outset, it was the empty weight and the wing loading that were the Me 210's Achilles' heel. With similar engines, in its third rendition the Me 210's empty weight was 5.6 metric tons compared to the 4.6 tons of the Bf 110. The wing area, however, was at 36 m^2—significantly smaller than the Bf 110's 38.4 m^2. The contractor must have knowingly accepted the resulting higher landing speeds. The decreasing climb performance can only lead one to conclude that the focus of development was on the light bomber/dive bomber, i.e. high speeds at low operating altitudes. The higher wing loading had manifestly reduced the service ceiling and climb performance, something which ran directly counter to the concept of the heavy fighter. The relatively small wings contributed to an increase in speed at low level by a few km/h, to be sure, but the loss in climb performance was of graver concern. A similar decision by Messerschmitt led to the failure of the Me 309 which, despite its more powerful DB 603, had poorer climb performance than that of the 109 with its DB 605.

Me 210 V-1 Through V-4

Messerschmitt data from 10/16/39:

Wing area V1:	34.4 m^2
Wing area V2 thru V4:	35.5 m^2
Weight V1 (empty):	5573 kg
Weight V3 (empty):	8873 kg
Weight V1 (gross):	8244 kg
Weight V3 (gross):	8873 kg
Fuel weight:	2016 kg, all in wings

In their layouts, the Me 210 V1 and V2 generally resembled the wind tunnel model. There were no major weight changes, other than the fuselage tank being dropped. The airplanes even had the outer wings with the different taper angle and (initially) the twin rudder configuration. Both exhibited the somewhat less aerodynamically refined split flaps as landing aids and had no armament. Over the course of the trials the Me 210 V1 saw its split flaps replaced by slotted ones.

During the design period of the Me 210 engineers at Messerschmitt attempted to move the oil coolers, which on the Bf 109 and Bf 110 were situated beneath the engines, to a more effective location. For the Bf 109 F and the new Me 210 an annular type of oil cooler was tried, located immediately behind the propeller. The spinner had a smaller diameter than the engine cowling, with the oil cooler located just behind the resulting gap. This arrangement did not prove successful, however, and only cropped up on the Me 210 V1 in its original form. Production Bf 109 Fs and Me 210s were fitted with larger spinners and, as was common, had their oil coolers fitted beneath the engines.

With *Dr.* Hermann Wurster at the controls, the Me 210 V1 flew for the first time on 9/2/1939. This was just twelve months after work began on the type in the design bureau under the direction of Walther Rethel and its subsequent transfer to the test design division under Hubert Bauer. It was fitted with a cockpit that did not as yet take into account the defensive armament (racing canopy). It has been reported elsewhere that *Dr.* Wurster called for the fuselage to be lengthened by a meter as early as completion of the first flight. On 10/12/39 the V1

above: The Me 210 V 1 had dual rudders, split flaps and a racing-type cockpit. The fabric tufts on the wings in this photo were attached to study airflow.

top right: Within the first year the oil coolers were moved underneath the engines. Problems with the undercarriage collapsing began with the V 1 and would haunt the type throughout its early life. Airflow studies using fabric strips were still being carried out at the time of this photo.

above right: This photo shows the V 1, carrying the registration code CE+BY (i.e. a year after its first flight), still flying with dual rudders. However, the split flaps have been replaced by slotted ones.

right: The instrument panel of the first prototype employed the folding center section, a feature designed for the type's intended dive bombing role. (all photos, Moor)

was flown by test center pilot Gustl Neidhard, who criticized its handling along the vertical axis (fuselage too short). On the other hand, his opinion of the type's stall characteristics was very favorable. Like the Bf 110 and the three subsequent V 2 through V4 prototypes, the V1 had automatic slats, which had a positive effect on the stall characteristics.

Some aviation publications claim that the V1 was fitted with the single rudder as early as 9/23/39 to counteract the type's poor stability. This is probably not true, since it would have required preparation beforehand. A new rudder can't be designed and finished in 20 days. On 7/15/1940 Willy Messerschmitt issued a report establishing that the Me 210 would have the single central rudder as provisionally fitted to the V2 and produced from the V5 onward. This indicates that the V1 still had the dual rudders at this stage, and it was the V2 that was provisionally fitted with the single rudder.

The V2 first took to the air on 10/10/39. With regard to its flexible weapons it had bubbled glazing in the aft canopy (military-style cockpit), although this was sometimes swapped out for the racing style canopy to

left: The oil coolers on the Me 210 V 1 were initially of an annular configuration around the propeller hubs. (Moor)

below: The V 2 was built with dual rudders. (Radinger)

study its effect on speed. At first, the V2 also exhibited the dual rudder configuration. In Messerschmitt documents the only reason for the single rudder layout being selected had to do with the armament configuration. There is no mention of its use in order to increase stability. Nevertheless, comparing the wind tunnel model with the V2 reveals that the single vertical stabilizer was larger than originally planned. General flight testing at the *E-Stelle* as well as at Messerschmitt revealed that the Me 210 suffered from unusual flight handling on takeoff. An investigation showed that the cause was a design flaw in the wing outline. Aviation publications mention that both the V2 and V3 were fitted with new outer wings. Perhaps these had the corrected outline. Once this error had been corrected, and following additional test flights both with and without slats, on 7/15/40 *Prof.* Messerschmitt declared the Me 210 to be finished from a flight handling standpoint. He left the issue of leading edge slats up to the RLM, which opted to dispense with them for cost and weight reasons.

Performance assessments with the Me 210 V2 with single rudder and a wing area of 35.5 m^2 (similar to the production version's 35.7 m^2) were carried out on 2/27/40, and in early June 1940 were used as the basis for calculating the maximum speed of the production version. Compared to the Bf 110, it was expected that the Me 210 would offer a 9% increase in flying speed at low level, a figure which mainly resulted from the 19% higher output of the DB 601 E engine. Since

this engine could also be installed in the Bf 110, the 210's main advantages were its longer range, ability to carry bombs, more modern equipment, and better defensive armament.

It was expected that in June 1940 the production version would have an empty weight of 6237 kg compared to the 5573 kg of the V2. The fixed tailwheel of the V2 would be retractable on the production version. The wing area would be increased from 34.4 m^2 to 36 m^2, the annular oil radiators exchanged for undernacelle coolers, the bulged aft canopy glass for flat panes, and the split flaps for cambered trailing edge flaps. Following general testing, the Me 210 V2 was primarily used for trials with the empennage and tests with the dive brakes. During one of these dive brake tests on 9/5/40, flutter built up in the elevator, eventually causing it to break and resulting in the crash of the machine. This event prompted the V3's fuselage to be reinforced with a corresponding increase in weight.

After initial static tests had concluded, the V3 was sent to Tarnewitz for weapons trials on 3/30/40. V4 was ready to take to the air some time prior to 7/1/40 and was utilized for evaluation of flight equipment. Both had the dual rudders, and at least the V3 was constructed with split flaps. During the first quarter of 1940 a new canopy design was developed that had flat rear panes and box windows, offering less drag and better visibility. It is currently not known whether it was available for the V3 and V4. The report quoted for the V2 indicates that the V3 already had the higher weight.

Me 210 V-5 Through V-16

While Messerschmitt and the RLM had planned three prototypes for the Bf 110, a total of 16 were envisioned for the Me 210. As no major problems were expected, the V5 through V16 were to fundamentally reflect production versions and would act as testbeds for components. The 12 prototypes were built between July 1940 and June 1941.

right: Like its predecessors, the V 3 was also initially fitted with a dual rudder and split flaps. (Nowarra)

As early as 15 July 1940, with Messerschmitt only having four prototypes in flight testing, the company assumed that there was very little work remaining on the design. However, test flights with Me 210 V9 on 18 and 19 December 1940 revealed critical stall handling and performance not equal to that of the Bf 110 E/N. These revelations were clear signs that the Me 210, contrary to the statement of 15 July 1940, was indeed in need of leading edge slats, yet no measures were taken. The differences between the V2's and V9's handling can probably be attributed to the fact that the V2 had a flawed outline with other unpleasant qualities, but stalling was not one of them. The provisional improvements to the V2's wing outline were then acceptable both with and without slats, while the production modifications were so different that it induced problems with stall handling. In addition to problems with flight handling there were others, which could be traced back to a flawed design in the landing gear. Abnormally high numbers of undercarriage failures delayed the testing program.

below: The V 2 was the first to be fitted with a single rudder. The defensive armament was a mockup and the cockpit canopy only an interim design. (Nowarra)

left: This test instrumentation was part of the Me 210 V 7's de-icing system. (Nowarra)

below left: The V 13 flew for a time with four-bladed propellers. (Moor)

bottom: The Me 210 V 10 suffered undercarriage failure on 16 June 1941. (Moor)

Me 210 V-17 and Other Prototypes

As a consequence of these unexpected problems, additional aircraft were pulled off the assembly line *sans* equipment and used for testing possible solutions. The V 17, for example, as factory serial number 101 was given a lengthened fuselage in October 1941 and was employed from February 1942 onward as a testbed for stall handling. It was later fitted with the DB 605 as the prototype for the C-series and soldiered on in further trials. The evaluation programs and prototypes involved are, as far as is known, provided in the appendix.

Me 210 A

The General Staff's planned variants and roles for the Me 210 fluctuated over time. The following list, therefore, incorporates differences for the same variants, based on the time. The data stem from type descriptions and manuals. According to Delivery Plan 17 b from June 1940, Me 210 production was to begin in July 1940 and peak at Messerschmitt's plant alone at a rate of 45 per month by September 1941.

By extending the fuselage, NE+BH became the prototype Me 210 V 17. (Radinger)

Me 210 A-0, Heavy Fighter and Dive Bomber

There were no known differences between the Me 210 A-0 pre-production versions and the Me 210 A-1. The number of pre-production aircraft built is probably 85. In documents, the designation Me 210 A-01 through A-85, as well as Me 210 A-1 and even Me 410 A-1 crop up in association with factory serial numbers 017 through 101. The Me 210 A-0 designations are derived mainly from test pilot flight logs at the various test centers. As a rule, they later appeared as modified airframes under the designation A-1.

Me 210 A-1, Heavy Fighter and Dive Bomber

(Description from 1941)

Engine:	2 x DB 601 F
Performance:	2 x 1350 hp
Propeller:	VDM-VS
Fixed armament:	2 x MG 17 1x MG 151 1 x MG 151/20
Flexible armament:	2 x MG 131remotely operated
Ordnance:	1 x 1000 kg or 2 x 500 kg or 2 x 250 kg 8 x 50 kg in bomb bay
Electronic systems:	FuG X, Peil G V, FuBl 1 EiV 1 a, FuG 16
Fuel:	2500 liters
Crew:	2 men
Wingspan:	16.338 m
Length:	11.183 m

Me 210 A-1, Heavy Fighter and Dive Bomber

(Description from 1942)

Same as 1941, but

Propeller:	VDM 9-12078, variable pitch
Fixed armament:	2 x MG 131s planned in place of the MG 17s 2 x MG 151/20
Additional armament:	mod pack for two MG 151s and an MG 151/20 could be substituted for the 500/XII racks
Fuel:	an additional 2 x 900 liters in drop tanks and 700 liters in the bomb bay could be carried
Electronic systems:	additional FuG 25 and autopilot

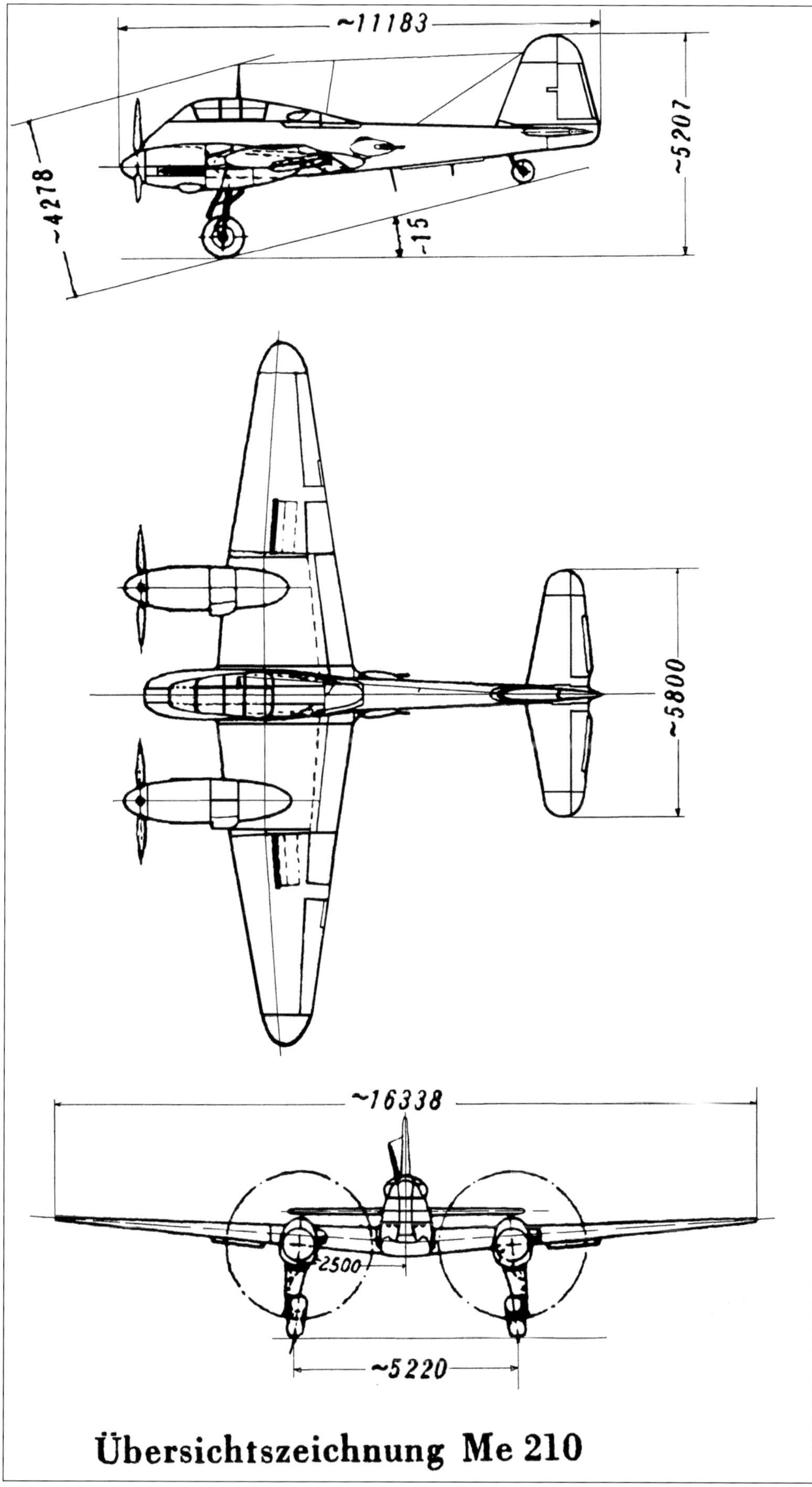

Messerschmitt drawings for the Me 210 A-0/A-1.

right: This picture shows the camouflage pattern on W.Nr. *102 (PN+PA). (Moor)*

right and below: During the winter of 1941 W.Nr. *139 (VS+SC, S9+DL) served as a conversion trainer with* Schnellkampfgeschwader 210 *at Landsberg am Lech. The tailwheel retraction arm has malfunctioned. (Petrick)*

In Delivery Plan 17 b from 6/26/40, the assembly of the prototypes was established as running from July through December 1940. The first 100 Me 210s were to be delivered without change and provided to the flight schools. The next 300 were to be sent to an airbase with depot facilities, where they would be reconfigured for low level strike operations. Part of this conversion would involve the Me 210 being armored at key points on its airframe. Starting with the 401st machine the modifications would be incorporated on the assembly line. Any major changes would not appear until the second variant was built starting in August 1942. These changes were, however, not to affect the intended production in the type's fundamental role as a light bomber. Although the extension to the fuselage was discussed in this meeting, it was not an item for action. Modifications were already underway at the Landsberg and Gablingen airfields prior to production being interrupted in the spring of 1942. This conversion was planned for two *Geschwader* to be equipped with the type by 5/1/1942. On 3/10/1942 those Me 210s undergoing modification were designated the Me 210 S (q.v.)

Me 210 A-1 (lang), *Stukazerstörer* (dive bomber heavy fighter) (1942/43)

(The classification "lang" [long] is used here by the authors; it was not an official designation)

The problems that had originally cropped up in the Me 210's development were, in part, rectified with the first variant, something that led to a delay in production initiation. Other changes were to have been incorporated in the second variant from August 1942 onward. However, the serious problems with spin handling led to suspension of any new production in May 1942. The existing machines were, after a break of several months, be corrected with necessary modifications. Those machines delivered after July 1942 were also designated Me 210 A-1s and exhibited the following improvements:

- The fuselage between the wing and the empennage was lengthened by 950 mm to eliminate yaw oscillation, and the tendency to ground loop during takeoff and landing, as well as the problem with spinning
- The dive brakes were moved from the inner wing to the outer wing sections to alleviate problems with elevator control
- The elevator was internally counterbalanced
- The turbocharger air intake was modified (round instead of square) and produced no interference with engine air intake
- The tendency for sudden stalls and the problem with spinning was cured by the fitting of leading edge slats
- Automatic dive recovery system and defensive armament were improved
- Armor for crew and engines was available for production models
- Cockpit was fitted with a roll bar

Noticeable is the fact that the wing geometry of the modified Me 210 A-1 was, as far as can be ascertained, no different than the initial version. It would be expected that the additional mass of the lengthened fuselage would have caused the center of gravity to shift aft and, as a result, the wing (or at least parts of it) would then have been moved back in order to get the wing's lift as close to the center of gravity as possible. This measure was probably unnecessary, since the additional armor for the cockpit and engines compensated for the extended fuselage's shift in the center of gravity.

The following data mainly come from the manual for the Me 210 A-1 from June 1943. It identifies the Me 210 A-1 as a *Stukazerstörer*, or heavy dive bomber fighter. In the Me 210 aircraft type sheet from 7/20/44 the Me 210 A-1 is listed as a high speed bomber. This takes into account the fact that the Me 210 A-1 was almost exclusively used as a *Zerstörer* or high speed bomber. By 1943 nearly all types had ceased to operate in the dive bombing role.

Type:	twin-engined all-metal cantilever low wing monoplane
Fuselage:	extended and strengthened behind the cockpit
Canopy:	with roll bar and modified glazing, glass plate in nose enabling the pilot to see the ground when the bomb bay doors are open
Wings:	running through the fuselage, with dive brakes under outer wing sections instead of on centerwing undersides, with automatic leading edge slats
Undercarriage:	hydraulically retractable, rotating through 90°
Vertical stabilizer:	single
Tailplane:	non-adjustable
Engine:	2 x DB 601 F
Performance:	2 x 1350 hp

Oil coolers: located under engines
Radiators: located under wings, adjustable louvers
Propeller: VDM-VS, 3.4 m diameter with electro-mechanical automatic pitch
Autopilot: Patin PKS 11
Systems: cockpit heating
ESK 2000b electronic narrow film camera or automatic camera
Fixed armament: 2 x MG 17
2 x MG 151/20
Flexible armament: 2 x MG 131 in remotely operated barbettes
Weapons system: 1 1000 XII rack or 2 500/XII racks or two 500/XIIC racks in fuselage, 4 ETC 50/XIId under wings, bomb panel
Ordnance: 1 x PC 1000 or 1 x PC 1000 RS or 1 SC 500 or 2 SC 240 or 2 SD 250 or 2 AB 250 or 8 SC 50 with hardpoints in fuselage bomb bay and 4 SC 50 or 4 SD 50/70 or 4 AB 23 SD 2 under wings
8 x SC 50 kg on multiple racks on Racks I and II
Armor: cockpit, engines and radiator
Electronic systems: FuG X, FuG 16, FuG 25, Peil G V, FuBl 1
Life raft: 2 man, in aft fuselage
Fuel: 2 x 410 + 2 x 630 + 2 x 170 = 2420 liters in wings
Oil: 2 x 70 liters aft of the engines
Crew: 2 men
Wingspan: 16.4 m
Length: 12.15m
Height: 3.7 m
Wheel base: 5.22 m
Tailplane span: 5.8 m
Main wheel: 1015 x 380
Tail wheel: 500 x 180
Tail wheel: retractable
Weights
(gross, as *Zerstörer*): 9.69 t
(gross, as *Stukazerstörer*): 10.69 t with 2 x 500 kg bombs
(empty): 7.27 t as *Zerstörer* and *Stukazerstörer*
Wing loading: 295 kg/m^2 max
Max. speed (as *Zerstörer*): 463 km/h at sea level
573 km/h at 5900 m
Max. speed (*Stukazerstörer*): 450 km/h at sea level
538 km/h at 5200 m
Landing speed: 188 km/h
Dive speed: 650 km/h at low level, max.
Climb rate (as *Zerstörer*): 6000 m in 13min
8000 m in 22 min
Climb rate (*Stukazerstörer*): 6000 m in 17min
Service ceiling (w/ 9 t): 9150 m
Service ceiling (w/ 10.3 t): 9150 m
Range (as *Zerstörer*): 1820 km with 2400 liters
Range (as *Stukazerstörer*): 1440 km with 2070 liters

The Me 210 A-1 with long fuselage was created exclusively in Germany (Messerschmitt Augsburg) through modification of existing short-frame Me 210 stock or airframes in advanced stages of production during the time period from July 1942 through March 1943. As a percentage of available Me 210 A-1s with short fuselage was also immediately converted into Me 410s and further numbers were already destroyed, the total production of the long-frame Me 210 A-1 was significantly smaller than that of the short-frame version. Precise numbers are not known, but it can be concluded that approximately 180 Me 210 A-1 (*lang*) were produced from the 354 Me 210 A-1s finished with the shorter fuselage from the Regensburg and Augsburg production lines, with another roughly 30 nearly completed airframes (possibly those of the sub-contracting company) being finished as long-frame aircraft. The original factory serial numbers and registration codes were retained after conversion, and the authors have determined that mention of the Me 210 A-1 designation in test pilot flight logs and from loss reports after July 1942 refers to the converted Me 210 A-1 and have had to estimate the totals based on this. According to acceptance documentation from the BAL oversight office only 166 Me 210s were converted (see Me 410 A-1).

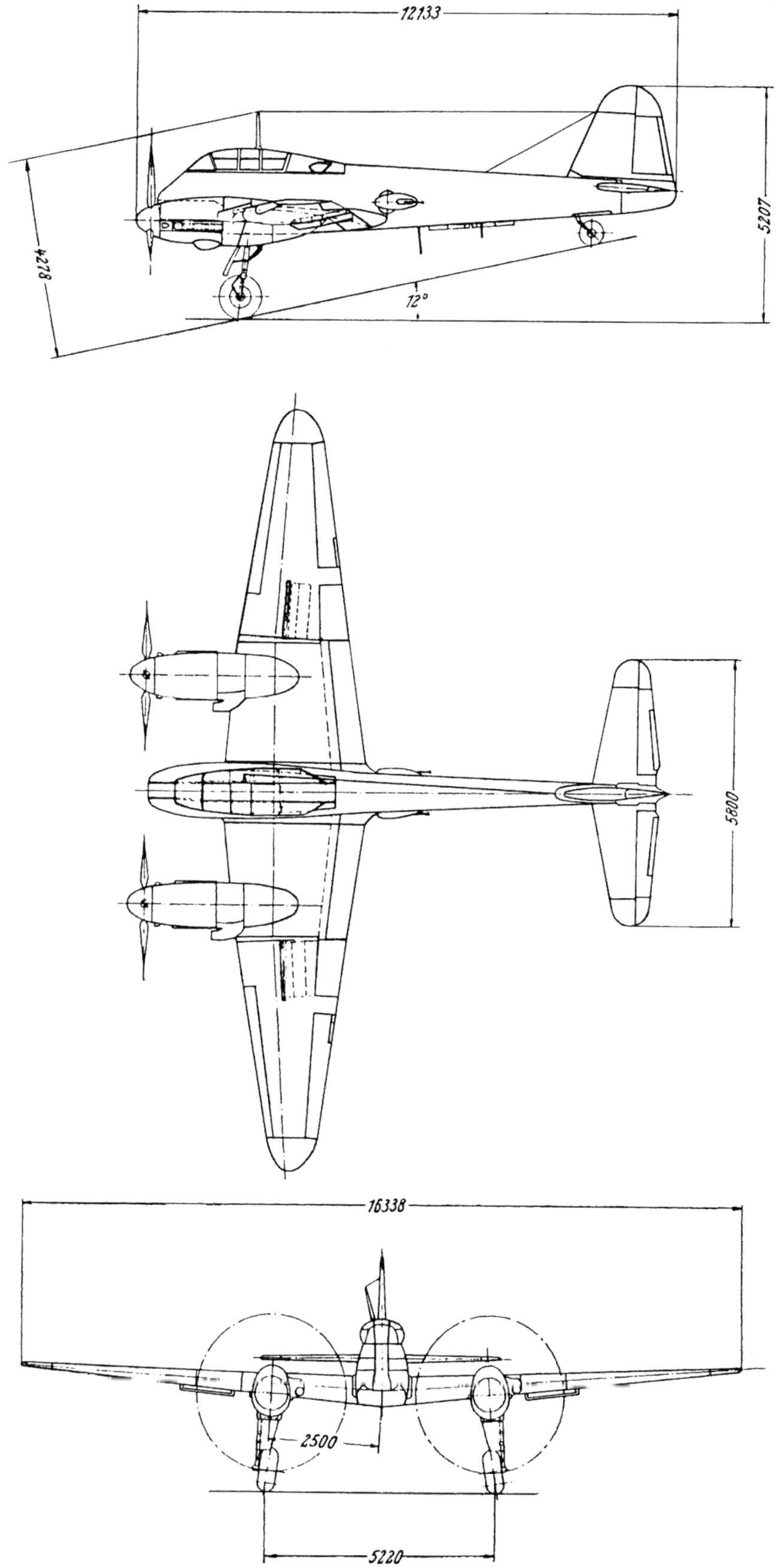

Flugzeugmusterblatt in Dreiseitenansicht

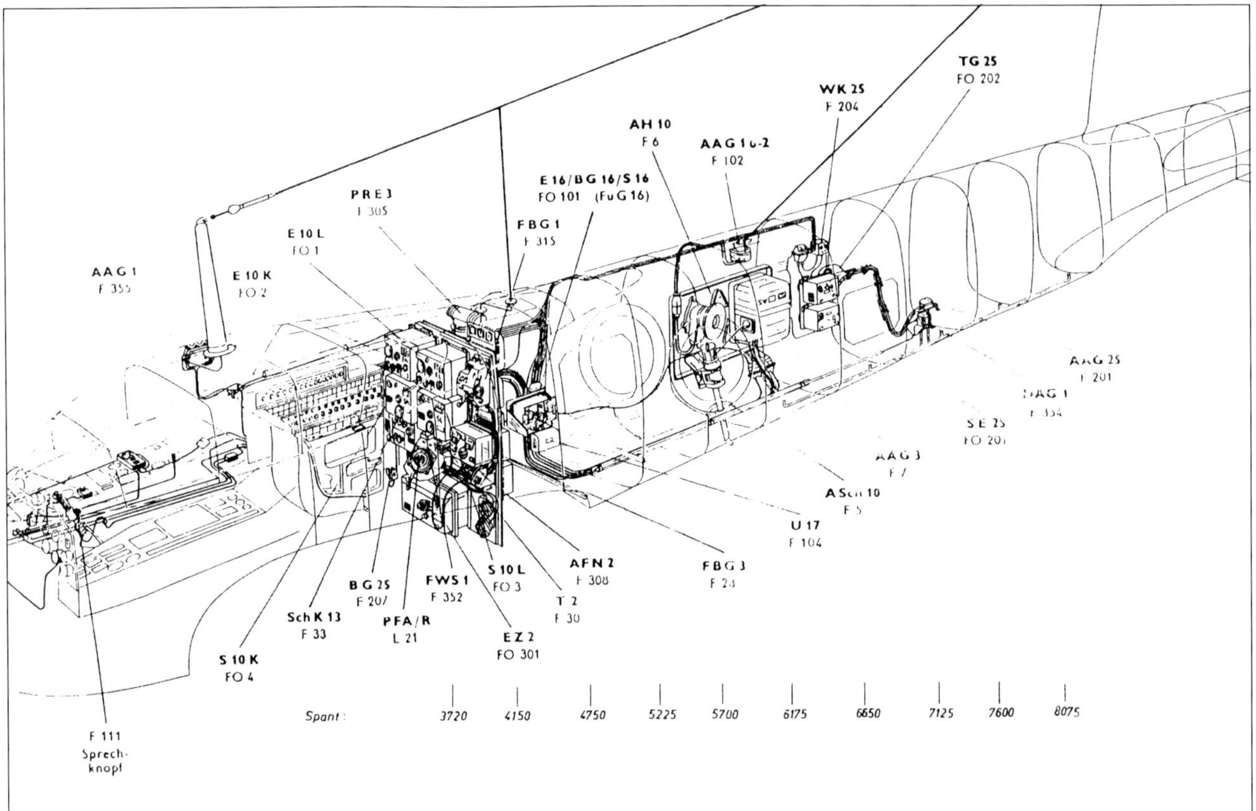

Lageplan 1

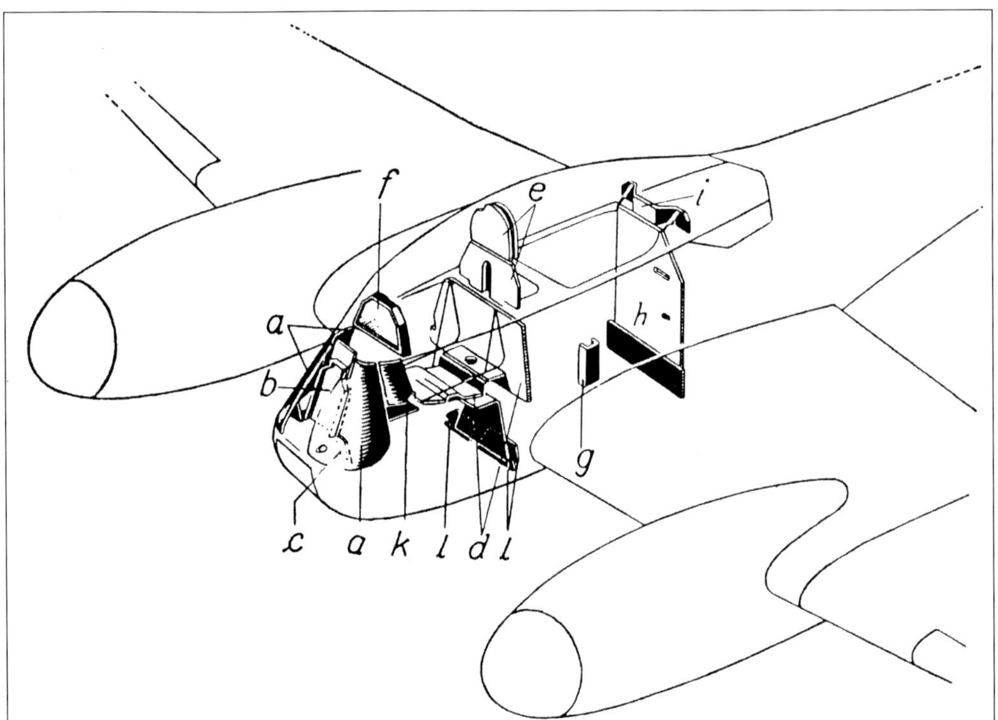

a Panzerplatten für Seitenwände
b Panzerplatte für Rumpfspitze
c Panzerplatten an Seitensteuerpedalen
d Panzerplatten für Führersitz
e Panzerplatten für Kopfschutz des Flugzeugführers
f Panzerscheibe
g Panzerplatte für Leuchtmunitionskasten
h Panzerplatten für Beobachterraum hinten
i Panzerplatte für Kopfschutz des Beobachters
k Panzerplatte im Führerraum
l Panzerplatte im Bombenraum

Anordnung der Panzerung im Rumpf

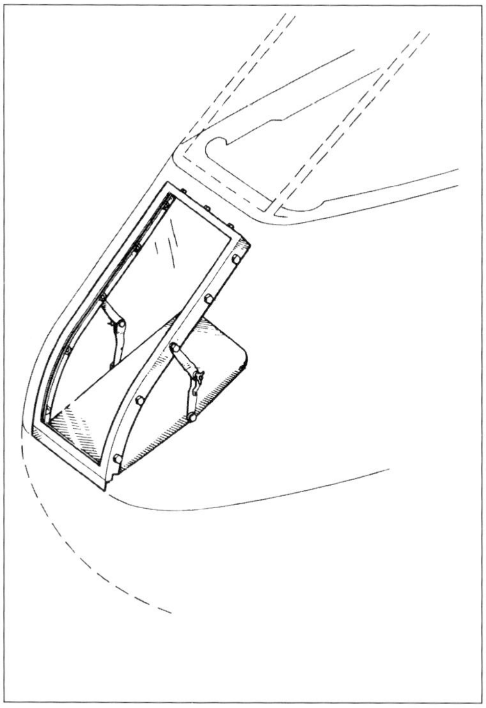

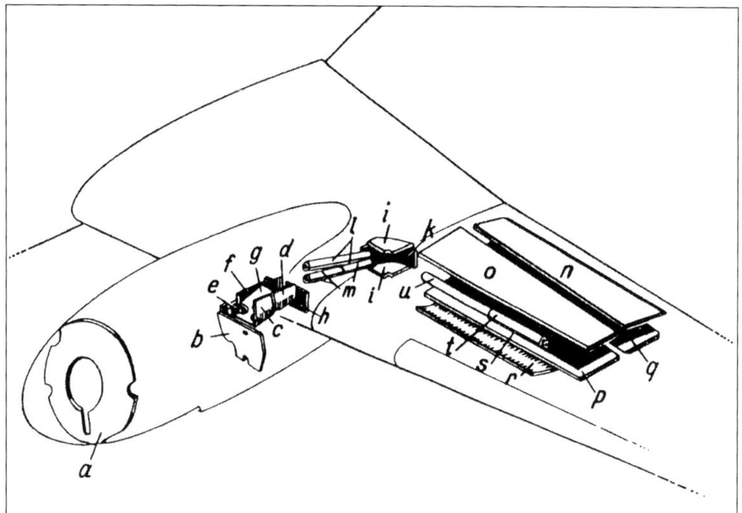

Übersicht der Panzerung des linken Triebwerkes

left: The folding armor behind the nose glazing was only used during heavy fighter missions.

Tabelle über Inhalt und Einbauort der Triebwerksbehälter

1 a	Kraftstoff	445 Ltr.
1 b	Kraftstoff	628 Ltr.
1 c	Kraftstoff	189 Ltr.
1 d	Schmierstoff	70 Ltr.
1 e	Drucköl	14 Ltr.
1 f	Kühlstoff	15 Ltr.
1 g	Einspritz	0,5 Ltr.

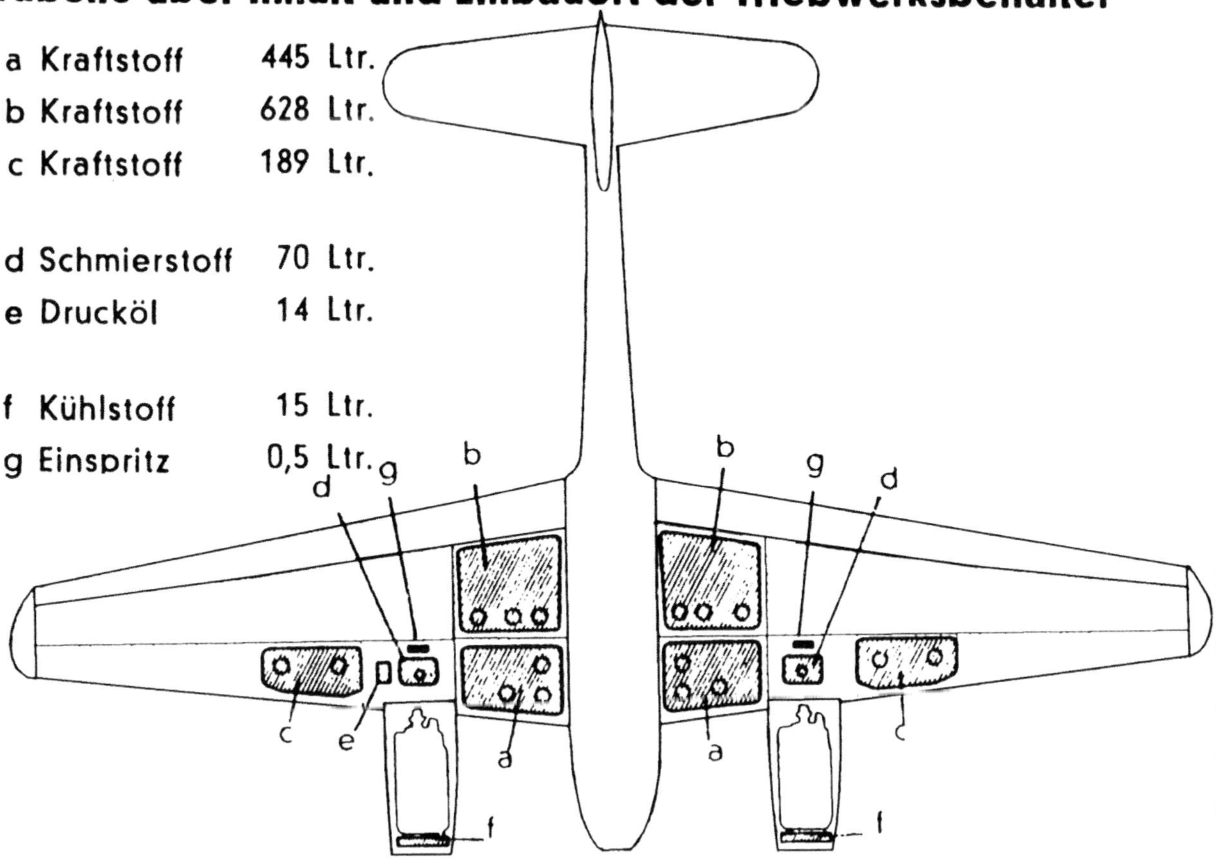

Abb. 1: Anordnung der Triebwerksbehälter

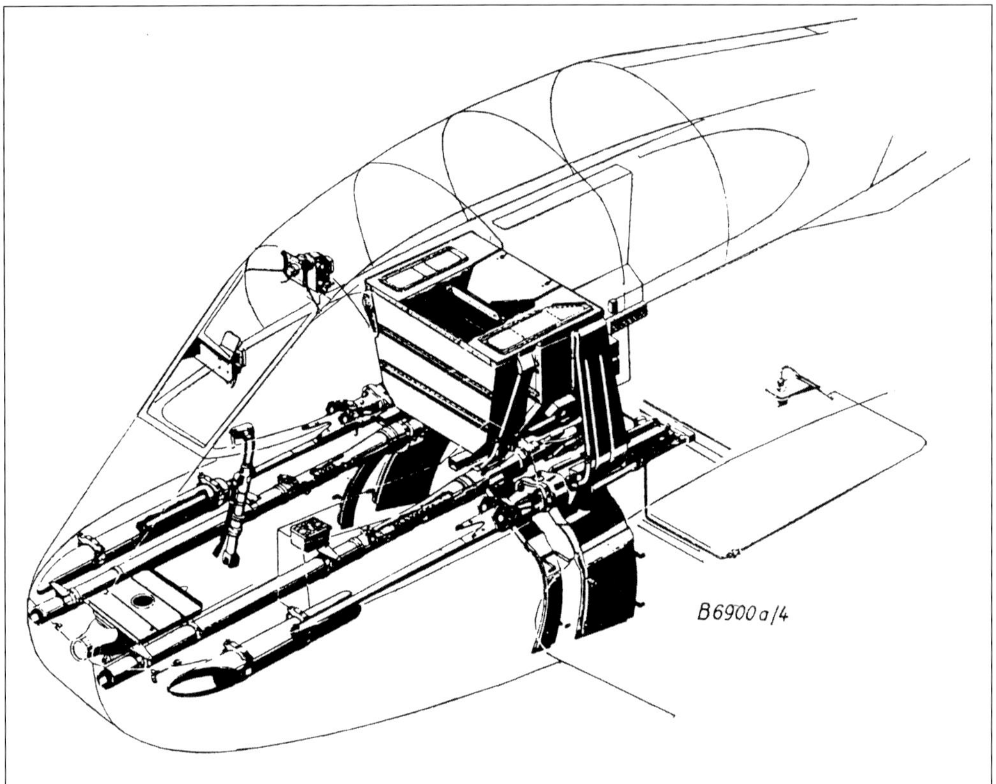

Übersicht der starren Bewaffnung

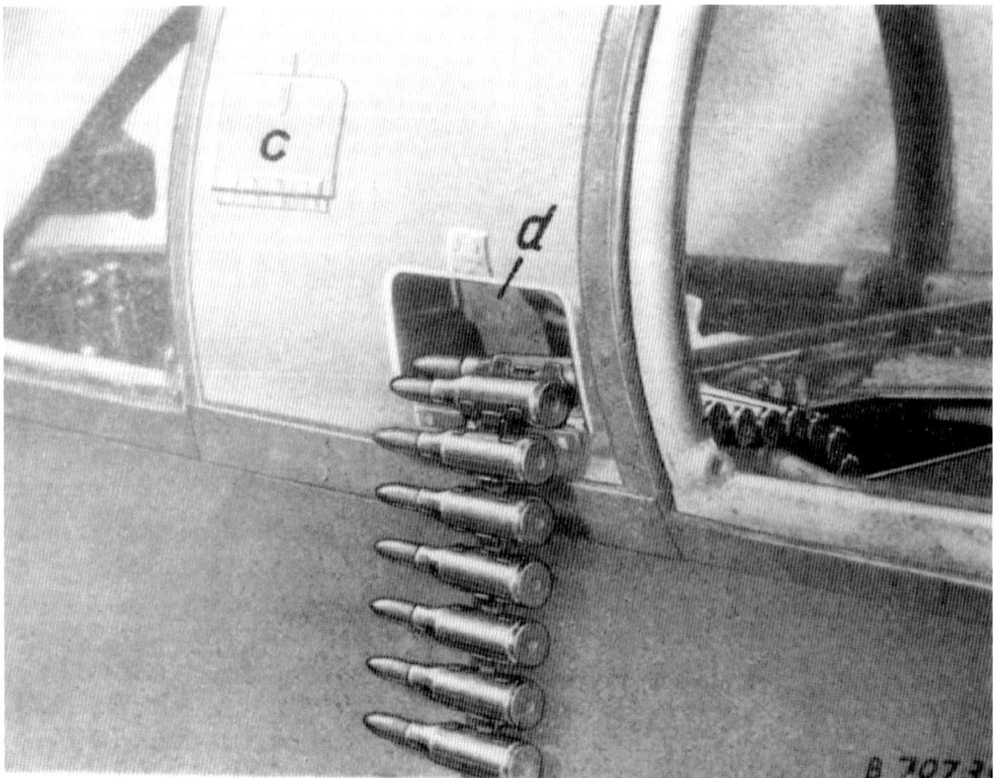

c für MG 17-Gurt d für MG 151/20-Gurt

Klappen im Kabinenmittelteil

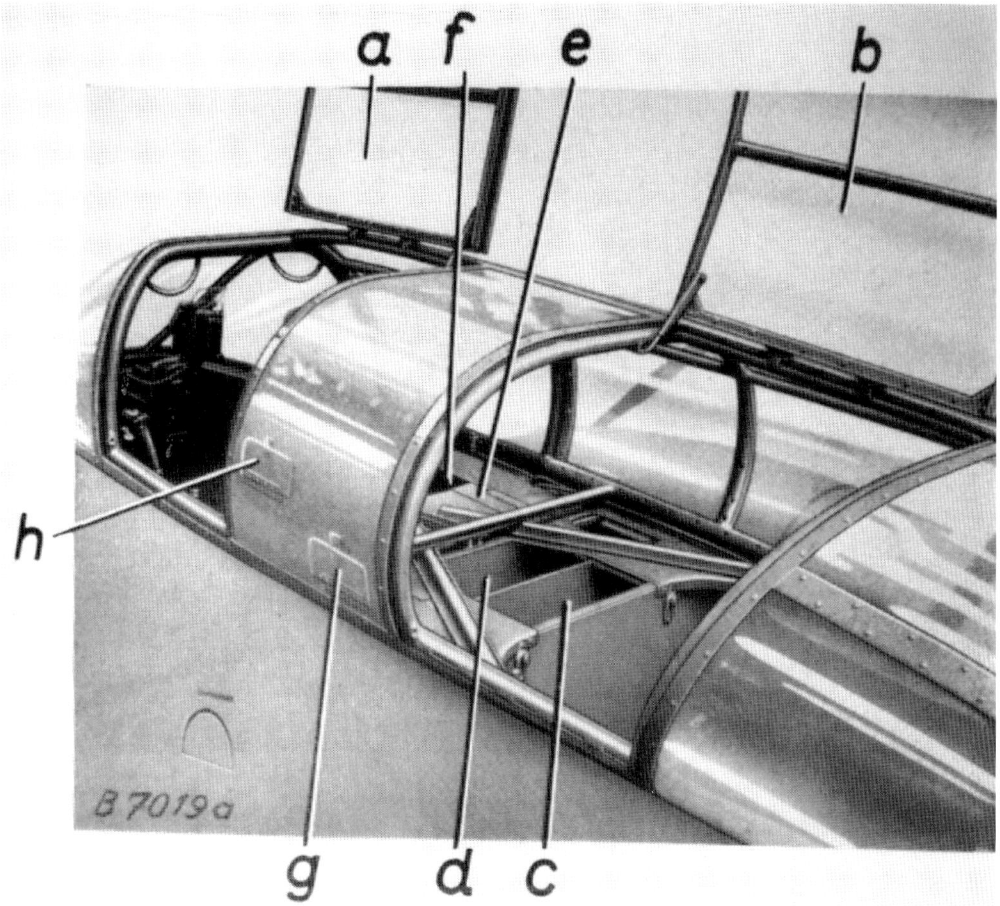

a = Einstiegklappe zum Führerraum
b = Einstiegklappe zum Funkerschützenraum
c = Munitionskasten für MG 151 (links)
d = Munitionskasten für MG 151/20 (rechts)
e = Munitionskasten für MG 17 links
f = Munitionskasten für MG 17 rechts
g = Klappe zum Einbringen der Munition für die MG 151
h = Klappe zum Einbringen der Munition für die MG 17

Abb. 3: Kabinenaufbau der Me 210

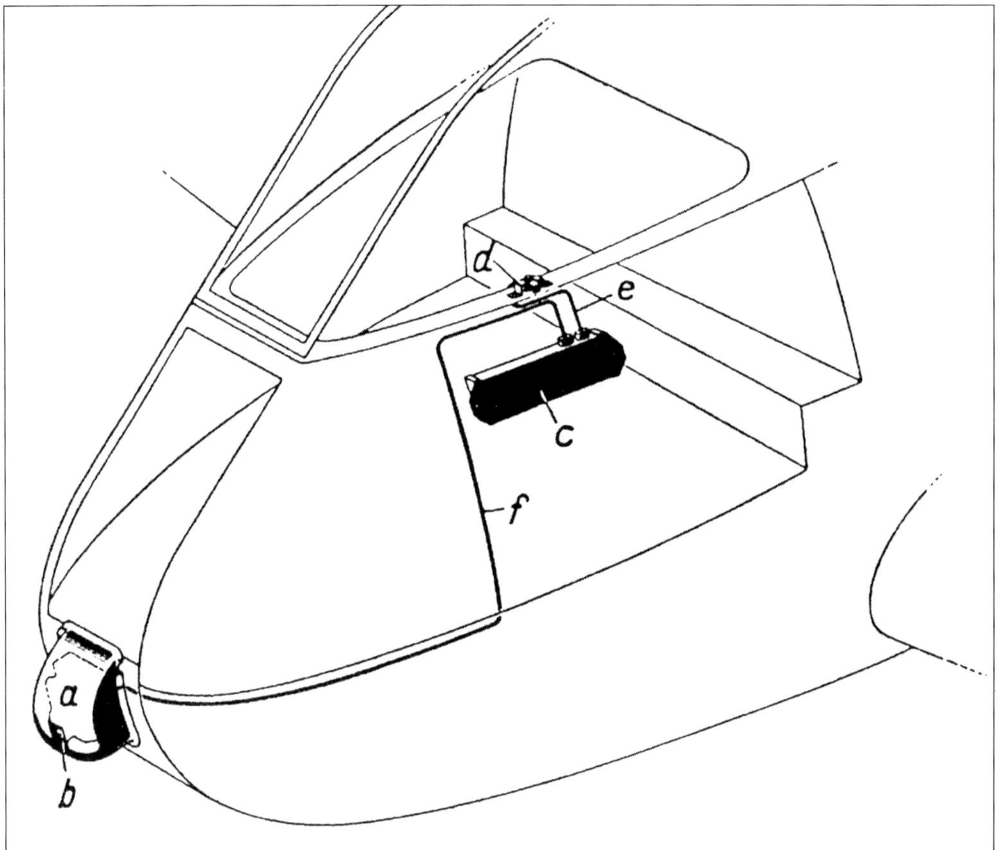

a Verkleidung der Kammerbefestigung
b Kleinbildkammer Robot II
c Batteriehalterung mit Batterie
d Knopfhalterung mit Auslöseknopf
e Leitung von Batterie zum Auslöse-knopf
f Leitung von Batterie zum Auslöse-magnet

Übersicht der Anlage für die Kleinbildkammer Robot II

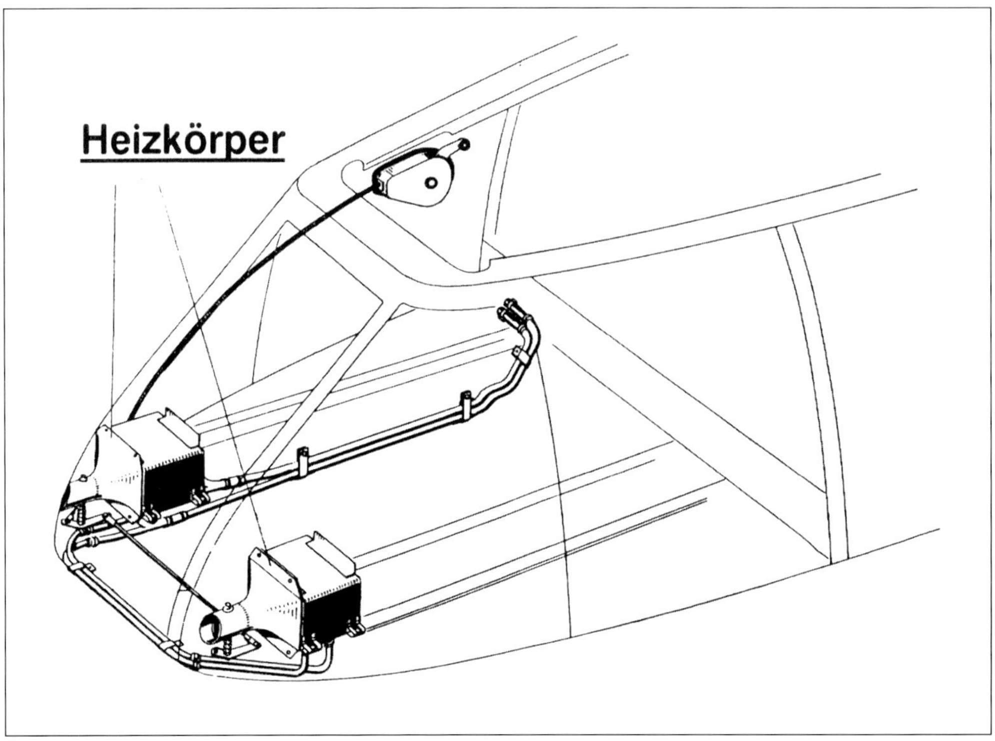

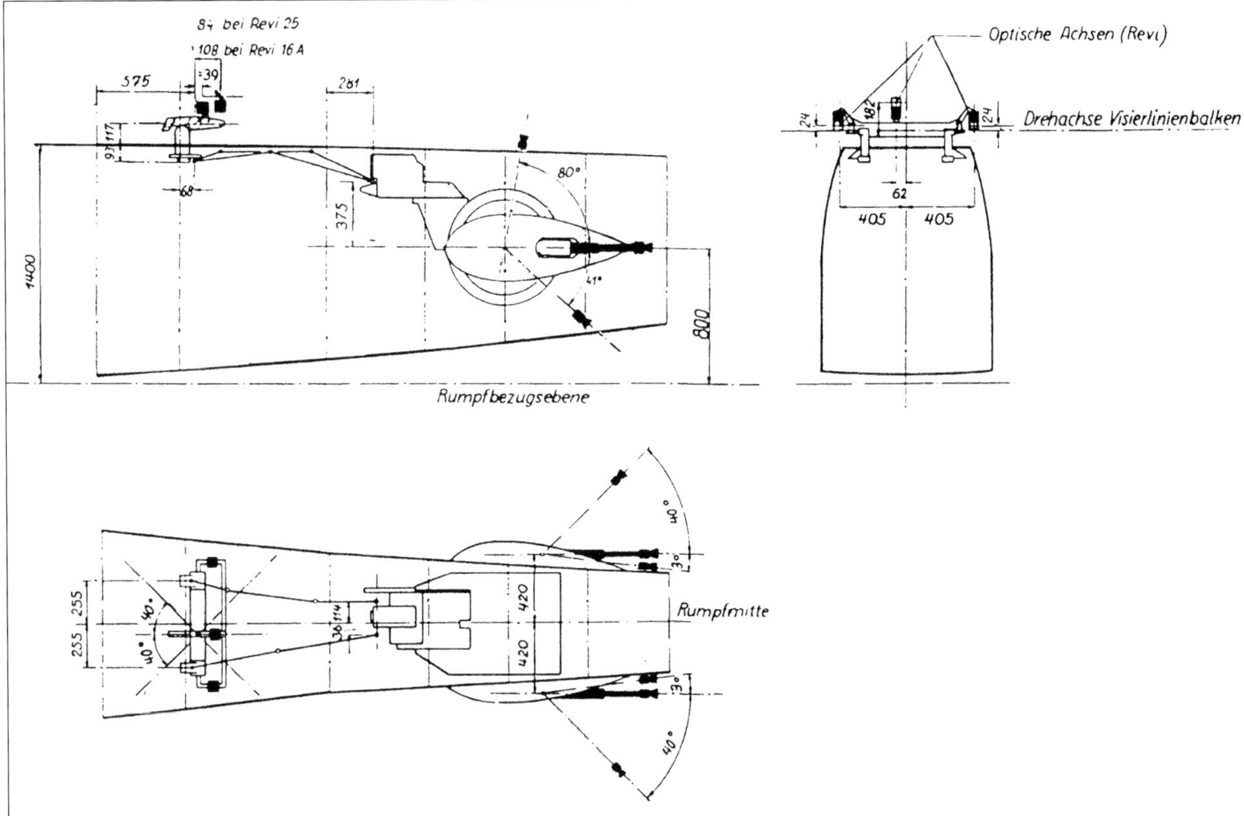

Visierdatenblatt der MG 131

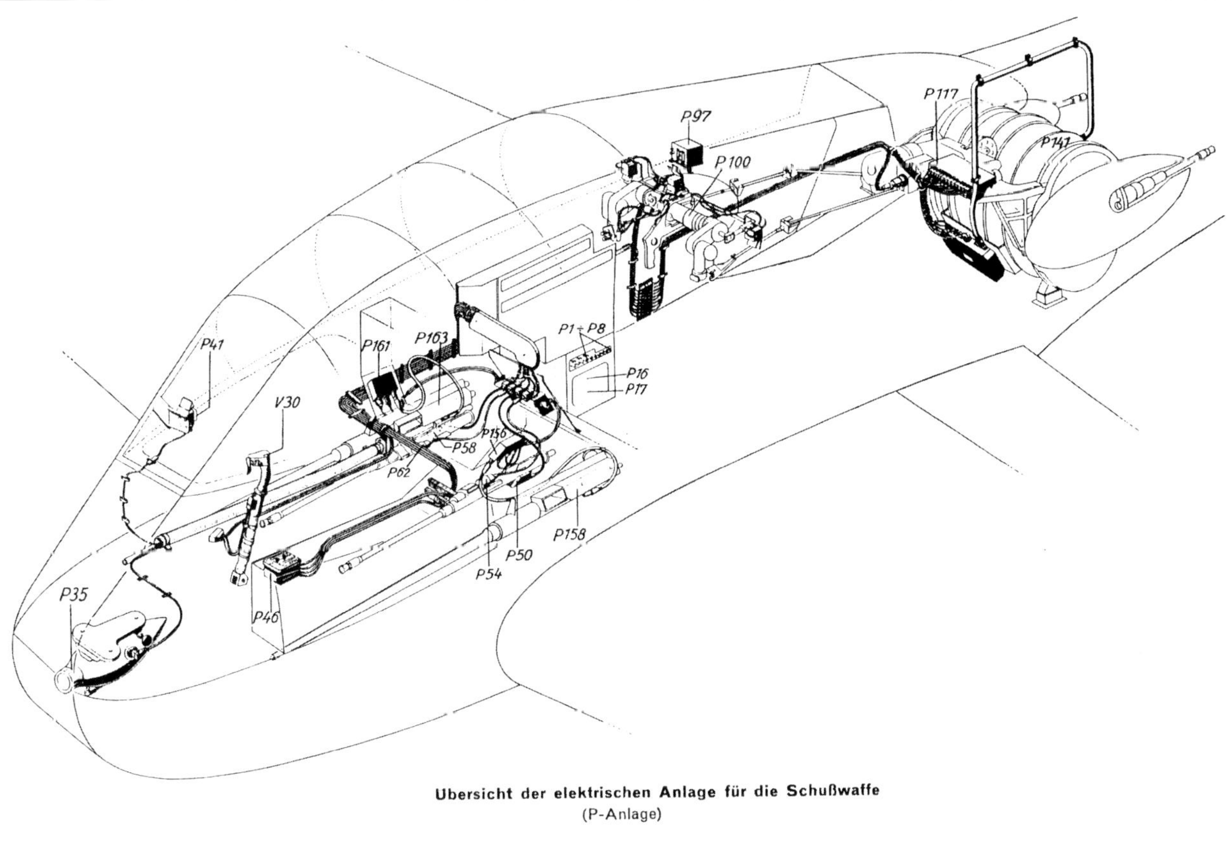

Übersicht der elektrischen Anlage für die Schußwaffe
(P-Anlage)

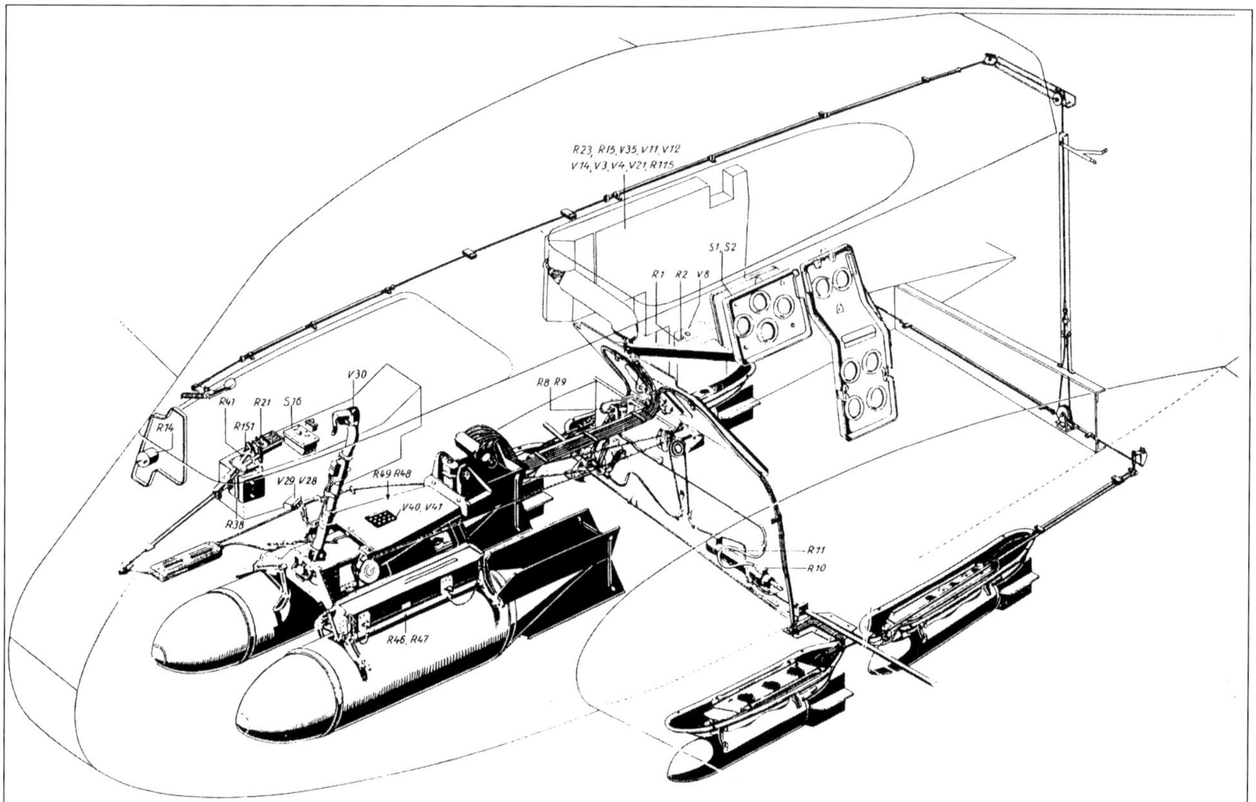

Übersicht der elektrischen Anlage für die Abwurfwaffe
(R- und S-Anlage)

below: W.Nr. *63 following conversion. (Moor)*

left: By the time of the Me 210 A-1's delivery, the dive brakes had become unnecessary. (Radinger)

below: Pilot's compartment of the Me 210 A-1 with the armor plating configuration of the heavy fighter mode.

1 Riegel für Schlechtwetterfenster
2 Doppelladedruckmesser
3 Absperrhahn für Horizont
4 Gitterschauzeichen für Fahrtmesser
5 Fahrtmesser
6 Horizont
7 Schwenkbares Gerätebrett
8 Hebel für Kabinenheizung

a) Führergerätebrett

1 Sauerstoffwächter
2 Druckmesser für Sauerstoff
3 Scheinwerferschalter
4 Druckknopfschalter für Triebwerksgerätebrettbeleuchtung
5 Hauptschalter für Vollsteuerung
6 Schalter für Staurohr
7 Schalter zum Abschalten der einzelnen Vollsteuerungsgetriebe
8 Schalter für Gerätebeleuchtung
9 Schalter für Kennlichter
10 Wechselschalter für Verstell-Luftschrauben
11 Druckknopf für Höhenatmer-Notauslösung
12 Drehumschalter für Kühlstoffkühlerregulierung
13 Verdunkler
14 Flaschenfernventil

d) Gerätebank rechts

1 Starterzüge
2 Preßluftnotventile
3 Brandhahnhebel mit P 1 und P 2
4 Trimmräder mit Anzeigegeräten
5 Schalter für Druckölanlage
6 Hebel für Kerzenabbrennung
7 12-Lampen-Gerät
8 Behälterumschalthebel
9 Schalter zum Abschalten der Vollsteuerung (Kuppelschalter)
10 Meßstellenumschalter für Kraftstoff-Vorratsanzeiger
11 Daumenschalter an Gashebeln
12 Kraftstoff-Vorratsanzeiger
13 Merkleuchten
14 Schalter für Kraftstoffpumpen

1 Doppeldruckmesser für Kraft- und Schmierstoff
2 Drehzahlmesser
3 Schmierstoff-Eintrittstemperaturmesser
4 Stellungsanzeiger für Verstell-Luftschraube
5 Kühlstoff-Austrittstemperaturmesser

h) Triebwerksgerätebrett rechts
(links spiegelbildlich)

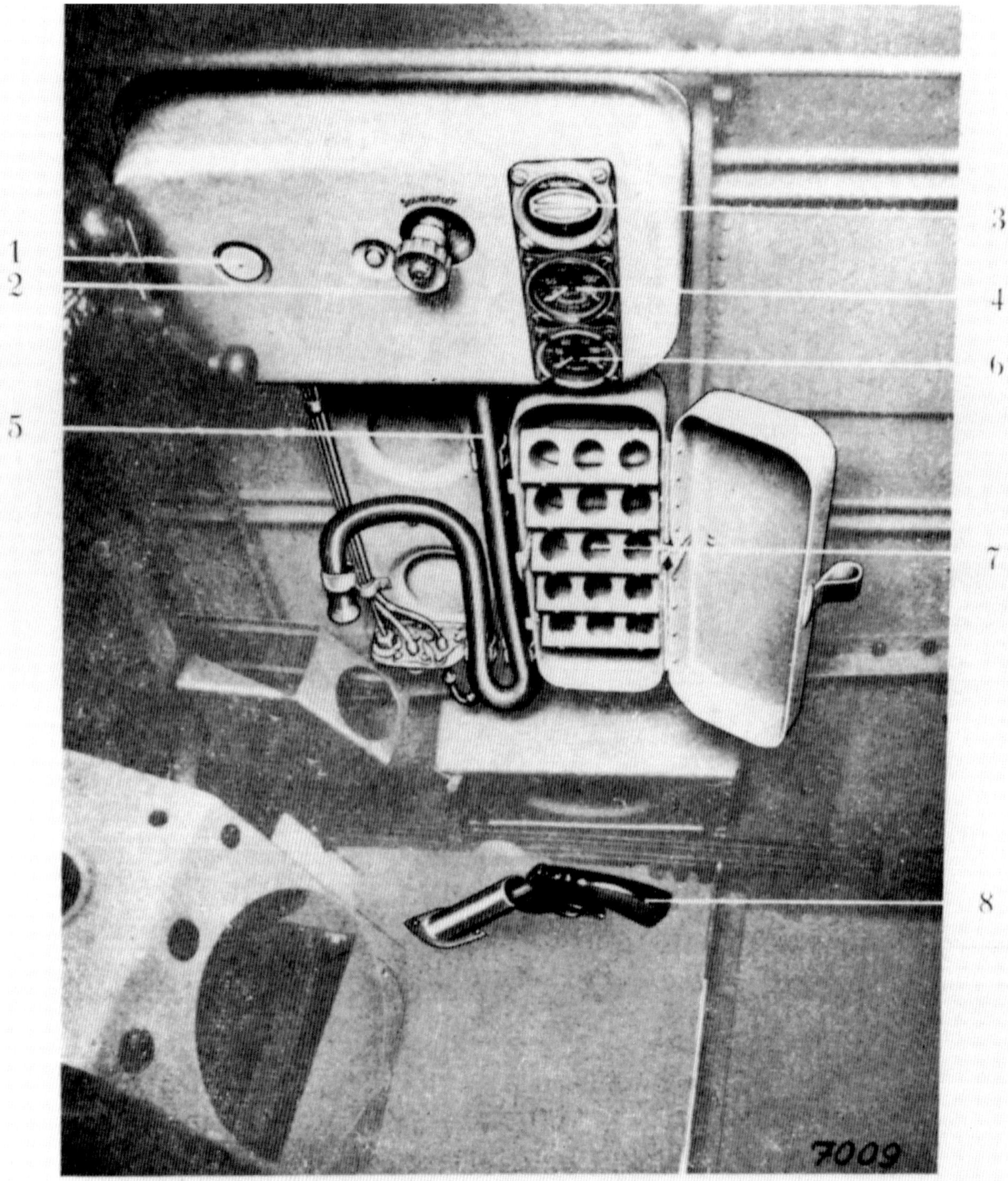

1 Druckknopf für Höhenatmer-Notauslösung
2 Flaschenfernventil
3 Sauerstoffwächter
4 Druckmesser für Sauerstoff
5 Schlauch
6 Druckmesser für Preßluft
7 Leuchtpatronenkasten
8 Leuchtpistole

e) Gerätekasten im B-Stand links

a Hauptschalter für MG 151
b Hauptschalter für MG 17
c Selbstschalter für MG 151
d Selbstschalter für Abzug MG 151

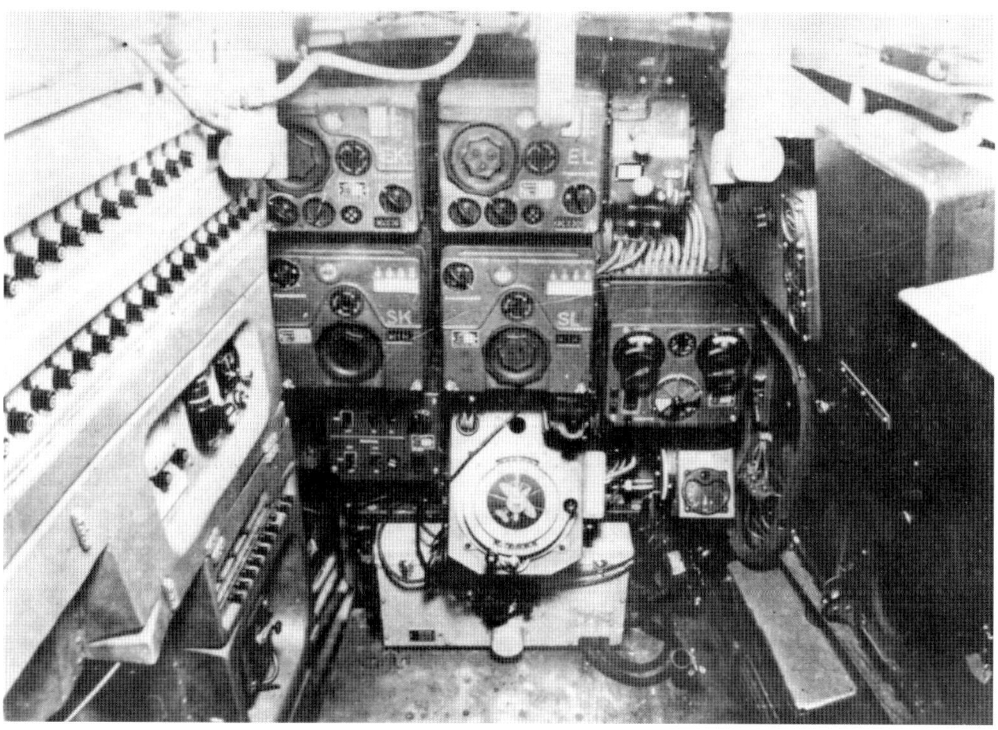

left: Radio equipment at the aft end of the cockpit.

right: Sighting mechanism and control system for the defensive armament.

below: Only a single SC 500 bomb could be carried. Here one is being lifted into the bomb bay, complete with shackles attached.

Situated between the bomb bay and the cockpit was a window enabling the pilot to keep the target in sight.

above: The block and tackle used to hoist these two SC 250s into the bomb bay is anchored to the tailwheel. (Petrick)
opposite page, top: The ETC 50 racks beneath the inner wing sections were only used on the Me 210. (Creek)

right: The General Staff was frustrated with the fact that dive bombing was not possible when carrying a load of eight SC 50s, as the bombs would fail to release. (Mankau)

opposite page, bottom: The pane of armored glass can be seen to good effect in the III./ZG 1 aircraft closest to the camera, photographed just prior to a mission from Trapani. (Petrick)

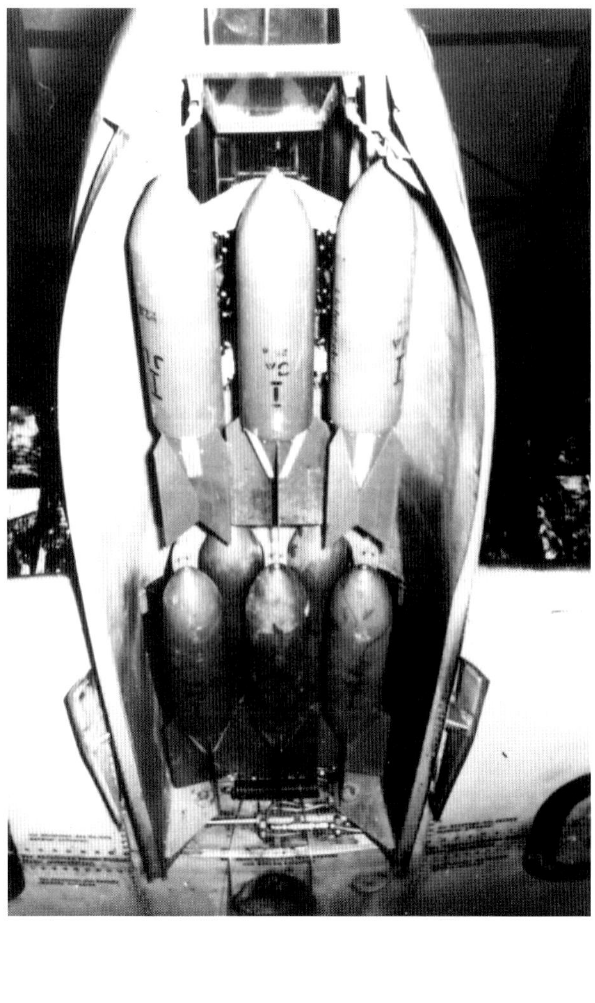

AS

Me 210 A-2

There was no manual for the Me 210 A-2 series mentioned in some publications, nor have the authors ever found a reference to this type in any manual or other document. The airplane Nowarra called the Me 210 A-2 (factory serial number 2350), which was sold to Japan, was in fact the Me 210 V22, tested in October 1942 at Rechlin using the DB 605 engine.

It may be possible that an Me 210 A-2 with extended fuselage and DB 601 powerplant was intended for production prior to the time construction was halted, and would have been an interim solution between the short Me 210 A-1 and the longer Me 210 C-1 with DB 605 (second production lot).

Me 210 B, Recce Version of the Me 210 A

Me 210 B-1, Reconnaissance (Description from 1941)

As A-1 (1941), but

Camera:	in bomb bay, 2 Rb 75/30 or 50/30 or Rb 20/30 in any configuration
Fixed armament:	1 x MG 151 1 x MG 151/20
Ordnance:	6 x LC 50 F in bomb bay

Me 210 B-1, Strategic Reconnaissance (Description from 1942)

As B-1 from 1941, but

Ordnance:	500/XII racks swapped out for racks with 6 ETC 50s for carrying flares
Fuel:	strategic recce with increased range, 2 x 900 liter external tanks, minus auxiliary fuselage tank

According to the C-Amt program, from 1 November 1940 the reconnaissance version of the Me 210 was to have been produced at the Gothaer Waggonfabrik sometime from June 1941 onward as a follow-on to the Bf 110 C-5. By March 1942 it was expected that 156 aircraft would have been delivered. A proposal by Mtt AG in August 1941 recommended that Mtt itself would build 102 Me 210 B-1 recce variants from October 1941 through April 1942, and a further 190 Me 210 D-1s with DB 605s by the end of 1942. In late September 1941 the delivery timetable was pushed back by two months. In fact, the BAL lists only show four to six Me 210 recce planes, which were taken on charge between October 1941 and January 1942. Serial number 198 was the prototype and underwent testing in early 1942. The authors have found no mention of the type in loss reports and flight logs. Thus, these may have been pre-production aircraft with small-frame fuselages. As a result of the delays, according to GL minutes from 5/23/41 production of the Me 210 B-1 was not to have begun until the second production lot, i.e. those with the lengthened fuselage, starting in September 1941. Following termination of production and its restart, the Me 210 B-1 was no longer carried on production lists.

Me 210 B-2, Tactical Reconnaissance (Description from 1941)

As A-1 (1941), but

Camera:	motorized hand camera
Ordnance:	not more than 2 x 250 kg

Me 210 C

The C series was similar to the A, but was powered by the DB 605.

Me 210 C-1, Heavy Fighter and Dive Bomber (Description from 1941)

As A-1, but

Engine:	2 x DB 605
Ordnance:	potential for carrying 1 x 1800 kg on external rack beneath bomb bay

In August 1941 Messerschmitt planned on building 282 Me 210 C-1s from March through December 1942. In September the planned target had grown to 945 airframes, which were to be produced from March 1942 to October 1943. The longer fuselage was most likely to have been incorporated in the design. The aircraft program from 2/1/1942 called for the DB 605 to be trial fitted in airframes 145 and 161 in February and March 1942. As a result of the general delay, Me 210 C 1 production would probably not have started before August 1942. In any event, the cancellation of production invalidated any plans.

Me 210 C-1 (*lang*), Heavy Fighter Dive Bomber (1943)

As Me 210 A-1 (*lang*), but

Engine:	2 x DB 605 B
Performance:	2 x 1475 hp

Following the halt in production and its subsequent restart, on 8 April 1942 the *Generalluftzeugmeister* intended to have the Me 210 A-1 conversions only delivered through May 1943, and even then still powered by the DB 601. It was planned to follow these with the DB 605 powered Me 210 C-1, as in Hungary. Messerschmitt was to have delivered all converted Me 210 airframes by the autumn of 1943. Since, however, the DB 605 initially proved extremely unreliable and was mainly needed for the Bf 109 and Bf 110, German production of the Me 210 C-1 with that engine occurred only in very limited quantities. There is only evidence to support less than ten airframes. In its place, the Me 410 with the DB 603 was converted from existing airframes starting as early as the spring of 1943.

Me 210 Ca-1, Heavy Fighter Dive Bomber

As Me 210 A-1 (*lang*), but

Engine:	2 x DB 605 B
Performance:	2 x 1475 hp
Electronic systems:	FuG X, FuG 16, Peil G V, FuBl 1
Weights (gross)	
(as *Zerstörer*):	9.706 t
(as *Stukazerstörer*):	10.706 t with 2 x 500 kg bombs
Weight (empty):	7.283 t as *Zerstörer* and *Stukazerstörer*
Wing loading:	296 kg/m² max
Max. speed	479 km/h at sea level
(as *Zerstörer*):	578 km/h at 6500 m
Max. speed	466 km/h at sea level
(as *Stukazerstörer*):	553 km/h at 5200 m
Landing speed:	200 km/h
Dive speed:	650 km/h at low level, max.
Climb rates	
(as *Zerstörer*):	6000 m in 11.5 min
(as *Stukazerstörer*):	6000 m in 14.5 min
Range	1730 km with 2400
(as *Zerstörer*):	liters
(as *Stukazerstörer*):	1370 km with 2070 liters

The Me 210 Ca-1 was the license-built version of the C-1 intended for Hungary, which did not make use of the GM 1 system.

According to Weber and Lajos, the cooperation between the Hungarian company of Manfred Weiss Flugzeugwerke and the Messerschmitt AG stemmed from talks between the Hungarian War Ministry and the RLM in early 1941. A result of these meetings was that manufacturing facilities would first be set up in Hungary, then Me 109 Fs, Me 210s, and DB 605s would be produced. It was intended that half of the Me 210s built in Hungary would be sent to Germany, and the other half Hungary would retain for its own use. The Hungarian War Ministry ordered 210 Me 210s on 6/26/1941. Production began in May 1942, although it initially involved only final assembly of parts shipped in from Germany. Maximum capacity would be reached in September 1943, according to plan. The first license-built machine, with registration code RF+PA, was completed in December 1942 and flown on 12/28/1942. The test pilots to be used for the initial flights had already trained on an Me 210 purchased from Germany in 1941. Parts assembly of the Me 210 Ca-1 was terminated in late April 1944 as part of the emergency fighter program and in favor of the Me 109. Production continued for a time using existing parts from inventory, so that the last Me 210 Ca-1 rolled off the assembly line in September 1944.

In 1985 Kováts Lajos published a complete list of Me 210 Ca-1s built in Hungary, to include factory serial numbers and registration codes. The total number amounted to

270, although a percentage of these was destroyed in bombing raids while yet at the factory. 36 machines are absent of registration coding, so that there are 92 German and 143 Hungarian registration codes. According to serial numbers (those supplied to Germany were given special RLM serial numbers), the *Luftwaffe* received 100 Me 210 Ca-1s. BAL lists apparently show only 54 being accepted. It is clear from the listings that somewhere around the 200th machine between the blocks for Hungary, which have continuous serial codes, there are gaps that are identical in numerical quantity to the blocks for Hungary. It can therefore be concluded that the *Luftwaffe*, as planned, was given half of the Me 210 Ca-1s built. As it could no longer make use of these from about mid-1944 onward, some of them were handed back over to Hungary.

below, and bottom: This heavy fighter's zenith had passed well before the Hungarians modeled their Me 210 Ca-1s after the Me 410 A-1/U4 by fitting them with cannons and rockets.

Me 210 Ca-1, Heavy Fighter

Like the Germans with the Me 410, Hungary also tested an Me 210 with a large caliber cannon. Initiated by the War Ministry on 2/14/1944, a heavy fighter was developed that was armed with two MG 151/20s in place of the MG 17s and a 36 M 40 mm Bofors cannon in the bomb bay, as well as two three-tube 140 mm rocket launchers under the wings. Z0-03, with the nose typical for a recce version, is documented as having been converted. Its modification began on 3/3/44, and in October a firing demonstration was made before the acceptance committee of the aviation research institute. In the report on this demonstration, dated 10/31/44, 30 additional conversions were called for. According to Weber at least three further conversions were made.

Me 210 Ca-1, Night Fighter

In Hungary the Me 210 Ca-1 was also used in the night fighting role, with standard production versions being initially employed. Then a three-seat conversion in 1944 made use of a Hungarian radar system. This operated with an EC-103 scope on a wavelength of 55 cm. In normal conditions range was 5 to 10 km, with a maximum of 18 km. The antennas were 1.5 m long and affixed to the nose. The machine was tested with some success during the summer of 1944.

Me 210 Ca-1, Command Platform

There was a project in Hungary which called for an additional bench in the bomb bay for a person lying prone. This project was similar to modification pack 22, which envisioned installation of a sighting system in the bomb bay with access for the radio operator. This version was to have functioned as a command and control platform, and even progressed to the mockup stage. It is possible that both projects were identical.

Me 210 D, Recce Version of the Me 210 C

Me 210 D-1 (1941)

Reconnaissance as B-1 (1941) but

Engine: 2 x DB 605

According to Messerschmitt plans from August 1941, 190 of the Me 210 D-1 variant were to have been constructed between February and December 1942. For reasons that are already known, this never materialized. The authors are not aware of a single example of the Me 210 D-1 with short fuselage being built.

Me 210 D-1 (*lang*)

Reconnaissance version as D-1 (1941) but with modifications along the lines of the Me 210 A-1 (*lang*).

There is proof that the Me 210 V17 (*W.Nr.* 101) was converted to Me 210 D-1 (*lang*) standards in the winter of 1942 and tested during the summer of 1943. No other aircraft are known.

Me 210 Da-1, Reconnaissance

As D-1 (*lang*). According to Weber, Hungary bought an Me 210 D reconnaissance variant from the *Luftwaffe* (possibly that listed under Me 210 D-1 above) in December 1942 in order to use it as the basis for developing a strategic reconnaissance platform. As the Me 210 Da-1, the Hungarian version was nearly identical to the D-1, but supposedly carried three aerial cameras in the bomb bay in place of the original two. The space for the third camera and its mount was made by dropping the MG 17s and bomb racks. According to Hungarian information two such aircraft were built (Z0-06 and Z0-07), none of which were sent to Germany. The Hungarians either built or were planning to build three tactical reconnaissance planes that, according to Weber, were to have had a crew of three. No further information is available.

Me 210 D-2, (1941), Tactical Reconnaissance

As B-2 (1941), but

Engine: 2 x DB 605

Me 210 E-1 (1941/42), *Zerstörer* and Dive Bomber

As A-1, but

Engine: 2 x DB 603

In September 1941 Messerschmitt planned on beginning deliveries of an Me 210 with DB 603 starting in April 1943. These plans called for an initial total of 451 machines to be supplied by March 1944. The capped rate of 70 aircraft per month throughout 1944 indicates that further deliveries were planned. Somewhat later, this variant received the designation Me 210 E-1. Trial fitting of the DB 603 in Me 210 *W.Nr.* 027 was, according to the aircraft program of 2/1/1942, to have taken place in March 1942. The first flight was delayed until 8/26/1942, however. This project spawned the Me 410 A-1, and the prototype became the Me 410 V1.

Me 210 F, Recce Version of the Me 210 E

Me 210 F-1 (1941/42), Reconnaissance

As B-1 (1941/42), but

Engine: 2 x DB 603

This project became the Me 410 A-3.

Me 210 F-2 (1941/42), Tactical Reconnaissance

As B-2 (1941/42), but

Engine: 2 x DB 603

Me 210 S-1 (1942), Strike Aircraft

As A-1 (1942), but

Ordnance: 1 x 500 kg or
2 x 250 kg or

	8 x 50 kg in bomb bay and 4 ETC 50/VIII or 4 *Rost* 24 SD 2 under inner wing sections
Fuel:	without 2 x 170 liter tanks in outer wings
Armor:	pilot and observer, frontal for engines and radiators, cutouts for undercarriage

In the aircraft program from 2/1/42, airframes with serial numbers 157 and 162 were named as prototypes for the Me 210 S, and reputedly entered flight testing in April and March of that year, respectively. At a GL meeting on 10 March 1942, those Me 210s undergoing conversion that had previously been designated strike variants were assigned the designation Me 210 S. As can be seen from the data, the additional weight of the armor had to be offset by less fuel capacity and bomb payload. Further differences included the RAB bombing system, which permitted the Me 210 S-1 to drop twelve 50 kg singly or as a salvo. Only the two prototypes for the Me 210 S-1 were built, and these were subsequently reconverted back to their original state. The armor, however, in part later became production standard for all Me 210s and Me 410s.

Me 210 S-2 (1942), Strike Aircraft

As S-1, but

Engine: 2 x DB 605

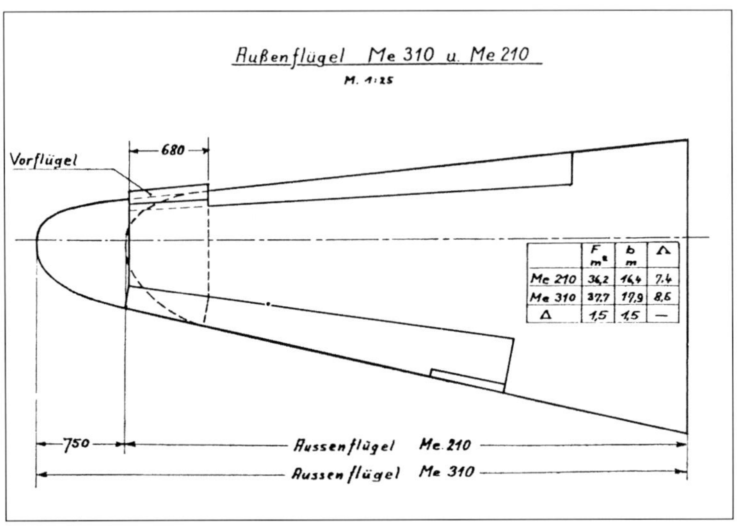

Me 210 Trainer

As Me 210 A-1 (*lang*), but with third seat and second set of controls in place of fixed armament.

From 1943 through 1944 Blohm & Voss took 48 long Me 210 A-1s and Ca-1s no longer fit for combat duties and converted them into trainers for the Me 410. It is not known if these were given a specific designation.

Me 310

As Me 210 E, but

Fuselage:	lengthened and with pressurized cockpit
Equipment:	modified
Wingspan:	17.9 m

In early 1941 Messerschmitt not only began development of a faster Me 210 series with more powerful engines (Me 210 C, Me 210 E), but also focused on a follow-on design with the goal of increasing the type's service ceiling. As this involved more sweeping changes, this variant was given an entirely new designation (Me 310). The C-Amt program from 10/1/41 mentions the Me 310 V1 and V2 with DB 603 A engines, for which some subassemblies had already been built. Completion deadline had not yet been established. By this time production of the Me 210 A-1 had already begun, but no prototype of the Me 210 with DB 605 or DB 603 had yet been planned. On 2/1/42 the Me 310 was still in the subassembly stage. The program had yet to be organized and was still unclear. The Me 210 prototypes for installation of the DB 605 and DB 603, however, were just two months away from being finished. On 11/1/1942, at the behest of the RLM, the aircraft program shows that all work on the Me 310 was to have ceased.

Nevertheless, at least one set of wings was built and tested in August and September 1943 on Me 210, *W.Nr.* 179 (VN+AQ). 179 was a testbed, and not one of the Me 310 prototypes that had been started. These test flights were not part of any Me 310 program, but were focused on the flight handling using larger wings with a view toward increasing the Me 410's high altitude performance. The trials showed that the stall handling with extended wingspan and longer leading edge slats was even better than with the standard production Me 210. Without the slats, however, handling was more pronounced and unpleasant than with the early versions of the Me 210 without slats. It was decided that, even with the larger wings, the slats should be retained.

Me 410

Messerschmitt was interested in the DB 603 from the moment the RLM sanctioned the engine in February 1940. Once the Me 210 V17 had been fitted with the longer fuselage in October 1941, in 1942 (although prior to break in production) the company generated the Me 210 E-1, F-1, and F-2 projects based around the DB 603. The Me 210 E-1 was planned as a standard follow-on development of the Me 210 A-1 and was, like the second production lot for the Me 210 A-1, to have been built with the longer fuselage. In this instance, the longer fuselage was needed to compensate for the higher engine weight. As this was still not sufficient, the sweep of the outer wings was moved forward as on the wind tunnel model, now giving a constant sweep across the entire wing's leading edge. The Me 210 E (Me 410) was not, as has often been claimed in publications, a hastily improved Me 210 with short fuselage that Messerschmitt shook out of his sleeve, so to speak. As early as 1 February 1942, i.e. prior to the interruption in production, the C-Amt's aircraft program made mention of an Me 210 with factory serial number 027 that in April 1942 was to be built with a test fitting of the DB 603. Its first flight, however, did not occur until 8/26/1942. After the machine reached 525 km/h during its evaluation at Rechlin and displayed good flight handling, *Generalfeldmarschall* Milch directed that it be designated the "Me 410." The Me 410 designation appears in RLM minutes for the first time on 9/9/42. Once production had resumed the Me 210 could only be delivered in relatively small numbers, as its engines were more urgently needed for the Bf 109 and Bf 110. With production of the DB 603 just beginning, the *Generalluftzeugmeister* could then have the Me 410 built in quantity alongside the Bf 110. To the General Staff and the GL, the Me 410 seemed so important that they left the Do 217 without engines in order to get more Me 410s. Even production figures for the Ju 88/188 were reduced in favor of the Me 410.

Me 410 A

A type overview put together by Messerschmitt at Oberammergau on 31 May '44 identified the variants Me 410 A-1 through A-3 as converted airframes and the B-1 through B-8 versions as new builds. A data sheet from the Messerschmitt AG dated 4/13/43 on the Me 410 B-1 also lists this type as a new build. Similar information can be found in publications as well. Nevertheless, this claim is not entirely accurate. Since, according to a statement by *Oberstabsing.* Alpers to the *Generalluftzeugmeister* on 6/19/42, there were 354 Me 210 A-1s completed, 108 unassembled, and a further 98 in

below: The Me 410 V1 was born by redesignating the Me 210 testbed (W.Nr. 027) *for the DB 603 powerplant. (Nowarra)*

above: The Me 410 V3 also stemmed from an old Me 210 (W.Nr. 055). *(Nowarra)*

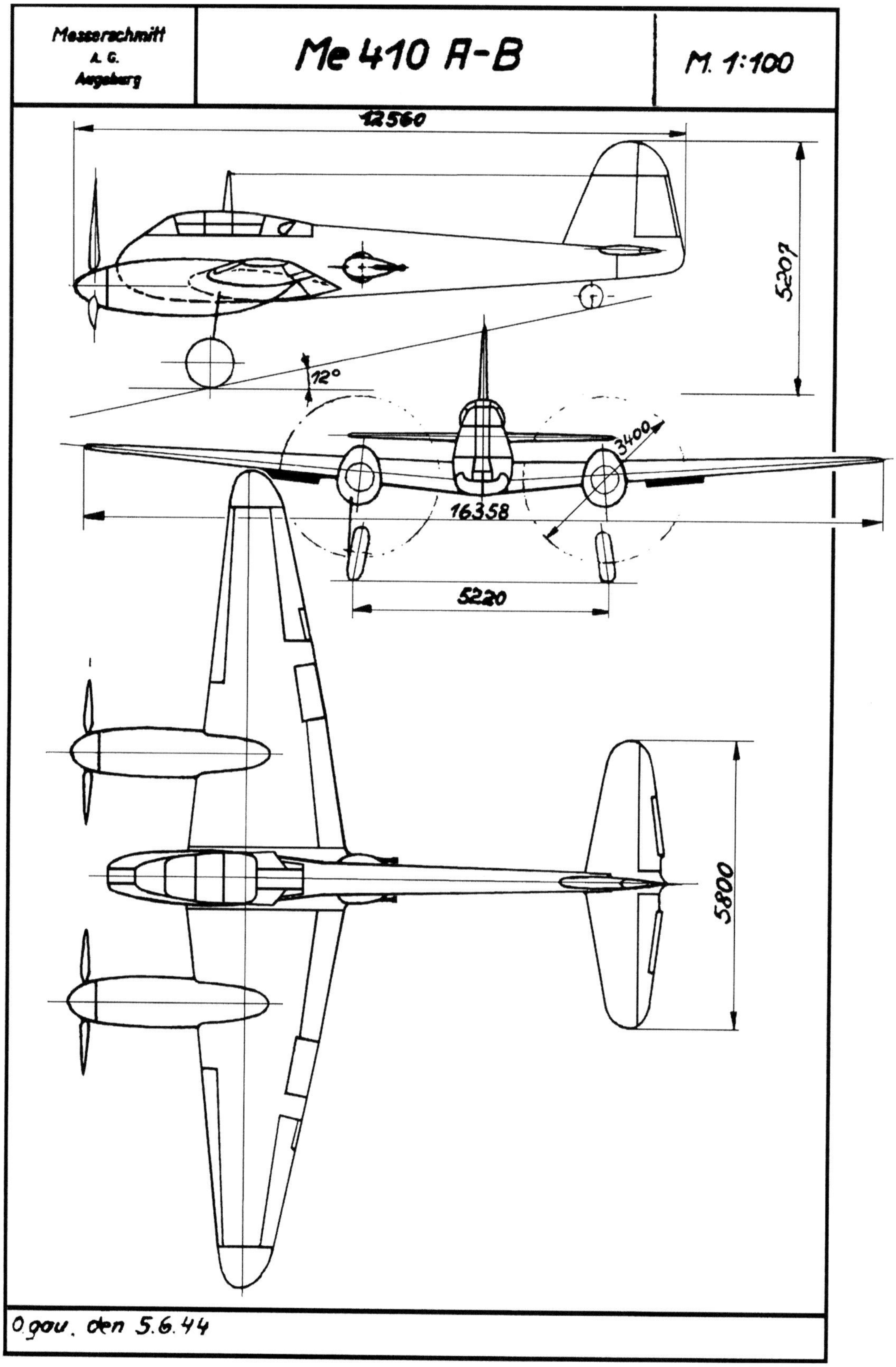
Messerschmitt
A. G.
Augsburg
Me 410 A-B
M. 1:100
12560
5207
12°
3400
16358
5220
5800
O.gau. den 5.6.44

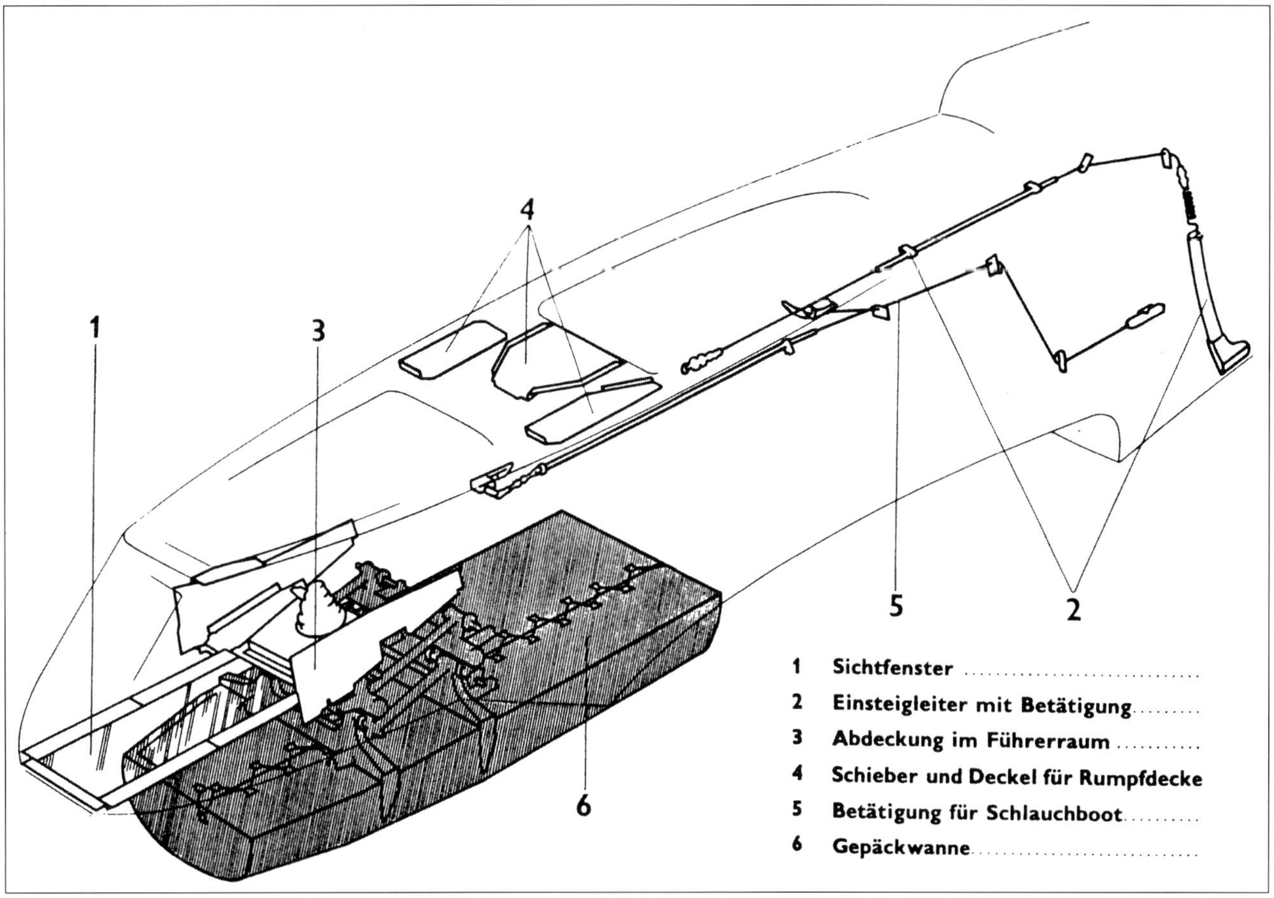

above: A baggage pack could be fitted for long-range ferry flights.

left: A baggage pack being loaded into the bomb bay. (Petrick)

the initial stages of production, i.e. a total of 540 existing airframes; thus, these could not have comprised the basis for the long frame Me 210 A-1s and the approximately 780 Me 410 As. To be sure, the Me 410 A includes the converted airframes, but it also constitutes identical looking new builds as well. Since the Me 410 B was to have had a few additional modifications compared to the Me 410 A that could not be implemented soon enough, the A series ran longer than originally planned. Production of the Me 410 A took place exclusively at Messerschmitt up

(Bundesarchiv *Koblenz*)

to early 1944, with Dornier also supplying the version from January 1944 onward.

Me 410 A-1, High Speed Bomber

Data is mainly derived from the Me 410 A-1 manual.

As Me 210 A-1 (*lang*), but

Wings:	outer section sweep same as inner section
Engine:	2 x DB 603 A
Performance:	2 x 1750 hp
Propeller:	VDM-VS, 3.4 m diam.
Weapons system:	as Me 210 A-1, but the wing ETC 50s were soon dropped
Sight:	Stuvi 5 B
Electronic systems:	FuG 10 (later FuG 10 P), FuG 16, FuG 25, Peil G V, FuBl 1(later FuBl 2 f)
Wingspan:	16.35 m
Length:	12.48m (12.56 m is also mentioned)
Height:	4.28 m
Weights	
(gross):	11.3 t with 2 x 500 kg bombs
(empty):	6.7 t
Wing loading:	312 kg/m^2 max
Max. speed	485 km/h at sea level
(at max. wt):	575 km/h at 6300 m
Max. speed	490 km/h at sea level
(at 9.5 t):	590 km/h at 6300 m
Landing speed:	230 to 250 km/h
Dive speed:	650 km/h at low level, max.
Climb rates	
(at max. wt):	6000 m in 13min
	8000 m in 22 min
(at 9.5 t):	6000 m in 9 min
Service ceiling	
(w/ 11.3 t):	8400 m
(w/ 9.5 t):	1000 m
Range (w/ 11.3 t):	approx. 1350 km with 2400 liters, at 6400 m
Endurance:	approx. 2.75 hrs

According to logbook entries and loss reports, from December 1942 until around May 1943 there were about 135 Me 410 A-1s built, either through conversion or completion of existing short frame Me 210 A-1s. Original serial numbers and registration codes were retained in the process. As Messerschmitt did not sequentially follow serial numbers when undertaking the conversions, instead seeming to have selected the machines arbitrarily, the compilation of references after December 1942 must be relied upon to verify documentation entries. Yet because loss reports are known to contain errors and do not necessarily include all aircraft, there is still some uncertainty. Approximately 25 converted machines cannot be classified with any degree of accuracy into the Me 210 or Me 410 categories. The lists from the production oversight office (BAL) showing accepted airframes is not an accurate source either. According to it, from January through May 1943 there were 88 converted *Zerstörer* and 25 modified reconnaissance versions taken on charge. If we add together the converted Me 210s (166) and Me 410s (113) that, according to BAL, were accepted, we are still well shy of the 354 converted short frame Me 210s, not to mention the number of Me 210s completed. It is difficult to accept the claim that the nearly 100 missing aircraft all functioned as testbeds or were lost before being turned over.

The converted Me 410s had their engine gauges in the nacelle sides, as with the Me 210. As this arrangement did not prove effective, the gauges were moved into the cockpit, in the floor space in front of the control stick. Although the exact time of this change cannot be determined, it appears that it occurred by the summer of 1943 with the shift from conversion airframes to new-built ones, for there is documentary evidence that aircraft from the first new-build series (serial numbers 10xxx) had the new configuration.

The Me 410 A-1's main role was as a high speed bomber (*Schnellkämpfer*) for strikes against England. More precisely, it was to be used in high speed daylight raids on point targets, although priority was given to night attacks against enemy bomber airfields (long range night fighting). Due to its relatively high speeds, only a few of these aircraft were ever shot down on these raids. However, due to its layout the type was not ideally suited for this role. In the first place, it lacked a corresponding targeting system for strikes made from level flight: a *Lotfe* gyroscopic reflector bombsight. The bomb bay was too small, and could normally only accommodate two 250 kg bombs of any type. Two 500 kg bombs could be carried, but they had to be the narrow body type, such as the armor piercing SD 500, which was designed specifically for use against armored targets. Of the larger SC 500, filled with more explosives and developed for use against buildings, only one would fit into the bomb bay.

Lt. *Baak of* 14./KG 2 *flew this flame damper-fitted Me 410 A-1 over England during the fall of 1943. The machine has the engine instrumentation located beneath windows on the engine nacelles, seen just ahead of the turbocharger intake. (Baak)*

Sometime during the summer of 1944 the instruments were moved into the cockpit.

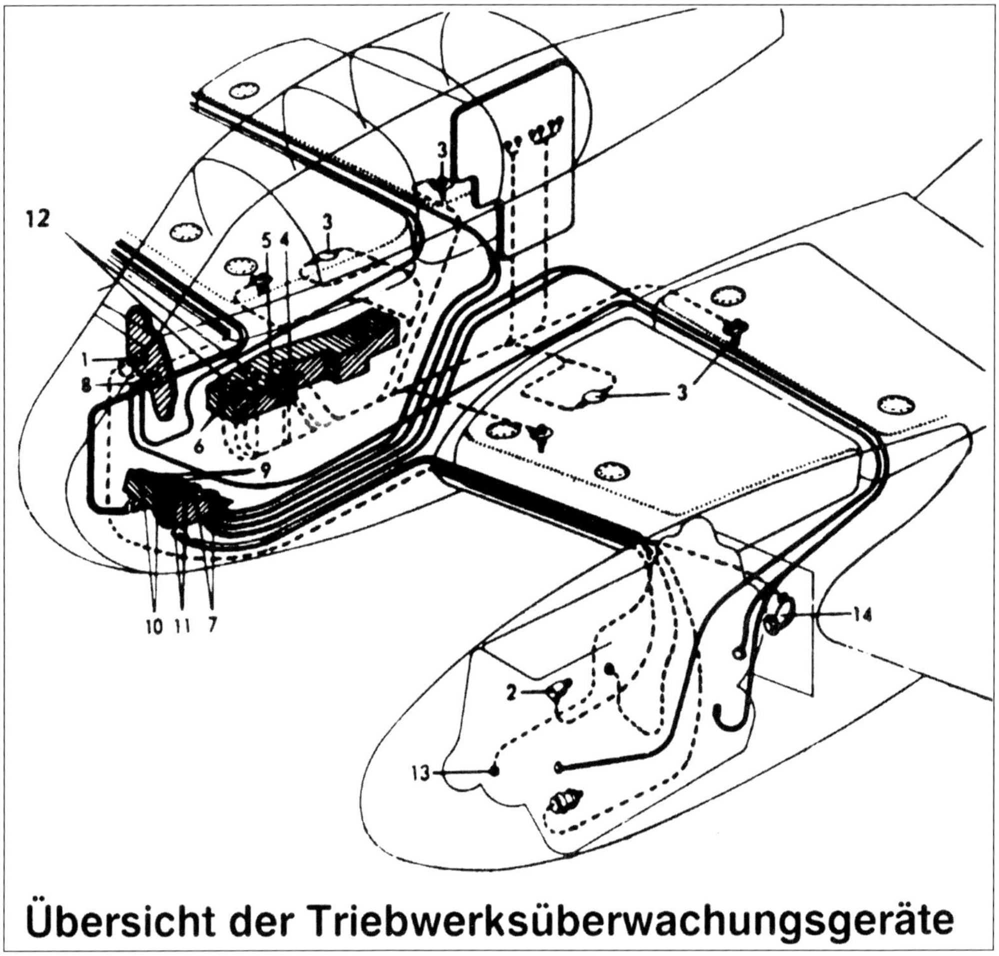

Dual pressure gauges for the lubricant and fuel, temperature gauges for the coolant and propeller pitch indicator were all now located ahead of the control column. (Radinger)

Operations were also flown with two SC 500s, but in this case the bomb bay doors could not close completely and resulted in a negative effect on airspeed and range.

In the opinion of the *General der Kampfflieger*, *Oberst* Peltz, the range was extremely poor for attacks against England, and what the machine offered was extremely bad. He would have gladly exchanged his Me 410 A-1s for Ju 88 S planes and given the Me 410 to the *General der Jagdflieger*, *Oberst* Galland. This idea was abandoned as the Ju 88 S was not available in sufficient numbers since, among other reasons, the RLM arranged for the Henschel Flugzeugwerke to switch production from Ju 88s to Me 410s, and both Hitler and Göring ordered the bombing of England to continue with all means available (see Me 410 A-1/U2).

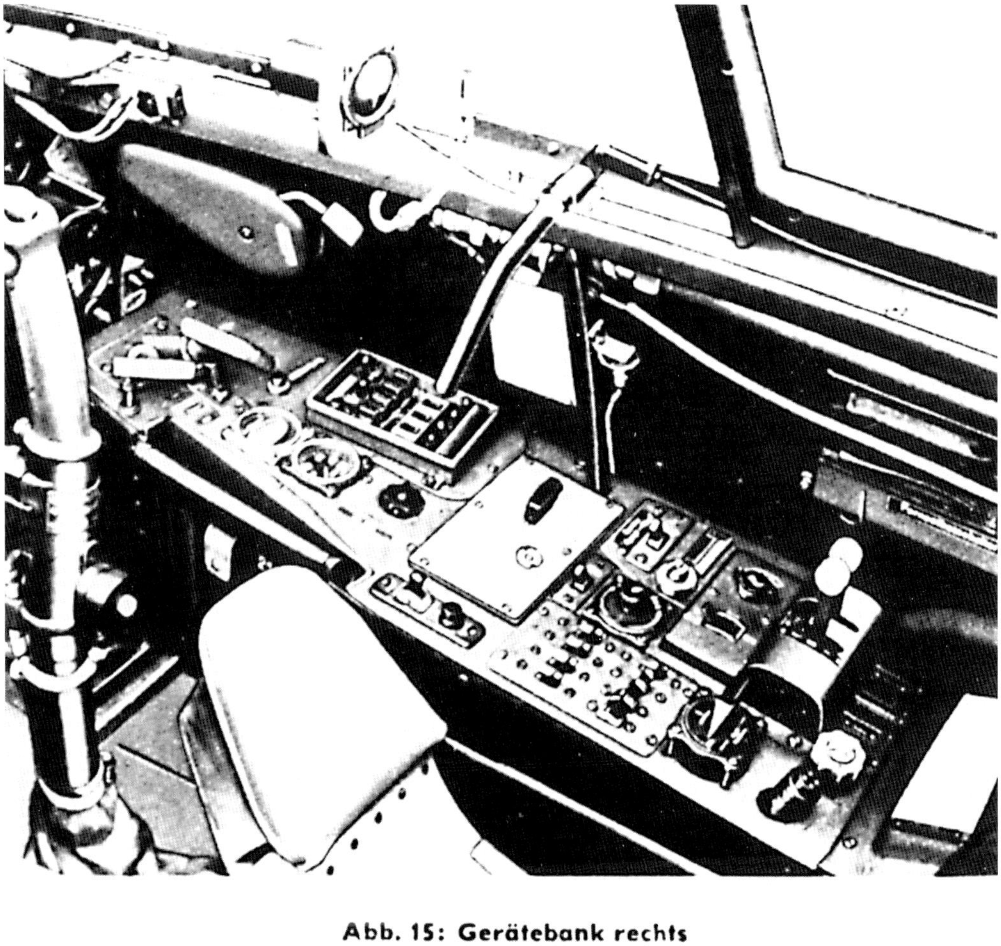

Even the layout of the right instrument panel was altered.

U5+KG of 5./KG 2 *has been kitted out with flame dampers for nighttime operations. Engine gauges are located in the cockpit. (Petrick)*

The window in the bomb bay and the additional covers indicate that this aircraft is an Me 410 A-1/U1 with RB 75/30 camera. Due to the instrument windows in the nacelles, this plane was formerly an Me 210.

Me 410 A-1/U1, Auxiliary Reconnaissance Platform

According to Me 410 A-1 manual, section 0, October 1943,
According to Messerschmitt type overview from 31 May 1944,
According to Me 410 aircraft type sheet from 20 September 1944:

As Me 410 A-1, but

Sight:	Revi C/12 D
Fixed armament:	2 x MG 151/20
Camera:	RB 20/30 or RB 50/30 or RB 75/30 in bomb bay

According to Messerschmitt type overview from 20 September 1944:

Fixed armament:	2 x MG 17 2 x MG 151/20
Ordnance:	2 x 2 ETC 50 racks under center wing section
Electronic systems:	FuG 10 P, FuBl 2F, TZG X, FuG 16, FuG 25a

According to Messerschmitt type overview from 31 May 1944:

Auxiliary Reconnaissance Platform with Bomb Doors

According to the Me 410 A-1 handbook, part 0, the photographic system was fitted into the bomb bay of the Me 410 A-1/U1. According to the Messerschmitt overview this version was fitted with bomb bay doors. On the other hand, there were conversion kits 30 through 32, which enabled the cameras to be fitted in the fuselage behind the EDL, and in the Messerschmitt description for conversion kits there is no camera installation in the bomb bay listed. According to statements from a former member of a reconnaissance unit, he first flew an Me 410 where the radio operator had to open the lens caps for the camera with a cable, and he believed the camera installation to have been in the aft fuselage.

In the book "*Aufklärer - Luftwaffe* Reconnaissance Aircraft and Units 1935-1945" by Bradley, Ketlay, and Wadmann, photograph no. 488 shows an Me 410 (VC+GG, *W.Nr.* 2257, formerly an Me 210 A-1) that has a glass plate in the forward nose floor, a round opening in the middle of the bomb bay door, and no MG 17s.

The similarity to our photo, the visible details, and the time frame lead the authors to speculate that the Me 410 A-1/U1 was only derived from converted Me 210s, with a camera in the center bomb bay and only two MG 151/20s as forward firing armament. The camera opening was probably capped off with a cable-controlled cover, and in the case of the RB 75/30 installation had an additional cover piece.

No information is available regarding numbers. The Me 410 A-1/U1 variant is included in the totals for the Me 410 A-1.

Me 410 A-1/U2, Auxiliary *Zerstörer*

According to Me 410 A-1 manual, section 0, October 1943,
According to Messerschmitt type overview from 31 May 1944,
According to Me 410 aircraft type sheet from 20 September 1944:

As Me 410 A-1, but

Wing: no dive brakes, no *Kutonase*
Sight: Revi C/12 D
Fixed armament: 2 x MG 17
2 x MG 151/20
2 x MG 151/20 with 200 rounds each sharing a single belt (first version) or 230 rounds each using two belts in *Waffenbehälter* 151 A gun pod
Armor: armored glass for pilot

Electronic systems: FuG 10 P, FuBl 2 f, TZG X, FuG 16

For the role of *Zerstörer* in 1942 the armament consisting of two MG 151/20s and two MG 17s was considered too weak. Even for the Me 210 the WB 151 A gun pod was developed to increase the fixed armament. The Me 410 *Zerstörer* version (Me 410 A-2) was to have two MK 103 cannons in place of the pod. With delays in MK 103 production, however, an interim solution was found by creating the Me 410 A-1/U2 auxiliary *Zerstörer*, which would take the gun pod. With it, an Me 410 A-1 high speed bomber

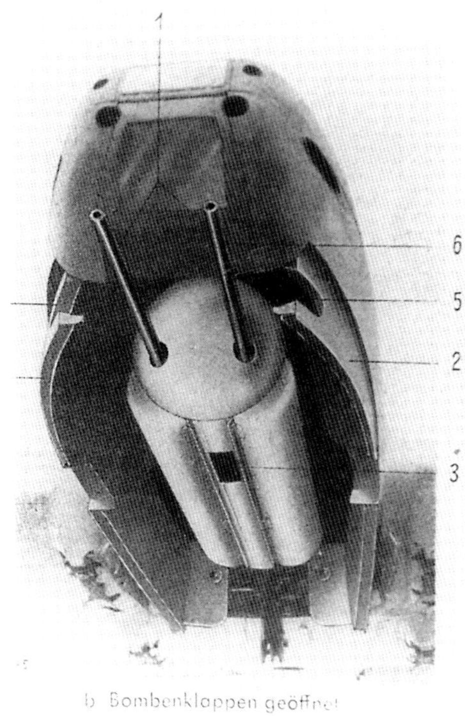

The WB 151 A weapons pack, comprising two MG 151/20s, was the most obvious modification to the Me 410 A-1/U2.

could metamorphose into a *Zerstörer* in less than ten hours.

The number of modified airframes is not known, but in the *Luftwaffe*'s view it was too small. Production began in June 1943 with 10 units. In July 1943 the RLM intended to have just 100 of the 400 Me 410s expected in 1943 to be built as Me 410 A-1/U2 *Zerstörer*. As was mentioned with the Me 410

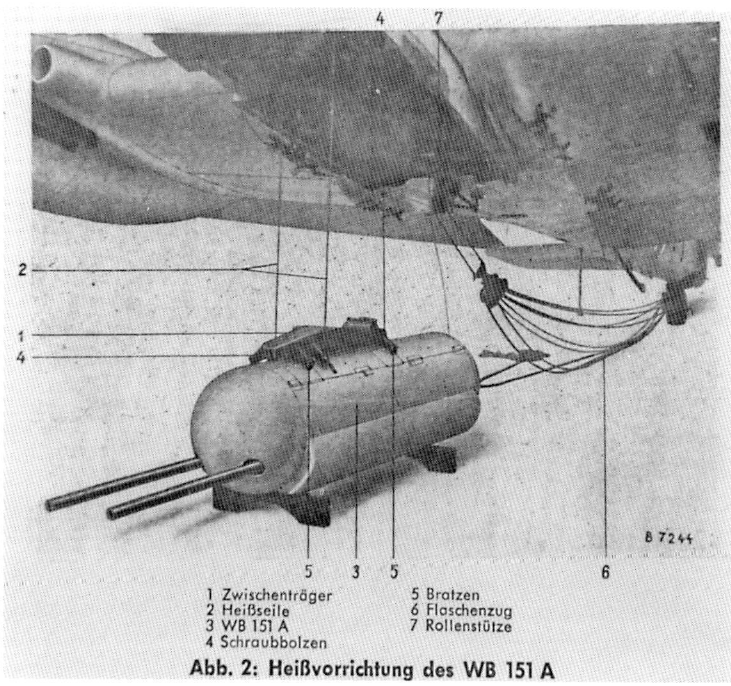

opposite page, top: As the two MG 17 and four MG 151 guns were considered to provide inadequate firepower, a temporary solution was to fit the Zerstörer *with two tubes for the 21 cm* Wurfgranate *beneath the outer panels of the wings. (Price)*

right: This Me 410 A-1/U2 built by Dornier in 1944 is armed with two MG 17s, four MG 151s, and two twin-tube packs. (Petrick)

opposite page, bottom: 2N+DD of Stab III./ZG 1 *was caught on film at Diepholz in August of 1943. It no longer had the engine instrumentation in the nacelles and boasted the brand new* Nebelwerfer *tubes. (Petrick)*

A-1, the *General der Kampfflieger* was unhappy with the Me 410 and would happily have given them to the *General der Jagdflieger*. In turn, he would have been able to use the 410 with the gun pod as daytime heavy fighters and thus have freed up the Bf 110 G-2 for use as a night fighter. The RLM even implemented this measure in the autumn of 1943, but in late October of that year the *Reichsmarschall*, probably at the behest of his master, instructed the Me 410 to continue in its role as high speed bomber, with priority given to building the type in this variant. As a result, the number of Me 410 A-1/U2 *Zerstörer* variants remained low for several months, i.e. production was about 10 *Zerstörer*/month. This gives a (generous) estimate of about 100 aircraft, calculated from the entire production time of the Me 410 A-1 (in addition there was the Me 410 a-1/U4 *Zerstörer*). The operational use of the Me 410 A-1/U2 was planned for a group from ZG 26 (I./ZG 26 and for two groups from ZG 76. On 8 May '44 the Messerschmitt Company wrote to the L. Hansen Company, instructing them that all Me 410 A-1 high speed bombers were to be converted to Me 410 A-1/U2 heavy fighters. The number of airframes affected by this is unknown. Yet because only I and II Groups of KG 51 flew the Me 410 A-1, the total would have been about 100 aircraft. A further clue as to the number of Me 410 A-1s operating in the *Zerstörer* role can be derived from the data in loss reports of ZG 26 and ZG 76 (where losses were determined to be anything from 10% to 100%). By February 1944 approximately 40 reports had appeared with a total of 165, whereby as a rule the reports did not distinguish between the Me 410 A-1, Me 410 A-1/U2, and the Me 410 A-1/U4.

Me 410 A-1/U3

As there were the U1, U2, and U4 conversions, it is safe to assume that the U3 was also at least a project. Unfortunately, the authors are not aware of any documentation describing this version. We speculate that this may have been the single seat version with GM 1, of which 30 units were reputedly built after the Me 410 A-1/U2 and prior to the production of the Me 410 A-1/U4.

Me 410 A-1, Single Seat *Zerstörer* with GM 1 System

As Me 410 A-1/U2, but

Crew:	pilot only
Fixed armament:	2 x MG 17 2 x MG 151/20 2 x MG 151/20, each with 230 rounds in WB 151 A gun pod
Flexible armament:	no FDSL barbettes, GM 1 tank in place
Armor:	only against frontal attack
Electronic systems:	FuG 16 Z
Weight:	1800 kg reduced

Two of several studies showing the Me 410 fitted with the GM 1 boost system. The upper variation was realized in the Me 410 A-3/U1 and Me 410 B-3/U1. The lower variation was tested, unsuccessfully, during the winter of 1943/1944 with a WB 151 A and GM tank in Reich defense operations.

On 8 March 1943 the RLM had a meeting in which it was believed that the Americans would shortly be appearing at altitudes above 10000 m. A countermeasure in the form of a single seat Me 410 was proposed that, by removing the aft armament and the radio operator, would be lighter by some 380 kg. Desired weaponry consisted of two MG 151/20s and two MK 103s. Research would be conducted into using wingtip extensions to increase altitude even further. The DB 603 was to be used, and mention was made that conversion to GM 1 was underway.

On 9/14/43 the RLM reported the existence of a single seat Me 410 presently undergoing conversion. It was to be lighter by about 1800 kg and would have the 500 kg GM 1 system, enabling it to fly for one hour at altitudes of 10.5 to 11 km. The lightened Me 410 was also discussed on 9/21/43. But this lightweight plane was only the first step. The second step involved GM 1 and improved firepower (only two MK 103s and two MG 151s).

A production rate of 10 -15 *Zerstörer* planes per month was planned for the *Zerstörer* version of the Me 410 A-1/U2 on 11/15/43. The ultimate goal for 1945 was 100

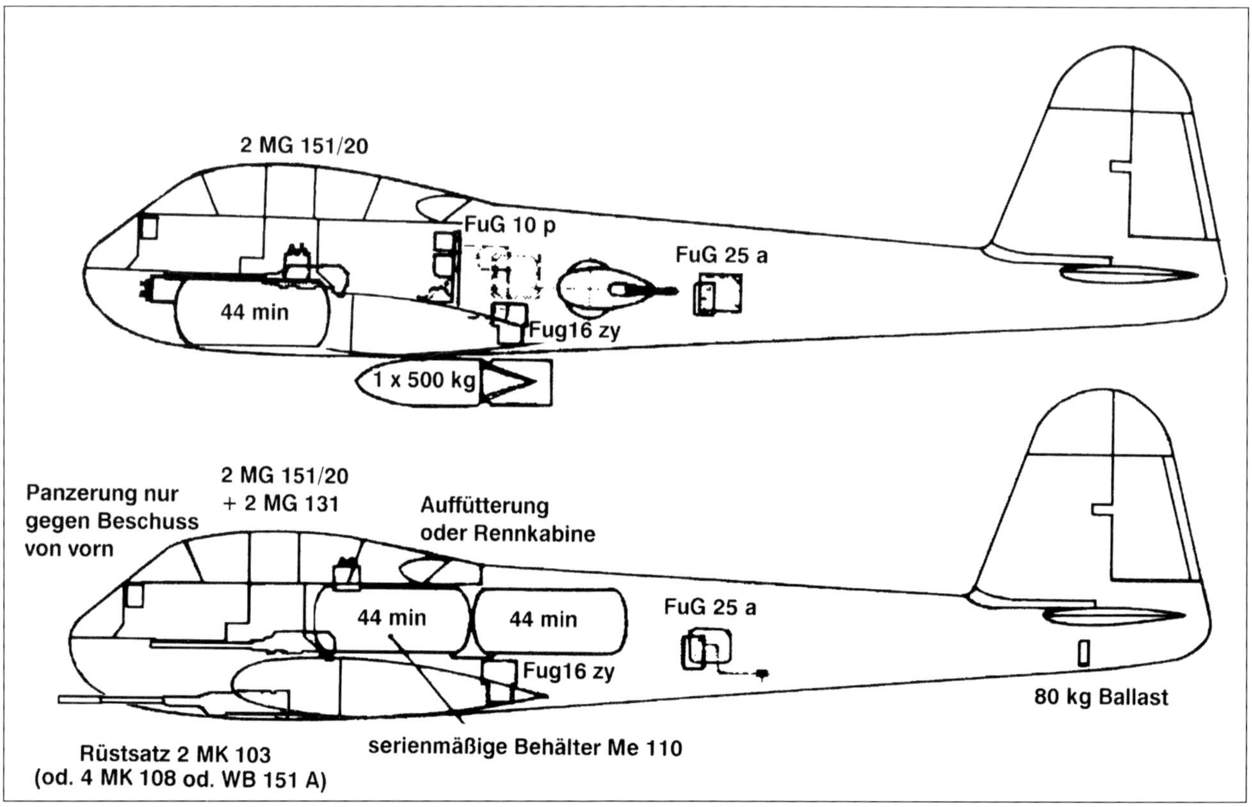

Zerstörer/month (Me 410 A-2). 50% of A-2 heavy fighters were to be kitted out with the KWK 38, and 50% with two MK 103s, with the entire series configured as single seaters with GM 1 and new canopy. On 30 November 1943 the Me 410's overall production in its latter stages was reduced to 150/month. Galland continued to call for 100 Me 410s with forward firing MK 103s and the GM 1 system aft and, in the event the heavy guns were adopted (KWK 39), 150 units per month.

According to the recollections of *Zerstörer* pilot Fritz Buchholz of II./ZG 26, operations using the single seat Me 410 took place in February 1944 under the supervision of *Hauptmann* Tratt (on 2/11/44 with twelve aircraft). However, he claims the weight saving measures had been undertaken in order to boost speed by 20 km/h and considers the idea absurd. According to him, missions were flown both with and without *Dödel*. His memoirs make no mention of the GM 1 system. In March 1944 the group converted to the Me 410/U4.

On 3/31/1944 the *Generalluftzeugmeister* declared that agreement had been reached on building a single seat Me 410 with GM 1 system. 30 had already been built, and now it was being said that they were not wanted anymore.

This variant of the Me 410 did not prove effective, as the improved high altitude performance was no longer needed and the pilots did not like flying without the defensive armament. Chronologically, the single seat Me 410 followed the Me 410 /U2 and preceded the Me 410/U4 on the assembly lines, so that it is entirely possible it was given the designation Me 410 A-1/U3, although we have no hard evidence of this. It is also not clear from the above statements whether, as the GL intended, the machine in fact had the GM 1 system.

This machine from II./ZG 26 (W.Nr. *10117) flew from Hildesheim as a single-seater without any rearward firing armament. It was probably fitted with the GM 1 system. (Petrick)*

Me 410 A-1/U4, *Zerstörer* with 5 cm KWK

According to the manual for Me 410 A-1 weapons (part 8A), as of November 1943:

As Me 410 A-1, but

Sight:	Revi C/12 D
Fixed armament:	2 x MG 17
	2 x MG 151/20
	1 x 5 cm BK

According to the ME 410 A-1/U4 manual (part 8A) weapons system with 5 cm BK, as of April 1944:

Sight:	Revi 16 B, later ZFR-4A
Fixed armament:	2 x MG 151/20
Electronics systems:	FuG 10 P, FuG 16, FuG 25 a, TZG X, FuBl 2 f

According to the Me 410 aircraft type sheet from 20 September 1944: the Me 410 A-1/U4 is not listed, in its place was the Me 410 B-1/U4. This is a case of a mixup between the two.

As there are photographs of the Me 410 A-1/U4 showing the aircraft with both open and covered ports for the MG 17, there were probably two variations on the type.

As early as 10/20/42 *Generalluftzeugmeister* Milch called for 3.7, 5, and 7.5 cm installations in bombers and heavy fighter aircraft to be undertaken with urgency, with the main focus to engage tanks using these large caliber weapons. Over the course of development, however, it seemed sensible to use these for attacking bombers as well. The *Flak 18*, *Flak 43*, and the 5 cm KWK were explored for the Me 410. Preference was given to the KWK, which would have to be modified from a single shot gun to accept a fully automatic shell feeder mechanism. An example was fitted at Lufthansa's Staaken facility in August 1943. At the end of September 1943 the General Staff called for an initial batch of 50 aircraft to be equipped with the cannon, thereafter to continue at a rate of 20 per month. Following a promising 8 week evaluation period, the starting pistol was fired for full scale production in October 1943. However, that month Galland drew attention to the fact that at an engagement range of 1000 m only two hits could be expected if the 22 rounds carried were fired at the planned rate of 60 per minute. He saw the KWK as a stopgap measure, since it was designed as a single shot weapon, and pushed for a greater rate of fire, e.g. with the MK 103. In spite of this, Galland hoped for deliveries of 150 per month. The guns were installed in the Me 410 by Auto-Union, Chemnitz, in and around Oberpfaffenhofen. The first aircraft were completed in late December 1943, but suffered from teething troubles. The belt, in particular, became stretched, and the shells themselves were not always true to size, so that sometimes the gun jammed after a single shot. Nevertheless, Milch stood by his decision to field the machines. Approximately 30 aircraft were delivered in January 1944, but could not be declared operational until around mid-February due to problems with the weapon. Following this, there began a program to retrofit the airframes with better weapons. By the end of February it was determined that, for the most part, the problems had been alleviated and the cannon fired normally. The first kills were scored around this time. In early March 1944 the three squadrons (4, 5, and 6 *Staffel*) of II./ZG 26 were equipped with the improved Me 410 A-1/U4, i.e. 3 x 12 aircraft plus HQ planes. At the time, deliveries were planned at a rate of 30 *Zerstörer* per month. From the outset, intentions were to deploy the Me 410 A-1/U4 only under a protective fighter umbrella; however, sufficient numbers of fighters needed for this protection were lacking. As the presence of enemy escort fighters increased, so did the risk of using the Me 410 with KWK. And when it became obvious that Galland had been right, and that at the standard engagement range of 400 m the KWK offered no advantages over the MK 103, it was soon decided to reduce the original totals requirement. On 6/9/44 the inventory of II./ZG 26 stood at 53 aircraft. There was no intention of building more than would be needed to maintain the numbers of this group. This required a production rate of 15 airframes per month. The assumption was that either the MK 103 or a quad pack of MG 151/20s would replace the KWK. Exact production figures are not known. However, as just 30 machines were complete by around

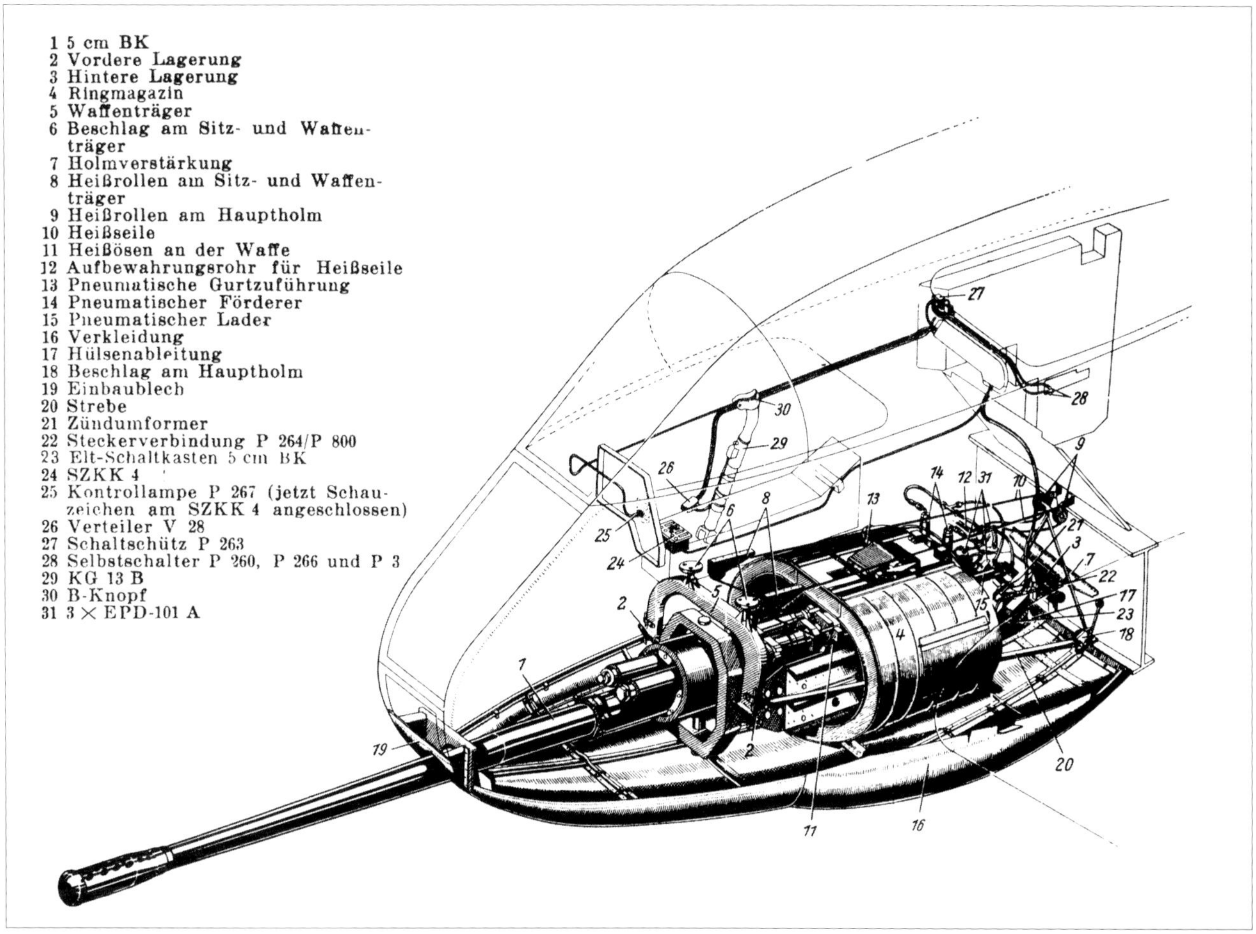

1 Rollenbock
2 Flaschenzug
3 Heißseil
4 Heißösen der Waffe
5 Holzbock

Abb. 11: 5 cm BK, Heißvorgang

the end of February 1944 and deliveries of Me 410 B-2s began in May, the total number produced can be reasonably estimated at around 60.

Me 410 A-1 with *Flak 43*

Studies into the use of the 3.7 cm anti-aircraft gun ran parallel to development of the Me 410 with BK 5. The *Flak 18*, however, was destined primarily for the Bf 110, while the Me 410 would be given priority for the BK 5. In early 1943 work began on building an Me 410 with *Flak 18*, but in June of that year *Erprobungskommando 25* complained that in the Me 410 the radio operator found it impossible to reload the *Flak 18*. Only the twelve rounds in the magazine could be fired. This was due to the fact that on the Me 410 the *Flak 18* was situated beneath the pilot, while on the Bf 110 it hung underneath the radioman's compartment. On 8/3/43 at a meeting with the RLM, Galland stated that he believed the MK 103 would be adequate to cover any circumstance. At this time, *Erprobungskommando 25* was installing *Flak 18* guns in the Me 410 at Vechta. The RLM only discussed the *Flak 18* in conjunction with the Me 410. In fact, however, the gun was indeed fitted into Me 210 V24 (*W.Nr.* 2347, GE+KS). In addition to the Revi

opposite page, top: As these planes are not fitted with the ZFR gunsight, they are most likely Me 410 A-1/U4s. The muzzles for the MG 17 are covered. (Petrick)

right: The Flak 43 *was belt-fed, meaning that the magazine feeds protruding from the side of the covering were dispensed with. (Baak)*

*opposite page, bottom: Forced landing of Me 410 A-1/U4 (*W.Nr. *420464, 3U+AM) on 21 June 1944 near Stettin. Notice the ZFR 4 gunsight. (Petrick)*

gunsight, the aircraft was also fitted with the ZFR, but had no MG 17 and no aft armor. It was planned to use a racing style canopy and GM 1, with the FDSL 131 being dropped in the event that altitude proved inadequate. In April 1944 the machine was based at Tarnewitz, but then the trail grows cold.

On 10/29/43 Galland reported that in his area of responsibility two Me 410s had been equipped with the *Flak 43*. In conjunction with this, the ZFR 4 gunsight had proven to work superbly and should be supplied as quickly as possible. *Erprobungskommando 25* completed the first installation of the *Flak 43* in October 1943. According to an RLM report on 11/12/43, two examples of a lightened Me 410 with GM 1, *Flak 43*, and ZFR gunsight were flying: one at Rechlin and one with *Erprobungskommando 25.* In its October work status report, *Erprobungskommando 25* reported that the *Flak 43* installation in the Me 410 was pushed back in favor of the Bf 110.

In March 1944 the evaluation detachment handed over the two Me 410s armed with anti-aircraft guns to ZG 1 (Königsberg-Neumark) for operational trials. By this time there was no longer any interest in the single seat Me 410 with GM 1 system. The two Me 410s with *Flak 43* were therefore converted back to their original configuration prior to being handed over. In June 1944 the evaluation detachment reported that three Bf 110s and two Me 410s with *Flak 43* flew operationally on 5/17/44. Of these, two Bf 110s and an Me 410 were shot down on their first mission. The pilot and radio operator of the Me 410 were killed as a result. The subsequent fate of the second Me 410 is unknown.

Me 410 A-2, *Zerstörer*

According to the 1943 identification sheet from the Rechlin test center:

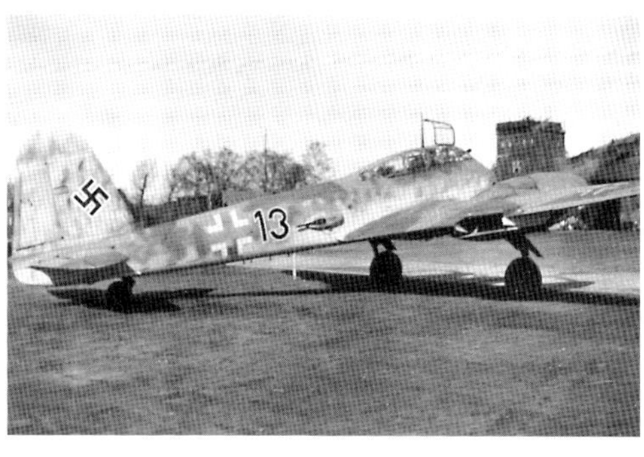

right: This Me 410 A-1 with Flak 43 *(*W.Nr. *10241) was shot down on its first operational sortie on 17 May 1944 near Parchim. (Baak)*

As Me 410 A-1, but

Wings:	no dive brakes or *Kutonase*
Sight:	ZFR 4
Fixed armament:	2 x MG 17 with 1000 rounds each
	2 x MG 151/20 with 350 rounds each
	2 x MK 103 with 100 rounds each
Ordnance:	system dropped

*above: This Me 410 A-3 (*W.Nr. *10259) was a true Me 410 build and originally flew with the registration code of F6+OK with* 2(F)/122. *It was captured on 27 November 1943 at Salerno and underwent thorough testing in England. (Nowarra)*

opposite page, top: The cameras were housed in the forward part of the fuselage, with the aft section reserved for illumination flares. (Lichler)

*left: This Me 410 A-3, captured at Trapani in August of 1943, was originally an Me 210 A-1 (*W.Nr. *018, D1+NN). It flew with* 2(F)/122. *(Nowarra)*

opposite page, bottom: On this Me 410 A-3 (FA+AH of 1./Aufkl.Gr. 121*) only the camera compartment's front panel is glazed. (Petrick)*

Weights

(gross):	11.03 t
(empty):	7.94 t

The Me 410 A-2 is not listed in the manual on armament systems for the Me 410 A-1 (part 8A), November 1943, the Messerschmitt type overview from 31 May 1944, nor the Me 410 aircraft type sheet from 20 September 1944.

The Me 410 A-2 was initially planned as a true *Zerstörer* version of the Me 410 with two MK 103s installed on the production line, and basically looked like the Me 410 A-1. In late 1943 it was then planned to make the *Zerstörer* a single seater and produce it with either the MK 103 or BK 5 and GM 1 system. By early 1944 the single seat idea had been dropped and the A-2 took on its original form again. As stated in the manual for the ZFR 4 gyroscopic gunsight, the ZFR was planned for use in this *Zerstörer* version. But since there were delays with the MK 103, the A-series terminated before the cannon's production even began. The Me 410 A-2 was dropped, with the Me 410 B-2 later being built in its place. The Me 410 A-1/U2 was built as a stopgap filler between the two types.

Me 410 A-2/U4, *Zerstörer* with 5 cm KWK

The manual on the Me 410 A-2/U4 (effective November 1943) was published in January 1944, whereas the one for the A-1/U4 was not available until April 1944 (effective April 1944), and then as a replacement for the A-2/U4. The latter manual no longer made reference to the A-2/U4. As the Me 410 A-2 was not yet in production in January 1944 and later was dropped altogether, there was also no Me 410 A-2/U4 and the manual was replaced.

Me 410 A-3, Reconnaissance

According to Messerschmitt's type overview from 31 May 1944: reconnaissance platform with camera pod.

According to the Me 410 aircraft type sheet from 20 September 1944: reconnaissance platform with camera aperture gondola.

According to Rechlin test center identification sheet from 1943 and the manual for Me 410 A-1 armament (part 8A), effective November 1943:

As Me 410 A-1, but

Camera:	in enlarged bomb bay, two Rb 75/30 or 50/30 or Rb 20/30 cameras in any combination
Fixed armament:	2 x MG 151/20
Ordnance:	6 x LC 50 F in bomb bay on special bomb pylons
Electronic systems:	FuG 10 P, FuG 16, FuG 25 a, TZG X, FuBl 2 f
Weight (gross):	10.3 t
Weight (empty):	7.7 t
Wing loading:	285 kg/m^2 max.

According to BAL there were 25 converted Me 410 reconnaissance variants accepted. What is not explained is whether these were Me 410 A-1/U1s or Me 410 A-3s created from Me 210s. In addition, BAL shows 20 new Me 410 reconnaissance versions being taken on charge, but these are fewer in number than identified through factory serial numbers.

Me 410 A-3/U1, Reconnaissance

According to Messerschmitt type overview from 31 May 1944:

As Me 410 A-3, but reconnaissance version with camera in the aft fuselage and GM 1 system in bomb bay. These components were originally intended for the Me 410 B. With the delay of this variant it is possible that a handful of machines from the A-series were modified.

Me 410 B

In a list of valid variants for the Me 410 drawn up by Messerschmitt on 31 May 1944 at Oberammergau, the Me 410 B-1 through B-8 were shown as new builds with DB 603 A engines, as opposed to the Me 410 A-1 through A-3/U1 conversions. The designation "new build airframe," however, had already appeared in a data sheet from the Messerschmitt AG dated 4/13/43. As was stated in the section dealing with the Me 410 A-1, there were hardly enough Me 210s to have provided the stock for converting all Me 410 As, and the production run apparently continued longer than originally anticipated on 4/13/43. There were, as a result, also new build Me 410 A-1s.

As early as mid-February 1943 the Me 410 was an intended recipient of the fighter/heavy fighter standard powerplant, although it had not yet been developed. The Me 410 B series was, according to plans from 4/13/43, to still have been fitted with the DB 603 G (octane rating 95, C3 fuel) as part of the standardized powerplant, the same engine that was to have been used with the Me 309. The DB 603 G had a larger turbocharger and better high altitude performance. In a meeting held on 6/3/43 it was established that the DB 603 E, designed for using the B4 fuel, was not suitable for the Me 410. The changeover would go directly from the DB 603 A to the G model, which would be driving the rapid variable pitch Me P6 propeller.

Development of the standardized powerplant, however, did not proceed at the desired pace. On 10/5/43 the old DB 603 E was once again planned for the Me 410 with wing mounted radiators, while the standardized powerplant would still utilize the DB 603 G as before. The DB 603 E was pushed back from January 1944 to April, with the standardized engine expected in October 1944. This meant that the Me 410 C series with Me P6 propeller and the fighter/heavy fighter engine would be in production by early 1945.

But this production startup was postponed as well. As a result, like the A-series before it the Me 410 B had to make do with the DB 603 A when production began in May 1944. In the Messerschmitt type overview from 31 May 1944 the DB 603 A is listed as the engine for the Me 410 B series.

On 5/12/44 an RLM report stated that the DB 603 A with G turbocharger was to enter production as a stopgap solution. Messerschmitt was expected to get 140 units in June and 240 in July for the Me 410. Plans called for switching to the DB 603 E in September. The change of engines was also mentioned in Study 1033 from 6/29/44. According to the study, the DB 603 A powered Me 410 would cease production in October 1944. During the transition period from August through October the bulk of Me 410s would be supplied with the DB 603 Aa, a DB 603 A with G turbocharger. This was then to be replaced by the DB 603 E until the production series terminated in August 1945. The Do 335 was to take over the role hitherto served by the Me 410. It is unknown whether or not any of the Me 410s actually received the DB 603 A with G supercharger. With the Me 410 being redlined on 7/1/44 as part of the *Blitz* streamlining program, it would seem improbable that Messerschmitt would continue to make any type of modifications to the engines with the intent of fitting the larger turbocharger. The authors assume that those Me 410s produced in the last two months and delivered by September 1944 had no changes made to them. In the RLM's aircraft type sheet from 20 September 1944 only the DB 603 A is mentioned for the Me 410 B.

According to various evaluation reports, the Me 410 B was intended to make use of the *Kutonase*, deicers, a high altitude oxygen system, and a strengthened undercarriage. In addition, there was a large number of conversion kits projected that would broaden the type's operational spectrum even further.

The war situation and the development programs, both of which were continuing longer than expected, led the *Luftwaffe*'s leadership to change its planning rather quickly in 1944. This had a telling impact on the Me 410 B series in particular, as descriptions were based on a specific point in time. Publications have often overlooked this fact, leading to what appears to be contradictions. For example, initial descriptions of the Me 410 B show it being powered by the DB 603 G, whereas in fact only the A-model engine was ever installed. The authors have attempted to reflect the different information here, as far as is known.

Me 410 B-1, High Speed Bomber

According to Messerschmitt performance sheet from 4/13/43 (however, as mentioned above, the DB 603 G never materialized):

As Me 410 A-1, but

Engine:	2 x DB 603 G
Performance:	2 x 1740 hp
Cooling:	47 dm^2
Propeller:	VDM-VS, 3.4 m diameter
Fixed armament:	2 x MG 17 2 x MG 151/20
Flexible armament:	2 x MG 151 remote controlled barbettes
Weights (gross):	11.3 t with 2 x 500 kg bombs
(empty):	8 t
Max. speed (at max. wt):	501 km/h at sea level 630 km/h at 8100 m
Climb rate (at max. wt):	6000 m in 13 min 8000 m in 23 min
Service ceiling (w/ 11.3 t):	9500 m
Endurance:	approx. 2.5 hrs

According to Messerschmitt type overview from 31 May 1944:

High Speed Bomber with DB 603 A, New Build

Engine:	2 x DB 603 A
Fixed armament:	2 x MG 131 2 x MG 151/20
Undercarriage:	reinforced
Equipment:	high altitude oxygen system
Fuel:	additional 2 x 300 liter outer wing fuel tanks
Electronic systems:	FuG 10 P, FuG 16, FuG 25a, TZG X, FuBl 2 f
Performance:	as Me 410 A-1

The order went out in early May 1944 to convert all Me 410 A-1s and B-1s to the Me 410 A-1/U2 *Zerstörer* standard. Dive brakes, as far as possible, were to be left off. As the Me 410 B-1's production was just getting underway at the time, it is doubtful that any high speed bomber version of this type ever made it to the *Luftwaffe*. There is also no mention of this version made in any loss reports.

Me 410 B-1/U2, Auxiliary *Zerstörer*

According to Me 410 aircraft type sheet from 20 September 1944:

As Me 410 A-1/U2, but

Fixed armament: 2 x MG 131
2 x MG 151/20
2 x MG 151/20 in WB 151 A gun pod
Undercarriage: reinforced
Equipment: high altitude oxygen system

There are no Me 410 B-1/U2s to be found in any loss report. It can be assumed that this version never existed, as those Me 410 B-1s that were on hand were delivered as B-2s. The Me 410 B-1/U2 was, therefore, listed as Me 410 B-2/U2.

Me 410 B-1/U4, *Zerstörer* with 5 cm KWK

Not listed in the Messerschmitt type overview from 31 May 1944 and in the Me 410 A-1/U4 manual, part 8 A weapons system with 5 cm BK, but mentioned as a *Zerstörer* in a communiqué to the L. Hansen Company on 5/17/44.

According to the Me 410 aircraft type sheet from 20 September 1944:

As Me 410 A-1/U4, but

Fixed armament: 2 x MG 131
2 x MG 151/20
1 x 5 cm BK

There are no Me 410 B-1/U4s to be found in any loss report. It can be assumed that this version never existed, as those Me 410 B-1s that were on hand were delivered as B-2s. The Me 410 B-1/U4 was, therefore, listed as Me 410 B-2/U4.

Me 410 B-2, *Zerstörer*

According to Me 410 A-1 weapons systems (part 8 A), as of November 1943:

As Me 410 A-2, but

Sight: Revi 16 B
Fixed armament: 2 x MG 131, 600 round each
2 x MG 151/20, 350 rounds each
2 x MG 151/20 in WB 151 A gun pod, 230 rounds each

As the Me 410 B-2's predecessor (the A-2) was expected to get the MK 103 early on, this information from the manual is difficult to explain. It is possible that the MK 103 was not mentioned for security reasons, for the Me 410 A-2 was not listed either. The possibility also exists that for the Me 410 B-2 the MK 103's availability was not a foregone conclusion.

According to Messerschmitt type overview from 31 May 1944: *Zerstörer* with two MK 103s

According to the Me 410 type sheet from 20 September 1944:

Sight: ZFR-4A
Fixed armament: 2 x MG 131, 500 round each
2 x MG 151/20, 350 rounds each
2 x MG 151/20 in WB 151 A gun pod, 100 rounds each

The Me 410 B-2 was finally the long awaited heavy fighter with two MK 103s. Deliveries began in June 1944 with approximately 45 units being supplied. Its armament was most certainly effective against enemy bombers. However, by the time they appeared on the scene enemy bomber formations were flying exclusively under fighter protection provided by escorts, and the Me 410 B-2 never quite fully lived up to expectations. Production numbers were never very high, partly because the reliable MK 103 was just entering production when, a month later, the Me 410 was redlined. According to planning, in early May 1944 II./ZG 26 was projected to be equipped with the BK 5 and II./ZG was to be armed with the MK 103 version. I./ZG 26 and I./ZG 76 were still flying with the WB 151 A gun pod, but these were soon expected to be replaced with the MK 103. Out of the

left: The Me 410 B-2 was armed with 2 MK 103 cannons on the production line, as well as having the ZFR 4 *gunsight. (Petrick)*

320 Me 410 B-2s, only about 100 were flown with the MK 103. The others had either the WB 151 A as the Me 410 B-2/U2 or the 5 cm BK as the Me 410 B-2/U4.

Unlike the plans, which called for a single seat Me 410 with GM 1, the Me 410 B-2 was to be operated from the outset by a two-man crew with armor and defensive

left: An Me 410 B-1 of ZG *76 with drop tanks. (Chapman)*

below: Werknummer *710340 and the WB 151 reveal that this is a Dornier-built Me 410 B- 2/ U2. (Petrick)*

opposite page, bottom: Reminiscent of the Bf 110's M1 conversion kit, the Me 410 was also fitted with two MG 151s beneath the fuselage. However, this was a field modification and had no official conversion kit designation. Stab II./ZG 26 *operated this machine during the summer of 1944. (Petrick)*

weaponry. The differences from the Me 410 B-1 weren't great: the ordnance tub was replaced by a 2 x MK 103 pack; nose window, dive brakes, and *Kutonase* were dropped; and armor windscreen and plating were affixed in front of the pilot. The Stuvi 5 B was replaced by the ZFR 4 gyroscopic gunsight.

Me 410 B_V-2, *Zerstörer*

As Me 410 B-2, but according to Messerschmitt type overview from 31 May 1944: *Zerstörer* with 2 x MK 103s and simplified air-to-air communications system. On 3/24/44 the RLM reported that streamlining commissions had been set up to determine what was actually needed for aircraft and what should be dropped. The simplified communications system was a result of these efforts.

Me 410 B-2/U1, *Zerstörer* with 5 cm KWK

According to the Me 410 A-1/U4 manual, part 8 A, weapons system with 5 cm BK, also applicable to the Me 410 B-2/U1, from April 1944

Sight:	ZFR-4A
Fixed armament:	2 x MG 131
	2 x MG 151/20
	1 x 5 cm BK

As for the A-1 (see Me 410 B-2/U1 and U4), the Me 410 B-2 was originally to have had another designation for this modified version. Loss reports, however, do not record any Me 410 B-2/U1s. Apparently the old designations were indeed carried over.

Me 410 B-2/U2, Auxiliary *Zerstörer*

According to Messerschmitt type overview from 31 May 1944: New Build Aircraft

As Me 410 B-2, but with MG 151s in place of the MK 103. Since there were insufficient quantities of MK 103s available when the Me 410 B02 entered production, a stopgap heavy fighter was built, again making use of the WB 151 A. With units operating four groups of Me 410s, of which two flew the Me 410 B-2/U2, of the approximately 320 Me 410 B-2s built probably 160 were fitted out as U2s. About 10 Me 410 B-2/U2s appear in loss reports.

*above: In May 1945 this Dornier-built Me 410 B-2/ U4 (*W.Nr. *710458) was found parked next to the* Autobahn *leading to Munich. (Crow)*

Me 410 B-2/U4, *Zerstörer* with 5 cm KWK

According to Messerschmitt type overview from 31 May 1944: *Zerstörer* with BK 5.

According to Me 410 aircraft type sheet from 20 September 1944: As Me 410 B-2 with 2 x MK 103s and two external *Schloss* 2000 racks, variant not planned.

According to the manual for the ZFR 4 gyroscopic gunsight, Me 410 A-1/U4s and Me 410 B-2/U4 with BK 5s were fitted with the ZFR 4 sight in place of the Revi C/12 D or Revi 16 B in order to improve accuracy. A Dornier memorandum from 7/17/44 regarding new armament boresighting reveals that Dornier built roughly 53 Me 410 B-2/U4s with the KWK. The Me 410 B-2/U4 can also be found in loss reports. The B-2 series of aircraft with the KWK were subsequently designated Me 410 B-2/U4. The manual probably contains an error or refers to an outdated status.

Loss reports indicate that a few more Me 410 B-2/U4s were made from Messerschmitt aircraft. At a production rate of about 15 to 20 per month and with only II./ZG 26 using the type, it is doubtful that much more than 80 were built in total. Some of these were probably converted over to the MG 151 quad pack in the bomb bay.

Me 410 B-2 with 6 MG 151/20s

Arming the stopgap heavy fighters with two MG 131s and four MG 151s was seen by the *Luftwaffe* as being inadequate. Once

above: This fitting of four MG 151s in an MK 103 weapons pack was deemed most favorable and was planned as a production feature shortly before the Me 410 assembly line came to a halt. The photo was taken at III./ZG 1 in the summer of 1944. (Petrick)

the BK 5 and 23 cm air-to-air mortar had been decided on, the ultimate goal became equipping the *Zerstörer* with two MK 103s.

In early May 1944 ZG 26's second group was flying with the BK 5. The other *Zerstörer* groups still had to make do with the WB 151 A. In order to increase the firepower for the auxiliary *Zerstörer* planes, units installed additional MG 151/20s in the Me 410. As these installations were homemade, they were afforded no conversion kit designations. We are not sure where some authors have come up with designations such as Me 410 B2/U2/R4. Prompted by these installations, the RLM initiated formal development. There was a heavy version of the quad pack the units flew with. The test center derived both a heavy and a light version from this, with work being done in July 1944. Partly as a result of the Me 410's cancellation, the quad pack was probably never fully developed, and the only ones extant were the conversions the units undertook. The following versions are known to have existed:

2 x MG 151/20 under the fuselage of the Me 410 B-2/U2;
2 x WB 151 A side by side in the bomb bay;
Quad pack in the bomb bay with bulged nose compartment of the Me 410 B-2/U4
Quad pack in the bomb bay with flat nose compartment of the Me 410 B-2.

It is not known how extensively the field units modified their A-1/U2, A-1/U4 or B-2/U2, and B2-U4 airframes, nor are accurate numbers available.

Me 410 B-3, Reconnaissance

According to Messerschmitt type overview from 31 May 1944: New Build Aircraft.
According to Me 410 aircraft type sheet from 20 September 1944:

As Me 410 A-3, but reconnaissance version with camera bay and the improvements of the B-series (also see Me 410 B-7).

Me 410 B-3/U1, Reconnaissance

According to Messerschmitt type overview from 31 May 1944:

As Me 410 B-3, but with camera system in the tail and GM 1 system in the bomb bay (see Me 410 B-7).

On 12/17/43 Messerschmitt released performance sheets for an Me 410 B reconnaissance variant for daylight operations with a fuselage bay in place of the bomb bay doors and GM 1 fuel boost for 37 or 45 minutes, or a 650 liter fuel tank in the bomb bay. The description fits the Me 410 B-3/U1 or B-7. As the Me 410 reconnaissance version with GM 1 indeed existed and the Me 410 B-7 did not appear in any loss reports, this was most probably the B-3/U1.

Me 410 B-5, Torpedo Bomber

According to a Messerschmitt abbreviated type description from 1/10/44:

As Me 410 B-2, but

Engine:	1 x DB 603 A and 1 x DB 603 D or 2 x DB 603 A
Fuel:	additional 630 liter self sealing tank in the bomb bay, i.e. total of 3060 liters optional additional 700 liter self sealing tank in place of the FDSL barbettes, i.e. total of 3760 liters optional underwing drop tanks
Armament	
Fixed	2 x MG 151/20
Flexible:	2 x MG 131 in FDSL barbettes or 700 liter auxiliary fuel tank
Ordnance:	1 LT 5 b 800 kg or 1 LT 5 i 760 kg or 1 Lt 5 u or 2 BT 400 a 400 k or 2 BT 200 a 200 kg or 2 BT 1800 kg or up to 1800 kg of bombs on two *Schloss* 2000/13 mounts in fuselage depressions behind the main wing, and 4 BT 200 a 200 kg or 4 SC 250 a 250 kg on the outer wings

The bomb load was planned to counter any invasion. The fuel load had to be limited for payloads over 900 kg so that, because of the tires, the takeoff weight would not exceed 11.5 metric tons.

Targeting systems:	Revi 16 B or TSA 2 with ToKG, without ASKR
Equipment:	additional instrument panel with altimeter, airspeed indicator, drift adjustment, dial switch for ordnance release system, four indicators torpedo control panel deicer and *Kutonase* planned for mid-1944 on production models
Electronic systems:	As B-2, but trailing antenna for increased range
Armor:	frontal only
Speed (max, at max wt):	455 to 484 km/h at sea level 541 to 578 km/h at 6600 m, depending on load
Range with 6 BT 200:	1660 km with 2660 liters at 5000 m
Range with 6 BT 200:	2180 km with 3660 liters at 5000 m
Range with 1 BT 1800:	1260 km with 2000 liters at 5000 m
Range with 1 LTF 5:	2580 km with 3760 liters at 5000 m

Performance data and the abbreviated description were documented by Messerschmitt on 1/10/44 at Oberammergau. On 2/4/44 the RLM felt that the Me 410 was capable of functioning as a torpedo bomber at extremely low altitudes (toss release with the TSA *Tiefsturzanlage* low level dive bombing system), assuming that electronic range finders would become available. The Me 410 B-5, however, was not listed in a description of valid aircraft types from 31 May 1944, nor did it show up as a follow-on development. But it had to have been pulled from the program by 18 June 1944 at the latest, as that is when Göring ordered all production of bombers, torpedo bombers, etc.

opposite page, top: A better approach aerodynamically was the installation of MG 151 quads in the weapons pack of the U4 version. This machine belonged to 2./ZG 26, a squadron which formerly flew with the BK 5 cannon. This fact indicates that the quad pack seen here is a modification. (Petrick)

below: Side view of the Me 410 B 5 planned for early 1944.

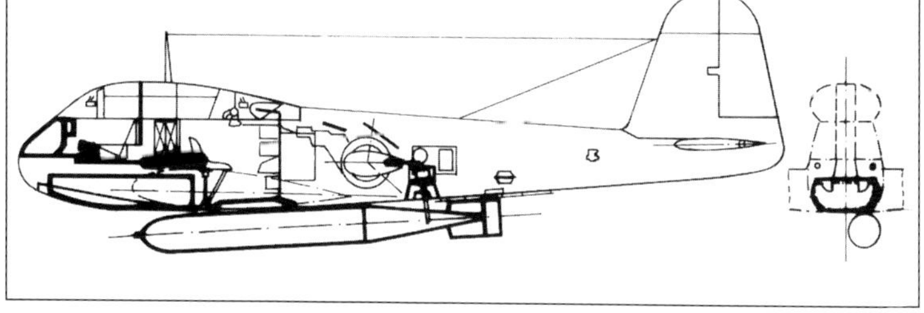

to cease. It is also not mentioned in the aircraft type sheet from 20 September 1944.

Me 410 B-6, Naval *Zerstörer*

As Me 410 B-2, but:

Electronic systems:	FuG 200 with *Zaunkönig* wideband antenna

Aviation publications describe the Me 410 B-6, of which only a few examples are known to have been delivered, as a *Zerstörer* for attacking shipping targets. Now, a weapons suite of two 3 cm cannons is not bad to be sure, but it would be insufficient for most ships. There was no ordnance planned and, for reasons of weight, would not have been possible in any case.

As GL minutes reveal the Me 410 was intended to provide cover for friendly submarines, so it is more likely that the Me 410 B-6's role can be found here. Fitted with the FuG 200 it would have been able to maintain contact with the submarine, and the MK 103s would have permitted it to engage enemy aircraft at great distances. When the *U-Boot* harbors in France were lost during the Normandy invasion, the Me 410s equipped with the FuG 200 (not all of which had the MK 103) were used in the Baltic in the air-sea rescue role.

In the RLM's aircraft type sheet from 20 September 1944 and the Messerschmitt AG's type overview from 31/5/44 the Me 410 B-6 is not shown.

Only this single example of a B-6 series aircraft is known to have existed, belonging to Seenotgruppe 80 *and put on display in England after the war. (Imperial War Museum)*

Me 410 B-7, Day Reconnaissance

According to the Messerschmitt type overview from 31 May 1944:

Equipment:	simplified
Camera systems:	in fuselage tail

On 2/29/44 the *Generalluftzeugmeister* proposed abandoning the reconnaissance version of the Me 410 as part of the streamlining measures being undertaken at the time. The Me 410 B-3 had a complicated camera pod, and the B-3/U1 a simplified camera arrangement for the same operational role. Since the B-3's camera pod offered no real advantages and in fact hindered fitting a GM system, there was a push for a new reconnaissance version in the form of the Me 410 B-7, identical to the Me 410 B-3/U1 that would have the camera in the aft fuselage and would be equipped with the GM 1 system. Production was never initiated as a result of the Me 410 program being canceled. It cannot be verified that the GM 1 system was actually intended for the Me 410 B-7, but it is likely.

Me 410 B-8, Night Reconnaissance

According to the Messerschmitt type overview from 31 May 1944:

As Me 410 B-7, but with flare illuminators in the bomb bay and behind the main spar.

Me 410 C

Using the technical guidelines for the *Kampfzerstörer* (bomber destroyer/heavy fighter) from 7 August 1942 as a basis, Messerschmitt began development of a follow-on to the Me 410 with the designation Me 410 C. In February '43 the Me 410 entered into that circle of aircraft that would be powered by the fighter/heavy fighter standardized engine with forward radiators. It was established in March that the DB 603 G would form the basis of this powerplant. It was planned in June that production of the Me 410 using the standardized powerplant would begin on 1 January 1945, and development of the Me 410 with standardized powerplant was considered a closed matter.

The new Me 410 C series was also to have had a new forward fuselage with redesigned cockpit and DF installation. On the

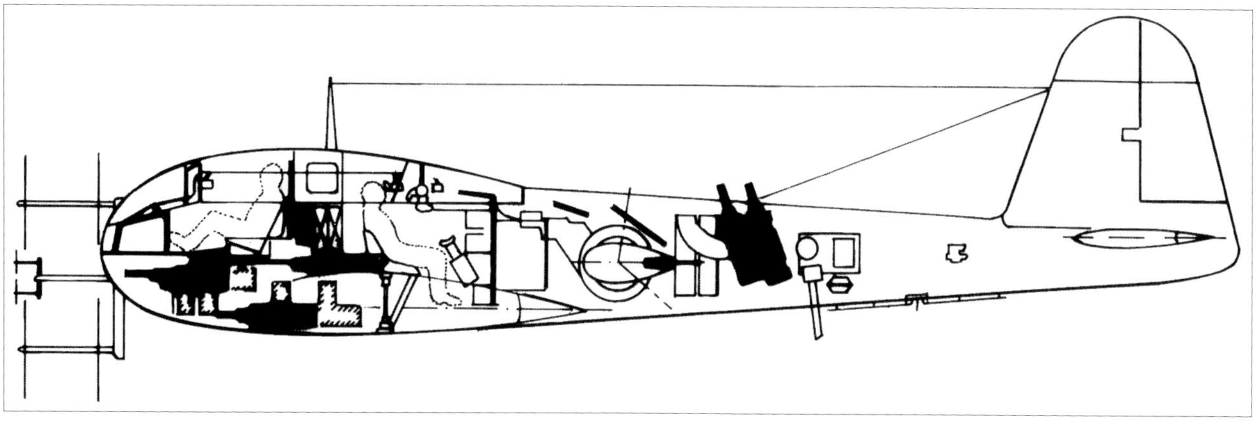

In addition to the known B-series sub-variants, Messer-schmitt also planned several modifications to the basic C-series design. One example is this drawing of a night fighter, armed with four MK 108s in addition to the two forward-firing MG 151s and two MK 108 schräge Musik *guns.*

other hand, the wings were modified only insofar as was necessary to accept the standardized powerplant. The wingspan and profile was the same as for the B-series, according to an aircraft comparison study prepared by Messerschmitt in 1945. Messerschmitt planned a whole series of modern weapons installations. However, on 30 November 1943 the Me 410's star began falling. The Do 335 had proven to be a very promising design, was expected to enter production in limited numbers in August 1944, and was envisioned as the replacement for the Bf 110 and as a supplement to the Me 410. In addition, due to material shortages the planned numbers of Me 410s was reduced to 150, and a new series with wooden wings was in the planning stages (see Me 410 D). On 2/1/1944 the RLM proposed using the me 410 with the small air-to-air X 4 missile, which was reflected in the armament data for the Me 410 C-2. At the same time it became clear that the DB 603 E, the basis for the fighter/heavy fighter engine, would not be available for the Me 410 before the end of 1944. As early as 2/25/44, Milch told the RLM that the Me 410's production should terminate in early 1945, but even by then this decision was old news. On 2/29/44 the RLM proposed to continue building the Me 410 exclusively as a *Zerstörer* and dropping the Me 410 C in favor of the Me 410 B. On 5/10/44 the Oberbayrische Forschungsanstalt Oberammergau (Upper Bavarian Research Institute Oberammergau) sent the VDM documents for the calculations and design of propellers that listed the Me 410 as a heavy fighter with the DB 603 E/F. In these, the wingspan was still shown as 16.24 m. A type overview released by Messerschmitt on 31 May 1944 no longer carried the Me 410 C. Therefore, plans for producing this version had been abandoned months before the Me 410 was redlined.

Me 410 C-1, High Speed Bomber

According to the Messerschmitt type overview from 31 May 1944 and aircraft comparison study from 7/23/45:

As Me 410 B-1, but

Fuselage: new forward section, new cockpit with direction finding system
Equipment: simplified

(According to Messerschmitt comparison study from 7/23/45)

Bomber Destroyer
Engine: standardized with DB 603 E
Fixed armament: 2 x MG 17
2 x MG 151/20
Ordnance: 8 x 50 kg internal
2 x 500 kg external
Conversion packs: 2 x MK 108 upward firing behind FDSL barbettes and
1 BK 5 cm or
bombs 1 x 1800 kg or
optional 1 x LT 950 kg
Max. speed: 602 km/h at 6400 m
650 km/h with water methanol system
Range: 1350 km at 6400 m
Endurance: 2.25 hrs
Max. pressure altitude: 6400 m
Service ceiling: 8900 m
Climb rate: 8000 m in 19 min

Messerschmitt C-2, *Zerstörer*

According to the Messerschmitt type overview from 31 May 1944:

As Me 410 B-2, but

Fuselage: new forward section, new cockpit with direction finding system
Equipment: simplified

According to Messerschmitt aircraft comparison study from 7/23/45 and information from Obb Forschungsanstalt Oberammergau from 5/10/44

Engine: standardized with DB 603 E
Propeller: 3-bladed, 3.4 m diameter
Wingspan: 16.24 m
Fixed armament: 2 x MG 17 or 2 x MK 108 and
2 x MG 151/20
Ordnance: optional 2 x 300 canisters or bombs or
2 x "X4" missiles
Conversion packs: 2 x MK 108 upward firing behind FDSL barbettes and optional
WB 151 A or
4 x MK 108 fixed or
1 BK 5 cm or
1 *Wurfgerät* 21 cm or
2 x MK 103 flexible or
2 x 2 or 3 WG 21 cm
Max. speed: 495 km/h at sea level
620 km/h at 8100 m
670 km/h with water methanol system
Takeoff speed: 210 km/h
Landing speed: 198 km/h
Dive speed: 750 km/h max.
Range: 1750 km at 6400 m
Endurance: 2.8 hrs
Max. pressure altitude: 6400 m
Service ceiling: 8900 m
Climb rate: 8000 m in 19 min

Messerschmitt C-3, Reconnaissance

According to the Messerschmitt type overview from 31 May 1944:

As Me 410 B-7, but

Fuselage: new forward section, new cockpit with direction finding system
Equipment: simplified

Me 410 D

On 30 November 1943 the RLM was told that *Reichsmarschall* had reduced the Me 410's final production stage from 400 to 150 due to material shortages. In addition, the Me 410 was to be built with wooden wings from the third quarter of 1945 onward in order to produce as many aircraft as possible with the available supplies of aluminum. It was subsequently decided to fit the Me 410 D with larger wings and tanks. In early 1944 the RLM lost interest in the Me 410 entirely, for it was on 2/25/44 that Milch told the RLM about his desire to terminate Me 410 production in early 1945 as scheduled, but that this could possibly be extended. Although Messerschmitt drew up a type overview on 31 May 1944 that showed the Me 410 D still in development, on 5/28/44 the RLM was already saying that the Me 410 would be terminated, and that therefore there was little reason to make a big deal out of a wooden wing design with steel spars. Continued development of the wing itself was desirable, however, since it might prove important for the Me 262. On 6/2/44, about a month before production was halted, the RLM killed the Me 410 D with extended wooden wings. On the one hand, the reason for the disinterest was the Do 335 which, as a *Zerstörer*, offered much better performance, and on the other hand, the RLM was increasingly giving priority to the Me 262 and Ar 234 jets, which could more capably fill the Me 410's roles.

Me 410 D-1, High Speed Bomber

Me 410 D-2, *Zerstörer*

Me 410 D-3, Reconnaissance

According to the Messerschmitt type overview from 31 May 1944:

As Me 410 C-1, C-2, C-3, but

Wing: increased span wooden design
Engine: fighter/heavy fighter engine
Undercarriage: dual wheeled with new retraction sequence

The authors have included a Messerschmitt overview of the Me 410 A - B with a 36 m² area and wing radiators, as well as a follow-on development with 44 m² and the DB 603 E/F standardized powerplant. Based on this, the following data was projected for the Me 410 D:

Max. speed: 502 km/h at sea level
637 km/h at 8100 m
Climb rate: 8000 m in 19 min
Service ceiling: 10700 m
Range: approx. 1850 km with 2800 liters, at 7700 m

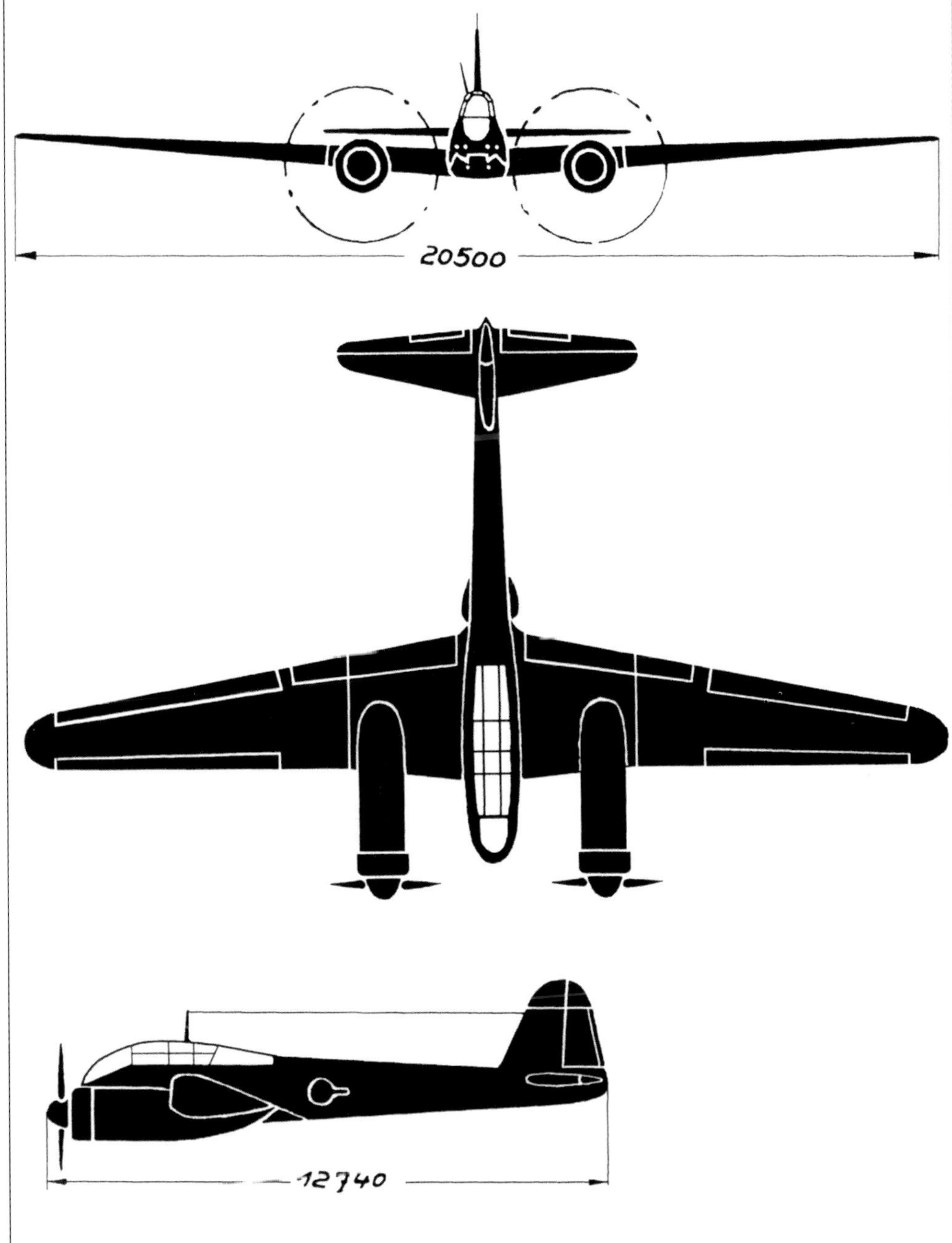

Me 410 Weiterentwicklung

Me 410 H, High-Altitude *Zerstörer*, Torpedo Bomber, Bomber

According to RLM minutes regarding structural requirements, from 2/12/44:

As Me 410 B-2, but

Wing:	rectangular center section between inner and outer panels
Engine:	2 x DB 603 A
Fixed armament:	2 x MK 108 2 x MG 151/20 2 x MK 103 as modification pack
Wingspan:	23 m
Wing area:	46.5 instead of 36.6 m^2
Weights (gross):	13.4 t with 2 x 500 kg bombs or 2 x MK 103
(empty):	9 t
Wing loading:	288 kg/m^2 max
Max. speed (at max. wt):	530 km/h at sea level 630 km/h at 6500 m
Dive speed:	850 km/h max.

From the summer of 1943 onward there were fears within the RLM that enemy bombers would be appearing at higher altitudes, and a quick solution was sought for a way to counter this threat. New developments were out of the question due to the great urgency involved, and efforts were made to meet this requirement by modifying existing designs. The first steps saw the use of the GM 1 system in the Bf 109, Bf 110, and Me 410 as well. In addition, the DB 605 AS/D and DB 603 E/F/G were fitted with larger turbochargers. Although this made the engines suitable for higher altitudes, because of their stubby wings the fighters were not able to attain the altitudes one had hoped for. On 28 August 1943 the RLM reported that research was being made into a high altitude variant of the Me 410 with extended wings. Solutions were being sought for other primary types as well, most of which envisioned attaching longer wing tips or fitting rectangular center sections into the wings. However, these extended lifting arms placed greater stress on the wing roots, meaning that the larger machines had to be handled more carefully. Based on this need, Messerschmitt developed the Bf 109 H, the Bf 110 H, and the Me 410 H. On 1/25/44 a meeting took place at Augsburg between representatives of the RLM, wherein the structural guidelines for the Me 410 H were laid out. Messerschmitt had already drawn up the design and made performance calculations beforehand. However, development was broken off shortly thereafter. This was probably a result of the RLM as early as the spring of 1944, assuming that the Me 410's production would terminate at the beginning of 1945. The subject of longer wings was not broached for the remainder of the type's production life. The Me 410 H was no longer listed in the type overview Messerschmitt prepared on 31 May 1944.

Me 410 with 1 or 2 TL

With its decision to have turbojet engines (TL) developed, for reasons of redundant security the RLM contracted with two companies. Junkers was to proceed with greater caution on the understanding that the Jumo 004 engine would be heavier as a result. BMW entered into development with greater haste, but nevertheless reached the goal at about the same time Junkers did, offering a smaller yet nearly as powerful engine in the form of the BMW 003. Since the jet-powered Ar 234 and Me 262 aircraft developments were being designed around the less-risky Jumo 004, the RLM was faced with the prospect of the BMW 003 going into production in early 1944 without an airframe available to take it. It was thus decided to hang the engine on existing aircraft in an effort to boost maximum speeds by up to 100 km/h, well aware that this would mean a significant reduction in range. On 9 July '43 the RLM reported that the aviation industry was tackling such projects on a wide scale. About two months later, on 27 August, there was discussion on the speed boost using turbojets on the Ju 88 and Me 410. Major sticking points for the Me 410 were felt to be the higher weight, the reduced cruising speed, and the drop in range. Without countermeasures, it was feared that the Me 410 would drop like a brick with the 540 kg increased weight of the jet engine combined with its high landing speeds. The rear guns, armor, and if necessary the second crewman would have to be tossed overboard. It was assumed that endurance would be reduced from two hours twenty minutes to just barely two hours. The *General der Jagdflieger* would need to be asked about this. On 27 August 1943 the General Staff's *6. Abt.* called for priority to be given to fitting the BMW 003 to aircraft performing air defense duties in the following order: Me 410; Ju 188 R and *Zerstörer* G; and Ju 388 J. The existing production resources, i.e. 1000 engines per month, were to be utilized fully once the definitive test results were in. Work in this area was to be given highest priority due to its critical nature.

In October 1943 Messerschmitt produced a drawing of just such a design study. The obvious drawbacks and the anticipated introduction of the Ar 234 and Do 335, however, led to development work being abandoned. And, as early as 1943 a better use was found for the BMW 003: mounting four of them on the Ar 234 C. This aircraft could be realized with less expense than a modified Me 410 and was ultra modern at its inception, whereas the Me 410 would have remained a revamped old crate with many drawbacks.

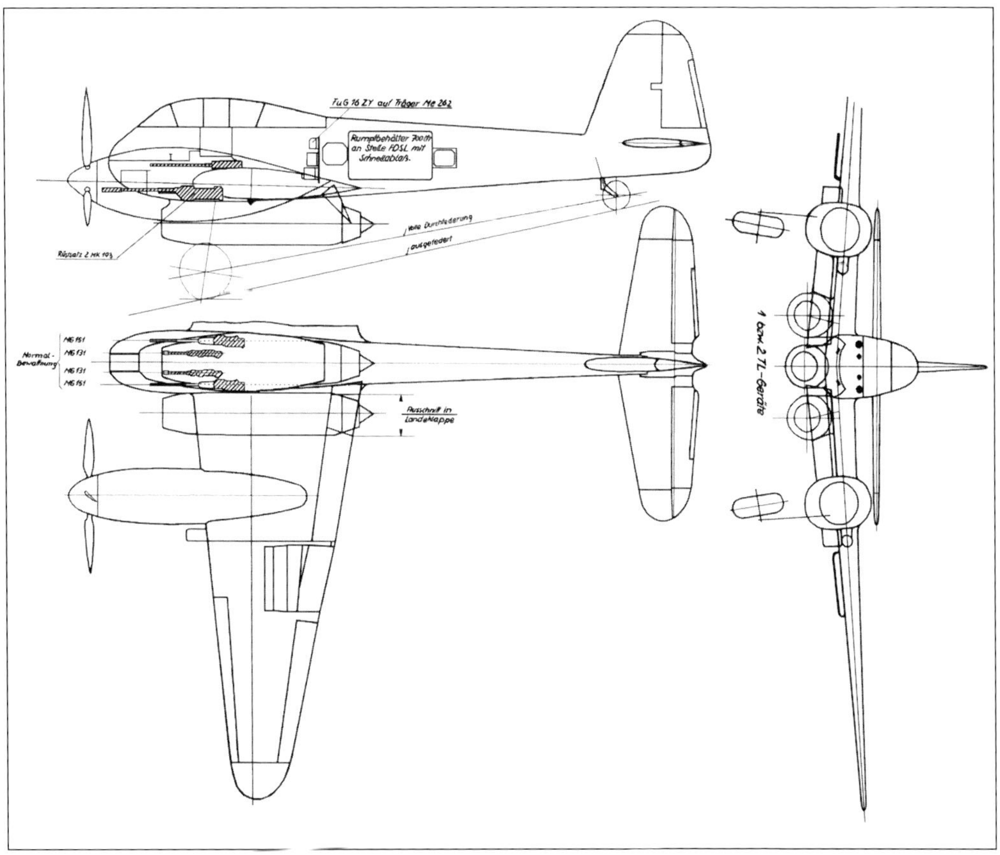

Project blueprints for the Me 410 fitted with one or two jet engines.

Me 610 *Zerstörer*

In October 1942 the Command Staff assumed that the Me 410 was to be a high speed bomber, and called for the Me 610 to be developed as a *Zerstörer* as soon as possible. The RLM also mentioned the Me 610 in November of that year, but after that the designation disappeared. On 26 February 1943 it was decided to produce the *Zerstörer* version as a sub-type of the existing production series (possibly using mod pack 221/103), chronologically following the high speed bomber version. Thus the way was paved from the Me 610 to the Me 410 A-2.

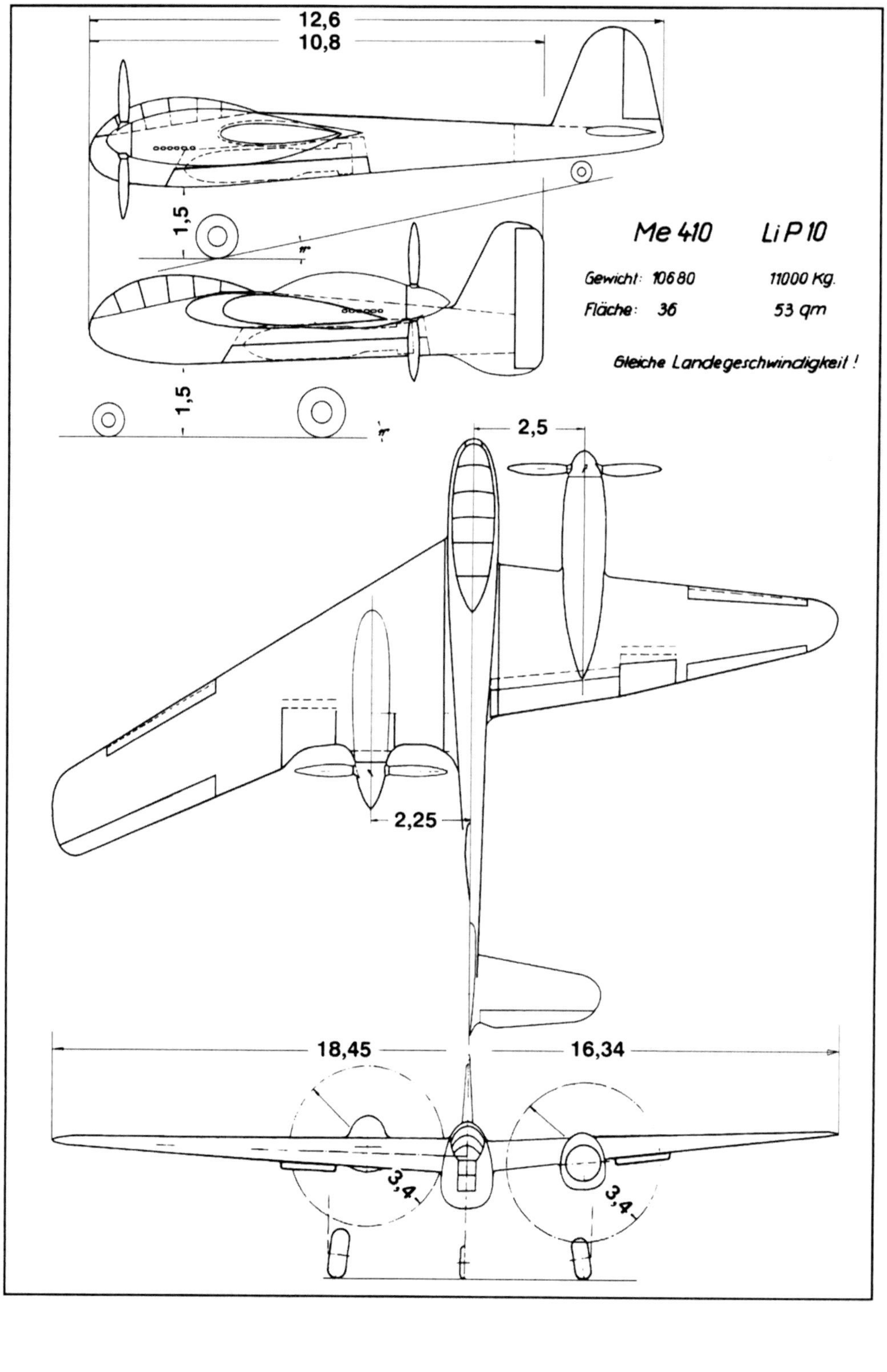

Comparison of the Li P 10 with an early design for the Me 410 C.

Li P 10, Tailless Counterpart to the Me 210/410

Type: twin-engined all-metal cantilever low-wing monoplane of flying wing design
Engine: 2 x DB 603
Propeller: VDM metal pusher type, 3.4 m diameter
Wingspan: 18.45 m
Length: 10 m
Max. speed (as fighter): 682 km/h at maximum pressure altitude
Landing speed: 170 km/h
Service ceiling: 12100 m
Service ceiling (w/ 10.3 t): 9150 m
Range (as fighter): 2480 km

In early 1942, when the problems with the Me 210 became apparent, Alexander Lippisch (then a designer at Messerschmitt) proposed an alternate tailless design to the RLM, which initially supported his efforts. The Li P 10 was first envisioned with the DB 606 dual engine driving a pusher propeller via an extended shaft. Due to unanticipated problems with the extended shaft, the project was reworked into a design with two single DB 603 engines situated on the wing trailing edge, also driving pusher propellers. The Li P 10 was to have made use of some of the Me 210's components. For further information, see Me 329.

Me 329, Tailless Counterpart to the Me 210/410

Type: twin-engined all-metal cantilever low-wing monoplane of flying wing design
Fuselage: with cockpit, weapons bay and bomb bay
Cockpit: pressurized, with ejection seats
Wings: two-piece, with steel spar and anti-icing system
Undercarriage: hydraulically retractable, with nose gear
Vertical stabilizer: single, with Flettner tabs
Tailerons: in outer wing sections
Engine: 2 x DB 603 or 2 x Jumo 213
Radiators: located in wing ahead of engine
Propeller: VDM metal pusher type, 3.4 m diameter, also functions as dive brake
Fixed armament: 4 x MG 151/20 in fuselage
2 x MK 103 in wings
Flexible armament: 1 x MG 151/20 in tail barbette (FHL 151) or 2 x MG 131 in FHL 131, either with periscope sight
Ordnance: up to 2500 kg under fuselage or
up to 1000 kg under wing root fairing
Armor: radiator
Electronic systems: standard for its class
Life raft: 2 man, in aft fuselage
Fuel: 2500 liters in wings
Oil: 2 x 85 liters aft of the engines
Crew: 2 men
Wingspan: 17.5 m
Length: 7.71 m
Weights (gross, as fighter): 9.52 t
(gross, as bomber): 12.15 t with 2500 kg of bombs
Weight (empty, as fighter): 6.82 t
Wing loading: 295 kg/m^2 max
Max. speed (as fighter): 685 km/h at maximum pressure altitude
Landing speed: 170 km/h
Service ceiling: 12500 m
Service ceiling (w/ 10.3 t): 9150 m
Range (as fighter): 2520 km with 2400 liters

The Lippisch design was in principle similar and contemporary to one by *Dr.* Wurster, the Me 329. The project draft dated from 15 March 1942 and envisioned the type as a heavy fighter, escort fighter, dive bomber, strike fighter, and armed reconnaissance platform.

Prof. Messerschmitt preferred the Me 329 and had a 1:1 scale mockup built. At his request (TDM file memorandum from 9/2/42) performance comparison calculations were made for these two designs, as well as for the Me 410 using a standard base. These showed that the tailless design enjoyed advantages in the areas of top speed, service ceiling, and range (technical report No. 80/42 from 12/1/42).

Theoretically, the Me 329 had better performance figures than the Me 410, but would have been hard pressed to enter production before 1945.

Aside from its flying wing construction, the project is of interest for another reason: Messerschmitt borrowed some key features from the Ar 240. These included a periscope as the better choice for acquiring targets and sighting the defensive armament, and all bombs were now carried externally. This offered greater flexibility in the choice of caliber and meant that a bomb bay would not be wasted space on the return flight.

However, because of the developmental risk and the anticipated length of development, and in view of the fact that the Me 410 had resumed production in the interim (whereby much of the Me 210's tooling, jigs, and components could be utilized), the project was canceled in late 1942/early 1943.

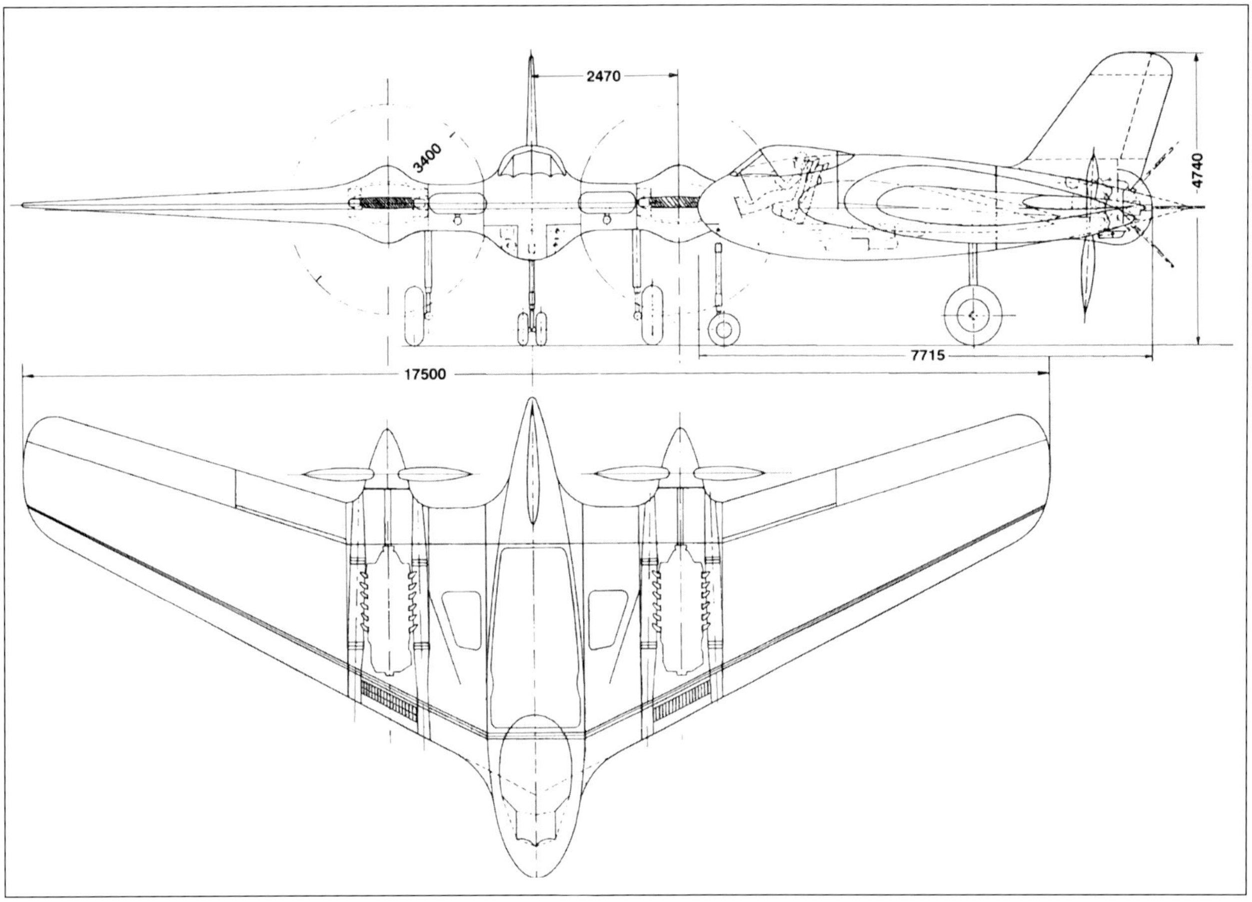

Me 410 Conversion Kits
(as of 15 May 1944)

The following overview stems from the Messerschmitt AG. Of note is the absence of the camera pod for the Me 410 A-3. It is probable that this was no longer a current variant at the time the list was prepared, as the cameras were subsequently to have been installed in the aft section of the fuselage (Me 410 B-7/8). Conversion kit 18, GM 1 tank, is shown here as still in design, but in fact it did go into operation. The variant with the GM 1 tank in place of the FDSL barbettes is not shown here, as it had already been replaced. The weapons packs with four additional MG 151s were field modifications, and at this stage the final details were not yet being worked on by Messerschmitt.

Nr.	Einbaugegenstand	Ausbau	Mehrgewicht [kg]	Geschwindigkeitsverlust [km/h]	Stand der Fertigung oder Konstruktion am 15.5.44
1	WB 151 A, je 300 Schuss	-	290	0	Vorhanden
2	2 MK 103, je 100 Schuss	Bombenklappen	584	1	Vorhanden
3	4 MK 108, je 100 Schuss	Bombenklappen	582	0	In Konstruktion
4	1 BK 5, 22 Schuss	Bombenklappen	650	15	Vorhanden
5	Drehling 6 WG 21 cm	Bombenklappen	1000	20	In Konstruktion
6	2 x 3 WG am Außenflügel	-	850	20	Vorhanden
7	Abwurfanlage innen 2 x SC 250 od. 2 x SD 500 od. 1 x SC 500 od. 1 x SD 1000 od. 1 x SB 1000/410	-	100	0	Vorhanden
8	Schlossrahmen 8 x 50 8 x SC 50 od. 8 x L-Bomben od. 8 x BL-Bomben	-	38	0	Vorhanden
9	Abwurfanlage außen 2 x SC250 od. 2 x SC 500 od. 2 x BT 400 od. 1 x LT 950 od. 1 x SC 1800 od. 1 x BT 1800 od. 1 x Qu-Rost	Boden	97	Bis 30	Vorhanden
10	Abwurfanlage Mittelflügel 4 x SC 50 od. 4 x BL-Bomben	-	35	25	Vorhanden
11	Abwurfanlage im Außenflügel 4 x SC 50	-	40	25	Im Entwurf

Nr.	Einbaugegenstand	Ausbau	Mehrgewicht [kg]	Geschwindigkeitsverlust [km/h]	Stand der Fertigung oder Konstruktion am 15.5.44
12	Abwurfanlage im Außenflügel 4 x SC 250 od. 4 x BT 200	-	40	30	Im Entwurf
13	Gerät X4	-	320	15	Im Entwurf
14	Kraftstoffzusatzbeh. 2 x 300 Ltr.	-	450	25	Vorhanden
15	Kraftstoffzusatzbeh. 2 x 900 Ltr.	-	1480	25	Vorhanden
16	Kraftstoffzusatzbehälter im Bombenraum	Bombenklappen	562	0	In Konstruktion
17	Kraftstoffzusatzbehälter anstelle FDSL	FDSL	358	0	Im Entwurf
18	GM -1 Behälter 45 min für 2 x 300 PS	2 MG 131 + 2 MG 151	178	0	In Konstruktion
19	WM - Behälter 225 Ltr. bei jetziger Hauptschalttafel	Boden	265	5	Im Entwurf
20	WM - Behälter 225 Ltr. bei neuer Hauptschalttafel	Boden	265	0	Im Entwurf
21	BZA oder TSA 2 oder ToKG	-	50	0	Vorhanden
22	Lotfe 7 D (nur Führerflugzeug)	Bombenklappen + 2 MG 131	-51	8	Attrappe gebaut
23	FuG 202 od. 212	-	80	20	Im Entwurf
24	2 MK 103 gesteuert, 170 und 180 Schuss	2 MG 131 + 2 MG 151	348	2	Im Entwurf
25	1 BK 5 Gesteuert, 22 Schuss	2 MG 131 + 2 MG 151	178	15	Im Entwurf
26	1 BK 7,5 starr, 12 Schuss	2 MG 131 + 2 MG 151	478	10	Im Entwurf
27	2 MK 108 gesteuert, je 150 Schuss	2 MG 131 + 2 MG 151	-122	5	Im Entwurf
28	2 MK 108 hinter FDSL, je 150 Schuss	-	380	2	In Konstruktion
29	2 MK 108 gesteuert, je 150 Schuss	FDSL	298	3	Im Entwurf
30	Bildgerät RB 20/30	-	160	0	Vorhanden
31	Bildgerät RB 50/30	-	160	0	Vorhanden
32	Bildgerät RB 75/30	-	160	0	Vorhanden
33	Nachtbildgerät NRB 35/25	-	90	0	Vorhanden
34	WM - Behälter, 220 Ltr. für 30 min	-	270	0	Im Entwurf
35	Schulflugzeug	2 MG 131 + 2 MG 151	-372	0	Vorhanden
36	Panzerung für Schlachtflugzeug	-	550	4	Im Entwurf
37	Folienbehälter I = 65000 Stück II = 24000 Stück III = 15000 Stück	-	III = 300	III = 15	Im Vorentwurf

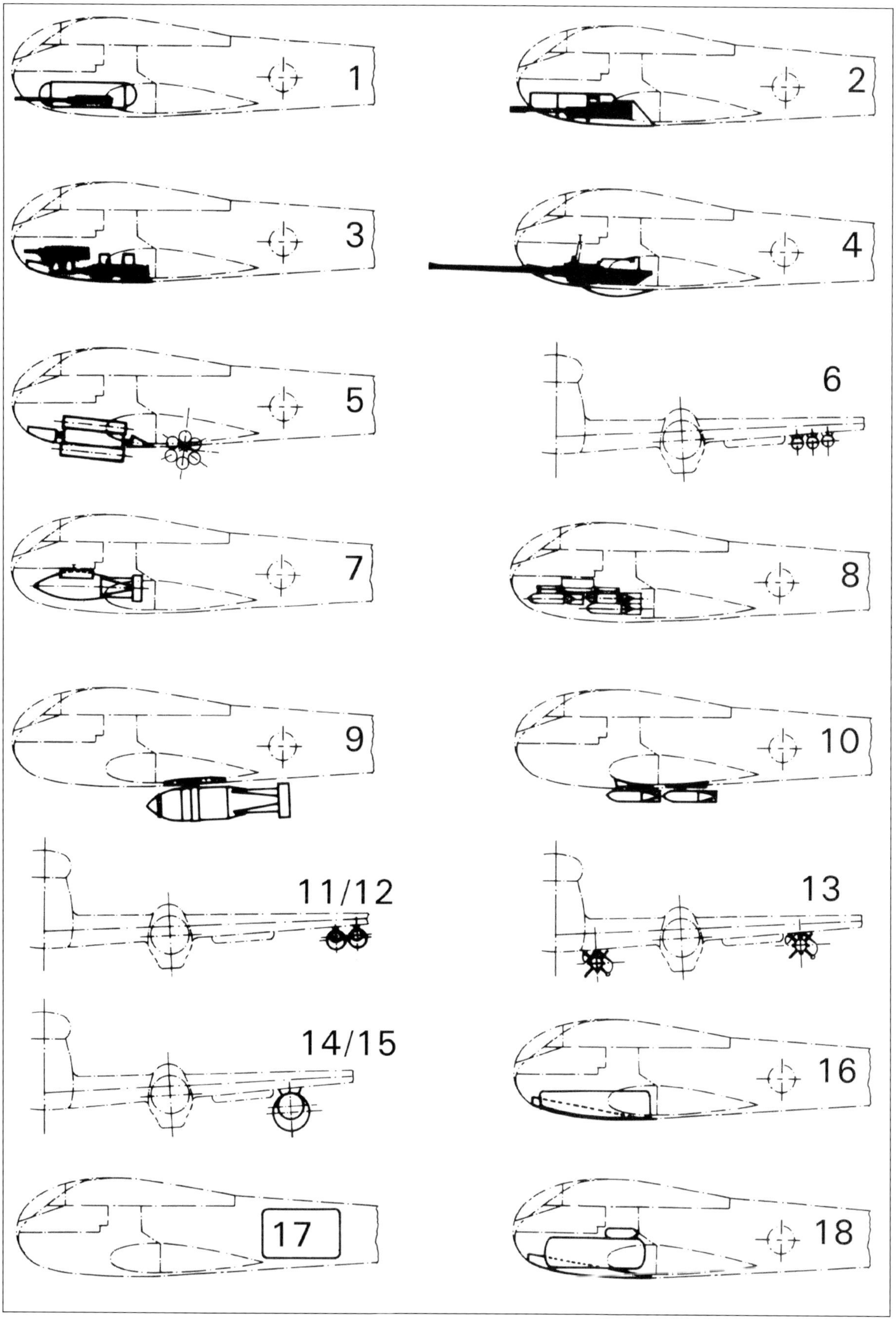

Drawings for conversion Kits 1 through 18.

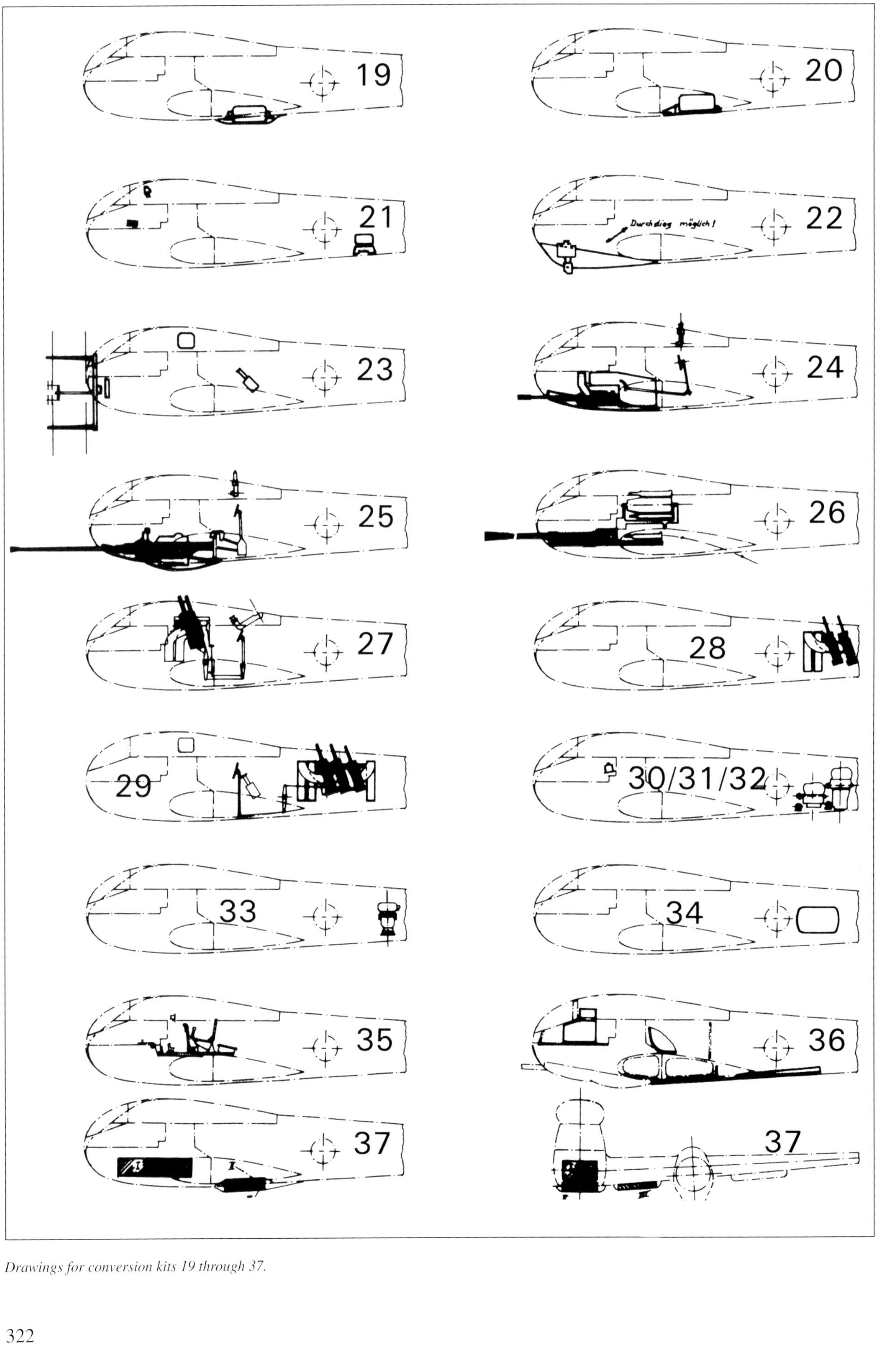

Drawings for conversion kits 19 through 37.

Variants, Serial Numbers, Quantities

The following list is derived from *C-Amt* programs, loss reports, flight log entries, and other reports. However, it is only an attempt at reproduction since the dates, particularly from 1944/45, are not available in their entirety. Coded factory serial numbers (*Werknummern*) after mid-1943 prevent an exact determination of the actual size of these number blocks. These blocks may have been longer at either the front or the end, and small gaps also cannot be ruled out. Comparison of these numbers derived from the dated listing with those aircraft actually taken on charge by the BAL *Bauaufsicht* reveals a satisfactory agreement, particularly when one takes into account the fact that a part of these aircraft remained at the manufacturer's for testing purposes or were destroyed before being turned over. (The BAL list is only available after 9/39, so that the number of aircraft delivered before then are estimates taken from *Luftwaffe* inventory reports.) Total quantity for the Bf 110 based on factory numbers is 6043, and according to BAL it is approximately 5930.

354 of the short body Me 210 version were completed and 108 never assembled, for a total of 462. The BAL reported taking on charge 183 short body Me 210s, 169 converted Me 210s, 88 converted Me 410 A-1s, and 25 converted Me 410 A-3s, for a total of 465. This agreement is also satisfactory. A portion of the short bodied Me 210s was also modified but, as these had already been accepted, did not show up as new aircraft in the BAL listing. Others were lost during testing or destroyed in training. As a result, the two sources do not agree with regard to overall numbers of converted aircraft.

For new-build Me 410s it appears that some blocks are too small. 970 aircraft according to factory numbering are listed in comparison to the BAL's 1010.

Loss reports for the Me 410 B show incongruities in the assignment of series designators. The redesignation within the Bf 110 D series should be taken into account.

Abbreviations for manufacturer data are based on those of the *C-Amt* from 1940 and indicate: Mtt = Messerschmitt AG Augsburg; BFW = Bayerische Flugzeugwerke Regensburg; GWF= Gothaer Waggonfabrik AG Gotha; Miag = Mühlenbau und Industrie AG Braunschweig; FW = Focke-Wulf Flugzeugbau GmbH Bremen; and Fi = Gerhard Fieseler Werke GmbH Kassel.

Messrs. Luther and Jordan bought the aircraft section from Miag in 1941 and renamed the new company Luther-Werke Luther & Jordan Braunschweig (identified as "Luther" in the listing). Miag continued to appear in some official documentation throughout 1942, but on 1 January 1943 Miag was no longer carried as an active producer on the RLM's listings.

On 1/1/43 the BFW was called Messerschmitt GmbH Regensburg. The abbreviation "Du" stands for Manfred Weiss Flugzeugwerke, Dunai.

Muster Baureihe	Werknummer von	Werknummer bis	Herstell-er	Produktio von	Produktio bis	Stück	Summe Baureihe	Summe Muster	Summe BAL
Bf 110 V	868	870	Mtt	36	36	3	3	6043	bis 8.39:
Bf 110 A-0	910	916	Mtt	7.37	3.38	7	7		
Bf 110 V7 / B-0 / B-1	917	942	Mtt	4.38	1.39	24	88		98 V/ A/ B + ca.
Bf 110 B-1	1731	1792	GWF	10.38	10.39	62			70 C
Bf 110 C-1	943	986	Mtt	1.39	3.39	44	195		
Bf 110 C-1	1344	1401	Mtt	4.39	9.39	58			
Bf 110 C-1	1793	1822	GWF	11.39	1.40	30			9.39 bis
Bf 110 C-1	2045	2052	GWF	1.40	2.40	8			2.45:
Bf 110 C-1	2619	2636	FW	9.39	11.39	15			
Bf 110 C-1	2801	2840	Miag	4.39	39	40			5762
Bf 110 C-2	2053	2147	GWF	1.40	3.40	95	359		
Bf 110 C-2	2637	2638	FW	11.39	11.39	2			davon
Bf 110 C-2	2885	2892	FW	11.39	11.39	8			ca. 2240
Bf 110 C-2	3203	3245	FW	12.39	4.40	43			G-4 und
Bf 110 C-2	3487	3563	Miag	5.40	7.40	77			494
Bf 110 C-2	3000	3133	Mtt	9.39	1.40	134			Aufkärer
Bf 110 C-4 +5 C-6	2148	2174	GWF	5.40	6.40	21	155		
Bf 110 C-4	2190	2194	GWF	6.40	7.40	5			
Bf 110 C-4	2215	2224	GWF	7.40	7.40	10			
Bf 110 C-4	2275	2284	GWF	7.40	9.40	10			
Bf 110 C-4	3246	3300	FW	4.40	7.40	55			
Bf 110 C-4	3564	3617	Miag	7.40	8.40	54			
Bf 110 C-5	2175	2189	GWF	6.40	6.40	15	100		
Bf 110 C-5	2195	2214	GWF	7.40	7.40	20			
Bf 110 C-5	2225	2244	GWF	7.40	7.40	20			
Bf 110 C-5	2255	2274	GWF	8.40	8.40	20			
Bf 110 C-5	2285	2309	GWF	11.40	1.41	25			
Bf 110 C-6	2152		GWF	5.40	5.40	1	12		
Bf 110 C-6			GWF	5.40	6.40	5			
Bf 110 C-6	2249	2254	GWF	7.40	7.40	6			
Bf 110 C-7	2245	2248	GWF	7.40	7.40	4	39		
Bf 110 C-7	3618	3652	Miag	8.40	9.40	35			
Bf 110 D-0	3134	3148	Mtt	3.40	4.40	15	83		
Bf 110 D-0	3152	3162	Mtt	4.40	4.40	11			
Bf 110 D-0	3166	3202	Mtt	4.40	5.40	37			
Bf 110 D-0	3311	3418	Mtt	7.40	9.40	20			
Bf 110 D-0 / D-1	3799	3809	FW	7.40	8.40	11	21		
Bf 110 D-0 / D-1	3301	3310	FW	7.40	7.40	10			
Bf 110 D-0 / D-3	3810	3816	FW	8.40	8.40	6	12		
Bf 110 D-0 / D-3	4207	4212	FW	8.40	8.40	6			
Bf 110 D-1 / D-4	3149	3151	Mtt	4.40	4.40	3	6		
Bf 110 D-1 / D-4	3163	3165	Mtt	4.40	4.40	3			
Bf 110 D-2	3311	3418	Mtt	7.40	9.40	73	73		
Bf 110 D-3	3311	3418	Mtt	7.40	9.40	16	254		
Bf 110 D-3	3653	3720	Miag	9.40	11.40	70			
Bf 110 D-3	4213	4380	FW	9.40	3.41	168			
Bf 110 E-1	3419	3462	Mtt	8.40	10.40	45	334		
Bf 110 E-1	3471	3486	Mtt	11.40	12.40	16			
Bf 110 E-1	3817	3889	Mtt	10.40	12.40	73			
Bf 110 E-1	3895	3995	Mtt	1.41	3.41	96			
Bf 110 E-1	4013	4116	Mtt	5.41	8.41	104			

Muster Baureihe	Werknummer		Hersteller	Produktion		Stück	Summe Baureihe	Summe Muster	Summe BAL
	von	bis		von	bis				
Bf 110 E-2	2310	2314	GWF	2.41	3.41	5	322		
Bf 110 E-2	2350	2354	GWF	4.41	4.41	5			
Bf 110 E-2	2375	2384	GWF	4.41	4.41	10			
Bf 110 E-2	2425	2434	GWF	6.41	6.41	10			
Bf 110 E-2	2540	2554	GWF	11.41	12.41	15			
Bf 110 E-2	2639	2654	GWF	12.41	1.42	16			
Bf 110 E-2	3463	3470	Mtt	10.40	11.40	8			
Bf 110 E-2	3721	3798	Miag	12.40	3.41	78			
Bf 110 E-2	3890	3894	Mtt	1.41	1.41	5			
Bf 110 E-2	3996	4012	Mtt	4.41	4.41	17			
Bf 110 E-2	4381	4400	FW	4.41	4.41	21			
Bf 110 E-2	4401	4532	Miag	4.41	12.41	132			
Bf 110 E-3	2315	2349	GWF	2.41	3.41	35	200		
Bf 110 E-3	2355	2374	GWF	4.41	4.41	20			
Bf 110 E-3	2385	2424	GWF	4.41	5.41	40			
Bf 110 E-3	2435	2539	GWF	6.41	10.41	105			
Bf 110 F-2	2655	2659	GWF	12.42	1.42	5	190		
Bf 110 F-2	4533	4598	Luther	3.42	5.42	65			
Bf 110 F-2	5011	5030	Luther	7.42	8.42	20			
Bf 110 F-2	5044	5108	Luther	8.42	9.42	65			
Bf 110 F-2	5114	5132	Luther	11.42	11.42	20			
Bf 110 F-2	5154	5168	Luther	11.42	11.42	15			
Bf 110 F-3	5001	5010	Luther	6.42	7.42	10	43		
Bf 110 F-3	5031	5043	Luther	8.42	8.42	13			
Bf 110 F-3	5109	5113	Luther	10.42	11.42	5			
Bf 110 F-3	5169	5184	Luther	11.42	12.42	15			
Bf 110 F-4	2660	2724	GWF	12.41	1.42	65	279		
Bf 110 F-4	4601	4620	GWF	5.42	5.42	20			
Bf 110 F-4	4628	4821	GWF	6.42	12.42	194			
Bf 110 G-0	4621	4627	GWF	6.42	6.42	6	6		
Bf 110 G-2	5133	5148	Luther	12.42	12.42	15	797		
Bf 110 G-2	5185	5251	GWF	1.43	2.43	55			
Bf 110 G-2	5255	5259	GWF	3.43	3.43	5			
Bf 110 G-2	5601	5640	GWF	7.43	8.43	40			
Bf 110 G-2	6100	6102	Luther	2.43	2.43	2			
Bf 110 G-2	6105	6155	Luther	2.43	3.43	51			
Bf 110 G-2	6161	6218	Luther	3.43	4.43	58			
Bf 110 G-2	6229	6268	Luther	4.43	5.43	40			
Bf 110 G-2	6248	6303	Luther	6.43	6.43	20			
Bf 110 G-2	6319	6339	Luther	6.43	6.43	21			
Bf 110 G-2	6360	6429	Luther	7.43	8.43	70			
Bf 110 G-2	120002	120117	Luther	8.43	11.43	120			
Bf 110 G-2	120163	120191	Luther	9.43	10.43	30			
Bf 110 G-2	130038	130100		12.43	2.44	60			
Bf 110 G-2	150072	150140		7.43	9.43	70			
Bf 110 G-2	170063	170077		2.44	3.44	15			
Bf 110 G-2	210001	210010	GWF	10.43	10.43	10			
Bf 110 G-2	210087	210094		10.43	10.43	10			
Bf 110 G-2	410092	410100		10.43	10.43	10			
Bf 110 G-2	420001	420038	GWF	12.43	1.44	40			
Bf 110 G-2	420110	420129	GWF	1.44	1.44	20			
Bf 110 G-2	500001	500030	Luther	12.43	12.43	30			
Bf 110 G-2	710005	710008	GWF	10.43	10.43	5			

Muster Baureihe	Werknummer		Herstell er	Produktio		Stück	Summe Baureihe	Summe Muster	Summe BAL
	von	bis		von	bis				
Bf 110 G-3	4828	4853	GWF	1.43	1.43	26	172		
Bf 110 G-3	4894	4919	GWF	3.43	3.43	26			
Bf 110 G-3	5381	5420	GWF	5.43	5.43	40			
Bf 110 G-3	5481	5520	GWF	6.43	6.43	40			
Bf 110 G-3	5681	5720	GWF	8.43	9.43	40			
Bf 110 G-4	4854	4893	GWF	1.43	2.43	40	2293		
Bf 110 G-4	5252	5254	GWF	3.43	3.43	3			
Bf 110 G-4	5301	5380	GWF	3.43	4.43	80			
Bf 110 G-4	5421	5480	GWF	5.43	6.43	60			
Bf 110 G-4	5521	5600	GWF	6.43	7.43	80			
Bf 110 G-4	5641	5680	GWF	8.43	8.43	40			
Bf 110 G-4	6102	6104	Luther	2.43	2.43	3			
Bf 110 G-4	6156	6160	Luther	3.43	3.43	5			
Bf 110 G-4	6219	6228	Luther	4.43	4.43	10			
Bf 110 G-4	6269	6283	Luther	6.43	6.43	15			
Bf 110 G-4	6304	6318	Luther	6.43	6.43	15			
Bf 110 G-4	6340	6359	Luther	6.43	7.43	20			
Bf 110 G-4	110024	110093		4.44	7.44	70			
Bf 110 G-4	110123	110132		5.44	8.44	10			
Bf 110 G-4	110150	110176		5.44	7.44	25			
Bf 110 G-4	110421	110440		6.44	6.44	20			
Bf 110 G-4	110503	110510		12.44	12.44	10			
Bf 110 G-4	140000	140087	GWF	1.44	3.44	90			
Bf 110 G-4	140192	140229	GWF	3.44	4.44	30			
Bf 110 G-4	140292	140364	GWF	4.44	6.44	72			
Bf 110 G-4	140638	140680	GWF	6.44	7.44	40			
Bf 110 G-4	140756	140766	GWF	8.44	8.44	10			
Bf 110 G-4	160120	160194	Luther	12.44	12.44	74			
Bf 110 G-4	160574	160675	Luther	12.44	1.45	100			
Bf 110 G-4	160750	160800	Luther	2.45	4.45	50			
Bf 110 G-4	160847	160848							
Bf 110 G-4	180090	180136		2.44	3.44	50			
Bf 110 G-4	180336	180408		3.44	4.44	70			
Bf 110 G-4	180526	180594		11.44	1.45	70			
Bf 110 G-4	180810	180850		1.45	2.45	40			
Bf 110 G-4	440004	440165	Luther	3.44	5.44	120			
Bf 110 G-4	440244	440358	Luther	5.44	7.44	115			
Bf 110 G-4	441083	441127		5.44	7.44	40			
Bf 110 G-4	480092	480145	GWF	1.44	3.44	50			
Bf 110 G-4	480160	480188	Luther	3.44	4.44	30			
Bf 110 G-4	720001	720083	Luther	8.43	9.43	80			
Bf 110 G-4	720151	720272		9.43	10.43	100			
Bf 110 G-4	720380	720418		11.43	12.43	40			
Bf 110 G-4	730001	730122	GWF	4.44	5.44	120			
Bf 110 G-4	730201	730391		6.44	1.45	190			
Bf 110 G-4	740000	740084	GWF	9.43	10.43	84			
Bf 110 G-4	740114	740238	Luther	10.43	12.43	120			

Muster Baureihe	Werknummer		Hersteller	Produktion		Stück	Summe Baureihe	Summe Muster	Summe BAL
	von	bis		von	bis				
Me 210 V	001	016	Mtt	9.39	6.41	16	16	16	
Me 210 A-0/ 1	017	100	Mtt	1.41	4.41	84	354	354	183
Me 210 A-1	101	270 ?	Mtt	5.41	5.42	144			
Me 210 A-1	2251	2350	BFW	10.41	5.42	100			
Me 210 A-1	3001		Fi			0			
Me 210 A-1	4001		Miag			0			
Me 210 A-1	5001		GWF			0			
Me 210 A-1	8151	8176	Luther	2.42	2.42	26			
Me 210 A-1 lang	020	260	Mtt	7.42	1.43	130	212	212	169
Me 210 A-1 lang	2251	2350	Mtt	9.42	3.43	50			Umbau
Me 210 A-1 lang	8151	8176	Mtt	12.42	1.43	26			
Me 210 A-1 lang	11051	11056	Mtt	3.43	3.43	6			
Me 210 Ca-1	316001	316026	Du	4.43	11.43	26	114 Luftw.	272	105
Me 210 Ca-1	150011	150098	Du	11.43	8.44	88			Neubau
Me 210 Ca-1	2.001	269.159	Du	3.43	9.44	138	158		
Me 210 Ca-1	210.216	261.151	Du	6.44	9.44	20	Ungarn		
Me 410 A-1 + A-3	017	270	Mtt	12.42	4.43	100	160	160	113 Umbau
Me 410 A-1	271	304	Mtt	3.43	4.43	35		Umbau	davon 25
Me 410 A-1	2253	2344	Mtt	12.42	4.43	25			Aufklärer
Me 410 A-1	10011	10050	Mtt	7.43	7.43	40	508	970	1010
Me 410 A-1	10101	10120	Mtt	7.43	8.43	20		Neubau	Neubau,
Me 410 A-1	10171	10200	Mtt	8.43	8.43	30			davon 110
Me 410 A-1	10230	10270	Mtt	8.43	9.43	40			Aufklärer
Me 410 A-1	10300	10315	Mtt	9.43	9.43	16			
Me 410 A-1	120001	120027	Do	1.44	3.44	27			
Me 410 A-1	120092	120172	Do	2.44	4.44	80			
Me 410 A-1	420001	420041	Mtt	9.43	10.43	40			
Me 410 A-1	420082	420104	Mtt	9.43	10.43	25			
Me 410 A-1	420188	420202	Mtt	10.43	11.43	15			
Me 410 A-1	420283	420299	Mtt	11.43	11.43	17			
Me 410 A-1	420402	420509	Mtt	11.43	1.44	108			
Me 410 A-1	420622	420640	Mtt	1.44	2.44	19			
Me 410 A-1	420653	420683	Mtt	5.44	5.44	31			
Me 410 A-3	170001	170043	Mtt	10.43	11.43	43	109		
Me 410 A-3	170087	170152	Mtt	2.44	5.44	66			
Me 410 B-2	410047	410102	Mtt	6.44	9.44	55	319		
Me 410 B-2	410208	410226	Mtt	9.44	9.44	20			
Me 410 B-2	470092	470140	Mtt	5.44	6.44	49			
Me 410 B-2	710310	710383	Do	5.44	6.44	74			
Me 410 B-2	710399	710406	Do	5.44	6.44	7			
Me 410 B-2	710444	710473	Do	5.44	6.44	30			
Me 410 B-2 (B-3)	130351	130379		7.44	7.44	30			
Me 410 B-1, B-2, B-3	150083	150136	Mtt	7.44	7.44	54			
Me 410 B-3	190121	190132	Mtt	6.44	6.44	11	34		
Me 410 B-3	190157	190179	Mtt	6.44	7.44	23			

Prototypes and Testbeds

Muster	Motor	Werknr.	Stkz	Bemerkungen
Hs 124 V1	Ju 210			Erstflug im Sommer 1936, keine Einzelheiten bekannt
Hs 124 V2				vermutlich umgebaut auf BMW Sternmotoren
Hs 124 V3				vermutlich mit Blechbug
FW 57 V1	DB 600			Erstflug im Sommer 1936, keine Einzelheiten bekannt
FW 57 V2	DB 600			Fertigstellung nicht belegt
FW 57 V3	DB 600			Fertigstellung nicht belegt
Bf 110 V1	Ju 10 D	868	D-AHOA	Erstflug 12.5.36, allgemeine Flugerprobung in Augsburg, 10.37 Erprobung in Travemünde
Bf 110 V2	Ju 210 D	869	D-AQYE	Erstflug 24.10.36, allgemeine Flugerprobung in Augsburg
Bf 110 V2	Ju 210 D	869	D-AQYE	2.37 Erprobung in Rechlin
Bf 110 V3	DB 600	870	D-ATII	Erstflug 24.12.36, allgemeine Flugerprobung in Augsburg
Bf 110 V3	DB 601 A	870	D-ATII	7.40 Erprobungsträger, 11.40 an Reparaturwerk
Bf 110 A-0	Ju 210	910	D-AISY	1.38 allgemeine Flugerprobung in Augsburg
Bf 110 V4	Ju 211	910	D-AISY	3.39 Erprobung Jumo 211 in Rechlin
Bf 110 A-0	Ju 210	911	D-AAHI	3.38 allgemeine Flugerprobung in Augsburg, 2.1.39 Erprobung in Rechlin
Bf 110 V5	Ju 210 G	911	D-AAHI	7.40 – 10.41 bei Arado, Erprobungsträger mit Ar-Visier-Einbauten, Attrappe
Bf 110 V8?	Ju 210 G	913	D-AIJO	27.12.38 bei Messerschmitt, 7.40 Erprobungsträger, Fertigstellung für den Einbau des Gerätes 3302
Bf 110 A-0		915	D-AUDU	9.38 bis 1.39 bei Messerschmitt
Bf 110 V6	DB 601 A	915	D-AUDU	7.40 Eprobungsträger., 100 Stunden-Erprobung abgeschlossen, 11.40 Verschrottung, 2.41 bis 5 41 unsymmetrische Belastungsversuche, Standschwingversuche
Bf 110 A-0	Ju 210 G	916	D-AYGE	9.40 Erprobungsträger bei Messerschmitt
Bf 110 B-0 /V7	Ju 210 G	917	D-AEDO	19.4.38 bei Messerschmitt, Musterflugzeug für Bf 110 B
Bf 110 B-0 V8?	Ju 210 G	918	D-ADVO	10.39 Erprobung der Luftschraube Me P 6
Bf 110 B-0	Ju 210 G	918	D-ADVO	7.40 – 9.40 Musterflugzeug für Änderungsanweisung und Einbau des Gerätes 3302
Bf 110 B-0	Ju 210 G	918	D-ADVO	11.40 Abgabe an Fa. Junkers
Bf 110 B-0	Ju 210 G	919	D-AAZI	20.7.38 Propellereinstellung in Rechlin
Bf 110 B-1	Ju 210 G	920	D-ADJD	3.39 Erprobung Trommelgerät TG 65 mit 8 RZ 65 Raketen
Bf 110 B-1	Ju 210 G	926	PV+AA	3.40 und 10.40 Schießflüge in Travemünde

above: A new antenna mount was tested on this Bf 110 F-4 at the Erprobungstelle *Werneuchen. (Petrick)*

below: This Bf 110 G-4 was put to use as a testbed for the FuG 101 and FuG 216. The MG 17s had to be removed to make room for the antenna system of the FuG 216 Neptun. *(Petrick)*

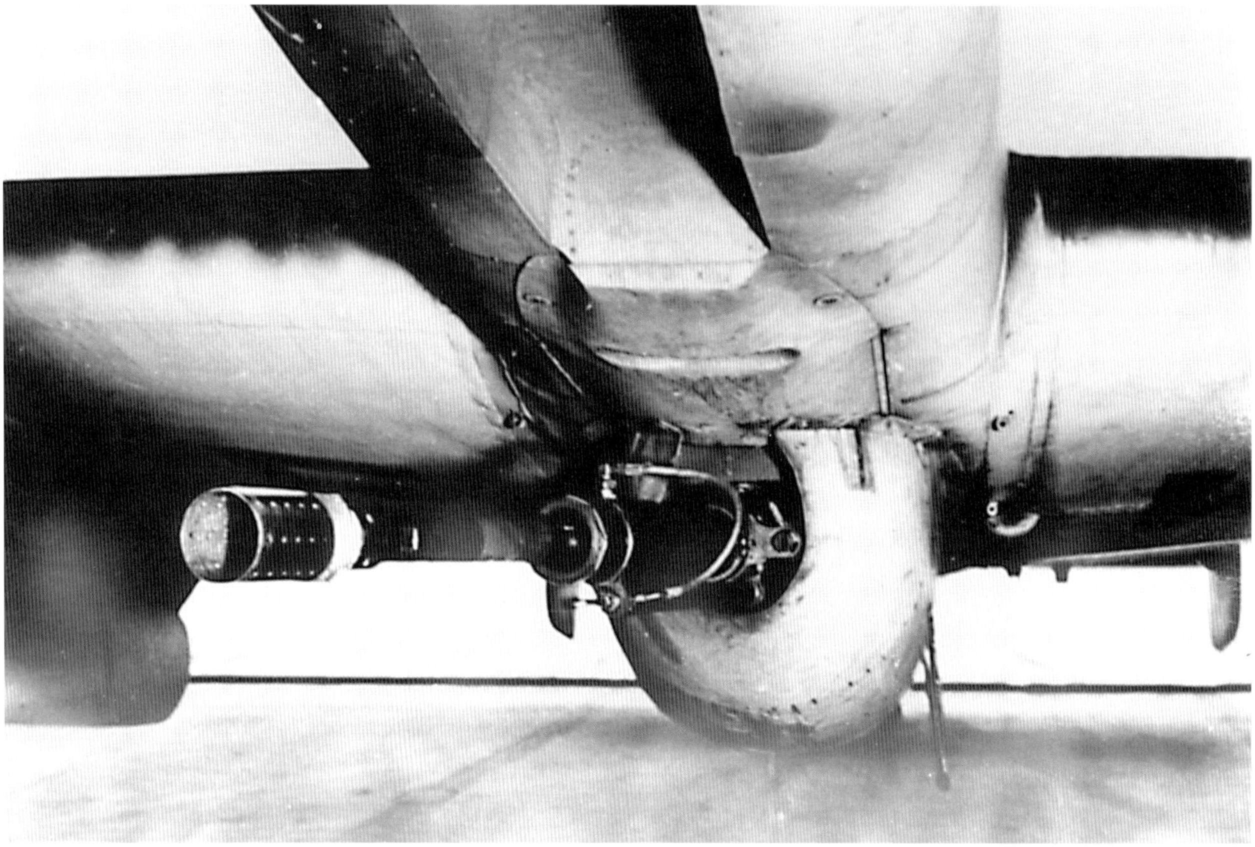

above: Erprobungskommando 25 *tested this Bf 110 G with a semi-fixed MK 101 in August of 1943. The radio operator had limited movement of the weapon, increasing its accuracy. (Radinger)*

below: Me 210 A-1 (W.Nr. *102, PN+PA) was used for diving trials. (Moor)*

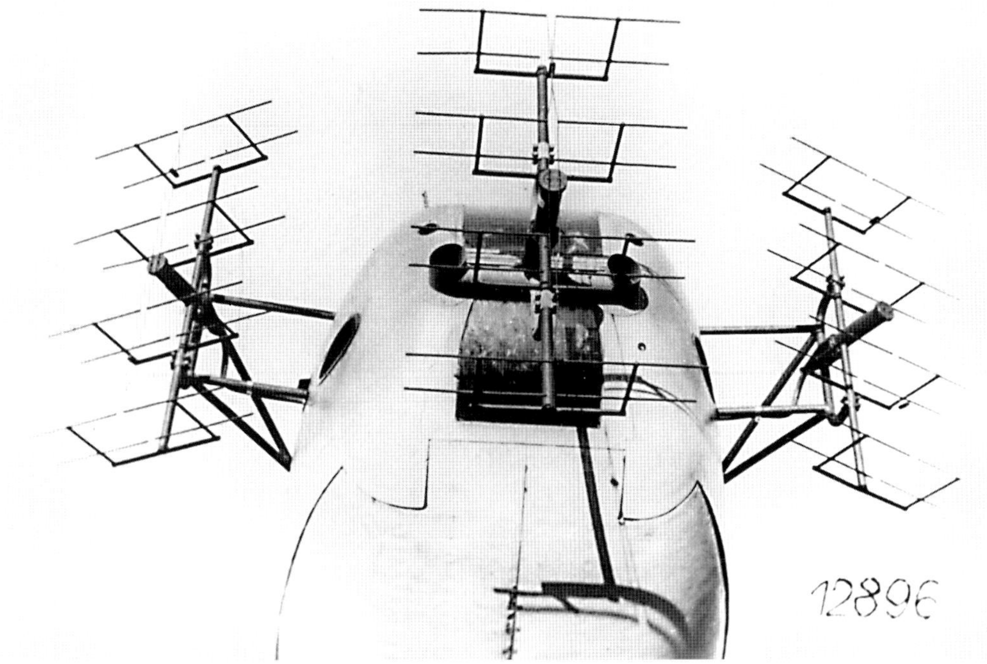

Abb. oben:
Im Mai 1943 erfolgte der Einbau eines „Hohentwiel“ durch DLH in die Me 210 A-1 (W.Nr. 2319, DF+ER) (Nowarra)

left: In May of 1943 the DLH fitted a Hohentwiel *system in this Me 210 A-1* (W.Nr. *2319, DF+ER)*

left: During the spring of 1943 a Flak 18 *was installed and tested by the* E-Stelle *Tarnewitz in an Me 210 A-1* (W.Nr. *2347, GE+KS). The limited number of rounds contained in the horizontally-mounted magazine led to the development of the* Flak 43. *(Schliephake)*

*above: At the end of the general testing phase the Me 410 V 2 (*W.Nr. *023, DI+NS, formerly an Me 210 A-0) served as a testbed for the 5 cm* Bordkanone, *evaluated by the DLH at Staaken. (Nowarra)*

below: This photo of the Me 410 V 3 clearly shows the rough transition from the wide canopy to the narrow fuselage. (D'Amico-Valentini)

above: Me 410 V 18 (W.Nr. *10115, TF+ED) was used to test the MK 103. (Radinger)*

below: Erprobungsstelle *Tarnewitz tested the WG 21 triple gun using this Me 410 A-1* (W.Nr. *420416) in February 1944. (Nowarra)*

above, below, and opposite page above: This Me 410 A-1 (W.Nr. *420090, PP+VG) was used to test various torpedoes at the* E-Stelle *Gotenhafen in 1944. These photos show an LT 950 with the L 10* Friedensengel, *enabling the drop range to be increased. (above and below: Nowarra, opposite:* Deutsches Museum, *Munich)*

below: Me 410 A-1 (W.Nr. 2300, BN+CY) was photographed at Daimler-Benz in Echterdingen in October 1943, where it was testing the development of the DB 603 G fighter/ heavy fighter engines. With the radiators shifted ahead of the engine, a counterweight had to be installed in the tail. (Petrick)

right: This variant had both the turbocharger air intake and the flame dampers integrated into the nacelle. (Petrick)

right: This photo shows yet another variant. (Daimler Benz AG)

Engines and Powerplants

Definitions

While the terms have been used interchangeably throughout this book, technically the term "engine" refers to the basic units supplied to the airframe manufacturers by the engine manufacturers. By themselves, these engines were incapable of running due to the fact that they lacked cooling systems.

The term "powerplant" encompassed the cowlings, propellers, radiators, etc. These were originally built by the airframe manufacturer, with the engine manufacturer providing a portfolio consisting of maximum permissible oil and coolant temperatures, maximum loss of pressure in oil lines, etc. This allowed the airframe manufacturer to locate oil coolers and coolant radiators on the airframe as desired.

Fighter/Heavy Fighter standard engines/powerplants were complete units ready for operation, supplied by the engine companies to the airframe manufacturers, and included the cowling and all necessary coolant and operating fittings. The background behind the procurement of standard engines was, in the main, simplification of production. Primarily, though, it now gave the engine manufacturer the responsibility for proper installation and the ability to properly dimension the radiator.

Engines for the *Zerstörer* Prototypes

Because of the difference in their undercarriage lengths, larger propellers could be fitted to the heavy fighters (Bf 110) than to the fighters (Bf 109). These larger propellers required a lower rpm rate when producing the same amount of thrust, yet because the engines had the same maximum permissible rpm rating, of necessity heavy fighters were required to have different gearing than fighters. This resulted in variants of the same engine that essentially differed only in the gear reduction from engine to propeller rpm.

Jumo 210

The water-cooled Jumo 210 was born in 1931 (preliminary study) as an internal initiative by the Junkers Company, and adhered to the design guidelines set down by the *Reichswehrministerium* in 1929. As a result of the Ministry's streamlining measures it remained the only 20 liter engine to be used by the *Luftwaffe.*

Jumo 210 A, 1935 onward

Carbureted engine with 19.7 liter piston displacement, with low-altitude supercharger:

Performance at sea level:
680 hp (briefly for 5 min)
610 hp (combat for 30 min)
545 hp (constant)

Jumo 210 B/C

As Jumo 210 A, with supercharger for 2.7 km rated altitude:

Performance at sea level:
600 hp (briefly for 5 min)
540 hp (combat for 30 min)
480 hp (constant)

Performance at 2.7 km:
640 hp (briefly for 5 min)
575 hp (combat for 30 min)
510 hp (constant)

Variants B and C had different gearing, reducing the maximum engine rating of 2700 rpm to 1543 propeller rpm for the Jumo 210 B and 1700 rpm for the Jumo 210 C.

Jumo 210 D/E, 1936 onward

As Jumo 210 B/C, but with two-stage supercharger:

Performance at sea level:
680 hp (briefly for 5 min)
610 hp (combat for 30 min)
545 hp (constant)

Performance at 2.7 km: 640 hp (briefly for 5 min)
575 hp (combat for 30 min)
510 hp (constant)

Jumo 210 Da/Ea, 1936 onward
As Jumo 210 D/E, with modified supercharger gearing, with 3.7 km rated altitude:

Performance at sea level: 720 hp (takeoff for 1 min)
690 hp (briefly for 5 min)
620 hp (combat for 30 min)
550 hp (constant)
Performance at 3.7 km: 680 hp (briefly for 5 min)
615 hp (combat for 30 min)
545 hp (constant)

DB 600
The desire for increased speed soon led to the 30 liter engine—originally intended only for bombers—being considered for the heavy fighter types as well. The first 30 liter engine was the carbureted DB 600, although this only found its way into the *Luftwaffe* in very limited numbers.

Based on the *Reichswehrministerium's* guidelines of 1929, Daimler-Benz internally developed a liquid-cooled 12-cylinder inverted V 30 liter engine. The initial version was the F4, two prototypes of which were running in 1931. The F4 B, a follow-on development, was the prototype for the DB 600, for which the company was awarded a developmental and production contract in 1933 for six engines. The DB 600 was the only German liquid-cooled engine in the 30-liter class for many years. 2281 examples of this engine were ultimately built.

DB 600 A/B, 1934 onward
Carbureted engine with 33.9 l displacement and low-level supercharger:

Performance at sea level: 1000 hp
(briefly for 5 min)
Performance at sea level: 900 hp
(combat for 30 min)
Performance at sea level: 800 hp
(constant)

Versions A and B had different gear reductions, the DB 600 A for the Bf 109 and the B for the Bf 110.

DB 600 C/D
As DB 600 A/B, but with high altitude supercharger rated at 4 km:

Performance at sea level: 950 hp
(takeoff for 1 min)
Performance at 4 km: 910 hp
(briefly for 5 min)
Performance at 4 km: 850 hp
(combat for 30 min)
Performance at 4 km: 800 hp
(constant)

DB 600 G/H, 1936 onward
As DB 600 C/D, but with improved performance:

Performance at sea level: 1050 hp
(takeoff for 1 min)
Performance at sea level: 920 hp
(briefly for 5 min)
Performance at sea level: 775 hp
(constant)
Performance at 4 km: 1050 hp
(briefly for 5 min)
Performance at 4 km: 800 hp
(constant)

BMW 132 Dc, Radial (carbureted), from 1937
with 27.7 l displacement, high altitude supercharger, maximum pressure altitude 2.6 km:

Performance at sea level: 880 hp
(takeoff for 1 min)
Performance at sea level: 800 hp
(briefly for 5 min)
Performance at sea level: 720 hp
(combat for 30 min)
Performance at sea level: 580 hp
(constant)
Performance at 2 km: 945 hp
(briefly for 1 min)
Performance at 2.5 km: 870 hp
(briefly for 5 min)
Performance at 2.9 km: 790 hp
(combat for 30 min)
Performance at 3.8 km: 655 hp
(constant)

In addition to the inline engines, Henschel also proposed a radial engine for use in its Hs 124, but by then the Hs 124 was no longer being considered as a bomber destroyer.

First-Generation *Zerstörer* Engines:

Jumo 210

Jumo 210 G, 1937 onward
As the Jumo 210 Da, with fuel injection and 3.8 km rated altitude:

Performance at sea level: 730 hp (takeoff for 1 min)
Performance at 3.8 km: 670 hp (combat for 30 min)

Prior to the Bf 110 B entering production Junkers switched over to building the Jumo 210 in its G version with fuel injection.

DB 601, 1937 onward
As the DB 600, 33.9 l displacement, with fuel injection:

The DB 601, which saw widespread use, was effectively a fuel-injected DB 600. The first test engine with fuel injection (F4 E) ran in 1935, and an initial contract for 150 engines followed in February 1936. Production began in November 1937, ending in 1943 after a run of over 19,000 engines built.

DB 601 A/B, 1937 onward
With continuous high altitude supercharger for 4 km maximum pressure altitude:

Performance at sea level: 1100 hp (takeoff for 1 min)
Performance at 4 km: 960 hp (combat for 30 min)

The DB 601 A was installed in the Bf 109 and the DB 601 B in the Bf 110.

DB 601 Aa/Ba, 1937 onward
With continuous high altitude supercharger for 5 km maximum pressure altitude:

Performance at sea level: 1175 hp (takeoff for 1 min)
Performance at 5 km: 1000 hp (combat for 30 min)

DB 601 N, 1940 onward
As DB 601 Aa, but with improved compression, C3 fuel:

Performance at sea level: 1275 hp (takeoff for 1 min)

Second-Generation *Zerstörer* Engines:

The following engines were originally intended for the Me 210 and Ar 240. However, since the Bf 110 continued in production longer than first planned, it too was fitted with the improved performance version of the DB 601, as well as the DB 605.

DB 601

DB 601 E/F, 1939 onward
As the DB 601 A/B, improved version, increased rpm, 4.9 km maximum pressure altitude:

Performance: 1350 hp (takeoff and emergency for 1 min)
1200 hp (combat for 30 min)
1000 hp (constant)

DB 605
Like the DB 601 with nearly the same installation dimensions, follow-on development, 35.7 l displacement, increased rpm and larger supercharger, as well as crossed firing sequence. The RLM viewed the DB 605 as a diseased powerplant, since it often failed during its first months in production and led to many fatal accidents. By 1944 even the DB Company would gladly have dropped it in favor of the much better DB 603. Nevertheless, since RLM planning called for the Bf 109 and Bf 110 to be produced in large numbers through 1945, with the greatest monthly output achieved by the end of 1944 manufacture of the DB 605 was forced to continue, along with work on improving it. As a result, in mid-1944 it was fitted with the blower from the DB 603. The RLM would also have liked to replace the DB 605 with the Jumo 213 E. This failed, however, due to the fact that the Bf 109 and Bf 110 would have needed fundamental design changes, causing interruptions in production. Approximately 42,400 DB 605s were built.

DB 605 A/B, 1941 onward
A and B with different reduction gearing:

Performance at sea level: 1475 hp (takeoff and emergency for 1 min)
Performance at sea level: 1310 hp (combat for 30 min)
Performance at sea level: 1075 hp (constant)
Performance at 5.7 km: 1355 hp (emergency for 1 min)

Performance at 5.7 km: 1250 hp
(combat for 30 min)
Performance at 5.7 km: 1080 hp (constant)
Performance at 10 km: 790 hp
(emergency for 1 min)

DB 605 AM, 1944 onward
As A, with water-methanol injection for improved performance at low levels:

Performance at sea level: 1800 hp
(takeoff and emergency for 1 min)

DB 605 AS/BS, 1944 onward
As A/B, with high altitude supercharger (from DB 603) for 8 km maximum pressure altitude:

Performance at sea level: 1435 hp
(takeoff and emergency for 1 min)
Performance at sea level: 1275 hp
(combat for 30 min)
Performance at sea level: 1040 hp (constant)
Performance at 8.0 km: 1200 hp
(emergency for 1 min)
Performance at 7.8 km: 1150 hp
(combat for 30 min)
Performance at 5.7 km: 1040 hp (constant)
Performance at 10 km: 925 hp
(emergency for 1 min)

Pre-production series for DB 605 D as this was not able to go into series production quickly enough. A and B had different reduction gearing.

DB 605 C
As A, but rotating clockwise and with different reduction gearing.

DB 605 D series, 1944 onward
As DB 605 A, with the larger blower of the DB 603, higher compression, oil slinger, 7.6 km maximum pressure altitude:

Performance at sea level: 1435 hp
(takeoff and emergency for 1 min)
Performance at sea level: 1275 hp
(combat for 30 min)
Performance at sea level: 1075 hp (constant)
Performance at 8.0 km: 1280 hp
(emergency for 1 min)
Performance at 7.8 km: 1200 hp
(combat for 30 min)
Performance at 5.7 km: 1040 hp (constant)
Performance at 10 km: 930 hp
(emergency for 1 min)

DB 628 A, 1943
As the DB 605 A with two-stage blower, one of which was located ahead of the engine, air intake behind the propeller, with blower air cooler beneath the engine. 11 km maximum pressure altitude.

Performance at sea level: 1600 hp
(takeoff and emergency for 1 min)

Although the engine performed satisfactorily, only about 150 were built, as flight performance proved disappointing (flown in the Bf 109 V54). It was believed that the blower air cooler drew off the engine's surplus power due to its increased drag. The DB 605 AS and DB 605 D were used instead, as these also provided improved altitude performance.

Junkers Jumo 211
The rapid expansion of the *Luftwaffe* and the demand for improved performance led to Daimler-Benz being unable to provide sufficient production capacity on the one hand, and the Jumo 210 unable to offer adequate performance on the other. As a result, Junkers was awarded a contract by the RLM in 1934 for the development of a 35 liter engine. The resulting Ju 211 was, in essence, a long nosed version of the Jumo 210. The Jumo 211 was initially fitted into bombers, while the DB 601 was mounted in fighters and heavy fighters.

Junkers Jumo 211 A/D, 1939 onward
Fuel injected engine with 35 l displacement, 5.2 km rated altitude.

Performance at sea level: 1200 hp
(takeoff and emergency for 1 min)
Performance at sea level: 950 hp
(combat for 30 min)
Performance at sea level: 800 hp
(constant)

This engine was the standard engine for the Ju 87, Ju 88, and He 111.

Junkers Jumo 211 F, 1941 onward
As the Jumo 211 A, improved, higher rpm, 5.3 km rated altitude:

Performance at sea level: 1340 hp
(takeoff and emergency for 1 min)
Performance at sea level: 1060 hp
(combat for 30 min)

As the Jumo 211 A fitted in the Ju 87, Ju 88, and He 111. Because of the planned shift to the Ju 188 with Jumo 213 as the medium bomber in 1944, this engine was available in large numbers and was to have been used for the Ta 154.

Junkers Jumo 211 N, 1943/44
As Jumo 211 F, boosted performance, 5.2 km rated altitude:

Performance at sea level: 1450 hp
(takeoff and emergency for 1 min)

The Ju 88 C's poor flight performance and the impossibility of getting sufficient numbers of BMW 801s for the better performing Ju 88 *Zerstörer* (Ju 88 R) led to an improved version of the Jumo 211 (a design that had actually already been written off) as the engine of choice for the Ju 88 C. The Ju 88 G was instead powered by the Jumo 213. In late 1943 the engine was also planned for the Ta 154 A then in development, and installation in the Bf 110 was also explored but not followed through due to the large number of changes necessary. By the time the Ta 154 A was ready for production in 1944, the Jumo 211 N was no longer up to meeting the tasks required of this airframe. This resulted in the planned number of Ta 154 As being sharply reduced in favor of variants that would be powered by the Jumo 213. Only in 1944 were there plans to produce a small batch of Ta 154 As using the more powerful Jumo 211 N, with production ceasing in early 1945. However, this never happened, as the Ta 154 was stricken from the production list due to its lack of promise.

Junkers Jumo 213
The Jumo 213 was fundamentally similar to the Jumo 211, but had a higher rpm and other improvements. From 1942 until the war's end approximately 9000 of the type were built. The Jumo 213 was developed in 1942, but it took until 1944 before production actually spun up. The Jumo 213 was not supplied to the airframe manufacturers as an engine, but as a complete powerplant, and was chiefly used in the Fw 190 D (fighter engine) and Ju 88/Ju 188 (bomber engine).

Junkers Jumo 213 A-1, 1944 onward
As the Jumo 211 F, improved, increased rpm:

Performance at sea level: 2100 hp
(with MW 50 injection for 10 min)
Performance at sea level: 1900 hp
(takeoff and emergency for 1 min)
Performance at sea level: 1750 hp
(combat for 30 min)

The Jumo 213 A was installed in the Fw 190 D, Ju 88 G, and Ju 188. It was also tested in the Ta 154. The cost of installing it in the Bf 109 and Bf 110 was estimated and determined to be too high in light of the engine's limited remaining production lifespan. The RLM and Junkers planned for switching from the Jumo 213 A to the Jumo 213 E as quickly as possible.

DB 603
Daimler-Benz had offered the RLM the DB 603 as early as 4 September 1936 and was awarded a developmental contract just a few weeks later. On 11 March 1937 the RLM had the contract voided. Development continued at the company's own expense, and a prototype engine found itself on the test bench in 1939. The war caused the RLM to change its thinking, and on 3 February 1940 a contract was confirmed for the first 120 engines. Full-scale production began in 1941. The engine was mainly installed in the Me 410 and He 219, and proved to be a reliable powerplant. The Do 217 also received limited numbers of this engine, but only when production levels permitted. Since the Me 209, Me 309, and He 177 B never materialized and the Me 410 and Do 217 ceased production in 1944, in the fall of 1944 the situation arose, whereby there was temporarily no suitable taker for the DB 603, while at the same time large numbers of the "sick" DB 605 were being built. It wasn't until 1945 that widespread use was again projected for the Do 335 and Ta 152 C.

DB 603 A/B/C, 1942 onward
Engine with 44.5 l displacement, 5.7 km maximum pressure altitude, clockwise rotation.

Versions A through C with different gear reduction, DB 603 C with long end shaft.

Performance at sea level: 1750 hp
(takeoff and emergency for 1 min)
Performance at sea level: 1580 hp
(combat for 5 min)
Performance at sea level: 1375 hp (constant)
Performance at 5.7 km: 1620 hp
(emergency for 1 min)
Performance at 5.7 km: 1510 hp
(combat for 5 min)
Performance at 5.4 km: 1400 hp (constant)

Performance at 5.0 km: 1170 hp
(min cruise)

DB 603 A, July 44 onward
As DB 603 A 1942, but with Riedel starter, modified blower:

Performance at sea level: 1750 hp
(takeoff and emergency for 1 min)
Performance at sea level: 1590 hp
(combat for 5 min)
Performance at sea level: 1390 hp (constant)
Performance at 5.7 km: 1680 hp
(emergency for 1 min)
Performance at 5.7 km: 1590 hp
(combat for 5 min)
Performance at 5.5 km: 1450 hp (constant)

DB 603 AA, July 44 onward
As DB 603 A 1944, but with the larger blower of the DB 603 E:

Performance at sea level: 1670 hp
(takeoff and emergency for 1 min)
Performance at sea level: 1510 hp
(combat for 5 min)
Performance at sea level: 1325 hp (constant)
Performance at 7.3 km: 1450 hp
(emergency for 1 min)
Performance at 7.2 km: 1370 hp
(combat for 5 min)
Performance at 6.9 km: 1280 hp (constant)

The DB 603 AA was an interim step to the DB 603 E, and is believed to have been built for only a few months in 1944.

DB 603 D/E/F, 1942
Originally as the DB 603 A/B/D, but rotating counterclockwise. For stability reasons, Messerschmitt always wanted the Me 410 to be fitted with a clockwise rotating and a counterclockwise rotating engine. Due to technical reasons with production, though, the counterclockwise rotating engine was never built in series. The war situation prevented the building of production materials for the engines and propellers.

DB 603 G/H/J, 1942
Originally like the DB 603 A/B/C, but with improved performance due to C3 special fuel and higher compression:

Performance at sea level: 1900 hp
(takeoff and emergency for 1 min)

These engines, designed for the C3 fuel, never materialized because fuel supplies initially did not reach the desired level and later fell through altogether.

DB 603 K/L/M, 1942
Originally like the DB 603 G/H/J, but counterclockwise rotating.

Third-Generation *Zerstörer* Engines:

Junkers Jumo 213

Junkers Jumo 213 E-0, 1944 onward
As the Jumo 213 A-1, with three-stage supercharger, 9.2 km maximum pressure altitude:

Performance at sea level: 2050 hp
(with MW 50 injection for 10 min)
Performance at sea level: 1730 hp
(takeoff and emergency for 1 min)
Performance at sea level: 1580 hp
(combat for 5 min)
Performance at sea level: 1320 hp (constant)
Performance at 9.0 km: 1320 hp
(emergency for 1 min)
Performance at 9.0 km: 1260 hp
(combat for 5 min)
Performance at 8.8 km: 1060 hp (constant)
Performance at 7.8 km: 900 hp
(min cruise)
Performance at 13 km: 760 hp
(emergency for 1 min)
Performance at 13 km: 1140 hp
(with GM 1)

The Jumo 213 E was only fitted in small numbers into the Fw 190 D and Ta 152 H. Until the Ta 254 was abandoned, it was also planned for this *Zerstörer*, as well as for the Ju 88 G.

DB 603

DB 603 AE, July 1944 onward
As DB 603 AA 1944, but with C3 fuel:

Performance at sea level: 1750 hp
(takeoff and emergency for 1 min)
Performance at sea level: 1575 hp
(combat for 5 min)
Performance at sea level: 1370 hp (constant)
Performance at 7.4 km: 1625 hp
(emergency for 1 min)
Performance at 7.4 km: 1520 hp
(combat for 5 min)
Performance at 7.0 km: 1410 hp (constant)

DB 603 AM, July 1944 onward
As DB 603 A 1944, but with C3 fuel and MW 50 injection boost:

Performance at sea level: 2250 hp (takeoff and emergency for 1 min)
Performance at sea level: 1510 hp (combat for 5 min)
Performance at sea level: 1325 hp (constant)
Performance at 3.7 km: 2100 hp (emergency for 1 min)
Performance at 5.7 km: 1510 hp (combat for 5 min)
Performance at 5.4 km: 1400 hp (constant)

DB 603 AAM, July 1944 onward
As DB 603 AA 1944, but with C3 fuel and MW 50 injection boost:

Performance at sea level: 2250 hp (takeoff and emergency for 1 min)
Performance at sea level: 1450 hp (combat for 5 min)
Performance at sea level: 1290 hp (constant)
Performance at 7.2 km: 1900 hp (emergency for 1 min)
Performance at 7.2 km: 1370 hp (combat for 5 min)
Performance at 6.9 km: 1280 hp (constant)

DB 603 E/F, 4/43
As DB 603 A/D, but with higher maximum pressure altitude resulting from special supercharger, nosewheel anchor eyelets, different propeller settings (braking blades), higher weight, longer gearbox, fitted oil slinger:

Performance at sea level: 1750 hp (takeoff and emergency for 1 min)
Performance at sea level: 1580 hp (combat for 5 min)
Performance at sea level: 1375 hp (constant)
Performance at 6.3 km: 1590 hp (emergency for 1 min)
Performance at 6.3 km: 1490 hp (combat for 5 min)
Performance at 6.0 km: 1390 hp (constant)

Since the DB 603 E and F engines were never produced in their original form, these were redefined in April 1943. The DB 603 E through K engines were assigned to the Me 309, but were also planned for the Me 410, He 219, and Do 217. With the cancellation of the Me 309 these engines also became superfluous, resulting in yet another redefinition.

DB 603 E, 10/1943
As DB 603 A, but with 7.4 km maximum pressure altitude resulting from the larger supercharger of the DB 603 Gl:

Performance at sea level: 1800 hp (takeoff and emergency for 1 min)
Performance at sea level: 1500 hp (combat for 5 min)
Performance at sea level: 1330 hp (constant)
Performance at 7.4 km: 1480 hp (emergency for 1 min)
Performance at 7.4 km: 1380 hp (combat for 5 min)
Performance at 7.0 km: 1270 hp (constant)

As the engine for the DB 9-8603c fighter/heavy fighter standard powerplant the DB 603 E was planned for the Me 410 C, among others, but when the Me 410 C and D were redlined it was to have been mounted in the Me 410 B for the duration of its production life.

DB 603 E-2, 1944 onward
As DB 603 E 1943, but with 6.4 km maximum pressure altitude:

Performance at sea level: 2000 hp (takeoff and emergency for 1 min)
Performance at sea level: 1710 hp (combat for 5 min)
Performance at sea level: 1540 hp (constant)
Performance at 6.4 km: 1740 hp (emergency for 1 min)
Performance at 6.4 km: 1550 hp (combat for 5 min)
Performance at 6.4 km: 1300 hp (constant)

The DB 603 E-2 was installed in the Do 335 as the forward engine.

DB 603 G/K, 4/43
As DB 603 E/F 4/43, but with different compression, C3 special fuel and different supercharger reduction gearing:

Performance at sea level: 1750 hp (takeoff and emergency for 1 min)
Performance at sea level: 1580 hp (combat for 5 min)
Performance at sea level: 1375 hp (constant)
Performance at 7.0 km: 1600 hp (emergency for 1 min)

Performance at 7.0 km: 1475 hp (combat for 5 min)
Performance at 6.5 km: 1350 hp (constant)

DB 603 G/K, 10/1944
As DB 603 E/F 1944, but with different compression (C3 special fuel) and different supercharger reduction gearing:

Performance at sea level: 1900 hp (takeoff and emergency for 1 min)
Performance at sea level: 1575 hp (combat for 30 min)
Performance at sea level: 1375 hp (constant)
Performance at 7.0 km: 1650 hp (emergency for 1 min)
Performance at 7.0 km: 1480 hp (combat for 30 min)
Performance at 6.5 km: 1355 hp (constant)
Performance at 10 km: 1100 hp (emergency for 1 min)

DB 603 LA-0, 1944
As DB 603 E 1944, but follow-on development, 9 km maximum pressure altitude:

Performance at sea level: 2100 hp (takeoff and emergency for 1 min)
Performance at sea level: 1800 hp (combat for 30 min)
Performance at sea level: 1500 hp (constant)
Performance at 9.0 km: 1760 hp (emergency for 1 min)
Performance at 9.0 km: 1500 hp (combat for 30 min)
Performance at 8.6 km: 1240 hp (constant)

DB 603 LA-1, 1944
As DB 603 LA-0, 1944, but with modified blower, 11 km maximum pressure altitude.

DB 603 N, 1944
As DB 603 LA 1944, but follow-on development, 11 km maximum pressure altitude:

Performance at sea level: 2750 hp (takeoff and emergency for 1 min)
Performance at sea level: 2400 hp (combat for 30 min)
Performance at sea level: 2180 hp (constant)
Performance at 11.0 km: 1950 hp (emergency for 1 min)
Performance at 11.0 km: 1590 hp (combat for 30 min)
Performance at 11.0 km: 1320 hp (constant)

Standard Powerplants

In order to avoid the incessant battles between the engine and airframe manufacturers on the issue of radiator and feed lines, the RLM decided to assign responsibility for the entire powerplant, including the cowling and radiator, to the airframe manufacturer. Aircraft manufacturers were to be included in the developmental process. Due to the differing speeds, a standard fighter/heavy fighter engine was to be developed for the fighters and *Zerstörer* types, while for the slower bombers and transports a standard bomber/transport engine would be created. The two types differed mainly in the diameter of the radiators affixed ahead of the engines, with the standard fighter/heavy fighter engine having a smaller diameter. The Messerschmitt Company attempted to push through a standard fighter/heavy fighter engine with an especially small diameter, over the objections of engine manufacturers as well as other aircraft designers. As a result, the Me 209 V5 operated at engine temperatures that were far too high, and even with the Do 335 the radiator diameter proposed by Messerschmitt (Do 335 V1) had to be enlarged to the dimensions called for by DB. As a result of the forward mounting of the radiator and frontal armor the standard engines were heavier than other engines up to that point in time, since the latter had radiators located in other areas of the airframe. This shift in the center point of gravity meant that the standard engines could not simply be swapped out with older-type engines on aircraft already in the inventory. At the very least, this necessitated lengthening the fuselage. Center of gravity problems in test aircraft were alleviated by adding weight to the extreme aft end of the fuselage.

DB 9-8603 B 1944
Standard fighter/heavy fighter powerplant including radiator, engine cradle arms, cowling plating and armor, test engine using DB 603 E.

DB 9-8603 B-1 1944
Standard fighter/heavy fighter powerplant including radiator, engine cradle arms, cowling plating and armor, production version using DB 603 LA, planned for the He 219 and Me 410.

DB 9-8603 B 1944
Standard bomber/transport powerplant including radiator, engine cradle arms, cowling plating and armor, test engine using DB 603 A.

Bibliography

Books

Aders, Gebhard: *"Geschichte der deutschen Nachtjagd"*

Balke, Ulf: *"Der Luftkrieg in Europa"*

Becker, Hans-Jürgen: *"Schwere Jäger und Zerstörer der Luftwaffe 1933-1945"*

Blume, W.: *"Arbeiten und Gedanken über die bewegliche Bewaffnung der Flugzeuge"*

Bornemann, K.: *"Eine neuartige bewegliche Waffenanlage"*

Cescotti, Roderich: *"Kampfflugzeuge und Aufklärer", vol. 15 from the series "Die Deutsche Luftfahrt"*

Dierich, Wolfgang: *"Die Verbände der Luftwaffe 1935-1945"*

Ebert, H.J., Kaiser, J.B,; Peters, K.: *"Willy Messerschmitt - Pionier der Luftfahrt und des Leichtbaus", vol. 17 from the series "Die Deutsche Luftfahrt"*

Green, William: *"Warplanes of the Third Reich"*

Hahn: *"Deutsche Geheimwaffen 1939 - 1945"*

Held, Werner: *"Die deutsche Tagjagd"*

Held; Nauroth: *"Die deutsche Nachtjagd"*

Held; Nauroth: *"Messerschmitt Bf 110"*

Irving, David: *"Die Tragödie der Deutschen Luftwaffe"*

Kens; Nowarra: *"Die deutschen Flugzeuge 1933 - 1945"*

Kosin, Rüdiger: *"Die Entwicklung der deutschen Jagdflugzeuge" vol. 4 from the series "Die Deutsche Luftfahrt"*

Lange, Bruno: *"Das Buch der deutschen Luftfahrttechnik"*

Pohlmann, Hermann: *"Chronik eines Flugzeugwerkes 1932 - 1945, B & V, HFB"*

Ries, Karl: *"Dora Kurfürst und rote 13", vols. 1 through 4*

Ries, Karl: *"Markierungen und Tarnanstriche der Luftwaffe im zweiten Weltkrieg", vols. 1 through 4*

Ries, Karl: *"Luftwaffe Photo-Report 1919 - 1945"*

Ries, Karl: *"Luftwaffenstory 1935 - 1939"*

Ries; Galland; Ahnert: *"Die Deutsche Luftwaffe 1919 - 1945"*

Schliephake, Hanfried: *"Flugzeugbewaffnungen"*

Sengfelder, Günter: *"Flugzeugfahrwerke"*

Smith; Gallaspy: *"Luftwaffe Camouflage & Markings 1933 - 45" vol. 2 and 3*

Smith, Kay: *"German Aircraft of the Second World War"*

Trenkle, Fritz: *"Bordfunkgeräte - Vom Funksender zum Bordradar", vol. 7 from the series "Die Deutsche Luftfahrt"*

Vajda; Dancey: *"German Aircraft Industry and Production 1933 - 1945"*

v. Chlingensperg: *"Über die Abwehrbewaffnung der Me 210" in reports to the deutsche Akademie der Luftfahrtforschung 1942, no. 82* von Gersdorff, Kyrill et al.: *"Flugmotoren und Strahltriebwerke", vol. 2 from the series "Die Deutsche Luftfahrt"*

Magazines and Publications

Aircraft No. 2 (Feist, Dario): *"Luftwaffe in Action"*

Aircraft No. 1148 (Punka George): *"Messerschmitt Me 210/410 in Action"*

Air Show (Kocent-Zielinski, E.): *"Messerschmitt Me 210 Ca-1 - ein ungarischer Lizenbau"*

Flugzeug 5/97 - 3/98 (Mankau, H.): *"Ar 240/440"*

Kováts, Layos: *"A Dunai Repülögépgyár RT. Története"*

Luftfahrt international Vol. 1: *"Zielfernrohr ZFR 4 A"*

Luftfahrt international Vol. 15: *"Henschel Hs 124 Mehrzweckflugzeug"*

Modell Magazin 11/81 through 4/82 (Mankau, H.): *"Die große Hornissen-Story"*

Modell Magazin 11/82 (Chapman, R.): *"Me 410-Nachtrag"*

Modell Magazin 4/83 (Schmidt, A.): *"Die Me 210 made in Ungarn"*

Profile No. 167 (Smith, Richard): *"The Messerschmitt Me 210/410 Series"*

Scale Models (Jenkins, Paul): Feb. and Mar. 1979: *"Messerschmitt Me 210/410"*

Waffen-Arsenal S-43 (Dabrowski, H.-P.; Petrick, P.): *"Zerstörer Me 210"*

Waffen-Arsenal S-56 (Griehl M.,): *"Nachtjäger über Deutschland 1940 -45"*

Waffen Revue 114 through 117: *"Geheimwaffe RZ 65"*

Wydawnictwo Militaria (Ledwoch, J.): *"Messerschmitt Me 210/Me 410"*

Test Reports and Meeting Minutes

10. Staffel JG Richthofen report from 11/26/39 re: Me 110 testing for night fighting

Mtt letter to Miag Mühlenbau und Industrie AG: Lutherwerk, from 6/18/40 re: Me 110 D

RLM letter to Mtt re: Bf 110 F with DB 601 F from 12/15/41

Mtt letter to RLM re: Bf 110 F with DB 601 F from 1/5/42

Mtt minutes re: Bf 110 with Jumo 211 F engines of the Ta 154 from 9/18/43

MTT VT directive 1570 from 11/6/41: Barrage Balloon Protection for the Me 210

Mtt test report No. 210 15 E 42 from 8/7/42 alternative armament for Me 210 (MG 81 Z and MG 151)

RLM/Mtt minutes from 11/26/42 installation of DB 603 standard engine in the Me 410

Mtt flight testing 8/14/43, research into water radiator for the Me 410.

Mtt technical report No. 93/43 from 12/1/43, drag measurements on Me 210/410 model

Mtt minutes from 2/1744, installation of ZFR 4 in Me 410 with BK 5 and MK 103

Mtt flight report from 2/2/42, icing flights with Me 210 V 13

Mtt memorandum Me 410 69/43 from 6/25/43, Me 410 de-icing status

Mtt testing bureau memorandum from 8/31/43: Me 410 de-icing matters

Mtt testing bureau minutes from 10/27/43 Me 410 de-icing system

Steno minutes of *Reichsluftfahrtministerium* meetings at or with the participation of *Generalluftzeugmeister* Milch from 1941 to 1944, documents from the Federal Archives in Freiburg

Mtt data sheet Me 410 B 1 from 4/13/43

Mtt performance Me 410 B day reconnaissance aircraft with fuselage gondola and GM 1 in bomb bay from 12/17/43

Mtt condensed assembly description Me 410 torpedo bomber with increased range from 1/10/44

Mtt aircraft comparison Me 410 C-1, Me 410 B-2, Me 410 C-2 from 7/23/45

RLM minutes from 1/25/44, structural requirements for Me 410 H

Mtt project description Me 329 from 3/15/42

Manuals, etc.

Fl.T.S Jüterbog Lehrgr. Einweisung Bf 119 B, C

Messerschmitt vorläufige Betriebs- und Rüstanleitung Bf 110 C

L.Dv. 578/1a Bf 110 B-1/C-1 Bordfunkanlage as of Feb. 1940

L.Dv. 578/1a Bf 110 B/C Schusswaffe as of Dec. 1938

L.Dv. 578/1a Nachtrag 1, Bf 110 E Schusswaffe as of Feb. 1941

L.Dv. T2100 G-2 bis G-4/Wa Bedienungsvorschrift Waffenanlage

L.Dv. T2413/1 Nachtrag 1 Zusatzanlagen Bf 110 D as of Nov. 1940

L.Dv. T 2413/1 Nachtrag 2 Zusatzanlagen Bf 119 E as of Jul. 1941

L.Dv. T2413/1 Nachtrag 3 Höhenatmeranlage as of Oct. 1941

L.Dv. T2413/1 Nachtrag 6 Bf 110 C-1, C-2, C-3, C-7, D-2, D-3, E-1, E-2 als Tiefangriffsflugzeuge as of Oct.1942

L.Dv. T2413/1 Nachtrag 8 Zusatzanlagen Bf 110 F-2 bis F-4 as of Mar. 1942

L.Dv. T2413/7 Bf 110 E-1 und E-2, Stromlaufplan

D.(Luft) T579/6 Bf 110 Abwurfwaffe

D.(Luft) T2110 8B Heft 1 Abwurfwaffe Bf 110 E as of May 1941

D.(Luft) T2110 9D Bordfunkanlage Bf 110 C-2 bis C-7, D-0 bis D-4, E-1 bis E-4 as of Jul. 1942

D.(Luft) T2110 E/Bo Abwurfwaffe

D.(Luft) T2110 E und F/Wa starre Rückwärtsbewaffnung

D.(Luft) T2110/Trop Bf 110 Trop as of Aug. 1941

D.(Luft) T2110 F/Fl Bedienungsvorschrift as of Mar. 1943

D.(Luft) T2110 F und G/Wa Beiheft 2, Rüstsatz M1, 2 MG 151/20

D.(Luft) T2110 F-2 as of Jun. 1942 - Teil 0 (Allgemeine Angaben), Teil 1 (Rumpfwerk), Teil 2 (Fahrwerk), Teil 4 (Steuerwerk), Teil 6 (Triebwerksanlage), Teil 7 (Triebwerksbedien- und -versorgungsanlage), Teil 8A (Allgemeine Ausrüstung), Teil 9B (Bordnetz)

D.(Luft) T2110 F-3 as of Mar. 1943 - Teil 0 (Allgemeine Angaben), Teil 8B (Abwurfanlage), Teil 8F (Rüstsätze), Teil 9E (Lichtbildanlage)

D.(Luft) T2110 G/Fl Bedienungsvorschrift as of Mar. 1943

D.(Luft) T2110 G-2 bis G-4/Wa Bedienungsvorschrift Schusswaffenanlage as of April 1943

D.(Luft) T2110 G-4/Wa Bedienungsvorschrift Schrägeinbau 2 MG /FF as of Jul. 1944

D.(Luft) T2110 G-2 as of Nov. 1943 - Teil 8A (Schusswaffenanlage), Teil 8A (Schusswaffenanlage) Beiheft 1 2 MK 108, Teil 8C Heft 1 Rüstsatz M5, Teil 9A (Allgemeine Ausrüstung)

D.(Luft) T2110 G-2/R1 as of Jul. 1943 - Teil 0 (Allgemeine Angaben), Teil 1 (Rumpfwerk), Teil 8A (Schusswaffenanlage)

D.(Luft) T2110 G-3 as of October 1943 - Teil 0 (Allgemeine Angaben), Teil 9A (Allgemeine Ausrüstung)

D.(Luft) T2110 G-4 as of August 1943 - Teil 0 (Allgemeine Angaben), Teil 7 Beiheft 1 (Betriebsstoffzusatzanlagen Bf 110 G-4/U8), Teil 8F (Rüstsätze)

Chef TLR Flugzeug-Baureihen-Blatt Bf 110 G/H

Messerschmitt Me 210 Bedienungsvorschrift - Fl, Mar. 1941

L.Dv. T2210 A-1/Bo, über die Abwurfwaffenanlage für Me 210 A-1

L.Dv. T2210/Wa - as of Nov. 1942 - Me 210 Bedienungsvorschrift Waffenanlage

L.Dv. T2210/Wa - N.f.D. - Me 210 Schusswaffenanlage

D.(Luft) T2210 A-1 Me 210 A-1 as of April 1943 - Teil 0 (Allgemeine Angaben), Teil 1 (Rumpfwerk), Teil 2 (Fahrwerk), Teil 3 (Leitwerk), Teil 4 (Steuerwerk), Teil 5 (Tragwerk), Teil 6 (Triebwerksanlage), Teil 7 (Triebwerksbedien- und -versorgungsanlage), Teil 8A (Schusswaffenanlage), Teil 8D (Kutonase), Teil 8E (Lichtbildanlage), Teil 9D (Bordfunkanlage)

Me 210 replacement parts list, excerpts
Flugzeugtypenblatt Me 210 dated 2/1/1942

D.(Luft) T2210 Ca-1 Me 210 Ca-1 Teil 0 (Allgemeine Angaben), Teil 6 (Triebwerksanlage)

D.(Luft) T2410 A-1 Me 410 A-1 as of Jul. 1943 - Teil 0 (Allgemeine Angaben), Teil 1 (Rumpf), Teil 3 (Leitwerk), Teil 4 (Steuerwerk), Teil 5 (Tragwerk), Teil 6 (Triebwerk), Teil 8, Heft 1-3 As of Nov 43 (Schusswaffenanlage me 410 A, B),

D.(Luft) T2410 A-1/U4 Me 410 A-1/U4 as of April 1944 - Teil 8A (Schusswaffenanlage mit 5 cm BK), Teil 9B (elektrisches Bordnetz)

E-Stelle Rechlin: Flugzeugmuster Me 210 A-1, recognition sheet 1942
E-Stelle Rechlin: Flugzeugmuster Me 410 A-1, A-2, A-3, recognition sheet 1943
E-Stelle Rechlin-Bericht 334 from 19.1.43: "Schnellbombervergleich Me 410, Ar 440, Ju 88 S, He 219"

Conclusion

The RLM and the *Luftwaffe* were able to establish the basic criteria for the lightweight fighter and the medium bomber relatively quickly, and from these guidelines created the Bf 109 and He 111 as the primary and successful examples of these two classes of aircraft. The definition and acquisition of the *Zerstörer*, however, was another matter. Without a clear focus of purpose, this aircraft class ultimately proved to be fraught with disappointment.

After an initial search that also considered heavy and slow airplanes being fitted with turrets, in 1936 a decision was made in favor of the Bf 110, which in its original form was conceived as a heavy fighter. Yet the contractors began having doubts about the concept itself even before the Bf 110 entered production. According to its newly defined role, the *Luftwaffe* was expected to destroy the enemy's air forces and industry in enemy territory early on in any conflict. To this end, the heavy fighters were to have sufficient penetration range to be able to destroy point targets by dive bombing and then, thanks to their performance and firepower, provide protection for the bombers over their targets. However, because of the increased load resulting in poorer flight performance compared to short-range single-engined fighters, it was soon felt that rear-firing defensive armament was indispensable.

The new role definition spawned the Me 210, which differed from the Bf 110 mainly in its increased range and bomb bay for two 500 kg bombs, as well as its improved defensive firepower. According to initial planning, the Me 210 was to have replaced the Bf 110 on the assembly line some time after 1941. Follow-on improvements, however, ensured the Bf 110 was able to fulfill the new tasking required of the *Zerstörer* class. Drop tanks and hardpoints were developed to meet these requirements, and these started appearing on the type around the spring of 1940.

The *Luftwaffe* felt the Bf 110 was ill-suited for its intended role, as evidenced by the construction contract for the Me 210. This, combined with the lack of a heavy four-engined heavy bomber and a *Luftwaffe* that was not yet fully up to strength, makes one wonder today how Germany could have allowed itself to prosecute a war that inevitably involved England.

Once the feared inferiority of the Bf 110 manifested itself so plainly in the Battle of Britain, with increasing frequency the *Luftwaffe* began employing the type as a high speed bomber and dive bomber against ground targets. In conjunction with this, the type was also given a new lease on life in the night fighting role, where it proved to be most effective through the early months of 1944. During the time span from mid-1943 through mid-1944 the high speed bomber mission was abandoned in favor of daytime attacks against the enemy's four-engined bombers.

The same situation as encountered over England occurred when enemy single-seat fighters began appearing in the skies over the *Reich*, and by mid-1944 *Zerstörer* operations were compelled to cease in defense of the *Reich* as well. Furthermore, such missions were in effect uneconomical from the outset, as the Fw 190 had the same number of guns and required far fewer resources in men and materials, while also facing the enemy with better flight performance. The advantage of the Bf 110 and the Me 410 was in their potential for poor weather operations, but by 1944 the *Luftwaffe* could no longer afford specialized aircraft, not to mention the fact that by then there were insufficient numbers of trained pilots available for such a role.

The Bf 110 proved effective as a night fighter as long as it was used in a confined operational area under the direction of ground control. For free-ranging night fighter operations—increasingly popular from 1944 onward—it found itself lacking the necessary range. As a result, the Ju 88 and He 219 began replacing the type more and more throughout 1944.

The Me 210 was the intended replacement for both the Bf 110 and Ju 87 but, because it was rushed into production too quickly, it suffered from two main faults that made its flight handling entirely unacceptable: it was too short; and the leading edge slats—absent from the initial design—were absolutely necessary. Göring's order to cancel production was premature; with the changes the new Me 210 proved to be a viable aircraft, although by the time production resumed its performance was no longer up to par.

With its more powerful engines, the Me 410 would have been effective against allied daylight bombers from 1943 through the spring of 1944, but Göring ordered the type to be sidelined in virtually ineffectual night bomber raids against England. It was not until the spring of 1944 that the airplane started predominantly being used in the defense of the *Reich*. Like the Bf 110, with the appearance of enemy fighters it could only operate over the *Reich* with its own fighter protection, and in this case two Fw 190s were more effective than a single Me 410 with a Bf 109 flying escort. The Me 410 was unsuitable as a night fighter due to its high wing loading. As a result, the Me 410's production came to a close in the summer of 1944. The Bf 110 survived the Me 410 by just a few months due to the fact that, on the one hand, He 219 and Ju 88 G production did not reach intended levels soon enough and, on the other hand, the Luther and Gotha manufacturers were as yet unable to switch over to the Ta 152 C since it had not yet been fully developed.

Generally speaking, the RLM seemed to play a poor hand when it came to choosing aircraft. Single-seat fighter production concentrated almost exclusively on the Bf 109 in 1943, whereas at this time most pilots preferred the Fw 190. The RLM considered the He 111 to be an outdated interim solution as early as 1938, a type which was to be replaced by the Ju 88 and He 177. Yet in operations over England and Russia the pilots much preferred the robust He 111 over the Ju 88. During the war the He 111 proved to survive the longest of all combat aircraft, and had it been given the more powerful Jumo 213 would have been an effective airframe in 1944 as well. But because the RLM only had the type built from 1944 onward as a combat transport (He 111 H-20) with the restrictive underbelly racks, from that time on it was effectively unusable as a bomber. The Ju 88's dive bombing capability was no longer desired by the *Geschwader* after early 1943, but with the BMW 801 engines the type proved excellent in the role of *Zerstörer* for maritime operations, as a night fighter, and as a high-speed bomber. With regard to the Bf 110, even as it was going into production the *Luftwaffe* was no longer convinced of the type's effectiveness, and the Me 210/410 never fully lived up to expectations.

With today's hindsight, the *Luftwaffe* should have abandoned Bf 110 production with the F model and replaced it with the Fw 190. Production of the Me 210/410 should never have resumed after Göring's order to stop it, and in its place the Ju 88 C, S, R, and G should have been built as night fighters and high-speed bombers. The bomber role of the Ju 88 and Ju 188 could then have been fulfilled by an improved version of the He 111, and this would have enabled Messerschmitt to have the production capacity for the Me 262. However, in light of the enemy's material superiority, even by shifting production priorities around nothing would have changed the ultimate outcome of the war.